San Diego Christian College
2100 Greenfield Drive
El Cajon, CA 92019

Magic Flutes & Enchanted Forests

Magic Flutes & Enchanted Forests

THE SUPERNATURAL IN EIGHTEENTH-CENTURY MUSICAL THEATER

David J. Buch

The University of Chicago Press   Chicago & London

DAVID J. BUCH is visiting professor in the Committee on Theater and
Performance Studies at the University of Chicago.

The University of Chicago Press, Chicago 60637
The University of Chicago Press, Ltd., London
© 2008 by The University of Chicago
All rights reserved. Published 2008
Printed in the United States of America

17 16 15 14 13 12 11 10 09 08   1 2 3 4 5

ISBN-13: 978-0-226-07809-0 (cloth)
ISBN-13: 978-0-226-07810-6 (paper)
ISBN-10: 0-226-07809-4 (cloth)
ISBN-10: 0-226-07810-8 (paper)

Library of Congress Cataloging-in-Publication Data
Buch, David Joseph.
p.   cm.
Magic flutes & enchanted forests: the supernatural in eighteenth-century musical
theater/David J. Buch.
Includes bibliographical references and index.
ISBN-13: 978-0-226-07809-0 (cloth : alk. paper)
ISBN-13: 978-0-226-07810-6 (pbk. : alk. paper)
ISBN-10: 0-226-07809-4 (cloth : alk. paper)
ISBN-10: 0-226-07810-8 (pbk. : alk. paper)
1.   Musical theater—Europe—History—18th century.   2.   Supernatural in
musical theatre.   3.   Music and magic.   4.   Mozart, Wolfgang Amadeus, 1756–1791.
Zauberflöte.   I.   Title.   II.   Title: Magic flutes and
enchanted forests.
ML1720.3.B83 2008
782.109'033—dc22   2008010681

♾ The paper used in this publication meets the minimum requirements of the
American National Standard for Information Sciences—Permanence of
Paper for Printed Library Materials, ANSI Z39.48-1992.

CONTENTS

ILLUSTRATIONS

Color Plates (following page 212)

Black-and-White Figures

PREFACE

Un opéra doit être un conte de fées. Je trouverai asseʒ ailleurs des pièces raisonnées et touchantes, qui parleront à la raison et à l'âme. Ici, je veux un monde étrange et de fantaisie.

LOUIS SÉBASTIEN MERCIER, "Poèmes lyriques," *Tableau de Paris* (commentary 654), Paris, 1783

Modern scholarship often specifies two broad categories for classifying eighteenth-century opera: serious and comic. This distinction only had limited currency in the eighteenth century outside of Italy and is not very useful for works after about 1760, even in Italy. For France it is almost deceptive. French tragic operas usually had happy endings, and horrific, disturbing works such as André-Ernest-Modeste Grétry's *Raoul, Barbe-bleue* were called *opéra-comique*.

One also reads of a threefold scheme—heroic, comic, and pastoral—which was used by some seventeenth-century writers.[1] This scheme may work well for many operas in that century, but for the next it is still far too reductive, neglecting the generic nuances of the period's own vocabulary. More inclusive is a fivefold distinction consisting of four acknowledged categories received by eighteenth-century writers who produced librettos: (1) mythology, either pastoral or heroic, (2) history, usually with heroic themes, (3) epic romance, and (4) comedy. A new kind of story, based on fairy tales and legends, developed during the eighteenth century. French writers linked it to the "marvelous" of mythology and epic romance. This term already had a long history in discussions of literature and opera, mostly regarding issues of verisimilitude during

---

1. Pierre Perrin, attempting to synthesize modern practice with classical poetics, advanced these three categories for French opera in the seventeenth century. Commentators invoked them again in accounts citing classical authority, including Mably, *Lettres*, and Batteux, *Les beaux-arts*. Harris, "Eighteenth-Century Orlando," 106, cites them without attribution as the sole categories in opera. She offers the same view in her *Handel and the Pastoral Tradition*, where she mentions occasional magical elements as details in these three categories. I will demonstrate that most commentators in the eighteenth century did not restrict themselves to these categories, especially French writers, who provided a more nuanced taxonomy for the marvelous. Trowell, "Libretto (ii)," mentions the marvelous and the supernatural only briefly without exploring the literary background of the librettos.

the classicist-modernist controversy. During the seventeenth century marvelous events and characters might occur in any of the four categories, reflecting the continuing connection of magic with nature. At the beginning of the eighteenth century, however, the term "marvelous" merely designated a kind of effect, one created by magical, superhuman, or divine events—an important aspect of certain operas but not a defining quality. By the end of the century, however, magic opera was acknowledged to be a distinct genre by as influential a composer and commentator as Grétry.[2] A new opposition had taken shape: the natural (nonmagical) versus the supernatural (magical).

A number of factors contributed to this new opposition. First, the theater reflected the social and intellectual characteristics of Enlightenment thinkers, whose notion of the natural carried a scientific and ideological association that excluded superstition, magic, and religion. No such clear opposition had existed in the seventeenth century, when magic still could be conceived as allied with nature. Second, some recent additions to the literary canon in Europe led to a new kind of "exotic marvelous" on the stage, specifically fairy tales, fantastic oriental stories, and popular legends. Thus the magical, supernatural, and the marvelous categories grew more distinct from the natural categories in both literary and musical content throughout the century. Mozart's *Die Zauberflöte* (*The Magic Flute*) can serve as an example. Most modern discussions of the genre of this opera offer contrived notions like "Masonic opera" and "magic opera buffa," or stress the mixing of genres.[3] Although mixed genres had a place in eighteenth-century theater, modern discussions ignore the literary background, the theatrical traditions, and the musical conventions that decisively contributed to the character of operas such as *Die Zauberflöte*, which do not fit neatly into any conceivable mixture of heroic, comic, and pastoral types. There is something essential that is missing in this formulation, in regard to both music and librettos. One finds that missing element in a forgotten chapter in the history of music; an investigation of it explains much, including the musical devices created to depict the supernatural in the eighteenth century. These would have a profound impact on musical rhetoric far beyond that of supernatural opera.

✳

The term "marvelous" was first used in the French Renaissance to designate wondrous and exceptional tales, as in the titles of Rabelais's books and the *mer-*

---

2. Grétry, *De la vérité*, 1:18, mentions "la magie" along with "tragédie," "comédie," and "drame" as suitable poetic genres for operas.

3. Jackson, "Palella, Antonio," generically describes *Die Zauberflöte* as a subspecies of *opera buffa* that he calls "'magic' opera." German-language scholarship has placed the opera in an indigenous singspiel tradition. Geyer-Kiefl, *Die heroisch-komische Oper*, sees the opera as an example of a special category mixing the serious and comic genres.

veilleux faicts extolled in French chapbooks. In Italy the "marvelous" (*meraviglioso*) referred to a poetic style associated with Giambattista Marino and meant to inspire wonder and admiration in the listener or reader, literally "to make one marvel."[4] In the seventeenth century this meaning became linked to a category in faculty theories where "marvelous" meant the power to overwhelm reason with wonder and bedazzlement.[5] This power is the essence of the theatrical concept of the "marvelous", an effect on the audience derived from a magical or divine presence or event.[6] Divine events and characters had long been a topic of discussion in literary theory, dating back at least to Aristotle, who allowed them only in epic poetry.[7] During the "Paper War of the Ancients and Moderns" in the seventeenth century, French writers of tragedy such as Racine mostly condemned the theatrical use of the "marvelous" and relegated it to what he regarded as that modern abomination of classical theater called opera.[8] French theorists from the camp of the ancients similarly derided it, notably Boileau, who found little virtue in opera.[9] Thus it is no coincidence that modernists first invoked French fairy tales in order to assert a claim to both modernity and nationalism and to rival the prestige and authority of classical mythology.[10]

Around the turn of the eighteenth century Italian reformers of opera succeeded in almost banishing the "marvelous" in one genre, *dramma per musica*, where it would remain suspect for several decades. But it had an allure that continued to appeal to European audiences. As we shall see, even Italian opera continued to depict the "marvelous," and by the 1750s this element would return decisively to the Italian stage.

The term "marvelous" did not really specify an operatic style before about 1750, although by about 1740 it was being used to describe the difference between spoken tragedy and opera.[11] The meaning changed during a controversy concerning its validity, the War of the Buffoons (1752–54), waged against traditionalists by the encyclopedists and *philosophes*. In the following few years the term carried new associations as two distinct camps took shape, those who condemned the "marvelous" and those who advocated its use. For writers such as Denis Diderot, Jean-Jacques Rousseau, and Friedrich Melchior Grimm,

4. See Mirollo, *Poet of the Marvelous*, 24–25, 117–18, and 166–74 for a summary of the Italian conventions.

5. Jensen, *Muses' Concord*.

6. For example, see Hedelin d'Aubignac, *La pratique du théâtre*. Garlington, *"Le merveilleux,"* 484, discusses this treatise.

7. Aristotle, *Poetics*.

8. See Barthélemy, "L'opéra français."

9. Boileau [Despreaux], "Dissertation sur Joconde,"310–11.

10. Magné, *Crise de la littérature française* and "Le chocolat et l'ambroisie."

11. Saint-Mard, *Réflexions*, uses this term to distinguish lyric from spoken tragedy. It is employed in the same way in Batteux, *Les beaux-arts*. For details, see Kintzler, *Poétique de l'opéra français*, 259ff.

who made up the reformist camp in the French paper wars, the "marvelous" came to mean the supernatural, an illusory, childish, unnatural, and unbelievable effect.[12] Their fellow encyclopedists Louis de Cahusac and Jean-François Marmontel refuted this charge and defended the "marvelous" as a universal topic and an important decorative element.[13] The "marvelous" now became associated with a particular musical style, one linked to scenic decoration. By the time Marmontel first used the phrase *le théâtre du merveilleux* to designate a broad theatrical category of the supernatural that contrasts with "simple nature" (1787),[14] the period of ideological debate about the "marvelous" in France was over. The supernatural had prevailed, as the epigraph to this preface demonstrates.

While these controversies raged, the "marvelous" and the supernatural continued to appear as elements in traditional operatic genres; they actually became the distinguishing characteristics of several newer genres, such as French *féeries,* Italian *fiabe teatrali,* and German *Märchenopern.* These form a distinct tradition that differs from the earlier theater of the "marvelous," with its aristocratic plots derived from mythology, pastorals, and epic romance. While both have archetypal characters, situations, and plots, in the newer genres the stylized and formal language of the older stage traditions gave way to a more direct and simple language. Such works evince more magical thinking, that is to say, irrational beliefs associated with childhood, and they often treat Enlightenment themes with a penchant for supernatural and improbable events in the lives of everyday people. They derive these aspects from a variety of sources, including the more traditional ones (scripture, chivalric romance, pastorals, mythology, and commedia dell'arte), as well as unconventional sources such as oriental literature, fairy tales, and legends, especially devil stories. The new theater of the "marvelous" would also eschew the essential function of the old one—reifying the divine right (*jus divinum*) of the aristocrats who patronized it. Rather, it increasingly came to subvert that ancient ideology and the social order it supported.

This new notion of the "marvelous" also influenced the older traditions of court opera and ballet, in both French and Italian varieties. Composers set newly revised librettos of Philippe Quinault; the "marvelous" returned to Italian opera; Christoph Willibald Gluck's revamped marvelous operas triumphed in Paris; and new, large-scale operatic settings of fairy tales became popular, as did horrific effects in theater music. The "marvelous" regained its place of

12. See Garlington, "*Le merveilleux*"; Grimm, "Poème lyrique"; and Diderot, *Entretiens sur le fils naturel,* 155–56.

13. These two authors treat the term in the *Encyclopédie.* Marmontel wrote the article "Merveilleux" (3:906–8); Cahusac wrote "Ballet" (2:42–46), "Decoration, opéra" (4:701–2), and "Feérie" (6:464). Also see Marmontel, *Poétique françoise,* 2:329 ff., and Cahusac, *La danse ancienne et moderne,* 3:65–71.

14. Marmontel, "Opéra."

prominence on the lyric stage, as evidenced again by the epigraph. Thus the controversies were ultimately resolved in the last quarter of eighteenth century, when the supernatural flourished in all of Europe's operatic venues. Its legacy survived in opera from Weber to Wagner and beyond.

As for music, the Enlightenment's application of new standards for debate and judgment, with the movement's rigorous appeal to "nature," led to a critical separation of music from its earlier magical associations. Composers developed a distinct representational category of magical and supernatural musical topics (or better, perhaps, a musical "decor") that was now distinguished as such in contemporary commentary. Thus, as with librettos, one should differentiate between the general magical character of music prior to the eighteenth century and this new category of the theatrical "marvelous" in the 1750s and beyond. During the late seventeenth and the eighteenth centuries the magical association of music was replaced by a rational view of music as sonic decor for the theater, in which distinct devices were associated with the magical and illusory in musical depiction. Thus the eighteenth century's theater of the "marvelous" acquired characteristic topics in musical rhetoric, with mimetic devices to suggest the fantastic in both vocal and instrumental music.

Cahusac noted the intimate connection of a particular style of music with the "marvelous," which he said required "un ton d'enchantement qui fait illusion . . . une musique qui peint" (1756).[15] Here he draws an important distinction between enchantment per se and an illusory "tone of enchantment," a decorative concept actually linked by Cahusac to painting. In reviewing marvelous and supernatural scenes, one should attempt to identify music that Cahusac might recognize as imparting the illusory tone of enchantment. It is one of the paradoxes of music history that this most mimetic of all musical styles attempts to imitate not nature but the supernatural, reflecting the ambivalence toward the metaphysical in the so-called Age of Reason.

Theatrical Context

The distinctive qualities of the "marvelous" in the eighteenth-century theater had its roots in the previous period. Superhuman events and characters from religion and classical mythology dominated a long tradition of European stage productions made for the aristocracy, such as operas, *feste*, and *azioni*.

Although writers such as Machiavelli and Thomas Hobbes attempted to construct a rational basis for monarchy, the supernatural basis of the aristocratic social system—the divine right—remained fundamentally unchanged. In medieval Christian tradition God assigned individuals to immutable social stations. The investiture of secular power in the Christian emperors belonged to the church, and the divine right of kings came from scripture. When super-

---

15. Cahusac, "Féerie." Cahusac develops this idea in "Ballet" and "Decoration, opéra."

human characters appeared in stage productions for the nobility, they were representations of that same nobility, as they would like to be seen. These characters were also affirmations of the divine authority of the ruling class.

The high-minded stage productions at court, however, stand in contrast with another well-established tradition, the low comic theater derived from the Italian commedia dell'arte. In Paris this tradition was practiced at the Théâtre-Italien and the Théâtre de la Foire; in Vienna, at various theaters that staged comedies. These pieces also had prominent supernatural elements, albeit in a different context. The supernatural aspect there was not an affirmation of the established political order with the high moral rectitude and virtue associated with a divinely invested aristocracy, but one directed more to the everyday world of common people through comedy, parody, and social critique. This kind of comedy stood authority on its head, often by having a supernatural being present magic power as a gift to a powerless character, who then corrected the corruption of the powerful and aided the innocent. Such transformations may have been all but impossible in real life, but they could be imagined when the spirit of the Enlightenment demanded a demonstration of its social and political principles. Owing to the rigid and "unnatural" system of social class, a member of the lower class could affect socially and politically powerful individuals only by having recourse to magic. One finds examples of this kind of supernatural in the ubiquitous musical stage works based on an old story popularized by Charles Coffey's *The Devil to Pay, or the Wives Metamorphosized* (London, 1731). Here a magician transforms two wives, having them wake up in each other's beds. One is an abused but good-hearted peasant, the other an abusive wealthy bourgeoise. One magical event is thus the pivot point of the plot. The middle-class moral depends on magic to effect a demonstration of natural principles. Thus magic is really a rational element in a plot of this type, and the victory of the lowborn can be convincingly achieved only through the intervention of a magic implement given by a powerful magician or sorceress. This is what the eighteenth-century French writers Pierre-Jean-Baptiste Nougaret and Marmontel meant when they asserted that magic could be verisimilar and tell us much about life.[16] While eighteenth-century magic taxed logical explanation, it also furthered rapid social (and sometimes political) change on the stage. The touch of a magic wand reversed the fate of an impoverished prince, and magic could quickly elevate a member of a lower social class and enable him or her to affect events and characters of a higher social order. The use of magic here resulted in some good, either for the characters or for the audience's sense of moral rectitude. Magic imparted social change, and the beneficent fairy, magician, or genie in the eighteenth century was often a divine agent of natural wisdom and justice, an embodiment of the spirit of reason. Only such a character could set an ambitious social experiment into play.

16. Nougaret, *De l'art du théâtre*, 215–18. (Page numbers here and in other citations refer to the 1971 edition.)

The commedia dell'arte was the first genre to widely exploit this use of magic, and it was the first venue for fairy tales and the newer oriental fantasies adapted in the theaters of the Parisian fairs. The new marvelous theater of the eighteenth century soon was a pan-European phenomenon, and older genres began to reflect this spirit, with fairies and genies supplanting mythological beings. Playwrights and librettists treated controversial philosophical themes—for example, the importance of experience versus nature. Critiques of religion favored the worship of nature, the most common expression of which was with romantic love. As the notion of natural magic became a contradiction in terms, Enlightenment thinkers made magic and the supernatural suspect by its association with a corrupt social order that employed illusion and superstition. They associated religious practice, magic, the occult, and superstition with fantasy and childish thinking. But playwrights and librettists transformed both Christian and pagan traditions in popular entertainment. New literary genres such as gothic novels also absorbed the marvelous material of legend and fairy tale, and these in turn influenced the theater.

Opera was originally a creation of the Counter-Reformation, a mixture of pagan mythology and the Christian concept of the "marvelous" that was first developed in epic romance poetry. The French seventeenth-century modernists asserted that the Christian "marvelous" was superior to that of classical antiquity, which had provided a model once thought impossible to equal. French fairy tales, from an unspecified agrarian and prelapsarian past, became the modernists' rival mythology. Then came the demonstration of universal cultural claims in the form of oriental fairy tales. These included tales from Arabia, Persia, China, and even the Americas. With the dissemination of these tales, myth, legend, and fantasy were acknowledged as universal human attributes whose allegories applied to all peoples. Behind this acknowledgment stood the ideology of the Enlightenment and its claim to rationality, cultural universalism, progressivism, and the possibility of human perfection. This claim formed the ideological background to the most important changes in the eighteenth-century concept of the "marvelous."

It is perhaps no coincidence that tales from the Islamic golden age piqued the curiosity of both philosophers and contemporary theatrical audiences. Both cultures shared an admiration for rational thought and attempted to resolve the tension between reason and religious belief in their imaginative literature, where fantasy and magical forces operated freely.

Disregard of the Fantastic on the Stage

Historians often refer to the eighteenth century as the Age of Reason and the Enlightenment, when superstition, the occult, and the supernatural were all but banished, even when Christian in origin. This characterization derives from the writings of the *philosophes*, who saved their most severe criticism for unquestioned belief or magical thinking. But to characterize an age by one ideology, no matter how prevalent, is to distort history. Conflicting and contra-dictory views of religion and secular philosophy existed in the eighteenth century, along with widespread resistance to Enlightenment ideals.

With the secular forces of the Enlightenment removing faith as the final mediation of Christianity, late seventeenth- and eighteenth-century thinkers completed the dissolution of magic from the natural world, a world that was now complete without divinity or magic. But art is distinct from philosophy and theology. Fantasy (a term covering the broadest category of fictive creations of the imaginative faculty that are dependent not on reason but on strangeness and caprice) resonates with audiences as entertainment, even in societies that honor skepticism and shun superstition. Art and literature transform outdated notions into allegory for expressive and aesthetic purposes. The new distinction between the natural and the supernatural allowed for the categories of the "marvelous" and the fantastic in art and literature, categories associated with irrationality and illusion. Mystery, miracle, and magic found a new home in the numinous art of the lyric theater and its music of the "marvelous," where the divinity, the magician, the demon, and the ghost continued to reside, despite their banishment from the real world. The music of the Enlightenment even developed a distinct imagery for the supernatural.

Unfortunately not even a single book has been devoted to this operatic tradition since 1896.[17] Moreover, a number of dubious assumptions in the literature have contributed to an inaccurate view of the "marvelous" and the supernatural:

1. Derisive attitudes toward this kind of fantasy, apparent from the seventeenth century, continue to the present day.[18] Classicists such as Boileau first derided the "marvelous" as vulgar, associating it with childishness and low genres. Critics during the Enlightenment began to savage the aristocratic genres for their use of unbelievable events and characters. The values of these critics have been taken over by modern scholars. More recent values that favor reality-based theater also have worked against a sympathetic reading of this type of material. One should keep in mind that all dramatic arts require the suspension of disbelief. Audiences willingly participate in theatrical illusion and sacrifice the reality principle because fantasy allows for a safe distance from which to broach topics that would be disturbing if presented in a more

---

17. Schmidt, *Zur Geschichte der Märchen-Oper,* is a brief doctoral dissertation discussing only a small portion of fairy-tale operas. More comprehensive treatments of fairy-tale settings deal with a limited repertory, e.g., Crosby, "Fairy Tale." Few of these discussions take broad theatrical traditions into account.

18. E.g., Palisca, *Baroque Music,* 141–42, judges the marvelous in Roman and Venetian opera as "bauble," facilely dismissing it from discussion or analysis. Likewise, Graham Sadler's articles in NGO and his "Rameau," 262, delegates Rameau's opera *Zoroastre* to a lower status simply because it "makes excessive use of the supernatural."

explicit manner due to their uncomfortable social and psychological implications. Many eighteenth-century ruling elites used oppressive tactics to keep civil society in order. Austria (in the eighteenth century still the seat of Holy Roman Empire) and pre-Revolutionary France, for instance, both maintained a stringent police force that exercised tight control, enforcing strict censorship of books and theatrical performances. Vienna, in addition, supported a particularly oppressive religious censorship. Those who held opposing views were thus forced to resort to more subtle means to put across their ideas. The more controversial the topic, the greater the need to distance it from everyday life when presenting it onstage. For this purpose nothing served better than fairy tales and similar fantasies.

2. The false notion that the Enlightenment stage banished the supernatural in favor of the natural and the rational is widespread,[19] thanks to an unquestioning acceptance of the ideological polemics of thinkers like Diderot, Grimm, and Rousseau.[20] In fact the supernatural enjoyed popularity as writers pressed popular fantastic narratives into service as polemics. While the fantastic was being challenged in the religious and political life of the period, it came to be reconstructed in the theater.

The anthropologist Bernard McGrane writes of Enlightenment thought as having divested the non-European of certain demonic qualities, replacing the mere lack of Christian identity with the presence of ignorance and superstition, thus opening a wider door to a view of diverse cultures.[21] Hence it is not surprising that the new marvelous theater of the eighteenth century should treat the exotic cultures of oriental tales, as well as the indistinct agrarian past of indigenous European fairy tales. Both served as an examination of culture itself, a concept created in part by French nationalism in *le grand siècle*. Here magic, superstition, and spirit ruled once again after being banished from the real world, a reality verified only through scientific methods.[22]

The tension between reason and fantasy is one of the characteristic forces

---

19. Modern scholars commonly express this idea, e.g., Bartlet, "Pièce à machines," who notes the "virtual disappearance of magic and gods as prime movers in the action" of opera in the late eighteenth century. Similarly, Heartz, *"Les Lumières,"* 237, states that "Opéra comique inherited from the Théâtre de la Foire a certain amount of magic or mythological content, but the 'merveilleux' receded as the new type of libretto took shape, in favor of common everyday settings and plots."

20. Rousseau, "Opéra," in "Ecrits sur la musique," 948–62. Rousseau's polemics were integrated in historical writing and became accepted as fact by such writers as Charles Burney. Part of his discussion of opera in "The Progress of the Music of Drama," in Burney, *General History*, 555, is a literal translation from Rousseau. (Page numbers here and in other citations refer to the 1935 edition.)

21. McGrane, *Beyond Anthropology*.

22. This new role for magic is evident in Emanuel Schikaneder's citation of Masonic references in *Die Zauberflöte*, which is a somewhat naive attempt to bridge the gap between fantasy and Enlightenment reason. The new concept of the marvelous returned religious and mythological arche-

in the marvelous and magical plots of the eighteenth century, and it attends most theoretical discussions of the topic. It lurks in the theatrical works themselves, where one finds critiques of reason and of magical thinking; a proposed reconciliation of these two seemingly opposing spheres is frequently present in some form.

3. The notion prevails that the libretto and a theatrical work's literary aspect were mere pretexts for the display of masterful musical composition and virtuoso performance. This view has discouraged study of the literary aspect in favor of source studies, formalistic analyses of music, and ideological critiques. All have worked to the detriment of what would have been the most obvious aspects of a work for the stage in the eighteenth century: its literary components, its theatrical efficacy, and its use of musical convention.

4. In twentieth-century scholarship, nationalistic and ideological projects (even some with racial overtones) took precedence over the kind of pan-European view that was needed for a full account of theatrical practice.[23] Although the bases of these views no longer hold sway, some ideas have survived as received wisdom.[24]

5. The classification of fairy tales as "children's literature," "women's narratives," and "folk" material, not products of serious writers and composers but expressions of less sophisticated or even "primitive" art, has been unfortunate and persistent. This view also applies to so-called oriental literature, which has been regarded as exotic and primitive, with consequences for reception comparable to that of the fairy tale.

6. Another common notion equates stage machinery with the term "marvelous." This idea ignores the different functions of magic in court opera, particularly the affirmation of the divine basis of the ancien régime, or the fairy tale's mask of innocence that hides erotic material and biting social commentary.

7. The word *Zauber* continues to be used generically in German scholarship to classify theater works, as in the assertion that the *Zauberstück* descended di-

---

types to the theater in a form closer to the lives of contemporary audiences. More than a recondite subtext, this material evoked popular sentiment as part of the work's dramatic theme.

23. This is apparent in the publications of Otto Rommel and Robert Haas. Rommel's magisterial *Die Alt-Wiener Volkskomödie* evinces a nationalistic agenda and stresses a kind of *Volksgeist* when emphasizing the indigenous German-language singspiel over the clear evidence that German opera was mostly a derivative of Italian, French, and English models. Glossy and Haas, *Wiener Comödienlieder*, xiii, also see German musical theater as an expression of the German *Volk:* "In der 'Zauberflöte' hat dann die Wiener Volkstradition der großen deutschen Kunst eine unvergängliche Blüte beschert, das volkstümliche Theaterlied ist darin dauernd verklärt" (In the *Zauberflöte* the Viennese *Volk* tradition bequeathed an immortal blossoming to great German art; the popular theater song is enduringly transfigured in it).

24. Bauman, *North German Opera*, who provides the most comprehensive study to date on the subject of north German opera, presents evidence of the Italian, French, and English derivation of singspiel. Bauman's book has made a considerable contribution to my discussion of German opera.

rectly from the modern category of "baroque drama" (usually traced to Jesuit school plays).[25] This terminology is based on aesthetic distinctions in art history rather than an understanding of literary sources and musical traditions. The word magic also carries ideological content here, opposing older magic to modern, "enlightened" reason. In reality, these stage works treated contemporary issues rather than merely providing scholars with "baroque" references to decipher centuries later. Discussions of genre in the eighteenth century in fact rarely employed the term *Zauber*. In addition, various other non-German conventions heavily influenced the German "magic" theater, particularly French comedy.[26]

8. In the case of the best known work of this type, Mozart's *Die Zauberflöte*, highly speculative discussions of Masonic and other arcane programs have tended to dominate the treatment of this subject.[27] Many writers have even claimed that the entire topic of the theatrical "marvelous" is irrelevant to the "deeply hidden" meaning of the opera that its creators conspired to conceal.[28]

Thus an important chapter in eighteenth-century opera history has received little attention in modern scholarship. I have written this book to enter the matter into the dialectic of scholarly debate, claiming not a definitive treatment, only a necessary first step. In addition, by delineating the tradition of the "marvelous" as a subject in theatrical music, I hope to make a contribution to our understanding of the general topics of eighteenth-century musical rhetoric.[29]

Objectives, Limitations, Terms, and Organization

My interest in this subject began with research on the literary origins of *Die Zauberflöte* and extended to its musical and theatrical tradition. In a sense this book is an account of the roots and development of those traditions. A substantial section on *Die Zauberflöte* concludes the chapter on Mozart's operas, along with a detailed analysis of the supernatural episodes in the score. As my inves-

25. Rommel, *Die Alt-Wiener Volkskomödie.*

26. This is the subject of Kirk, "Viennese Vogue."

27. These include political, Masonic, Rosicrucian, kabbalistic, and gnostic interpretations, among others. See Emil Karl Blümml, "Ausdeutungen der 'Zauberflöte,'" for an overview. See also Chailley, *La flûte enchantée*, I. Grattan-Guinness, "Counting the Notes"; Nicolas Till, *Mozart and the Enlightenment*, 294–313; Irmen, *Mozart;* and Perrotta, "Gnostiche 'Ethos.'" *Mozart Jahrbuch 1997*, 45–67.

28. Brophy, *Mozart the Dramatist*, 143, refers to the "neutral or nonsensical (the 'fairy-tale') façade presented to outsiders—to cloak an utterance in code." Friedrich, *Die Magie*, asserts that magic was significantly rarer in the eighteenth century than it was earlier. Older accounts such as Abert, *W. A. Mozart*, 2:755–60, give emphasis to the magical *Maschinenkomödie.*

29. Although Ratner, *Classic Music*, offers the most complete account of rhetorical topics in music to date, he does not discuss the marvelous or supernatural.

tigation continued, *Die Zauberflöte* came to assume a smaller role. I found it necessary to argue for a more serious treatment of the eighteenth century's tradition of the "marvelous," demonstrating how fairy tales, legends, and oriental stories influenced theatrical texts in this period. Modern scholarship had not identified important literary sources, neglecting essential distinctions in genre and rarely placing individual works within the appropriate classification. The recurrent themes in these texts also needed to be acknowledged, as did their significant social, intellectual, and aesthetic dimensions.

My treatment therefore begins with literary sources, because this element almost always preceded the music, and because so many more librettos survive than do their musical settings. The most difficult questions here concern the generic classification of this large body of works.[30] At first the variety of loosely related marvelous and fantastic theatrical works seemed difficult to categorize, for new issues regarding the classification kept emerging while I examined the sources. Although contemporary commentary was helpful, I found it more useful to make distinctions based on eighteenth-century concepts: genres such as the fairy story, the false magic story, the fairy tale (the distinction between these types will be discussed later), and, in music, the categories of the "marvelous" and the terrifying.

The supernatural in the eighteenth century was a pan-European phenomenon with strong influences from non-Western sources, for example, the "Arabian Nights." Studies that focus on a single national tradition have limited our understanding and failed to appreciate the many reciprocal influences. This is especially true of French popular theater, whose impact has been consistently underestimated in the secondary literature on opera.

The geographic scope of this study is France, Italy, and German-speaking areas. Although fantasy-related genres were not exclusive to these areas (evidence of their influence may be seen in England, Scandinavia, Spain, Portugal, Greece [Corfu], and eastern European countries), I have focused on those European centers whose primacy for the operatic tradition is well established. A few exceptions have been made for works that influenced this tradition.

The time frame encompasses the period from the late seventeenth century through 1791, the year of Mozart's *Die Zauberflöte*, which I see as a turning point in the history of the "marvelous" on the European stage, one that inaugurated a new and distinct period for the supernatural. With the rapid and broad success of this opera, works of the fantastic proliferated. E. T. A. Hoffmann's view of Mozart as one of the first romantic composers seems especially compelling in regard to this singspiel. The subject of fantastic operas from

---

30. The variety of sources complicates the taxonomic aims of modern scholarship, which too often seems to assume that theoretical constructs precede practice. Eighteenth-century commentators used generic classification mostly for general descriptive purposes and rarely to advance a coherent poetic scheme.

1792 through the early nineteenth century deserves close study, but is beyond the scope of this book.

The introduction reviews the literary, theatrical, and musical background to the theater of the "marvelous" before the eighteenth century. There I delineate the origins of the particular supernatural topics favored by eighteenth-century writers. This material provides general background and is not intended as an exhaustive review. The focus of this book concerns works developed in the eighteenth century, and these receive more detailed analyses. The settings of Greek and Roman myths and of Ariosto's and Tasso's epic poems changed in the eighteenth century, reflecting contemporary influences such as fairy tales; but the plots associated with them were from the seventeenth century, and as such they are not the subjects at hand. The development of supernatural musical conventions is of greater importance for this study. The segments of this book devoted to music explore these conventions in detail.

Chapters 1 through 5 treat the influential operatic traditions of the eighteenth century, French, Italian, and German. Although, for reasons of space, I cannot take up every theatrical work in this period with supernatural content, most of the influential ones find a place here, especially those works that received significant attention by contemporaries. Because the French tradition provided the basic materials for many German and Italian texts, it is the first one I discuss. The broad scope of the discussion demonstrates the extensive use of magic and the supernatural in the eighteenth-century theater, as do the appendices at the end of the book.

Originally I had hoped to restrict myself only to operas, acknowledged even in the eighteenth century as the natural locus of the "marvelous." However, it soon became clear that this limitation was arbitrary and distorted the broader theatrical context provided by comedies, pantomimes, farces, ballets, and even a few relevant "heroic" works. Operas were the lyric expression of contemporary trends in drama and comedy; viewing them in isolation or as mere pretexts for musical expression obscures their literary context.

My approach to music expands the application of the topics in musical rhetoric and examines accepted conventions in musical settings and audience expectations. Like analyzing visual imagery, identifying topics in opera is especially compelling because the text confirms the musical allusions.

A number of closely related terms are used in a restricted manner in the discussions in chapters 1–6. As defined above, the term "fantasy" delineates the broadest category (see p. xvi); the term "magic" suggests mysterious powers from superhuman forces, often but not always malevolent. The "marvelous" designates the effects of wonder and bedazzlement derived from a magical or divine presence or event on the stage; this interpretation changes around 1750, when the supernatural becomes a clear counterpart to the natural, representing all that is magical, divine or superhuman.

I selected the phrase "Magic Flutes and Enchanted Forests" for the title

because these are among the most frequently encountered references in supernatural operas. Both represent some of the conventions inherited from
the seventeenth century. Flutes and recorders have a long history in scenes of
enchantment; composers frequently used them for moments of magic sleep,
spells, trance, and the descent of a deity. The enchanted-forest motif is likewise
commonplace from epic romance, particularly the Armida episode in Torquato
Tasso's *Gerusalemme liberata* (1575), as well as in numerous fairy tales. Other
supernatural topics, such as the Don Juan story, are subsumed within the subtitle of this book.

I have restricted the musical examples to material that is not readily available in modern editions. Thus the discussions of music by Handel, Rameau,
Gluck, Mozart, and Haydn do not include many musical examples. This decision was necessitated by the paucity of music in modern edition by lesser-
known composers and by the number of musical examples required to illustrate aspects of their music.

❋

As theatrical versions of fairy tales enjoyed continued success, they contributed to the broad dissemination of fantastic material and helped to define a national character for several European regions. The violent and vivid depictions of terrifying events often bore the appellation *terribile* (Italian) or *terrible*
(French), and these contributed to the aesthetics of the sublime. The musical idioms associated with terror and the sublime would later be developed in works
like Carl Maria von Weber's *Der Freischütz* and Richard Wagner's *Der fliegende
Holländer;* they also found their way into instrumental music, especially symphonies, overtures, and piano concertos in the minor keys. Beethoven's impassioned and violent expression would not have been possible without the legacy
of the "marvelous" and the terrifying in opera.

The most familiar figures of the fantastic genres survive into the present day in film and literature. The fairy Mélusine, Beauty and the Beast, Cinderella, Aladdin, Sleeping Beauty, Bluebeard, and the sorcerers of the Harry
Potter books remain archetypes in the popular imagination, where *un monde
étrange et de fantaisie* continues to attract audiences. This book is the story of
their birth in the theater and their intimate connection to music.

Acknowledgments

A Professional Development Grant (1996–97) and several Summer Fellowship
Awards from the University of Northern Iowa supported some of the prelimi-
nary research for the book. Wayne State University also provided funds to help
with publication costs. Alena Jakubcová, Kathleen K. Hansell, and Marita P.
McClymonds generously shared the results of their primary source research,
as did Michel Noiray, who advised me on this project from its earliest stages

and provided insights for more than a decade. Our discussions have informed this book in essential ways. He, along with John Rice and Peter Branscombe, read the first draft and provided detailed commentary and critique. John Rice and Marita McClymonds helped immensely on the final draft. Special recognition must go to Kathleen K. Hansell, a dedicated editor who oversaw this project from the first draft to the final manuscript. This book is dedicated to Lucia and to the individuals mentioned above; each steadfastly believed in the value of this project and encouraged me to continue.

ABBREVIATIONS

Secondary Sources

Bauer 1955 Anton Bauer, *Opern und Operetten in Wien*. Wiener Musikwissenschaftliche Beiträge 2. Graz: Hermann Böhlau, 1955.

Bauer-Deutsch Wolfgang Amadeus Mozart, *Mozart: Briefe und Aufzeichnungen*. Edited by Wilhelm Bauer, Otto Erich Deutsch, and Heinz Eibl. 7 vols. Kassel: Barenreiter, 1962–75.

Deutsch Otto Erich Deutsch, *Mozart: Die Dokumente seines Lebens*. *Neue Mozart-Ausgabe*, Series 10, Werkgruppe 34. Kassel: Bärenreiter, 1961.

Hadamowsky Franz Hadamowsky, *Die wiener Hoftheater (Staatstheater), 1776–1966: Verzeichnis der aufgeführten Stücke mit Bestandsnachweis und täglichem Spielplan*. Vol. 1, *1776–1810*. Vienna: Georg Prachner, 1966.

IO *Italian Opera, 1640–1770*. Edited by Howard Mayer Brown and Eric Weimer. New York: Garland, 1977–84.

IOL *Italian Opera Librettos, 1640–1770*. Edited by Howard Mayer Brown and Eric Weimer. New York: Garland, 1978–79.

NGO *The New Grove Dictionary of Opera*. Edited by Stanley Sadie. 4 vols. London: Macmillan, 1992.

Pirker 1927 Max Pirker, *Teutsche Arien, welche auf dem Kayserlich-privilegirten Wienerischen Theatro in unterschiedlich producirten Comoedien, deren Titul hier jedesmahl beigeruket, gesungen worden. Cod. ms. 12706–12709 der Wiener Nationalbibliothek*. Vienna: Strache, 1927.

Rommel 1935 Otto Rommel, *Die Maschinenkomödie*. Deutsche Literatur in Entwicklungsreihen, Reihe Barock, Barocktradition im

Österreichisch-Bayrischen Volkstheater 1. Leipzig, 1935; reprint, Darmstadt: Wissenschaftliche Buchgesellschaft, 1974. (Page numbers refer to the 1974 edition.)

Rommel 1952   Otto Rommel, *Die Alt-Wiener Volkskomödie*. Vienna: Anton Schroll, 1952.

Sartori   Claudio Sartori, *I libretti italiani a stampa dalle origini al 1800*. Cuneo: Bertola & Locatelli, 1990.

Stieger   Franz Stieger, *Opernlexikon*. 4 vols. Tützing: Hans Schneider, 1975.

TdlF   Alain-René Lesage and [Jacques-Philippe] d'Orneval, *Le théâtre de la foire, ou l'opéra-comique . . . aux foires de S. Germain et S. Laurent*. 10 vols. Paris, 1721–37; reprint in 2 vols., Geneva: Slatkine, 1968. (Page numbers refer to the 1968 edition.)

Library Sigla

Note: A = Austria; B = Belgium; D = Germany; F = France; GB = Great Britain; US = United States

A-Wgm	Vienna, Gesellschaft der Musikfreunde
A-Wn	Vienna, Österreichische Nationalbibliothek
A-Wst	Vienna, Stadt- und Landesbibliothek
A-Wt	Vienna, Österreichisches Theatermuseum
B-Bc	Brussels, Conservatoire Royal, Koninklijk Conservatorium
D-B	Berlin, Staatsbibliothek
D-Dlb	Dresden, Sächsische Landesbibliothek
D-F	Frankfurt, Stadt- und Universitätsbibliothek
D-Mbs	Munich, Bayerische Staatsbibliothek
D-Hs	Hamburg, Staats- und Universitätsbibliothek, Carl von Ossietsky
H-Bn	Budapest, Országos Széchényi Kónyvtára, Music Division
I-Fc	Florence, Conservatorio Luigi Cherubini
F-Pn	Paris, Bibliothèque Nationale de France
F-Po	Paris, Bibliothèque-Musée de l'Opéra
GB-Lbl	London, British Library
US-Wc	Washington, D.C., Library of Congress

Theaters

BT	Hofburgtheater (Vienna)
CG	Covent Garden (London)
KT	Kärntnertortheater (Vienna)
KTH	King's Theater, Haymarket (London)

LHT	Little Haymarket Theater (London)
LT	Theater in der Leopoldstadt (Vienna)
PO	L'Académie Royale de la Musique [L'Opéra, Paris]
QT	Queen's Theater, Haymarket (London)
Th.-It.	Théâtre-Italien
WT	Theater auf der Wieden or Wiednertheater (Vienna)

Genres

c	*comédie, commedia*
dg	*dramma giocoso*
dm	*dramma per musica*
K	*Komödie*
kO	*komische Oper*
L	*Lustspiel*
Mk	*Maschinenkomödie*
O	*Oper*
oc	*opéra-comique*
os	*opera seria*
opr	*Operette*
pant	pantomime
rkO	*romantisch-komische Oper*
rO	*romantische Oper*
Sch	*Schauspiel*
spl	singspiel

Appendices

Note: The appendices give the title, genre, composer, theater, and date of premiere, when known, of all sources known to the author.

anon = anonymous
mus. = music by
carn. = carnival
C.-Fr. = Comédie-Française
pant = pantomime
past = *pasticcio*
Th. = Théâtre, Theater
Th.-It. = Théâtre-Italien
tl = *tragédie lyrique*
tm = *tragédie en musique*

Precedents & Sources of Magic & the "Marvelous"

The eighteenth-century theater in Europe inherited material from a variety of sources characterized by fantastic events and superhuman characters, including mythology, religious texts, and what the nineteenth century would call "folklore," a category that refers to narrated and legendary material coming from outside the purely literary sphere. Playwrights and librettists relied heavily on Greco-Roman mythology and classical literature. Homer, Aeschylus, Euripides, Ovid, and Virgil transmitted epics, myths, and pastoral stories featuring superhuman creatures, oracles, and horrific occurrences. The Orpheus legend, with its pastoral setting, chthonic episodes, and intercession of deities, is perhaps the most common Greek myth in opera (Ovid, *Metamorphosis*, books X–XI, and Virgil, *Georgics*, book IV, lines 453–527). Homer's *Odyssey* transmitted in written form the myths of Telemachus, the sorceress Circe, and the hero Ulysses. The sorceress Medea came from the myths of the golden fleece (Euripides, Apollonius's *Argonautica*, and book VII of Ovid's *Metamorphoses*). Ovid and Virgil recounted the myths of Scylla and Glaucus, Hercules, and the Athenian king Theseus. The first two myths include chthonic scenes.[1] The myths of Alcestis (Euripides) and Semiramis (found in various Roman writers) include the appearance of a ghost. The *Oresteia* (Aeschylus) and the story of Iphigenia (Euripides) had Orestes tormented by the Furies. Transformation figured prominently in the myth of Pygmalion, a king of Cyprus who created an ivory figure of a beautiful woman brought to life by Aphrodite. Along with the more somber sacrificial mythology, pastoral and satyr stories also featured transformations, magicians, sorceresses, and superhuman creatures.

1. The Greek-derived term "chthonic" denotes the mythic underworld of classical antiquity. I prefer it here to the Latin-derived "infernal" because of the common association of the infernal with Christian hell (e.g., Dante). The English term "underworld" is more neutral and therefore useful in other contexts.

Traditions from the Middle Ages and the Renaissance

One of the first Western literary traditions of the "marvelous" is that of the satirical writing in ancient Christian and Byzantine literature associated with Menippus, including Petronius's *Satyricon* and Apuleius's *Metamorphoses*, also known as *The Golden Ass*.[2] Menippean satire mixed the past with the present and future, the dead with the living, the real with the unreal, and the underworld with the earthly and upper realms. The uncanny, the unnatural, and the divine are characteristic features of this literature. For example, in his *Enneads* (third century; translated into Latin c. 1480), Plotinus described the magical animation of statues (a device that would reappear in the eighteenth-century theater).

An even more significant medieval tradition is epic romance or chivalric poetry, with its superhuman characters and magicians who both aid and fight knights and crusaders. *Romans de chevalerie*, the *chansons de geste*, and other medieval poems told of fairies, dwarfs, sylphs, gnomes, and genies governing the elements.[3] The literature and fables of the Middle Ages also had fairies such as Viviane, Melior, Mélusine,[4] Manto, Morgana, Morgue, Orva, Urgande, and La Déconnue.[5] Intimacies between imaginary beings and mortals, such as fairies coupling with princes and genies mating with princesses, may have been modeled on similar events in classical mythology. The giants of classical mythology returned in the *romans de chevalrie* and then in popular festival imagery. In local legends their bodies were associated with such natural formations as rivers and islands. Orderic Vital, the eleventh-century Norman historian, recounted the vision of the priest Goshelin, who in 1091 saw the Elf [or Erl] King's army on the march. The Elf King is sometimes described as a giant carrying a mace and leading a procession of the damned. Legends and tales of utopian lands date back at least to the Middle Ages. The *Dit de Cocagne* (Cockayne in early English literature) told of a fabulous land of idleness and luxury. The anonymous thirteenth-century *Aucassin et Nicolette* described a place called Torelore, a world turned inside out where the king bears the children while the

2. Lucius Apuleius of Madaura (born c. 123 A.D.), educated in the Greco-Roman tradition, later turned to the Egyptian occult. His *Golden Ass* is the story of a man transformed by a witch into an ass. After much suffering he is transformed back into his human form when he witnesses an ecstatic vision of the goddess Isis.

3. See Schreiber, *Die Feen;* Maury, *Les fées du moyen-age;* Keightley, *The Fairy Mythology;* Kurtz, *Studies in the Marvelous,* 69–244; and Harf-Lancner, *Les fées au moyens âge.*

4. Mélusine is the fairy of Gaelic legend (Brittany and Poitou). Her legend dates back to an oral tradition, first recounted in the fourteenth-century as a poem by Couldrette and in a prose setting by Jean d'Arras (c. 1387), and was first printed in Geneva in 1478.

5. The fairy Morgana appears in medieval French legends and Arthurian tales. She is the sister of King Arthur and has been instructed in the magic arts by Merlin. She may be derived from Mourgue of "La chronique de Geoffroi de Montmouth." See Storer, *Un épisode littéraire,* 236.

queen fights the wars. Utopias and social inversions continued to be an important theme in literature and theater.

Attempting to synthesize the disparate mystical and legendary traditions of various religions, Renaissance humanists transformed the forbidden magic of the Middle Ages into the somewhat more systematic notion of the "occult." Marsilio Ficino translated the *Corpus Hermeticum*.[6] In his *Liber de nymphes, sylphis, pymaeis et salamandris et de caeteris spiritibus*,[7] Theophrastus Paracelsus (1493–1541) detailed the elemental beings of air, earth, fire, and water as sylphs, gnomes, salamanders, and undines. Henry Cornelius Agrippa's *De occulta philosophia* of 1533 provided the first broad survey of Renaissance magic. In France the Neoplatonist Psellos studied texts on demonology and influenced poets such as Pierre de Ronsard, Giordano Bruno, and Tommaso Campanella. Roger Bacon continued exploring occult subjects.[8] References to occult magic appeared in supernatural episodes of eighteenth-century theater.[9]

Renaissance thought did not separate medicine, astrology, and "natural magic," and the quest to identify the sympathy between phenomena was a goal of Renaissance science. The distinction between sinful, chaotic, ceremonial magic and natural magic allowed the Renaissance commentators to embrace the latter in a manner that medieval thinkers would have found impossible because of the scriptural association of magic with the profane. The figure of the Renaissance *magus* updated the medieval magician and invoked the legendary Arthurian sorcerer Merlin,[10] who operated within the boundaries of Christian morality. From the common street theater of the commedia dell'arte to the

6. The Hermetica, based on the Pythagorian tradition with some gnostic influences, were Neoplatonic writings from the second century A.D. Hermes, the putative author of over a dozen treatises, claims to expound the mysteries of the Egyptians in the period of Moses. Although Moses received the sacred revelations, the Egyptians were the custodians of secular wisdom and divine revelations about the physical world. Hermes' heliocentric universe names light and the sun as the source of life. The secret forces of magic are available to a chosen few initiated into the world beyond surface phenomena. See Koyré, *Mystiques, spirituels, alchemistes*, and Yates, *Giordano Bruno*.

7. *Werke Theophrastus Paracelsus*, ed. Will-Erich Peuckert (Basel/Stuttgart: Schwabe [1964–68]) 5, *Panophische magische und gabalische Schriften*.

8. For a discussion of Renaissance magic, see Walker, *Spiritual and Demonic Magic*, and Garin, "Magic and Astrology," Garin, *Science and Civic Life*. A discussion of musical aspects of the magical occult in the Renaissance may be found in Tomlinson, *Music in Renaissance Magic*.

9. References to cabalistic magic occur in *Le Comte de Gabalais et les peuples élémentaires*, a divertissement by Pierre-François Godard de Beauchamps (Sceaux, 1714); *La statue merveilleuse*, by Lesage (Paris, 1719); *Le jeune vieillard*, by Louis de Fuzelier, Alain-René Lesage, and Jacques-Phillipe d'Orneval (Paris, 1722); *Roger de Sicile, surnommé le roi sans chagrin*, by Lesage and d'Orneval (Paris, 1731); and *Ninna*, an anonymous two-act Italian pantomime (Paris, 1747).

10. The Renaissance *magus* believed his tradition dated back to distant antiquity. Most of his sources in fact date no earlier than the second century A.D.

sumptuous operas and ballets of the royal courts, the magician was to become a familiar figure on the stage.

✳

Epic French and German poems transmitted medieval chivalry to Renaissance Italy. Rusticiano of Pisa refashioned the French *Tristan* and *Palamède* into the *Meliadus* in 1275, and Dante and his contemporaries mentioned characters from French chivalric romance. Epics were turned into prose and abridged during the fourteenth century, then printed beginning in the fifteenth century.[11] The fascination at Italian courts with Carolingian legends inspired a new interpretation of medieval chivalric fantasy in epic romance poetry. These sources provided the heroes, fairies, and supernatural beings that peopled the epic poems of the late fifteenth and the sixteenth century. Similar characters also appeared in Spanish and Portuguese sources as well as in fantastic Italian tales, particularly the publications of Straparola and later Basile.[12]

Two medieval French poems, *Renaus* (Rinaldo) and *Aspremont*, were especially important influences on the Italian tradition. Arthurian legends also supplied enchantments, magicians, superhuman creatures, and magic objects.[13] Early Italian versions of the Roland legend include Luigi Pulci's mock-heroic *Il Morgante maggiore* (Florence, 1483). Here the naive and loyal giant Morgante displays brute force and voracious appetites. Pulci contrasts Morgante with the evil and cynical semi-giant Margutte. Teofilo (Girolamo) Folengo's macaronic poem *Baldus* (Venice, 1511, written under the suggestive pseudonym Merlini Cocai), typifies the Italian heroic-comic tradition. This poem, mixing legend with history and mythology, included fairies, giants and other fantastic beings. François Rabelais drew freely on the same material.

Italian epic poetry reinterpreted medieval romance, offering the same sprawling series of adventures, coincidences, and surprises. Idealized quests were at the center of long, convoluted plots, whose themes revolved around love, illusion, and magic. Heroes found themselves lost, then enchanted, as they searched for a person or a precious object such as the Holy Grail. Parts of these poems were serviceable as theatrical plots.[14] Struggles with giants for the prize of a beautiful nymph, appearances by demons and dwarfs, and transport to an enchanted palace became the subjects of the French court ballets in the late sixteenth century.

---

11. See Doutrepont, *Les mises en prose des épopées*.

12. Giovanni Francesco Straparola's *Piacevoli noti* (Venice, 1550–53; Rome/Bari: Gius. Laterza, 1975) is the first large Renaissance collection of fairy tales. Basile, *Il pentamerone*, written in a Neapolitan dialect, was an influential source in the eighteenth century.

13. See Gardner, *Arthurian Legend*.

14. See Mamczarz, "Quelques aspects," 189; Barbier, "La pastorale," 270; and Champion, *Ronsard*, 209–10.

Three Italian epic romance poems from the Renaissance provided basic materials for marvelous ballets and operas: Matteo Boiardo's *Orlando inna-morato,* Ludovico Ariosto's *Orlando furioso,* and Torquato Tasso's *Gerusa-lemme liberata.* A fourth source was Spanish-Portuguese in origin, Garcí Ro-drêguez de Montalvo's *Amadis.* Boiardo combined a complex web of materials in the sixty-nine stanzas of his enormous unfinished epic *Orlando innamorato* (Ferrara, 1482–83). Drawn from history and from legends surrounding Char-lemagne's defense of Christian Europe against Islam, the poem tells of the love of the austere Christian knight Orlando for the beautiful Angelica, a princess from Cathay (India). Among the numerous subplots are those of Ruggiero, the pagan king fated to become a Christian in spite of the efforts of the magi-cian Atlante, and of Ranaldo (= Rénaud, Rinaldo) and his sister Brandiamante (= Bradamante). The poem includes mythical creatures, magic devices, and the ogres and monsters of Greek and Celtic origin.

Many of Boiardo's characters and events reappeared in Ludovico Ariosto's *Orlando furioso* (Ferrara, 1516–32),[15] which combined classical sources, Car-olingian and Celtic legends, and contemporary references. Ariosto included three evil practitioners of magic among his cast of characters: the sorcerer At-lante and the sorceresses Alcina and Morgana (he mentions the magician Zoro-astro in canto 31). Atlante, Ruggiero's supporter, holds captive all the beautiful women of his region in an enchanted castle. Mounted on his flying hippogriff, he carries a magic shield that renders unconscious those who are struck by its beam. Both of these magical items will be taken and used against him by Bra-damante, who possesses a magic ring that counteracts all other magic spells and can render its wearer invisible. She gives Atlante's hippogriff and shield to her beloved Ruggiero, who is transported to the island of the beautiful Alcina. The fairy Melissa (Bradamante's protector), in the disguise of Atlante, rescues Ruggiero. Logistilla, who like Melissa is a beneficent sorceress, teaches him to master the hippogriff. Merlin is the last of the three good magicians Ariosto in-cluded to balance the three evil masters of sorcery.

Ariosto's mythical beings are ghosts, giants, demons, sprites, monsters, sea and land orcs, and fantastic (sometimes winged) horses. Magic implements in-clude swords, armor, Atlante's shield, a ring that counteracts other spells or renders its wearer invisible, a horn whose sound renders all hearers helpless with terror, a net that entraps its victim with the slightest touch, a liquor that makes one invincible, a golden spear that guarantees victory in battle, an herb that restores sight to the blind, and a book that can be used to conjure demons and sprites.

The most concentrated episode of sorcery is that of the evil enchantress Al-cina, who captures men in her enchanted palace and hides her ugliness behind a seductive spell of beauty (cantos 6–8). Quasi-historical characters such as

---

15. Ariosto, *Frenzy of Orlando.* On the influence of *Orlando* on the French theater, see Roth, *Der Einfluss.*

Ginevra, the daughter of the king of Scotland, also appear in operas, but they need not be associated with the supernatural. At the end, the descent into hell of Rodomonte, the king of Algiers, prefigures the later *Don Juan* comedy.

Torquato Tasso's *Gerusalemme liberata* (1575) is a rhymed stanzaic epic poem from the period of the Counter-Reformation. Although Tasso reduces religion mainly to external processions, preaching, and acts of contrition, the conflicts in the complex plot reflect both the battles with the Turks and the Roman Catholic conflict with the Protestants.[16] The crusades of the Middle Ages served Tasso as a parallel to the Counter-Reformation. Thus Tasso's poem is more theological than Ariosto's epic. His heroes seek to separate falsity and illusion from (theological) truth.

Set during the First Crusade, when Christian knights attempted to recapture Christ's sepulcher from Islamic control, Tasso's epic constructs a web of fantastic elements. Ismeno, a renegade Christian, becomes a sorcerer and steals the miraculous statue of the Virgin, placing it in a mosque in order to protect the Muslim status of Jerusalem. In the course of events and with numerous battles, Satan spreads his demons to thwart the Christian advances. One of these demons approaches the Syrian sorcerer Idraote, suggesting that he send his beautiful niece Armida to charm the knights through magic. The Saracen sorceress succeeds in seducing those knights who are unattached to a specific feudal lord and imprisons them in her castle. Ismeno creates an enchanted forest populated with shrieking devils. No one but Rinaldo can penetrate it without falling into a terrible state of fear. A Christian sorcerer informs the knights that Rinaldo is being held in the magic garden of Armida's island of pleasure. They venture forth to retrieve him. Showing him his own image and family history in an enchanted shield, they shame him into returning with them. Armida begs him to stay, and when he refuses she destroys the magic garden and flies away in her chariot. With the help of the Christian sorcerer, Rinaldo liberates the enchanted forest. The poem ends with Armida's conversion to Christianity after being dissuaded from suicide by Rinaldo.

Borrowing directly from Ariosto, whom Tasso admired, *Gerusalemme liberata* has similar supernatural elements: infernal spirits, sorcerers (Ismeno, Ascalon), sorceresses, a magic chariot, a magic shield, and an enchanted forest. Like Alcina, Armida traps Tancred in a magic garden and palace. The Arabic name Almanzor also appears here, a name that became common in theatrical fairy tales of the eighteenth century.

Amadis is a pseudo-medieval legend based on Spanish and Portuguese sources and recounted in a chivalric romance by Nicolas Herberay des Essarts. The legend was expanded in a novel by Garcí Rodrêguez de Montalvo (c. 1470) and others who continued Montalvo's four books after his death (the number rose to twenty-five books by 1615). *Amadis de Gaula* (the 1540 French translation) tells the story of Amadis, the son of King Perion of France. Amadis ex-

---

16. Tasso, *Jerusalem Delivered*.

periences numerous encounters with various enchantments, including that of the sorceress Urganda, in his efforts to obtain the hand of his beloved Princess Oriana, the daughter of the English King Lisuarte.

In the Renaissance, pastoral genres, based on models from classical mythology, were related to epic poetry.[17] With their amorous initiation of innocents, pastoral plots often included magical events and superhuman characters.

Fables and Tales

Superhuman and magical elements were common in popular literature as well as in "high" literary genres. The popular literary tradition derived material from legends, fables, fairy tales, and oriental collections, all of which appealed less to the literary inclinations of the highly educated elite than to those attracted to lighter entertainment.[18] Until the rise of the chapbook (a modern term for small volumes of popular tales, ballads, and the like, sold by traveling dealers called chapmen), such works were usually written or published only after the higher classes had taken an interest in them. Giovanni Boccaccio's *Decameron* (Florence, 1351–53) figures among the most celebrated examples derived from popular tradition. The collection comprises a hundred *novelle* (short stories) told by seven young women and three young men, ten on each day, to amuse themselves as they remain outside of Florence in an attempt to escape the Black Death (c. 1348). The *Decameron* (the title was derived from a Greek compound meaning "ten days") is a diversionary set of stories narrated in an elevated, literary Italian. It offers satire on love, fortune, ingenuity, and the vices. Boccaccio mixes tragic and heroic themes in a human comedy where the divine and the "marvelous" are as much an object of awe as of folly.

Collections of tales in imitation of Boccaccio's proliferated in Italy. Giovanni Francesco Straparola's tales from Venice were especially significant (see below). Short tales and fables were also common in France in the sixteenth century (Rabelais) and the seventeenth (La Fontaine). Niccolò Machiavelli's *Novella di Belfagor arcidiavolo* (before 1520) provides a good example of a fantastic tale thought to be of Asian origin. In this early comic devil story the archdemon Belfagor is sent to Earth after an infernal council to determine whether marital life is really as terrible as the condemned souls report it to be. After he experiences it firsthand, he decides to return to hell for an easier existence.

Cheaply produced prints of anonymous popular literature began to be widely disseminated by about 1550, and this *littérature du colportage* persisted until the middle of the nineteenth century.[19] The *merveilleux faicts* of medieval chivalric romances were among the most common stories in French chap-

17. Greg, *Pastoral Poetry;* and Poggioli, *Oaten Flute.*

18. Delaporte, *Du merveilleux,* 10ff.; and Christout, *Le merveilleux et le "théâtre du silence,"* 280–304.

19. Nissard, *Histoire.* See also Andries, *La bibliothèque bleue.*

books, where Huon de Bordeaux, Holger the Dane, Roland, and Pierre de Province were familiar heroes. German-speaking areas and England preferred the darker legend of Faust.[20] Utopian stories such as *le pays de Cocagne* and Hans Sachs's *Schlaraffenland* were also the subjects of popular literature and fable. Mikhail Bakhtin has observed that chapbooks transmitted many similar adventures, especially *Guyon de Bordeaux* and the *Travels and Voyages of Panurge, Pantagruel's Disciple, to Unknown and Wondrous Islands* (1537). In his version of the Pantagruel story and in his *Gargantua* of 1534 (based on chapbooks such as *The Great Chronicles of Gargantua* [1532] and Folengo's poem *Baldus* [1517]), François Rabelais recounts numerous tales of magic and exotic lands, such as *L'isle sonnante* (book 5). Gargantua is a giant created by Merlin, and Pantagruel is a devil who became Gargantua's son in Rabelais's account. Rabelais turns popular legends into symbolic satires with carnivalesque imagery,[21] inverting the social order in a *monde renversé* where gluttony and idleness are held in high esteem, virtues are considered sinful, and authority is stood on its head. This "low literature" of Europe's fairs and carnivals also left its mark on the popular Italian theatrical tradition, the commedia dell'arte. These in turn return to the anonymous *littérature du colportage*, such as *The Gay Story of the Feats and Adventures of the Italian Comedian, Harlequin* (Paris, 1585), where the dreams and visions of Arlequin include a descent into hell.

Aside from occasional stories found in chronicles, histories, almanacs, and other periodical literature, the earliest fairy-tale collections published in Europe come from Italy. The largest Renaissance collection is Straparola's *Piacevoli notti* (2 vols., Venice, 1550–53).[22] Straparola (perhaps a pen name) drew upon numerous sources, including Apuleius, Brevio, and the Neapolitan Girolamo Morlino, the author of some eighty Latin tales. At least fifteen fairy tales among the seventy-three stories here show close similarities with those from Arabian, Persian,[23] and other distant sources not widely disseminated in the West until the eighteenth century.[24] These use plot elements later found in "Beauty and the Beast," "The Talking Bird," "Riquet à la Houpe" (*notte* 2, *favola* 1), "Puss-in-Boots" ("Soriana," *notte* 11, *favola* 1), and "Peau d'Ane" ("Tebaldo," *notte* 1, *favola* 4). Straparola characterizes this writing as literature in the "low style," claiming nothing in regard to the originality of their invention. Each tale (called a *fabula docet*) has a clear moral. In Straparola's stories we

20. For example, Spiess, *Historia*, and Christopher Marlowe, *Dr. Faustus* (1594, 1604, 1616).

21. Bakhtin, *Rabelais*, introduced the concept of the "carnivalesque," where inversions of the normative social structures were commonplace. Bakhtin cites carnival parades of the sixteenth century that featured the fantastic images of monsters, dragons, palaces, carnivorous devils, and giants.

22. Straparola, *Facetious Nights*. For recent research on the context of Straparola's tales, see Mazzacurati, "La narrativa di G.F. Straparola," and Bottigheimer, "Straparola's *Piacevoli Notti*."

23. Armeno expresses the Venetian interest in fantastic Persian tales in his *Peregrinaggio*.

24. See the notes by W. G. Waters in Straparola, *Facetious Nights*, 4:277–309. (Page numbers here and in other citations refer to the 1909 edition.)

find almost all of the major elements of the later fairy tale, including enchanted animals, magic rings, the dead returned to life, devils, witches, fairies, wizards, and astrologers. Like Boccaccio's *Decameron* and other collections of *novelle*, *Piacevoli notti* has a frame story. Immensely successful, the *Piacevoli notti* occasioned some twenty editions before it fell out of favor. In 1624 it was placed on the Inquisition's Index Librorum Prohibitorum. Its legacy continued into the next century with Basile's Neapolitan tales and *contes de fées*, which became popular at the end of the seventeenth century in France.

The Seventeenth Century

Belief in magic became less prevalent in learned circles as the scientific revolution challenged belief in the occult. The influence of the Protestant Reformation contributed to this attenuation as well. John Calvin furthered the dissolution of the mystical mediation of Catholicism, reducing that mediation to a single item, faith, and opposing it to superstitious belief. Weber described this principle as a "disenchantment of the world" that created a new kind of natural order no longer penetrated by divine beings and forces.[25] This world was verified only by science, which dissolved the connections Renaissance humanism had attempted to synthesize among religion, pagan mythology, mysticism, and science. Although the uneducated majority of Europe's population in the seventeenth century continued to believe in prophecy, witchcraft, magic, and conjuring,[26] the scientific literature of the seventeenth century became independent of magic and the occult, leaving the supernatural to fantastic literature.

One minor genre of this kind of literature would prove significant in later years: Italian fairy tales. Giambattista Basile's *Lo cunto de li cunti, overo Lo trattenemiento de li peccerille* (The Story of Stories or the Entertainment of the Little Ones) is the second major collection of fairy tales published in Europe. The original (Naples, 1634–36) is in Neapolitan dialect; a translation by the Apulian priest Pompeo Sarnelli into standard Italian appeared as *Il Pentamerone, ossia La fiaba delle fiabe* (The Five Days, or The Fable of Fables [Naples, 1674]). This wording refers to the frame story, wherein a Moorish slave girl usurps the place of a princess. After her marriage to the prince, ten different women entertain the newlywed couple, each telling one story for five consecutive days (making fifty in all). The rightful princess narrates the fiftieth tale on the last day (her own true story) and wins back her rightful position.

The original title is one of the earliest references to fairy tales as children's literature. The elevated language of Boccaccio is less apparent in Basile's prose, and oriental fantasy and magic are more pronounced than in the tales of Stra-

---

25. See Weber, *Sociology of Religion* and *Protestant*. Also see Berger, *Sacred Canopy;* and Thomas, *Religion and the Decline of Magic.*

26. See Bila, *La croyance à la magie;* Cocchiara, *History of Folkore*, 45–67; and Friedrich, *Die Magie im französischen Theater.*

parola. Among these tales are stories that will appear in Perrault's French collection at the end of the century and will provide plots for comedy, ballet, and opera:

1. "Sole, luna e talia" (day 5, no. 5) = "La belle au bois dormant"
2. "La gatta Cenerentola" (day 5, no. 6) = "Cendrillon"
3. "Ninnillo e Nennella" (day 5, no. 8) = "Le petit poucet"
4. "Cagliuso" (day 2, no. 4) = "Le chat botté"
5. "Le tre fate" (day 3, no. 10) and "Le due pizzette" (day 4, no. 7) = "Les fées"
6. "L'orsa" (day 2, no. 6) = "Peau d'âne"

The land of Cockaigne is mentioned in "Le sette cotennine" (day 4, no. 4).

Basile's translator, Pompeo Sarnelli, published a guide to regions around Naples that recounted local fairy tales, legends, and stories associated with various sites and monuments.[27] Some of these tales—for example *L'augel belverde*—were adaptations of Basile's stories. In their turn, Sarnelli's stories provided Carlo Gozzi with some of the motifs in his theatrical tales of the 1760s.[28]

Magic and the "Marvelous" in French Literature

French sources often drew a distinction between the Christian "marvelous" and its pagan counterpart, with its demonology, witchcraft, spirits, oracles, and tales attributed to midwives. In his *Démonomanie des sorciers* (1581) Jean Boudin claimed that thousands of sorcerers were active in France, and Gabriel Naudé (1625) provided a catalog of illustrious individuals who practiced magic.[29] In his popular novel *Le Comte de Gabalis, ou Entretiens sur les sciences secrètes* (1671),[30] Nicolas-Pierre-Henri Montfaucon de Villars derived information on elemental beings from Paracelsus's *Liber de nymphes, sylphis, pymaeis et salamandris et de caeteris spiritibus*. Montfaucon's book delineates intermediary or elemental beings; it is the source of Pope's sylphs in *The Rape of the Lock* and numerous other literary works.[31] The Silesian mystic Jakob Böhme (1545–1624) transmitted the same material to German readers in his *Aurore, oder Morgenröte im Aufgang* (1634; frequently reprinted up to 1730).[32]

---

27. Sarnelli, *Posilecheata*. Sarnelli used the name Mesillo Reppone in this publication.

28. See chapter 4 and Calvino, *Italian Folktales*.

29. Naudé, *Apologie*.

30. Montfaucon de Villars, *Le comte de Gabalis*.

31. Seeber, "Sylphs and Other Elemental Beings." The false-magic comedy *La pierre philosophale*, by Thomas Corneille and J. Donneau de Visé (1681), makes references to Gabalis, and it also influenced Nodot in his *Histoire de Mélusine*.

32. Böhme, *Sämtliche Schriften*, vol. 1.

Although sixteenth-century French literature and theater alluded to super-human characters from medieval sources (the fairy Mélusine was mentioned by Rabelais, and fairies and magicians commonly appear in plays), the pastoral novels, fables,[33] and theater of the *grand siècle* show evidence of a renewed interest in these subjects. Mythology and chivalric romance suited the refined interests of the social world of the salon to which this literature appealed.

Six French translations of Ariosto's *Orlando furioso* were published between 1554 and 1615.[34] The themes from epic romance continued to have currency in European literature, and seventeenth-century French writers borrowed heavily from the magical aspects of epic romance and pastoral poetry. In his pastoral novel *L'astrée* (Paris, 1618–27),[35] Honoré d'Urfé described a magic fountain and a magic mirror, drawn from the poetry of Ariosto and his contemporaries.

Although fantastic oriental literature was first widely published in the early eighteenth century, European knowledge of Asian cultures was clearly evident well before this time.[36] Oriental stories were available in the late Middle Ages through sources such as the twelfth-century *Roman des sept sages*.[37] By the seventeenth century there was a growing interest in the Orient as an exotic counterpart to European society. Both real and imaginary recollections of voyages were popular reading,[38] for example Jean-Baptiste Tavernier's trip to Turkey (1676) and John Chardin's voyages to Persia and the Indies (1686). The first mandarins arrived in Paris in 1684, and in that same year Giovanni Paolo Marana's *Espion turc* enjoyed an enormous success.[39] Charles Dufresny's *Les amusements sérieux et comiques d'un Siamois* (Paris: C. Barbin, 1699) depicted the diversions of Siamese culture shortly before the publication the *Arabian Nights*.[40] Jean de La Fontaine drew upon Ariosto, Boccaccio, Machiavelli, and others in his *Contes et nouvelles en vers* (1664; reprinted in 1665, 1666, 1671, and 1674) and his *Fables choisies, mises en vers* (1688). Writers adapted a few of La Fontaine's stories for theatrical works.[41]

The knowledge of earlier Italian fairy tales and oriental stories, acquired

33. Particularly in the fables of La Fontaine and La Motte. For details see Delaporte, *Du merveilleux*. For information on François de la Moche Fénelon's late seventeenth-century fairy-tale fables (pub. 1721), see Storer, *Un épisode*, 257, 266.

34. Mamczarz, "Quelques aspects," 187.

35. D'Urfé, *L'astrée*. The magic mirror also appears in d'Urfé's five-act verse setting with choruses of the *fable bocagère Silvanie, ou la morte vive* (Paris, 1627).

36. Dugat, *Histoire des orientalistes;* Martino, *L'orient;* and Dufrenoy, *L'orient romanesque*.

37. Misrahi, *Le roman des sept sages;* also *Les sept sages de Rome;* and *Le roman des sept sages de Rome: A Critical Edition*.

38. Hazard, *La pensée européenne*, 14–18.

39. Martino, *L'orient dans la littérature française*, 284.

40. Galland, *Les mille et une nuits* and *Les mille et une nuits: Contes arabes*.

41. For example, *La fée Manto, ou Le chien qui secoue des pierreries*, an anonymous one-act pantomime (St. Laurent, 15 August 1746), based on a *conte* by La Fontaine, "Le petit chien qui secoue

through trade, colonial ties, and political contacts, seems to have influenced the earliest *contes*.[42] Thus one cannot always make a clear distinction between "indigenous" European stories and those from outside the continent. In his *Lettre sur l'origine des Romans* (1670) Pierre-Daniel Huet represents fairy tales as expressions common to all eras and peoples.[43] Although references to *contes de fées* and *contes de la mère l'oye* occur throughout the seventeenth century, French fairy tales seem to have remained an oral tradition until the 1690s, when publishers first printed collections for the Paris court and the salon society.[44]

Chivalric romance remained the most popular genre in chapbooks. The Mélusine legend appeared in these popular publications beginning in 1624.[45] Parodies of chivalric novels were first published as early as 1675. One finds no actual fairy tales or oriental stories in surviving chapbooks before the eighteenth century, although such publications were ephemeral, and not all of the prints survive.

Most European fairy tales derive from the popular French collections printed for the educated reader. These are the sources that were frequently

---

de l'argent des pierreries." For a list of theatrical adaptations of La Fontaine's *contes* and fables see Brenner, *Dramatization of French Short Stories*, 6–13.

42. See Shah, *La magie orientale*, and Schuhl, *Le merveilleux*. Examples of authors claiming direct influences include d'Aulnoy, who claimed to have heard the story of *Finette Cendron* from an "old Arabian slave." A seventeenth-century manuscript today housed in Paris, Bibliothèque de l'Arsenal (Ms. 3186: *Ouvrages de Monsieur L. de Choisy qui n'ont pas été imprimés*), contains an oriental story entitled *L'histoire de la princesse Aimonette*. See Mazon, "Une collaboration inattendue." For details see Martino, *L'orient dans la littérature française*, and Storer, *Un épisode*, 224–25, 248–51.

43. Pierre-Daniel Huet, *Traité de l'origine de Romans* (Paris: Claude Barbin 1670; reprint, Stuttgart: Metzler, [c. 1966]; modern ed., Paris: Nizet, 1971).

44. Storer, *Un épisode*, offers a chronology of French fairy-tale publications from 1690 to 1923. The earliest of these include L'Héritier [de Villandon], *Œuvres meslées;* d'Aulnoy, *Les contes des fées* and *Contes nouveaux;* Bernard, *Inés de Cordoue;* La Force, *Les contes des contes;* Perrault, *Histoires ou contes* (later editions used the term *Contes de ma mère l'Oye*); Castelnau, *Contes des fées* and *Nouveaux contes des fées;* Le Chevalier de Mailly, *Les illustres fees;* and Préchac, *Contes moins contes.*

45. The prose setting by Jean d'Arras (c. 1387) was first printed in Geneva in 1478 and reprinted in the sixteenth and the seventeenth centuries. The Geneva edition of the poem was reprinted twice, in 1677 in Troyes and in 1692. Early seventeenth-century prints include chapbooks such as *Mélusine* (Troyes: N. Oudot, 1624) and an anonymous "novel" by one M. L. M. D. M., *Le roman de Mélusine* (Paris: 1637). Salvaing de Boissieu, *Septem Miracula Delphinatus: Gratianoploi* (1656), includes a Latin poem titled "Melusina." Two publications of the Mélusine legend based on Jean d'Arras survive in the *Bibliothèque bleue de Troyès* (Paris, 1677 and 1692). The version by Jean d'Arras was also published in the setting arranged by Nodot (cited above). Early French fairy-tale collections also mention Mélusine, especially Prechac and Catherine Bédacier (Madame Durand). For details, see Storer, *Un épisode*, 231–32.

translated, providing the models that later writers would use for more ambitious literary projects. The most popular of these collections was Charles Perrault's *Histoires ou contes du temps passé* (1697). The context for Perrault's collection was France's burgeoning nationalism under Louis XIV and the assertion of equality with the prestige of classical antiquity in the Quarrel of the Ancients and the Moderns. The Quarrel centered on several literary issues. The novel was the most important of the modern genres in dispute, but the value of *contes* was also debated. Writers first invoked the tales as narrations from the postclassical world, much like medieval romance, and *contes* would serve as examples of an indigenous French mythology to rival that of classical antiquity.

The earliest French publications designated these stories as an old tradition of oral narrative whose natural milieu was the nursery, where "grandmothers and wet nurses" recounted fantastic moralizing tales to children. The common generic name for such tales in the seventeenth century, well before any publication appeared with that name, was *contes de ma mère l'Oye* (Mother Goose stories).[46] Asserting an obscure, ancient heritage in their first published collections, Perrault and Mademoiselle L'Héritier also made claims to modernity and appeals to nationalism.

Basile's characterization of fairy tales as children's literature in the title of his collection (1634) found an echo in France. Madame de Sévigné recommended them as narratives for children, and in 1677 she wrote of *contes* at Versailles; one of these has a setting on the Green Island, where a beautiful princess was raised by fairies.[47] Both Perrault and L'Héritier specify *contes* as narratives for children, and L'Héritier indeed recounts that she herself heard them as a child. The first print to use the title was the Comtesse d'Aulnoy's *Les contes des fées* (Paris, 1696). Supporting the notion of fairy tales as "children's literature" is the didactic moral found in most stories,[48] along with stereotypical, one-dimensional characters (either good or evil), the use of magical thinking, and a simple language stripped of the refinements associated with more sophisticated literature such as pastoral stories. French fairy tales, usually set in some vague, prehistoric agrarian past, evince a tone of nostalgia for a lost age of innocence.

The marvelous aspect in a fairy tale often differs from that in classical mythology, chivalric romance, and the pastoral genres. Mythological and heroic plots offered meditations on use of the divine right of kings; representations of magic and the supernatural in these plots reflect that power. If it was an admonishing or moralizing plot, aristocratic characters might function maliciously,

---

46. Delaporte, *Du merveilleux*, 33, 38–39; and Storer, *Un épisode*, 9–17, 224–59.

47. Sévigné, *Lettres*, 2:320 (6 August 1677).

48. Morals were acknowledged even in the earliest French sources. For details, see Storer, *Un épisode*, 225 ff.

reminding the audience or reader of the responsibilities of the ruling elite that are attendant upon divine right. (Perhaps the best example of this kind of plot is the Don Juan story.) By contrast, fairy tales usually are not closely linked to religion and the aristocracy and contain far less of this kind of allegory.

The origin and function of fairy tales remains a matter of speculation and differing opinion. Writers influenced by psychoanalytic thought, anthropology, and folklore continue the universalistic view, considering fairy tales an archetypal form of narrative that transcends individual cultures. They date the earliest sources back to ancient Egypt.[49] Folklore studies offer divergent theories on the origins and transmission of narrative tales. Stith Thompson's research offers an impressive account of themes and elements from across a broad cultural spectrum,[50] supporting the theory that fairy tales present a common set of archetypal characters and plots in diverse periods and geographic areas.

Recent commentary associated with the "new historicism" has challenged the universalistic view by pointing to a more specific social context that accounts for both characters and plot. Although authors of fairy tales claimed that their stories were transmitted by peasant wet nurses to the children of the higher classes, "new historicists" remind us that fairy tales actually flourished in the precious world of the late seventeenth- and eighteenth-century salon. The reading aloud of tales in salons was a cultivated form of social activity for the upper classes. Robert Darnton, who draws a distinction between orally transmitted peasant stories and those published beginning in the late seventeenth century,[51] notes that villagers' oral narratives depict the brutal world of the peasant, with no real view of childhood in mind. Nor is there any trace of a sympathetic, patient narration by parents or guardians. Their stories offer few of the morals that Perrault provided and even fewer of the abstractions that the *philosophes* embedded in their *contes*.

No doubt daily existence in a French village was distinct from aristocratic and even bourgeois life in Paris. But because no collections of peasant stories from this time have survived, there is little concrete evidence that the stories created for the entertainment of Parisians were drastically different from those of peasants. Darnton's suppositions about the nature of seventeenth-century peasant stories are highly speculative and are based on accounts of peasant life

---

49. For bibliographical studies of research on the fairy tale, see Röhrich, *Sage und Märchen;* Ranke et al., *Enzyklopädie;* Lüthi, *European Folktale;* Grätz, *Das Märchen*. Recent studies include Barchilon, *Le conte merveilleux français;* Delarue and Tenèze, *Le conte populaire français;* Robert, *Le conte des fées littéraire*. For recent English-language studies, see Barchilon, "Uses of the Fairy Tale"; and Zipes, *Brothers Grimm*.

50. Aarne, *Types of the Folktale*, and Thompson, *Motif Index*.

51. See Darnton, "Peasants Tell Tales." Darnton dismisses Sigmund Freud's and Bruno Bettelheim's psychoanalytical interpretations of fairy tales. For an informed discussion of French social structure see Fritz, *L'idée de peuple en France*.

in the late nineteenth and early twentieth century. He assumes that their lives were fundamentally the same as those of their counterparts in the previous two centuries because this was a "long and stagnant period" in Europe. Such assumptions do not constitute evidence, especially in view of the changes to rural life during and following the industrial revolution.

There is much evidence of brutality, unhappy endings, and cruelty in the early fairy-tale material in books and on the stage. The Pierrots, Arlequins, Hanswursts, and other lowborn *zanni* types in commedia dell'arte plays are all tricksters of the sort Darnton describes in his essay. But their manipulations are the object of humor for Parisian audiences, and not for the rural residents of the French countryside.

The eighteenth century marks the beginning of children's literature and drama in Europe, which utilizes fairy tales along with other literary and pedagogical genres.[52] Most fairy tales are at least on one level "children's literature" in that they have the goal of "improving the listener" through the narrative instruction of a clear moral to the "unsocialized" child.[53] Fairy tales share this trait with fables. The simplicity of fairy tales is also consistent with children's literature, as seen in the central narrative line and the one-dimensional characters (often cast in contrasting pairs with good or evil natures, or with wise or foolish dispositions). The narrative function of "female" domestic literature glorified story telling in the salon and the nursery. The notion of these stories as "narrations by wet nurses" and "Mother Goose" suggests a concept of childhood as a distinct period when the imaginative powers are most potent. In functioning as an outlet for fantasy the new *contes* redefined the irrational, relegating magical thinking to the natural state of childhood.

The growing notion of the nobility of rustic life as a romantic antithesis to courtly or urban life certainly influenced these stories, which often began in rural villages at the edge of an enchanted forest. Vague agrarian settings evoke a sentimental nostalgia for the simpler past of mythic memory (tales were almost never specific as to their time).[54] The function of the central moral in fairy tales made them vehicles for Enlightenment allegory as well, where the "improvement" of the audience replaced that of the child.

Perrault's Fairy Tales

Charles Perrault's publication of the *Histoires ou contes du temps passé* in 1697 would become the most frequently reprinted fairy-tale collection in the eigh-

---

52. Genlis, *Théâtre*, includes three fairy-tale comedies.

53. Perrault's dedication of his *Histoires* specifies that each story contains one clear moral. See Delaporte, *Du merveilleux*, 95.

54. Jameson, "Magical Narratives," has pointed to the tendency of magical narratives to find an audience in times of social change, especially when pressures from the loss of rural life are felt.

teenth century. Writers adapted some tales almost immediately to the Parisian stage, and by the end of the century these were even cited as ideal theatrical sources.[55] Perrault's collection includes the following eleven stories:

1. *Cendrillon, ou La petite pantoufle de verre* (Cinderella, or the Glass Slipper) is a well-known story of an ill-treated and ragged stepdaughter whose fairy godmother grants her a night at the royal ball, where she appears as a princess.

2. *La belle au bois dormant* (The Sleeping Beauty).[56] A princess is cursed by a fairy to fall asleep until a prince can awaken her. Informed of these events by a dwarf with seven-league boots, a good fairy comes to the palace and creates an enchanted forest around the castle to protect the princess. A century later a virtuous prince awakes her, falls in love, and becomes her spouse.

3. *Le petit poucet* (Little Thumb). Driven by famine, the diminutive son of a poor woodcutter encounters a cannibal ogre. He outwits the ogre, stealing his seven-league boots and treasure, and saves his family from starvation.

4. *Le chat botté* (Puss-in-Boots). This tale, which also appears in Basile and Straparola's collections, is the story of the son of a poor miller whose only inheritance is a clever cat. The animal promises his master that if provided with boots and a small satchel, he will reward the man handsomely. Having received what he has requested, the cat embarks on a series of adventures that ultimately reward his young master with nobility and the hand of beautiful princess.

5. *Riquet à la houppe* (Riquet of the Tuft) is one of at least three similar *contes* in contemporary prints, including *Ricdin-Ricdon* of L'Héritier (the basis of the operas *Rosanie* and *Azélie*) and *Riquet à la houppe* by Mademoiselle Bernard. An ugly and lame hunchbacked prince named Riquet has but a single tuft of hair on his head. As a recompense for his ugliness, a beneficent fairy endowed Riquet at his birth with charm and good sense. He was also given the power to bestow that same good sense on whomever he loved. The same fairy then made a beautiful princess stupid and granted her the power to make handsome the man who most pleases her. This turns out to be Riquet, whom she agrees to marry in order to overcome her stupidity. The princess gains good sense and Riquet is transformed into a handsome man.

6. *La Barbe-bleue* (Bluebeard) is the tale of a rich landowner with an ugly blue beard. He had been married several times; his former wives' whereabouts are unknown. He manages to ingratiate himself with his less affluent neighbor, whose daughter he wishes to marry. After the wedding he leaves on a short trip, giving his new wife a set of keys to the palace doors but forbidding her to open the door to the closet with the smallest key. Her curiosity gets the better of her and she opens the door to the forbidden closet, where she finds the bodies

55. This is suggested in the anonymous *Bibliothèque universelle des romans*. Also see Lebègue, "Le merveilleux magique."

56. There exist a number of precursors for this story, including Basile and other sixteenth-century sources. See Soriano, *Les contes de Perrault*, 126–34.

of Bluebeard's murdered wives. Like her, they had failed the test of obedience. In her distress, she drops the key, and her husband discovers her transgression when he returns. He condemns her to death but she keeps stalling him until her brothers arrive. They kill Bluebeard as he tries to escape.

7. *Les fées* (The Fairies) uses a common theme, found twice in Basile (*Le tre fate* and *Doie pizzelle*). A cruel woman has two daughters, one good and the other evil. The good daughter shows generosity to a poor old woman—a fairy in disguise. In return for her kindness, the fairy enchants the girl. With every good word she speaks her mouth will produce a precious jewel. Upon seeing this gift the mother orders the other daughter to show similar kindness to old women in the hopes of further reward. The fairy now appears as a rich lady. When the evil daughter speaks to her rudely, the fairy curses her so that each time she speaks her mouth will spew vermin and vipers. When she returns and her mother sees the results, she throws out both daughters. The good daughter meets and marries a prince while the evil daughter dies alone in the woods.

8. *Le petit chaperon rouge* (Little Red Riding Hood). Perhaps the best-known of Perrault's stories, the original version has the wolf inviting Little Red Riding Hood into bed before it eats the child.

In addition to the prose *contes*, Perrault includes three *contes* in verse:

9. *Peau d'âne* (The Donkey's Hide) in the only Perrault tale not known to have been set for the stage in the eighteenth century.

10. *Les souhaits ridicules* (The Ridiculous Wishes) is a popular tale with numerous precedents from the twelfth through the sixteenth century.[57] The deity Jupiter grants a woodcutter three wishes. He foolishly wishes for a plate of eel; after being reprimanded by his wife he thoughtlessly wishes she were mute, and this wish is granted. He is forced to use his last wish to restore the power of speech to his wife.

11. *Griselidis*. The tale concerns a prince who is troubled by what he considers the unfaithfulness and deceptions of women. He marries a young and beautiful shepherdess named Griselidis and they have a daughter. Then the doubts and suspicions of the prince return. He decides to test Griselidis with a series of terrible trials. But Griselidis persists in her self-composure, and finally the prince is convinced of his wife's virtue.

Magic in the Theater before the Eighteenth Century: Italy

The approximately 600 surviving synopses of the commedia dell'arte plots reveal numerous superhuman characters and marvelous elements.[58] The *mago* or

---

57. Ibid., 107–12.

58. For synopses in modern edition see Pandolfi, *La commedia dell'arte*. For a review of literature see Heck, *Commedia dell'arte*.

the *negromante* (sorcerer) figured among the stock characters, along with astrologers, sorceresses, fairies, oracles, spirits, and ghosts. Commedia dell'arte
plots offered the earliest theatrical adaptations of fairy tales,[59] as well as disseminating another source of theatrical magic throughout Europe, Ariosto's
Orlando furioso.[60]

These Italian comedies employed two types of magic plots. In the first,
magic plays a minor role, most often in the form of a magician who helps characters at critical moments, less frequently as an encounter with an oracle. In
the second, magic and magicians are central. Kathleen Lea notes that one of
the most common plots has lovers and their comic companions shipwrecked
upon a strange arcadian island where they meet up with a powerful magician
who reigns there.[61] Although the magician intrigues against the visitors, in the
end he learns that he is related to one or more of the strangers. He renounces
magic and returns with them to "civilized" European society. Examples of this
plot, which bears a resemblance to Shakespeare's *The Tempest*, include *L'arbore
incantato* (The Enchanted Forest), *Il gran mago* (The Grand Sorcerer), *Li tre
satiri* (The Three Satyrs), and *L'Arcadia incantata* (Arcadia Enchanted). A related plot is the false-magic story, where a ruse is played on a gullible character
using feigned magic.

Unlike early Italian *intermedi* and opera, the commedia dell'arte employed
magic not to bedazzle and inspire awe or admiration (a primary goal of the
"marvelous"), but to allow the lowborn to achieve powers that otherwise
would be impossible for them. In this respect the comic-"marvelous" is very
much the opposite of its counterpart in more serious court opera. Rather than
a social affirmation of the connection of nobility with the divine, comedy subverts that order by awarding superhuman powers to commoners, effecting a
reversal of the usual social roles.

The Don Juan story is another popular marvelous *scenario*,[62] dating back
to early Jesuit morality plays. The first established source is an anonymously
published Spanish play attributed to Tirso de Molina (a pseudonym for Gabriel Téllez), *El burlador de Sevilla y convidado de piedra* (Barcelona, 1630).[63]
Italian comedy troupes adopted the story as *Il convitato di pietra* (The Stone
Guest), beginning in Naples around the same time. Seventeenth-century com-

59. Lea, *Italian Popular Comedy*, 1:189 and 2:431–32, identifies elements from Straparola's fairy
tales. Also see Lea, "Bibliography of the Commedia dell'arte."

60. See Mamczarz, "Quelques aspects." These adaptations ranged from one or two episodes
to as many as sixteen of the poem's cantos in a *scenario* in the Locatelli collection Rome, Biblioteca
Casanatense, F. IV, 12–13, now codices 1211, 1212.

61. Lea, *Italian Popular Comedy*, 2:444.

62. For accounts of the Don Juan legend in the theater, see Macchia, *Vita avventure e morte;*
Pirrotta, *Don Giovanni's Progress;* Russell, *The Don Juan Legend;* and especially Weidinger, "*Il
Dissoluto punito.*"

63. Alonso de Córdova y Maldonado's *La venganza en el sepulcro* is yet another example of a fantastic seventeenth-century Spanish play.

media dell'arte manuscript sources preserve at least three Don Juan comedies, a *Convitato di pietra* setting in *Gibaldone comico di varij suggetti* (Naples, Biblioteca Nazionale, shelfmark XI AA.41, part ii, no. 14), another in the Ciro monarca collection in Rome's Biblioteca Casanatense (no. 24). A third Don Juan *scenario*, entitled *L'ateista fulminato*, survives in the same source (no. 4).[64]

References to the titles of the earliest works for the Italian string-operated puppets (*fantoccini*) and hand puppets (*pupi, pupazzi,* and *burattini*), staged by Filippo Acciaiuoli in Venice, suggest a close parallel between the marionette repertory and the commedia dell'arte.[65] Burlesques such as *Ulisse in Feaccia* (1681) and *Il Girello* (1682)[66] included superhuman characters and situations taken from mythology, epic romance, and legendary material.

Italian Opera

The representation of superhuman power in opera owes much to Renaissance court festivities and *intermedi,* where magic and divinity were associated with the aristocratic patrons who sponsored them. Archetypal characters from mythology most often represented these forces, along with the magician, a character found in biblical, classical, medieval, and Renaissance sources. The magician possessed powers that were symbolic of the superhuman power of the prince, and spectacular magic is a frequent allegorical and political symbol in Renaissance festivities.[67]

The most popular supernatural subjects in seventeenth-century Italian opera include Orpheus, the sorceresses Medea and Circe,[68] Hercules, and

64. Performed by the troupe of Pedro Osorio and Gregorio Laredo. Osorio Giliberto made a translation into Neapolitan dialect (lost) and an undated version by Giacinto Andrea Cicognini, printed anonymously in several Italian cities. Other *Il convitato di pietra* plays include one by Tiberio Fiorilli (before 1640), another by Giambattista Andreini (before 1651), and yet another by Onofrio G. di Solofra (before 1652). See Spaziani, *Don Giovanni dagli scenari,* 99–134.

65. See Leydi and Leydi, *Marionette,* and Minniear, "Marionette Opera."

66. Based on Acciaiuoli and Melani's popular *dramma musicale burlesco* of the same name (Rome, 1668), discussed below.

67. Greene, "Magic and Festivity."

68. Seventeenth-century operas that use Homer's sorceress Circe as a subject include *Circe delusa,* a *dramma musicale,* by Virgilio Puccitelli, music by [?] Scacchi (Warsaw, 1648); *La Circe,* a *dramma per musica,* by Cristoforo Ivanovich, with music by Pietro Andrea Ziani (Vienna, 9 June 1665), also set with music by Giovanni Domenico Freschi (Venice, 1679–80, music lost); and *Circe abbandonata da Ulisse,* a *dramma* by Aurelio Aureli, with music by Bernardo Sabadini (Piacenza, 1692). Giacinto Andrea Cicognini based his *Il Giasone,* a *dramma musicale* (with music by Cavalli, Venice 1649), on the Jason and Medea myth. Others heroic operas on Medea include *Medea placata,* by Giovanni Faustini (Venice, c. 1662), composer unknown; *Medea in Atene* (with prologue), by Aureli, with music by Antonio Giannettini (Venice, 1675); and *Gli Argonauti in Colcos,* by Aureli, with music by Giannettini (Venice, 1675).

Ulysses.[69] A variety of librettos have oracle scenes. Incantation episodes, favored in the commedia dell'arte, were also common in Italian opera,[70] along with magic sleep scenes,[71] as well as appearances of ghosts.[72] The Orpheus myth served as the basis of Angelo Poliziano's *La fabula d'Orfeo* (Mantua, 1480),[73] which influenced the earliest opera librettos. Many scholars consider Ottavio Rinuccini's *L'Euridice*, with music by Jacopo Peri, to be the first opera (Florence, 1600). This libretto was set again, to new music, by Giulio Caccini (Florence, 1602). *L'Orfeo*, the *favola* (with prologue) by Alessandro Striggio, set to music by Claudio Monteverdi (Mantua, 1607), is perhaps the best-known of all early operas.[74]

Hercules (or Alcide) goes to the underworld in various operas, including Alceste, Ercole, and Alcide operas. An underworld scene was featured in Giovanni Andrea Moniglia's *Ercole in Tebe*, a *festa teatrale* for the marriage of Cosimo de' Medici III (performed in Florence on 8 July 1661), with music by Jacopo Melani. Aureli revised Moniglia's *Ercole in Tebe* as a *dramma per musica* with music by Giovanni Antonio Boretti (performed in Venice at SS. Giovanni e Paolo on 12 December 1670). Alcide sings in an underworld scene in *La lotta d'Hercole con Acheloo*, a *divertimento drammatico* in one act with a text by Ortensio Mauro (based in turn on Ovid's *Metamorphoses*) and set to music for the Hanover court in 1689 by Agostino Steffani. The myth of the Herculean hero Bellerophon (Hesiod, *Theogony*), who slew the monster Chimera with the aid of Pegasus, was the subject of *Bellerofonte*, with libretto by Vincenzo Nolfi

69. Ulysses operas include Giacomo Badoaro and Monteverdi's *Il ritorno d'Ulisse in patria* (Venice, 1640) and Badoaro's *L'Ulisse errante* (Venice, 1644), based on the *Odyssey*, with music by Francesco Sacrati (lost).

70. See Rosand, *Opera in Seventeenth-century Venice*, 268, 342–46, and Susan Shimp, "Women, Magic, and Incantation."

71. For example, Alessandro Striggio and Claudio Monteverdi's *L'Orfeo*, and Giovanni Francesco Busenello and Monteverdi's *L'incoronzione di Poppea*, Venice, 1643, act 2, scenes 10–11.

72. For example, Busenello and Francesco Cavalli's *La Didone*, Venice, 1641.

73. For details on Poliziano's drama. see Rosand, introduction; and Pirrotta, *Music and Theatre*.

74. Other settings include *Il pianto d'Orfeo*, a *favolette* by Gabriello Chiabrera, composer unknown (Florence, 1608); *Orfeo dolente*, set as five intermedi by Chiabrera [?], with music by Domenico Belli (Florence, 1616); *La morte d'Orfeo*, a *tragicommedia pastorale* with music by Stefano Landi (Venice, c. 1619); *L'Orfeo*, a *tragicommedia* with prologue by Francesco Buti, with music by Luigi Rossi (Paris, 1647); *L'Orfeo*, with music by Carlo d'Aquino (1654); *L'Orfeo*, a *dramma per musica* by Aureli, with music by Antonio Sartorio (Venice, 1672). *L'Orfeo*, with music by Giuseppe di Dia (Palermo, 1676); *L'Orfeo*, with music by Francesco Della Torre (1677); *La lira d'Orfeo*, a *trattenimento musicale* in one act by Nicolò Minato, with music by Antonio Draghi (Vienna, Laxenburg Park, 1683); and *Amor spesso inganna*, a *dramma per musica* by Aureli, with music by Sabadini (Piacenza, 1689). Although it was written by a French composer and produced in Paris, André Campra's *Orfeo nell'inferni* is an Italian *intermedio* inserted into his *comédie-lyrique Le carnaval de Venise* (Paris, 1699).

and music by Francesco Sacrati (Venice, 1642). *Il pomo d'oro,* Antonio Cesti's massive *festa teatrale* for the wedding of Leopold I to Princess Margareta of Spain (text by Francesco Sbarra; performed at the Vienna Hoftheater on 12 and 14 July 1668), was based on the myth of the Judgment of Paris.[75] The opera includes a plethora of mythological characters in elaborate scenes set in Hades, the heavens, and the palaces of various deities.

Epic Romance in Opera

Episodes from Italian epic romance supplied materials emphasizing the "marvelous" for numerous plays with music, beginning with *La cortesia di Leone a Ruggiero* by Giovanni Cosimo Villifranchi (printed in Venice 1600), as well as for operas. Ariosto's *Orlando furioso* provided the basis for at least twenty-three seventeenth-century Italian operas.[76] Their composers included Francesca Caccini, Luigi Rossi, and Francesco Cavalli.[77] Many have marvelous episodes. Tasso's epic poem *Gerusalemme liberata* was also a source of magic in opera; Tim Carter lists eight seventeenth-century settings of the Armida and Rinaldo episode and four settings of the Erminia episode.[78] Composers included Michelangelo Rossi and Benedetto Ferrari.

Ferrari alloyed commedia dell'arte, epic romance, myth, and fairy tales in his "serio-comic *favola*" *La maga fulminata* (The Sorceress Struck Down by Lightning), with music by Francesco Manelli (lost) for the Teatro S. Cassiano, 1638.[79] The divinities Jupiter, Mercury, Echo, Pallas (or Athena), and Pluto interact with human characters and the sorceress's comic old servant Scarabea. Superhuman ensembles include invisible spirits, sirens, and enchanted knights. The anonymous *Rosaure, imperatrice di Constantinople,* performed by the Troupe Italienne at the Théâtre du Petit Bourbon (20 March 1658), was one of the few Italian court operas staged during the minority of Louis XIV. Like *La maga fulminata,* this libretto included elements of Italian comedy, medieval chivalric romance, exotic orientalism, magic, and quasi-historical characters.[80]

Between 1650 and 1670 Italian librettists introduced the exotic Orient to opera librettos in Venice. The intermingling of mortal and superhuman char-

75. Schmidt, "Antonio Cesti's *Il pomo d'oro*"; and Schmidt, "*Pomo d'oro, Il.*"

76. Carter, "Ariosto, Ludovico." Rosand, "Orlando," reviews the operas that used Ariosto's Orlando story in the seventeenth and early eighteenth centuries.

77. Döring, *Ariostos* Orlando Furioso, 331–33, discusses selected examples.

78. Carter, "Tasso, Torquato." For another account, see Balsano and Walker, *Tasso, la musica;* and Tim Carter, review.

79. Libretto, Venice: Antonio Bariletti, 1638. The libretto for the revival was printed as well (Bologna: Gio. Battista Ferroni, 1641; copy in US-Wc, Schatz 5888).

80. Synopsis from Desboulmiers, *Histoire anecdotique et raisonné,* 1:44–48. Joseph Dominique Biancolelli's manuscript in F-Pn, Ms. Rés. 625, includes notes on the production.

acters continued to parallel the *scenari* of the commedia dell'arte in one of the most popular of these comic operas, *Il Girello*. This *dramma musicale burlesco* (also described as a *dramma per musica* in the 1682 libretto) by Filippo Acciaiuolo, with music by Alessandro Stradella (prologue) and possibly Jacopo Melani as well, was probably created for a commedia dell'arte troupe in Rome (Palazzo Colonna, 4 February 1668).[81] *Il Girello* had numerous performance runs in other Italian cities.[82] Its plot owes much to the comic tradition, with its low characters, magic, and political satire and allegory. The opera, which begins with several underworld scenes, concerns a magician who gives Girello an enchanted cloak allowing the wearer to exchange his appearance with that of another character, and a magic root whose touch will transform another person's appearance into that of Girello.

The tradition of Don Juan comedies seems not to have inspired an operatic setting until *L'empio punito*, a *dramma musicale* by Filippo Acciaiuoli and Giovanni Apollini, with music by Alessandro Melani (Rome, 1669). The opera was performed in masks and set in a pseudo-classical Macedonia with the new names for the standard characters (Don Juan becomes Acrimante).[83] Another Don Juan opera was *Il convitato di pietra*, an *opera tragica* in three acts by Andrea Perrucci (Naples, 1678).

The "Marvelous" and Theatrical Music in Italy

Opera is rooted in humanistic thought, where music by its very nature is magical and mystical. Music was thus a fitting theatrical expression for otherworldly topics, although there is no special category or type of magical music. Italian humanists such as Marsilio Ficino linked song to divine expression. One finds a similar idea in the anonymous manuscript from about 1630, *Il corago:* "musical speech is more to be associated with the concept of the superhuman than the concept of ordinary man."[84] The author indicates that musical expression was most appropriate for "astral and fluvial spirits." Similarly, Giovan Battista Andreini delineates two different approaches to music in his *La centaura* (Paris, 1622), modeled on the fourth-century rhapsody by Chaeremon with the same title. The first approach has music performed when the (mostly mortal) characters recognize they are making music; the second has music performed in a

---

81. See Weaver, "*Il Girello*."

82. Various printed librettos survive., e.g., US-Wc, Schatz 8198 (Venice: G. F. Valvasense, 1682). Manuscript scores survive in the Vatican (Chigiana Ms. Q.V. 56), the British Library (Add. 14204), the Biblioteca Estense (Mus. E. 181), and the Conservatory of San Pietro a Majella in Naples (shelfmarks 32.3.21 and 33.5.33).

83. Macchia, *Vita avventure e morte*, 207–99, provides the complete text.

84. *Il corago, o vero, Alcune osservazioni;* passage translated in Bianconi, *Music in the Seventeenth Century*, 174–75.

magical manner, where a divine character's normal speech occurs through music.[85] Early baroque conventions of musical magic on the stage associate aristocratic power with divinity, and the "noble elegance" of court ballets certainly reflected the earthly expression of divine aristocratic privilege.[86] By the end of the century theatrical divinity had fully appropriated the musical elegance of courtly dance, with its graceful rhythm, conjunct melodic motion, and consonant harmony.

Music enhanced the spectacular effects and theatrical illusions of stage machinery. Battle scenes, magical scenic and character transformations, and the imitation of natural and divine events all found a place in these extravagant productions. The role of music in them was decorative and not often mimetic; it was rarely the sole object of the audience's attention. Decoration necessitates formulaic requirements rather than highly distinctive or individual expression. The music in and of itself connoted a magical presence by virtue of its inherent allegorical nature; one did not have to resort to the suggestion of a real experience that a special category of musical imagery would necessitate.

Four general traits of the music of the "marvelous" in the seventeenth century may be delineated, although these traits cannot be said to be exclusive to otherworldly characters and scenes:

1. Elegant instrumental music is often associated with divinities, the superhuman, sleep or trance, and magical appearances. The connection between the aristocracy and the divine is confirmed by a common style in music for superhuman characters and the nobility. Seventeenth-century Italian, French, and English stage productions indicate such music. Elegance is of course a relative term, designating music that is more lyrical and sensual than that which precedes and follows it; often the timbre is brighter and the sonority more consonant. It creates a distinct sonic moment of grace, suggesting nobility and an elevated expression. The indication of "soft music" is common in English opera, for example Purcell's "Soft Symphony" in *Circe*, played as the heavens open and Cupid appears. The ubiquitous magic sleep scenes in baroque opera also emphasize the soporific effects of music.

2. Composers exaggerated this elegant style in the distinctive vocal music for imposing and evil superhuman characters, such as magicians, sorceresses, genies, fairies, ghosts,[87] and oracles. Invocations, the magic conjuring

---

85. MacNeil, "A Modern *Centaur*," discusses the mixed genre found in antiquity and represented by the centaur. This symbol returns in the early seventeenth-century theater.

86. This basically decorative function of music is most obvious in the French *ballets de cour*, where elegance dominates. Commentators on the ballet such as Mersenne, Saint-Hubert, de Marolles, Ménéstrier, and de Pure spend very little time discussing music but consistently require that the music please the listener and suit the subject of the *entrée*.

87. For example, the ghost scene in Busenello and Cavalli's *La Didone* (1641).

of spirits, and similar pronouncements in Venetian opera were often cast with poetic rhythms that stress the antepenult (Italian *sdrucciolo*),[88] and sometimes bore other peculiar musical features such as unusual hexachord modulations.[89] Ensembles with groups of supernatural characters such as witches' covens, demons, and dances for imps or elves were also common.

3. In scenes with otherworldly characters and events, composers occasionally selected instruments and sonorities borrowed from church music and earlier court spectacle. They scored such Hadean scenes with the regal and ceremonial trombones; one finds examples in Florentine spectacles and *intermedi*, such as *La pellegrina* of 1589. This characteristic was taken over in court operas, from Monteverdi's *L'Orfeo* to Cesti's *Il pomo d'oro*. The trombones then seem to disappear from opera until Gluck, if we are to believe the scores and archival records of orchestral players (wind players commonly performed on a variety of instruments often not noted in archival documentation, and military bands were at times hired to augment the theater orchestra). Their reemergence is associated with a very different type of expression in the second half of the eighteenth century.

4. Specific tonal areas for scenes of horror or unearthly events may have been chosen for their distinctive qualities. For example, Purcell uses C minor for some otherworldly scenes and F minor for scenes of horror.[90] Such practice seems to have been more a personal trait than a matter of convention until the eighteenth century.

Although music retained a measure of its traditional transcendental association in late seventeenth-century opera, composers devised their scores chiefly as a decorative component. As with stage design and costume, the chief aesthetic goals were illusion, bedazzlement, and elegance. By the middle of the eighteenth century one can perceive a still clearer break in the association of magic and music, apparent both in theory and practice. As the scientific revolution fostered the separation of magic, mysticism, and alchemy from science, music became the object of rational analysis. Only then did composers begin to develop a distinct musical expression for magic and the "marvelous."

Intermedi and Early Court Opera

Early court opera derived its vocal idioms, scenic spectacle, and instrumental accompaniment from *intermedi*—musicodramatic entertainments inserted between acts of plays. The effusive and virtuoso vocal style, with its extravagant, instrumental-like embellishment, was well suited to the pronouncements of the goddess Harmony and the Sorceress in the Florentine *intermedio* of 1589,

---

88. See Rosand, *Opera in Seventeenth-Century Venice*, 268, 342–46.
89. Shimp, "Women, Magic, and Incantation."
90. This was first observed in Moore, *Henry Purcell*, 52.

La pellegrina.[91] This style and its association with magic figured prominently in the genre. In his dialogue *Il desiderio* Bottrigari described a multicolored *intermedio* orchestra,[92] which Robert L. Weaver has divided into three topical categories dating back at least to 1475: the pastoral, the Olympian (or celestial), and the infernal. One finds crumhorns, bagpipes, and, later, recorders in pastoral scenes, while celestial scenes have lutes, recorders, viols, harpsichord, and cornetts. Composers of Florentine *intermedi* from 1539 to 1589 commonly scored infernal scenes with trombones (usually four) and low-pitched viols. The trombones, associated with regal and ceremonial solemnity, appeared in both infernal and celestial settings.[93] These instruments suggest the otherworld—the solemn afterlife of Greek myth rather than the horrific Christian hell.[94]

The surviving music of *La pellegrina* provides insight into the instrumental tradition of the Florentine *intermedi*. Furies arrive to music for four trombones, and Cristofano Malvezzi adds flute and cornett to the trombones in his *sinfonia* "The Harmony of the Spheres." The combination appears again when the Fates join with the sirens for a chorus. The fourth *intermedio* has a sorceress and a Hadean scene scored with four *viole da gamba*, four trombones, and a *lirone*. Viols, trombones, and a *lira* accompany the underworld spirits in the sixth *intermedio*, while the celestial spirits have harps, citterns, and viols.

A similar topical approach to instrumentation appears to have been used in early court opera, for example Monteverdi's *L'Orfeo* (1607).[95] The underworld "marvelous" figures in acts 3 through 5. A regal organ, five trombones, two bass violas da gamba, and a violone accompany the chorus of underworld spirits in act 3. A *sinfonia* for brass in a dense seven-part texture follows this chorus. The next *sinfonia* has low-pitched strings and regal, the same instruments specified in act 5 when the music returns to accompany the descent of Apollo. (Thus the music is not directly identified with Apollo until his entrance in act 5.) Here Apollo enchants Charon to make him fall asleep, allowing Orpheus to cross the Styx—one of the first known instances of magical sleep music in opera. The low strings evoke languor; they will continue to do so in the seventeenth century. The low-pitched strings, trombones, regal, and cornetts are consistent with the depiction of Hades in the *intermedi*.

The incantations by Orpheus are significant, especially the aria "Possente

91. Walker, *Musique des intermèdes;* Weaver, "Sixteenth-century Instrumentation," *Musical Quarterly* 47 (1961): 363–78; Weaver, "The Orchestra in Early Italian Opera"; and Brown, *Sixteenth-century Instrumentation*. For a summary of these items, see Spitzer and Zaslaw, "Orchestration."

92. Bottrigari, *Il Desiderio.*

93. I will distinguish Hadean from Christian infernal topics, particularly in the eighteenth century. The former refers to the solemn underworld of classical mythology, while the latter refers to the horrific hell of Christianity.

94. Both chamber and church music used sackbuts and cornetts in the first half of the seventeenth century. The use of these instruments declined in the second half of the century, although a few composers continued to write for ensembles of trombones (see chapter 3).

95. See Beat, "Monteverdi and the Opera Orchestra."

spirto." Here sustained bass notes over an ornamented and subtle melody, drawing upon earlier Italian improvised traditions of monody and divine song, suggest a kind of magical trance. Act 4 occurs in Hades with Pluto and Proserpina. She sings in a normal recitative, while his bass voice has some short passages of repeated notes. The duet of Apollo and Orpheus as they rise in the sky is remarkably elaborate in its vocal ornamentation, perhaps owing to its magical function as well as to the capabilities of the singers.

Similar instrumentation appears in Florentine operas based on Ariosto's *Orlando furioso*,[96] as evidenced by the surviving score for Francesca Caccini's *La liberazione di Ruggiero dall'isola d'Alcina* (1625).[97] For some of the magic scenes Caccini has indicated three violins and basses, four viols with four trombones, and *organo di legno, e strumenti di tasti*. This is the combination for the ritornello that accompanies Ruggiero's encounter with the enchanted plants Alcina uses to capture knights and lovers. (The special handling of this scene will be a feature of Alcina operas for the next two centuries.) A five-part mixed contrapuntal chorus of enchanted plants, accompanied by five viols, *arciviolata*, and *organo di legno, e strumenti di tasti,* is preceded by a short solo for one of the *piante incantate*. In adherence to the aesthetics of early opera, in which music is superhuman by its very nature, no specific kind of divine or magical music is to be discerned in this score.

Roman operas treated the lives of saints, biblical stories, and epic romance,[98] using spectacle and stage machinery. Although Michelangelo Rossi's *Erminia sul Giordano* (1633) included Tasso's sorceress Armida, the three Furies, and a chorus of demons, there is no specific music for transformations or machinery.[99] Magical events and characters do not appear to have received special musical treatment in the arias or vocal ensembles. In spite of the fantastic episodes and characters in Luigi Rossi's *Il palazzo incantato, ovvero La guerriera amante* (1642),[100] the composer makes no stylistic differentiation between earthly and otherworldly characters or events. Francesco Buti included Hadean and Olympian scenes in his libretto for *L'Orfeo* (Paris, 1647), but Luigi Rossi's score indicated no specific instruments associated with the underworld. Neither does the recitative style of superhuman characters significantly differ from that of mortal ones. In one striking choral scene, however (act 2, scene 9), Euridice is put to sleep with instrumental ritornellos whose melodies lull in gentle conjunct motion.

96. The earliest of these are *Angelica in Ebuda* (G. Chiabrera, 1615) and *Lo sposalizio di Angelica e Medoro* (A. Salvadori and M. Da Gagliano, with music by Jacopo Peri, 1619).

97. Caccini, *La liberazione*. The modern edition is by Doris Silbert.

98. Murata, *Operas for the Papal Court*.

99. A facsimile of the printed score (1637) is published in the series Bibliotheca musica bononiensis, 4/12 (Bologna: Forni [1969]).

100. A facsimile edition is published in IO 2 (1977), and the libretto is reproduced in IOL 8 (1979). An earlier Ariosto opera is *Il ritorno d'Angelica nell'India*, by Ottavio Tronsarelli, with music by Cignani (Rome, 1626 or 1628).

Public Opera in Italy

Venetian public opera houses, for reasons of economy, reduced the size of the instrumental ensemble, using mainly strings; most surviving scores for these theaters do not specify instruments. Winds appear only in isolated numbers, and "cornettos, trombones, harps, and organs more or less disappeared."[101] Cavalli's *Rosinda* (1651) offers one rare designation of a musical instrument associated with magic, a *chiamata de la magica tromba*.[102] More typical is the simple descriptive *sinfonia* marked "infernale" in Cavalli's *Ercole amante* (Paris 1662), with no special characteristics to distinguish it as such.

Two types of magical scenes, sleep and incantation, were well established as operatic conventions by midcentury.[103] Susan Shimp has shown how Domenico Mazzocchi employed unusual modal change for an incantation by the sorceress Falsirena in his *La catena d'Adone* (Rome, 1626).[104] Shifts of affect occur through abrupt changes in mode (really hexachord). Cavalli's *Il Giasone* also includes an incantation in the underworld scene that ends the first act, Medea's "Dell'antro magico."[105] A slowly rising triadic instrumental introduction leads to the sorceress's hypnotic incantation of repeating notes in dactylic rhythms with a few triadic gestures and no florid writing at all. Cavalli gives Medea a restricted melody line of repeated notes and simple triads that obey the accents of the spoken text. For most of the piece the harmony consists of only two chords, what we would call E minor and C major. Ellen Rosand notes that although *Il Giasone* is not the first opera with such an incantation, it provided a prototype for subsequent incantation scenes.[106] Strophic recitative, though dated by this time, is still employed for superhuman characters such as those in Cavalli's *Ormindo* (1644). In his opera *Erismena* (Venice 1655), Cavalli has the Iberian slave Aldimira sing a conjuring aria, "Vaghe stelle," as she casts a spell over Erismena, who has fainted. Thus by the middle of the century one finds the beginnings of a theatrical style for musical incantation, using such techniques as strophic recitative, abrupt hexachord changes, repeating notes in *sdrucciolo* rhythms, and rising triadic motion.

Operas that employed these techniques continued to be produced in the second half of the century. Francesco Lucio's *Il Medoro* (Venice, 1658) in-

101. Spitzer and Zaslaw, "Orchestration," 3:721.

102. Tarr and Walker, "'Bellici carmi.'"

103. Rosand, *Opera in Seventeenth-century Venice*, 338–42. Stein, *Songs of the Mortals*, 113, cites the play *El jardin de Falerina* (1648–49), which has a musical incantation scene.

104. Shimp "Women, Magic, and Incantation," also cites incantation scenes in *La maga fulminata* (1638) and *La virtù de' strali d'amore* (1642). Rosand, *Opera in Seventeenth-century Venice*, 343–44, also gives a number of other underworld scenes in seventeenth-century Venetian opera from 1642 to 1670.

105. Cavalli, *Il giasone*.

106. Rosand, *Opera in Seventeenth-century Venice*, 268–70, 342–46; and Walker, "Cavalli," 159. Osthoff, "Musica e versificazione," discusses the use of *sdrucciolo* accent in underworld scenes.

cludes an invocation for the sorcerer Atlante, "Del nero Baratro, mostri tartarei, udite i magici scongiuri orribili," with the slowly ascending triadic motion and *sdrucciolo* rhythms.[107] In Antonio Sartorio's *L'Orfeo* (Venice, c. 1672–73) Euridice's ghost appears to Orfeo in a dream. The music is a measured recitative for the four eleven-syllable lines, with elaborate, decorative motion over a slow-moving bass. In the underworld scene Pluto's (bass) decision to restore Euridice to life begins with a short *sinfonia* of repeated chords, somewhat reminiscent of the instrumental introduction to Medea's invocation in Cavalli's *Il Giasone*. Carlo Pallavicino's music for *La Gerusalemme liberata* (Venice, 1687) introduces a novel approach in treating Armida: the sorceress sings the most ornate coloratura arias in the opera, rendering her musically distinct.[108] This device will be used more frequently in the eighteenth century, most famously in Mozart's music for the Queen of the Night.

Italian Comic Opera

Magical elements were also present in Italian comic opera of the period. The most popular of these, *Il Girello* (1668),[109] has two incantation scenes. Accompanied by a chorus of spirits, Pluto (bass, with a tessitura down to low D) sings an incantation, "Odi cocito oscuro deità," in slowly ascending triadic motion, with initial *sdrucciolo* rhythms, and descending octave leaps, suggesting conjuring through this unusual vocal gesture, which will become a distinguishing characteristic. The opera has another incantation for the magician that begins with the text "Mostri terribili, furie d'averno, spiriti invisibili." Like Pluto's aria, this begins with an opening ascending triadic gesture in the voice, followed by wide, descending vocal leaps. In contrast, the first Don Juan opera, *L'empio punito*, with libretto by Filippo Acciaiuoli and Giovanni Apollini and music by Alessandro Melani (Rome, 1669), has little to distinguish it from operas with no supernatural material.[110]

Later Court Operas and drammi per musica

Later court operas displaying aspects of the "marvelous" in Italy and Vienna were occasional works; they were distinguished from public opera by designations such as *festa*, *azione teatrale*, or *componimento*. Here superhuman characters and otherworldly scenes served as allegories for aristocratic patrons. One may infer the link from earlier court opera to the *festa* by the particular instrumentation of the *intermedio*, which reappears in later festive operas in Italy and

---

107. For a facsimile edition see Aureli and Lucio, *Il Medoro*.

108. Pallavacino, *La Gerusalemme liberata*.

109. I consulted the manuscript in the British Library (Add. 14204).

110. See the discussion in Pirrotta, *Don Giovanni's Progress*, 25–38, and seven musical examples from the score in Rome, Biblioteca Apostolica Vaticana, 203–22.

Vienna, where it seems to have become a self-consciously archaic approach by the 1660s. Act 3 of Jacopo Melani's *Ercole in Tebe* (1661),[111] for example, consists of a series of underworld scenes in Pluto's court. Scene 7 (6 in the libretto) begins with a chorus of monsters, "Terribili, orribili spiriti d'Erebo." Melani scores the ritornello for a Hadean ensemble of cornetts, trombones, and continuo: the music is regal and ceremonial in its consistent consonance and deliberate triple meter. The last scene in act 3 has another two choruses of monsters set for three low-pitched vocal parts. The concluding chorus, "Or mentre scherzano gli Amori," is almost identical in key, meter, orchestration, and style to "Terribili, orribili spiriti d'Erebo."

Because Giovanni Antonio Boretti's *Ercole in Tebe* (Venice, 1670) is a *dramma per musica* for the public theater, the score is less detailed in instrumentation than that of a *festa teatrale*.[112] When at the end of act 1 the mountain collapses and the scene is transformed into the mouth of Hades, a *sinfonia* in A minor evokes a regal, ceremonious atmosphere with dotted rhythms. The score indicates no instruments, but the clefs suggest a string ensemble.

Antonio Cesti's extravagant four-hour *Il pomo d'oro* (1668) is perhaps the last opera to use the *intermedio* ensemble. A prologue and three of the original five acts survive intact.[113] Documentation offers a rare, detailed description of the instrumental forces for this exceptional work,[114] with a large festive ensemble that included flutes, cornetts, trumpets, trombones, and bassoons added to the strings and array of continuo instruments. The Hadean scenes (act 1, scene 1, and act 2, scene 6) are accompanied by cornetts, trombones, bassoon, and regal. This ensemble provides the ritornellos to Proserpina's aria in A minor (act 1, scene 1) with block chords evoking the awesome solemnity of the underworld. The same combination of winds (without the regal) appears again in act 2, scene 6, set at the entrance to Hades, where another triple-meter ritornello in block chords sounds between the verses of the boatman Charon's lament. The Furies Megaera, Tisiphone, and Alecto appear for an ensemble with Charon. Their music is courtly and gracious, with polyphonic exchanges of florid motives. The wind ritornello (cornetts, trombones, and bassoon) for Charon's subsequent aria uses archaic imitative polyphony with suspensions, as the boatman rejoices at the prospect of more deceased voyagers. The writing here is somewhat reminiscent of the Venetian instrumental works of Giovanni Gabrieli, written for similar forces. It suggests an archaic reference associated with the marvelous elements of past Italian court opera. Other fantastic scenes

111. Manuscript scores survive in F-Pn, Vm⁴ 11, and US-Wc, and B-Bc. For a facsimile edition see IO 4 (1978); for the libretto see IOL 5 [= vol. 55], (1978).

112. A manuscript score survives in the British library. For a facsimile see IO 6 (1977); for the libretto see IOL 5 (= vol. 55), (1978).

113. Some extracts from the missing acts survive in Modena. See Schmidt, "Antonio Cesti's *Il pomo d'oro*." Acts 3 and 5 both have celestial scenes with supernatural characters.

114. Cesti, *Il pomo d'oro.*

also recall older court *intermedi* and operas. The theorbo and *graviorgano* accompany Juno's appearance before Paris, and there is a sleep scene for Oenone (act 4, scene 1), to gentle music for viols and *graviorgano*.

In his early Neapolitan *drammi per musica*, Alessandro Scarlatti suggests the superhuman by evocative *recitativo obbligato*, recalling string accompaniments for the divine voice in the composer's oratorio, *Cain, overo Il primo omicidio*, or to the voice of Christ in his *St. John Passion*. Recitative in late seventeenth-century French opera has similar accompaniment that will continue in the eighteenth century. Toward the end of the century Italian composers began to use a particular accompaniment in arias to suggest otherworldly expression. One example is an unusual aria for Hercules in Agostino Steffani's *La lotta d'Hercole con Acheloo* (1689),[115] "La cerasta più terribile," with dramatic tremolo strings and two changes of meter (**c**, 3/4, and 3/2). Although Steffani's writing may seem modest, the use of evocative accompaniment here is one of the first examples of an approach that will become a significant new expressive device in eighteenth-century opera.

The "Marvelous" in the French Theater

Ernst Friedrich's survey of the sixteenth- and seventeenth-century French theater documents the wide use of transformations, alchemy, soothsaying, astrology, and magic spells, with magicians and superhuman characters taken from epic romances, legends, and mythology.[116] The magic episodes of Orlando, Alcina, and Logistilla from Ariosto's *Orlando furioso* appear in numerous plays, ballets, and operas, either to instill virtue or for parody. Ariosto's magic mirror, enchanted wells of love and forgetfulness, magic rings, and the test that requires drinking without spilling from the magic cup occur in a variety of stage productions. Likewise, elements from Tasso's *Gerusalemme liberata* also figured in various theatrical genres:[117] the sorceress Armide, the magician Ismen in the enchanted island, and various transformations and magic events. Writers also plundered fantastic characters and events from *Amadis de Gaule*, particularly the sorceress Urganda.[118]

Friedrich cites some seventy-five French theatrical works in the seventeenth century with magical elements, thirty-nine of which had pastoral texts.[119] Pastorals offered metamorphoses, magicians and witches who conjured demons

---

115. Facsimile ed. in Handel Sources 9. Excerpts in Steffani, *Ausgewählte Werke*.

116. Friedrich, *Die Magie im französischen Theater*. A brief summary of seventeenth-century magic in the theater may be found in Lebègue, "Le merveilleux magique."

117. Beall, *Le fortune du Tasse;* and Simpson, *Le Tasse*.

118. A rarer medieval romance served as the basis for *Le ballet de Pierre de Province et de la belle Magdelonne* (21 February 1638). The text is reproduced in Lacroix, *Ballets et mascarades*, 5:181–97. (Page numbers here and in other citations refer to the 1868 edition.)

119. The pastoral in the seventeenth century derives from the late Renaissance models, which in turn was based on classical models. Pastoral dramas are a modern genre. See Greg, *Pastoral Po-*

or created images to cast a spell, earth spirits, nymph-sorceresses, oracles, magic rings that transformed one, and magic salves. Fairies frequently appeared in pastoral stories in the sixteenth and seventeenth centuries, such as Piérard Poullet's *pastorale* based on the Mélusine legend, *Clorinde, ou le sort des amants* (1598). Oriental references are also apparent in the pastoral genres. Friedrich observes that Arabic-sounding names evoked the exotic Orient in pastorals. Alcindor, for instance, is a character in Honorat de Bueil, Marquis de Racan's *Les bergeries, ou Artenice* (1618). Guérin de Bouscal's *La Doranise* (Paris 1634) includes supernatural beings on the island of Lydia and an Arab prince named Crysante. Jean Millet's *Pastorale, ou Tragicomédie de Janin, ou de La Hauda* (performed in Grenoble in 1635; published in Grenoble, 1636, and in Lyon, 1650) has a magic flute whose tones set listeners dancing. This is one of the earliest instances of a magical instrument that affected the auditor in this manner.

French comedies came in a variety of forms, some closely related to the classical pastoral tradition, others derived from Italian comedy. All of these might partake of the same magical elements found in tragic and pastoral genres. Philippe Quinault's *La comédie sans comédie* (1654) includes a two-act setting of *Armide et Regnault,* based on Tasso's characters. Thomas Corneille's comedy *La pierre philosophe* (1681) employs mythology with elemental beings (gnomes, sylphs, undines, and salamanders).

Spanish models also provided sources for French comedies. Jean de Rotrou based his *La bague de l'oubli* (performed at the Théâtre de l'Hôtel de Bourgogne in 1628; published in Paris in 1635) on the Spanish comedy *La sortija del olvida* by Félix Lope de Vega Carpio (Madrid, 1619), who borrowed elements from earlier models. Rotrou has Guarini's magician, Alcandre, providing the hero, Leandre, with a magic ring (derived from Ariosto) that causes the wearer to lose all memories. Perhaps the best-known Spanish comedy, the *Don Juan* play, became a staple at the Parisian fairs beginning about 1658.[120] Examples include various versions of *Le festin de pierre* by G. D. Biancolelli (from a copy by T. Gueullette), Dorimond (pseud. for N. Drouin; Lyon, 1658), and Villiers (pseud. for Claude Deschamps, 1659). The best-known of the seventeenth-century comedies is the richly layered and ironic comedy by Molière (1665). Other versions of the story include *Le nouveau festin de pierre, ou l'Athée foudroyé,* by Rosimond (pseud. for Claude de la Rose, 1670), and the anonymous *Le festin de pierre . . . Edition nouvelle* (Amsterdam, 1683).

Italian troupes in Paris produced commedia dell'arte beginning in the sixteenth century. The magicians Zoroastre and Merlin are among the cast in the oldest printed fair piece, *Les forces de l'amour et de la magie,* a *divertissment comique en trois intermèdes* by Maurice Vondrebeck and Charles Alard (per-

---

etry; and Clubb, "The Making of the Pastoral Play." On the French pastoral tradition in the theater, see Marsan, *La pastorale dramatique.*

120. See Spaziani, "Don Juan à la foire," ; and Balmas, *Il mito del Don Giovanni.*

formed at the St. Germain fair, 3 February 1678).[121] Zoroastre executes magic to conjure monkeys and demons and to levitate a goblet. Numerous arche-typal plots with magical episodes occur in Evaristo Gherardi's *Le théatre ita-lien* (1694),[122] the earliest published collection of comedies (with songs) staged at the Hôtel de Bourgogne by the Comédiens Italiens du Roy. Gherardi was the leading Arlequin in the Théâtre Italien. His collection became influential in German-speaking areas, especially Vienna, where local German comedy troupes adapted the plots. These comedies often included magical elements, either limited to a few episodes (e.g., *Arlequin Prothée*, 1683, and *La naissance d'Amadis*, 1694) or in a larger role (e.g., *La descente de Mezettin aux enfers*, by Jean-François Regnard, 15 March 1689). The latter begins with Mezzetin in the stomach of a whale while Colombine and Pierrot are riding a large fish (scene 2, lines 333–72). The final scene occurs in hell with Proserpina and Pluto. An-other comedy, *Mezzetin, grand Sophy de Perse* (scene 2, lines 373–420), by De-losme de Monchenay (10 July 1689), has Mezzetin as a wandering knight who is captured by the sorceress Mélisse. Pierrot arrives to rescue him by providing a talisman that negates her magic powers and conjured monsters. The one-act comedy *La baguette de Vulcain*, by Jean-François Regnard and Charles Du-fresny (10 January 1693, performed as the third act of *Les Chinois*),[123] adapts the characters Roger, Bradamante, Melissa, and Angelica from Ariosto's *Orlando furioso* (scene 4, lines 280–314). This critique of the hypocritical morals and customs of modern French society includes an enchanted giant, a mysterious grotto, a sleeping beauty, various transformations, an oracle, and a magic wand.

Claude-Ignace Brugière, sieur de Barrante, and Charles Dufresny invoked Perrault's fairy tales in their one-act comedy *Les fées, ou Les contes de ma Mère l'oye* (2 March 1697).[124] Rather than a dramatic setting of the actual fairy tale, the character Dancourt ridicules aspects of modish literature in a sophisticated comedy that centers on the subject of arranged marriages; the text jabs at the

---

121. Reproduced in [Poitevin], *Le théâtre de la foire*, 11–22. Moland, *Molière et la comédie ita-lienne*, 143, cites an earlier example of a fairy comedy entitled *L'amor nello specchio*, by Giovanni Battista Adreini, leader of the Fedeli troop, published in 1622.

122. Gherardi, *Théâtre italien*.

123. Scott, *Commedia dell'arte in Paris*, 373, notes that it "is certainly derived from *Orlando furioso* with the wand borrowed from the baguette de Lyon as described in the *Mercure galant*, Nov. 1692–January 1693." Parfaict and Parfaict, *Dictionnaire des théâtres de Paris*, 6:306, note that it mixes "mythologie, Romans des Chevalerie, des faits récents." But only the names derive from Ariosto, not the action. The comedy was apparently successful and was revived with new scenes on 28 October 1718.

124. Gherardi, *Le théâtre italien*, 6:659–82. Only the title *Les fées* was taken from a tale in Perrault's popular collection of the same year. Scott, *Commedia dell'arte in Paris*, cites Louis Bian-colelli as an author along with Dufresny. The engraving for *Les Fées* shows Arlequin with the magic wand, along with the fairy (she also holds a wand), the enchanted snail (with Mezzetin in-side the shell), the butterfly (with the nymph La Chanteuse), the clock, and the lantern, all in the fairy's palace.

artificiality of courtly manners and the pretensions of *le grand monde*. The plot is therefore worth recounting: A fairy has sent Prince Octave to find the abducted Princess Ismenie, who has been chained up in a cave by the sultan of the ogres in an attempt to force her to marry him. Octave and the fairy's valet, Pierrot, arrive in a flying chariot at the cave of the cannibalistic ogres. Octave finds her but is soon captured by the ogres. Octave's servant, Arlequin, escapes with the help of the fairy who protects the honor of young maidens up the age of fifteen years and six minutes. Arlequin tells the fairy that Ismenie's father, King Croquignollet, learned from a fairy that his daughter would be taken by the ogres, only to be rescued by a young prince. He locked his daughter away in a tower, but an ogre with an enchanted ring and seven-league boots has abducted her. Now Ismenie is about to exceed the maximum age. The fairy informs Arlequin that she has transformed Octave into a rock to save him from the ogres. She gives Arlequin a magician's robe and magic wand that can transform people into rocks and create an urn full of gold. In scene 5 the ogre orders the nurse to narrate a fairy tale to put Ismenie to sleep. Then the grand ogre arrives and demands that Ismenie marry him or be executed. He performs a dance with terrifying grimaces and beats the other ogres with his club. Ismenie tries to escape, but the ogre captures her. Arlequin transforms her into a rock before the ogre can harm her. He waits until the ogres leave, conjures the urn with the gold, and disenchants Octave and Ismenie. Ismenie demands that her father give his consent to her marriage, and Arlequin then makes King Croquignollet appear from out of the urn to agree. Arlequin then uses his wand to transform the scene into the magnificent fairy palace where he disenchants a variety of characters to entertain them, each offering social commentary.

Traveling marionette troupes settled in Paris around 1650 and eventually found an audience at the Parisian fairs. The acrobats J. B. Archambault and the Féron family formed a company in 1668 at the fairground of St. Germain, then at St. Laurent in 1670. Dominique de Normandin (called La Grillé) established the marionette company Le théâtre des Pygmées, called the Troupe Royale des Pigmées (named for its four-foot puppets) in 1676 at the Marais du Temple. They were soon known as the *bamboches* (based on the Italian *bamboccio*), and their success caused the opera house to seek their suppression in 1677. The following year the troupe moved to fair at St. Laurent and produced La Grillé's *pastoral enjouee meslee d'ornamens singuliers & divertissans Les amours de Microton, ou Les charmes d'Ocran*—one of the earliest surviving marionette plays.[125] As would be the case in the eighteenth century, the plot is strongly derivative of commedia dell'arte magical plots: Orcan is a magician who uses his wand to invoke demons, transform a cypress tree and vases, and make statues dance. Cupid appears in act 3, as do a large dragon, four sprites, and eight demons in act 4. In act 5 a magic charm does the opposite of whatever one asks, and a

---

125. The printed *argument* survives in F-Pn, bound with *Les pygmées* (Paris, n.d.), shelfmark Res. Yf. 418–19, microfilm m.9164.

magically set table materializes. There are songs for the statues, a demon, and a magician, along with various dances for supernatural characters.

Magic in Court Ballets and Opera

Myth, the "marvelous," and magic played important roles in the ballets originated by the French court in the 1560s and developed through the next two centuries.[126] The lavish allegorical *Circé, ou Le ballet comique de la royne* of 1581 celebrated the magical powers of Homer's enchantress; the epic poems of Tasso and Ariosto provided subjects for later ballets. The *Ballet de Monseigneur le Duc de Vendôme* (12 January 1610 at the Louvre) is one of the first to use Ariosto's sorceress Alcina, who transforms twelve Christian knights into naiads. Armida and her demons appear in Etienne Durand's *Ballet de la délivrance de Renaut* (1617). Two years later Tasso's sorcerer Ismeno is a central character in *L'aventure de Tancrède en la forêt enchantée* (12 February 1619).[127] Isaac de Benserade and Lully also exploited Tasso's epic in *Le ballet des amours déguizés* (15 February 1664). The subject of the *Ballet des fées des forêts de St. Germain* (11 February 1625) was the medieval fairy world. *L'intermède d'Ascanio Pio de Savoie* (1628) unites Ariosto's episode of Bradamante and Roger with that of the fairy Mélissa and the magician Atlante in his enchanted garden. A magic wand appears along with stage machinery.[128] The *Ballet des alchemistes* (19 February 1640) mocks those in search of the philosopher's stone. Hermes Trismegistes appears dressed as philosopher and holding a magic wand; he then introduces four of the most celebrated alchemists of the world.[129]

The twenty-fourth entrée of the *Ballet du Roy des festes de Bacchus* (2 May 1651) depicts "les fées qui enchantent des esprits folets" (the fairies who enchant the scatterbrained spirits). The scene appears in one of the seventy-five illustrations made for a sumptuous copy of the text (see plate 1). Benserade, Molière, and Lully collaborated on the *Ballet des plaisirs de l'Isle enchantée* of 1664, a sumptuous *comédie-ballet* for Versailles (7–12 [or 14] May 1664). On the third day the *Ballet du palais d'Alcine* showed the sorceress holding captive knights enchanted in her palace. The fairy Mélisse provides a magic ring that dispels the enchantment and reduces the palace to ashes by means of fireworks ("en cendres par un feu d'artifice").[130]

Contemporary French commentators often describe opera as the natural locus of the "marvelous," meaning the *tragédie mise en musique*, a genre

---

126. Prunières, *Le ballet de cour en France;* Isherwood, *Music in the Service of the King;* McGowan, *L'art du ballet de cour;* and Christout, *Le ballet de cour de Louis XIV.*

127. Lacroix, *Ballets et mascarades,* 2:161–98, reproduces these early texts.

128. Mamczarz, *Les intermèdes comiques italiens,* 191.

129. Cited in Ménéstrier, *Des balets anciens et modernes,* 81–82. (Page numbers here and in other citations refer to the 1972 reprint.)

130. See Isherwood, *Music in the Service of the King,* 265–70.

derived from the court ballets and Italian opera and produced by the Royal Academy in Paris. These productions regularly included sleep scenes, incantations, enchantments, and the final intervention of a deus ex machina, all long-established elements in Italian opera. Like the ballets, French court operas had superhuman characters and divinities from mythology and epic romance, along with fantastic and underworld scenes. Jean-Baptiste Lully and Philippe Quinault played a critical role in establishing these kinds of operas as a national idiom. They based their last three operas on epic romance. The characters in *Amadis* (18 January 1684), the Portuguese-Spanish romance, included the fairy Logistilla, the magician Arcalaus, the sorceress Urgande, sirens, river deities, fairies, earth spirits, forest spirits, and a dragon. *Roland* (8 January 1685), with its fairy choruses and dances, recounted the story of a noble warrior-knight whose passion for Angélique causes him to forget the higher claims of honor and glory. She possesses a magic ring that makes her invisible. Lully and Quinault's last opera, *Armide* (15 February 1686), was based on *Gerusalemme liberata*. Furies, demons and other underworld deities, the magician Hidraot, and his niece Armide figure among its superhuman characters.

An operatic tradition was established (and expanded) in the operas of Lully's successors, Marc-Antoine Charpentier, Pascal Collasse, Henry Desmarets, André Cardinal Destouches, André Campra, and Marin Marais. Works such as Destouches's *Issé* (1697) achieved distinction almost equal to those of Lully. Homer's enchantress was the subject of Desmarets' *Circé* (1694), and the myth of Medea was the basis of Thomas Corneille's *Médée*, with music by Charpentier (1683). Orpheus also appears in the theater of *le grand siècle*. Charpentier set the myth twice, first in *Orphée descendant aux enfers*, a dramatic cantata (1683), and then in *La descente d'Orphée aux enfers*, a two-act *opéra* (1685–86). Other examples include *Orphée*, a *tragédie en musique* by Michel du Boullay, with music by Louis Lully (1690); the anonymous *intermède* titled *Orphée* found in the tragedy *Alexandre* (1690); and Campra's *Orfeo nell'inferni* (1699), mentioned earlier.

The Musical Language of the "Marvelous" in French Opera

French opera drew heavily upon the tradition of court ballet,[131] developing its existing musical style. In the second half of the seventeenth century ballet composers started employing descriptive music to accommodate the growing taste for the exotic and the grotesque.[132] This continued in opera, where dramatic action was more important than it had been in the ballets. The role of physical gesture in ballet and pantomime certainly played a part in the development of

131. Buch, *Dance Music from the Ballets de cour.*

132. See Lecomte, "L'orientalisme." Although there is less here on music than on decor, costumes, and plots, this is an important study that traces the interest in oriental exoticism back to Renaissance spectacles, demonstrating its development in court ballet.

the musical style of the "marvelous." Although Italian opera also influenced early French opera, Parisian composers wrote more descriptive marvelous music for storms, battles, dei ex machina, and magic transformations.

French instrumental ensembles comprised a large string band; a wind band with trombones,[133] cornetts, and shawms that performed in theatrical, equestrian, and concert venues of the court; and foundation instruments such as lutes, harps, and keyboards. Composers employed other instruments more rarely and for special effects. When opera replaced ballets in the French court of the 1670s, the recorders, oboes, bassoons, and, more rarely, trumpets became a regular part of the orchestra (which also had a continuo complement). The winds both doubled the strings and performed independent parts.

In the "first age of the operatic marvelous" Lully set both mythological stories and epic romance in his *tragédies mise en musique,* although nothing in the music differentiates the two.[134] As in the earlier ballet repertory, the affect is almost always elegant. This requirement had both a social and an aesthetic context: the society privileged elegance and decorum as the hallmarks of nobility, whose lineage was tied to divinity. Musical decorum demanded that even monsters be given elegant music. Within the limitations of this noble elegance, Lully employed musical devices to suggest the pictorial imagery and enhance the actions created by stage machinery for magical scenes and characters. These episodes ranged from short continuo passages for scenic transitions to larger instrumental pieces for ensembles with certain melodic, textural, and instrumental conventions. A few rests might suggest horror or dread; rapid sixteenth notes were sufficient to denote fear, fury, or frantic motion; abrupt rhythms and string flourishes implied magic and astonishment. An ensemble of recorders, strings, and trumpets can suggest the power and glory of the gods, or their anger. In *Amadis* (1684; act 4, scene 5) the sorceress Urgande arrives on a flaming rock with a dragon. Although there is no corresponding key change, the deity arrives to the sound of an elegant five-part *symphonie.* In Urgande's following recitative she uses her magic wand, and the mode abruptly changes to minor.

Rapid scales and repeated notes, rhythmic variety, and dotted rhythms accompanied monsters, demons, magicians, and scenic transformations. Low-

---

133. The trombones were apparently not associated with the underworld in the French theatrical tradition, as they were in Italian court *intermedi* and operas.

134. For the "first age of the operatic marvelous" I am borrowing the notion of "the three ages of opera" from Grétry, whose book *Les trois âges de l'opéra* (1778) discussed the eras of Lully, Rameau, and Gluck. On the expressive content of Lully's music, see La Gorce, "L'opéra sous le regne de Louis XIV." Also see Wood, "Orchestra and Spectacle," based on the author's "Jean-Baptiste Lully" and her articles on Desmarets and *Circé* in NGO. Also see Bouissou, "Mécanismes dramatiques." These authors do not trace the origins of Lully's style in either Italian opera or French ballets.

pitched sonorities, dissonance, pictorial imagery, and unusual instrumental and vocal combinations were also common in such scenes.[135]

Unlike the staid ceremonial sonorities and timbres of the Italian operatic *inferno*, Lully's "entrée des démons" in the ballet *Flore* (1669) and dances for "divinités infernales" in the opera *Persée* (1682; act 2, scene 10) evoke Hades with repeated rapid ascending and descending scales and a heavy accent on the first beat of the measure. Storm music is rare in Lully, but the composer uses rapid scales and whirlwind effects in the violins to suggest tempests, for example in the prologue to *Cadmus et Hermione* (1673) and in act 1 of *Alceste* (1674).[136] At the end of *Armide* (1686) Lully depicts the destruction of the sorceress's palace and the shaking of the edifice with a twelve-measure ascending bass line, along with the repeated rhythmic figure | ♩ ♫ ♩ ♩ |, imitating his earlier "subterranean noise."

Lully sometimes employed his most elegant instrumental music for magical scenes, for example the three-part string music as Médée changes the scene from a frightful desert filled with angry monsters into an enchanted island in *Thésée* (1675; act 4, scene 3). A brief chromatic descent in the bass, along with a short modulation, enhances the transformation.

Although enchanted sleep scenes were a convention in earlier Italian opera, it appears that Lully developed the association of the recorders with enchantment and magical sleep. The oft-cited prelude and air for *le sommeil* in *Atys* (1676; act 3, scene 4) is but one example. The recorders in Lully's earlier works also suggest enchantment, for example in *Thésée* (1675), where these instruments perform the "Air de l'isle enchantée" (act 4, scene 7). Caroline Wood points to a direct precedent for the sleep scene in *Atys* in a similar episode in a *comédie-ballet* titled *Les amants magnifiques* (1670), which features lulling stepwise motion in continuous slurred note pairs, scored for recorders in a slow to moderate tempo. The "symphonie agrëable" also utilizes the recorders, like the "soft music" of Italian and English scenes of enchantment, for example the "symphonie des enchantements" in *Amadis* (1684; act 2, scene 7).

As in Italian opera, the bass voice denotes authoritative magic characters such as sorcerers, oracles, spirits, giants, ghosts, and mythological deities. There are exceptions, such as the "voix derrière le théâtre" (an offstage tenor voice) in *Bellérophon* (1679), and bass voices may represent normal human au-

---

135. *Le Mercure galant*, November 1713, 46, describes dissonance as "servant d'ombres au tableau" and warns that overuse diminishes its force, impugning the Italians for this excess.

136. The last category of Wood's essay concerns tempests and earthquakes. The author doubts that Lully ever attempted such a scene. Wood found the first tempest in Collasse's 1689 *Thétis et Pélée* (act 2, scenes 7–9), which indicated the use of sound effects by a *batterie de tambour*. Marais wrote a hundred-measure storm in *Alcyone* (1706). Collasse, Campra, Desmarets, Stuck, Bertin, Lacoste, Salomon, Matho, and Rameau all composed music to depict the violent expressions of nature.

thoritative characters as well. As noted in chapter 1, these conventions were flexible and not limited to depicting otherworldly events and characters.

There are oracle scenes in three of Lully's operas, *Psyché* (1678), *Bellérophon* (1679), and *Phaéton* (1683), and these long remained popular. Almost two-thirds of Parisian grand operas included oracle scenes during the next thirty years. Ghost scenes often relied on the same devices. For example, in the ghost scene in Lully's *Amadis* (1684), when the shade of Ardan Canile appears to the evil enchantress Arcabonne, the music is in a low register in the key of C minor (a rare key for Lully). The unrelieved quarter-note pulse and quasi-monotone declamation in simple rhythms also make this episode somewhat unusual.

Lully employs repeated motives in the transformations of Proteus in *Phaéton* (1683; act 1, scenes 7–8), which occurs during a prelude and recitative, when low-pitched strings accompany the monotone of the bass's vocal line. The composer also portrays invocation, a feature frequently encountered in Italian opera. In *Thésée* (1675), act 3, scene 7, he provides an instrumental segment followed by Medea's conjuring of the demons of eternal night. The composer uses the French overture style, a musical expression of nobility. Lully's sorceress and demons must have been more elegant and noble than frightening, judging by their music. Octave leaps and melodic figures spanning an octave occur in the initial vocal gesture, which is a kind of bold clarion call.

Lully also provides vocal ensembles of superhuman characters. The Fates in act 4 of *Isis* (1677) sing in three-part homophony with melismatic vocal writing in a slow, solemn tempo with continuo accompaniment. In the underworld divertissement of *Alceste* (act 4, scenes 4–5), a four-part male chorus (TTBB) imitates the barking of the three-headed guard dog of Hades, Cerberus, with untexted, rapid repeated chords supported by a loud sustained pedal in the continuo part.

French composers of the last fifteen years of the century expanded the musical language that Lully had established, differentiating magical and otherworldly aspects with more pictorial devices. They developed a vivid accompanied recitative for magical scenes, with low-pitched sustained string accompaniment that paralleled similar devices in Italian serious opera. New vocal styles also conveyed more ominous expression for oracles, ghosts, and other superhuman characters. The occasional use of archaic styles for these scenes began a tradition that would develop more fully in the next century.

A few examples will serve to illustrate this expansion. *David et Jonathas*, a sacred opera with a libretto by Père François Bretonneau, set by Charpentier for Paris (Collège de Louis-le-Grand, 28 February 1688),[137] includes an oracle scene in the prologue where Saul consults a prophetess who summons an evil magic power. A slow, eerie *symphonie* for muted strings has each part entering in succession, creating an archaic allusion to older sacred counterpoint enhanced by inversion; an unusual "modal" sequence of chords (F–D–

---

137. Charpentier, *David et Jonathas*.

flat–B-flat minor–G minor–F minor, etc.); and a series of suspensions. In the next recitative the prophetess invokes darkness as a short *symphonie* for muted strings in B-flat imitates the trembling of the earth. With no significant melodic motion, Charpentier constructs this piece as a series of repeated chords in eighth-note rhythms with a brief harmonic progression. The prophetess then continues her recitative, now accompanied by ascending scales in the strings, announcing the arrival of the demons she invoked in her previous recitation. A short, forceful *symphonie* in E-flat for strings, with similar eighth-note scales, follows as the demons arrive. She now summons the ghost of Samuel with a slow, declamatory recitative in E-flat accompanied by sustained, low-pitched, muted strings. Her invocation is interrupted when the demons enact a pantomime to a contrapuntal passage for strings. Failing at first to arouse the ghost, she tries her invocation again, and the ghost of Samuel (bass) appears (scene 4). The ghost sings a recitative in G minor, accompanied by a *basse de viole* and two *basses de violone* with continuo. Set in a pseudo-archaic style that starts with an almost fauxbourdon-like half-note motion, this movement contrasts with the simple recitative of Saul, set to continuo. The composer accompanies the ghost's strangely stark singing with unusual modal harmony of B-flat and G minor, atypical inversions, and Renaissance-style suspensions. Charpentier constructed this passage from short segments in the bass, with ascending and descending tetrachords and a rising chromatic line.

Charpentier's *Medée*, his only *tragédie en musique* (performed 4 December 1693),[138] includes another archaic reference in act 3, scene 5, when Medea performs her incantation in a large scene complex (act 3, scenes 5–7), beginning with a long prelude in G minor for low-pitched strings with bassoons and continuo. The counterpoint here is reminiscent of late Renaissance fantasies for viol consort, an archaic style. Similar music, now with muted strings, accompanies Medea's first incantation ("Noires filles du Styx, divinités terribles, quittez").

Desmarets's *Circé* (1694) is worthy of special note.[139] Its magical sleep segment (act 3, scene 3) begins with an instrumental *symphonie* for two recorders and five-part muted strings. A repeating rhythmic pattern, the remote key of F minor, and the low-pitched accompaniment have an eerie, soporific effect.[140] The chorus of Nightmares is especially striking, with its unison bass voices singing frequent leaps. Supernatural unison bass voices would be used similarly in the eighteenth century. In act 4, scene 5 the ghost of Elphenor (bass) appears and sings with a low-pitched five-part string accompaniment. His slow, somber melodic line has ominous repeated notes set against repeated rhythmic motives.

Destouches's *pastorale-héroïque Issé* (1697) offered a new kind of oracle

---

138. Charpentier, *Medée*.

139. A print (Paris: Ballard, 1694) survives in the F-Po, shelfmark A 35.

140. Wood, "Orchestra and Spectacle," 39.

scene that would be the object of admiration and imitation (see chapter 2).[141] In the large scene complex in act 3, scene 5, the High Priest and his subordinates consult the enchanted oaks in the forest of Dodonne, whose rustling leaves foretell the future. The scene begins with a solemn march in A minor that uses an archaic style reminiscent of the polyphonic pavanes of the late Renaissance. The strongest dissonance occurs on upbeats before important moments of arrival, a characteristic of *entrées* in court ballets.[142] The High Priest then sings an air, followed by a chorus that marks a departure from the Lully style: it has an imitative opening. The five-part string orchestra mostly doubles the four vocal parts save for the highest viola, which participates in the imitation. Next, a prelude introduces the invocation of the High Priest. Again the instrumental introduction employs an archaic style for the five-part string music, marked "très gravement." The opening motive is the old canzona rhythmic figure. Strict and free imitative entries support a gradually ascending top voice, after which a short instrumental passage introduces the invocation, an *air* using imitative three-part accompaniment, "Arbres sacrés, rameaux mistérieux." The following chorus, "Chênes divins, parlez tous," another invocation, has an imitative middle section. The response to this conjuring is an instrumental passage with soft ("doux") and conjunct parallel thirds that Lully exploited for his magic sleep music. Here it suggests the breeze in the forest of enchanted oaks. Act 4 has a magic sleep scene with recorders, based on *Atys*. This music becomes the accompaniment for the High Priest when he announces that the oracle will speak. The oracle itself is strikingly original in its marvelous effect. Sung by a tenor in a slow-moving recitation limited to the range of a fourth and frequent repeated notes, the pronouncement is accompanied by sixteenth notes in the continuo instruments, punctuated by chords in the six-part string orchestra.

Several marvelous episodes are noteworthy in Destouches's *Amadis de Grèce* (1698).[143] The composer provides instrumental pieces in fast tempos for magic scenes, as in Lully's operas. The fast tempo also figures in the chorus of magicians, who sing a bass melody in unison with repeated notes, accompanied by low-pitched strings. This style recalls the similar chorus of Dreams in Desmarets's *Circé* (act 4, scene 8), a possible model for this chorus and the *chœur de démons* in act 3, scene 3, whose melody is also a unison bass line with repeated notes. The lengthy prelude to act 5 is distinct from the others in the opera. Chromaticism, pedal point, and a low tessitura contribute to the setting of the scene, a terrifying cavern where Mélisse performs her enchantments. In act 5, scene 1, Mélisse conjures the ghost of the prince of Thrace. A brief transition

141. Published in Paris by Ballard in 1697, 1708, and 1724. Ballard published the full score ("Partition généralé,") in 1724.

142. See Buch, *Dance Music from the Ballets de cour.*

143. Printed in reduced score (Paris: C. Ballard, 1699, F-Pn, Vm² 155). For a facsimile of the 3rd ed., see Destouches, *Amadis de Grèce.*

in the continuo links Mélisse's invocation to an instrumental passage evoking the spread of a black vapor when the ghost arrives. When the ghost declares that Mélisse will not succeed, the repetitive accompaniment figures recall the obsessive rhythms of Desmarets's scenes of horror and awe.

The "Marvelous" in Late Seventeenth-century German Opera

Seventeenth-century German theater also includes an array of magical material not unlike that of Italy and France.[144] One of the particular traditions associated with the supernatural in the German (and English) imagination is Faust. Theaters offered productions based on this popular legend in various German-speaking cities during the eighteenth century.[145] Jesuit theatrical productions stressed the religious and miraculous aspects of the "marvelous" by means of devils, demons of vengeance, ghosts, sorcerers, the occult, transformations, stage machinery, and magic.[146] The Jesuits had their own precursor to Don Juan in the Ingolstadt Jesuit drama (1615).

The influence of magical elements from French and Italian sources is evident in German opera. The earliest German Orpheus opera was J. J. Löwe von Eisenach's singspiel *Orpheus aus Thracien* (1659). Johann Philipp Krieger's operas usually employed mythological and legendary materials (for example *Orpheus und Euridice* [Eisenberg, 1683] and *Der wahrsagende Wunderbrunnen* [1690]). Operas based on the myth of Jason and Medea include *Jason,* a five-act singspiel on a text by Friedrich Christian Bressand, with music (lost) by Johann Sigismund Kusser (Brunswick, 1692). Reinhard Kaiser's singspiels for Brunswick utilize similar subject matter, for example *Circe, oder Der Ulysses* (1695, lost) and *Orpheus* (1689; rev. 1699; Hamburg, 1709). At least two of Keiser's operas for Hamburg's Gänsemarkt, *Procris et Cephalus* (1694) and *Hercules und Hebe* (1699), exploit mythological subjects, and did similar operas at Hamburg by Johann Wolfgang Franck. Johann Hugo von Wilderer composed fantastic Italian operas for Düsseldorf and Heidelberg (with instrumental movements and dances by Georg Andreas Kraft) such as *Giocasta* (1696). Few sources for these operas survive, and the musical component must remain a matter of speculation. Manuscripts from eighteenth-century revivals and revisions of these works can provide limited information on the techniques used by these composers for magical scenes (see chapter 5.)

144. Flemming, "Le merveilleux."

145. Dabezies, *Le mythe de Faust*, cites the following performances: Graz, 1608; Dresden, 1626; Prague, 1651; Danzig, 1668 and 1679; Munich, 1669; Bremen, 1670 and 1690; and Basel, 1696.

146. Flemming, *Geschichte des Jesuitentheaters*.

CHAPTER ONE

L'Académie Royale de Musique

Until the Revolution, the French royal court continued to sponsor elevated, "marvelous" genres (mostly ballets and operas), where decorum prevailed in mythological allegories that justified the aristocratic social order. Here the marvelous plays a traditional role as the affirmation of divine right. These productions were almost always formal, ceremonial, and stoic, except for an occasional comic episode or short divertissement that might exploit the grotesque. *Tragédie en musique*, a heroic sphere of drama treating conflicts of love and glory or honor versus passion, concerned the affairs of the aristocracy. Thus mythology continued its reign at the official theaters patronized by the royal court. Both in revivals of older repertory and in new settings, Orpheus, Jason and Medea,[1] Circe, Iphigenia, and their kin made frequent appearances. Epic romance also figured in the repertory, whether in full settings of episodes from Ariosto such as Antoine Danchet's *Alcine*, with music by Campra (1705), or in the use of isolated elements and characters. Tasso also continued to be plundered as a source of marvelous episodes in the texts of ballets and operas,[2] as did the chivalric tale *Amadis*.

In addition to mythology and epic romance, the theater also absorbed new literary sources, both in *grand* and *petit* genres. New subjects for the grand genres included fashionable fairy stories and "oriental" tales, beginning with Stuck and Mennesson's *tragédie en musique*, *Manto la fée* (1711).[3] Subsequent

---

1. Russo, "Visions of Medea," provides a comprehensive listing of the Medea operas in France, including some of the comic parodies from the fair theaters.

2. See Frati, "Torquato Tasso in musica."

3. The librettist Mennesson's first name is unknown; he is thought to have died in 1742. Christout, *Le merveilleux et le "théâtre du silence,"* 284, singles out two principal styles of *la féerie*: the comic-burlesque and the fantastic. The former had roots in the ballets of the seventeenth century, where sumptuous, ethereal fantasy sought to surprise through extravagance. The latter appeals

tragédies en musique have more diverse supernatural elements, as do *ballets-héroïques*, *pastorales-héroïques*, and other grand genres performed at the Royal Academy. The ballets of 1730–60 also exploited *le merveilleux féerique* for its erotic allure, for example François Rebel and François Francœur's highly successful "ballet féerie" *Zélindor, roi des Silphes* (17 March 1745; see plate 2). In all of these productions fairies and genies assumed roles formerly assigned to the superhuman characters of traditional mythological and pastoral genres. Librettists based grand operas on oriental tales but not on indigenous fairy tales associated with children's literature.

Literary Debates and Poetics of the Grand Genres

Although the classicists condemned opera for its use of the marvelous, partisans of modernity such as Charles Perrault argued that the nationalistic and Christian references in modern genres made them morally superior to classical subject matter. As a modern theatrical genre, similar to the *conte*, opera must go beyond the bounds of the natural rather than slavishly imitate it.[4] The writer Houdar de La Motte, an early eighteenth-century apologist for the marvelous in opera, glorified the genre as the modern successor to tragedy.[5] Jean Terrasson similarly delighted in the replacement of the mythological gods with the fairies and genies of the "moderns."[6] But the debates about the efficacy and appropriateness of opera mostly revolved around the attitude toward illusion's "rape of the senses." Moralist commentators such as Saint-Évremond condemned opera and the illusions of the senses,[7] claiming that the intellect forms a secret resistance to such illusions, rendering them ineffective. Rationalist and moralist critics, on the other hand, associated illusion with deceit. Supporters of opera such as Rochemont answered these charges by asserting that the effect of all fiction is to create illusion, a device with an old heritage based on magic.[8] Jean-Baptiste Dubos tried to mitigate the problems associated with illusion and verisimilitude in the theater by demanding that the supernatural adhere closely to nature.[9] Drawing on Aristotle's *Poetics*, he put forth imitation (or mimesis) of nature in music as the measure of verisimilitude.

---

to the fantasies of childhood and animism by the use of contrasts. French fairy tales belong to the second category.

4. Perrault, *Parallèle des anciens et des modernes*, 3:283: "Dans un opéra . . . tout doit être extraordinaire et au-dessus de la nature. Rien ne peut être trop fabuleux dans ce genre de poésie; les contes de veille . . . en fournissent les plus beaux sujets et donnent plus plaisir que les intrigues les mieux conduites et les plus régulières." See Parker, "Pastoral Drama."

5. Antoine Houdar de La Motte, "Second discours sur la tragédie," *Œuvres*, 4:88.

6. Terrasson, *Dissertation critique*, 1:396.

7. Saint-Évremond, "Sur les opéra."

8. De Rochemont, *Réflexions d'un patriote*, 129–30.

9. Dubos, *Réflexions critiques*, 154–56.

In arguing that mimesis is the basic principle uniting the arts, Dubos observed that dramatic context determines verisimilitude. He maintained that preludes and *ritournelles*, when outside the scenic context and devoid of a libretto, sound "insipid," and "bad" (*mauvaise*). It is only a relationship to the action that gives such music meaning.[10] The idea of the real tempest moves the audience, not the actual music. Without a context where word, idea, or emotion can be identified readily, music only puzzles the literary-minded individual whose aesthetic understanding is based on mimesis. Dubos discusses some of the most fantastic episodes of *tragédie en musique*, such as the ghost scene in Lully's *Amadis*, the oracle episode in Destouches's *Issé*, magic sleep enchantments, and the restoration of Orlando's sanity by the fairy Logistille in Lully's *Roland*. Such scenes are only believable when they sound the way we imagine they should.

Like many issues in the Quarrel of the Ancients and the Moderns, the matter of opera and verisimilitude came to no real resolution. However, the debate allowed for new approaches to the old questions. Voltaire asserted that because the very basis of opera is bizarre and magnificent spectacle, with its demons, magicians, fairies, monsters, appearing and disappearing palaces, the application of classic poetic rules to opera is as inappropriate as introducing dancing and demons in classical tragedy.[11] Callières, Boileau, Perrault, L'Héritier, and Terrasson all drew a clear contrast between the mythological marvelous and the fairy-tale marvelous.[12] By 1741 the Abbé de Mably was distinguishing two types of fables in Quinault's opera librettos, the ancient and the modern, the first corresponding to the pagan deities, the second to magicians from the more modern Christian epic romance.[13] Louis de Cahusac and other defenders of the marvelous would later take up this twofold distinction.

For Toussaint Rémond de Saint-Mard (1741) the marvelous element and divertissements were the exception to the classical rules of tragedy and should be allowed only in opera.[14] Charles Batteux designated a "grand genre" of the marvelous, restricting it to opera.[15] Thus the marvelous and the fairy world were now concepts associated particularly with grand opera, and as Catherine Kintzler notes, the term "marvelous" came to mean *tragédie en musique*.[16] In Batteux's *Cours de belles-lettres* (1747) the marvelous aspect indeed became the justification for opera's continuous singing.[17]

By the middle of the eighteenth century a kind of reconciliation was evident

10. Ibid., 155.

11. François Marie Arouet de Voltaire, preface to *Œdipe* (1730), in *Œuvre* (Paris: Garnier, 1877), *Théâtre*, 1:47ff.

12. For citations, see Magné, "Le chocolat et l'ambroisie," 97.

13. Mably, *Lettres*, seconde lettre, 49. Cited and discussed in Kintzler, *Poétique de l'opéra*, 261.

14. Saint-Mard, *Réflexions sur l'opéra*.

15. Batteux, *Les beaux-arts*, tome 1, chap. 8, p. 274.

16. Kintzler, *Poétique de l'opéra français*.

17. Batteux, *Cours de belles-lettres*.

in practice as well as theory. As interest in rules derived from antique theory dwindled, the theater of the marvelous continued violating most of the classical strictures. Fairies, magic, and classical mythology were seamlessly combined with little concern for literary tradition.[18] Indeed, distinctions among eighteenth-century genres tended to reflect the current social order more than a consistent poetic system.[19] But the questions about verisimilitude and marvelous effects were not simply disregarded; rather, they reappeared in an entirely different context, one of far greater controversy and political moment. In this debate commentators such as Rousseau, Grimm,[20] and Noverre would cede marvelous and supernatural aspects to theatrical dance,[21] reserving their most severe objections for opera at the Royal Academy.

Music and the Marvelous in the Grand Genres, 1700–1733

For much of the seventeenth century, as discussed above, music had retained an essential association with the marvelous, and composers had little need to create specific techniques to suggest magic or divinity until late in the century. With no clear distinction between the broad categories of the natural and the supernatural, music retained an association with the mystical, the mysterious, and the divine. The notion of natural or white magic, as practiced by a beneficent sorcerer, persisted in literature and the theater throughout the period.

It was not until the eighteenth century that all magic would be commonly seen as something outside nature, or, as Jean-François Marmontel and his contemporaries called it, "supernatural" (*surnaturel*). Once the Enlightenment completed the dissolution of music's connection to magic, the view of music itself changed. Theory became another systematic scientific activity, based solely on natural laws. No longer magical or divine in and of itself, music to theorists such as Jean-Philippe Rameau could be explained in purely rational terms, and composers developed musical devices to suggest both natural and supernatural topics. As discussed in the preface, these devices were decorative in nature, the sonic equivalent of the staging. Rather than attempting to cre-

18. The combination of mythology with "la féerie" is the subject of the *avertissement* for Rameau and Marmontel's *pastorale héroïque Acante et Céphise* (Paris: Delormel & Fils, 1751).

19. In France the period's commentators concentrated first and foremost on the plot and style of the text in musical theater; it is in this context that they often cite the source(s) of the story. Music usually figured among the secondary, decorative elements, along with costumes, stage designs, and machinery. Although the amount of detail in such commentary varied, discussion was often limited to determining whether the music fit the story and noting any perceived defects.

20. Grimm, "Poème lyrique," in *Encyclopédie;* reproduced in Grimm, "Poème lyrique," in *Encyclopédie méthodique*, 1, 3e partie, 102. See the preface for details.

21. This reconciliation is discussed in Kintzler, *Poétique de l'opéra français*. An important exception is Noverre, *Lettres sur la danse*. In *lettre* viii (1978, 197), he attacks the marvelous, even in the ballet. But this Rousseauian diatribe appears to have been opportunistic, for Noverre continued to choreograph dances with fantastic content.

ate "enchantment," composers depicted the illusory scene with an appropriate "tone of enchantment" (Cahusac; see preface), as in a painting or set design. Thus late seventeenth- and early eighteenth-century composers created a category of devices for the magical and the superhuman to enhance dramatic effects in theatrical music. Changing tastes in the later eighteenth century required a heightened degree of realism to make those effects believable, and opera expanded its vocabulary of topics and allusions for invocations, transformations, ghost scenes, and oracles.

Composers for the eighteenth-century stage gradually mastered and manipulated the decorative aspects of theatrical music. Decoration in turn necessitated formulas based on inherited techniques for depicting magical events and superhuman characters. In the course of the eighteenth century composers not only developed these older techniques, they also devised new ones.

Serious operatic genres in eighteenth-century France retained the association of magic and divinities with their earthly counterparts, the nobility. French elegance, the hallmark of aristocratic and divine characterization, continued to govern the decorative musical style. However, the developing pictorial imagery in instrumental pieces and in the accompaniment to vocal numbers is particularly noteworthy for its departure from the almost ubiquitous decorum and grace of French style. Moreover, physical movement and gesture in ballet and pantomime (essential components in French productions) certainly influenced stage music.

Thus the period when composers developed devices to depict magical and marvelous events on the stage must be considered an important episode in the history of musical mimesis. But in assessing these techniques one should bear in mind Dubos's observation: musical representation is not independent of context, for mimetic conventions are not fixed or invariable. Musical images derive their identity from the theatrical situation, which determines the choice of key, melodic style, harmony, texture, rhythm, dynamics, and timbre.

At least seven elements of the marvelous musical style in the first half of the eighteenth century may be delineated:

1. Traditional and new uses of instrumental music to accompany stage machines, transformations, magic, storms, the sudden presence of darkness or light, states of trance, and similarly remarkable events in a plot. Instrumental *sinfonie* and *ritornelli* signaled magic in *intermedi* and court opera. French *tragédie en musique* had its short instrumental ritornellos and preludes, often leading to recitative. Short sections with continuo accompaniment only could also provide musical sound effects, guiding the singers and musicians through the workings of the stage machinery into the next scene. Composers such as Rameau and the team of Rebel and Francœur composed especially elaborate music to accompany stage machinery.

Elegant music continued to be associated with divinities and their earthly counterparts, the aristocracy. Of course, elegance in music is a relative term.

Here it designates more lyrical, metrical, and formal episodes than the music that precedes and follows it; often the timbre is brighter and the sonority more consonant as well. It creates a distinct moment of grace, suggesting nobility with an elevated expression. English sources indicate "soft music," while the French specify a "douce symphonie" or "aimable concert." Such music can also accompany transformations, sleep, trance scenes, and other magical events. Trumpets can depict the brilliance of a divinity and the startling effect of a sudden supernatural appearance.

2. Exaggerated, emphatic expressions for imposing or evil superhuman characters, such as magicians, sorceresses, genies, and fairies. (See the examples below from Rameau's *Zoroastre*.) The most common of these conventions were:

    a. *Alla zoppa* syncopation,[22] which disrupts the normative beat pattern with rhythms that suggest agitation and disturbance: | ♪♩ ♩ ♩ ♪|

    b. Extremely rapid scale passages (both ascending and descending), suggesting anger, flight, or sweeping motion. These were also evocative of physical gestures in ballet and pantomime.

    One of the most frequent conventions involves a triplet or quadruplet to a quarter or half note: ♫ or ♫ . These accompany all kinds of emphatic expressions, including powerful jolts, animal sounds, howling, and the horrific sounds emanating from infernal regions.

    c. Octave-and-unison sonority for emphatic motivic or melodic figures suggesting terror or merely underlining a special passage. Other examples of octave-and-unison gestures include descending arpeggios with emphatic dotted rhythms for added force. This sonority, devoid of harmonic color, could also evoke the "hollow" or empty aspect of a scene or mental state.

    d. Harmonic aspects, also figuring in the repertory of emphatic expression. The choice of key, the use of minor mode and diminished chords, harmonic ambiguity, and quick changes of mode were all devices that suggested force and extreme emotion. Rameau was especially skilled in the use of harmony for marvelous effects.

3. References to otherworldly events and characters through instrumentation and sonority. Two distinct trends develop: the first from older opera and church music traditions, and the second—with a new, more vivid naturalism—first appeared in France shortly after Lully's death. New instrumental combinations and sonorities continue to mark the exotic quality of marvelous operatic orchestration.

4. Ensembles of superhuman or magical characters, for example witches' covens, monsters, and sprites. Examples range from ogres in early *opéra-comique* to Rameau's three Fates in *Hippolyte et Aricie*.

---

22. For a discussion of this "limping" (*zoppa*) figure, see Ratner, *Classic Music*, 85.

5. The use of accompanied recitative in French opera, as discussed in the introduction.

6. Distinctive vocal writing for magical and superhuman characters. The most popular was a kind of incantation with a chantlike melody, recalling the treatment of a cantus firmus, or chorale-like writing. These "intonations" were reserved for magicians, spirits, oracles, and similar characters (early examples are cited in the introduction). Conjuring and incantation may also employ normal recitative, as in Rameau's *Zoroastre,* or fanfare-like gestures, suggesting a clarion call of sorts, also in Rameau's *Zoroastre* and in *Les Boréades.* Distinctive vocal writing can also make a supernatural character stand out in relief from normal mortals, through the use of simpler and more emphatic melodies. This tradition dates back to early Venetian opera and its incantation scenes. The use of descending octave leaps in the vocal line of a magician, sorceress, or superhuman character, first found in late seventeenth-century English and French opera, becomes a pan-European operatic convention in the eighteenth century.

Modern writers often use the term *ombre* or *ombra* (meaning shade or specter) to refer to underworld scenes or to the earthly appearance of ghosts in opera. This word is problematic, for it conflates several different traditions that were not always related. There are, for instance, ghost scenes in Lully's operas and those of his successors at the Royal Academy. In some cases these are similar to oracle scenes; in others they are not. Often they call for special treatment, as discussed in the introduction. In the eighteenth century ghost scenes in French operas occurred mostly in those based on the Iphigenia or Alcestis myths.

7. The use of particular keys for horrific effects. Composer continued to cultivate these associations, with keys such as C minor, F minor, and E-flat beginning to be favored for magical or horrific scenes. They often set infernal scenes in E-flat, a key Charpentier (c. 1692) found to be "cruel and hard."[23]

To this discussion I would add one further observation, namely that composers employed these conventions in different ways and with differing degrees of efficacy. The chronological discussion below will highlight the various individual approaches to musical expressions of the marvelous and the supernatural, giving special attention to composers who developed these techniques in distinctive ways.

❋

Composers of the generation of Destouches, Aubert, and Campra developed the vocabulary of Lully's musical language, expanding oracle, storm scenes,[24]

---

23. For a review of key characteristics, see Steblin, *History of Key Characteristics.*

24. Marais wrote a hundred-measure storm episode in his *Alcyone* (1706).

stage-machine music, and *bruits* of various kinds (subterranean and aerial rumbling were the most common). Elegance still dominates this fundamentally decorative style, with its musical depiction of horror, terror, and catastrophe derived from Lully's rapid string figurations, abrupt rhythmic changes, and dotted rhythms. Composers still employed both short continuo sections and longer preludes and *ritournelles* for scene transitions. They continued to favor the bass voice for authoritative magic characters such as magicians, oracles, ghosts, and deities, as for example in Michel de la Barre's *La Vénitienne* (1705; act 2, scene 2) and Marais's *Alcyone* (1706; act 4, scene 4). But the music of this generation was more pictorial than that of Lully.

Although recorders and flutes still suggested enchantment (the term "douce symphonie" often accompanies this scoring),[25] compositional techniques grew more complex. In his *Tancrède* (1702) Campra adds recorders when Tancrède enters the enchanted forest. A *symphonie agréable* with recorders continues the sonic suggestion of enchantment. In *Alcina* of 1705 (act 5, scene 2), Campra introduces the recorders as Alcina transforms lovers into trees. (Stuck included similar instrumental movements in *Manto la fée* [1711], as did Jean-Baptiste Mathau in his prologue to *Arion* [1714].) These "enchanted" recorder ensembles (and the string symphonies that occasionally accompany magic events) differ from their predecessors in their close-voiced interweaving polyphony with chains of suspensions and accented dissonance.

Instruments are also used in new ways. In Campra's setting of Danchet's *Alcine* (15 January 1705),[26] the marvelous still evokes the elegance associated with nobility through conjunct, symmetrical phrases in consonant sonority. But when La Gloire descends in the prologue, the trumpets double the strings, adding a brilliant and ceremonial quality to the appearance of the god of glory. An "aimable concert" commences when Mélanie magically rises out of the sea (act 2, scene 1), accompanied by the genies of the fairy Mélisse who have been transformed into *tritons et néréides*. The startled exclamations of the admiring Athlant and Crisalde are accompanied by an elegant *ritournelle* for strings, alternating with passages in parallel thirds for two oboes supported by a bassoon.

Along with new instrumental combinations, the post-Lully generation employed imitative texture for the marvelous scenes. The opening of act 4 of Campra's *Alcine*, set in a magic cavern, begins with an elegant imitative *ritournelle* for strings. Elegance dominates even a storm scene (act 4, scene 3), with terrifying monsters and ghosts, all suggested simply by an increase in the surface rhythm. When the enchanters appear (act 4, scene 5) the instrumental pre-

25. The occasional specification of a "flûte allemande" as opposed to a "flûte" indicates a transverse flute. Composers employed trumpets and drums for special effects, along with musettes and other unusual instruments.

26. Only the short score survives, Paris: Ribou [1705] (RISM C704). I consulted the copy in the Newberry Library, Chicago, IL.

EXAMPLE 1.1 Louis de Lacoste, *Philomèle*, act 2, scene 3, "Prélude pour la descente de Minerve"

lude seems like a ceremonial procession, reminiscent of a French overture. The second scene of act 5 uses instrumental music to emphasize a dramatic change: lightning and a terrible din (represented by rapid eighth-note motion in the violins) yield to elegant music for recorders as Alcine's captives are freed by the beneficent powers of Mélisse.

Louis de Lacoste's score for *Philomèle* (libretto by Pierre-Charles Roy; 20 October 1705) has four traditional marvelous episodes that show a subtle flair for originality.[27] The pastoral *symphonie pour l'Amour* has two *flûtes allemandes* and one violin part. The divertissement in act 2, scene 3 includes a "prelude for the descent of Minerva" in C major, where Lacoste created a delicate elegance with three-part, close-voiced texture and parallel thirds (see ex. 1.1). A light, floating quality derives from his circuitous melody, repetitive phrasing, consonant harmony, and high tessitura. The succeeding duple-meter dance in D major for the Furies recalls Lully's depiction of terror, with its rapid sixteenth-note passages, abrupt rhythmic figures, and dotted rhythms. But Lacoste's Hadean dance is more contrapuntal than those of Lully. A brief departure from the elegant style occurs in the "vîte" D minor prelude to act 4, scene 3, where Jealousy appears with a dagger. Disruptive, irregular rhythms erupt in a striking chromatic segment. The following chorus of Furies has male voices (TTB) for the representation of female deities, a grotesque device used by Rameau and other composers later in the century.

When it premiered on 20 January 1711, *Manto la fée* introduced a new kind of libretto, one that portrayed the fairy world. Jean-Baptiste Stuck (called Batistin) provided the music for Mennesson's libretto:[28] Spurned by her beloved Prince Licarcis, Manto abducts Ziraine, the Syrian princess with whom the

27. Reduced score (Paris: Christophe Ballard, 1705), F-Po, shelfmark A.68 B1, B2, B3.
28. Reduced score (Paris: Christophe Ballard, 1710).

prince has fallen in love. Ziraine, however, loves Prince Iphis, the long-lost son of Manto. Merlin's powerful magic eventually resolves the intrigues. Subterranean scenes and a pantomime combat with a dragon figure among the numerous supernatural events. The commentator Rochemont described Stuck's style as including "musical beauties of a new taste,"[29] perhaps referring to the preference for contrapuntal textures, or perhaps the pictorial musical imagery. These elements are apparent at the beginning, when a magic cloud transports the fairies Manto and Ismène to a palace in Syria, accompanied by an imitative *ritournelle* for strings with fanfare motives. In fact, the composer provides mood-setting preludes in all the acts. When in act 2 Merlin and Iphis, riding on a sea monster, arrive on Manto's desolate island, the composer provides a processional march in the elevated style with imitative texture. Act 4 begins in a dark subterranean cavern; the prelude, marked "gravement," suggests a slow, noble march. A *symphonie* marked "gai" begins the fifth act, another imitative piece, here evoking Manto's enchanted castle and garden.

Stuck employed a variety of descriptive music for the scene transformations. Some scenes include traditional brief continuo preludes, but others have more elaborate instrumental settings, as when Manto causes the winds to howl as her aerial spirits abduct Ziraine in a cloud (act 1, scene 5). A prelude represents the dark whirlwind with sixteenth-note scales and repeated notes. Similar music occurs when the spirits and winds struggle in a pantomime (act 3, scene 8: *bruit pour les vents aeriens*), and during the combat episodes in the final act (scene 4). In act 4 a *ritournelle* for recorders begins as a dark cave changes to a magnificent room, with deities arranging themselves for a *fête galante*. The music has fully imitative part-writing, with a chain of suspensions and complex harmony, features associated more with older church music than with French opera (see ex. 1.2). Even the heroine, Ziraine, reacts with astonishment at the unusual sound. Thunder announces the final transformation as the enchanted castle disappears and Merlin arrives with Ziraine and a hundred captive beauties. A polyphonic *ritournelle* for strings and recorders in A minor evokes this event, and the recorder ensemble continues in close-voiced polyphony and chains of accented suspensions.

Other magical operas at the Academy at this time were less inventive than *Manto la fée*. Although Joseph-François Salomon's successful setting of Pellegrin's first libretto, *Médée et Jason* (24 April 1713, with four revivals, 1713–49),[30] includes music depicting magical events with descriptive symphonies and fantastic dances, the music seems somewhat conservative in style. For example, in act 5, scene 1, Médée invokes the three Furies (alto, tenor, bass), and they join her for a quartet. The style here seems more suited to the elegant

29. Rochemont, *Réflexions d'un patriote*. Stuck's earlier opera *Méléagre* (1709) utilized Italian vocal and instrumental styles, and these could have been the new musical beauties that Rochemont observed.

30. Salomon, *Medée*.

EXAMPLE 1.2 Jean-Baptiste Stuck, *Manto la fée,* act 4, scene 1, *ritournelle*

tradition of court ballet than that in recent Hadean episodes. The *bruit sou-terrain* recalls the first part of a French overture rather than an underground rumbling of contemporary French opera, and the composer renders a terrifying noise as fast repeated notes, as Lully did. Médée's incantation scene (act 2, scene 1) employs a rather simple recitative invocation in the declamatory style, followed by a short, unpretentious "symphonie effrayante" accompanying the whirlwind of clouds that transports Médée with her magicians and demons. At the end of act 4 Salomon suggests a thunderstorm with a rapid sixteenth-note prelude for "toutes les basses," a short continuo segment that leads to a chorus where sailors express their terror, accompanied by a four-part orchestra depicting the winds and thunder with repeated-note motives. One harmonic device is particularly noteworthy: in act 2, scene 2, Médée transforms the pleasant countryside to a "hideous place, where the greatest crimes of Médée are formulated," and a short descriptive *symphonie* modulates from B-flat major of the previous recitative to a somber G minor. Marked "doucement," this music utilizes the dotted rhythms and rapid scale figures of the French overture. B-flat returns for the first *air des magicians* and an abrupt four-part chorus of magicians and demons accompanied by "furious" string figures.

Destouches's setting of Pierre-Charles Roy's libretto *Sémiramis* (4 December 1718) further demonstrates the composer's gift for vivid musical depiction in scenes that represent magic.[31] When Zoroastre (bass) conjures an enchanted palace in act 3, scene 3, the composer provides a prelude and lyrical recitative, accompanied by a string ensemble scored in the low range (violins, violas, bass viols, and contrabass), a device of the post-Lully period for oracular pronouncement. The prelude is in free imitation with chromatic harmony. Zoroastre's emphatic bass voice has a series of descending phrases with numerous leaps. For the two magical scene transformations the composer employed the same imitative instrumental interlude with sixteenth-note descending figures, performed "détachez." In the fifth scene of act 4 the oracle appears and sings its decree in a slow-moving bass voice with frequent repeated notes, the monotone of post-Lully oracles. A plaintive G minor suits the low-pitched string accompaniment.

Pellegrin revisited the Rinaldo and Armida encounter (made famous by Lully) in his *tragédie lyrique Renaud, ou La suite d'Armide,* with music by Desmarets (5 or 14 May 1722).[32] Audiences and critics did not like the opera, perhaps owing to the continued popularity of Lully's *Armide* and the inevitable comparison. Here the marvelous seems more akin to Lully, however, than in Desmarets's earlier *tragédies en musique.* The final *entrée* is in fact a *passacaille,* perhaps intended to recall Lully's *passacaille* in *Armide,* when the sorceress commands her demons to raise an enchanted palace. Although there are many indications of marvelous effects in the libretto, only some have musical depiction, and these are rather conservative and even reverential toward Lully's version. For example, when Armide and Mélisse arrive in a magic vessel in the second scene of act 2, Desmarets accompanies their entrance with a short "doux" prelude in close-voiced, imitative texture, set for two violins (doubled by winds) with continuo. Act 5 includes a short segment with thunder, depicted by conventional rapid sixteenth-note runs. In the act 4 divertissement Armide summons her demons with an *invocation magique,* for which Desmarets provided a brief instrumental prelude with dotted rhythms and short, brisk scale figures, recalling the opening of a French overture.

La reine des péris, a *comédie persanne* in five acts and prologue, written by

31. Reduced score, Paris: Ballard, 1718 (F-Pn, Vm² 270).
32. Reduced score, Paris: Ballard, 1722 (F-Pn, Vm² 276).

Louis Fuzelier, with music by Jacques Aubert (10 April–4 May 1725), was a rare comedy at the Royal Academy.[33] Nonetheless, aside from the exotic setting (Ginnestan, the home of the *peris,* the favorable genies of the Turks and Persians) and oriental customs depicted in the story, both the text and music are in the form and style of the *tragédie en musique,* with little to distinguish it from earlier works with texts based on classical mythology or chivalric poetry. Perhaps Fuzelier designated this a comedy owing to the exoticism of the oriental fairy tale rather than the standard plot and characters: French operatic stereotypes with Persian names and costumes. With one exception, exoticism is not evident in the music either, which remains in the noble style typical at the Royal Academy. From the overture to the recitatives, *airs,* and divertissements, there is little to distinguish the sonority, melody, rhythm, and harmony in this "oriental" opera. A few marvelous episodes do, however, employ more expressive music. In act 2, scenes 4–5, the queen dismisses her genies and they vanish to the music of a *symphonie* in G major. She immediately revives Fatime with her magic wand and at this point in the recitative the mode changes to G minor. Transformations use short continuo passages, reminiscent of Lully's scenic changes. The fourth act begins on the Isle of Inconstancy with an imitative *symphonie* in E minor. Scene 4 is a divertissement for Inconstancy and her attendants. Aubert depicts these divinities with abrupt changes in rhythm, dynamics, and phrasing during the "Air des zephirs et de l'Inconstance." The *air chinois,* following the unremarkable "Marche des Chinois, Péris, et Arabes" (act 5, scene 6),[34] is Aubert's single attempt at musical orientalism. The libretto describes a chariot decorated in the Chinese fashion and a Japanese palace, a mixture of "Asian" styles; the melody and bass line (see ex. 1.3) have unusual short, repetitive motives with rhythms such as 𝄃 𝅘𝅥𝅯𝅘𝅥𝅯𝅘𝅥𝅯 𝅘𝅥𝅯𝅘𝅥 𝅘𝅥𝅯𝅘𝅥 𝅘𝅥 𝄀.

Pirame et Thisbé is Rebel and Francœur's first operatic venture, a *tragédie en musique* on a libretto by Jean-Louis-Ignace de La Serre after Ovid's *Metamorphosis* (15 October 1726).[35] The composers basically adhered to the post-Lully generation's penchant for colorful pictorial imagery and counterpoint. The opera's mythological prologue includes a *prélude pour la descente de Vénus.* To accompany the floating stage machine the composers supplied a close-voiced, high-pitched trio scored for two recorders and violins (one line in the reduced score) in D minor, introducing the recitative of Glory (la Gloire), also scored with two flutes (see ex. 1.4). Suspensions evoke a seemingly weightless, otherworldly state.

In act 2, scene 5, Zoroastre unleashes wind and thunder with a furious interlude for flutes and strings performing descending sixty-fourth-note runs.

---

33. The libretto was published (Paris: Veuve de Pierre Ribou, 1725), as was a reduced score (Paris: The author, 1725). Cahusac singled out the work along with *Manto la fée* in "Féerie," 464.

34. Here I disagree with Weller, "Aubert, Jacques," who states that this work "does not attempt exotic effects."

35. Reduced score (Paris: Carfour & Boivin, 1726), F-Pn, shelfmark X.910.

EXAMPLE 1.3 Jacques Aubert, *La reine des péris*, act 5, scene 6, "Air chinois"

The composers depict the descent to hell with a simple descending bass line. In act 4 Zoroastre (bass) begins a divertissement, invoking "the spirits of the air and the earth" in G minor with a rapid triple-meter, imitative *ritournelle*. The next prelude, for recorder and violins, introduces the homophonic chorus of the spirits. This rapid duple-meter prelude in B-flat major has dizzying figuration, with descending sixteenth-note runs and a final thirty-second-note flourish that elides into the chorus. A triple-meter *air pour les esprits aeriens* in B-flat

EXAMPLE 1.4 François Rebel and François Francœur, *Pirame et Thisbé*, prologue

follows the chorus, with appropriately airy sixteenth-note figuration. One particularly effective moment occurs in the final act. The stage slowly becomes illuminated as E minor changes to E major. The brief combat with the monster is accompanied by a prelude in E major with thirty-second-note figuration, leading to the triumphant ending.

Thus Rebel and Francœur are transitional composers, beginning their operatic careers with a masterful demonstration of the conventions of French grand opera during first two decades of the century. They would become more adventurous in their later compositions for the Academy, with a new approach to musical depiction often attributed today solely to the innovation of Rameau (see below).

The Second Age of the Marvelous, 1733–74: Rameau and His Contemporaries

Rameau and his contemporaries expanded the French conventions of the marvelous. At first attacked by the old guard for deviations from tradition, in a few years it became apparent that Rameau had actually breathed new life into grand opera, helping to sustain interest in the genre and keeping at bay the growing Italian influence that was so successful elsewhere in Europe. Eventually Rameau achieved acceptance as a legitimate heir to the tradition of *tragédie en musique* and thus he then became the target of reformers whose agenda included a revolutionary vision of the theater, propelled by new social and philosophic ideas. With the success of Gluck in Paris in the 1770s, Rameau's innovations seemed old-fashioned and timid when compared to the force, violence, and passion of a new kind of opera, a "third age of the marvelous" at the Royal Academy.[36]

Two aspects of Rameau's background seem significant in assessing his contributions to opera. First, his broad knowledge of musical technique and practice, owing in part to his activities as a theorist and commentator, influenced his compositional approach. In addition, his experience as a composer for the fair theaters of Paris, where an experimental spirit was necessary, may also have influenced the broadening of his musical vocabulary for the stage. Rameau expanded traditional French conventions of the marvelous: sweeping instrumental motives, vocal incantation, storm scenes, subterranean or aerial *bruits,* enchanted music for flute or recorder ensemble, and exalted marches. All of this Rameau derived from Lully and his followers. But in his first opera for the Royal Academy, *Hippolyte et Aricie* (1733), Rameau added significantly to the mimetic conventions of the marvelous. In dances, *entr'actes,* and short, contrasting segments of instrumental music, he provided vivid "sonic images" for choreographic expression and for the appearance of superhuman characters and events. In vocal numbers it was the accompaniment that often displayed the mimetic elements. Rameau also anticipated his marvelous events before they occur, using instrumental figures that forecast the next episode in the plot. For music accompanying stage machines Rameau used more complex orchestration and texture both in extended pieces and in brief, contrasting preludes that served as "sonic images." Even in his first opera Rameau heightened the violent effects of thunder, swelling waves, and similar events.

Much of Rameau's vocal writing maintains the grandiloquent style of the *tragédie en musique.* Incantations are delivered in the manner of the clarion call, with moderately paced, bold rhythms and wide melodic leaps. Variety in vocal expression is still a matter of subtle gradation. Unlike Lully's immediate successors, Rameau was not inclined to use monotone recitation or evoke the cantus firmus style. Nor are characters sharply defined as individuals by their vocal style, with the exception of the occasional use of coloratura. As such, Rameau's overall vocal writing is as stylized as Lully's or that of his followers.

Critics viewed this intensification of the earlier style music as "baroque" and artificial. But Rameau was a distinctly individual composer who departed from convention. He expanded the use of counterpoint started by his predecessors Destouches and Desmarets. His choruses featured more complex textures than those of his predecessors, with imitation and staggered entries. Extensive polyphony is also apparent in some instrumental dances, ballets, and vocal ensembles.

36. See introduction, n. 134.

One should regard Rameau's occasional extended coloratura for characters with supernatural powers, expressing an almost demonic intensity, as another imaginative and effective aspect of his theatrical music. Indeed, this approach contrasts with the customary restrained vocal style of *tragédie en musique*. But the melodic style of the solo vocal pieces is less adventurous in marvelous scenes than the accompaniments, and Rameau developed a more predictable approach to oracular pronouncement than Desmarets or Destouches. Reinhold Hammerstein has studied Rameau's settings of invocations and oracles.[37] Providing examples from *Hippolyte et Aricie, Castor et Pollux* (1737), *Le temple de la gloire* (1745), *Les fêtes d'Hébé* (1739), *Les fêtes de Polymnie* (1745), and *Zoroastre* (second version, 1756), he shows how Rameau devised a set of procedures from earlier conventions. Contemporaries recognized these procedures as distinctive and original.[38] Rameau set off the brief oracle segment within the scene complex from the surrounding music by providing different meter, key, dynamics, and vocal style. Rameau's vocal line for oracular pronouncement employs a simple syllabic setting, adhering to the metrical declamation of the spoken text, sometimes in an anapestic meter that suggests a quasi-archaic psalmody and its double verse structure. On occasions when the expression intensifies, Rameau accompanies the voice with either continuo alone or a special string accompaniment playing sustained notes, often for low-pitched instruments such as the *basse de violone* and the bassoon. When accompanied by the strings playing double stops, the effect is a soft (*doux*) sustained sound, the favored device of Italian recitative for similar scenes. The composer differentiated between the report of an oracle or a divine pronouncement and the actual event in real time on the stage. He also distinguished Olympian oracles from the Hadean type. The latter are horrific in nature, more extreme in affect, and lower in range of voices and instruments. They were never marked "doux."

Perhaps from his experience with parody and grotesque music at the fair comedies, Rameau created some unusual vocal ensembles for superhuman characters. He selected male voices for the female Fates (*parques*) in the two remarkable trios from *Hippolyte et Aricie* (composed in 1733, but not performed in the original production). The first (act 2, scene 4) serves as an oracle, with a syllabic treatment accompanied by the low strings. The second trio (act 2, scene 5) has three segments: an introduction with dotted rhythms, an enharmonic section expressing terror, and the actual prophesy. Rameau set the prophetic segment in his usual calm oracular manner, with simple rhythms, continuo accompaniment, and "doux" diatonic homophony.

37. Hammerstein, "Invokation—Göttersprach—Orakel." Hammerstein does not take into account either Caroline Wood's research on post-Lully French opera or Charpentier's remarkable setting of the oracle scene from the prologue of the sacred opera *David et Jonathas* (1688). Composers set oracle scenes with similar devices over a half a century before Rameau.

38. Laurent de Béthizy, *Exposition*, 290, praises Rameau's use of sustained notes in the accompaniments of invocations, and Decroix relates these to the organ in *L'ami des arts*, 106.

Rameau's orchestration is richer and more varied than that of earlier composers. Graham Sadler has described, in addition to novel orchestral combinations (e.g., the bassoons and clarinets in *Zoroastre* and *Acante et Céphise*), instances of Rameau's exceptional use of instruments and original approach to scoring.[39] Many of these features occur during supernatural episodes, with storm scenes and magic transformations receiving imaginative orchestral effects. Examples include Rameau's unusual divisions of the string sections for certain passages in *Hippolyte et Aricie*, such as the "shaking of the sea waters" (*frémissement des flots*, act 3, scene 9) and the second trio of the Fates (act 2, scene 5). Multiple stops in the strings often coincide with marvelous events and expressions. Examples include thunder in *Castor et Pollux* (act 5, scene 4), with its low pitches on open strings, and the solemn recitative accompaniment with sustained double-stops (act 5, scene 6), a device from earlier eighteenth-century *tragédies en musique*.[40] Rameau also gave the winds virtuoso passages in the *bruit* segments, for example the flutes in *Hippolyte et Aricie* (act 4, scene 3). The oracular birdsong of *Naïs* (act 2, scene 6), scored with two *petites flûtes*, two *grandes flûtes*, and continuo, is but one example of Rameau's simulations of nature. He could also signal the marvelous by unconventional combinations of instruments, for example trumpet, flutes, and strings for the "descent of Venus and Mars" in the prologue of *Castor et Pollux*.

Although Rameau's placement of instrumental pieces in opera was traditional, the content of that music could be unconventional. In both *Zoroastre* and in *Les Boréades* the composer replaced the prologue with a three-movement overture to suggest a dramatic series of events. When Rameau's librettist Cahusac described mimetic *symphonies* that produce agreeable illusions, he was perhaps referring to Rameau's descriptive instrumental writing. In *Hippolyte et Aricie* Aricie's sleep scene in an enchanted garden (act 5, scene 3) has the violins playing conjunct pairs of sighing motives while the "magic" flutes play languishing sustained notes and expressive trills. The brief, choreographically inspired "Vol des zéphirs" (act 5, scene 7) is a sonic image of flight. Elaborate divertissements are more closely linked to the dramatic action than in earlier French opera, as in the bloody sacrifices of *Zoroastre* or the events in *Les Boréades* (see below). Rameau's novel use of key and harmony as expressive devices connected to a dramatic situation seems related to his interest in theory. His most vivid depictions of terror employ enharmonic alterations, for example the polyphonic trio of the Fates (act 2, scene 5) from *Hippolyte et Aricie*. When dis-

---

39. Sadler, "Rameau and the Orchestra," offers a detailed analysis of this aspect of Rameau's composition, avoiding the faulty conclusions of past discussions based on the unreliable *Jean-Philippe Rameau: Œuvres complètes*. However, Sadler's commentary in NGO evinces occasional disdain for the supernatural elements in Rameau's stage works.

40. Notably, Desmarets, *Circé* (1694), and Destouches, *Issé* (1697), up to Montéclair, *Jephté* (1732).

cussing his theoretical principles, Rameau described this ensemble as a depiction of horror through enharmonic means.[41]

Whether a novel technique is entirely original or was influenced by others is not always apparent. Even if we consider Rameau a highly original composer, he was not alone in developing new expressive techniques for supernatural events on the stage in the 1730s and 1740s. An analysis of selected music by Rameau, followed by a discussion of music by his contemporaries, will detail instances of the experimental approach to the representation of fantastic scenes that seems to have been common at the time.

Some Selected Works by Rameau

Little remains of Rameau's music for fair comedies. He set vaudeville airs and provided incidental music in Alexis Piron's *opera-comique L'Endriaque* (1723), a send-up of chivalric romance with numerous magical events.[42] He also contributed to at least three other comedies by Piron while attempting to secure major operatic commissions in the later 1720s. Thus Rameau certainly had some experience by the time he set his first *tragédie en musique, Hippolyte et Aricie*. Olympian and Hadean oracles fill this much-criticized text, as do divine invocations and conjuring. The prologue has magical appearances of several divinities. For example, in scene 2 Diana invokes Jupiter (with a sustained string accompaniment) to help her resist Cupid. An instrumental prelude for the descent of Jupiter follows, a solemn marchlike piece with pompous dotted rhythms. Rameau loosely based the trios of the Fates in the underworld (act 2, scenes 4–5) on Lully's Fates in act 4 of *Isis* (1677), using the same key; three-part homophony (the three characters sing as one in their prophecies); a slow, solemn tempo; and continuo accompaniment. Although Lully's harmony seems restrained, Rameau's remarkable enharmonic language in the second trio is right at the limits of the chromatic language of the period.

For the next twenty years Rameau produced music with originality and skill to evoke magic and enchantment on the stage of the Royal Academy. His next opera, *Castor et Pollux* (1737; text by Pierre-Joseph Bernard; substantially revised in 1754), marshals some of the contrapuntal novelties of *Hippolyte et Aricie* with more conventional elements. The prologue offers standard musical images: a magical descent for Venus and Mars in a cloud chariot is accompanied by a "douce symphonie," with trumpet fanfares suggesting the martial deity and flutes and strings evoking his erotic counterpart. When Jupiter (bass) descends in act 2, Rameau employs the aristocratic dotted rhythms of a French overture. Act 3 begins at the entrance to the underworld, where Télaïre

41. Rameau, *Erreurs*, 59–60. "Toute l'horreur qu'elles annoncent se trouve peinte dans un *genre diatonique enharmonique*."

42. A volume will be devoted to this opera in the new *Opera omnia* (Paris: G. Billaudot).

sings Apollo's oracle with Hadean musical references: rapid, agitated marvelous figures depict lightning and thunder. But when Phébé invokes underworld demons, Pollux and Télaïre attempt to stop them in a complex contrapuntal trio, "Sortez, sortez d'esclavage." The demons (a male chorus) block Pollux's way to Hades singing forceful contrapuntal choruses (although they dance to lively, elegant music with rapid figuration). Act 4, set in the Elysian Fields, has an extensive divertissement of ethereal *ombres heureuses,* whose music is both graceful and contrapuntal. Rameau scored their dances and chorus with the flutes playing conjunct duplets, a convention of soporific enchantment. The powerful and extended *bruit* for strings in act 5 depicts the thunder signaling the arrival of Jupiter. A graceful "symphonie mélodieuse," scored with flutes, serves as stage-machine music when the deity descends. When Jupiter orders a scene transformation, Rameau sets his words as an oracle, with accompaniment by sustained low strings. He highlights the pronouncement with brilliant string figures to suggest the clearing of the clouds and the movement of the sun through the visible zodiac over Mount Olympus. Divinities from the heavenly sphere join Jupiter for the final divertissement of the opera, where the composer once again employs brilliant string figuration. Each scene in act 5 seems a distinct sonic picture of scenic contrast.

Two years later Rameau set *Dardanus,* a text by Charles-Antoine Le Clerc de La Bruère (19 November 1739). Rather than striking out in new directions, this opera seems to consolidate the composer's skills in a more conventional manner. *Dardanus* begins with an allegorical prologue about Venus and Cupid, including a magic sleep scene. In act 2 the magician Ismenor reveals the extent of his supernatural powers with a forceful invocation that causes an eclipse of the sun. Double stops on the sustained strings accompany a disjunct vocal line, with its fanfare-like clarion call. An incantatory chorus of magicians continues the occult ceremony. Venus and her Dreams visit Dardanus in act 4 and Dardanus battles a sea monster, set to storm music.

Rameau's first collaboration with Cahusac was also the composer's first experience setting an oriental fairy story with exotic elements. *Les festes de Polimnie* (12 October 1745), a *ballet-heroïque* commissioned in celebration of the battle of Fontenoy,[43] consists of a prologue and four entrées, like the *opéra-ballets* at the Royal Academy. The third and last entrée is *La féerie,* an oriental fantasy, and here the composer provided vivid and distinctive marvelous effects using harmony and rhythm. A short, fast prelude heralds the magic descent of the fairy Oriade with her ward Argélie, a "sonic image" made of rapid sixteenth-note figures for oboes, strings, and continuo. Perhaps the composer selected the key of D minor to enhance the scene's setting—a somber, deserted forest. The tempo, rhythm, and figuration suggest the motion of the descending machine (see ex. 1.5). In scene 5 the fairy's son Zimès is sleeping to the sound of a duple-

---

43. Only a reduced score was published (Paris: Ballard, n.d.). The edition in *Œuvres complètes* 13:316–422 is an unreliable reconstruction.

EXAMPLE 1.5 Jean-Philippe Rameau, *Les festes de Polimnie, la féerie,* "Descente d'Oriane et de Argélie"

meter prelude in C minor, scored with flutes. Argélie arrives with her nymphs to the same music, followed by a vocal *air* and "Danse des nymphes." The scene then changes to the fairy's garden, and Rameau prepares this transformation by moving from C minor to C major when Argélie sings of love. A short prelude modulates to G major as Zimès awakes to the enchanted song that Argélie and her nymphs sing in praise of Cupid. His bedazzled exclamation might serve as an emblem for the marvelous: "Quels accords importuns! Où suis-je? Quel séjour?" (What troublesome chords! Where am I? What abode?). This scene prefigures the remarkable awakening scene in *Pygmalion* of 1748.

Cahusac's next libretto for Rameau was an Egyptian *opéra-ballet, Les fêtes de l'Hymen et de l'Amour, ou Les Dieux d'Egypte,* commissioned for the wedding of the dauphin in 1747 (revised 9 July 1754) and consisting of the three *entrées:* Osiris, Isis, and Canope. The second *entrée* has a pagan sacrifice scene with a high priest and chorus invoking the water god Canope. Suddenly the stage darkens and a "noise similar to thunder" occurs. The music, for the most part, seems skillful but unadventurous until the Nile overflows and Canope appears in a chariot drawn by two giant crocodiles (recalling the worshipped beast in the *opéra-comique L'Endriaque*). An unusually large ten-part chorus accompanies this spectacular use of stage machinery.

Cahusac and Rameau's next collaboration, *Zaïs,* a *pastorale-héroïque* (1748),[44]

44. Published in reduced score (Paris: Delormel, n.d.), edited in *Œuvres complètes* 16.

fully developed the pastoral mode, an association often linked to this kind of
fairy story. Rameau's interest in the musical representation now turned to the
ambitious overture, which represents the primordial separation of the four elements and the formation of the universe out of the void. Rameau created an unusual variation on the French overture, with a slow introduction rather than a
procession or a march. (Rebel and Francœur had done much the same in *Zélindor, roi des Silphes;* see below.) Abrupt motives, staggered phrases, and unusual
harmonic progressions mark an original style that Rameau would exploit again
in his last opera, *Les Boréades* (act 5, scene 1). The faster contrapuntal section in
triple meter has rapid figures for *petites flûtes,* representing aerial spirits. The
numerous mimetic *symphonies* are now very economical, more vividly depicting images such as a flaming whirlwind and torrents of fire. Flutes highlight
the brisk string scales to suggest lancing flames. During the storm music (act 2,
scene 4; and act 4, scene 1), rapid repeated notes in the low strings depict thunder, and fast ascending scales for strings and flutes evoke lightning. Magical
scene transformations are not reflected in the music, but Rameau employed
his particular accompanied recitative for the oracle scene (act 4, scene 1). The
"Chœur des sylphides" (act 1, scene 2) is a stunning, ethereal ensemble for female voices, with a striking string prelude and accompaniment.

In 1748 Rameau and Ballot de Sauvot adapted Antoine Houdar de La
Motte's arrangement of the legend of the Cyprian king and sculptor *Pygmalion.* This *acte de ballet* became one of the composer's most popular works for
the stage.[45] Rameau developed an original musical means to portray the magical transformation in scene 3, when the statue awakens. A dramatic change of
key, from G major to E major, occurs for "une symphonie tendre et harmo-
nieuse," and the stage becomes more illuminated. Thomas Christensen has
suggested that this may be a demonstration of Rameau's idea of the *corps sonore,*
the putative source from which human beings learned to create music.[46] In fact,
Rameau may have even been attempting to depict animation through the experience of music, a power attributed to music since antiquity. Chromatic modulation, new orchestration "à demi jeu," and an ascending major triad depict the
mysterious force (love) that transforms the statue and creates the new light on
the stage. The first movements of the statue are represented in the next section,

45. Rameau's next *acte de ballet* was *La guirlande, ou Les fleurs enchantées* (1751), on a text by
Marmontel. The score contains mostly elegant decorative music for this aristocratic and idyllic
fairy story about a pair of magic garlands that stay fresh as long as the lovers remain faithful. The
modern edition in *Le pupitre* is based on a printed reduced score, manuscripts, and the printed libretto (F-Pn, Rés. Yf. 762).

46. Christensen, *Rameau and Musical Thought,* 218–31, discusses this segment in the light of
"sensationalist" theories, some of which draw on the analogy of the animation of a statue. He views
the unfolding of the upper partials of the E major triad and the disposition of the F major triad in the
subsequent chorus as corresponding to the initial proportions of Rameau's *corps sonore* and a "musical allegory of Lockean sensationalist psychology" (231). Incidentally, Rameau uses the same triadic
disposition for the strings and winds in Apollo's magic appearance in act 5, scene 5 of *Les Boréades.*

marked "lent," a series of soft, brief flute motives interspersed with Pygmalion's exclamations of surprise. Rameau then depicts the subsequent descent of the statue with a pair of descending triplets. For the first tentative steps of the statue he composed a march constructed from a descending tetrachord in half notes. The statue then speaks the lines "Que vois-je? Où suis-je? Et qu'est-ce que je pense," describing a process of growing consciousness, starting with perception, then moving to thought.

Perhaps Rameau's most ambitious *tragédie en musique* to date was another collaboration with Cahusac, *Zoroastre* (1749; revised 1756).[47] Cahusac stated that he departed from convention by turning to Persian sources for the oriental fairy-tale plot concerning the sorcerer Zoroaster, who by 1749 was a familiar figure on the French musical stage.[48] The tragic element concerns the passion of love, which drives people to commit ignoble deeds. Zoroastre is a tenor, and the villainous cultic priest Abramane is a bass. Both characters have choruses for the attendants, Zoroastre with his magicians and Abramane his subordinate priests. A fairy and genie appear in act 3, graceful and elegant supernatural characters. But for all the novelty of its libretto, the score of *Zoroastre* seems rather tepid. Rameau derived some of the music from the unperformed opera *Samson,* which he had written with Voltaire in the early 1730s. This might explain the old-fashioned music in certain passages, although the composer also adapted two recent pieces from the *Pièces de clavecin en concerts* (1741).

The overture of the 1749 version replaced the prologue, beginning with storm music in the "Dorian" D minor,[49] changing to a pastoral D major section, and ending with a fast section in duple meter with bustling sixteenth-note figures. The composer then supplied standard magical scenes that seemed to demonstrate his lack of interest in breaking new ground. Act 2 opens with a sleep scene scored with flutes. Among the instances of magical stage-machine music is the descent of Zoroastre in his chariot (act 3). Here Rameau provided four measures of rapid ascending scales in octaves.

As in his earlier invocations, Rameau favored recitative. In act 1 the sinister Erinice invokes the Furies, and Amélite implores the gods for support. The Furies appear at the end of the act in a three-part male ensemble (TTB), like

47. A reduced score was published around 1749 (Paris: Veuve Boivin, n.d.). The first modern edition of the 1756 revision is *Zoroastre: Tragédie lyrique de L. de Cahusac,* restored by Gervais. Based on the manuscript score (F-Pn, Vm⁷ 376) and parts (F-Po, Fonds La Salle 2), this score is highly edited, with the ornaments fully written out. For a modern edition of the 1749 version, see Rameau, *Zoroastre (version 1749).* An edition of the 1756 version will appear in the same series.

48. For a synopsis of both versions, see Graham Sadler, "Zoroastre," NGO 4:1244–46. As with *Die Zauberflöte,* commentators have interpreted the opera as a Masonic allegory, owing to the fact that Cahusac was a Freemason and the story occurs in Egypt. This interpretation, as in the case of Mozart's opera, is speculative.

49. Rameau characterized D minor with the same attributes as the Dorian mode (grave and serious), and the contemporary German theorist Johann Mattheson made a direct correspondence between them. For details, see Steblin, *History of Key Characteristics,* 39, 45–49.

the Fates in *Hippolyte et Aricie*. The music, marked "vîte," has rapid sixteenth-note accompaniment. Act 2, scene 5 contains an oracle scene where La Voix (a high tenor) warns Zoroastre of the coming danger, but the scene contains little to distinguish itself. Zoroastre has invocations in acts 2 and 5, and the villain Abramane invokes flames and thunder with a contrapuntal chorus in act 4. After some dances, Abramane and Erinice call upon their demons (singing coloratura passages on the word "volez"), and they appear as a three-part male chorus accompanied by furious scales in the strings. An extended divertissement ends the act as Vengeance arrives and her demons dance a ballet. The Furies sing a contrapuntal ensemble with Vengeance, accompanied again by rapid sixteenth-note figures. The climactic end of the opera has Abramane and his army attacking Zoroastre. The music depicts a storm with thunder and a battle, along with invocations by the Zoroastre and Abramane. But all of these events seem tame in comparison to the most effective dramatic moments in earlier works. Perhaps this gave Rameau greater impetus to completely revise the work in 1756 and produce a much more memorable opera.

Rameau's experimental spirit and novel approach to harmony, texture, rhythm, and the orchestra (and to a lesser degree, the vocal writing) seem to have been most inspired in scenes of magic and enchantment. Rather than a result of interest in abstract theory, as some others have argued, the composer appears concerned with mimesis and the potential of sonic images to enhance a theatrical moment. To some degree this approach is also evident in supernatural episodes of Rameau's contemporaries.

Contemporaries of Rameau

Works based on fairy-tale texts appeared at the Royal Academy well before Rameau, and most of the music was conservative. This would continue to be the case in the 1730s. The marvelous episodes in Fleury's ballet, *Les Génies, ou Les caractères de l'amour,* with music by Mademoiselle Duval (1736) recalls Lully's orchestration, with its strings, continuo, and flutes (or recorders) for moments of enchantment.[50] The ballet begins with an invocation, an accompanied recitative with rapid violin figures, for the magician Zoroastre (a bass). Zoroastre exclaims, "Quels bruits, quels doux accords, quelle clarté nouvelle!" (What noise, what sweet chords, what new brightness!) when the flutes enter. There is nothing in the vocal writing to suggest magic power and no musical accompaniment for the lifting of Ismène in the chariot of the genies (act 3, scene 3).

Jean-Baptiste Niel provided a little more dramatic music for Michel de Bonneval's *Les Romans* (1736),[51] where three of the *entrées* have marvelous mate-

---

50. The libretto was published (Paris: J. B. C. Ballard, 1736), F-Pn, Musique, D. 2765, and Imprimé, Yf. 724. A reduced score was also published (Paris: The authors, n.d.), F-Pn, Musique, D-3765.

51. Reduced score (Paris: Boivin [c. 1736]), F-Pn, Musique, D 11880, and other copies. In its first performance run, this *ballet-héroïque* consisted of a prologue and three entrées, *La bergerie, La*

rial. The continuo line contains descriptive elements, the flutes have a magical association, and short, pictorial *symphonies* depict supernatural events such as storms, a *bruit terrible,* and a subterranean *bruit.* A number of transformations, pronouncements, and magical events occur without any musical accompaniment at all. The *entrée* "La féerie" contains mostly elegant music, even for the *airs* for the elemental spirits. In scenes 3 and 4 two short pictorial *symphonies* have rapid runs in octave sonority that depict a *bruit* interrupting the fairies and Princess Eglantine. The motives are doubled at the octave below by the continuo ("toutes les basses"), as Démogorgon and his genies arrive and the startled fairies exclaim their surprise and scatter. When the fairy Logistille appears, rapid scales depict another *bruit terrible,* and fast, repeated sixteenth-note figures in the strings and continuo serve as accompaniment for her pronouncements. "Le roman merveilleux" includes an example of machine music as well. This plaintive, gentle segment for flute and strings in D minor (with touches of expressive dissonance) accompanies the arrival of Minerve and a scene transformation, serving as a prelude and *ritornelle.*

The librettist Jean-Jacques Lefranc de Pompignan's *ballet-héroïque Le triomphe de l'harmonie* (1737, with music by François-Lupien Grenet), has an initial *entrée* entitled "Orphée" with some notable orchestral effects that remind one of Rameau's vivid sonic images.[52] The scene in "L'enfer" with Pluto, Le Styx, and the chorus of demons and Furies begins with a slow, triple-meter "Prélude pour le Styx" in A minor, scored with contrabasses and bassoons. The music imitates the churning waters of the Styx as the violins play increasingly longer scale figures. Le Styx (bass) sings one line, "Coulez mes flots coulez et pouvantez le ombres," ending with a thirty-second-note run marked "sur l'extrémité de la mesure." The accompanied recitative for Pluto (bass) includes a pair of flutes. A chorus of demons in A minor is followed by a duet with Le Styx and Pluto in D minor, leading to a furious chorus with sixty-fourth-note scales accompanying the text "Qu'un supplice affroiable punisse le coupable et vanne les enfers." The first musical indication of Orphée's approach to Hades is a high-pitched, elegant A major instrumental interlude for two flutes and violins. The three-part "Prelude pour l'arrivée," a brief "sonic image" in G minor, signals a scene transformation as the chorus of demons and Furies exclaim "Quels accords?" in response to hearing this otherworldly music.

Toward the middle of the eighteenth century a new, *galant* musical style was in fashion. Simpler than the earlier baroque style, this music was primarily homophonic, with accompanying figuration in the broken-chord style of the Alberti bass and gracious ornaments on the periodic phrases to soften the melodic contours. This style came to be employed in the musical depictions of the marvelous. One of the earliest French stage works to employ it was François-

---

chevalerie, and *La féerie.* A fourth was added for the performance on 23 September 1736, called *Le roman merveilleux.*

52. The score was published (Paris: The author, n.d.), F-Pn, Musique, D. 5018.

EXAMPLE 1.6 François Rebel and François Francœur, *Zélindor, roi des silphes*, overture

Augustin Paradis de Moncrif's one-act *ballet féerie* or divertissement *Zélindor, roi des sylphes,* with music by the team of Rebel and Francœur (1745),[53] composers whom Cahusac considered masters of the marvelous. Like Rameau, they provided vivid, descriptive music with colorful orchestration and instrumental segments. The overture, in G minor and scored for flutes, bassoons, strings, and continuo, replaces the pompous, marchlike first section of the older French overture with a slow introduction, recalling a mood-setting prelude. Another unusual feature is the extended pedal passage on the dominant that leads to the second section, marked "gay." The new *galant* style is evident in this sec-

53. Published score (Paris: Madame Boivin, le Sieur le Clerc, 1745), F-Pn, Musique, L. 9977.

EXAMPLE 1.6 (*continued*)

ond section, with its characteristic ornaments (especially the graceful triplet
figures), short contrasting episodes, and alternating triplet and duplet figures.
The surfeit of embellishment here seems to suggest the fantastic world of the
sylphs (see ex. 1.6). The instrumental airs and preludes are descriptive, often
using repeating motives, such as the "Air pour les sylphes et salamandres." The

composers used loud, rapid sixteenth-note passages for dramatic marvelous episodes, such as in scene 4, the "Prélude pour les génies élementaires."

Jean-Marie Leclair's score for d'Albaret's *tragédie en musique Scylla et Glaucus* (1746),[54] after Ovid's *Metamorphoses,* contains numerous marvelous episodes, particularly the scenes involving Circe, deities of the underworld, nymphs, and a marine deity. The composer depicted supernatural events with vivid mimetic devices, especially in the accompanied recitative in acts 2 through 5. The accompanying figuration for marvelous episodes is faster and contains longer rapid scale passages than other segments. The prologue, set in the temple of Venus, includes a four-part *bruit de tonnerre* with fast repeated notes and rapid scales, suggesting lightning. Leclair wrote triadic fanfare figures in the triple-meter "Symphonie pour la descente de Minerve" for two trumpets, *timballes*, bassoons, five-part strings, and *basse* (in D major, marked "gay"). The "descente de Venus" in her chariot follows, scored for a three-part wind ensemble (two oboes and bassoon) and continuo in B minor. The unusual key and the wind instruments are both distinctive features. Increasingly composers would choose various kinds of wind ensembles to convey enchanted moments such as these.

Leclair lavished special care on the supernatural scenes. Circe appears in act 2 accompanied by a dramatic C minor prelude marked "gracieusement" and "lent et marqué," with suspensions and stark dynamic contrasts. As the sorceress summons the chthonic deities during an accompanied recitative in the "underworld key" of E-flat (act 4, scene 3; see ex. 1.7), the set changes to an erupting Mount Etna. The instrumental introduction begins with a series of extended rapid ascending scales in the violins, perhaps representing flames. The composer accompanied these figures with brief descending scales in the bass. A short episode of chromatic chords creates an eerie sense of unease as the moon appears. The ominous vocal line ("Noires divinités de la rive infernale") has wide leaps, outlining an initial descending octave. As is the case with most invocations to underworld deities, this one elicits a response: a "Chœur de démons" and two "Airs de démons" in E-flat. This first dance has extended thirty-second-note ascending scales and suspensions, and the second is a lengthy piece with running figuration. In scene 6 Hecate, the goddess of incantations, presents Circe with a poisonous herb to murder Scylla, her action accompanied by a continuo line with repeated thirty-second notes marked "tremissent." The mimetic *symphonie* in D major (act 5) that depicts the barking of monsters and the chasms is a violent ballet with long ascending and descending thirty-second-note scales in the flutes, strings, and bassoons; abrupt leaping motives; arpeggios; and repeated sixteenth-note figures.

Rebel and Francœur set Leclerc de La Bruere's *ballet-héroïque Le Prince de*

---

54. A manuscript survives in F-Po, shelfmark A. 158a, with numerous performance changes in red crayon. A printed score also survives (Paris: The author, Boivin/Le Clerc, n.d.). D'Albaret's first name is unknown; see Zaslaw, "Leclair's 'Scylla et Glaucus,'" 900.

(*continued*)

EXAMPLE I.7 (*continued*)

Noisy (Versailles, 13 March 1749)[55] with techniques similar to those used in *Zélindor, roi des sylphes*. The librettist and composers disregarded the satiric content of the original *conte* in favor of a serious plot that emphasized marvelous elements such as the pagan celebrations, a scene in act 1 for the gnomes, and the deception and murder of the evil giant Moulineau. A relatively large wind ensemble of flutes, *petites flûtes*, oboes, horns, and bassoons augments the strings and continuo as dark orchestral colors are exploited, often in low tessitura.

The overture has an unusual episodic form, and the unpredictable, almost capricious variety of motives, the extensive wind writing, and the fashionable *galant* triplets and ornaments all seem to suggest the fantastic world of a fairy

55. A full score was printed after the revival at PO on 16 September 1760 (Paris: The authors, n.d.) with some divergences from the libretto. An earlier version of this fairy-tale story, set by Jean du Mas d'Aigueberre, was staged at the Comédie-Française on 4 November 1730; no sources survive.

tale. A brief slow introduction leads to a faster section with fanfare motives and a mixture of triplets and duplets, often in antecedent and consequent phrases but sometimes more free. A cadential section then leads to a short, slow transition and a final segment in a bustling triple meter. The fanfare motives here are reminiscent of horn calls, with the rhythm.

There are numerous instrumental preludes and interludes. *Ritournelles* begin the acts, setting the mood and scene with sonic imagery. The pagan worship ceremony (act 1, scene 4) begins with an instrumental prelude in A minor for low strings and bassoons marked "très doux," with slurred duplets in conjunct motion for the violins and the bassoons in parallel sixths (this is called a *symphonie mystérieuse* in the libretto). The pagan ceremonial music in act 1 also includes a solemn processional, the "Air pour l'adoration du Guy." Act 2 begins in Moulineau's garden. A prelude in C minor sets the dark mood with wide melodic leaps, abrupt thirty-second-note scales, and persistent quarter-note rhythm in the bass. The *ritournelle* that starts act 3 in the temple of Truth is the most contrapuntal music in the ballet. Like the episode for the armored men in *Die Zauberflöte,* this oracle scene invokes the *stile antico* of sacred music. As Poinçon reads the inscription, the bassoons interject short figures. Demons suddenly transport his beloved Alie. The accompanied recitative here has marvelous sixteenth-note violin figures accompanied by flutes, bassoons, and bass punctuating the interjections of Poinçon, who exclaims "Quels sons!" Poinçon then banishes the demons, and a prelude depicts the furious rush into the inferno. The libretto mentions a second *symphonie mysterieuse* for the moment when Poinçon asks the oracle if Alie loves him. Here the composers provide a four-measure segment scored for strings, bassoon, and continuo. The oracle then answers to the same string, bassoon, and continuo accompaniment: "Alie has chosen the Prince of Noisy." An E minor prelude for the magical scene transformation features brisk ascending scales for the two violin parts and two oboe parts supported by continuo with basses. Alie reacts by exclaiming: "Quels sons brillants!" and the prince sings: "Quelle clarté nouvelle."

In act 2, scene 3, music scored with flute enchants Moulineau, putting him to sleep. The druid chorus then urges the hero, Poinçon, to murder the sleeping giant. Violent music erupts, and a sharply descending motive describes the act of murder, followed by an abrupt change of key after his death. The three-part gnomes' chorus with the druid (act 1, scene 1) is the most exotic of the vocal ensembles, with bassoon and strings accompanying the voices (TTBB). Two dance *airs* for the gnomes follow. The accompaniment is in a low range, with the strings and bassoons matching the low-pitched voices. The "Air pour les génies et pour les fées" (act 3, scene 5), scored for violins and bassoons, has ascending thirty-second-note scales in the bass, expressing a powerful, deep force.

Thus Rameau's contemporaries shared the master's experimental spirit and interest in creating varied, startling, and sometimes original music for supernatural events. It appears that magic episodes often inspired the musical imaginations of these composers to produce their most novel effects, creating and then varying the sonic language of the supernatural to delight and surprise their audience, long acquainted with the conventions of the "theater of the marvelous."

The Supernatural and Musical Expression, 1750–91

By the middle of the eighteenth century the notion that music was divine or magical had become a relic of the past, and the marvelous in the theater became identified with the supernatural. Only when composers, theorists, and critics could define music in purely rational terms and divest it of its mystery could they construct a distinct category for magical topics. Once the supernatural was accepted as a legitimate decorative and expressive element, it became demystified and was subject to skillful manipulation. This new approach to the topic of the supernatural would contribute to a related aesthetic principle in the early nineteenth century, the sublime.

By expanding the range of traditional musical practices with new techniques for portraying magical and otherworldly topics, French composers in the second half of the century were able to reinterpret earlier representational conventions as found in Italian arias and French opera. They applied these techniques to instrumental music, accompanied recitative, and vocal ensembles. To enhance expression they experimented with new instrumental colors, more daring harmonies, and new styles of vocal writing. At the same time, the use of older musical techniques, mostly from church music, became a more significant source of supernatural expression than in the past. Chantlike recitation, chorale-like settings, old-style polyphonic textures, and disjunct melodies that suggested baroque contrapuntal "subjects" contributed to a kind of musical antiquarianism evoking the otherworldly. A new expressive mode, also derived from contemporary Italian arias, employed much more vivid and violent music for infernal and stormy episodes. Powerful orchestral effects, augmented with brass and later timpani, imparted frightening and anguished expressions, such as hellish bellowing and blaring. This style, it should be stressed, is not that associated with the noble Hades of earlier opera, but rather with the horrific inferno of the Christian hell and the Last Judgment. Composers and librettists often designated it by the term "terrible," a word also used in discussing the sublime. The continuing influence on French opera of physical movements from ballet and pantomime must have contributed to the repertory of musical gestures in the terrifying style as well, although this aspect is difficult to assess with precision.

Certainly, music that elicits terror and abandons elegance and pleasure to pursue more disturbing emotions violates Cahusac's "agreeable illusion" in musical decoration. Combining such moments of terror with segments of noble elegance effected a kind of early musical expression of the sublime, and it antedates another remarkably effective combination, that of comedy and terror. (The new "terrifying" style can also be recognized in a variety of non-operatic contexts, especially instrumental music.) When considered in the light of theoretical discussions and theatrical context, the musical style that represented terror, divinity, and magic is a clear precursor to that used to suggest the sublime.

Certain literary impulses behind newer librettos also contributed to the growth of the musical language of the supernatural in the lyric theater. English "gothic novels," for instance, reflected a new fascination with violence and horror, also present in the musical theater, both in serious operas such as Salieri's *Les Danaïdes* (1784) and Luigi Cherubini's *Lodoïska* (1791), as well as in comic works such as André Ernest Modeste Grétry's *Raoul, Barbe-bleue*.

✳

The function of music as a decorative device directly linked to stage design and machinery is apparent in scores with verbal cues indicating how the music participates in scene transformations and other events in the plot. Composers continued to associate elegant "soft" music with beneficent divinities and their earthly counterparts, the nobility, as well as with sleep, trance, and magical transformations. Magicians, sorceresses, genies, and spirits, by contrast, often received more exaggerated and emphatic expression. Among these special effects were *alla zoppa* syncopation, suggesting terror, agitation and disturbing movement; rapid scale passages describing various events and emotional states; rapid scale figures, providing powerful jolts, animal sounds, hellish howling, and horrific threats from the Furies; the latter could also depict sword fights, swirling motion, confusion, supernatural winds, storms, lightning, infernal scenes, and terrifying apparitions. Composers often combined octave-and-unison sonority with bold scale figures and broken chords to signal drama and tension. The minor modes, diminished chords, harmonic ambiguity, and quick changes of mode also contributed to musical terror.

Earlier experiments with new instrumental combinations by Rameau and his contemporaries had made orchestration a clear indicator of the supernatural, and composers continued to suggest otherworldly events and characters through timbre and sonority. In addition to flutes, trumpets, and horns, the trombones suggested infernal imagery in the scores of Gluck and his successors at the Royal Academy.[56] Another important resource was greater use of accompanied recitative to achieve a powerful dramatic force through vivid mimetic devices and a free approach to musical form and style in longer and more complex scenes. The new genre of melodrama indeed owes much to this kind of recitative. Other novel vocal techniques included distinctive writing for supernatural characters—a resource that continued to be developed in the later eighteenth century. One such is a kind of incantation with chantlike, cantus

---

56. An early "magic" use of a pair of trombones occurs in *The Enchanter, or Love and Magic*, an afterpiece in two acts by David Garrick with music by John Christopher Smith (Drury Lane, 13 December 1760): the "Dead March," scored for flutes, strings, two trombones, and timpani.

firmus, or chorale-like recitation (or intonation), often used for magicians, spirits, oracles, priests, mysterious voices, and deities. Conjuring and incantations could also employ normal recitative melody with fanfare-like gestures, suggesting the clarion calls of older French operatic incantation. Vocal writing could make a character stand out in relief from normal mortals. This effect was sometimes achieved with simpler, bolder vocal lines; more rarely, composers would use coloratura for this purpose. Another device, descending octave leaps in the vocal line of a magician, sorceress, or supernatural character, was first seen in late seventeenth-century English and French opera but became a pan-European convention in the eighteenth century. Finally, special vocal ensembles of supernatural characters such as spirits, Furies, witches, and sprites regularly appeared in supernatural operas.

The use of particular keys for their affective association continued throughout the century.[57] Antonio Salieri, for one, remarked that he would choose the key of a piece in his operas by looking at the text, as had his teacher (Leopold Gassmann).[58] For infernal scenes composers in the later eighteenth century most often selected E-flat major. To Georg Joseph Vogler the key suggested the dark (1778) and night (1779). For C. F. D. Schubart (c. 1784) three flats represented the trinity, and thus the key had a Christian association.[59] In his *Orphée et Euridice* (1774) and subsequent operas at the Royal Academy, Gluck often composed scenes of terror or awe in E-flat. Composers also used the relative minor of E-flat, C minor, for scenes of terror. Described as gloomy and plaintive in the late seventeenth century, C minor maintained this association from Rameau through the nineteenth century. On the other hand, composers did not employ the key of D minor consistently for terror until later in the eighteenth century, as in the infernal allusions of Salieri's *Les Danaïdes*. The long association of D minor with grave or sacred expression had its origins in the Renaissance theory's Dorian mode.

Grand Genres in the Second Half of the Century: Rameau after 1750

With his imaginative approach to harmony, tone color, and compositional virtuosity, by midcentury Rameau had become the leading composer at the Royal Academy. The theatrical works of the last thirteen years of his remarkable career reveal even greater mastery and achievement. By 1750 fairy stories and fairy tales had begun to heavily influence the repertory at the Royal Academy, and Rameau and his librettist Marmontel emphasized this fairy world in an *acte de ballet* titled *La guirlande, ou Les fleurs enchantées* (21 September 1751)

---

57. See Steblin, *History of Key Characteristics*.

58. See Thayer, *Salieri*, 45.

59. Schubart, *Ideen zu einer Ästhetik*, 261–62. Lesueur, *Exposé*, 19–20, states that E-flat has religious qualities.

and a *pastorale-héroïque* titled *Acante et Céphise, ou La sympathie* (19 November 1751).[60] In *Acante et Céphise* the librettist and composer again dispensed with the old-style celebratory prologue, favoring an overture that serves similar ends but in a purely musical fashion.[61] Rameau sets elegantly ornamented *airs* for the enchantment scenes and lively ballets for malevolent characters with bursts of sixteenth-note accompanimental figures. He employs his particular style of obbligato recitative for oracular pronouncement. The plot concerns the trials of young lovers, helped by the fairy Zirphile. When Zirphile tells the lovers of the magical "sympathy" charm she will grant them, Rameau gives her a sustained six-part string accompaniment in the style of an invocation. Along with imitative choruses Rameau provided a homophonic fairies' chorus in act 1. Several scene transformations receive special instrumental music. When Zirphile gives Acante the magic bracelet in act 1, her fairies dance to enchant the lovers with the "le charme de la sympathie" (hence the subtitle of the work). The music here is an extended minuet-like dance in Rameau's most elegant style, with complex, fussy rhythms and ornaments. The evil genie Oroès (baritone) has an enchantment scene as well in the first act. He waves his magic wand to four measures of old-style magic flute music, a sonic image of enchantment.

Act 2 of *Acante* includes several solemn oracle scenes, in one of which Oroès consults Cupid as to how he can break the bonds between the lovers. He hears a short pastoral *annonce* for two oboes and bassoon that heralds the arrival of a troupe of lovers with the priestesses of Cupid. For her pronouncement the high priestess of Cupid sings an obbligato recitative with sustained strings divided in six parts with a solo flute. When Oroès and his genies fail to break the bond of Acante and Céphise, Oroès invokes his *aquilons* (north winds) to abduct them into the clouds. Rameau accompanied this action with a *simphonie* marked by rapid sixteenth-note figures in the strings and oboes.

In act 3 the *aquilons* take the lovers to a frightening desert. A short prelude introduces a rapid, homophonic, three-part invisible chorus commenting in their singing on the barbarous death of the lovers, while the monsters and serpents hurl themselves at Acante and Céphise, their actions depicted in sixteenth-note accompaniment figures of the strings and oboes. The lovers ask for divine help, and Oroès descends in a chariot of fire, depicted by four measures of stage-machine music with a descending melodic phrase and a rapid scale fig-

60. This commissioned court opera celebrated the birth of the Duke of Bourgogne. The print (Paris: Boivin, Le Clerc, n.d.; F-Pn, X. 856, H. 709) is a reduced score. For a modern edition of the full score, see Rameau, *Achante et Céphise, ou La Sympathie.*

61. The overture is in two parts. The first has two subsections, the "vœux de la nation" and the "feu d'artifice." The music of the first is in C minor, triple meter, for flutes, horns, bassoon, strings, and continuo. The second section is in C major, duple meter, with fanfares for clarinets, trumpets, horns, strings, continuo, and *timbales.* This section uses cannon fire to enhance the effect of the celebratory fireworks.

ure. To close, the genie conjures his demons for a divertissement that includes a frenetic ballet with Lully-like "demonic" sixteenth-note accompaniment.

Zoroastre, 1756

Cahusac and Rameau heavily revised *Zoroastre* for the 1756 staging, emphasizing the fairy-tale theme of trial and initiation: Amélite, Zoroastre's beloved, has been abducted and imprisoned in order to undergo a trial to determine her virtue. Zoroastre is also tested to see if he will keep his faith when faced with the impending loss of Amélite. Rameau's tame music of 1746 has here been replaced by a dramatic score rich in contrasting, vivid imagery, and inventive orchestration. The printed libretto included an interpretation of the new tripartite overture that "serves as the prologue," suggesting the contrasting Manichean powers at war in the opera. The first section depicts the barbarous supernatural power of the sorcerer Abramane in a stormy C minor movement marked with violent repeated notes and rapid ascending scales. The flutes emit a plaintive effect (the sighing *gémissmens* of the oppressed people). The libretto states that the second part represents a lively and cheerful picture of Zoroastre's powerful beneficence.

Many of the other changes in the revised *Zoroastre* involve the opera's original supernatural scenes, including several invocations of deities. The Bactrian princess Erinice is now like Armide, a jealous lover spurned by the hero. In act 1, scene 5, Erinice invokes the Furies with a bold clarion-call recitative beginning in A-flat and modulating to C major, enjoining them to abduct Amélite. The Furies appear in a trio in D minor that modulates to F major to end the act. Such a broad traversing of harmonic territory is unusual in opera of this era. In act 2 Oromasés, the king of genies, conjures his Elemental Spirits to perform a large-scale divertissement. A *symphonie* introduces the incantation of the bass Oromasés, with descending leaps in his forceful vocal line. In scene 3 the Elemental Spirits arrive and begin to conjure, dazzling Zoroastre, who can only sing "Where am I?" The enchantments form an elegant divertissement as Zoroastre falls on and is enveloped by a magic cloud.

Standing outside these celebrations, Abramane and Erinice plot against their enemies (act 3, scene 1). His *air* has an unusual tonal progression, traversing the keys of G, B-flat, E-flat, G, C, A minor, and D. Abramane envelops Erinice in a cloud that makes her invisible. Scene 3 begins just before dawn with a kind of enchanted sleep scene scored with flutes. The ensuing large divertissement is a ceremony of sun worship, starting with an *entrée* depicting the sunrise, and features a solemn, multipartite "Hymne au Soleil," a sequence of marvelous dances, ensembles, and vocal solos. A *bruit souterrain et de tonnerre* then interrupts the celebration as darkness descends and Abramane appears in his chariot. He invokes the north winds to ravage the country. Zoroastre once more rescues Amélite, summoning his Beneficent Spirits with a clarion-call recitative. In anger Abramane's priests set Bactria aflame with subterranean fires in a noisy instrumental segment called the *embrassement,* and the act ends.

Abramane performs a pagan occult sacrifice in act 4, beginning with an invocation to the supreme master of evil. Lully's *Armide* seems to have served as the inspiration for the act because Hatred and Vengeance appear with the Underworld Spirits. The ambitious harmonic plan remains in the flat keys (most of the act is in E-flat or a closely related key). The polyphonic priests' chorus (SCTB) has trio episodes with three priests. Abramane begins the blood sacrifice, danced in a ballet-pantomime to an *air grave.* In scene 6 the demons sing a C minor chorus (CTB) along with Vengeance, Hatred, Despair, and the Furies. The deities continue to conjure, and Despair gives a bloody dagger to Erinice. Rameau underscores Erinice's *air* with two bassoons, which provide an eerie timbre. Vengeance presents a cudgel to Abramane to the sound of a fanfare; then Vengeance sings a diabolical coloratura. A dance for the underworld spirits, an elegant but complex *air vif,* is interrupted by *une simphonie effrayante* marked "vite." This becomes a stormy prelude for Vengeance, who announces success in conjuring the master of evil. The subterranean voice of Arimane (bass) emerges from the underworld, accompanied by low-pitched bassoons, cellos, and contrabass in the unusual key of B-flat minor. A C major *annonce* in act 5, scene 6 signals the concluding transformation as Oromasés appears as a deus ex machina in a brilliant cloud with his Elemental Spirits, restoring Amélite to the victorious Zoroastre. A ballet for the Beneficent Spirits continues the music of the *annonce* as they crown the triumphant pair, and a divertissement ends the opera with a celebration in the pastoral style. Here Rameau fully exploits the sharp keys for the first time.

The opera of Rameau that is most closely linked to epic romance is his late work *Les Paladins,* an anonymous *comédie-lyrique* attributed to Jean-François Duplat de Monticourt (12 February 1760).[62] Based on a fable by La Fontaine, *Le petit chien qui secoue de l'argent et des pierreries,* which was based in turn on Ariosto's *Orlando furisoso* (canto 18), the plot has the fairy Manto helping to unite the knight Atis with his beloved Argie. The libretto allows for Rameau's musical representations of lightning and thunder (act 1, scenes 1–2), as well as dances for superhuman characters. In act 1, scene 8, a *troupe des démons* appears and dances an *air de furie* with rapid repeated notes and furious ascending scales in octaves for the strings. Rameau also provided music for magical transformations, for example, when the fairy, disguised as a slave, appears in act 3, scene 2 to enchant the tiered towers (*pagodes*) that decorate the palace. The *pagodes* become animated and dance to an "Air pour les pagodes" for Anselme, a gavotte for strings and "magic" flutes.

With its ravishing instrumental music,[63] imaginative accompaniments, and intense expression, Rameau's final *tragédie en musique, Les Boréades,* ranks

---

62. Rameau, *Les Paladins.*

63. The three-movement overture in F major serves as the prologue, recalling the precedents

among his most impressive works for the theater.[64] The author of the libretto remains unknown, and the opera was not performed in the eighteenth century, although it apparently was rehearsed in April 1763. The composer achieved his most masterful balance of conventional and novel elements in the opera's substantial marvelous episodes. We still hear the customary two flutes during certain magical events, for example the pantomime showing the abduction of the Greek princess Oreithya. Here a five-measure instrumental segment with brisk string figures and short motives for the flutes (act 2, scene 6) initiates the divertissement. The flutes emerge again as the chorus anticipates the arrival of Apollo. Rameau has the flutes perform conjunct pairs of thirds in alternation with the strings as a burst of light appears. Cupid descends as the flutes and violins play the motives together in the final *ritornelle*. The deity then sings his obbligato recitative with Rameau's oracular six-part sustained strings, presenting an enchanted arrow to Alphise, the queen of Bactria (and the opera's leading role).

Other examples of descriptive instrumental music include the gradually building storm scene. In act 3, scene 4 Rameau accompanied the impressive *aquilon* chorus with an orchestral tempest consisting of furious repeated notes and arpeggios (act 3, scene 4). He represents magic whirlwinds in an accompanied recitative with rapid sixteenth notes, scored for flutes, strings, and bassoons. The *entr'acte* to act 4 for the winds ("Suite des vents") is a long storm piece with rapid figuration for flutes, bassoons, and strings that introduces another chorus. One of the most evocative ballets occurs in act 4, scene 4, a "Gavotte pour les heures et les zéphirs," with the strings imitating the ticking of a clock (*horloge*) while the *petites flûtes* play descending triplet motives supported by duplets in the bassoons.[65] Act 5 likewise begins with a remarkable contrapuntal prelude depicting the impotent gasps of the subterranean winds with strangely disconnected and breathless phrases that stretch contemporary mimetic conventions to their limits (Rameau used similar phrases in his overture to *Zaïs*). This introduces a chorus of the winds with solo interjections for Boréas, the chief wind deity. The chorus continues with these unusual disconnected phrases.

The climax of the opera occurs when Abaris, the lover of Alphise, interrupts a long torture scene, using his magic arrow to break the evil spell and invoke Apollo (act 5, scene 4). Two flutes play in the accompanied recitative as the arrow touches the innocent princess. The key changes from G minor to D major, and majestic descending triadic figures depict the descent of Apollo and the surprised reactions of the Boréas and his chorus of winds ("Quel éclat!"). Apollo (baritone) then sings a recitative accompanied by flutes and

---

of *Zoroastre* and *Acante et Céphise*. It consists of an introductory section, a minuet-like segment, and a final section in the hunting style with gigue rhythms.

64. See Bouissou, *Jean-Philippe Rameau: Les Boréades*. A facsimile of the autograph and a modern edition of the libretto are available (Paris: Stil, 1982).

65. The text recalls the magic *horloge* scene in Louis Fuzelier's early *opéra-comique Mélusine* (1719).

strings. Abaris uses his magic arrow once more as he touches the princess; the two flutes again play their solo material. In another recitative Apollo invokes a magic transformation of the scene. An ascending D major chord for the winds and strings, reminiscent of Rameau's *corps sonore*,[66] further dissipates the previous sonic distress as the scene changes and the final graceful divertissement celebrates the victory of virtue.

Les Boréades is a culmination of Rameau's art, combining the mastery of French operatic tradition with an original, inspired approach to enchantment on the stage. The virtuoso use of texture, timbre, harmony, and mimesis helps Rameau's score to achieve a unique dramatic force that would not be surpassed until Gluck's operas for the Parisian stage.

Gluck and the Third Age of the Marvelous in French *grand opéra*

By the early 1760s a French translation of Gluck's *Orfeo ed Euridice* by Antoine-Jacques Lablet de Morambert, published in 1764, had introduced the work to Paris.[67] French theatrical music would never be the same once Gluck's powerful music was heard on Parisian stages.[68] Yet the subject matter of the texts set to music hardly changed: mythology, epic romance, and fairy tale continued in the stage works of almost all composers at the Royal Academy, including Gluck, Piccinni, J. C. Bach, and Sacchini. In fact, librettists returned to the venerated texts of Quinault, reducing them to three acts without prologues. Ballets and parodies also drew upon Ariosto's epic as Alcina continued to be a familiar operatic role, along with Armide and Amadis.[69]

Grétry's "third age" of French opera, the last flowering of the marvelous associated with the ancien régime, commenced with Gluck and continued with admiring imitators such as Jean-Baptiste Rochefort and Gluck's great rival Niccolò Piccinni. Commentators actually coined the term *grand opéra* around 1782 to distinguish this new operatic style.[70] Gluck's importing of the Franco-

66. The "resonating body" of a string instrument by which Rameau sought to show the basis of all harmony. See p. 64.

67. Other settings of the Orpheus story include the *tragédie pastorale et lyrique Orphée aux enfers*, by H.-E. Jougla de Parasa, 1764 (F-Pn, Ms. f.f. 9246); *L'Orphée moderne*, attributed to a M. Montorcier for the Théâtre de l'Ambigu-comique (1772); *Orphée*, a *scène lyrique* in one act by L. Bursay (pen name of Louis Bruyas) (Marseilles, 1775); *Orphée*, a *drame héroïque* in five acts by Vénard de La Jonchère, (s.l., 1785); and an anonymous setting, *Orphée et Euridice aux enfers* (Wauxhall d'été, October 1786).

68. For details on the change in opera owing to Gluck's success in Paris, see Weber, "*La musique ancien*. This period is the subject of Rushton, "Music and Drama." See also Johnson, *Listening in Paris*, who credits the music of Gluck with the growth of *sensibilité*.

69. Comic works that use or parody material from *Amadis* include *Coraline et Camille fées*, by C. Véronèse, Th. it. (1758); *Matroco*, by Pierre Laujon, music by Grétry, (1777); and *Corisandre, ou Les fous par enchantement*, by Auguste-François Lebailly, music by Honoré-Langlé (1791).

70. Weber, "*La musique ancien*."

Italian synthesis (see chapter 3) into French opera at first inspired an association with the Parisian reform ideology of the 1750s, which demanded a musical theater without the emotional distance and stylized grandiloquence that had been the hallmarks of the *tragédie en musique*. Because he created original and moving portrayals of familiar characters such as Orestes, Armida, and Iphigenia, Gluck seemed to be the composer they desired; even Rousseau initially embraced his music.

The repertory at the Royal Academy before Gluck's triumph in Paris included numerous revisions of the earlier marvelous repertory.[71] Pierre-Monton Berton reworked the last act of Lully's *Armide* for the 1761 production. Berton and Jean-Benjamin (-François) de La Borde revised Quinault's *Amadis de Gaule* in 1771 without the prologue.[72] The last *tragédie-lyrique* of the "third age of the marvelous" may have been François-Joseph Gossec's *Sabinus,* on a text by Michel de Chabanon (1773; revised in four acts, 1774).[73] The composer employed the newer *galant* style and was apparently the first to use the trombones at the Royal Academy. But for all that, *Sabinus* is actually a tame, even conservative opera. Eclipsed by Gluck's *Iphigénie en Aulide* in 1774, the work was soon forgotten. The supernatural scenes include two pantomimes, marches, ceremonial scenes, a tomb scene, and magical transformation music in act 5, scene 7 with the indication "the genie of Gaul descends in all his glory." This brief sonic image is created with tremulous basses, strings playing soft arpeggios, sustained wind chords, and suspensions. Gossec depicts the descent of the genie by gradually falling pitch, slowly changing suspensions, rhythmic augmentation, and a long pedal. This segment leads to a short obbligato recitative for the genie (bass), accompanied by sustained, low-pitched strings.

❊

Gluck's second Parisian opera was a reworking and translation by Pierre-Louis Moline of Calzabigi's famous *azione teatrale* into a three-act *tragédie*

---

71. Large-scale spectacles with elaborate stage machines, fireworks, and similar devices were the specialty of Giovanni Niccolò Servandoni. Best known for the display that occasioned Handel's *Music for the Royal Fireworks* in London, Servandoni created popular "spectacles d'optiques orné de machines" from the late 1730s to the 1750s at the Salle des machines in the Tuileries. These included *La forêt enchantée* (31 March 1754), drawn from Tasso's epic romance, and *La constance couronnée* (27 March 1757), a mixture of Greek mythology and oriental fairy tale. For details, see Bergman, "La grand mode du pantomime."

72. The score of *Amadis* is in F-Pn, Mus. ms. D. 1034. Although the revision reduced the supernatural element, the episode when Urgande touches Arcabonne with her wand has an unusual modulation to depict the transformation (D–Dm–Gm–F–B°–Cm–F⁷).

73. An autograph score, in F-Pn, Ms. 1429, is a mixed collection of scenes, including sketches and revisions. A manuscript copy made in 1937–38 from these materials, shelfmark S.F.M. 17 (1–5), provides a more legible score. The overture is lost.

opéra, *Orphée et Euridice* (2 August 1774).[74] For this revision the composer borrowed music from several earlier works, including the *terrible* ending of his *Don Juan* ballet (see chapter 3), which provided ballet music for the Furies. Two years later Marie François Louis Gand (dit Leblanc), bailli du Roullet, translated and adapted Gluck's *Alceste* as a three-act *tragédie*.[75] Gluck revised a number of supernatural episodes. In act 3, scene 3, the striking three-part chorus of infernal deities (ATB) has the voices singing fifteen measures of the tonic against changing harmonies in F minor (reworked from an aria for Alceste). In act 3, scene 4, the *air* for an infernal deity (bass), "Caron t'appelle" (revised from the aria "Nume infernale" from the 1767 version), begins with a chantlike recitation. Gluck accompanies the vocal part with swirling sixteenth notes in the strings and a wind complement with a trombone. The following chorus of infernal deities has repeated notes in octaves in the "infernal" key of E-flat.[76]

Relying heavily on Quinault's libretto (without the prologue and some material from the individual acts), Gluck set *Armide* as a five-act *drame héroïque* in late 1777.[77] This was the composer's second original opera for Paris, and it caused controversy for the partisans of his rival Piccinni. The score is particularly rich in traditional and newer marvelous effects. Gluck even recycled his favorite invocation music from *Telemaco* in act 2, scene 2, a conjuring scene with Hidraot and Armide's duet "Esprits de haine et de rage."[78] In act 2, scene 4 Renaud is enchanted and falls asleep to magic flute music. Although the libretto calls for a solo naiad to appear, Gluck composed a polyphonic trio with echo effects for three female spirits (the naiad and two *coriphées*), "Au temps heureux où l'on sait plaire."

Gluck employed wind instruments for their otherwordly affect in scenes the French long associated with Lully. For Armide's aria "Ah! quelle cruauté de lui ravir le jour!" (act 2, scene 5), he has the winds providing an echo and a sudden change in sonority. A later segment of the aria serves as the incantation in which Armide charges her demons to transform themselves into zephyrs ("Venez, secondez mes desires"). The rapid staccato triplet figures in the accompaniment and the pizzicato bass line underline Armide's bold vocal com-

---

74. Modern edition ed. Ludwig Finscher in Gluck, *Sämtliche Werke*, Abt. 1, Bd. 6 (1967). For a list of the self-borrowed material, see Hortschansky, *Parodie und Entlehnung*, 314–15.

75. Modern edition published as *Alceste/Alkestis (Pariser Fassung von 1776)*, ed. Rudolf Gerber, in Gluck, *Sämtliche Werke*, Abt. 1, Bd. 7 (1957).

76. Based on a parallel ensemble, "Ma! qual suono," in the 1767 version. The *Journal de Paris*, August 1788, refers to the simple incantation of this chorus of underworld deities in *Alceste*, and the composer tells how he had "les priver de tout accent, réservant à mon orchestre le soin de peindre tout ce qu'il y a de terrible dans ce qu'ils annoncent" (deprived them of all pitches [or tones], reserving for my orchestra the task of painting everything terrible in what they are proclaiming).

77. Modern edition ed. Klaus Hortschansky in *Sämtliche Werke*, Abt. 1, Bd. 8 (1987), 2 vols.

78. See the discussion of Gluck's *Telemaco* (1765) in chapter 3.

mands. Gluck depicted the transformation in the final ritornello, a postlude serving as stage-machine music to accompany the zephyrs as they carry off Armide and Renaud to end act 2.

In act 3, scene 3 Armide invokes Hatred to appear from hell and aid her in overcoming her love for Renaud. Armide is human here, delivering an F major aria with whole-note wind accompaniment and an obsessive syncopated string motive:│ ♫ ⁷ ♩ ♩ ♫ │. In act 3, scene 4 Hatred and her retinue arrive to counteract Cupid's power over Armide. Hatred's Allegro in A major summons her retinue with a triadic fanfare motive, a kind of call to arms ("Plus on connaît l'Amour"), borrowed from a similarly otherworldly aria in Gluck's much earlier Italian opera *Ippolito* (1745) and recycled in *Telemaco* (1765) and *Les festes d'Apollo* (1769).[79] Magic conjuring continues in the pantomime, based on the fifth dance from Gluck's *Don Juan* ballet. (This music occurred in the ballet during the sword fight with the commendatore; in *Armide,* instead of swords Armide waves a magic wand in the air.) Hatred then tries to banish Cupid, singing a simple incantation borrowed from Circe's "Dall'orrido soggiorno" in *Telemaco.* The repeated notes impart a trancelike effect to support the declamatory rhythms of the melody. A short ballet leads to the duo and chorus "Sors du sein d'Armide." Gluck reworked both segments from the false hell scene *in L'ivrogne corrigé* (1760), a duo for the two characters disguised as Furies.

Most of act 4 is a large-scale magical divertissement, beginning with storm music in C major. Gluck provided music for two scene transformations in episodes involving a magic wand—a short prelude in C minor with ascending triadic gestures and dotted rhythms. Act 5 includes another large divertissement, now in the enchanted palace of Armide. One of the choruses for the Pleasures ("C'est l'Amour qui retient dans ses chaînes") has fanciful appoggiatura figures in the accompaniment, like those Mozart would use for the trio of the three boys in *Die Zauberflöte.* Gluck composed another short prelude with sweeping gestures in octaves as transformation music when the magic shield breaks Armide's spell and awakens Renaud. A long instrumental piece with trumpets and timpani, entitled "Terribile sinfonia," accompanies Armide's destruction of her enchanted palace, one of the most violent musical endings to date.

Gluck's final opera for Paris was *Iphigénie en Tauride,* a four-act *tragédie* on a text by Nicolas-François Guillard, after a spoken drama by Guymond de La Touche (18 May 1779).[80] Among Gluck's self-borrowings are several pieces he originally used for other magical representations. The first in *Iphigénie* is the invocation by the priestess (act 1, scene 6), based on earlier music

79. Hortschansky, *Parodie und Entlehnung,* 191–93. These earlier settings always had some relationship to otherworldly subjects, especially the original setting in *Ippolito,* where Theseus describes an image of a battle and the underworld ("Ah! già parmi, che d'armi").

80. Modern edition ed. Gerhard Croll in Gluck, *Sämtliche Werke,* Abt. 1, Bd. 9 (1973).

for various enchantresses, with one section derived from *Antigono* (1756), the second from Circe's aria "Je t'implore" in *Telemaco* (1765). Act 2, scene 3 is a large scene complex for the guilt-ridden Orestes, who believes that he has been responsible for the death of his friend Pylades in addition to the murder of his mother Clytemnestra. Here Gluck transformed a traditional supernatural episode into a psychological portrait, as the Furies become the conscience of a man almost driven mad by guilt. The scene starts with "terrifying" motives of dotted rhythms from Gluck's earlier ballet, *Sémiramis* (1765). This serves as a prelude to an angry recitative by Orestes, accompanied by furious scale figures in the strings when Orestes asks to be struck down by the gods. Orestes' mood changes, and he sings a lyrical arioso, "Le calme rentre dans mon cœur," describing his welcome peace of mind. But the Eumenides' motive begins in the orchestra, tormenting Orestes' conscience with the repetition of a syncopated, obsessive rhythmic figure that Gluck later inserted in the score: ♩♩ ♩♩. Gluck suggested that he was having the orchestra speak the Furies' words "il a tué sa mère" (he killed his mother).[81] In scene 4 the Furies assail Orestes again as the fateful dotted motives from *Sémiramis* return. This music forms the basis of the ballet-pantomime "de terreur," scored with trombones (as Ninias's ghost returns). A choral scene follows with the Furies assailing the pleading Orestes with fateful three-stroke motives,| ♫♩ ɣ | ♫♩ ɣ |, taken from Gluck's overture to *Sémiramis*. These motives return with a vengeance in act 3, scene 4, reinforced by trombone accompaniment, as Orestes describes to Pylades the Furies' torments.

The increase of intensity, terror, and violence in Gluck's "supernatural" scenes matched his powerful musical representation of the tender emotions and ceremonial solemnity. This combination proved irresistible to the French and served composers as a model for musical theater during the "third age of the marvelous." Like Rameau and his generation, these later composers found inspiration in the magic episodes of the librettos and responded with new musical corollaries for supernatural events.

Gluck's Successors, Imitators, and Rivals

Gluck's successors in Paris continued his expansion of the expressive musical vocabulary, mostly in their use of the orchestra. In the late 1770s and the 1780s composers had larger orchestral ensembles at their disposal, and they experimented with novel instrumental combinations. A more symphonic style is evident in Parisian operas of the 1780s, when composers wrote more extensive ensembles and longer finales. Although Gluck exploited the trombones selec-

---

81. Gluck's quote concerning the nature of these motives first appeared in the *Journal de Paris*. He inscribed these motives as an afterthought in the theater score, to show that Orestes was lying to himself. See Noiray, "La dramaturgie musicale," 45. Genlis, *Dictionnaire*, 2:12–13, also treats Gluck's views on this passage.

tively, Piccinni and Salieri used them for sheer volume within a larger brass complement. Salieri's heavy orchestration sometimes overwhelms a scene, particularly when other elements are repetitive or stagnant—as in, for example, the denouements of *Les Danaïdes* and *Tarare*.

For a number of reasons, Gluck ultimately disappointed the reformers and became the target of their enmity. For one thing, his operas were rich in the supernatural marvelous that was so distasteful to them; he even set Quinault's *Armide*, a libretto that personified the disdained operatic orthodoxy of Lully. Gluck's retention of older mimetic elements of the marvelous in music must have also been a sensitive point. It mattered little that the composer reinterpreted these devices with greater verisimilitude. Gluck's opponents found a new ideal in the Italian Piccinni, an unlikely but nonideological composer. Piccinni's music fit the demands for a more "natural" style, with periodic melody and unencumbered accompaniment. The Bohemian composer's melodies, on the other hand, often eschewing periodicity, now seemed to them unnatural, and his remarkable synthesis of disparate styles no longer appeared to be novel. Piccinni's French operas are freer in structure than his earlier Italian models, using more chorus and simpler mythological plots. By comparison to the librettos set by Gluck and others, Piccinni's significantly reduced the supernatural material. One might see Salieri as a midpoint between these two, restraining the dramatic intensity of Gluck's contrasts and exploiting the melodic periodicity of Piccinni.

The earliest successors of Gluck integrated his approach in different ways. Marmontel collaborated with the Belgian composer André-Ernest-Modeste Grétry to create the unsuccessful three-act *ballet-héroïque Céphale et Procris, ou L'amour conjugal* (Versailles, 30 September 1773; PO, 2 May 1775).[82] Act 3, scene 1 contains one of Grétry's invocations of the marvelous, wherein he uses a broad harmonic palette to enhance the musical imagery that Gluck had introduced to Parisian audiences. The prelude in E-flat with rapid string figures and tremolos sets the scene in a deserted terrain. Jealousy sings a forceful recitative with a few descending octaves, invoking a polyphonic chorus of demons. An episodic "Danse infernale" then begins with the Larghetto in E-flat, scored for blaring horns, oboes, clarinets, strings, and covered timpani. An initial fortissimo E-flat chord and a timpani roll are answered by a rapidly ascending scale, followed by repeated octaves in *alla zoppa* syncopation. Marvelous allusions continue as these motives recur against a descending harmonic progression with borrowed harmonies from the flat side of the tonal spectrum. In the next passage Grétry scores infernal horns against chromatic descending octaves in the bass, leading to a recitative segment with an abrupt juxtaposition of contrasting phrases. Stark octave gestures lead to rapid sixteenth-note figures, followed by octave leaps in jerky dotted rhythms between bass and soprano ranges. This sequence of conventions for depicting the supernatural oc-

---

82. Grétry, *Collection complète*, vols. 3–4.

curs while the music traverses the broad tonal area first of F minor and then of G minor. The opening eighteen bars return, and the dance ends with sweeping ascending gestures followed by a cadential passage in octaves before the final cadence in E-flat.

Piccinni's first Parisian opera was Marmontel's three-act revision of Quinault's *Roland* (27 January 1778).[83] The composer reduced the supernatural element to a few marvelous episodes such as the "Marche des insulaires orientaux" (March of the Oriental Islanders). Following traditional practice, the composer employs the winds in these scenes. For example, when the enchanted fountain of love appears in a forest, the audience hears a flute solo in A major, accompanied by strings and horns. The mad scene, set as an obbligato recitative in the key of F minor (ending in G minor), evokes the "terrifying" style with rapid scales and repeated notes as Roland imagines the Furies attacking him. The fairy Logistille appears to the sound of a sparkling "Andantino amoureux" in E-flat for solo flute, oboes, clarinets, horns, and strings. This elegant music, with its graceful periodic phrases and instrumental style, seems as much a wind serenade as a traditional evocation of the marvelous.

Jean-Baptiste Rochefort, a member of the Royal Academy and director of music for the Théâtre des Élèves de l'Opéra, composed fashionable *galant* music for Parisian pantomimes and ballets, all of it highly pictorial. His four-act pantomime *mêlé de danses Jérusalem délivrée, ou Renaud et Armide* (7 January 1779) is a virtual catalog of descriptive musical devices created to represent various events and characters.[84] Musical passages or short pieces accompany natural and supernatural transformations (often by magic wand or shield), with trap-door entries and exits, flying machines, and the destruction of Armide's palace. The music ranges from sentimental dances to military marches. Rochefort's three-act pantomime *La pantoufle*, a setting of Perrault's Cinderella,[85] also offers examples of his "terrifying" style, with decorative music whose effects are often clichés, such as the frequent sixteenth- and thirty-second-note figures for the many violent episodes. Repetitive and trite, this music nonetheless shows the degree to which a mimetic language of the supernatural had become accepted.

Johann Christian Bach's *Amadis de Gaule*, a three-act *tragédie lyrique* with libretto by Alphonse-Denis-Marie de Vismes du Valgay based on Quinault

83. The large print (Paris: The author, 1778) specifies this as an *opéra en trois actes*, F-Pn, Mus. Vm² 509, D 12.632, or X. 376. An extensive manuscript score with the final scenes missing survives in F-Pn, Mus. Vm⁶ 130. Mozart acknowledged the public approval of this opera to his father in a letter of 28 February 1778 but commented on its weaknesses as well, which included monotonous music and weak choruses.

84. Jean-Joseph Le Boeuf's libretto was printed ([Paris]: de Lormel, 1779) and an engraved score survives (Paris, 1779), F-Pn, Mus. Vm⁶ 130.

85. F-Pn Vm⁶ 132, *La pantoufle, ballet-pantomime*, is dated 17 May 1779 on the score. The author of the text is probably Pierre-Germain Pariseau, whose *La pantoufle de Cendrillon* premiered at the Théâtre des Élèves de l'Opéra on 13 September 1779.

(14 December 1779),[86] is a much more accomplished example of Gluck's influence (although Bach employs the periodic melody associated with Piccinni).[87] Unfortunately, the opera was a critical and commercial failure, and a revision did not improve the critical reaction. Yet *Amadis* is Bach's most ambitious opera, with masterful orchestration that differentiates characters and events. This was, for example, Bach's first use of piccolos and trombones. The choral writing is varied and demanding, with multiple soloists and staggered polyphonic entries, such as in act 1, scene 6, when Amadis encounters a hidden chorus of demons.

The numerous supernatural episodes use a broad range of expressive devices. Bach employed his version of the "terrifying" style in the complex E-flat double chorus for full orchestra with trombones after Arcabonne and Arcalus invoke the deities Discord and Hatred (act 1, scene 3). Noble expression of the marvelous permeates the "Cérémonie funèbres autour du tombeau," an elegant "Andantino gratioso" (act 2, scene 2). Special sonorities and harmonies also define the otherworldly realm. At the end of act 2, scene 2, for example, the sorceress Arcabonne calls forth the ghost of the dead magician Ardan Canil. Wind chords first indicate an unearthly presence, recalling the ascending triadic chords of Rameau's superhuman epiphanies. But here the harmony is not the major triad of Rameau's *corps sonore* but a fully diminished seventh chord, starting in the trombones and moving to the other winds (see ex. 1.8).[88] Bach employed a similar rising triad in the winds for the first indication of Arcabonne's fate in act 3, scene 6.

A prelude for winds and strings, with its rising tessitura coordinated with the movement of the harmonic progression, signals the magical appearance of the ghost in scene 3. Bach set the pronouncement as an obbligato recitative in which the ghost (bass) accuses the sorceress of betraying him and predicts that she will soon be condemned to hell. He sings the slow-moving recitative with repeated notes and accompanied by low-pitched strings, a standard device for ghosts since early in the century.[89] The unstable and eerie harmony seems un-

---

86. The music was published in full score (Paris: Sieber, n.d.), showing numerous changes from the libretto. For a facsimile with commentary see J. C. Bach, *Collected Works*, vol. 10. The libretto calls this a *Tragedie-opera en trois actes* (Paris: Lormel 1779). An *avertissement* comments on the cuts necessary for the "modern" composer. The libretto is reproduced in J. C. Bach, *Collected Works*, vol. 45.

87. Bach had arranged Gluck's *Orfeo ed Euridice* for Naples (4 November 1774). See the facsimile of the manuscript score in J. C. Bach, *Collected Works*, 11.

88. An alternate setting of this section exists in a manuscript in Po, shelfmark A. 274.b, 35–36, where string tremolos are either added or substituted for the winds.

89. Bach set an earlier oracle scene for tenor in his opera seria *Orione* (London, King's Theatre, Haymarket, 19 February 1763), act 1, scene 3, a more conventional obbligato recitative, in a short segment with four low-pitch sustained string parts. The key here is also E-flat, which shifts from D minor for the oracle's pronouncement. A facsimile is printed in J. C. Bach, *Collected Works*, vol. 4, and vol. 12, 94–95.

EXAMPLE 1.8 J. C. Bach, *Amadis de Gaule*, act 2, scene 2

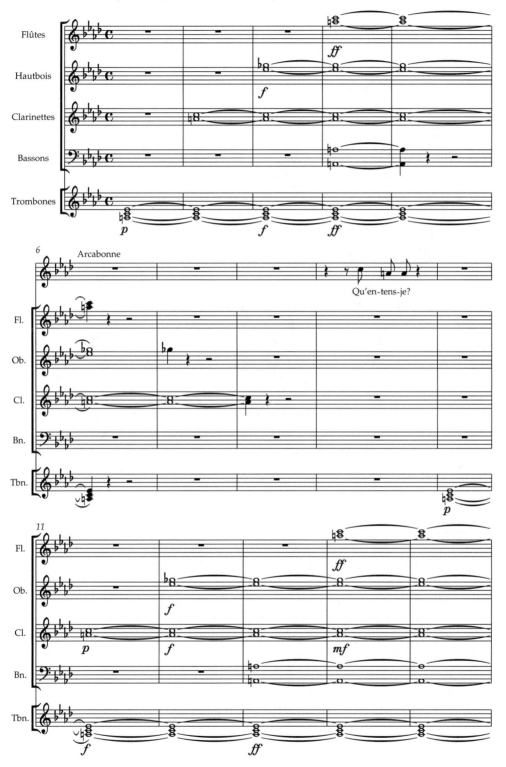

usual here, beginning and ending in E-flat minor but moving through A-flat, D-flat, F, and B-flat with shifting major, minor, augmented, and diminished sonorities.

All of the divertissements in *Amadis* have supernatural content. The longest of these occurs at the opera's conclusion. Arcabonne is startled when she hears diminished-seventh chords in the winds, reminding her of Canil's ghost and its terrible pronouncement. Summoned to hell by the ghost, she uses her dagger to commit suicide (in G minor, Mozart's "suicide key"). Suddenly the scene changes to the splendid palace of the fairy Urgande. The tone of Arcabonne's distressful recitative changes to a joyful D major as Urgande's retinue welcomes Amadis and Oriane. Urgande sings a short obbligato recitative with sustained string accompaniment. The subsequent music includes a pantomime trial scene where Amadis must overcome a short series of obstacles. The "Air pour le moment ou Amadis passe sous l'arc de loyaux amans" is a solemn and triumphant march for winds in B-flat, with exquisite consonant sonorities and periodic phrases (see ex. 1.9).

Unlike Bach's opera, Piccinni's *Atys* (2 February 1780), the third of his nine serious operas for Paris (based on a three-act revision by Marmontel of Quinault's libretto for Lully),[90] proved a major success and positioned the composer as a rival to Gluck. There is no magical transformation of Atys into a pine tree by Cybele at the end, as in Lully, but a more "verisimilar" suicide and mourning scene; indeed, a revival in 1783 substituted a happy ending. The only extensive marvelous episode in the opera is the celebrated dream sequence (act 2, scenes 3–4): an obbligato recitative in E-flat, marked "andante sostenuto," for flutes, clarinets, horns, and muted strings. The short ritornello has consonant sonority, conjunct melody, and repetitive dotted figures to suggest the soporific effect; the winds begin to play just as Atys falls asleep. The mode suddenly shifts to the minor when Morphée, the god of sleep, appears. The major mode returns with the imitative "Chorus of Dreams," accompanied with running sextuplets as the Dreams promise to calm the cares and charm the senses. Morphée then wakes Atys, with his obbligato recitative suddenly changing to C major accompanied by the sustained chords in the strings, now without mutes.

Piccinni's *Iphigénie en Tauride*, a four-act *tragédie lyrique* by Alphonse Du Congé Dubreuil (23 January 1781),[91] enjoyed considerable success in Paris and was revived in 1785 and 1790. The composer limited the marvelous element to one accompanied recitative at the end of the opera (act 4, scene 7), when the goddess Diane arrives to the sound of an "enchanted" ritornello in A for flutes, oboes, and strings. Although other scenes in the work include pictorial elements, such as the rapid scales, string tremolos, loud brass, syncopated figures,

90. Facsimile ed., Rushton, *French Opera*.

91. Printed score (Paris: Chez le Suisse de l'hôtel de Noailles, 1781); manuscripts in F-Pn, Po, Germany, and Italy.

EXAMPLE 1.9 J. C. Bach, *Amadis de Gaule,* act 3, scene 8, "Air pour le moment ou Amadis passe sous l'arc de loyaux amans"

and unstable harmony that accompany the bloody dream of Iphigenia in E-flat (act 1, scene 3), the violent storm scene (act 1, scene 4), and the anguished vision of Orestes in C minor (act 2, scene 2), in these the characters recount their dreams and visions in extended accompanied recitative, not as events occurring in real time.

François-Joseph Gossec's setting of Etienne Morel de Chédeville's *tragédie lyrique Thésée* (1 March 1782) also betrays the influence of Gluck in its marvelous episodes and solemn ceremonies.[92] In act 3 Medea summons her demons with an accompanied recitative in the infernal key of E-flat, scored with three trombones, horns, oboes, and strings. Her music is a clarion-call triadic invocation, based on the introductory motive in octave-and-unison sonority. Tension increases through the use of arpeggio accompaniment in the violins and sustained wind chords. The four-part chorus of demons (SATB) responds to her summons, repeating her incantation motive first in unisons and octaves, then in four-part texture as wind chords with trombones accentuate the words. The "Pantomime des démons" in C major, for full orchestra including trombones, features a variety of fantastic scale figures in the strings, bassoons, and bass. The dance ends with a chorus in C minor with "underworld" instrumentation and octave-and-unison sonority. Medea summons the Furies at the end of the act, and the scene transformation has a musical correspondence, beginning with the change of mode to C major. The score indicates that "La décoration change"; Gossec provided an effective musical transition with *smorʒando* phrases based on suspensions and sequential harmony over a dominant pedal. The effect is to hold back the musical momentum, allowing energy to gather for the coming event, in much the same way as a sonata form before the recapitulation (see ex. 1.10). Modulation also figures among Gossec's expressive devices. For example, Minerve appears at the end of the opera as a dea ex machina to a brilliant instrumental fanfare with trumpet and timpani in the new key of D major, which changes to C when Eglée, the king, Arcas, and the people give thanks to the goddess.

Antonio Sacchini's setting for Paris of Jean Joseph Le Bœuf and Nicolas-Etienne Framéry's revision of Pellegrin's three-act *tragédie-lyrique Renaud* (25 February 1783) has little in common with his earlier *Armida* (1772; see chapter 3), but it fully embraces the magical elements rejected by Piccinni.[93] Here the composer integrated the latest styles in French *grand opéra* with more mimetic devices and marvelous elements. Armide first appears in her chariot (act 1, scene 4) to the sound of a bustling instrumental prelude, an Allegro assai for trumpets, oboes, strings, and timpani. String tremolos and timpani rolls accompany the stage machines. The sorceress conjures the Eumenides during a pantomime (act 2, scene 9), set to articulated figures in the first violins and bass (see ex. 1.11), repeated in the winds, and accompanied by string tremolos. The composer suggests the subterranean stirring of the Furies with

---

92. The autograph manuscript in F-Po, shelfmark A. 290a, was lost sometime in the early twentieth century (only the "Partie de ballet" survives, A. 290b). F-Pn has a manuscript copy, Rés. 2360.

93. One printed score (Paris: The author, n.d.) in F-Pn, shelfmark D. 13.805, bears Sacchini's signature. Like Bach's *Amadis de Gaule*, this opera too was patronized by Marie-Antoinette and was a failure.

EXAMPLE I.II Antonio Sacchini, *Renaud*, act 2, scene 9

an abrupt key shift from G major to the infernal E-flat. A duet for Armide
and the magician Hidroat, her uncle, leads to a "Chorus of Divinities," which
sings an intonation of unison repeated notes. After the large *chœur général* in
the "terrifying" style, Armide invokes a hellish storm from the infernal deities
with bold, triadic clarion-call motives, accompanied by forte string tremolos in
C minor. A brief descending chromatic octave-and-unison passage in the

strings then introduces the C minor trio for the three Furies. Tisiphone, Alecto, and Megaera sing of the futility of resistance to fate in homorhythmic and imitative textures, accompanied by string tremolos and horns playing a pedal. As they exclaim "Entends sa foudre," Sacchini renders theatrical thunder with fast sixteenth-note tremolos and scale figures, along with blasts of horns and oboes. This pictorial style is also evident in the prelude to act 3, a scene in a desolate battlefield strewn with cadavers. This Allegro assai in C minor, with its dynamic contrasts, crescendos, rapid scales, and octave-and-unison passages, recalls the *terribile* "sinfonia tetra" of Sacchini's earlier *Armida*. In the final scene (a happy ending) Armide calls upon her spirits to transform the battlefield into her enchanted palace. Here *galant* instrumental music accompanying the stage machines (with conjunct, periodic melody, accompanied by staccato Alberti bass figures) both describes the transformation and introduces the genies' chorus, based on the same music.

Gluck's appointed successor, Antonio Salieri, began his Parisian career with controversy. The murders and final hell scene of Salieri's *Les Danaïdes*, a five-act *tragédie lyrique* on a text by Marie François Louis Gand Du Roullet and Ludwig Theodor Tschudi, after Calzabigi (4 April 1784),[94] shocked contemporary audiences and outraged critics. The plot concerns the Danaids, a corrupt family of ancient Greece led by their ruthlessly ambitious father, Danaus. He plots to murder his rivals, but the love of his daughter for one of them, Lincée (Lyncaeus), causes her to spare his life. Lincée then marshals his forces and slays the Danaids. As John Rice has observed, the D minor/D major overture and the horrific act 5 finale have distinct similarities to the overture and infernal music of Mozart's *Don Giovanni*.[95] After the Danaids die (accompanied by music in the terrifying style), an instrumental interlude serves as stage-machine music. The earth trembles, the palace collapses, and the scene changes to hell, where the Danaids endure torture. They watch as a giant vulture eats their father's bloody intestines, which lie strewn across the stage. This transition music consists of tremolos and blasts of the wind instruments (with three trombones) as the key changes from E-flat to the relative C minor. The Danaids sing "Quelle rigueur, quels tourmens inouis!," beginning in stark octaves and ending in close-voiced diminished chords in the dark key of C minor. A chorus of demons then sings an incantation in unison, "Jamais filles dénaturées vos supplices ne finiront," accompanied by sustained winds (including trombones), string tremolos, and chords in *alla ʒoppa* syncopation. The key here

---

94. Based on Calzabigi's libretto *Ipermestra, o Le Danaidi*. The print (Paris: Des Lauriers, n.d.) is fairly close to the manuscript (F-Pn, L. 2468). For details on the opera, see Rice, *Antonio Salieri and Viennese Opera*, 307–29. *Les petits spectacles de Paris*, 115, cites a five-act pantomime-parody of *Les Danaïdes* entitled *Les Adélaides, ou La mort des quarante-neuf cousins* at the Grands danseurs de corde in 1784.

95. John A. Rice, "Danaïdes, Les," NGO 1:1058. Dezède's *Alcindor* and Grétry's *Raoul, Barbe-bleue* also have similar D minor/D major overtures.

shifts to A-flat, then to F minor after a dominant seventh on C. The demons continue their chantlike infernal expression in F minor, first in octaves, then in unison, as the daughters alternate implorations to cease and horrific cries of "Ah!," set in close-voiced chords (see ex. 1.12). The harmony now moves to the major sixth (D-flat), then an augmented sixth, which resolves not to the dominant but to a B-flat seventh chord, the dominant of the new key, E-flat minor— an unusually remote tonality for this period. The minor mode changes to major for a series of cadential phrases with string tremolos, followed by triplet accompaniment, then *alla zoppa* figures. Salieri then shifts rapidly from E-flat to G minor and then C minor in preparation for the climactic cadence. The chord progression of that cadence, $i–VI–ii^{o6}_5–V–i$, is one that the Italian composer Vincenzo Righini had used to accompany the damnation of Don Juan in his *Il convitato di pietra* (1776), and again in the overture to *Alcide al bivio* (1790). Mozart would employ it for the moment of damnation in his *Don Giovanni* and in the Dies irae of his *Requiem*.

As potent as Salieri's music for *Les Danaïdes* might first appear on the written page, it is actually more noisy than disturbing. Salieri's music remains mostly in major keys, and its force is derived from the large-scale orchestration, the violent accompaniment figures, the mixture of vocal forces in the otherworldly unison chorus, and the gasps and exclamations of the Danaids. But a series of heavily decorated clichés remains under the weight of all the orchestral effects, whose repetition dissipates the tension. Salieri's harmony lacks imaginative scope and chromatic flavor. The topical range here is also more limited than Gluck's, Sacchini's, or certainly Mozart's, because Salieri integrates few elements from sacred music and instrumental idioms.[96]

Sacchini's three-act *Œdipe à Colone*, also on a text by Guillard (1786, 1787) contains one supernatural scene where the gods reject a ceremony of the priests (act 1, scene 5). The scene begins with the "Hymne et chœur de prêtres" in E-flat, called "Marche des Prêtres pendant l'Hymne" in the libretto and score. During this solemn ceremonial march the High Priest (bass) and a chorus of priests (TBB) beg for the approval of the divinities of Athens. (One wonders if Mozart was aware of this music when he set his scenes for Sarastro and his priests in *Die Zauberflöte*.) Sacchini accompanied stage thunder with rapid ascending scales in the strings and bass. The horns and oboes deliver hellish blasts as the divinities refuse to be appeased (a tenor singing one note on the word "Non"). The three Eumenides appear, and the altar ignites as general confusion spreads, portrayed by terrifying orchestral music with violent sixteenth-note ascending and descending figures.

96. In the next season (1777) Salieri attempted to follow up his success with another grand opéra for the Royal Academy, the *tragédie lyrique* in three acts *Les Horaces*, on a text by Nicolas-François Guillard. Its only marvelous material is a brief oracle scene in D-flat marked "un poco adagio" and scored with wind and string accompaniment (act 1, scene 1). The composer seems to suggest an otherworldly quality in the vocal line, with its repeated notes in a limited range.

EXAMPLE 1.12 Antonio Salieri, *Les Danaïdes*, act 5, scene 11 (finale)

The following year the Royal Academy mounted the three-act *tragédie lyrique La toison d'or* (The Golden Fleece), on a text by Philippe Desriaux, with music by Johann Christoph Vogel (5 September 1786, revised as *Médée de Colchos*, 1788).[97] The supernatural is a prominent element even in the C minor slow introduction of the terror-laden overture, with its full wind complement with trombones (leading to an Allegro maestoso in C major). In act 3, scene 3, the vengeful Medea has a furious "Grave e sostenuto" invocation in D minor ("Viens, viens, O divinités terribles"). The aria begins with a portentous descending string motive in dotted rhythms, followed by bursts of an ascending scale figure that lead to a repeat of the descending motive, now on the dominant. *Alla zoppa* syncopation, sustained chords, and diminished and augmented harmonies enhance the infernal topic. As is the case with similar incantations, a chorus of subterranean voices (SATB) follows, here an Allegro in F major scored with trombones. An oracle scene for the prophetic sibyl (soprano) in F major follows, for full orchestra with trombones, in which the sibyl foretells in recitative the dire consequences of Jason's marriage. The instrumental Allegro introduction starts with the old-fashioned canzona rhythm in the trombones and bassoons and continues with descending triadic figures in *alla zoppa* rhythms. When the oracle makes her pronouncement the tempo changes to Adagio; her melody includes a setting for the words "this is the torch of the Eumenides that burns over the altars" of a repeated incantation on the tonic. The oracle then sings of "perfidious oaths" to an ascending chromatic line. After Medea curses Jason as her betrayer, the opera ends with a large-scale, violent instrumental segment in D minor. With its tremolos and other terrifying features, the music is like the tumultuous final scene in *Les Danaïdes* and Mozart's second finale of *Don Giovanni*.

Salieri's next opera for the Royal Academy, the five-act *Tarare*, on a text by Pierre-Auguste Caron de Beaumarchais (8 June 1787),[98] was one of his greatest successes. Conforming to Diderot's notion of "intermediary genres," with comedy and tragedy combined, this opera also revived the traditional five-act format of the *tragédie lyrique*, but in an oriental setting. The opera has a special significance as a rare instance of a social allegory.[99] Salieri's busy score features extensive writing for wind instruments. Here the marvelous occurs in the overture, the allegorical prologue, and the final scene. The overture (unrelated to later material in the opera) is full of gestures that suggest the supernatural, such as trombones playing sustained notes and accompanied by rapid sixteenth-note scales. Swirling figures in the wind instruments during the storm music suggest violent vortices. The allegorical prologue includes a pantomime for the winds, set with trombones; the Genie of Fire (bass) waves a wand to transform

97. The printed score (Paris: Clochet, n.d.), F-Pn, D. 14188, was consulted.
98. For a modern edition see Salieri, *Tarare*.
99. See Betzwieser, "Exoticism and Politics."

the scene, and Nature (soprano) appears with her wand. Her recitative seems mortal rather than divine as she conjures the chorus of winds. She sings in the heroic style, with bold gestures, dotted rhythms, and rapid ascending scales. A graceful dance accompanies the chorus of ghosts (bass voices), preparing the appearance of the ghost of Urson (bass).

The most ambitious musical setting of a fairy-tale for the Royal Academy was *Alcindor*,[100] a three-act *opéra-féerie* on a text by Marc-Antoine-Jacques Rochon de Chabannes, with music by Nicolas Dezède (17 April 1788).[101] This throwback to traditional *tragédie en musique*, with deities, divertissements, a magic sleep scene, elemental spirits, and dance, seems "tragic" only as the last gasp of opera in the ancien régime. The librettist drew upon on *Les mille et une nuits* and the precious fairy-story tradition (see chapter 2).[102] Alcindor, the king of the Island of Gold, desires the glory of victory. Almovars, his genie-protector, wants to make him sensitive to the happiness of his people and devises a series of trials in order to help the young king acquire the virtue of enlightened leadership. Apparently this advice was too little too late: the Revolution soon did away with the French monarchy.

Instrumental preludes figure among *Alcindor*'s marvelous conventions, along with a *bruit souterrain* with rapid, repeated sixteenth notes, and supernatural ensembles such as the three-part gnomes' chorus and a four-part offstage "small chorus of Dreams." The overture begins with a dark, Maestoso introduction in D minor (see ex. 1.13) leading to the Allegro in D for winds, with its foursquare *contradanse* theme. The following segment offers a new theme with sweeping marvelous figures, tremolos, and *alla ƺoppa* syncopations. The opera's first number is an eerie ensemble for three gnomes (singing mostly in unisons) and Alcindor. After the octave-and-unison opening, the unison bass voices rise in a slow, chromatic incantation (see ex. 1.14). Alcindor disperses the gnomes and asks for the treasures promised to him by the enchanter Almovars. He then hears a magic *simphonie*, an Andantino in B-flat for flutes, horns, and strings, serving as the basis of the following chorus of Enchanted Dreams. The style is suggestive less of traditional magic sleep music than of a

100. Two texts survive (Paris: Delormel, 1787 and Paris: Ballard, 1787) in F-Pn, Musique, shelfmark 8° ThB 98. A manuscript score and parts are in F-Po, shelfmark A. 319 (I–III), shelfmark Mat. 18/6 (parts): the dance music is found in a manuscript in F-Po, *Recueil d'airs de ballet*, vol. 26. Drawings of the characters by Alexandre Moitte are preserved in London, Victoria and Albert Musuem, Harry A. Beard Collection, and are reproduced in Winter, *Pre-Romantic Ballet*, 130. The opera is discussed in Pitou, *Paris Opéra*, 2:21–23.

101. Rushton, "Floquet," reports that the opera was begun by Etienne-Joseph Floquet, who died in 1785. According to Fox, "Dezède," some of the dances may be by Floquet. No mention of this occurs in Charlton, "Dezède." Some sources attribute the dances to Pierre Gardel.

102. Vol. 4, "L'Histoire du Prince Zeyn Alasnam, et du Roi des Génies." For a modern edition see *Les mille et une nuits*, ed. Garnier, 2:404. Carlo Gozzi also drew upon this source in his *Zeim, re de' genj* (1765).

EXAMPLE 1.13 Nicolas Dezède, *Alcindor*, overture

Maestoso

EXAMPLE 1.14 Nicolas Dezède, *Alcindor,* act 1, scene 1

solemn march. In scene 11 Almovars (bass) arrives with a brief instrumental Andante consisting of a series of repeated cadential chords in the winds (oboes, clarinets, bassoons, and horns) and strings, a sonic image of enchantment.

The second act of *Alcindor* begins with a grotesque pantomime as the gnomes lead Alcindor and Zerbin into the oracular chamber. Dezède scored the music for low strings and winds (horns, bassoons, violas, and basses) and added oboes, clarinets, and violins to the orchestra when the gnomes bring in the young girls, augmenting the timbre as the pitch rises and the surface rhythm increases. In scene 14 Alcindor hears mysterious chords that announce the descent of Almovars and his genies from above. This is a short segment of "enchanted" wind music for oboes, clarinets, and bassoons, with sustained octaves in the horns.

In act 3, scene 4, thunder and lightning instigate a terrifying offstage chorus, which from inside a cave intones a promise of great fortune if Alcindor renounces the love of Azélie and returns to his realm as a ruler. Rapid figures and *alla ʒoppa* syncopations accompany the slowly rising chromatic unison vocal intonation for a chorus of basses ("Frémer, faible mortelle"), followed by the horrified reactions by the Azélie and Alcindor. Loud sustained chords for the orchestra, with trombones, announce the oracular voice (bass) heard from inside the cavern accepting their sacrifice and inviting them into the cave. His unaccompanied vocal line has repeated notes and prominent leaps. In scene 5 the offstage chorus demands that Alcindor obey the decree of heaven in an ensemble with *alla ʒoppa* figures scored with trombones. The cavern disappears, and the scene changes to Almovars's palace to music accompanying the stage machines: an Allegro marked "le jour." The key now modulates to D major, the trombones drop out, and the winds and violas play an eight-measure sustained tonic chord supporting sixteenth-note scale figures in the violins. Timpani rolls help build the crescendo along with syncopated rhythmic figures. Almovars appears seated on a throne near a golden statue. He tells Alcindor that his trials are over. When Alcindor asks about his loss of Azélie, Almovars strikes his wand on the statue, and two measures of ascending duplets in thirds (on a dominant chord) facilitate the transformation of Azélie, Osman, and Zerbin.

For all its descriptive features, Dezède's music lacks a personal, compelling means of communicating emotion, and the listener is at pains to identify with characters and their situations. As in the ballet music of Rochefort, mimetic and decorative principles dominate *Alcindor*'s busy score, which is rich in orchestral effects, dance, and divertissements but lacks harmonic variety and dramatic force. Dezède should not be counted among the masters of the "theater of the marvelous" in the final years of the ancien régime. By contrast, Gluck, Piccinni, Sacchini, J. C. Bach, and Salieri alloyed with varying degrees of efficacy the Franco-Italian synthesis, musical terror, and heightened emotion with the tradition of French *grand opéra,* making that nation's opera an equal to its admired Italian counterpart.

CHAPTER TWO

✦

Opéra-comique

In contrast to the *grand* theatrical genres, the *petit* genres were the sphere of *opéra-comique*.[1] Most of these had musical components; they ranged from one-act *parades*, performed on balconies over the fair theater's entrances in order to entice paying customers, to complex works in five acts. Comic works had a broad range of themes and forms as well. The ceremonial solemnity and formality of the official theaters became a target for parody in the *petit* theaters of Paris. Here playwrights relied on the lower literary genres such as the fable, the *conte de fées,* and the *conte oriental,* which had a kinship to fairy episodes of medieval romance. The term "comedy" did not always imply a humorous piece; rather, it usually concerned characters of social ranks lower than the aristocracy. "Comedy" might also designate a work that departed significantly from the rules of classical drama, or one that treated a subject in a modern setting. This is the broad meaning of the word *comédie* in the Comédie-Française. In any event, writers' treatment of subject matters in comic works was usually more realistic that that in other genres, even if such works included supernatural elements.

French comedy of the era often concerned the middle classes, rustics, and servants. This tradition, dating back to classical antiquity, had been developed in the commedia dell'arte,[2] where supernatural powers were granted to

1. Many manuscripts and prints from theatrical productions survive, including librettos, playbooks, synopses, and *arguments*. These include brief *canevas* or sketches of the action used by acting companies, full manuscript texts, printed librettos sold to audience members, and published texts in collected editions, dictionaries, histories, and periodicals. Although I have consulted most of the commedia dell'arte scripts in Parisian libraries preserving "fantastic" material, not all are listed here. I have attempted to be representative and include all of those that prominently featured fairy-tale, oriental, or legendary material.

2. French translations of *scenari* include Thomas-Simon Gueullette's translation of Joseph Dominique Biancolelli's eighty *scenari* (F-Po, Ms. Rés. 625, and F-Pn, f.f. 9328). See T.-S. Gueullette, *Notes et souvenirs.*

génix, En habits Sérieux,

FIGURE 2.1. *Génies en habits sérieux.* F-Pn (Opéra), Rés. D. 216 [o.4, fol. 64, (Cliché B.N. 75 C 74557). (Courtesy of Bibliothéque Nationale de France.)

the lowly comic servants. These archetypal survivors were conniving, fearful, hungry, and always poor. They delighted audiences with their clever use of magic power, usually inverting some social convention or challenging received wisdom that the pretentious bourgeoisie held as treasured truth. Although some eighteenth-century comedies are to some extent socially affirming, others are more seditious. Playwrights often differentiated the speech of characters from different social spheres, thus clearly maintaining their status. Magicians, sorceresses, fairies, and genies speak in an elevated and more formal aristocratic style, as in *Les lunettes magiques* and *Barbe-bleue.* Furthermore, such characters often wore the most lavish costumes (fig. 2.1) and danced to the most elegant music.

Unlike in serious, official opera, in the comic theater the marvelous subverts the social order. Magic powers allow commoners to assume princely roles and to further events in the plot that otherwise would be impossible owing to the period's rigid class system. It may seem ironic, but magic actually allows for the rational enlightenment of characters (and the audience), demonstrating the arbitrary nature of distinctions in social class. Comedies based on *contes orientaux* reveal that these principles are universal, operating in foreign as well as European cultures. The "comic marvelous" in the theater therefore had a powerful allure that spoke to the audience in a way that quotidian elements could not. It presented onstage the reification of wishes and "what if" thoughts: What if I had the power to read minds? What if I were invisible? What if I could assume the appearance of another? What if I could be king? For those who saw themselves as powerless, these wishes made for attractive thought experiments that provided pleasurable fantasy as well as suggesting the possibility of social change. Coffey's ubiquitous *The Devil to Pay* (London, 1731),[3] adapted in French by Michel-Jean Sedaine as *Le diable à quatre* (Paris, 1756), is perhaps the best-known example, with its magical event that triggers the plot (see preface).

Although not necessary components in comic genres,[4] magic and the marvelous nevertheless remained important features. Like their Italian predecessors, comic playwrights in France and the fair comedians (*forains*) combined satire, burlesque, and parody with fantastic elements from literature and legend, as well as violating the strictures of traditional theory, all the while ignoring the demands of verisimilitude and genre distinction. Their humor derived mostly from tensions inherent in controversial topics. The earliest comedies of Florent-Florent Carton Dancourt and Alain-René Lesage offered a succession of contrasting social types petitioning a character possessing magic power; all are held up for ridicule.

Magic in the eighteenth-century theater often enlightens the leading characters; fairies, genies, magicians, and sorceresses can serve as kindly benefactors with magic implements that unmask pretense, ill will, and deception. Here magic is a means of imparting truth, knowledge, and wisdom to the mortal protagonists, whose education frequently drives the main plot line of the story. The trials and tribulations of human heroes and heroines (along with their comic and cowardly companions) impart moral lessons. These protagonists encounter formidable obstacles, often in the form of evil giants (see plate 3), fairies, ogres, genies, or magicians (fig. 2.2). In the course of their quest they achieve critical knowledge and eventually attain their goals. Supernatural beings also serve as commentators on topical or social issues, often with satirical intent. Thus in Alexis Piron's *L'antre de Trophonius* (Foire St. Germain, Febru-

3. This ballad opera was based on Thomas Jovon's *The Devil of a Wife* (1686), which in turn is based on the story of Mopsa in Sidney, *Arcadia* (c. 1590]).

4. For a comprehensive contemporary survey of comic elements in literature see Le Roux, *Dictionnaire*, which mentions the marvelous only in passing. For a modern study on this topic see Isherwood, *Farce and Fantasy*. Pré, "Le livret d'opéra-comique," 360–65, adopts Christout's categories of *la comédie fantastique* and *la féerie*, designating the former as a plot with standard comic characters (peasants, shepherds, et al.) who encounter magic or the intervention of supernatural characters in the real world.

FIGURE 2.2. Anonymous copy of Nicolas Boquet, *Maquette de costume de magicien*. F-Pn (Opéra), Rés. D. 216 III, pl. 14 (Cliché B. N. 87 C 132146). (Courtesy of Bibliothéque Nationale de France.)

ary 1722), Mercury, the god of thievery, delivers mordant observations on the contemporary social scene.

In time the court and public theaters exerted reciprocal influences, and the distinction between low and the high genres became more blurred. Although standard genres such as tragedy, comedy, and pastoral continued in new theatrical productions, playwrights alloyed oriental or folk tales with topical satire, comic episodes, burlesque, or esoterica. From their earliest appearance, dramatic fairy tales almost always included comic characters and scenes.[5] The Royal Academy began staging occasional comedies, and comic style became more evident in some of its new repertory. Conversely, the comic theaters also turned to the stoic, serious style of the Royal Academy, if only in the form of parody. Thus the vivid ghost, tempest, and oracle scenes that distinguished opera in the 1690s appeared in comic genres of the early eighteenth century. By the middle of the eighteenth century, theater, art, music, and literature exploited greater violence and horror as well.

New Literary Inspirations

Shortly after the publication of the first French fairy tales (c. 1695–1700), the vogue for fantastic narratives gained impetus with printed collections of oriental tales, beginning in 1704 with Antoine Galland's free translation of Arabic stories, *Les mille et une nuits*.[6] François Pétis de la Croix's French adaptations of Persian stories appeared in 1710 as *Les mille et un jours*,[7] followed by Tartar tales translated by Thomas-Simon Gueullette in 1712.[8] At least since the time of Straparola (see introduction), oriental stories had been closely associated with fairy tales. Both had similar archetypal characters and plots, as well as a similar use of fantastic situations. But the new oriental tale did not emphasize the conflict between the religion and culture of the Orient and that of the West. Rather, it explored erotic and exotic themes of remote lands, often using a foreign setting to criticize and satirize contemporary European society by implication, a critique that would be uncomfortable or even seem seditious if broached more openly. In directing their attention to "oriental" societies, Europeans began to view themselves with more detachment, recognizing their similarities in other cultures. As culture itself became the subject of critique, French playwrights questioned Europe's notion of its exclusive authority, particularly its claim to universal morality.

Following the initial wave of publications of edited translations from authentic Eastern sources (1705–10), a number of French authors produced imitations (1710–25).[9] Disaffection began to influence these tales, and self-parody

5. Cahusac mentioned the new combination of comedy and the marvelous on the lyric stage beginning c. 1710 in the *Encyclopédie*. For details, see Anthony, *French Baroque Music*, 137.

6. Galland altered his sources to fit European taste, emphasizing the fantastic and avoiding the erotic elements of the originals.

7. Pétis de la Croix, *Les mille et un jours*.

8. T.-S. Gueullette, *Les mille et un quarts d'heure*. The magistrate Gueullette also wrote *Soirées bretonnes* in 1712, and preserved or arranged numerous commedia dell'arte plays. See J.-E. Gueullette, *Un magistrat du XVIIIe siècle*. The highly edited stories were pruned of "improper" erotic content and adapted to Europe's image of the Orient.

9. Chapbooks were another important means of disseminating fantastic literature, and in the series called *Bibliothèque bleue* chivalric stories remained the most popular. Among them the Me-

became a topic after about 1730, especially in the stories of Antoine Hamilton. By the 1740s a new type of oriental tale had emerged in print and on the stage, one that celebrated the sensations and details of erotic arousal (an emotion believed to diminish considerably after marriage). Not all oriental tales had supernatural content; some merely relied on improbable situations, presenting extreme emotions, unusual characters, and novel events that appalled, startled, and frightened the reader. (Perrault's *Bluebeard* is a good example.) Furthermore, both oriental and European fairy tales included as a distinct species a subcategory that we might designate the false-magic story. Here clever protagonists employ superstition and the fear of supernatural power to deceive gullible characters.

The following segment approaches the topic of magic and the supernatural on the French stage from two perspectives. First an analysis of key theatrical genres serves to draw the significant distinctions in content. Then a brief survey of repertories demonstrates the widespread use of the supernatural in virtually all of the *petit* theaters.

The Fairy Story

During the 1730s Parisian comic theaters staged a new kind of erotic fairy story, distinct in its *galant* style and content, which eschewed seriousness, pedantry, and formality to concentrate on the details of courtship and the arousal of erotic sensation. Unlike fairy tales—and here I am making an important distinction between "tales" and "stories"—these stories employed sophisticated language and precious poetic conventions. Oriented toward elite court society, fairy stories, unlike fairy tales, were rarely rustic or childlike. Pastoral settings and references to chivalric traditions were common in fairy stories, with knights, shepherdesses, arcadian locales, and even occasional deities from classical mythology. In many of these stories a fairy or genie typically rears a young aristocrat, who in finding a mate must overcome formidable obstacles resulting from the curse of a malevolent fairy or oracle. The good fairy or genie helps to bring about this union by enlightening the couple. The focus concerns the vicissitudes of love, the rules and dynamics of courtship, the problem of arranged marriages, and the slow progression of erotic attachment. These cautionary tales revel in the delicate details of sensation, attraction, and the eventual passionate union. The plots frequently contrast nature versus artifice in matters of love.

As for the fairies themselves, they are aristocratic in behavior and appearance (see fig. 2.3). They marry princes of royal blood and establish illustrious families, such as the eight seigneurs of Lusignan who claimed to be descendants of the fairy Mélusine.[10] The good fairy functions as a teacher, instruct-

---

lusine story appeared at least eight times in surviving French chapbooks published between 1624 and 1750.

10. For other examples, see Delaporte, *Du merveilleux dans la littérature française*, 93–94.

FIGURE 2.3. *Chœurs de fée*. F-Pn (Opéra), Rés. D. 216 III, fol. 7. (Courtesy of Bibliothéque Nationale de France.)

ing innocents in rational, mature thought. She helps mortals by her prescient knowledge of human affairs, displaying axiomatic truths not by an appeal to dogma or force (as the evil fairy does), but by applying sound abstract principles to the problems at hand. She sets in motion the events necessary to enlighten the naive, to persuade the closed-minded, and to educate the young. Led not by her passions but by reason, she is an ideal of a philosopher-teacher and of a beneficent, enlightened monarch who uses power for good. The plot demonstrates the truth of her enlightened values. Good fairies and genies, furthermore, offer elegant aphorisms concerning love and human nature. Their erotic experiments yield insightful observations on passion, pleasure, and the relations between the sexes. For example, Fonpré de Fracansalle's *Almanzor et Nadine* (6 December 1787)[11] treats "experience versus nature" in a critique of religion and a glorification of nature, with romantic love as its most direct expression. Wit and finesse mark the best of the genre, with a nuanced and precious approach to language and character. Dialogue may often contain social commentary, already characteristic of the French comic theater in the early eighteenth century.

Erotic tales of sexual initiation tantalized audiences with characters such as the innocent and sexually vulnerable nymph, the languishing and passive beauty, and the aggressive and Amazon-like enchantress, a predatory dominatrix type with appetites commensurate with her supernatural power. The young males, on the other hand, are naive characters in need of the fairy's instruction. The role of men in the refined society of women is a common topic here, with important lessons in submission, delayed gratification, and self-control.

Fairy Tales

The vogue of French fairy tales, beginning about 1695, quickly occasioned theatrical settings, such as Dancourt's three-act comedy *Les fées* (1699).[12] Later stage works based on fairy tales employ an affectation of naiveté and magical thinking associated with childhood. Although ostensibly directed toward children, the main audience for these stage works was adult. Writers adapted nine of Charles Perrault's stories for the Parisian stage multiple times in the eighteenth century, as well as fantastic oriental stories. *Les mille et un jours* and *Les mille et une nuits* provided Lesage the basis for some twenty-one plays,[13] while other oriental tales inspired the comedies of Fuzelier, Piron, and Gueullette. The major comic librettists of the next generation also adapted such tales as comic operas. Charles-Simon Favart, among the most notable, based his groundbreaking comic opera *Acajou* (1744) on Charles Pinot Duclos's tale "Acajou et Zirphile," from *Le cabinet des fées*.[14] This bizarre plot combines social commentary, eroticism, internal narration of fairy tales, and various supernatural devices in recounting the fate of Princess Zirphile, a vain and indifferent beauty who is beheaded. Her head is then transported to the

11. F-Pn, Ms. n.a.f. 2857, fols. 174–91. The author's first name is unknown.

12. Writers employed "Les fées" as a title in at least two productions, although Perrault's tale of that name was not the basis of the plots.

13. Lesage also integrated elements from these tales into his novel *Gil Blas de Santillane*, 287. He helped edit the "Persian Days" in Pétis de la Croix, *Les mille et un jours*. For a discussion of these sources see Luciani, *Carlo Gozzi*, 2:504–29. (The page numbers here and in other citations refer to the 1958 edition.)

14. *Le cabinet des fées.*

moon, where her faithful lover, Prince Acajou, uses a magic ring to restore her to life.

Like French fairy tales, *contes orientaux* served as Enlightenment allegories and erotic fantasies, treating some of the most troubling issues in French society: culture, nationalism, human nature, and the politics of love and power. Plots questioned whether these were natural or learned aspects. To attempt answers, writers explored subordinate social relationships such as rulers and the ruled, women and men, and slave and master. They depicted love as a natural phenomenon suppressed by the artificiality of rigid courtly manners. The popular topic of coquetry treated women's power over men and the use of sexual attraction as a tool of that power (e.g., *Le ballet des porcelains, ou du prince pot à thé*, 1739). Another common subject was universality in nationalism and culture, as was Rousseau's notion of the nobility of the savage and the natural versus the artificial in social organization. Social thought experiments occurred in fantastic lands, with magic used as a means to demonstrate universal principles.

Devil Stories, Utopian Fantasies, and False-magic Stories

In stories featuring the devil, playwrights drew on Machiavelli, Boccaccio, and La Fontaine, as well as Spanish plays and various legends, to create plots that remained popular throughout the eighteenth century, owing in part to their timely social critiques. Dancourt's comedy based on Lesage (in turn based on Spanish sources), *Le diable boiteux* (Comédie-Française, 1707), is perhaps the best-known example. Lesage then set his own novel as a *pièce en écriteaux, Arlequin invisible chez le roi de Chine* (Foire St. Laurent, 1713).[15] Theatrical adaptations of utopian plots with supernatural episodes such as *Le monde renversé* and *Le roi de Cocagne* also explored contemporary Enlightenment issues. Chicanery using the belief in magic is the central plot device in what I call the false-magic story, an old tradition dating back to fables. In one plot variant a man impersonates a sylph in order to deceive a naive young woman. In another an impoverished young swain has lost his beloved to a rich rival; to intimidate the rival and win back his beloved he disguises himself as a magician.

The Comédie-Française, the Théâtre-Italien, and the Fair Theaters

The Comédie-Française provided a venue for new theatrical material.[16] Dancourt first adapted (and ridiculed) Perrault's fairy tales there in his *Les fées*

15. The *pièce en écriteaux* was a strategy for avoiding the period's prohibitions on dialogue: the actors performed in mime only, while the verses they would have spoken were written on placards for the audience to see. See Isherwood, "Popular Music Entertainment," 305–6.

16. For a list of comedies given at the Comédie-Française, the Théâtre-Italien, and the fair theaters (some with plot summaries and commentary), see Parfaict and Parfaict, *Dictionnaire des théâtres de Paris;* the "scenario de Dominique Biancolelli" (translated by T.-S. Gueullettte), F-Pn, Ms. 9328; and Luigi Riccoboni, *Le nouveau théâtre italien* (Paris, 1733) and *Le nouveau théâtre ita-*

of 1699. Le Grand's *Le roi de Cocagne* (1718) presented the well-known utopian fairy tale about the land of Cockaigne. Germaine-François Poullain de Saint-Foix wrote one of the most successful and influential erotic fairy stories, *L'oracle* (1740). Rich in aphorism, nuance, and finesse of thought, this witty and sophisticated example of fairy erotica has a plot that allegorically treats social habits, love, and the role of men and sexual desire in polite society. Pierre-Claude Nivelle de La Chaussée used a Persian setting for his fairy tale *Amour pour amour* (16 February 1742), whose characters Zémire and Azor would reappear in the first operatic setting of the Beauty and the Beast story, Marmontel and Grétry's *Zémire et Azor* (1771).

Numerous French commedia dell'arte plays at the Théâtre-Italien retained traditional magic episodes, and playwrights revised earlier magical comedies such as the anonymous *Le naufrage d'Arlequin, ou l'Arcadie enchantée* (1740). Jean-François Deshayes based his *Arlequin génie* (1754) on the plot of Coffey's *The Devil to Pay*, apparently the first French adaptation of that widely used magic plot. Italian comedians also presented parodies of marvelous operas performed at the Royal Academy. Among the earliest plays to feature fairies were Meunier's *Les lunettes magiques, ou Les enchantemens* (1718) and Fuzelier's *La fée Mélusine* (1719). Fuzelier's plot is particularly rich in disguise and gender confusion; it commences after the estrangement of Raymond Lusignan from his fairy wife, Mélusine, and includes references to Ariosto's magic cavern and Orlando's lost reason. Here the fairy is a deceptive sorceress like Alcina or Armida, rather than the tragic heroine of Gaelic legend. The comic oracle episode features an astrological clock with musical chimes. French fairy tales (as opposed to elegant fairy stories) were also a favored subject at the Théâtre-Italien beginning with Jean-Antoine Romagnesi and Luigi Riccoboni's *Le conte de fée* (1735) and Coltelli (Michel Procope-Couteaux) and Romagnesi's *Les fées* (1736). Playwrights also updated utopian tales, as in Barthélemy-Christophe Fagan de Lugny's *L'île des talents* (1743), a spoof on the rage for "genius," set on an island where all the inhabitants are required to be talented, educated, and industrious.

By the 1740s theaters were staging longer, more convoluted magic plots, for example Dionisio Gandini's *Les métamorphoses de Scaramouche, ou La vengeance de Scaramouche* (1745). Along these lines, Carlo Antonio Veronese (= Véronèse) and his family produced successful comedies at the Théâtre-Italien. *Coraline esprit follet* (21 May 1744) marked the debut of Veronese's daughter Camille, admired by Casanova and others.[17] Her older sister Anna

---

lien, nouvelle édition. For discussions of the eighteenth-century Italian comedies in Paris, see Beagle, "The Théâtres de la foire," and Spada, *Domenico Biancolelli*.

17. According to Desboulmiers, *Histoire anecdotique*, 4:373, Carlo Antonio (Charles Antoine) Véronèse, a Venetian actor-playwright, first performed as Pantalon in Paris on 6 May 1744. He died in 1759. Desboulmiers, *Histoire anecdotique*, 7:214–18, gives Camille's real name as Giacomina-Antonietta Véronèse.

had performed the title role in *Coraline magicienne* (1744). Both actresses appeared as their stage personae, Coraline and Camille, in numerous magic comedies, creating a variation of the standard trickster, a female Arlequin. As a modern woman from the lower classes, she cleverly gains magic power and instigates the events in the plot. The anonymous *L'année merveilleuse* (1748) relies on the magical transformation of gender in several characters, and this device would appear occasionally in subsequent French comedies.

Owing to their peculiar and tenuous situation in the Parisian theatrical pecking order, the fair theaters were forced to adapt to quickly changing conditions during the first half of the eighteenth century. Necessity made this a period of experimentation for the *forains,* who maintained a flexible approach to their productions. Under pressure from the official theaters, these smaller stages restricted their music, dialogues, and actors at various times, adopting pantomime, monologue plays, marionettes, and singing. Early writers of fair plays, such as Louis Biancolelli, Dancourt, Charles Dufresny, Jean-François Regnard, Gherardi (1663–1700), Lesage (1668–1747), d'Orneval, Fuzelier, and Alexis Piron,[18] collaborated with composers such as Jean-Claude Gilliers, Jean-Joseph Mouret, Elisabeth Jacquet de La Guerre, and Rameau. The earliest fair repertory relied on the commedia dell'arte, and writers would continue to draw upon the Italian *scenari* throughout the century. Don Juan plays were popular in Paris since Molière's *Le festin de Pierre,* and these were recycled at the fairs with regularity, as were devil stories such as Lesage's *Arlequin invisible chez le roi de Chine* and the anonymous *pantomime anglaise Le docteur Faustus* (dated 1740, theater unknown).

As a guise for social criticism targeting the *grandes dames* and the bourgeoisie, with its corrupt lawyers and doctors, Lesage utilized material from *Les mille et un jours.* He based his first oriental fairy-tale comedy, *Arlequin Mahomet* (1714), on "L'histoire de Malek et Schirine." Similarly, Fuzelier, Lesage, and d'Orneval collaborated on a utopian fantasy and satire on French values entitled *Le jeune vieillard* (1722), based on "L'histoire des deux frères génies, Adis et Dahy." A magic mirror or statue that exposes sin and moral weaknesses was one of the most popular devices in the comic marvelous genres. Drawn from Galland's *Les mille et une nuits,* vol. 8 ("l'histoire du Prince Zein-Alasnâm et du Roi des genies"), Lesage was the first to use this device, in *La statue merveilleuse* (1719). It turns up in numerous productions throughout the century

18. For more information on Lesage and the fair theaters, see Barberet, *Lesage et le théâtre de la Foire;* Spaziani, *Il teatro minore de Lesage;* Brockett, "The Fair Theaters of Paris," 249–70; Striker, "Theater of Alain-René Lesage"; Laufer, *Lesage;* Grewe, *Monde renversé—théâtre renversé;* and Baggio, "Ambiguity of Social Characterization," 618–24. Campardon, *Les spectacles de la Foire,* 1:267, gives the first names Jacques-Philippe for d'Orneval. For recent research on Fuzelier, see Trott, "Louis Fuzelier et le théâtre"; Trott, "Pour une histoire des spectacles non-officiels." For information on Piron, see Chaponnière, *Alexis Piron,* and Maurice Barthélemy, "Alexis Piron et l'opéra-comique," 194.

in other countries as well, for example Gozzi's *Zeim, re de' genj*. Lesage and d'Orneval adapted the tale of Princess Turandot from "L'histoire des amours de Camaralzaman, prince de l'île des enfans de Khalédan, et de Badoure, princesse de la Chine" (nuits 211–21) for their *La princesse de la Chine* (1729), providing yet another model for Gozzi. One of the most exotic and fantastic of the fair plays is Piron's *L'Endriaque* (1723, with music by Rameau), which spoofs chivalry with episodes of cannibalism, human sacrifice, and a terrifying (but also ridiculous) crocodile-like monster.

Opéra-comique also drew on French fairy tales.[19] Fuzelier, Lesage, and d'Orneval turned to Perrault's "Le petit poucet" (Tom Thumb) for their *Arlequin roi des ogres, ou Les bottes de sept lieues* (1720); *La pantoufle*, attributed to one M[onsieur] Marignier (1730), is the first known staging of the Cinderella story. The first setting of *La Barbe bleüe* was a pantomime by Adrien-Joseph Valois d'Orville (St. Laurent, 3 July 1746). Marvelous episodes from epic romance also turn up in *opéra-comique*, both as central subjects and as parodies of grand genres. Lesage, d'Orneval, and Joseph de La Font exploited carnivalesque utopian themes in their popular *Le monde renversé* (St. Laurent, 2 April 1718), a "land of Cocaigne" satire on French culture. Merlin's flying griffin transports his two valets, Arlequin and Pierrot, to the strange land after crossing Europe and Asia. This piece is also an early example of an episodic social comedy, where a series of stereotypical characters are presented in consecutive scenes.

Parisian marionette plays should be considered a subgroup of *opéra-comique;* indeed, their texts can be differentiated from *opéra-comique* only by the phrase "represité aux marionnettes" on the title pages.[20] A review of the surviving sources demonstrates that the texts also derive from the commedia dell'arte tradition, with its superhuman characters and fantastic events. Mythology, epic romance, literature, fairy tale, and legend were frequently exploited in these plots, just as they were in *opera-comique*.

Although the chronological review that follows covers only a representa-

---

19. By 1760 French writers drew parallels between the *conte* and *opéra-comique*. Marmontel later devised a theory of literature that posited the *conte* as a comic counterpart to the epic. For details see Couvreur and Vendrix, "Les enjeux théoriques."

20. For details see Lindsay, *Dramatic Parody by Marionettes*, and Minniear, "Marionette Opera." I located the surviving *scenari* in F-Pn: *Polichinelle, Amadis*, a three-act *pièce* by Denis Carolet, "sur le Jeu de Marionnettes du St. Bienfait," St. Germain, March, 1732 (based on *Amadis de Gaule*); *L'île des fées, ou Le géant aux marionnettes* (St. Laurent, 12 July 1735), an anonymous parody of *Le conte de fée* (Théatre Italien, 26 May 1735); *Le songe agréable, ou Le rêve de l'amour*, anonymous (St. Laurent, 1735); *Polichinelle, roi des fées*, anonymous (St. Germain, 4 February 1737); *Le songe de Pierrot*, an anonymous *pièce de marionnettes* in prose with vaudevilles (1739); *Les métamorphoses de Polichinelle*, an anonymous one-act *pièce en vaudevilles, mélés de prose*, Jeu de Marionnettes de Bienfait, St. Germain, 1740; *Polichinelle gros Jean*, an anonymous parody of Quinault and Lully's *Roland* (St. Germain, 1744); and *Polichinelle, maître maçon*, an anonymous one-act *pièce* (St. Germain, 1744).

tive sampling of fantastic materials employed in *opéra-comique* during the Age of Reason, the impressive extent of magic and supernatural becomes obvious. For a more comprehensive list, the reader may consult Appendix A—a chronology of most French operas, ballets, comedies, pantomimes, and other plays containing supernatural episodes from 1699 to 1791.

Music and Magic in the Parisian Comic Theater, 1699–1730

Unlike the large extant repertory of the Royal Academy, only a relatively small amount of music survives from early eighteenth-century Parisian fair comedies. The music seems to have been ephemeral in nature; if preserved at all, it appeared in shorthand form, most often as melodies given at the end of a published volume.[21] A few pieces survive in short-score format. The large gaps in the chronology also make any conclusions tentative.

Although Jean-Claude Gillier composed original music for "low comedies," Mouret's various *recueils des divertissements* are the best sources for this repertory. These prints contain numerous airs, dances, choruses, and ensembles for genies, fairies, Furies, demons, and other superhuman characters. Often there is little to distinguish the music for marvelous scenes from that of more natural episodes,[22] but instances of pictorial musical imagery exist. Evidence of a grotesque musical style occurs in divertissements beginning around 1718. Some are clearly parodies of French *grand opéra*, and as such they are early instances of musical irony. For example, in *Belphégor* (see ex. 2.3) Mouret parodied the ghost scene from act 5 of Destouches's *Amadis de Grèce* (1698). Although elegance continued to be the rule for music at the Royal Academy, the comic theaters explored less noble expressions. A few surviving examples from these comic operas suggest that early scene complexes could be rather bizarre. Did the composers at the comic theaters devise more diverse styles

---

21. For a facsimile of the 193 vaudeville melodies from the 1810 edition of Lesage's *Oeuvres choisies*, see Spaziani, *Teatro della foire*.

22. Some of the music for Marivaux's *Arlequin poli par l'amour* (1720) was published in Mouret, *Quatrième recueil*, 89–97. F-Pn, Vm⁶ 46⁽⁴⁾, and some has been preserved in a 1914 manuscript (F-Pn, Ms. 8300) copied from a Philidor manuscript dated 11 March 1731 and entitled *Premier livre des divertissements des comédies . . . par Mr. Mouret.* The only surviving piece that appears to involve the marvelous is the "Entrée de lutins," a short, elegant dance with no special features to distinguish it from the other dances. The following three comedies have no musical corollaries to their marvelous effects at all: *La foire des fées,* a one-act pièce en vaudeville by Fuzelier, Lesage and d'Orneval (1722), with music by Mouret in his *Sixième recueil*, 17–28. F-Pn, Vm⁶ 46⁽⁶⁾. Specified music includes an overture, a *cantate récitatif,* an *air,* an *ariette,* two "airs pour les fées et les amans," and the final vaudeville (the music is mainly at the end). The "airs pour les fées et les amans" are unremarkable binary dances in minor keys. Other examples include *Le fleuve d'oubli* by Marc-Antoine Le Grand (1721), with music by Mouret in his *Cinquième recueil*, 85–94. F-Pn, Vm⁶ 46⁽⁵⁾, and Pierre-François Godard de Beauchamps, *Arlequin amoureux par enchantement* (1722), with music in Mouret, *Cinquième recueil*, 9–26; copy in F-Pn, Vm⁶ 46⁽⁵⁾.

to compensate for their limited vocal and orchestral resources? When one examines divertissements such as those for Mouret's *La Mélusine* (1719), one is tempted to answer in the affirmative.

The first known use of a *conte de fées* in the French comic theater, Dancourt's *Les fées,* included music by Michel de Lalande (1699).[23] The single example of a reference to what may be magic music in the libretto occurs at the end of the comedy, when the fairy Logistille arrives and Lalande adds trumpets and drums to the orchestra. But Lalande's surviving music indicates no typical conventions associated with the marvelous among the surviving songs, duet, and choruses in the divertissement and the *intermédes*.[24] The next relevant comedy with surviving musical materials comes from almost two decades later. Le Grand's *Le roi de Cocagne* (1718) included incidental music by Jean-Baptiste-Maurice Quinault.[25] The French overture and the divertissements show little evidence of musical imagery, even in the "Air des silphes" in act 2. Mouret's music in the divertissements of the anonymous comedy *Les lunettes magiques, ou Les enchantemens* (c. 1718) seems similar.[26] Although the genie has stately, regal music, his recitative and *air* show nothing distinctive. Likewise, the dance *airs* for the genies seem no different than others in the comedy.

Thomas Guellette's *Arlequin Pluton,* with music by Mouret (1719),[27] has extensive marvelous material, including monsters and scenes in hell. Supernatural musical imagery occurs in the first divertissement, a funeral for Arlequin. Although the episode is missing from the manuscript libretto, Jean-Auguste Jullien's synopsis in the *Histoire anecdotique et raisonnée du théâtre italien* (Paris, 1769) describes an infernal scene during which Arlequin's friends on earth celebrate his funeral with a "march and dances fitting the subject." Along with

23. Fontainebleau, 24 September and 24, 1, and 8 October. After seven performances at the Comédie-Française (20 October to 14 November), *Les fées* had another seven performances in October 1753 at Fontainebleau, with new *intermèdes* by Rebel and Francœur.

24. These include melodies for twenty-six movements printed in the libretto (1699) and reprinted at the end of vol.6 of *Oeuvres de théâtre de M. d'Ancourt*, F-Pn, ThB 3205). Some excerpts of Lalande's music, arranged as *symphonies*, are preserved in two manuscripts. Barbara Coeyman has identified movements arranged as two-part *symphonies* among two manuscript sources of Lalande's music in F-Pn, Rés. 582 (1703) and Rés. 581 (1733–45). For details see Coeyman, "Stage Works of Michel-Richard de Lalande," 241–57, 467–72. All are given in the thematic catalog at the end of her dissertation, 523–643.

25. A printed libretto (Paris: P. Ribou, 1719) survives along with a printed score (Paris, n.d.) The latter contains the overtures and divertissements (F-Pn, Rés. 1920, and Rés. 1922). The comedy was revised in 1781 with new music by Beaudron.

26. Mouret, *Premier recueil*, 119–28; copy in F-Pn, shelfmark Vm^6 47$^{(1)}$. There are also two airs printed in *Nouveau recueil des chansons choisies* 5.

27. The libretto survives in a manuscript copy in F-Pn, Musique (ThB 288 and two printed pages from the third divertissement, ThB 3880). The music for the divertissements appears in Mouret, *Premier recueil*, 101–18.

the more conventional pieces Mouret's print includes an "Air pour les affligéz" marked by abrupt musical changes that seem to reflect choreographic expression. This and other pieces in the print appear to be musical parodies of the official operatic style.

Mouret's music for Fuzelier's comedy *Mélusine* (1719) provides the first significant instance of music that suggests otherworldly affect in a comedy.[28] A good deal of the music for this comedy survives, and much of it is no different in style than that from other plays with no marvelous content, for example the conventional French overture and the unremarkable vocal *airs*. But some notable exceptions occur in the second divertissement, a grotesque comic scene where Arlequin has fallen into the hands of several hungry, cannibalistic ogres. Mouret supplied the low-pitched voices of the three-part trio (or chorus) of ogres with unusual chromatic harmony, occasional dissonance, and imitation as they musically drool over their fat human prey (see ex. 2.1). In subsequent solo sections each ogre in turn suggests an idea for preparing Arlequin as a meal. The third ogre's solo has a low-pitched string accompaniment that enhances its non-human expression.[29] The succeeding "Air pour les ogres" begins with elegant minuet-like phrases that become grotesque in the second half of the binary, with an unusual mixture of repeated-note motives.[30]

The third divertissement contains an oracle scene where the characters consult an *horloge* (an astrological clock of sorts).[31] Both in its distinctive trancelike expression and its exotic choice of instruments (carillon and bells),[32] the scene of "L'horloge de verité d'amour" seems to personify the illusory tone of enchantment that Cahusac would discuss some thirty-six years later. Mouret represents the clock with an atmospheric three-voice piece for carillon, creating an antiquated, religious, chimelike effect with suspensions, pedal point, echo, and repetitive, stagnant motives (see ex. 2.2). The *horlogeur* then sings a brief incantatory *air*, "Carilloneurs d'amour carillonés," with string accompaniment, where he commands the bell-ringers to chime the enchanted bells (*cloches*). The bells then respond with another strangely evocative instrumental piece whose motive recalls the coloratura phrase sung by the *horlo-*

28. Some of the music is preserved in Mouret, *Premier recueil*, 276–87. There are also two airs printed in *Nouveau recueil des chansons choisies* 5.

29. The manuscript of the text includes additional interjections for the ogres and Arlequin not in the printed version of the ensemble.

30. Other possible examples of grotesque style in dance include the two "Airs pour les chevaliers et les nains" in the first divertissement. The opening duple-meter dance in G major with dotted rhythms suggests the style of the gigue except for the missing measure at the end of the first strain. The contrasting short binary minor *air*, marked "vite," has an unusual asymmetrical phrase structure that abruptly thwarts expectations (4 + 4 + 2). Perhaps this reflects the choreography.

31. The text also differs here in printed score and the manuscript.

32. The bells may have been a mechanical instrument rather than a set. *Les spectacles des foires*, 160–61, mentions a musical clock of a M. Barbier le jeune called *l'horloge*, performing with two flutes and a "forte-piano."

EXAMPLE 2.1 Jean-Joseph Mouret, *Mélusine*, first divertissement

geur, a clever association that links the musical invocation (through the power of song) to the resulting magical event. The bell music is like the introductory music for carillon, with repetitive motives, nondirectional phrases, and a pedal. A dronelike fifth also enhances the static chiming effect. After the bells finish their magic music the *horlogeur* continues with his *air*. The unusual bell music seems to be based on standard carillon tunes similar to the one used for some Vespers services at St. Gervais in Paris. Louis Couperin's two arrangements of this tune have survived from the second half of the seventeenth

EXAMPLE 2.2 Jean-Joseph Mouret, *Mélusine*, third divertissement, "L'horloge de verité d'amour"

century.[33] A similar repetition of the short chime motives with suspensions, echo effects, and pedal (or organ) point imparts a trancelike static effect in both the Couperin pieces. The bells in the libretto and Mouret's score alike suggest an archaic, sacred association, one that is divine and magical in nature.

Mouret also supplied the music for Le Grand's *comédie-ballet Belphégor, ou La descente d'Arlequin aux enfers* (1721).[34] In an episode in the first divertissement, the "Entrée de paysans," the composer parodies two standard marvelous scenes from *grand opéra*. The first scene depicts a tempest, narrated by the chorus. The peasants sing a chorus, begging Bacchus for help; in response the deity sends a sprite flying through the air singing a dramatic arioso that parodies

33. The "Piesce par Mr. [Louis] Couperin pour contrefaire les Carillons de Paris et qui a toujours esté jouez sur l'Orgue de St. Gervais entre les Vespres de la Coussin et celle des Morts" and the "2e Air des Carillons" are found in F-Pn, Mus. Ms. Rés. F. 494, 71–76. This is the first volume of the manuscript collection compiled by Philidor l'aîné for the music library of Louis XIV. The first of Couperin's two "Carillons" is a two-voice piece written in five staves where the inner three parts are left blank. The second is a four-voice piece using the same bell motive found in the intoning of "les cloches" in *Mélusine*.

34. Some of the music was printed in Mouret, *Cinquième recueil*, 85–94. One air was printed in *Nouveau recueil des chansons choisies* 6, F-Pn, Weck. E. 3 (6). The story was also set as *Belphégor*, with music by Franz Beck (Bordeaux, 1789). Parts survive in Bordeaux's Bibliothèque municipale.

EXAMPLE 2.3 Jean-Joseph Mouret, *Belphégor*, first divertissement, "entrée de paysans"

a ghost scene (see ex. 2.3). The melody and obsessive accompaniment come directly from act 5 of Destouches's *Amadis de Grèce* (1698), where the ghost of the prince of Thrace appears and issues his decree.

For Louis Rustaing de Saint-Jorry's *Arlequin camarade du diable* (1722),[35] Mouret chose to provide mostly elegant French music, even for the sprites. The "Air comique pour les esprits folets" is a binary dance in G major (marked "legerement") with modal inflections of the minor seventh and a few asymmetrical phrases in the second strain. But Mouret's music for Fuzelier, Lesage, and d'Orneval's *Le jeune vieillard* (1722) includes marches in a more varied, descriptive vein.[36] The opening march in A minor is marked "grave," appropriate

35. Mouret, *Quatrième recueil*, 82–88. F-Pn, Vm⁶ 46⁽⁴⁾.

36. Mouret, *Cinquième recueil*, 39–60.

for the slow gait of the elderly characters at the center of the story. The march from act 2, "L'isle des vieillards," has a stately formality and decorum. The pair of binary "Airs pour les vieillards" are a contrasting set of dances, one pastoral (G major, 6/4), and the other a faster dance with *contredanse* rhythm. The contrast seems to derive from the dramatic function, with Mouret depicting the magic transformation of elderly characters into young persons. The composer employs the same device during a parallel scene in Jean-Baptiste Lacroix's divertissement in *L'amant Protée* (1728), a false-magic story about a putative fountain of youth.[37] In the "Ceremony of the Elderly, who enter the Fountain and leave Rejuvenated," the opening march, marked "lentement" in the minor key, starts with a languid suspended ninth. When the old people's youth is restored to them, the tempo of the music increases and the meter changes to cut time (marked "legerement"), beginning with an octave leap followed by rapid sixteenth-note passages.

In summary, Mouret's unusual music for supernatural events and characters suggests the beginning of a comic style for the small theaters in Paris. The style includes clever pantomime, grotesque expression, exoticism, archaic references, and parody of the pretensions of high society. All these elements will continue to be featured in comic operas, particularly those with supernatural episodes.

Opéra-comique, 1730–50

The innovations of the *opéra-comique* apparently inspired few significant additions to the already modest musical components at the Comédie-Italienne, the Comédie-Française, and the fair theaters. Although works of the comic marvelous such as *L'oracle* and *Acajou* were among the most popular in Europe, there appears to have been little in the way of musical imagery or marvelous devices exploited until after 1760. Some evidence points to hints of grotesque and parodistic features in isolated instances. Unfortunately there is little surviving music, and most early prints offer only reduced scores. Works during the 1730s that have some surviving music include the one-act prose comedy with divertissements *La sylphide*, by Pierre-François Dominique, called Biancolelli, and Romagnesi, with music by Mouret (1730).[38] A possible suggestion of the marvelous appears in first divertissement. Here an introductory instrumental piece marked "legerement," scored for two flute parts moving in conjunct parallel thirds and supported by one violin part, bears the style of enchantment and sleep scenes in serious opera. There is little in the *airs* for the sylphs, however, to differentiate them from those for mortal characters. An

37. Mouret, *Quatrième recueil*, 143–70.

38. A libretto was published (Paris: Delatour, 1730), and a manuscript survives in the Bibliothèque de l'Arsenal, Ms. M.762V. Some music was printed in Mouret, *Cinquième recueil*, 79–88. One air was included in *Nouveau recueil des chansons choisie 6*.

elegant, airy dance in two-part texture for flutes and violins is entitled "Air pour les silphes." Again marked "legerement," it has running sixteenth-note figuration.

Mouret's surviving music for the one-act comedy *Le conte de fée* by Romagnesi and Antoine-François Riccoboni (1735) is limited to the final divertissement and vaudeville, along with some incidental music.[39] Although the text itself is filled with fairy-tale elements, there seems to have been little in the music to depict them. The Mouret print offers a triple-meter, three-part "Entrée pour les génies" in G major, with fanfare-like triadic themes played "fort et piqué." The *entrée* leads to a coloratura da capo aria for a genie, scored for tenor voice, violin, and continuo accompaniment. The dances include an "Air pour un nain," a simple two-part giguelike dance in rapid tempo (marked "point viste"). Mouret offered a more tantalizing example of grotesque music in one *entrée* in Coltelli (Michel Procope-Couteaux) and Romagnesi's *Les fées* (1736).[40] Most of the music occurred in the final divertissement, the "Entrée pour la suite d'Amour," in which one finds a descriptive ballet entitled *Les animaux* in three-part texture and 6/8 meter, with unusual motivic musical gestures. This piece probably comes at the end of act 2, where Arlequin is surrounded by various animals that call to him, including an ass, a pig, a dog, and a cat, which chases him. The many apparent pantomimic figures imitate animal sounds: short slurred scale figures, abrupt juxtaposition of the repetitive motives, and leaps of an octave representing the braying of the ass. These grotesque features, unusual traits in a general ballet style that required an almost ubiquitous decorum and elegance, point the way to greater mimesis, which will soon be apparent in *grand opéra* and suggests an awareness of developments in contemporary Italian opera (see chapter 3).

Although there is no surviving music for the comedy *Les âges, ou La fée du Loreau* by Anne-Claude-Philippe de Tubières Grimoard de Pestels de Lévis, comte de Caylus (1739), the manuscript libretto contains descriptions of the music in each scene of the concluding ballet, *Le prince pot à thé*. Some are even provided with measure numbers.[41] One magic scene (act 1, scene 3), described on folio 18, indicates six measures of "musique magique" that commences with the arrival of the magician. The prince looks around as the music speeds up. Then the magician makes his circles with a wand, accompanied by a few measures of music repeated ad libitum. The magician touches the prince with the wand, and the music slows down to a "caractère de lenteur" as the spell takes effect, turning him into porcelain.

The most successful theatrical fairy stories in this period have some surviving music, but there is little indication of the marvelous in their scores. A late

39. Mouret, *Sixième recueil*, 197–210. F-Pn, Acq. 7927, film R. 7197.

40. Mouret, *Sixième recueil*, 263–74.

41. Ms. Arsenal 2748, fols. 1–16, then a copy on fols. 17–44. Also F-Pn f.f. 24343. This comedy has no music until the final ballet-pantomime.

print for the one-act prose comedy with divertissements *L'oracle*, by Germaine-François Poullain de Saint-Foix, with music by Nicolas Ragot de Grandval (1740),[42] contains unremarkable melodies for the divertissements. Another important fairy story is the three-act comedy in free verse with prologue *Amour pour amour*, by Pierre-Claude Nivelle de La Chaussée with music by Nicolas Ragot de Grandval (1742).[43] Some of the music for the divertissements survives in a print: an *air* for Zémire, two vaudevilles, and menuets.[44] Librettists wrote two sequels to this story, *L'amant statue* (1759) and *Zémire et Azor* (1771). Favart's popular *opéra-comique Acajou*, with music by Adolphe Blaise (1744), had numerous revivals and later revisions. The melodies of the *airs* and ensembles were printed in the 1763 libretto. The music shows no evidence of the marvelous style, but consists strictly of vaudevilles and simple *airs* and ensembles. These humble beginnings of the genre betray few of the important developments to come in the comic theater in the following decades.

The Supernatural at the Comédie-Française, Théâtre-Italien, and petit Theaters, 1750–74

Magical and supernatural episodes continued to be featured on the stages of the other theaters in Paris, with music providing an increasingly more significant element. The most prestigious theatrical venue, the Comédie-Française, produced erotic fairy stories such as Jean-Julien-Constantin Renout's *Zélide, ou L'art d'aimer et l'art de plaire* (26 July 1755). Another popular subject, the Pygmalion legend, appeared in numerous musical settings in the second half of the century. The best-known was Jean-Jacques Rousseau's *scène lyrique*,[45] set as a melodrama by Horace Coignet (Lyon, 1770; Comédie-Française, 1775).[46] These settings included music to accompany the supernatural scene where the statue awakes. In Coignet's version an elegant minuet-like "Amoroso" leads to three short segments where the sculptor sees the statue begin to move. Coignet forms these segments from a series of abrupt modulations. As the animated statue descends to Pygmalion the score indicates a D major Allegro in 6/8 meter, scored for muted strings and horns. This movement ends with an unusual modulation to B major. Cimador's *Pimmalione* also has music for the transfor-

---

42. (Paris: Prault fils, 1764), F-Pn, Mus. ThB 486B. The first libretto (Paris: Prault fils, 1740, F-Pn, 8° Yth 13088) contains no music. This story served as the basis for other fairy tales set for the musical stage, e.g., *Daphne and Amintor* in London and *Das Orackel* in German-speaking countries, and these sometimes included more descriptive music.

43. A libretto was published (Paris: Prault, 1742), then included in *Œuvres de theatre de Monsieur Nivelle*.

44. *Amusement des compagnies*, F-Pn, Musique, Rés. Vm⁷ 508.

45. For the original text and two musical settings, see Rousseau and Coignet, *Pygmalion*.

46. Also set by Franz Aspelmayr (Vienna, 1772), Anton Schweitzer (Weimar, 1772), and Georg Benda (Gotha, 1779). Simeone Antonio Sografi adapted the text as a short Italian opera with music by Giovanni Battista Cimador (Venice, 1790).

mation scene ("una soave Armonia" in the libretto), an "enchanted" ensemble of oboe, bassoon, and harp playing a minuet-like Andante in G major.[47]

Comic operas at the fairs in the 1750s apparently offered supernatural scenes with restrained musical accompaniment. Sedaine and Pierre Baurans's adaptation of Coffey's *The Devil to Pay* as *Le diable à quatre, ou La double métamorphose* updated a well-worn standard of the comic marvelous (St. Germain, 1756). But the score, by François-André Danican Philidor and Jean-Louis Laruette, shows little evidence of any allusions to the supernatural. There is no music to accompany the magician when he creates his spell and transforms the two female characters. This is also true of Louis Anseaume's adaptation of Perrault's Cinderella story as a one-act *opéra-comique, Cendrillon*, with music by Laruette (St. Germain, 21 February 1759).[48] For all the recitatives, vaudevilles, duets, trios, and choruses in the score, Laruette provided a modest musical component, with few effects to portray the supernatural events. The fairy's music contains only one instance to distinguish her from the human characters: two flutes provide rapid ornate figuration in her monologue and air in act 1, "Amour dont je ressens la flamme." There is even less differentiation in Charles de Lusse's short arias and duets for Jean-François Guichard's *L'amant statue* (St. Laurent, 18 August 1759),[49] an erotic pastoral fairy story where both the fairy and the mortal characters sing coloratura. *Opéra-comique* continued to use the marvelous elements of epic romance; for example, Rochon de la Valette and Marc-Antoine-Jacques Rochon de Chabannes's *La coupe enchantée* (St. Laurent, 19 July 1753), includes a fairy and a magical cup derived from Ariosto's epic poem.[50]

The Théâtre-Italien produced numerous musical comedies with supernatural episodes. Writers combined pastoral elements with *la féerie* in lengthy and convoluted Italian-style comedies, for example Pierre Prévost and Cazanove's *Les Thessaliennes, ou Arlequin au sabat*,[51] and Véronèse's *Arlequin génie* (both 1752). Véronèse and his family continued producing successful comedies with magical elements. A New Year's gift from Mercury, the magic cap of Jupiter that forces all who speak to him to tell the truth, is the chief magic device in Pierre-Antoine-Augustin de Piis and Pierre-Yon Barrè's [*Les*] *Etrennes de Mercure, ou Le bonnet magique* (1781). Beginning in the 1740s the generation of Favart enjoyed success with a new style of comedy, featuring exaggerated social types and a moralistic tone that replaced the ribald style of the past. Li-

47. See *Pygmalion*, 131–33.

48. (Paris: The author, n.d. [after 1762]), F-Pn, Vm⁵ 84, with the parts printed at end of volume.

49. The music is bound with the libretto in Lusse, *Ariettes*, F-Pn, Musique, 8 ThB 146(2).

50. (Paris: Duchesne, 1753.) For the many comic works that use or parody Ariosto see Roth, *Der Einfluss von Ariost's Orlando furioso*, 234–41.

51. Parfaict and Parfaict, *Dictionnaire*, 421, speculate on the identity of this author, possibly Giacomo Casanova.

brettists adopted the program for a mixed "reform" genre, calling such operas *drames lyriques*[52] and *comédie mêlée d'ariettes,* a compromise between the simple French vaudeville comedies and the more elaborate Italian opera. These works were mainly performed at the Théâtre-Italien. Favart, along with Nicolas Dalayrac, Sedaine, and Charles Collé, wrote many of the librettos, utilizing the marvelous as a central component of the plots. Examples include Jean Baptiste Dehesse's (dit Deshayes) *Arlequin génie* (1754), Favart's *La fée Urgèle* (1765), Marmontel's *Zémire et Azor* (1771), Favart's *La belle Arsène* (1773), Sedaine's *Alcine* (1785), Collé's *L'île sonnante* (1786), and Grétry's *Raoul, Barbe-bleue* (1789). The musical components of *opéra-comique* also changed considerably in the second half of the century, when composers such as Egidio Duni, Pierre-Alexandre Monsigny, Philidor, Grétry, and Gluck began providing more substantial and ambitious music.

Italian operatic styles made significant inroads in the Théâtre-Italien, especially after 1762, when the theater merged with the *opéra-comique.* Jean-François Guichard's *Le bûcheron, ou Les trois souhaits,* a three-act comedy *mélée d'ariettes* with music by Philidor (28 February 1763), was based on Perrault's popular fairy tale. A magic episode is the pivotal point of the plot: Mercury appears in a cloud to the rustic woodcutter Blaise, granting him three wishes. Two pieces in Philidor's score employ vivid depictions of supernatural events.[53] In scene 3 Mercury appears and tells the impoverished and henpecked Blaise that Jupiter has granted him three wishes. Mercury sings in obbligato recitative, preceded by four measures of stage-machine music as he arrives in his cloud chariot (see ex. 2.4). This short prelude is a brief sonic image, a burst of light, made up of descending triadic figures and short bursts of scales. Philidor accompanies his speech with sustained strings, the accompaniment of oracles, ghosts, and other superhuman characters. The second example is a septet in the comic style; here the enchanted Margot cannot speak but can only sing nonsense syllables. This is certainly the best-known example of the device later used by Mozart in *Der Stein der Weisen* and *Die Zauberflöte.*

Probably one of the most influential of Favart's librettos for the future acceptance of supernatural elements in comic opera was his four- act *comédie mêlé d'ariettes La fée Urgèle, ou Ce qui plaît aux dames.* Set to music by Egidio Duni, it was first performed at Fontainebleau (26 October 1765), then at the Théâtre-Italien (4 December 1765).[54] Favart based his libretto on Voltaire's *Ce qui plaît*

---

52. See Kopp, "'Drame lyrique.'"

53. The printed score (Paris: The author, n.d.), F-Pn, H. 814, has no overture. The overture is available, however, in the printed parts (also F-Pn). For details, see Charlton, "Overture to Philidor's *Le Bûcheron.*" Light, *galant,* Italianate music dominates Philidor's *ariettes,* duets, and ensembles.

54. The libretto was published (Paris: Christophe Ballard, 1765, and Paris: Veuve Duchesne, 1765), with the melodies printed at the end of the volume. An orchestral score was also printed (Paris: The author. n.d. [c. 1766]), F-Pn, Musique, H. 765.

EXAMPLE 2.4 François-André Danican Philidor, *Le bûcheron*, scene 3

aux dames,[55] in turn taken from Chaucer's "The Tale of the Wife of Bath." The original sources of this chivalric fairy tale indeed date back to the Middle Ages,[56] and Dryden adapted the story as one of his *Fables.* By the eighteenth century the archetypal characters and plot of the Loathly Lady were familiar to almost all of Europe. Set in the seventh century, this is the story of a knight who encounters a fairy (fig. 2.4) disguised as an innocent shepherdess. His virtue is then tested by having to solve a riddle. The moral is that external beauty is superficial. Recast by Favart into a *drame,* with *ingénue* characters and a contrast-

55. The libretto was published (Paris, 1764) under the pseudonym "seigneur de Ferney" in the *Contes de Guillaume Vadé,* an invention alluding to a mythical father of the late *forain* Jean-Joseph Vadé (1720–1757). Alexandre-Joseph-Pierre, vicomte de Ségur, set it as a one-act *opéra-comique, Ce qui plaît aux dames* (*pièce mêlée d'ariettes,* after 1789; Bibliothèque de l'Arsenal, shelfmark Ms. 94901).

56. Maynadier, *Wife of Bath's Tale,* specifies a number of sources that either pre-date or are contemporary to Chaucer's version. Other modern discussions on the sources of this popular story and the plays it inspired include Kiepert, *Fletcher's "Women Pleased";* Vogt, "'Wife of Bath's Tale'"; Seeber, "Le 'Conte de la Femme de Bath'"; Iacuzzi, *European Vogue of Favart.* Also see Smith, "Egidio Duni."

FIGURE 2.4. Nicolas Boquet, *La fée Urgèle*. F-Pn (Opéra), Rés. D. 216 (07), pl. 51, (Cliché B.N. 86 C 127608). (Courtesy of Bibliothéque Nationale de France.)

ing comic pair of lovers in the servants La Hire and Robinette, the work enjoyed an enormous success, as shown by the large number of later translations and adaptations.[57] Although Duni's score for Favart's *La fée Urgèle* (1765),[58] with its light, Italianate music, contains no trace of the marvelous, Favart's text would appear in numerous translations and become a touchstone for works to come, particularly in German musical theater. For the stages of Vienna, for in-

57. For instance, the Danish *Feen Ursel, eller Hvad der behager Damerne* (1783), an "Operetta" in four acts, transl. by J. H. Wessel (cited in Iacuzzi, *European Vogue of Favart*, 327). German versions include Schiebeler's *Lisuart und Dariolette* (1766, 1772, 1776, and 1782). See chapter 5 for details. There were also Polish and English versions of the opera.

58. The libretto (Paris: Veuve Duchesne, 1765) has melodies printed at the end of the volume. A printed score (Paris: The author, n.d.) survives in F-Pn, H. 765, but it lacks an overture, which survives in a piano reduction (Paris: Bignon, n.d.), F-Pn, Vm[7] 5839.

stance, elements from *La fée Urgèle* served as models for new fairy-tale librettos, notably in the works of Karl Friedrich Hensler and Emanuel Schikaneder.

In the later 1760s French composers of comic opera devoted more interest to supernatural scenes. Jean-Joseph Rodolphe's music for *L'aveugle de Palmyre* by François-George Fouques Deshayes, called Desfontaines (1767),[59] includes one striking depiction of a supernatural event, the restoration of Alibeck's eyesight (act 2, scene 4). Here Rodolphe provides a Maestoso *ariette* with bold violin figures. At the end of the act Alibeck sings a D minor invocation to nature marked "ariette grave," "Astre éternel et des mers brillant."

Although the title of Collé's *L'île sonnante*, with music by Pierre-Alexandre Monsigny (1767–68),[60] recalls François Rabelais's *Gargantua* of 1534 (fifth book, chapters 1–8), which tells a legend of a "sonorous island" populated by singing birds, according to the newspaper *Le Mercure de France* of February 1768 (p. 207) the plot was in fact derived from *Les mille et un jours*. The libretto is a utopian story with a new twist: the rage for music. Musical topics run through the clever plot, where both real and feigned magic occur. The story concerns the restoration of the love between an unfaithful sultan and his jealous wife. At the same time Collé cleverly addressed a frequent complaint about opera: the continual singing that strains verisimilitude. Collé created a society that requires all its inhabitants to sing rather than talk.[61] Allegorical references to music abound, including proper names and references to the new "scientific music." Some of the magical elements in the libretto have musical counterparts that ridicule the old connection of music to magic. The orchestra is unusually large for a fairy-tale *opéra-comique*, with instruments and musical style differentiating the characters.[62] In an imaginative twist Monsigny provided monophonic texture when the characters sing their normal conversations, as opposed to when they are forced to sing songs by royal edict. The composer also offered a fresh musical approach for the series of supernatural events in act 3. In scene 2 the magician Presto conjures an infernal spirit (bass)

59. It was based on the fairy tale *L'aveugle* by Marie de Mesieres de Laboras Riccoboni, in *Le cabinet des fées*, vol. 37, and *Nouveau cabinet des fées*, 18:266ff. The libretto was published (Paris: Veuve Duchesne, 1767); copy in US-Wc, Schatz 11572. A synopsis is found in Desboulmiers, *Histoire anecdotique*, vol .7. The score was published (Paris: La Chevardiere, n.d.); copy in F-Pn, Musique, H. 910. Also set by Francesco Uttini, Drottningholm, Sweden, 1768 (manuscript score in Stockholm, Royal Theater Library).

60. The libretto was published (Paris: G. Hérissant, 1768); copies in F-Pn, Rés. Yf. 3802 (3) (*Recueil d'operas-comiques*, xii), and US-Wc, Schatz 6576, 11727 (Paris: veuve Duchesne, 1771). The score was also printed (Paris: Herissant, n.d.), F-Pn, H. 912.

61. This idea may have been inspired by Bergerac, *L'autre monde*, in which the inhabitants of the moon all sing.

62. Célenie has two "mad" arias of special interest. The first is a two-part aria in act 2, scene 8, "C'est lui même?," where the second part changes briefly to minor mode as she pretends to be obsessed by an imaginary fly. In the next scene she sings another mad aria, "Sans se connoître on peut s'entendre," with five fermatas where she asks, "Vous entendez bien?"

EXAMPLE 2.5 Pierre-Alexandre Monsigny, *L'isle sonnante*, act 3, scene 2

(*continued*)

to a G minor Allegro grave, scored for flutes, strings, and continuo. The piece builds tension through a series of phrases with rising tessitura and increasing surface rhythm. A short hint of an archaic walking bass leads to repeated motives in the flutes, built of slurred thirds accompanied by *alla zoppa* figures in the strings and continuo (see ex. 2.5). The ritornello becomes the accompani-

EXAMPLE 2.5 (*continued*)

ment of the slow declamation in the gradually rising, then falling, vocal line, with a few chromatic intervals in the instruments. Other marvelous devices include widely leaping figures, ascending scales in the flutes and violins, and chromatic intervals in the later part of the vocal line. In scene 3 the infernal spirit ascends from a trap door. As he slowly rises he sings the gamut "ut re mi fa sol," starting in C major. He approaches Presto and his vocal scale descends. Presto now repeats the scale in C minor (see ex. 2.6). Marking the passage "grave," Monsigny indicated pizzicato for the whole-note rhythms in the string accompaniment with continuo. The composer invoked the divine magic of music and its ancient theory here through the medieval hexachord based on the plainchant hymn "Ut queant laxis."

EXAMPLE 2.6 Pierre-Alexandre Monsigny, *L'isle sonnante*, act 3, scene 3

EXAMPLE 2.7 Pierre-Alexandre Monsigny, *L'isle sonnante*, act 3, scene 4

In scene 4 of *L'île sonnante* the spirit receives the magic book and wand from Presto, then makes his incantations "around the stage." The scene begins with an instrumental prelude, scored for flutes, bassoons, strings, and continuo in C minor (see ex. 2.7). This Presto non troppo serves to accompany Presto's mimed actions. Built on a descending bass line, the progression is a series of mostly dominant and diminished chords that traverse related keys with a repeated dotted figure. When the dominant is reached the spirit sings another ponderous whole-note melody of solfège, marked by leaps of a descending seventh. *Alla zoppa* figures in the low strings and bassoons, a sustained low horn pedal, and suspensions in the violins now accompany the voice. The effect is

EXAMPLE 2.7 (*continued*)

(*continued*)

EXAMPLE 2.7 (*continued*)

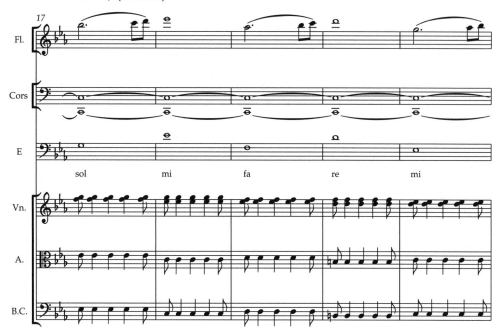

eerie and vaguely archaic. These solfège incantations are remarkably similar to contemporary examples of basic pedagogic exercises in scale harmonization, based on "the rule of the octave." Thus Monsigny may have been spoofing musical pedantry,[63] for the rule of the octave was indeed an "infernal" problem for the theorists such as Rameau. One further moment of musical magic occurs during the transformation in act 3, scene 7, when Henriette and Zerbin are released from their enchantment. Here Monsigny changed the mode from G minor to G major to enhance the magical moment and prepare their short duet as they awake from their spell.

Marmontel's four-act *comédie-ballet* on the story Beauty and the Beast, *Zémire et Azor,* was set by Grétry (16 December 1771)[64]—the composer's first fairy-tale opera. A Persian merchant named Sandor intrudes on the palace of Azor, a prince transformed by a fairy into an ugly beast. This spell can only be broken when Azor inspires the love of a virtuous beauty. In order to save Sandor's life, his beautiful daughter Zémire agrees to live with the beast. Azor

63. For example, see Dubugrarre, *Méthode,* 9–16. Christensen, "*Règle de l'octave* in Thorough-Bass Theory," discusses these in detail. I am indebted to Professor Christensen for pointing out the similarity.

64. Early versions of the fairy tale "La belle et la bête" include that of Gabrielle-Suzanne Barbot de Villeneuve, in *La Jeune amériquaine, et les contes marins* (The Hague, 1740), reprinted in vol. 26 of *Le Cabinet des fées.* Jeanne-Marie Le Prince de Beaumont's *La belle et la bête* was published in *Le Magasin des enfans, ou Dialogues entre une sage gouvernante et plusiers de ses élèves de la première distinction* (London: J. Haberkorn et alii, 1756). For full plot summaries and valuable commentary on this and other operas by Grétry, see Charlton, *Grétry,* 96–108.

displays a noble and virtuous character, and when he grants Zémire her freedom, she decides to remain with him. This act of love breaks the fairy's spell and transforms Azor back to a handsome prince. Azor's supernatural devices include a magic cloud that transports people, a magic mirror that allows one to see distant events, a troupe of dancing genies, and a magic ring.

Despite the studied simplicity and Rousseauian innocence of the score, Grétry includes some brief marvelous elements.[65] Among such features, as David Charlton notes, is the use of E major for the supernatural dances and for Azor's aria (Handel's favorite key for magical sleep). There is also a short "symphonie qui exprime le vol du nuage," which carries Ali and Sandor back to their Persian household. The running sixteenth-note figures of this stage machine music seem borrowed from traditional marvelous scenic transformations. The first section is a broad crescendo with static tonic harmony, followed by a diminuendo with passages of rapid chord changes bridged by a chain of suspensions.

Azor's dramatically static tripartite arias define his character as a conventional hero concealed behind a terrifying appearance. Ali, the comic servant, sings buffo parlando, especially in his act 4 aria. Like similar characters from *commedia per musica*, Ali trembles as he tells of the magic chariot drawn by winged serpents with gaping mouths, burning pupils, and menacing fangs. The well-known scene with the *tableau magique* (act 3, scene 6, see plate 4) features an offstage wind sextet (horns, clarinets, and bassoons) that accompanies the trio in which Sandor, Lisbé and Fatmé express sorrow over Zémire's absence.[66] Marked "en sourdine," the trio recalls similar instrumentation in the otherworldly scenes of supernatural operas. Grétry evokes an elegant (and perhaps nocturnal) serenade style through sweet, consonant sonority, short periodic phrases, and conjunct melody (see ex. 2.8). He also provides music for the magical scenic transformation at the end of the opera (act 4, scene 4). The bustling cadential phrase accompanies the spectacular transformation from a savage wilderness into an enchanted palace, with simultaneous sextuplet arpeggios and repeated-note quadruplets increasing the surface rhythm and dynamics in a brilliant sonic image.

Favart's *comédie-féerie La belle Arsène*, with music by Monsigny (6 November 1773),[67] exists in two versions, the first in three acts (1773) and the second in four (1775). The libretto, Favart's last, proved to be one of his most enduring

65. The printed score (Paris: Houbaut, 1772) served as the basis of the edition in Grétry, *Collection complète*, vol. 13. A second fairy-tale opera by Marmontel and Grétry, *Les statues*, was never completed.

66. The scene was imitated later in several operas, including Schuster's magic-mirror scene in *Rübenzahl* (see chapter 4).

67. The libretto was printed in 1772. The music survives in a printed score (Paris: Houbaut, 1775, without the overture), and printed parts (Paris: Houbaut, n.d.), among other printed sources.

EXAMPLE 2.8 André Ernest Modeste Grétry, *Zémire et Azor*, act 3, scene 6

works, with numerous adaptations and translations.[68] The *conte* was placed at the beginning of the libretto in order to establish the prudish character of Arsène and to give "the moral of the piece": to wish for better is the enemy of the

68. Other versions include: (1) Alexandre-Louis-Bertraud Robineau, called Beaunoir, *L'amant voleur, ou La bégueule*, a three-act prose comedy, Théâtre des Grands-Danseurs 1772 (1773), F-Pn, n.a.f 2858 (identical to *La bégueule*, a "canevas de parade" in F-Pn, shelfmark n.a.f. 2872), plays based on Voltaire's *conte La bégueule* of 1772; (2) Jacques Mague de Saint-Aubin, *La bégueule*, a two-act comedy with vaudevilles for the Ambigu-comique, 27 December 1781; (3) a parody for marionettes by Jacques Mague de Saint-Aubin, *La lingère*, a two-act prose comedy with vaudevilles, Théâtre de Petits Comédiens du Bois de Boulogne, 21 September 1781 (Amsterdam & Paris: Cailleau, 1782), cited in *Les petits spectacles de Paris*, 1786, 196; and (4) a manuscript in F-Pn (n.a.f. 2873), which contains two copies of a "canevas de parade," *La bégueule*, marked "Nicolet l'âné pour la foire St. Laurent." 5) *L'île d'amour*, an anonymous "comédie-féerie en un acte en prose," in F-Pn f.f. 9280, fols. 45–54; this must postdate *La belle Arsène* (1772). There are a number of translations in German, Dutch (as *De scoone Arsène*, 1789 by Bartholomeus Ruloffs, Wc, Schatz 6586, and by Jacob T. Neyts, n.d.), and Italian. Set in Danish as a four-act comedy *Arsène*, 30 January 1777, and with music by Thomas Christian Walter; another version was set by Adam Gottlob Thoroup as *Den skiønne Arsene* (10 December 1781, music of Monsigny adapted by Frigel; see the entry in Sonneck, *Catalogue*). Iacuzzi cites a Swedish four-act *Arsène* performed at Drottningholm (22 July 1779), transl. A. M. Malmstedt, and printed in Stockholm in 1779 (*European Vogue of Favart*, 329).

good. The chivalric plot, set during the reign of Henry II and Catherine de' Medici, concerns the efforts of the valiant knight Alcindor to win the heart of the beautiful Arsène, a spoiled and haughty young beauty. As usual, Monsigny composed *galant*, Italian-style music in his extensive score.[69] He seems to have reduced the marvelous allusions from those in *L'isle sonannte*, although Favart's story has significant supernatural content.[70] The music for the fairy Aline and her retinue suggests courtly elegance, an old allusion to the marvelous. The transformation scene is an accompanied recitative where the magical event is suggested by a crescendo, an acceleration of the surface rhythm, and a retransition back to the tonic for the ensuing *ariette*. The opera also includes an instrumental storm scene that occurs during an accompanied recitative, with rapid sixteenth-note figures and abrupt modulations.

Claude-Henri Fusée de Voisenon based *Fleur d'épine*,[71] a two-act *opéra-comique mêlée d'ariettes* (19 or 22 August 1776), on a 1730 satirical fairy tale by Antoine Hamilton.[72] An evil fairy named Dentue, who enjoys capturing virtuous beauties, is tormenting Fleur d'épine, the long-suffering daughter of Dentue's rival, the good fairy Seraine. Dentillon, Dentue's idiotic fop of a son, fails in his attempts to seduce Fleur, whose heart belongs to Prince Tartare. He comes to rescue her from the spell of a magic carillon. But all of this has been a test of virtue devised by Seraine, who serves as a dea ex machina and releases all the captives of Dentue at the end. The Italianate music, composed by Marie-Emmanuelle Bayon, has two striking musical elements to suggest the supernatural. The grotesque Dentue (baritone!) sings comic parlando, as does her son, the foppish Dentillon. Along with this unusual touch of gender confusion for comic effect, there is one more depiction of supernatural characters. In act 2, scene 8 the good fairy Seraine and her genies dance an elegant gigue, perhaps an allusion to the older tradition of the marvelous. Although the libretto indicates "une mélodie de sonnettes" (act 1, scene 4), no such music for bells appears in the printed score. At the start of act 2 the libretto also indicates a grotesque march for the relatives of Dentue's dwarfs, giants, hunchbacks, and cripples; this also was omitted from the score. These characters sing a chorus,

69. A printed score survives (Paris: Houbaut, 1775, without overture), as well as printed parts (Paris: Houbaut, n.d.), among other printed sources. See Fox, "*La Belle Arsène.*"

70. Not all fairy-tale operas at the Théâtre-Italien during this period had scores with vivid, pictorial music. Jean-Baptiste Moulinghem's revised setting of Favart's *Acajou* (1773) offers no more in the way of the marvelous than did Blaise's original in 1744.

71. The libretto was published (Paris: Duchesne, 1777) with melodies appended at the end, as was a score edition, *Fleur d'Épine: Comédie en deux actes* (Paris: Huguet [c. 1776]), F-Pn, Musique, Rés. F.358, and H. 954, which probably dates from 1776. There is also a collection titled "Airs detachés de Fleur d'épine" in F-Pn, shelfmark Y. 552. For general discussion see Sadie, "*Musiciennes* of the Ancien Régime," and Hayes, "Marie-Emmanuelle Bayon."

72. *Nouveau cabinet des fees*, vol. 10. The name *Fleur d'épine* appears in *Les mille et une nuits* and later in the *Le cabinet des fées* ("Sadak et Kalasrade," a *conte persan*). The name Tarare appears in this story and is also the title character in *Tarare* (Beaumarchais, music by Salieri, PO, 1787).

but as in other ensembles, there are few traces of anything resembling the marvelous or grotesque expression in their music.

The Théâtre de Nicolet, renamed the Théâtre des Grands danseurs du Roi in 1772, offered a repertory that used a wide variety of fantastic materials, including French and oriental fairy tales. Most of these pieces do not have surviving sources, but the titles of these anonymous one-act pantomimes indicate the subject matter, for example *Le palais des fées*[73] and *Les amours de la fée Carabosse, ou Le bouquet enchanté* (13 September 1779). A printed libretto (Paris: Claude Hérissant, 1764) survives for Laurent Dubut's two-act pantomime *Pierrot, roi de Cocagne* (1764). Here Pierrot is tricked into believing that he is the king of the land of Cocagne. Adaptations of Perrault's fairy tales and other marvelous texts figure among the manuscript sources of this theater's repertory. Don Juan comedies also were popular in Nicolet's theater.

Fairy-tale pantomimes, especially those based on Perrault's tales, were a specialty of Nicolas-Médard Audinot's Théâtre de l'Ambigu-comique, beginning with the first setting of *La belle au bois dormant*. Jean-François Mussot (called Arnould) arranged the fairy tale in 1770 as a *pantomime à grand spectacle* (also attributed to François Huguet, called Armand, and Nicolas-Médard Audinot).[74] A synopsis was printed for Mussot's third pantomime based on Perrault's fairy tale "Le chat-botté" (8 April 1772).[75]

False Magic

False-magic stories comprise an important subgroup of *opéra-comique* texts that used marvelous effects in music. This old comic tradition took on new importance in popular works such as Rousseau's *Le devin du village*. Here a false-magical incantation serves as a trigger in the plot, where a trickster manipulates naive individuals by abusing their credulity and willingness to accept the supernatural (the Enlightenment's critique of religion). In many instances the scores for these kinds of operas are indistinguishable from works that have no supernatural references at all. In other examples the musical components partake in parody of the marvelous scenes from French *grand opéra*, the home of invocation, stage machinery, and magic transformation. Thus one encounters a satirical picture of the marvelous at a time when *tragédie lyrique* had ossified.

Anseaume's one-act *Le soldat magicien*, with music by Philidor (1760),[76]

73. Brenner, *Bibliographical List*, gives the date as February 1755.

74. (Publ. Lyon: Olier, 1783). Other versions include an undated *comédie féerique* (F-Pn, Ms. n.a.f. 2873, fol. 137). It was revised on 5 December 1776, then again in Lyon 1783.

75. *Programme du Chat-Botté, pantomime, choisi devant sa majesté par les enfans de l'Ambigu-comique . . .* (Paris, n.d.) The Bibliothèque de l'Arsenal has two copies (shelfmarks R.f. 7.726 and R.f. Ra³ 248⁽²⁾). Audinot performed *Le chat botté* for the king at the l'Ambigu-comique theater in 1774.

76. Printed score (Paris: Leclerc, n.d.). For details on Philidor's opera, see Carroll, "François Danican Philidor."

concerns the Argants, a provincial bourgeois couple whose marriage is undermined by their character flaws. They mistreat a soldier who has been sequestered in their house, and he impersonates a sorcerer in order to teach them a lesson. As is usual, Philidor integrated Italian stylistic elements. In scene 14 he satirized the marvelous effects of *tragédie lyrique*, providing two false-conjuring scenes in which the soldier feigns bass incantations. The soldier-magician has promised to magically conjure up a large meal by the caterers of hell and he sings his first incantation, a "majestoso" G minor accompanied recitative, "O vous qui présidez aux repas des gourmands," with a rising triadic melody. The accompaniment suggests serious French opera, with its rapid scales in octave-and-unison sonority and its dotted leaping figures. The brief instrumental prelude is a sonic image of a magical fanfare. The soldier summons the demons of Proserpine's kitchen with a remarkable *air*, "Démons soumis à mes loix." Written in a mock-serious style, the *air* has a pompous vocal line that partakes of either the bold leaps of a clarion-call gesture or the ponderous repeated notes of resolute determination. Composers of serious French opera from Lully to Rameau employed both devices frequently. The accompaniment, too, is a direct reference to *tragédie lyrique*, with its obsessive violin figure punctuated by the occasional emphatic octave-and-unison gestures. Its humor resides in the use of the grand style for such a trivial ruse. Thus Philidor spoofed serious French opera while demonstrating his ability to write in the revered national style. With a *galant* and unpretentious vocal style and lively gigue rhythms, the soldier's following ariette in B-flat serves as a contrast—the War of the Buffoons reified.

The second incantation in *Le soldat magicien*, where the soldier makes a false spirit appear out of the chimney (Madame Argant's lover, covered with soot), begins with another serious accompanied recitative, "Invisible lutin, qui tapi dans un coin," and concludes with yet another pompous *air*. Opening with dotted figures from the French overture, Philidor accompanied the recitative incantation with strings playing dramatically rising triads in dotted rhythms, while the vocal line is declaimed in the ascending and descending leaps associated with *grand opéra*. The octave-and-unison accompanimental motive, heard through the entire texture, along with a final cadence culminating in a lower appoggiatura, sound as if they came directly out of the Royal Academy. The *air* that follows is a simple, straightforward piece with two unmistakable mimetic features from the repertory of the marvelous. First Philidor gives the soldier a rising triadic vocal line to repeatedly command the household spirit to leave. Ascending triadic figures accompany this melody, followed by emphatic octave-and-unison gestures, when the soldier-magician commands the infernal spirit to return to hell.

A more ambitious and satirical portrayal of the marvelous occurs in Antoine Poinsinet's *Le sorcier* (1764),[77] for which Philidor provided substantial

---

77. Printed score (Paris: Chevardière, n.d.).

preludes and more complex references to *tragédie lyrique*. The story concerns a soldier named Julien, who left his village sweetheart, Agate, two years earlier to go to war. Agate's mother has arranged a forced marriage to the underhanded Blaise, who has stolen the money that Julien entrusted to him. On the day of the wedding Julien returns and learns of these events. The village is expecting a visit from a sorcerer, so Julien decides to impersonate him with an exotic costume he has brought back from the Indies. Each character then appears before the false magician, and Julien exploits their selfish interests to win back his bride and his money.

A false-incantation episode (act 2, scene 7) is one of the high points of *Le sorcier*. Blaise asks the sorcerer if Agate will be faithful to him, and Julien replies with an incantation from *tragédie lyrique*, complete with instrumental prelude, a recitative ("Noirs habitants de la nuit éternelle"), a duet, and a mock chorus. The prelude is a brief sonic image, starting with abrupt terraced dynamics and concluding with *alla zoppa* syncopation. The subsequent accompanied recitative introduces a serious-style duet in E-flat in which the terrified Blaise reacts in a cowardly and comic manner. The ensuing duet has several supernatural allusions: Julien first falls into a trance as an Andante with sotto voce horns, oboes, and muted strings supports his exclamation "Quel transport me saisit soudain." The triplets in the strings cause Blaise to imagine, in a trembling voice with appropriate triplet accompanimental figures from *tragédie lyrique*, the earth trembling with a *bruit souterrain*. Then Julien provides the responding "chœur des démons," as he announces, in four different voice ranges (*fausset, haute-contre, basse-contre,* and *voix de basse,* as opposed to his own *voix naturelle*), the arrival of the devil. String tremolos (marked "senza sordini") in octave-and-unison sonority and dotted figures accompany the mock chorus (see ex. 2.9). A short comic ritornello in the Italian style marked "presto" introduces the accompanied recitative that serves as the devil's declaration to Blaise. This "devil" tells Blaise that he must return Julien's money if he has any hope of a successful marriage. He sings in a mock-serious bass voice, accompanied by sustained low strings. Here the score specifically instructs the singer to provide ornaments in the very style of the Royal Academy ("voix de basse avec toutes les charges qu'on fait à l'opéra comme port de voix, longue cadence, etc."). His decree ends with the declaration "Tu dois m'entendre" in unisons and octaves. In the subsequent duet Blaise is frightened into submission. This clever scene mocks the gullible audiences of serious opera as much as the naive Blaise.

Marmontel again collaborated with Grétry on the two-act *La fausse magie* (1774), an operatic comedy with one false-magic episode containing musical references to the marvelous.[78] The "Marche des bohémiens, accompagnée de cymbales, triangles et autres instruments singuliers" in act 2 is a solemn

---

78. There is also a substantial dream scene in E-flat. For details see Charlton, *Grétry,* 135–36.

EXAMPLE 2.9 François-André Danican Philidor, *Le sorcier,* act 2, scene 7

(*continued*)

EXAMPLE 2.9 *(continued)*

processional marked "andante maestoso." It leads to a four-part chorus of gyp-
sies that parodies an incantation with a veiled magic mirror. The scene starts
with a series of ominous rapid scales in the violins, the same device used by
composers for supernatural emphasis. The basses begin their conjuring with
the text "O Grand Albert descends des sept planètes," accompanied by an ascending triad doubled by unisons and octaves; the upper three voices answer in
unison and octaves, requesting they be given eyeglasses: "Mathieu Lansberg,
prête-nous tes lunettes."

Opéra-comique, Ballet, and Melodrama by Gluck and His Contemporaries

Well before the so-called reform period associated with Gluck, composers outside France such as Tomasso Traetta and Niccolò Jommelli were shaping a
more vivid musical language by integrating French elements into their Italian
operas, and contemporaneous ballets exploited the marvelous as a topic. But

it would be in the music of Gluck that the divergent styles of the Italian and French stage would find their most successful synthesis, if we judge success by the international dissemination of his music. The Bohemian-Austrian composer's career first led him to Prague, Vienna, Milan, and then London, composing chiefly Italian operas. He eventually settled in Vienna to compose for the French theater company. By 1759 he was collaborating with Gasparo Angiolini and Ranieri de' Calazibigi on pantomime ballets that required descriptive and pictorial music to accompany gestures both narrative and expressive in affect (the *ballet en action*). The widely traveled Jean-Georges Noverre also contributed to this genre, his works being produced in London, Stuttgart, Milan, Venice, Vienna, and Paris.[79]

Like his French counterparts, Gluck limited his use of descriptive music and marvelous effects in comic opera, but a few instances are significant. His second Viennese *opéra-comique* was an adaptation by Louis Anseaume of a well-worn "utopian" Parisian fair play by Lesage and d'Orneval (1718), *L'île de Merlin, ou Le monde renversé* (Schönbrunn, 1758; revived 1761). Although there is no evidence of marvelous material in the music to match that in the rather fantastic text, the overture has descriptive storm music that was later recycled in *Iphigénie en Tauride*.[80] The overture functions to prepare the first scene, which follows a tempest.

As in the earlier French settings of this text, Gluck's music for Sedaine and Baurans's adaptation of Coffey's *The Devil to Pay* as *Le diable à quatre* (Laxenburg, 1759) contains no incantation for the magician (here called *le Docteur*).[81] Bruce Alan Brown has noted that although the Vienna performance did not have the dance of the demons, there is an instrumental *sinfonia* between acts 2 and 3 to evoke the magical transport of Margot to the bedroom of the Marquise. In a later performance a canonic instrumental *entr'acte*, with string tremolos and diminished seventh chords, was added during the transmutation of the Marquise into Margot.[82]

Gluck added more marvelous devices in *L'ivrogne corrigé* (BT, 1760),[83] a false-magic story by Anseaume and Jean-Baptiste Lourdet de Santerre based on a comic opera by Lesage and d'Orneval, *Les trois commères* (1723), which was in turn taken from a fable by La Fontaine. In order to "correct" the

79. Various European cities performed Noverre's ballets, e.g., the choreographer's own mounting of his *Renaud et Armide* in Milan on 26 December 1775.

80. Edited by Günter Hausswald in Gluck, *Sämtliche Werke* 4, pt. 1. Also see B. A. Brown, *Gluck and the French Theater*, 219–24.

81. Edited by B. A. Brown in Gluck, *Sämtliche Werk* 4, pt. 3. The first known use of a matching musical depiction for this scene is in the version by Weisse and Hiller, *Die verwandelten Weiber, oder Der Teufel ist los* (Leipzig, 28 May 1766, see below).

82. B. A. Brown, *Gluck and the French Theater*, 224–32, suggests that these dramatic pieces were created to "circumvent the censor" and depict in music what could not be represented in the theater, bringing a vogue for demons and Furies on the Viennese stage.

83. Edited by Franz Rühlmann in Gluck, *Sämtliche Werke* 4, pt. 5 .

drunkenness of their friend, the characters impersonate Furies and demons in a mock hell scene.[84] The orchestra begins the A minor duet "Ah! si j'empoigne" (used later by Gluck for the appearance of the supernatural character Hatred in *Armide*) with an ascending triad in octave-and-unison sonority. Then the false Fury (an alto) sings her incantation in a monotone on the tonic while the horns emphasize unison tonic notes. The soprano Fury then joins in with rapid triplet exclamations on B, a dissonant interval of a second. The duet ends as it began, with octave-and-unison figures in the orchestra. When the false Pluto suddenly appears, Gluck abruptly modulates by a tritone (the *diabolus in musica*) to the key of E-flat, which Gluck will use for underworld scenes in *Orfeo ed Euridice* and other operas. This segment is an Andante *ritournelle* for strings with octave-and-unison sonority. After Pluto (a high baritone) sings his three lines ("Qui sont ces deux misérables?"), the soprano Fury replies in a hypnotic incantation with repeated notes.

The Viennese choreographer and impresario Franz Hilverding and the composer Joseph Starzer created independent *pantomime-ballets* based on French models, with unified plots, for the French theater in Vienna. These were often rich in marvelous effects. Their *La guirlande enchantée* (BT, 1757) contains a "Largo recita" in which the violins and continuo declaim the written inscription on the enchanted wreath in octaves, probably mimed by the Beneficent Genie: "La force de ces nœuds, le pouvoir de ces fleurs accomplissent les vœux, satisfont tous les cœurs."[85] Two oboe parts and the bassoon articulate the rhythm in this instrumental declamation with soft chords.

Gluck further developed this genre in collaboration with Hilverding's successor, Angiolini. Their first work, *Le naufrage* (1759), included a *sinfonia* strongly reminiscent of Rameau's "frémissement des flots" in *Hippolyte et Aricie* (each of the four string parts has a different rhythm), where diminished seventh chords and running figuration depict a violent storm at sea.[86] Gluck and Angiolini's three most ambitious *pantomime-ballets* were collaborations with Calzabigi: *Don Juan*, *Citera assediata*, and *Sémiramis*. The most successful of these was the first, *Don Juan, ou Le festin de pierre* (1761),[87] a work performed all over Europe and imitated in some thirty-five different ballet settings from 1762 to 1787 alone. The score includes extraordinarily violent music for the period, recalling the "terrifying" style of Italian composers such as Traetta and Jommelli (see chapter 3 for a discussion of this style in Italian opera). The Allegro furioso and the Allegro forte risoluto (nos. 4–5, both in D major) for the

---

84. See B. A. Brown, *Gluck and the French Theater*, 253–62.

85. See ibid., 166–67.

86. See ibid., 296–304.

87. Robert Engländer edited the music and program in Gluck, *Sämtliche Werke* 2, pt. 1, along with the *Sémiramis*. The full texts appear in Calzabigi, *Scritti teatrale*. See also Russell, "Libertine Reformed."

death scene of the Commendatore and the final two infernal dances use the new musical expression of terror. The first of the infernal dances is in D minor, a Larghetto with octave motives, sudden diminished chords, and a furious transition to the second dance, the "infernal" D minor, Allegro non troppo. This is the music Gluck later recycled as the dance of the Furies in *Orphée et Euridice* (Paris, 1774). The composer scored both dances for what was then an unusual combination of brass instruments (horns and alto trombone in the former, trumpet and alto trombone in the latter, along with oboes, bassoon, and strings), now associated with infernal imagery. (Whether the trombone was actually used in the 1761 production is not clear; there is no source that specifies the orchestration for 1761.) Calzabigi and Angiolini wrote in their program that Gluck had perfectly captured *le terrible* of the action in depicting the graveyard scene where the spirits drag Don Juan to hell. The term *terribile* is also found in earlier librettos such as *Ippolito e Aricia* of 1759 (see chapter 3). With recitative-like, halting motion, abrupt changes in affect, string tremolos, long crescendos, and brass suggesting the violent, loud bellowing of the inferno, this scene must have been startling to audiences in 1761. Angiolini and Calzabigi wrote in their program for the ballet *Don Juan* that its "imaginative subject is sublime." Most eighteenth-century commentators, however, considered the story depraved and its title character purely evil. Yet Count Karl Zinzendorf's diary indicates the enthusiastic reception of the ballet, especially the performance on 3 November, the traditional night for *Don Juan* performances, after All Souls' Day, when the Requiem Mass was sung.

One finds similarly vivid and contrasting music in *Sémiramis* (1765), a work based on Voltaire's version of the myth, whose famous ghost scenes provided the supernatural material in the story. The opening *sinfonia* begins with the emphatic wind chords and abrupt, obsessive, and forceful motives that suggest Semiramis's persistent guilty conscience. (Gluck would recycle this music in the pantomimic Furies scene in *Iphigénie en Tauride*, act 2, scene 4.) The *sinfonia* leads to a dream scene where the ghost of Ninus appears to Queen Semiramis. The contrapuntal D minor Andante, scored for bassoon and strings in the alla breve cantus firmus style, seems to be an allusion to sacred music. (Did Mozart recall this scene as he composed his contrapuntal D minor opening of the Requiem?) A D minor Allegro follows, with pulsating eighth notes, a series of dissonant seconds, and dramatic fermatas to depict the queen's emotions and cries. The ghost appears once more in act 3, interrupting a ceremony at the tomb. This scene begins with a hymnlike dance in G major, marked "affettuoso," ceremonial music in the solemn march style (no. 9). A pulsating G minor episode is next, with recitative-like writing for the interruption of the ceremony by the appearance of the ghost, who draws Semiramis into the tomb. Alternating Adagios and Allegros make up the violent final group of dances (nos. 12–15), representing the death of Semiramis with fermatas, recitative-like sections, and sweeping string scales.

Later French Comic Opera

Don Juan comedies and devil stories also continued to be produced in Parisian comic theaters, such as the pantomime *Le grand festin de Pierre, ou L'athée foudroyé* at the Théâtre des Associés (1787) and the comedy *Le festin de pierre de la foire* at the Théâtre des Grands-Danseurs (date unknown).

At least two of Perrault's fairy tales, "Cinderella" (1779/1785) and "Bluebeard" (1780), served as the subjects of pantomimes at the Théâtre des Elèves de l'Opéra. A *Cendrillon* was also performed at the Théâtre de Séraphin. The taste for gothic literature and medieval romance is evident in Parisian "comic marvelous" works of the 1780s. Alphonse-Maire-Denis Devismes de Saint-Alphonse's *Rosanie*, with music by Henri-Joseph Rigel for the Ambigu-Comique (1780), was based on a medieval fable, "The Marvelous Adventures of Richard and his Minstrel," arranged by L'Héritier as a *conte de fées* entitled "Ricdin, Ricdon" (*La tour ténébreuse et les jours lumineux, contes anglais*, 1705).[88] Rigel's music for this *comédie italienne mêlée d'ariettes* survives only in melodies for the airs and duets, and these are generally quite simple.[89] A large-scale work of a similar type is the racist *pantomime à spectacle, mêlée de dialogue, féerie en deux actes* entitled *Le prince noir et blanc* by Audinot and Mussot (1780).[90] In the following year Rigel set another medieval story, Jean-Pierre Claris de Florian's *Blanche et Vermeille* (1781). The surviving music appears to contain nothing for the supernatural episodes, which were perhaps omitted in the print.[91]

A throwback to the pastoral fairy stories of the 1740s is exemplified by Barthélemy Imbert's comedy with music by Marc-Antoine Desaugiers, *Les deux sylphes* (Hôtel de Bourgogne, 18 September 1781).[92] The music mostly

88. In some instances fairy tales provided only the names of the characters. The good fairy in *Arlequin recruteur* (1768), for instance, is "La fée Belle étoile," a name borrowed from d'Aulnoy, *Contes nouveaux*, while the ugly fairy Carabosse in *Arlequin et les fées* (1770) comes from her "La Princesse printanière," in *Les contes des fées*, vol. 2.

89. Rigel, *Airs détachés*, F-Pn, Musique, Y. 515. Rigel claimed that the "Air de l'enchanteur et des lutins" titled "Si jeune et tendre femmelle avoit mis dans sa cervelle que ricdon ricdon," an F major allegretto in 3/8, was composed by Richard Cœur-de-lion himself, along with some of the other melodies that he arranged. La Borde, *Essai*, 2, suppl., 6, lists Rigel's sources; see Charlton, *Grétry*, 230–31. The comedy met with only limited success and was revised as *Azélie* at the Théâtre de Monsieur, 14 July1790. Excerpts were printed (Marseilles, n.d.); these survive in Marseilles, Conservatoire de Musique et de Déclamation.

90. (Amsterdam/Paris: Cailleau 1782), F-Pn ThB 720.

91. Rigel, *Blanche et Vermeille*, F-Pn, L. 1342.

92. The *Almanach*, 1782, 155 (F-Pn, Fb. 19330), mentions the role of the fairy in this *nouvelle pastorale*. A printed orchestral score is preserved in F-Pn (Musique), shelfmark D. 2785 (1), *Les deux sylphes comédie sémi-lyrique, en un acte en vers, par M. A. Desaugiers* (Paris: The author, n.d.). Librettos are in F-Pn, ThB. 2864; FB 19328.33 (Paris: Bastien, 1781), and also US-Wc, ML 50.2. D5D2.

exploits contemporary Italian style, but with complex orchestral accompaniments and some noteworthy ensembles. The duet for the two sylphs and the trios for Zilla and the two sylphs recall the complex, modulating ensembles of the sylphs in Rameau's *Zaïs*, with similar wind obbligatos (oboes, bassoons, and horns or flutes). Florian's three-act *Le baiser, ou La bonne fée* is another fairy story, with music by Stanislas Champein (Hôtel de Bourgogne, 26 November 1782).[93] The act 1 finale includes a *Hymne à l'Amour* for vocal quintet, choruses, a *Marche religieuse*, and a magical appearance of the evil magician Phanor (bass) that leads to a trio (act 1, scene 5). In act 2 Phanor commands soldiers through a magic spell, set for solo voice and male chorus.

Gothic literature also influenced comic repertory, for example Antoine-Jean Bourlin's (called Dumaniant) *Urbélise et Lanval*, a *comédie-féerie ornée de musique et de chant* (Théâtre des Variétés-Amusantes, 1787) and Hyacinthe-Madeleine Dorvo's chivalric *féerie, Le chevalier errant, ou Le palais enchanté* (Théâtre Patriotique, 1788).[94] That same year the Théâtre de l'Odéon produced a similar *comédie-héroïque-féerie* by Pierre-Nicolas-André de Murville, *Lanval et Viviane, ou Les fées et les chevaliers*, an amalgam of fairy-tale elements, medieval romance, fairy story, and Arthurian legend. Much of Stanislas Champein's music for *Lanval et Viviane* is ceremonial, stressing the medieval spectacle with a military overture and instrumental interludes between text divisions.[95] These pieces include "Marche pour les candidates," an "Air pour les reception des candidates," a "Marche d'Artus," a "Marche de Roland," and the "Marche des Sarrazins." Champein also provided extensive music for the pantomimic battle scenes, for example the "Combat with the Dwarfs," with amusing indications of soft dynamics, "The Giants Advance," and the "Combat with the Giants."

Grétry's substantial setting of Michel-Jean Sedaine's three-act *Raoul, Barbe-bleue* (Théâtre-Italien, 2 March 1789), a loose adaptation of Perrault's fairy tale "Bluebeard,"[96] stresses the gothic element in a score that exploits the horrific, violent aspects of the text. Like several recent overtures to supernatural operas, Grétry's begins with a D minor largo introduction suggesting the dark and solemn aspect of the text; a D major Allegro maestoso follows in the bustling comic style (see ex. 2.10). As in Mozart's *Don Giovanni*, the violent finale returns to D minor, where Raoul is murdered in a pantomime-melodrama

93. The *Almanach*, 1782, 233–34, calls it a "féerie en trois actes, mêlée d'ariettes." The music survives in a reduced score, F-Pn, Mus. L. 3675. Champein later reworked this into an opera in three acts (1823–24), and the full orchestral autograph survives in F-Pn, Musique Ms. 8158, and Ms. 6464 (3).

94. Ms. F-Pn, Ms. f.f. 9273 (dated 1787), fols. 278–307.

95. The libretto was published (Paris: Prault 1788) and the music survives in a manuscript in F-Pn, Musique Ms. 8193 (most of the vocal airs were published in arrangements).

96. The score was printed (Paris: The author, n.d. [1790]).

EXAMPLE 2.10 André Ernest Modeste Grétry, *Raoul, Barbe-bleue*, overture

leading to a celebration in the contrasting major mode. The pantomime utilizes the "terrifying" musical style with appropriate harmonic and dynamic changes to describe the actions indicated in the score. An abrupt fortissimo signals Raoul's opening of his gruesome cabinet of corpses, and Raoul's wife is rescued with sudden Neapolitan chords. For the controversial scene in which the fathers of Raoul's former wives discover their daughters' bodies and murder Raoul, Grétry repeats the pantomime music rather than depicting the stabbing and death, as Mozart had done so effectively in the *introduzione* of *Don Giovanni*.

Even following the storming of the Bastille, the smaller Parisian theaters continued to produce operas on magical themes. An examples is Jean-François Sedaine de Sarcy's three-act *opéra parodié sur la musique italienne* (also described as an *opera bouffon*), *L'isle enchantée*, with a substantial musical score by Antonio Barolomeo Bruni (Théâtre de Monsieur, 3 August 1789). This opera is a reworking of Giovanni Bertati's well-known comic libretto *L'isola d'Alcina* (1772) and the anonymous farsa *La maga Circe* (Rome, 1778), with its shipwreck on an enchanted isle and parodies of national stereotypes (see chapter 4). No libretto survives for the French work, only a score and a synopsis.[97] The pictorial "Tempest, serving as the overture" in D minor begins with music in the terrifying style, with *alla zoppa* syncopations, abrupt dynamic shifts, sixteenth-note string figures, and bursts of sustained horns. This segment yields to a long decrescendo on the dominant, representing the calming of the storm created by the sorceress. But Alcine has little in her music to distinguish her from the mortal characters. As Grétry's did in his mute scene in *Zémire et Azor*, Bruni composed an "enchanted" wind serenade for pairs of clarinets, horns, and bassoons in the wings during the mimed scene in act 3 where a prison changes into a palace.

Exploiting supernatural scenes to a far greater degree is Honoré-François-Marie Langlé's score for *Corisandre, ou Les fous par enchantement*, a three-act *comédie-opéra* on a text by Antoine-François Lebailly (Paris Opéra, salle de la Porte Saint-Martin, 8 March 1791).[98] Elegant music dominates the magic episodes in the divertissements, colorful preludes establish the physical surroundings and enhance the transformations, and supernatural ensembles feature

97. *Almanach* (1790), 234. Here the date of the premiere is 26 January 1789. The music survives in a print: see Bruni, *L'isola incantata*, F-Pn, shelfmark Mus. D. 1610.

98. The music is preserved in an engraved score (Paris: le Duc, n.d.), F-Pn, musique, Vm² 572, D. 6635, called an *opéra-ballet*. A manuscript score also exists in F-Po, shelfmark A 339a-c, and parts: Mat. 18 [74 (1–104). An autograph of the ballet from act 3 is preserved in F-Pn, Mus. Ms. 2115, as does at least one dance in vol. 24 of the manuscript collection *Recueil de ballets* in F-Po, no. 18, "air de danse pour Corisandre de M. Langlé." (There are numerous disparities between the manuscript materials and the print.) The second theme of the overture is a traditional popular tune that dates back at least to the sixteenth century. The simple periodic phrases would also be used by Mozart for Papageno's "Ein Mädchen oder Weibchen" in *Die Zauberflöte* and would be recycled for the melody of the *Rondeau des visitandines* in the *opéra comique* of that name (7 July 1792).

grotesque elements, such as the male chorus in act 2 with two solo *coriphées* (tenors). A notable development in *Corisandre* is the extended scene complex that starts act 3, which constitutes one of the largest invocation scenes in the history of opera to this point. The act begins in Merlin's subterranean cave with an Andante larghetto entitled "La nuit," an instrumental prelude in E-flat for four-part string ensemble. The musical style suggests archaic polyphony with its suspensions and a degree of harmonic complexity unusual in opera (see ex. 2.11). This pianissimo duple-meter segment introduces the prelude-like dramatic Allegro moderato in B-flat minor, with *alla zoppa* syncopation and sweeping string gestures that leads to a recitative with string accompaniment for the magician Agramant. Agramant then commands his forces in an invocation, "Déployons nos charmes terribles des ombres, troublons le séjour" (We deploy our terrible enchantments of the shades, we disturb their rest), scored for three trombones and strings that support a vocal line with hypnotic repeated notes. Next the key changes to C minor for the *évocation*, marked "Grave," for the three-part male chorus, "Des bords du ténébreux rivage" (On

EXAMPLE 2.12 Honoré-François-Marie Langlé, *Corisandre*, act 3, scene 2

the banks of the dark coast), accompanied by trumpets, horns, three trombones, bassoons, and strings. Here the print of the score diverges from the manuscript, which leads directly to the oracle scene with the ghost of Merlin. The print extends the invocation scene with an obbligato recitative, an incantation for Agramant, "Sage Merlin, ombre sacrée, daigne éclaircir le sort de mon amour" (Wise Merlin, sacred shade, deign to make clear the fate of my love), supported by sustained string accompaniment. An arioso segment in triple meter, marked "Poco lento," leads to the *bruit souterrain* in C minor with repeated horn and trombone interjections; rapid ascending scale figures for piccolo; short, repeated violin and clarinet figures; bass and string tremolos; and broken thirds in eighth notes in the bassoons. Agramant interjects and asks in recitative, "Qu'entens? Le sage Merlin" (What do I hear? The wise Merlin) as the bass descends chromatically with augmented and diminished harmony.

Both print and manuscript versions continue with a scene for the ghost of Merlin, scored for trombones and basses in C major and marked "Un peu grave." The music here brings to mind early court opera, beginning with the repeated C major chords and followed by a slow, syllabic melody that features mostly repeated notes, accompanied by soft trombone chords and bass in a simple harmonic setting (see ex. 2.12). The act continues with a divertissement, beginning with an Allegro chorus in D minor, "O jour heureux," followed by the "Air des magiciens" in A major, a gigue scored for trombones, clarinets, bassoons, and strings. When the scene changes to Agramant's garden the music turns cheerful, with hunting, pastoral, and martial music in D and F major through the conclusion of the opera.

Langlé's score is illustrative of the increased substance of French music in the comic repertory, now approaching that of *grand opéra*. Along with the musical techniques developed by Gluck, Piccinni, Salieri, and their colleagues, the comic operas reveled in grotesque expression, satire, and parody—elements that had usually been missing from the official stage of the ancien régime. Aspects of this comic marvelous certainly derive from earlier *opéra comique*, such as the music of Mouret. But like the more serious operas of the Academy, influences also came from Italian opera with supernatural episodes—the topic of the following two chapters.

✦

CHAPTER THREE

Italian Serious Genres

Dramma per musica, 1700–1749

The numerous Italian critiques of opera, beginning around 1675, run the gamut from a broad condemnation of the entire genre to suggestions for improvements that would reform perceived excesses.[1] Although many arcadian reformers advocated abolishing the marvelous and supernatural elements entirely from opera, not all agreed. In his fifth dialogue on tragedy Pier Jacopo Martello has the pro-opera character (the "impostor") discussing the need to adapt the libretto to the machinery and the suitability of fairy tales (*favole*), rather than to an historical plot; he recommends the marvelous aspect over verisimilitude.[2] Martello's fifth dialogue may have inspired Benedetto Marcello's anonymously published satire *Il teatro alla moda* (1720).[3] There he discusses the "marvelous" as an element the librettist could introduce with oracles, evil auguries, and similar devices.[4]

In practice, Italian librettists rarely based *drammi per musica* on classical mythology or epic romance, and they rarely staged supernatural or magical events.[5] For spectacle, *dramma per musica* turned to natural phenomena such as storms, battles and military displays, processions, and sacrifice scenes. But festive genres such as the intermezzo, *pastorale*, ballet, *azione teatrale*, and *festa teatrale* still included supernatural elements. Pantomime ballets (1740–65)

---

1. See Freeman, *Opera without Drama*. The term "Arcadian" comes from the Roman "Arcadian Society," founded in 1690.

2. *Della tragedia antica e moderna* (Rome, 1715), in Martello, *Scritti critici*, 187–316.

3. Translated in Pauly, "Benedetto Marcello's Satire."

4. Luigi Riccoboni later criticized modern Italian opera for putting aside stage machinery and relying on history instead of fables, divinities, and pastoral. See Riccoboni, *Réflexions historiques*.

5. See S. Hansell, "Mythological Subjects."

frequently included mythological material and fantasy rarely encountered in *drammi per musica*.[6] The more elaborate ballets had magical scene transformations and aerial entrances. The supernatural elements in the ballets performed between the acts of operas eventually provided material for new operas. Magic occasionally turned up in *drammi per musica*, like Pallavicini's *Le fate* (Dresden, 1736; see below).

Even in *drammi per musica* without supernatural content composers supplied music to suggest imagined ghosts, monsters and magical powers. Thus marvelous musical imagery was exploited. Oracles pronounced terrible judgments, and angry princes and queens invoked unearthly terror in their singing. Ghosts were imagined in expressions of grief and guilt. The ghost or *ombra* scene seems to have become particularly popular in *dramma per musica* starting around 1730.[7] In these scenes a bereaved character imagines seeing the ghost of a loved one who is not really dead and, expressing grief or guilt, comments on the horrific illusion in a vivid, expressive aria.[8] An actual ghost occasionally appears only after about 1750, mostly in operas based on the stories of Iphigenia and Alcestis.

The political and nationalistic associations of fairy tales in France had little resonance in Italy, which had its own tradition of marvelous literature from mythology, pastorals, and epic romance, genres that included superhuman characters. Mythology provided the plots for many festive operas with characters such as Hercules, Jupiter, Mercury, Ulysses, Circe, Medea, Orpheus,[9] and Pygmalion's statue. Appendix B provides a selected list of Circe, Medea, and Orpheus operas from the years 1700 to 1791; many contain magical transformations and underworld scenes. The most common sources for Italian librettos with supernatural elements continued to be the poems of Ariosto and

---

6. K. Hansell, "Theatrical Ballet," 175–306. (Page numbers here and in other citations refer to the 2002 edition.)

7. Ratner, *Classic Music*, 24, asserts that in eighteenth-century opera, fantasia style was used for depicting the supernatural. He calls this style "ombra" and differentiates it from the "Storm and Stress style" (21), which he attributes to Klinger's literary use of the term in 1776. Allanbrook, *Rhythmic Gesture*, 361, further defines *ombra* as a style derived from hell scenes in sixteenth-century *intermedi* scored with trombones and discusses its use in the act 2 finale of Mozart's *Don Giovanni*. However, ghost scenes rarely used trombones, and underworld scenes in the sixteenth century used the brass in a different manner than in the second finale of *Don Giovanni*. Although there was no specific category of *ombra* designated by eighteenth-century writers, the historical categories of the marvelous and terror are missing from both Ratner's and Allanbrook's discussions. For a detailed study of ghost scenes, see McClelland, "*Ombra* Music."

8. For example, *Lucio Silla*, *Andromeda*, and *Vologeso*. See K. Hansell, "Opera and Ballet," 289–303, 335ff, 1017–51. After c. 1770 composers employed a new style for musical terror in ghost and other supernatural scenes.

9. See Harris, "*L'Orfeo:* Metamorphosis," and preface to Aureli and Sartorio, *L'Orfeo;* Sternfeld, "Orpheus," and "Orpheus, Ovid, and Opera."

Tasso.[10] At least fifty-eight eighteenth-century theatrical settings of Ariosto's *Orlando furioso* have been documented,[11] although they rework the plot extensively.[12] Magic, the supernatural, and spectacle were present in many of the period's productions based on Ariosto and Tasso's epic poems; most are listed in Appendix C.

Serious operas based on Ariosto include Carlo Sigismondo Capece's *L'Orlando, overo La gelosa pazzia*, with music by Domenico Scarlatti (Rome 1711, lost), which served as the basis of Handel's *Orlando* (London, 1733). Giovanni Alberto Ristori set Grazio Braccioli's *Orlando furioso* (Venice, 1713), as did Antonio Vivaldi (Venice, 1714). Ristori also composed the music for a *dramma per musica* by Stefano Benedetto Pallavicini that was inspired by epic romance, *Le fate* (Dresden, 1736; see below). Even Metastasio wrote two librettos based on Ariosto's poem, *Angelica* (1720) and *Ruggiero, ovvero L'eroica gratitudine* (1771). Although neither contains magic episodes, *Angelica* includes references in dialogue to the magic ring and bangle.

The Descriptive Musical Language of Italian Opera

Many Italian composers in the first two decades of the eighteenth century (such as Antonio Lotti and Carlo Pallavicino) belonged to an older generation whose craft was rooted in seventeenth-century practice, with a less mimetic and more detached approach to dramatic music. Others developed pictorial techniques and distinguished natural from supernatural events. In his Neapolitan operas Alessandro Scarlatti suggested the otherworld with evocative obbligato recitative, similar to the string accompaniments for the voice of God in his oratorio *Cain, overo Il primo omicidio*, or the voice of Christ in his *St. John Passion*. J. S. Bach used this same kind of recitative for the voice of Christ in his *St. Matthew Passion*. Italian opera and *feste* in the 1750s and 1760s, especially in Parma, Mannheim, Vienna, and Dresden, began to enhance the dramatic content with this kind of recitative.

The reformers' disdain for older Italian opera was based in part on the fact that their musical component often had no compelling relationship to the text. Perhaps in response to this concern, younger composers developed devices for musical representation of text, providing a repertory of topics for later devel-

10. Carter, "Tasso, Torquato," lists 8 seventeenth-century settings of the Armida and Rinaldo episode, and 43 eighteenth-century Italian settings. Also see Balsano and Walker, eds., *Tasso*, and Carter, review of Balsano and Walker, *Tasso*.

11. See Carter, "Ariosto, Ludovico."

12. Döring, *Ariostos "Orlando Furioso,"* lists numerous plays on 331–33. For a more detailed study of the operatic settings of Ariosto, see Collins and Kirk, *Opera & Vivaldi*, with articles by C. Peter Brand, Michael Collins, Sven Hansell, Ellen T. Harris, John W. Hill, Ellen Rosand, and Gary Schmidgall.

opment. Composers conveyed musical imagery and affect in the ritornellos, the accompaniments, and the expressive style of the vocal parts of ensembles and "simile arias" (a modern term).[13] For example, in his G minor *ombra* aria for tenor voice, "Io veggo qui d'intorno di quell'estinta salma l'immagine funesta" (I see around me the funereal image of that deceased body, *Ipermestra*, Rome, 1728), Francesco Feo employed characteristic descending octave leaps in the vocal line, along with octave-and-unison sonorities in the string accompaniment.[14] Vivaldi, Ristori, and Handel were among the most skillful masters of these practices, and their music warrants close examination. The significant contributions of these composers to the musical vocabulary of the eighteenth-century expression of the supernatural have not been generally acknowledged, much less studied. Yet by the second decade of the century these masters were creating vivid and engaging expression for supernatural (and natural) topics in vocal music, even more so than their French contemporaries, who continued to compose supernatural scenes.

Vivaldi

One of the earliest Italian composers to develop and systematically exploit a range of musical devices for effective presentation of supernatural images was Antonio Vivaldi, whose use of pictorial imagery is well-known from his programmatic concertos *The Four Seasons* (op. 8, nos. 1–4). But this repertory of images was developed in his vocal music. In Caio Silio's aria "Gelosia, tu già rendi l'alma mia" (act 1, scene 11) from Vivaldi's *Ottone in Villa* (Vicenza, 1713), the words "Dell'inferno assai peggior" have an unusually long and intense coloratura run culminating in a passage in octave-and-unison sonority. The ritornello employs tremolo figures in the strings. All of these devices will suggest infernal imagery throughout the century. Caio's aria "L'ombre, l'aure, e ancora il rio" (act 2, scene 3) presents a series of musical images in a masterful display of compositional skill: repeated-note motives, wavering figures in thirds in the strings and recorders, and echo effects. Vivaldi accompanied the words "Ahi quale orror" with tremolo figures in the bass. His later setting of Apostolo Zeno's *Griselda* (Venice, 1735) provides other fine examples.[15] In the middle section of Costanza's aria "Ombre vane, ingiusti orrori" (act 3, scene 5), Vivaldi suggests the character's horror at the cruelty of fate ("astri tiranni")

---

13. Strohm, *Italienische Opernarien*, 2:77, provides the most complete discussion of this repertory. Strohm embraces the modern category "ombre-aria" and gives three examples, one of which is the tenor aria from *Ipermestra*. Many discussions of this repertory have concentrated on musical form and theoretical analysis, with the result that the portrayal of text is of secondary importance, e.g., Westrup et al., "Aria."

14. See Strohm, "Italienische Opernarien," 77.

15. Vivaldi, *Griselda*.

with tremolos in the strings and octave-and-unison sonority in the voice and the accompaniment. Costanza's aria "Agitata da due venti" (act 2, scene 2) depicts a raging musical storm both on the sea and in the heart of the character though ascending and descending octaves and vocal coloratura, along with tremolo figures and sharp dynamic contrasts in the accompanying string ensemble.

Vivaldi's cantatas contain similar devices. A striking example is found in *Cessate, omai cessate* (RV 684), which concludes with a furious aria, "Nel'orrido albergo ricetto di pene." The accompaniment deploys short explosive scales in the bass line, rapid figuration, string tremolos, sharp dynamic contrasts, and octave-and-unison sonority. With these resources Vivaldi masterfully imparts the underworld imagery of the black shores of Acheron overflowing with innocent blood, cries for vengeance, and a raging ghost.

The best-known example of Vivaldi's marvelous operas is *Orlando furioso* (Venice, 1727; based on a partially lost 1714 version). Compared with Handel's *Orlando*, Vivaldi's score has far less instrumental music for magical or mechanical stage effects. But as in Handel's version there is significant imagery in the arias and in a few, special recitatives. The magical elements, such as the fountain, a potion that restores youth, the monster at Alcina's cavern (given a brief line in recitative for bass voice), and the magic ring, have no special musical devices. But Alcina has two vivid invocation arias: in act 3, mixing accompanied recitative with *arioso*, she calls forth the infernal deities; and at the end, she summons her Furies in a short aria with coloratura. Vivaldi set Orlando's mad scenes mostly in simple recitative, a short aria, or an *arioso* passage with octave-and-unison figures in the voice and the continuo part. The accompanied recitative includes some naturalistic devices as well: the shaking of the walls is depicted with string tremolos.

Italian Opera in Vienna and Southern Germany

Although supernatural episodes occur in later Viennese operas, the surviving scores for Andrea Stefano Fiorè's *Ercole in cielo* (Pietro Pariati, 1710),[16] Antonio Caldara's operas for Vienna, and Johann Joseph Fux's *feste, drammi,* and *componimenti* lack any evidence of music to depict magical events. Even Fux's score for *Orfeo ed Euridice* (1715) seems to offer little in this regard.[17] However, the scores of these operas do not often indicate instruments, which may have carried associations of magic or the underworld.

Johann Hugo von Wilderer composed Italian operas for Düsseldorf and Heidelberg. These included French features such as divertissements with ballets and descriptive instrumental music (composed by Georg Andreas Kraft).

16. The manuscript is preserved in A-Wn, shelfmark Hs. 17259.
17. Fux, *Orfeo ed Euridice.*

Examples include such *drammi per musica* as *Giocasta* (1696) and [*Nino, overo*] *La monarchia stabilita* (1703),[18] the latter based on the myth of Assyrian queen Semiramis. Act 2, scene 15 commences in a forest with the magician Targone using a magic book to conjure the devil. His invocation aria, "Farfarello, vieni, vieni, corri presto, Belzebù," is marked by a slowly ascending vocal line, with descending octave leaps and hypnotic repeated notes—a style consistent with that of earlier magic invocations in Italian opera. This musical style indicates the widespread acceptance of marvelous conventions outside Italy and France. The opera includes a magical appearance by the deceased Zoroastro returning in a cloud chariot as a deus ex machina.

Brunswick and Hamburg

Myth, epic romance, and the pastoral "marvelous" were frequent topics in operas produced in Brunswick and Hamburg, where librettos show little evidence of the reform that was being advocated in contemporary commentary elsewhere.[19] Georg Casper Schürmann's operas and pasticcios for Brunswick all include superhuman characters, as do the mythological operas by Reinhard Keiser for Hamburg's Gänsemarkt theater. Later operas and pasticcios performed in Hamburg continued the tradition, for example, Georg Philipp Telemann's *Ulysses* (1721) and Handel's *Admeto* (1730). The musical style of these operas is mainly derivative, based chiefly on Italian models with some French influence. That style remained consistent until the later 1730s. At first dominated by the da capo aria, the Italian operas that Handel, Graupner, Telemann, and then Hasse wrote for Germany in later years would capitalize on newer approaches to form and style. The music for these operas is not always intact; most of the complete scores were copied for the later productions. Keiser's operas seem typical in this regard. The scores to early works such as *Procris et Cephalus* (1694), *Circe* (1696), *Psyche* (1701), and *Minerva* (Keiser, 1703) are lost, although some individual numbers survive. (Keiser's German operas will be discussed in chapter 5.)

Magic and Stylistic Synthesis in the Operas of Handel

George Frideric Handel's maturation as a composer coincided with the development of the more vivid and expressive musical devices of the "marvelous" in French opera and the flowering of musical imagery and vocal display in Italian opera. Handel masterfully exploited all of these devices, including depictions of the "marvelous." Even his "historical" operas sometimes have magical scenes, for example act 2, scene 1 of *Giulio Cesare in Egitto* (1724), when

---

18. Manuscript score in A-Wn, shelfmark Hs. 17903. Kraft composed the overture and dances.

19. See Zelm, *Die Opern Reinhard Keisers*, and Lynch, "Opera in Hamburg."

Cleopatra enchants Caesar in a garden resembling the Palace of Virtue near Mount Parnassus. The sound of the first of two magical *sinfonias* of the Muses attracts the ruler of Rome. Handel designated two instrumental units in a seduction scene long associated with this libretto, and he scored the transformation into Parnassus with a rare combination of viola da gamba, harp, theorbo, oboes, bassoons, and muted strings.[20]

The main musical interest of Handel's operas resides in the solo arias, especially those large-scale virtuoso pieces that display the peaks of the composer's musical and emotional invention. The instrumental ritornellos in his arias occasionally function as music for transformations. Winton Dean and John Knapp argue that Handel did not convincingly use music for supernatural events until *Admeto* and *Orlando*.[21] And indeed, the presence of the magical *sinfonias* in *Orlando* must be reckoned as very special, as are the opera's vocal pieces with allusions to the "marvelous." Yet passages in the early operas suggest that Handel was aware of magical events in the plot and that the later works have precedents, especially in the vocal writing. Another fact supports this supposition: although Handel commonly borrowed preexisting materials, he reused very little when composing scenes with magical content. In the few instances of this self-borrowing, Handel derived material from numbers already in a supernatural context, an indication that Handel associated magical events and the use of mechanical stage with particular kinds of musical devices.

Handel's first "magic opera" became the composer's most popular during his lifetime. *Rinaldo* (Queen's Theatre, Haymarket, 24 February 1711) was revived five times and heavily revised for the last performance run on 6 April 1731.[22] The libretto is by Giacomo Rossi, based on Aaron Hill's outline of episodes from Tasso's *Gerusalemme liberata*, and concentrates on the enchantress Armida, who changes her form six times in the course of the opera. Other superhuman characters include the two sirens that sing a unison dance song in act 1, scene 3 and a Christian magician (alto) whose power resides in a magic wand. But although the opera requires stage machines and fantastic spectacle, most of the magical events take place in simple recitative with little or no special music. Military styles, suggestive of the Crusaders in the cast, are more

20. Handel's other vocal genres can also allude to the marvelous. *Semele*, a mythological oratorio of 1744, includes a short but stunning sleep scene at the beginning of act 3. The languid opening prelude for strings and woodwinds in low tessitura has an eerie set of sighing figures. Handel returned to this musical style shortly in the accompanying parts for the bass aria for Somnus, the god of sleep, in languid compound-duple meter.

21. Dean and Knapp, *Handel's Operas, 1704–1726*, 174. Dean, *Handel and the Opera Seria*, 77–99, was the first to discuss a genre of "magic opera" characterized by the use of sorcery, transformation, and machines. Dean discerns E major as Handel's key of sleep and offers the historical context of the conventions of Handel's operas.

22. Editions by Chrysander in Handel, *Werke*, vol. 58, and by Kimbell in *Hallische Händel-Ausgabe*, Ser. II, Bd. 4.

prevalent than references to magic, although the latter clearly dominate the libretto. The few instances of possible music to accompany stage machines include the introductory ritornello to Rinaldo's aria "Cara sposa" (act 1, scene 7, a Presto in A minor and 4/4 meter, with imitative texture), played while a cloud bearing fire-breathing monsters and two frightening Furies descends and then lifts off Almirena with Armida. The introductory ritornello to Armida's invocation "Furie terribili!" may also have had supernatural allusions (see below). But Armida, like Handel's later sorceresses, mostly has the music of a mortal woman rather than a superhuman character, featuring the same coloratura display as Handel's other *prime donne*. A forceful aria such as Armida's "Molto voglio, molto spero" (act 1, scene 5), for all its beauty and coloratura, could have been sung by any of his heroines.

One notable exception to the generally undistinguished character of these pieces is Armida's first aria in the opera, an angry invocation to the Furies in G minor, with the short text "Furie terribili! Circondatemi, seguitami con faci orribili" (act 1, scene 5).[23] The *sdrucciolo* poetic rhythms immediately signal something extraordinary, while the relatively long introductory ritornello, marked presto furioso, offers "furious" motives as a kind of instrumental response to Armida's contrasting vocal invocations. This ritornello articulates the individual sections of the aria, and it recurs in its complete form to close the number. The placement of the instrumental introduction in the score suggests that it accompanied Armida's magical appearance in the flying chariot drawn by two dragons. Thus it both underpins the spectacular appearance of the sorceress and reinforces Armida's extreme utterances. The ritornello culminates in repeated motives with octave leaps, one of the earmarks for magical characters and expressions (octave leaps also occur in a later vocal exclamation in this aria). The opening vocal gesture is a stark motive, marked "Adagio"; it encompasses a descending eleventh. Armida's first coloratura culminates in three descending octave leaps, the motive of superhuman and fateful pronouncements. It is repeated two more times in the orchestra. Handel also employs this gesture for emphatic expressions by human characters, as in Sesto's aria "Svegliatevi nel core" in *Giulio Cesare in Egitto* (act 1, scene 4). This motive will reappear in the supernatural contexts in the operas of Gluck, Anfossi, and Mozart; it is often an indicator of magical expression or invocation.

The aria of the Christian magician, "Andate, o forti," shows no evidence of the superhuman musical references (act 3, scene 2). The unison dance-song for two sirens, "Il vostro maggio de' bei verdianni, O cori amanti," has the quick rhythms of a gigue (the sirens sing and leap at the same time). The harmonic sallies into areas related to the tonic key of E minor suggest sensual delight in

23. Dean and Knapp, *Handel's Operas, 1704–1726*, 652, suggest a model for this aria in *Agrippina*, no. 35, Agrippina's act 2, scene 8 aria, "Pensieri." Baselt, *Händel-Handbuch* 1, does not list this as a model, and I see little similarity in these two arias.

movement rather than magical enchantment. Handel based both numbers on preexisting materials with no magical content.

Although cuts and alterations in the 1731 revision of the opera resulted in a reduction of both magic and spectacle, Handel added one scene in a magic grove. He reduced Armida's "Furie terribili!" and replaced her other three arias. He changed the role of the magician into a bass, altered his aria slightly, and transposed it down a sixth.

Handel's second magic opera was *Teseo,* a *dramma tragico* for the Queen's Theatre, Haymarket (10 January 1713). Nicholas Haym adapted the text from Quinault's *Thesée,* which in turn was based on Plutarch, Apollodorus, and Ovid's *Metamorphoses.*[24] This was Handel's only five-act opera, and it occasionally recalls *tragédie en musique,* with ballet, chorus, and spectacle. Like *Rinaldo, Teseo* includes numerous magical events in the libretto that Handel left to staging and spectacle rather than music. Although the sorceress Medea dominates act 2, most of her recitatives and arias in this act (and their earlier models) do not suggest superhuman expression. But in act 3, scene 5, Handel gives Medea a recitative and aria with a very different effect. She has transformed her palace into a horrible desert and surrounded the captive lovers Clizia and Arcane with monsters. The captives cry out to the gods for help in an accompanied recitative, then recoil at the sight of the "terrible specters." Medea returns and orders the lovers to be released in an F minor *recitativo orrido con stromenti,* "Ombre, sortite dall'eterna notte!" The unusual key, the sweeping ascending and descending gestures in the strings, and the octave-and-unison sonorities all suggest an otherworldly affect. Her vocal line also includes a portentous descending octave leap. In the following incantation aria in B-flat, "Sibillando e ululando," Medea conjures new plagues against her human rival, Agilea. Based on a similar model, the otherworldly aria "Oprida, oscura" from the cantata *Dunque sarà* (HWV 110), the initial triadic clarion-call vocal gesture recalls the declamatory invocations of the French "marvelous." In addition Handel gives Medea a long coloratura passage culminating in descending octave leaps, here accompanied by parallel thirds in the oboes and violins, a device of Handel's that would come to be used by a number of other composers in similar incantation scenes.

In act 4, scene 4, Medea calls forth the Furies with a short da capo aria in C minor, "Dal cupo baratro," whose "vivid and sinister" expression suggested to Dean and Knapp the dance style of Gluck's Furies in *Orfeo ed Euridice.*[25] Much of the unusual effect results from the unprepared vocal opening and the subsequent "demonic" coloratura. Scenes 6 and 7 also feature some slight

24. Edited by Chrysander in Handel, *Werke,* vol. 60. Forthcoming in *Hallische Händel-Ausgabe,* Ser. II, Bd. 6.

25. Dean and Knapp, *Handel's Operas, 1704–1726,* 241–42. Gluck's musical style for the Furies actually originates with his ballet-pantomime *Don Juan.*

touches of the "marvelous" in Teseo's music, first in the prelude to his arioso "Chi ritorna alla mia mente," a mood-setting device from *tragédie en musique*. Teseo's anger aria, "Qual tigre, qual Megera," invokes the Furies. In a kind of homage to French sleep scenes, Handel sets Teseo's aria "Deh, v'aprite, oh luci belle" (act 4, scene 7) with recorders doubling the muted violins; these instruments plays slow, slurred arpeggios over sustained pedals to suggest the soporific magic spell. In scene 6 Medea arrives in a flying chariot drawn by dragons. Her accompanied recitative has the rapid ascending string scales of the French "marvelous" when she summons the forces of hell. Then another French device, a short, transitional prelude in the continuo, signals Minerva's arrival as a dea ex machina. As Medea flies away the music modulates from G minor to G major, and *una Sinfonia di stromenti* serves as transformation music, yet one more French pictorial convention.

Handel's next marvelous opera was also drawn from a French tradition, albeit one based on a Spanish epic romance. *Amadigi di Gaula* (King's Theatre, Haymarket, 25 May 1715) was adapted from André Destouches's opera (1699), based in turn on Houdarde la Motte's *Amadis de Grèce*. The unnamed translator-arranger may have been Rossi or Haym.[26] As in the first two magic operas, there are fewer marvelous effects in the music than in the libretto, and magical events occur primarily in simple recitative. Three instrumental numbers and one obbligato recitative facilitate magical events in the plot. Melissa's infernal spirits appear in act 1, scene 2, accompanied with a brief *sinfonia* in an F major Allegro made almost entirely of sixteenth-note figuration. This is the kind of modest instrumental number one finds in similar scenes in *tragédie en musique*. For act 1, scene 6, Handel composed a *strepitosso sinfonia* in F major to suggest a darkening sky, thunder, and lightning. The composer marked the accompanied recitative in E minor for the ghost of Dardano, the prince of Thrace, "Adagio e staccato." Handel reworked this scene from an earlier arioso, "Se'l mio mal da voi dipende" in *Silla* (act 3, scene 4). A *sinfonia*, an appropriate triadic fanfare for trumpet and strings, indicates the magician Orgando's descent in a flying chariot as a deus ex machina and the change of scene from a cavern to a beautiful palace.

Although scholars do not usually classify it among Handel's magic operas, *Admeto* (31 January 1727), with a text based on Mauro's *Alceste*, after Aureli's *L'Antigona delusa da Alceste*,[27] contains a few scenes with magical elements. Here Handel employs minor keys (D minor, G minor) for the supernatural scenes, but without distinctive instrumentation. The first scene in act 1 has a somber "Ballo di larve con stili sanguinosi in mano" marked "Lentement," an elegant triple-meter binary dance in D minor with dotted rhythms that recalls

26. Edited by Chrysander in Handel, *Werke*, vol. 62, and by J. Merrill Knapp in *Hallische Händel-Ausgabe*, Ser. II, Bd. 8.

27. Edited by Chrysander in Handel, *Werke*, vol. 63. Forthcoming in the *Hallische Händel-Ausgabe*, Ser. II, Bd. 19.

the noble style of a sarabande. The voice of Apollo's statue (bass) sings an unremarkable simple recitative. Handel first depicts the underworld (act 2, scene 1) with an allusion to the French overture. The introductory G minor section has brisk ascending scales and one measure of octave-and-unison sonority. The ensuing contrapuntal Allegro employs a chromatic motive in the subject. During the simple recitative that follows, Hercules descends into the abyss to find Alceste tormented by the Furies. The Furies fly off and Hercules releases Alceste, leading her out of the inferno. Here Handel provides a contrapuntal *sinfonia* in G minor.

Orlando, composed for the King's Theatre, Haymarket (27 January 1734), contains the most vivid and varied music of all Handel's magic operas.[28] The character of Zoroastro,[29] created for the bass Antonio Montagnana, was first used in an early Venetian Orlando setting, *L'amorose furie d'Orlando* by G. A. Cicognini (Venice, c. 1640), where Astolfo cures Orlando of his madness (Ariosto actually refers to Zoroastro in canto 31 of his poem). *Orlando* was the closest Handel came to fully exploiting the French operatic style of musical depiction and the "marvelous"; it has the distinction of being Handel's first magic opera to employ horns and flutes, along with the oboes, strings, and continuo instruments found in the previous magic operas. He deployed a combination of low-pitched strings (two special violas, called *violette marine*, and a cello) to accompany the sleep scene of Orlando in act 3, recalling French accompaniment for similar magical scenes. There is relatively little borrowed material in this opera, and the music for magic scenes appears to be largely original.

The opera begins as Zoroastro reads Orlando's future by consulting the stars. The magician's accompanied recitative starts with an opening frequently used by Handel, two dotted *coups d'archet* on the tonic pitch, then another two on the dominant. The following contrapuntal material in B minor, with a walking bass and suspensions, vaguely suggests church music of the previous century (Mozart would later use similar material in his scene for the two armored men in *Die Zauberflöte*). Zoroastro sings his opening words, "Gieroglifici eterni," to repeated notes and a descending-octave incantation motive that

---

28. Edited by Chrysander in Handel, *Werke*, vol. 82, and by Siegfried Flesch in *Hallische Händel-Ausgabe*, Ser. II, Bd. 28. The libretto for this *dramma per musica* is anonymous. For background on this opera, see Dean, *Handel's Operas, 1726–1741*, 235–55.

29. The *mago* Zoroastro on the French musical stage dates back at least to 1678, *Les forces de l'amour et de la magie*, a "divertissement comique en trois intermèdes," the oldest printed Parisian fair play, by Maurice Vondrebeck and Charles Alard. The *mago* commonly appears in Semiramis and Ninus operas such as *Nino, overo La monarchia stabilita*, by J. H. Wilderer (Düsseldorf, 1703); *Sémiramis*, by Destouches (1718); Francesco Silvani's libretto *Semiramide* (1713); and *Ninus und Semiramis*, by Schürmann (Brunswick, 1730). He also appears as a character in J.-L.-I. de La Serre's *Pirame et Thisbé*, with music by Rebel and Francœur (1726), and in the 1732 ballet *Les génies, ou Les caractères de l'amour*, by Fleury de Lyon, with music by Mademoiselle Duval (1736). Zoroastre would be the central character in Rameau's opera of 1749, rev. 1756. For more information on this character, see Strohm, "Comic Traditions."

Handel had been employing at least since *Rinaldo* (1711) as a sign of the magical and of fateful pronouncement. Here it defines the music of the *mago* (magician). Burney describes this music as having "a wild grandeur in it of a very uncommon kind."[30] Although Zoroastro's music is as much a source for vocal display as any other in the opera, the composer provided the role with some distinctive qualities. In act 1 Handel adds two flutes to the string orchestra for the *sinfonia* as the magician waves a wand and his genies transform the scene to a palace. The music, a short and evocative triple-meter Andante, with conjunct pairs of sixteenth notes, is reminiscent of French sleep scenes. The magician sings a brilliant da capo aria with coloratura, "Lascia Amore e siegui Marte," and descending octave leaps figure prominently in the melody, terminating several emphatic phrases.

In act 2 Handel composed a most remarkable musical scene for the insane Orlando. In scene 10 Zoroastro's four genies abduct Angelica in a cloud chariot, depicted with a short passage for continuo and a sweeping final gesture as she soars into the air. Handel had used such a device for a similar scene in the French-influenced *Teseo*. Orlando then begins a long accompanied recitative with arioso sections. Here he imagines a variety of standard fantastic scenes from old court opera, in a kind of musical recall of past traditions.[31] First he summons in recitative the impious specters of the Styx. Likening himself to Orpheus when he attempted to gain entrance to Hades to retrieve Euridice, Orlando demands the return of his faithless lover, and an eighth-note pulse in this Andante arioso expresses the character's self-pity. Returning to recitative, he resolves to cross the river and enter the realm of affliction despite the opposition of the boatman, Charon. An irregular Andante in 5/8 meter depicts "ploughing through the black waves." Orlando then sees Pluto's smoke-blackened residence.[32] A 6/8 Andante section in C minor has the deluded Orlando describing the howling of Cerberus and the gloomy fury of Erebus in the *sdrucciolo* rhythms of Seicento opera, set to a hollow octave-and-unison accompaniment and thirty-second-note figures common in French marvelous opera. (Orlando's act 3 mad aria, "Già lo stringo," has a similar octave-and-unison accompaniment.) Returning to recitative, Orlando asks for the Fury named Medoro, who torments him, and he pictures Medoro in the arms of Proserpina. An Adagio segment with repeated notes depicts the weeping of this deity. Proserpina's tears touch Orlando's heart; in the concluding aria-

---

30. Burney, *General History of Music*, 2: 777.

31. Strohm, "Comic Traditions," views the opera as a fusion of the comic, tragic, pastoral, and magical, very much like Ariosto's original poem. Strohm reads Orlando's madness scene as a parody for Senesino, hence the irregular rhythms to help the singer act out the madness in the text with his gestures. Strohm traces this madness scene back to Lully's *Roland* (act 4, scene 1), especially the "Tempo di Gavotta" segment, and its numerous parodies, including Lully's own parodistic underworld scene in the divertissement of the fourth act of *Alceste*.

32. Burney, *General History*, 2:778, wrote that this is "a division in time which can only be borne in such a situation."

like sections in gavotte rhythms he implores her lovely eyes not to weep. This leads to a Larghetto segment based on the chromatic *lamento* bass motive, with coloratura on the word "awakening" (referring to the pity that is awakened even in this terrible realm). The gavotte music returns, and Orlando quickly changes his mood again. He sings, "Yes, yes, she should weep," because his heart has now become hardened to her enchanted spell. The word "enchanted" (*incantato*) is set with a long coloratura passage accompanied by rapid scales in the strings. A final furious ritornello with sixteenth-note scales serves as stage-machine music: Orlando rushes into the cavern, and Zoroastro sweeps him up in his arms and flies off with him into the air.

In act 3 the *mago* appears with his genies. In an accompanied recitative he commands the genies to transform the grove into a horrible cavern, with wavering figures in the strings. Zoroastro then sings a C minor bravura aria as an incantation for threatening storms ("Sorge infausta una procella"). Handel depicted the rising tempests both in the initial ascending vocal line and in the string figures. After the mad Orlando has his *furioso* accompanied recitative and duet scene with Angelica, he throws her into the cavern, and the scene changes to the temple of Mars (act 3, scene 8). Here Handel sets yet another marvelous scene with Orlando falling asleep. In the place of flutes, Handel designates two low-pitched *violette marine* and a cello to play sensual, sedate contrapuntal figures in conjunct motion,[33] which then accompanies Orlando's Larghetto arioso in E-flat. The magician then returns, and after some recitative segments he addresses the stellar divinities in a Larghetto incantation, "Tu che del gran tonante," accompanied by descending triadic motives in the strings. Here Zoroastro asks for the magic potion to cure Orlando's madness. A second magic *sinfonia* accompanies the magician as he waves his wand to make his genies descend with Jupiter's eagle bearing a cup of magic potion. With its airy counterpoint in moderate triple meter, its pianissimo dynamic, and its conjunct pairs of eighth notes, the music suggests the elegance of the French marvelous style and the "soft music" of magic scenes from seventeenth-century opera. A shorter version of this *sinfonia* recurs after a brief recitative exchange with the shepherdess Dorinda when the magician sprinkles the enchanted liquor on Orlando to restore his sanity.

Handel's last magic opera was *Alcina*, a *dramma per musica* for Covent Garden (16 April 1735). The anonymous libretto was based on Antonio Fanzaglia and Riccardo Broschi's *L'isola di Alcina* (1728, taken in turn from Ariosto's *Orlando furioso*, cantos 6 and 7).[34] As he had done in his early magic operas, here Handel allowed most of the fantastic events to be depicted without the

---

33. The *violetta marina* was a bowed instrument with sympathetic strings, probably similar to a viola d'amore.

34. Edited by Chrysander in Handel, *Werke*, vol. 86. Forthcoming in the *Hallische Händel-Ausgabe*, Ser. II, Bd. 33. For background on this opera, see Dean, *Handel's Operas, 1726–1741*, 312–34.

benefit of corresponding music, such as when the enchanted palace appears after thunder and lightning in act 1, scene 2. Handel gave the sorceresses, Alcina and her sister Morgana, a variety of arias, including incantation scenes. In act 2, scene 8, Alcina employs her magic with a furious accompanied recitative and an E minor da capo coloratura aria, "Ombre, pallide." This incantation aria has descending octave leaps in the vocal line and conjunct pairs of eighth notes in the violin accompaniments to suggest sleep or trance. As one of Handel's most imposing heroines, Alcina still emerges ultimately more human than supernatural.

Some of Handel's instrumental music may have been supplied for magical actions and transformations in *Alcina* as well. Unlike similar sections in *Orlando*, where there are independent instrumental numbers, this music occurs mainly in the instrumental ritornellos of vocal numbers. At the beginning of act 2 the composer evokes the scene of Alcina's wondrous palace with a short introductory instrumental largo in G minor. The librettist placed the divertissement-like sections, with their elegant ballet music and choruses, both within and at the end of acts. The second chorus (act 3, scene 6), "Sin per le vie del sole una gloriosa prole il volo sa drizar," has an introductory instrumental ritornello that may have functioned as magic music, because the libretto calls for the appearance of Alcina's palace with the magic urn. The musical style of this Andante in D major suggests a solemn march. The next choral ensemble, "Dall'orror di notte cieca," based on the aria "Cara pianta" from the cantata HWV 122, may also have functioned as transformation music (act 3, scene 10). The libretto has Ruggiero destroying the magic urn, causing the palace to collapse and the enchanted captives to resume their former human appearance.

Dresden

Seventeenth-century Dresden had long favored spectacular court operas based on mythology and epic romance.[35] A new opera house opened at the Redoutensaal in October 1717 with Antonio Lotti's spectacular *melodramma pastorale Giove in Argo*. Although Lotti is generally more restrained in his musical imagery than his younger contemporaries Handel and Ristori, his works did employ the larger instrumental ensembles associated with such spectacle, including oboes, recorders, bassoons, trumpets, and horns.

French influence and the Italian interest in projecting the character of aria texts in the vocal and instrumental components are evident in the coronation opera *Le fate* (Dresden, 10 August 1736), a *dramma per musica*, loosely based on

---

35. Examples include *Il Teseo* (Giovanni Andrea Moniglia, music possibly by Giovanni Andrea Bontempi, 1667), *Jupiter et Io* (Bontempi, 1673), and Carlo Pallavicino's *La Gerusalemme liberata* (1687).

Ariosto, by the librettist Stefano Benedetto Pallavicini.[36] The libretto recounts the adventure of Ruggiero on the island of the fairies Alcina and Melissa. The music, by Giovanno Alberto Ristori, includes da capo arias (many with coloratura writing), choruses, dances, and instrumental music.[37] The large ceremonial instrumental ensemble calls for flutes, oboes, *corni di caccia*, and bassoons in addition to the strings and continuo instruments. Italian influence is evidenced in the magical incantation of Alcina's dwarf Doro (bass), a da capo aria marked "Spiritoso" in D major with string accompaniment. As he waves the magic wand in circles, his vocal line has both descending octave leaps and triadic clarion-call figures, along with octave-and-unison sonority, dramatic fermatas, and rapid scales in the accompaniment. Doro's striking music calls to mind that of Handel's *mago* Zoroastro (see ex. 3.1). Doro conjures his demons for a "Ballo di demoni in figuri orribili," a D major Prestissimo with running sequential motives in contrapuntal texture, triadic motion in the strings, and repeated notes in the horns. This is perhaps the first known instance of a new use for the horns in an *orribile* infernal scene. Unlike the ceremonial and solemn expression of the brass in earlier *intermedi* and court operas, this blaring brass suggests the terrifying infernal imagery of the Christian hell. It proves too horrific even for Doro, who, in an accompanied recitative, uses his wand to conjure less vile spirits. The subsequent "Ballo di demoni in figura di donne" is an elegant rounded-binary form with flutes and oboes (the latter doubling the strings). Designated "transformazione," the music follows the first accompanied recitative in act 2, scene 1, as the fairy Melissa disenchants Astolfo out of the myrtle tree. This is a short Allegro made up of sixteenth-note string tremolos with harmonic motion over a tonic in repeated sixteenth notes, recalling French pictorial *symphonies*. Scene 9 is the denouement, with the fury of Alcina depicted in an accompanied invocation with sixteenth-note figures and rapid repeated notes.

Midcentury Developments, 1750–70

Around 1750 several cities or courts with interests in French musical theater began reincorporating supernatural events, along with ballet, chorus, and pantomime, into operatic productions.[38] Most of these efforts took place outside Italy (with the exceptions of Parma and Turin), specifically Mannheim, Stutt-

---

36. Libretto: Dresden: vedova Stössel, 1736 (US-Wc, Schatz 8817). Ristori also set *Orlando furioso* to a libretto by Grazio Braccioli (Venice, 1713). A manuscript score survives in Turin, Biblioteca Nazionale Universitaria.

37. The heavily damaged manuscript survives in D-Dlb (shelfmark Mus. 2455-F-5).

38. They also modified traditional formal procedures (e.g., the exit aria), expanded scene complexes, created ensembles of various size and scope, experimented with chorus and aria combinations, and intensified programmatic obbligato recitative.

EXAMPLE 3.1 Giovanni Alberto Ristori, *Le fate*, act 1, scene 8

Doro
Violini
Viola
Basso

Quan-ti di-se-gna in a - ria   la   ne-ra ver-ga cir - co-li.

Tan - ti ap-pa-rir qui   spi - ri - ti

veg-gan-si dal pro - fon-do, dal pro - fon-do, dal pro - fon - do   mon-do di Bel - ze -

- bù.   Su,   su,   su,   su!

gart, Vienna, and Berlin, where conditions allowed for greater latitude.[39] It was a decade or more before the efforts to achieve a Franco-Italian synthesis began having an effect on operatic repertory within Italy. Once this occurred, opera in Europe became more international in its musical resources; by the end of the century, national distinctions were far less pronounced, and European composers had established techniques for the expression of terror, the "marvelous," magic incantation, and otherworldly elements.

Theoretical discussions justified these new practices. In the "Osservazioni sull'opera in musica" printed in his libretto *L'Armida* (Milan, 1771), Giovanni De Gamerra defended the use of flight, flying chariots, and scene transformations in opera, claiming they were the "pleasant illusion that forms the theater's chief delight . . . the state of enchantment."[40] In his influential treatise (1755), Francesco Algarotti, Frederick the Great's dramaturge from 1747 to 1753, advocated a mixture of French and Italian operatic practice.[41] It does not come as a surprise, then, that the two opera examples at the end of his treatise include supernatural episodes. Ranieri de' Calzabigi, on the other hand, first initially derided the marvelous element, adopting the classicist criticism and some of the arguments from the War of the Buffoons (1755).[42] In the next few years, however, he would change in both theory and practice, and indeed used marvelous effects in his own stage works. In a letter of 6 May 1771, Calzabigi wrote of the prevalence of librettos by Metastasio in Italy and Vienna and the corresponding disdain for those based on the fantastic material in Ariosto. He expressed dismay at Metastasio's elimination of this material in the opera *Il Ruggiero,* an epic romance that necessitates "fantastic characters, the treating of enchantments, chivalrous adventures, and the machinations of the demons and the fates."[43] In the *Lettre sur le mechanisme de l'opéra italien* (Naples/Paris: Duchesne/Lambert, 1756), long attributed to Josse de Villeneuve but perhaps

39. See Heartz, "Operatic Reform at Parma," and *Music in European Capitals,* 443ff. Also see McClymonds, "Mannheim, *Idomeneo,* and the Franco-Italian Synthesis,", and "Verazi, Coltellini, and the Mannheim-Vienna Connection." For a discussion of developments at Turin see Butler, *Operatic Reform at Turin's Teatro Regio.*

40. *L'Armida* (Milan: Giuseppe Galeazzi, 1771, 46–47, US-Wc, Schatz 11309). See K. Hansell, "Opera and Ballet," 46–49.

41. Algarotti, *Saggio sopra l'opera.* For details on the influence of Algarotti, see Heartz, "Operatic Reform at Parma." Recent research by McClymonds and Butler on the influence of Algarotti's "reforms" has demonstrated connections between Berlin and Turin.

42. Calzabigi, "Dissertazione su la poesie drammatiche del Sig. Abate Pietro Metastasio [Paris: 1755]," in *Scritti teatrali,* 1:139–46. Calzabigi charges that the use of the marvelous in opera confuses the epic with the dramatic genre and claims that Quinault would eliminate the marvelous if he were writing in the present day. He criticizes Quinault's successors for supernatural elements included as concessions to the rabble.

43. K. Hansell, "Opera and Ballet," 49. The letter is found in Donà, "Dagli Archivi Milanesi," 292.

by Ranieri de' Calzabigi, the author defends marvelous episodes as the appropriate setting for theatrical music and praises Italian accompanied recitative as a vehicle for its expression.[44] Reform-minded writers continued to deride marvelous effects, and now they could cite Rousseau's polemical account of opera history in support of their opinion. Thus Stefano Arteaga's history of Italian opera asserted that the "apparatus of mythology was abandoned . . . and gods and devils were banished from the theater."[45] Yet my own examination of the repertory suggests a situation at variance with this reformist view. The many genre designations for works that include supernatural elements testify to the presence of supernatural materials across a wide spectrum of Italian lyric theater.[46]

※

Three divergent approaches to Franco-Italian operatic synthesis that Francesco Algarotti espoused in *Saggio sopra l'opera in musica* (1755) inspired the reemergence of the supernatural in serious opera starting at midcentury.[47] One approach employed a translated French model with a mythological subject, underworld scenes, scene complexes with dance and chorus, and a deus ex machina to facilitate a happy ending. Carl Heinrich Graun's *Le feste galanti* (Berlin, 1747) and *L'Europe galante* (Berlin, 1748) and Tommaso Traetta's groundbreaking operas for Parma *Ippolito ed Aricia* (Parma, 1759), *I Tindaridi* (Parma, 1760), and *Enea nel Lazio* (Turin, 1760) were of this type, as were Gluck's *Alceste* and the *Fetonte* settings by Graun (Berlin, 1748, the first Berlin opera with supernatural elements) and Niccolò Jommelli (Stuttgart, 1753 and 1768). The other approach added French characteristics (scene complexes, chorus, and dance) to Italian genres, but with limited supernatural content. These operas employed programmatic obbligato recitative and natural spectacles such as battles, storms, battles, sacrifices, and imagined or even real ghost scenes. They also might incorporate pantomime ballet and chorus. Operas of this type include Graun's *Ifigenia in Aulide* (Berlin, 1748) and *Orfeo* (Berlin, 1752), Traetta's Turin and Mannheim operas as well as his Viennese *Ifigenia in Tauride* (1764), Jommelli's *Enea nel Lazio* (Stuttgart, 1755) and *Pelope* (Stuttgart, 1755), and Gian Francesco De Majo's *Ifigenia in Tauride* for Mannheim (1764). Viennese theaters chose a third approach, employing formal innova-

44. See Heartz, *Haydn, Mozart and the Viennese School,* 158–64.

45. Arteaga, *Le rivoluzioni del teatro musicale italiano.*

46. Among the Italian genre designations of eighteenth-century works that contain fairy-tale material are *commedia per musica, divertimento per musica, dramma giocoso, dramma [comico] per musica, dramma serio-comico, drama serio-giocoso per musica, dramma tragicomico, farsa, farsetta, fiaba teatrale,* and *intermezzo.*

47. McClymonds, "Algarotti and Voltaire in Berlin," argues that these differing approaches belonged to the same movement.

tion within the tradition of the festive theatrical piece that continued to incorporate marvelous mythological elements. It fell to Marco Coltellini, a fellow Livornese and disciple of Calzabigi, to assist Calzabigi by providing the librettos for these *feste teatrali*, one of which was set by Gluck.

Mythology provided many plots for these operas. The myths of Orpheus and Hercules (set by Metastasio) served in spectacles for the Habsburg court, and Voltaire's adaptation of the myth of Semiramis offered a model for a number of theatrical works that included a ghost scene, such as Giampietro Tagliazucchi and Graun's *Semiramide* (Berlin, 1754).[48] Ghost scenes also occur in the three different *Enea nel Lazio* or *Enea e Lavinia* productions for Stuttgart, Parma, and Turin, and there are imagined ghosts in more traditional *dramma per musica*. Tasso's *Armida* was also a favored subject for opera in the second half of the century. Composers such as Georg Christoph Wagenseil, Traetta, and Salieri set this opera based on Quinault's libretto for Lully.[49]

Feste, azioni teatrali, *and* drammi per musica *in Italy, Vienna, and Berlin, 1750–70*

In 1750 Wagenseil arranged a *pasticcio* for a Viennese *festa teatrale* on the Orpheus theme, *Euridice,* with arias by Andrea Bernasconi, Baldassare Galuppi, Hasse, Ignaz Holzbauer, and Jommelli.[50] The bulk of marvelous content occurs in the scene complex set in the underworld (act 2, scene 8), where Wagenseil combines aria with recitative, ensemble, and chorus in an early manifestation of musical terror. At a subterranean cavern at the gates of Tartarus (the section of Hades reserved for the wicked), Orpheus (castrato) dismisses his retinue of shepherds in a short, simple recitative. Now alone, he begins an accompanied recitative, marked Adagio and introduced by solemn blasts of the two horns in the infernal key of E-flat. The section proceeds with descriptive music as the strings suggest the howling of the guard dog Cerberus in octave-and-unison leaps ("Behold the horrid gates where Cerberus stands guard"). Rapid violin scales suggest the irate Furies, chordal tremolos depict the "horrendous laments" and the trembling of Ixion as he turns on the wheel, and descending chromatic scales in unisons and octaves describe the falling rock of Sisyphus. Finally, alternating C-sharps and Ds in sixteenth notes suggest the receding waters of Tantalus's torment in wavelike musical motion.

Orpheus decides to try his musical powers and sings a G minor aria, "Numi, che impero avete," in gentle siciliano rhythms, accompanied by flute and pizzicato strings imitating Orpheus's lyre. Pastoral in allusion and tragic in key, his

48. Ballet also used this plot, e.g., Gluck and Gasparo Angiolini's *Sémiramis* (Vienna, 1765).

49. After 1769 Anfossi, Jommelli, Sacchini, Naumann, Mysliveček, and Haydn set versions of the Armida story more directly from Tasso's poem, establishing familiar musical conventions for the characteristic supernatural episodes (see below).

50. Facsimile edition of the manuscript score (A-Wn, Hs. 18032) ed. Weimer, IO 75.

song causes the gates of Hades to open. A solemn homophonic C minor "Coro di spiriti infernali" (SATB), marked "Grave e lento," with the text "Fuggi mai, fuggi da questo Regno," has rapid string motives in octaves and unisons, along with infernal blasts by the horns. Diminished chords and a final pedal all contribute to the otherworldly effect as the demons try unsuccessfully to repulse Orpheus, who resumes his aria.

In the same year (1750) Wagenseil arranged another Viennese *pasticcio*, *Armida placata*, adding music by Luca Antonio Predieri, Hasse,[51] Giuseppe Bonno, and Girolamo Abos. Like other marvelous operas in this period, the manuscript score (A-Wn, Mus. Hs. 18021) restricts pictorial music to arias and instrumental segments in the accompanied recitative. The most striking example is Erminia and Armida's exchange (act 2, scene 10), when the sorceress, accompanied by four-part strings and continuo, summons her infernal forces. The instruments play octave-and-unison sonority, tremolos, chromatic inflections, dotted rhythms, and brief rapid thirty-second-note scales in the bass and the violins. Some of the octave-and-unison scale figures depict thunder, lightning, and the horrible monsters that Armida describes.

Carl Heinrich Graun's supernatural operas for Berlin evince few instances of the "marvelous."[52] In his *L'Armida* of 1751 (libretto by Leopoldo de Villati, after Quinault),[53] the music for supernatural characters such as L'Odio (Hate) and Armida are indistinguishable from that of the mortal characters. In his *Orfeo* (Villati, after Michel Du Boulair, 1752),[54] Pluto (tenor) sings only nondescript da capo arias. The instrumental music is the vehicle for the most vivid expression. The opening *sinfonia* is in the infernal key of E-flat. The triple-meter Larghetto in D major, used as a ritornello in Pluto's accompanied recitative (number 11), suggests an enchanted sleep through its conjunct motion in thirds with muted strings. Apollo (soprano) arrives in the *scena ultima* of act 3, beginning with a largo in E-flat for strings and horns, elegant and light machine music to accompany the magical appearance of the deity.

Traetta's contribution to the development of the musical style of late eighteenth-century opera is more significant. His five-act *Ippolito ed Aricia*, a *tragedia* by Carlo Innocenzo Frugoni, based on Pellegrin (Parma, 9 May 1759),[55] integrates French-style choruses, elegant ballet music, descriptive instrumental pieces, and pictorial accompaniment for vocal segments with the

51. The British Library has a print of Hasse's *Rinaldo und Armida*, "eine dramatische Cantate," by Christopher Petri (Leipzig: The author, 1782), a piano-vocal score, shelfmark F. 386.(1.). The text appeared in the 1778 *Musenalmanach*.

52. These include *Fetonte* (1748, Villati, after Racine), *Ifigenia in Aulide* (1749, Villati, after Racine), *Angelica e Medoro* (1749, Villati, after Ariosto), and *Semiramide* (1754, Giampietro Tagliazucchi, after Voltaire).

53. A manuscript survives in Berlin's Staatsbibliothek, Mus. ms. 8226. A duet and trio were published in Graun, *Duetti, terzetti*, vols. 2 and 3.

54. A manuscript survives in Berlin's Staatsbibliothek, Mus. ms. 8228.

55. Facsimile of the Berlin manuscript ed. Weimer, IO 77.

conventional simile arias and virtuoso singing of *dramma per musica*. Especially noteworthy is the terrifying underworld scene in act 2, scene 1 (here the word *terribile* actually appears in the libretto to describe the *sinfonia* in scene 5 at the entrance of Hades with Tisiphone, the Fury who torments Theseus).[56] Here a chorus of avenging chthonic deities performs a kind of concluding divertissement during which the three Fates announce their prophecy. Pluto sings his accompanied recitative with numerous expressive devices to depict the text. The words "honor," "aristocracy," and "divinity" receive majestic dotted rhythms, and the "moaning and trembling" of subterranean rivers and the rising of the divinities of Erebus at Pluto's command also occasion appropriate musical devices. Traetta gave his vocal line the descending octave leaps of a magician's invocation. The key shifts to E-flat when the deities sing their chorus, "Plutone il chiede, Pluton si vendichi," with octave-and-unison figures and rapid ascending string scales as they mention the monsters and fury of Pluto. Articulated figures suggest the palpitations of fear in the text. A short *sinfonia* for strings announces the arrival of the divine messenger Mercury in scene 5 with majestic dotted rhythms and bright G major sonorities. This prepares the Fates' oracle scene, introduced by a "brieve sinfonìa maestoso, e terribile," a six-measure passage initiating the arioso of the Fates. The accompaniment has rapid repeated notes in the strings, marked "sotto voce" and accompanied by the horns playing first sustained notes, then a fanfare in thirds.

Instrumental music announces the arrival of Proserpina and her retinue (this was not in Pellegrin's original text). The *sinfonia* here is a more complex example of magical music, an Allegro in D with repeated sixteenth-note figures in the violins. Figures in the oboes and horns suggest infernal blasts of motives that continue in the following homophonic chorus, "Sparve l'empio mortal." In act 5, scene 3, Aricia has an accompanied-recitative sleep scene set in a "gran giardino delizioso," scored for muted strings and marked "sotto voce." Her "reeling from weariness" brings forth rapid repeated sixteenth notes, and the following *cavata* (a short aria without da capo) mimics the calm breezes that put her to sleep. More stage-machine music follows as *una dolce sinfonia* announces the arrival of Diana. An Allegro in G for strings, oboes, and horns (whose figures suggest an association of the goddess with the hunt) features a variety of short, rapid motives in polyphonic texture, with brief scalar bursts, dotted repeated notes, and dotted descending octave leaps.

Jommelli, Traetta, and Musical Terror

Niccolò Jommelli and the Italian composers in his generation (c. 1740–70) experimented with the dramatic use of accompanied recitative, pictorial instrumental music, and the integration of chorus, dance, and stage machines, all French conventions associated with the "marvelous." Slightly later Traetta

56. Facsimile ed. H. M. Brown, IOL 14, 24.

was writing similar music for Parma (*Ippolito ed Aricia*, 1759) and Mannheim. Both composers employed increasingly powerful musical effects. Shunned by arcadian reformers of serious Italian opera, the "marvelous" reappeared in the genre by 1755. Jommelli and Verazi's *Enea nel Lazio* and *Pelope* (1755) were both influenced by the French mimetic approach.[57] In Parma, Traetta also set translations of Rameau (*Ippolito ed Aricia* and *I Tindaridi*), and in Mannheim, *Sofonisba* (1762), with ballet music, chorus, and extensive orchestral music.

Perhaps the most significant new musical devices to appear in these works were those engaged to express emotions associated with terror. As mentioned above, we find the term "terribile" in the libretto of Traetta's *Ippolito e Aricia*. This word has a long history in aesthetics and the visual arts that dates back to Aristotle's *Poetics*.[58] Although Continental writers mentioned such concepts as terror only in passing, English writers such as Edmund Burke, James Addison, the critic John Aikin, Anna Letitia (Aiken) Barbauld, James Beattie, and Nathan Drake discussed these ideas in more detail,[59] relating terror to the sublime, a concept going back to Longinus. The Aikin treated the aesthetic category of the terrible in still greater detail (1773),[60] citing oriental fairy tales and modern tales of horror as the optimal mixture of terrible with marvelous effects.

One encounters terms designating these affects in various scores and librettos with supernatural topics. For instance, in their program for Gluck's *Don Juan*, Calzabigi and Angiolini praise the composer who "perfectly captured the terror [*le terrible*] of the action" in depicting the graveyard scene where the spirits take Don Juan to hell. Gaetano Martinelli's libretto *Le avventure di Cleomede* (Lisbon, 1772; music by Jommelli) calls such music "orribile armonia." Numerous other examples can be cited, but perhaps the best-known is Leopold Mozart's letter to his son dated 29 December 1780. Here Leopold advises young Wolfgang to choose "very deep wind instruments to accompany the subterranean voice [statue of Neptune or Poseidon]" in *Idomeneo* and suggests effects that "almost inspire terror" (*bis ins Schröckliche*).[61] Gluck, quoted in the *Journal de Paris* (August 1788), used the French term *terrible* to describe the Furies scene in his Parisian *Alceste*.

Musical terror on the stage first achieved prominence in the occasional productions known as *azioni teatrali* or *feste teatrali*, which employed vivid musi-

57. See McClymonds and Heartz, "Opera Seria," NGO 3:702.

58. Giorgio Vasari (1551) used *terribile* or *terribilità* six times while describing Michelangelo's "Last Judgment" fresco in the Sistine Chapel. For Vasari this was a most significant attribute of the artist's style. See Vasari, *Vite scelte*, 424–26.

59. Burke, *Philosophical Inquiry*, section vii, "Of the Sublime," printed in Adams, ed., *Critical Theory*, 310; Beattie [and Barbauld], *Dissertations*, and *Essays;* Addison, "On the Pleasures"; and Drake, *Literary Hours*.

60. Aikin, "On the Pleasure Derived," 119–26.

61. See Bauer-Deutsch 3, no. 572, 73–75.

cal depiction of horrific scenes.[62] Using spectacle, mythology, allegory, ballet, pantomime, descriptive orchestral music, and machines in long scene complexes with chorus and soloists and flexible recitative and aria mixtures, the genre became more dramatically charged than contemporary heroic opera. In this respect, the underworld scene in Wagenseil's *Euridice*, discussed above, seems a precedent for the underworld scene in the second act of Gluck and Calzabigi's *Orfeo ed Euridice* (1762).

Composers devised a designated "terrifying" musical style for depicting violent storms, Furies, flying dragons, infernal scenes, and similar horrific episodes. By the middle of the eighteenth century, rapid scale passages, sustained bursts in the brass instruments, disruptive *alla zoppa* syncopation, diminished chords, minor keys, tremolo,[63] octave-and-unison sonority, and sharply contrasting dynamics were the typical devices of musical terror. These techniques also appeared in choruses with chantlike monophonic writing (both in unison and in octaves) and repeated-note declamation. Modern commentators often refer to this style as "Sturm und Drang," particularly in discussions of instrumental music.[64] But contemporaries used instead terms related to terror in describing this music; the term "Sturm und Drang" was unknown at the time. In fact, the literary movement that gave rise to the it came after the period when this music was first popular (the late 1750s and early 1760s).

Not only did the early 1760s prove decisive for the musical expression of terror in theatrical music, but also, by this time composers in Vienna were integrating more French elements as well. Hasse's *festa teatrale* on a text by Metastasio, *Alcide al bivio* (1760, for the wedding of Joseph II to Isabella of Bourbon-Parma) is an allegorical opera sponsored by Empress Maria Theresa.[65] Like the future emperor, the young Hercules (Alcide) must choose between two paths. The correct path of virtue is difficult, while the path of pleasure is apparently easy but deceptive. Hasse employs French pictorial devices and adapts them to the Italian idiom with considerable mastery. Raymond Monelle notes that Hasse differentiates musically between the paths of virtue and pleasure, where the latter receives "una soave armonia di flauti, e di cetere," a *sinfonia* with flutes, oboes, and *cors anglais*, in an elegant 3/4 Andantino.

62. See Monelle, "Gluck and the 'festa teatrale.'" .

63. The terms in the scores include *tremulandi, tremulo* in Naumann's *Orpheus og Eurydike*, 1786, and *tremondi* in the Berlin manuscript of *Der Stein der Weisen*, 1790.

64. Chantler, "*Sturm und Drang* Style," situates the term in the history of ideas rather than the history of musical style.

65. Facsimile ed. H. M. Brown, IO 81. Libretto, IOL 11. Metastasio's supernatural text would receive six other settings in the century, including one by Paisiello (1780). Dmitri Bortniansky's setting for Venice (1778) actually quotes Gluck's "Che farò senza Euridice?" and includes violent storm music in the minor mode (score in Lbl). Paisiello also quotes Gluck's Furies scene in *Socrate immaginario* (1775), as does Carl Ditters von Dittersdorf in his singspiel *Betrug durch Aberglauben, oder Die Schatzgräber* (text by Friedrich Eberl, KT, 3 October 1786), where a band of chimney sweeps impersonates the Furies.

Hasse deployed the "terrifying" style in scene 10, where Alcide confronts specters, genies, and monsters during an accompanied recitative. Starting in G minor, this scene has contrasting tempos, meters, and styles, including recitative, dance, instrumental interludes, and aria, all leading to the triumphal chorus at the end of the scene, when Alcide has succeeded in his trial. The scene proceeds from Alcide's opening trepidation to his encounters with various genies; the composer employs the martial style for the virtuous genies, then the pastoral style for the chorus of the genies of pleasure. The visions of pleasure suddenly yield to those of horror as a Presto begins in C major and moves to B-flat. Hasse has Alcide marvel at the horrible apparitions while changing key from B-flat to E-flat to C minor to G minor to F, as if each new vision required another key to impart its horror. Alcide describes a vapor that creates darkness as the tonality progresses from B-flat to C minor, accompanied by tremolos in the strings and continuo against a widely spaced wind chord (flutes, oboes, and horns). These three measures are marked "piano." A sudden forte occurs as the strings leap a tenth in their sixteenth-note tremolos. Alcide then describes "all the horrors of the Tartarean nights" created by Erebus. When he mentions Erebus we hear the infernal key of E-flat with more tremolos in the strings. The bass then moves from the tonic E-flat to E-natural, the leading tone of F, as Alcide notes the blackness that obscures his steps, and the tremolos and wind chords marked piano begin again. Sudden rapid string scales rise by an octave and the tonality moves to F minor as Alcide speaks of the fiery thunderbolts and shooting flames that now appear. More string bursts occur as Alcide hears shrieks around him. The key rapidly changes from F minor to C minor to G minor to D minor to F to F-sharp as he describes sphinxes, chimeras, and livid monsters. These visions evoke rapid octave-and-unison scales, string tremolos, and piercing widely spaced chords in the wind ensemble for another twenty measures of accompanied recitative.

Alcide resolves to face the threat of death and enters the flames. The key then settles back to G minor with a fanfare in the strings built from ascending triads. A Presto *sinfonia* follows with rapid string tremolos set against chords in the oboes and horns. This leads to a passage that accompanies the transformation from darkness to the illuminated Temple of Glory. A final chromatic rise in unisons and octaves introduces an F major chorus, marked "Allegro ma non troppo." The 3/8 meter and light triplets evoke the elegant "marvelous" for the virtuous hero, as the deus ex machina descends—Juno's messenger, accompanied by another graceful *sinfonia*.

In the following year Traetta set *Armida*, an *azione teatrale per musica* to a text by Giovanni Ambrogio Migliavacca and Giacomo Durazzo after Quinault (BT, 3 January 1761).[66] The overture, in D major, begins with a set of majestic ascending chords articulated by fermatas. After a long pause the Presto

---

66. I consulted the three-act version for Vienna (1780) in the manuscript in F-Pn, Mus. ms. D. 9015 (1–2). See Heartz, "Traetta in Vienna."

EXAMPLE 3.2 Tommaso Traetta, *Armida*, sinfonia

begins with a theme made up of repeated eighth-note figures (see ex. 3.2). The association of these two elements with the supernatural may have influenced Mozart's use of both in the overture to *Die Zauberflöte*, whose introduction features an episode where three supernatural ladies fall in love with an unconscious prince, just as Armida does with Rinaldo.

The score includes coloratura arias for both Armida and Rinaldo. Armida's aria "Io non cerco ed io non amo," in B-flat (act 1, scene 2), actually starts very much like the Queen of the Night's act 1 aria, another intriguing link to Mozart's singspiel. One of the most familiar marvelous scenes in Armida operas is the *scena ultima,* where the sorceress destroys her palace and flies away in her chariot. Here the scene is an accompanied recitative in E-flat, with an inserted cavatina in C minor marked "Allegro agitato." Armida's final recitative includes furious instrumental music to depict the tragic fate of the sorceress, augmented here by blasting horns.

The most vivid imagery in Traetta's next Viennese opera, Coltellini's *Ifigenia in Tauride* (1763),[67] occurs in act 2, scene 4, a scene complex built with a series of connected sections for chorus and soloist (Orestes, a castrato). Written in the infernal key of E-flat and scored with oboes, horns, strings, and continuo, the scene begins with a slow four-part chorus of Furies singing sotto voce to the sleeping Orestes. He asks what they want of him, and the chorus erupts with a violent, accusatory Allegro in the "terrifying" style, accompanied by rapid thirty-second-note string figures ("Vendetta che per gli empi riposo non v'è"). The tempo slows again as Orestes begs for pity. The key suddenly changes to D major for an Allegro strepitoso chorus, with busy imitative counterpoint for the words "tornate più implacabili a tormentarlo ognor" (return more implacably, to torment him forever). Another dejected utterance by Orestes ("Ah! Ah! perdono crudel genitore") incites the Furies once more with violent music as the scene concludes.

Gluck's Serious Operas: From azione *to "Reform Opera," 1761–67*

In the year after Traetta's *Armide,* Gluck and Calzabigi collaborated on their *azione teatrale Orfeo ed Euridice.* This and other works by Gluck, especially *Alceste,* were remarkably influential, and composers all over Europe imitated them. By the end of the century Gluck was associated with the notion of reform in eighteenth-century opera. In truth the composer had no contact with the radical French reform polemics of Diderot, Grimm, and Rousseau in the 1750s. But although Gluck did not create operatic reform, he was active at the right place and time to receive substantial credit for doing so.

Modern music history has too often defined the operatic reform of the second half of the century mainly in terms of a new style associated with Gluck and his librettist Calzabigi in the 1760s. In truth, the path they took was already laid out. Along with other reformers, they adapted older French-style tragic texts, often with substantial supernatural content. Gluck and his followers expanded the use of the orchestra; enhanced scenic effects; linked cho-

---

67. Facsimile of the Florence manuscript ed. H. M. Brown, IO 47. For a modern edition of the Furies scene see *Ausgewählte Werke vom Tommaso Traëtta* in *Denkmäler der Tonkunst in Bayern* 25, 14/1 Jahrgang, ed. Hugo Goldschmidt (Leipzig: Breitkopf und Härtel, 1914), 26–98.

rus, ensemble, instrumental music, ballet, and pantomime more closely to the
drama; and extended scene complexes. Composers replaced most of the simple
recitative with dramatically varied accompanied recitative, and they created
arias as much for dramatic efficacy as for vocal display. They also developed
multiple-affect arias with heightened dramatic expression.

But even before the so-called reform period of Gluck's operas, Jommelli
and Traetta had experimented with many of these same elements.[68] Traetta's
Ifigenia in Tauride was in fact the first serious opera in Vienna to incorporate
French elements. Gluck's own innovations actually developed from conventional sources. Bruce Brown has offered a detailed account of how Gluck's
interest in ballet and *opéra-comique* influenced his putative "reform of opera."[69]
The usual list of reform attributes cited in textbooks neglects the aspects that
the composer himself stressed. Gluck concentrated on the inner life of his characters rather than the stereotypes of traditional serious opera. He reduced textural complexity, preferring the sensual and emotive associations of sound to
intricate compositional virtuosity. His expressive range extended from the tender and touching sentiment of French comic opera to an especially explosive
and violent expression of musical terror, with broad contrasts in close proximity.[70] Gluck's musical expression of terror, first apparent in his ballets, exploited
the trombones, instruments that in the previous century had been associated
with the underworld in mythological *intermedi* and court operas but had been
used only in sacred music for the past eight decades.[71] Along with the low-
pitched strings and other wind instruments (particularly the cornett), trombones had suggested solemn or regal ceremony. There was little to distinguish
the musical writing for the trombones. Yet their low range and sonority made
them stand out. In church music composers often included three trombones to
double other parts or to act as a kind of choir in *concertato* opposition to other
groups of voices or instruments. On occasion the trombone was a solo instru-

68. Heartz, "Traetta in Vienna." Also see Haas, *Gluck und Durazzo*.

69. B. A. Brown, *Gluck and the French Theater*, 358–81.

70. Gluck's desire for dramatic continuity extended to song as well, causing him to reject the
periodic quality of Italian melody that the Piccinnists later demanded. This became the rallying
cry of his enemies, who raised the nonideological Piccinni as their ideal. For some of the primary
source writings from this paper war, see Leblond, *Mémoires*. For an analysis of the ideological
agenda behind these positions, see Isherwood, "The Third War." For a detailed discussion of the
musical aspects of the war, see Rushton, "Theory and Practice of Piccinnism."

71. Composers of Austrian church music and oratorio who used the trombone include Caldara
(for example, *Joaz*, 1726), Fux, Albrechtsberger, L. Hoffmann, Wagenseil, L. Mozart, M. Haydn,
and W. A. Mozart, among others. These composers did not use the instrument in opera, however, until after Gluck in 1760 (*Don Juan*). In Fux's religious music the instrument depicted texts
associated with death and suffering. For details, see Hanlon, "The Eighteenth-Century Trombone"; Selfridge-Field, "The Viennese Court Orchestra"; van der Meer, *Fux als Opernkomponist*;
and Winkler, "Die Bedeutung des Posaune."

ment with varying degrees of virtuosity. But Gluck's trombone writing both suggests the traditional solemnity of the underworld and enhances the expression of terror, surpassing the intensity of any of his predecessors.

Trombones and cornetts are rare in surviving opera scores from the 150 years between Monteverdi's *L'Orfeo* and Gluck's Viennese stage music of the 1760s, though they were certainly present in Viennese church music and oratorio. Perhaps these instruments were more common in Hadean scenes of *feste teatrali* than the surviving documentation would suggest. German translations of the Bible often associate the trombone with the last judgment (*letzte Posaune*), and the "Tuba mirum" of the Dies irae chant in the Requiem mass was an image of terror. Unfortunately we have little evidence of these instruments outside German-speaking areas. Were they present but not specified? Horn or trumpet players may well have doubled on trombones without being identified as trombonists. Court records in Vienna between 1698 and 1741 reveal the names of a dozen hired court trombonists,[72] and composers such as Fux, Georg Matthias Monn, Balthasar Schmid, Georg Reutter, Leopold Hoffmann, Johann Ernst Eberlin, Leopold Mozart, Johann Georg Albrechtsberger, and František Tůma used trombones in their sacred music. But we do not find the instruments in their secular compositions of this period.

Gluck continued to associate certain keys with the supernatural, especially those that accommodate his wind combinations. B-flat is one of the keys found in invocation or incantation scenes (where it was also used by Anfossi and Mozart), E-flat for infernal scenes, and D minor, G minor, and C minor for demonic force, death, and tempests.

❋

Although Gluck frequently borrowed from his own music, he composed an entirely new setting for *Orfeo ed Euridice*, Ranieri de' Calzabigi's three-act *azione teatrale per musica* (Vienna, 5 October 1762).[73] The extensive supernatural effects begin at the end of act 1, when Orpheus implores the gods in an accompanied recitative, then vanishes amid lightning and thunder. Twelve measures of furious instrumental stage-machine music for strings depict this event, with rapid sixteenth-note octave-and-unison figures, repeated notes, and sweeping arpeggios.

Act 2 of *Orfeo* begins in the underworld as somber dotted *coups d'archets* introduce the opening *ballo* in E-flat, a free Maestoso in alla breve meter (𝄵) for strings, oboes, and horns. This leads to a three-measure harp solo using simple arpeggios as Orpheus plays his lyre. A terrifying chorus of monsters and Furies in C minor suddenly erupts (marcato 3/4), with a ternary *ballo* in C minor interpolated into the chorus. Repeated slurred string figures

---

72. Hanlon, "The Eighteenth-Century Trombone," 1:55.

73. Gluck, *Sämtliche Werke*, Abt. 1, Bd. 1.

depict the howling of hell's multiheaded guard dog Cerberus in the text. Although such texts commonly evoked vivid musical depiction, Gluck's supernatural musical imagery would become the most common model for future underworld scenes.[74] The *ballo* returns, leading to the harp solo that now provides the accompaniment to the song of Orpheus, with interjections by the defiant chorus accompanied by cornett, two trombones, and two violin parts producing hellish bellowing and repeated figures: ♪ . Further short aria-like segments alternate with the increasingly soft choruses as Orpheus pacifies the monsters and Furies with his singing. The scene then changes to a pastoral locale, where an elegant F major *ballo* (in the Parisian version this is the "Air des ombres heureuses") and Orpheus's arioso-like accompanied recitative with chorus "Che puro ciel" set a calmer and more rustic mood.

In Gluck's next work for the stage, *Telemaco, ossia L'isola di Circe* (BT, 30 January 1765), a two-act *dramma per musica* by Coltellini after Carlo Sigismondo Capece,[75] the composer employed a number of noteworthy devices for the supernatural episodes. In act 1 he gave the oracle a chantlike intonation with string accompaniment, and he distinguished the sorceress Circe by a powerful aria, "Se per entro alla nera foresta." This aria was based on Sofonisba's aria "La sul margine di Lete" from *Sofonisba* (1744). Gluck had previously recycled this music twice, first for Zeus's aria "Saprò dalle procelle" in *Le nozze d'Ercole e d'Ebe* (1747), then for Vitella's aria "Getta il nocchier talora" in *La clemenza di Tito* (1752). He would use this music once again for the conjuring duet with Hidraot and Armide (act 2, scene 2), "Esprits de haine et de rage," in *Armide* (1777).[76] This stunning coloratura display piece became a model for later invocation arias. To contrast with the coloratura, Gluck accompanied the bold and simple melodic vocal phrases with running parallel thirds. Sforzato wind blasts with octave-and-unison motives add to Circe's emphatic pronouncements. One segment of this aria may have inspired a similar episode in the second section of Mozart's second aria for the Queen of the Night in *Die Zauberflöte*. Both have running parallel thirds in the orchestra while the vocal line unfolds in bold and simple melodic lines; wind sforzando blasts and octave-and-unison motives add emphasis. At the end of *Telemaco* Circe transforms the scene into a desert as she flies away in her chariot, invoking a chorus of demons and singing in a kind of recitation. Once again Gluck repeats a chord three times to signal an otherworldly force, as he did in the ballet *Sémiramis* (1765) and would do again in the opera *Iphigénie en Tauride*.

Gluck's remarkable achievement, the three-act *tragedia Alceste*, to a text by

74. Mozart possibly drew upon this model when he set his underworld tableau in *Die Zauberflöte* (act 2, scene 28).

75. Modern edition in Gluck, *Sämtliche Werke*, Abt. I, Bd. 2.

76. For a detailed discussion and list of Gluck's self-borrowings, see Hortschansky, *Parodie und Entlehnung*, 88–100, 188–91.

Calzabigi (BT, 16 December 1767),[77] deserves its place as an important milestone in opera history. More than any earlier work, *Alceste* fully exploits the expressive innovations of the last two decades, breaking down the traditional boundaries between the supernatural world of the *azione teatrale* and the humanistic goals of reform *dramma per musica*. The opera has several supernatural episodes. The trombones in the overture suggest the otherworld, and scene 4 of act 1 is an invocation for the *gran sacerdote* set for three trombones, bassoons, and horns. A solemn march introduces the oracle, which sings in chantlike intonation accompanied by three trombones, oboes, bassoons, and strings. The oracle then calls forth the backstage chorus of basses with the same otherworldly orchestration as in act 1, scene 4, leading to Alceste's great supernatural invocation aria, "Ombre, larve," with its *alla zoppa* syncopation, triadic bass figures, sforzandos, and fluid series of changing affects.[78]

Act 2 commences with Alceste entering a dark forest to meet the deities of the underworld. Here Gluck evokes the solemn, ceremonial Hades of early Italian *intermedi* and opera. An underworld unison chorus responds to Alceste by chanting a D minor monotone recitation on a unison bass tonic note. The spirits appear and surround Alceste, intoning their hypnotic recitation in a dramatic exchange. The chorus "Dunque vieni" continues the unison vocal sonority, but now with melodic leaps accompanied by rapid string scales punctuated by dotted unison motives on a single pitch in the brass. She entreats the gods with an elegant and poignant aria, "Non vi turbate," whose restrained expression continues for the following infernal pantomime. When the underworld deities return in act 3, they again sing a unison chorus. Gluck accompanied Apollo's appearance in a cloud chariot with magic entry music in G major, a marchlike Andante for flutes, oboes, horns, bassoons, and strings that recalls the traditional "marvelous" of French opera.

✳

Gluck's contemporaries were also developing new techniques, though they were usually employed in more limited ways. Eleven months before *Alceste* another Bohemian master of this period, Josef Mysliveček, set underworld and Olympian scenes in Giuseppe Bonechi's *dramma per musica Il Bellerofonte* (Naples, 20 January 1767).[79] In this operatic version of the myth of Perseus, Bellerophon encounters a test of his resolve in the second act (scene 9), when he confronts monsters in the dark forest near the seashore. This episode, rendered as a Maestoso accompanied recitative in the infernal key of E-flat, has descriptive instrumental music for oboes, horns, and strings to depict terrify-

77. *Alceste (Wiener Fassung 1767)*, in Gluck, *Sämtliche Werke*, Abt. 1, Bd. 3.

78. Franz Xaver Gerl imitated this aria in his "In finstrer Höhlenkluft verschlossen," sung by the evil spirit Eutifronte in *Der Stein der Weisen* (Vienna, 1790). See chapter 5 for details.

79. I consulted the manuscript in F-Pn, D. 8199-8200 ("Napoli 1769").

ing visions. A "horrifying nimbus" receives an E minor Allegro segment with thirty-second-note figuration, and an allusion to trembling has rapid staccato repeated notes. After his large-scale multipartite aria of resolve, Bellerophon asks for divine help in another vivid accompanied recitative. His answer appears in the form of "divine" instrumental music, an elegant F major Andante marked "sempre sotto voce" and scored for two flutes and strings with triplet motives in the accompaniment. Minerva magically appears with her chorus to the sound of this music.

Unlike *Il Bellerofonte*, *Orfeo ed Euridice*, and *Alceste*, many contemporary mythological operas in Vienna, Naples, and Stuttgart did not differentiate the natural from the supernatural realm, or divine from mortal characters. In this sense these operas are throwbacks to the seventeenth century, when the presence of music alone signaled divine characters and events. Florian Leopold Gassmann's *Amore e Psiche*, another Coltellini court spectacle, comes between Gluck's *Telemaco* and *Alceste* (BT, 5 October 1767).[80] The opera has only two mortal characters (one of whom will become divine), and the action is almost entirely supernatural. Although the colorful, woodwind-rich score betrays the influence of Gluck, the music evinces no contrast between the divine and natural spheres; magical transformations occur in unremarkable recitative.

Jommelli's setting of Verazi's *Fetonte* (Stuttgart, 11 February 1768) is an even more conservative score, with numerous exit arias.[81] Although Jommelli also chose not to distinguish the divine from the mortal, he accompanied a few of the transformations with evocative stage-machine music. The first scene change begins with terrifying underground rumbling, the collapse of the sacred altar at Tethys's cavern, and the chaotic scattering of priests. D minor yields to D major as a long crescendo passage with sustained notes in the horns, flutes, and oboes commences the bustling thirty-bar sonic image of magical transformation to the lush realm of the marine Titaness, depicted with elegant triplet and ornamental figures. Act 3, scene 6 has Phaeton riding in Helios's chariot, igniting the skies with a fire that soon spreads to the earth. This long accompanied-recitative segment, part of the impressive ensemble finale, has passages of instrumental music to suggest Phaeton's ride, the spread of the swirling flames, a deep vortex, and Jupiter hurling his thunderbolt to strike down Phaeton and plunge the chariot and horses into the sea. In this segment Jommelli shows himself a master of dramatic recitative closely coordinated to the supernatural events on the stage. Haydn would develop this resource even further, and in both comic and serious genres.

80. Verazi's text was adapted from Villati's libretto (Berlin, 1753), which was taken from Ovid's account of Phaeton (*Metamorphoses*, II). Facsimile of the Naples manuscript, IO 87.

81. *Fetonte: Dramma per musica* in *Denkmäler deutscher Tonkunst*, 1. Folge, Bd. 32–33, ed. Hermann Abert (Leipzig, 1907); 2nd ed., ed. Hans J. Moser (Graz and Wiesbaden: Breitkopf & Härtel, 1958), 2 vols.

Dramma per musica, 1770–79

The influence of the Franco-Italian synthesis became pervasive during the 1770s, and Gluck's works were particularly admired. Marco Coltellini adapted Calzabigi's *azione Orfeo ed Euridice* as a *tragedia* in three acts, with new music by Antonio Tozzi (Munich, 1775) modeled after Gluck.[82] Although Tozzi employed many of the same devices that Gluck did, such as the barking of Cerberus, his is a more conventional "number opera," with coloratura arias and simple recitative. The underworld scene (act 2, scene 6) begins not in the E-flat of Gluck's Hades but in Handel's "magic" key of E major. Ferdinando Bertoni also set Calzabigi's *Orfeo ed Euridice* as a three-act *dramma per musica* (Venice, 1776), and it enjoyed considerable success.[83] Bertoni's score has numerous parallels to Gluck's, but the brass instruments, flutes, chalumeaux, English horns, and bassoons are absent here. The vocal writing is more florid and demanding, and the effects of the "marvelous" are more subdued.

Although history has favored Gluck, other skilled composers enjoyed sustained success as well. Consider that Traetta's *Ifigenia in Tauride* was produced in Italy as often as Gluck's *Orfeo* or *Alceste*. Certain Italian courts in fact industriously pursued new operas, particularly those based on mythology and epic romance. For example, the Florentine court of Archduke Leopold of Austria staged the latest operas from a variety of locales. Traetta's *Ifigenia in Tauride* (1767) was soon followed by *I Tindaridi* (1777) and Gluck's *Orfeo ed Euridice* (1771). Antonio Sacchini's *Armida* was mounted in 1772, as was Jommelli's in 1775. Florence produced De Gamerra and Sacchini's *Perseo e Andromeda* (London, 1774) in 1775 with new music by Giuseppe Gazzaniga. Francesco Bianchi set Frugoni's libretto *Castore e Poluce* (*I Tindaridi*) in 1779. The court staged a *pasticcio* on Coltellini's *Amore e Psiche* in 1780, and Bianchi set Gaetano Casori's new libretto *Venere e Adone* in 1781. In 1786 Angelo Tarchi set Coltellini's *Ifigenia in Tauride* for Florence, and in 1787 Gluck's *Alceste* was finally produced there. In the 1780s the repertory of Milan (where the Habsburgs also ruled), long a city with conservative Italian tastes, began adopting similar operas, as did some theaters in Venice, Naples, and other locales.[84]

---

82. Ms. in F-Pn, Rés. 1818 (1–3), and D-Mbs, Mus. Mss. 2592. Tozzi also set a number of other comic and serious supernatural operas. His *Il paese della Cuccagna* (Bologna, 1771) is lost; his *Rinaldo* (Venice, 1775) is discussed below. Two of Tozzi's magic operas were composed for Barcelona: *Lo scherzo della magia, ossia La casa incantata* (1785) and *Zemira ed Azor* (probably 1791, on a libretto attributed to Da Ponte and based on Marmontel).

83. See S. Hansell, "Ferdinando Bertoni's Setting." The score was printed in Venice c. 1776. For a facsimile see *Bibliotheca musica Bononiensis*, sezione 4, n. 5 (Bologna: Forni, 1970). The work was performed in Padua and London, as well as other Italian and German cities.

84. See McClymonds, "Opera Reform in Italy," and "The Role of Innovation." For a full appreciation of the dissemination of Franco-Italian opera in this period see Sartori, *I libretti italiana*, 1:3–223.

Paisiello and Mozart's generation (c. 1760–91) brought still more dramatic and violent expression into serious opera while employing all of the accoutrements of the "marvelous."[85] In the 1770s and 1780s *Armida* operas became more common in Italy. Fairy-tale material also made its way into Italian opera, again through French influence. Later Italian comic opera and especially the shorter genre of the *farsa* adapted the latest comic French material, some of it supernatural, to the Italian idiom. By the 1780s the striving for greater theatrical verisimilitude meant violence depicted on the stage and more extreme musical expression,[86] evident in music for *ombra* scenes, where a character imagines the presence of a ghost.[87]

Armida *and* Rinaldo *in the 1770s*

Among the most frequently staged opera texts of the 1770s were those derived from the story of Armida and her tragic love for Rinaldo.[88] Composers particularly favored librettos by Jacopo Durandi (*Armida*) and Francesci Saverio De Rogatis (*Armida abbandonata*). At least five scenes in these texts have supernatural content: the arrival of transformed spirits of Armida as Rinaldo sleeps (act 2); the encounter with Armida's seductive representative (often Zemira or Ismene); Ubaldo's use of a magic shield to destroy the spirits that hold Rinaldo captive; Rinaldo's dramatic encounter in Armida's enchanted garden, where he must resist his feelings of love for the sorceress and destroy the magic plant that sustains her power; and, if there is no *lieto fine* in the libretto, the final destruction by Armida of her palace, followed by her flying away in a chariot pulled by fire-breathing dragons. Composers developed special musical devices for these episodes. Pasquale Anfossi set Durandi's *Armida* (Turin, 1770) using extensive coloratura for both supernatural and mortal characters.[89] Anfossi's instrumental music for magic scenes is more distinctive, particularly the two instances of *orrida armonia* in act 1. These scenes have descriptive *sinfonias* (perhaps staged as pantomimes) for strings, horns, oboes, and bassoons, reminiscent of those by the composers that created the Franco-Italian synthesis. Simple harmonies highlight the string tremolos, piercing interjections for the wind instruments, and rapid sweeping string figures. A second *orrida armonia*, with similar effects, follows. For the sleep scene (act 2, scene 9) Anfossi provides a sensual serenade-like Adagio for strings, marked "dolce" (see ex. 3.3). The static tonic pedal in the bass and the lulling thirds in the violins suggest

---

85. See McClymonds and Heartz, "Opera Seria."

86. See McClymonds, "'La morte di Semiramide.'"

87. See K. Hansell, "Opera and Ballet," 289–303, 1017–51.

88. Note that Cimarosa's *L'Armida immaginaria* (1777), however, was not based on Tasso but is instead a comedy without any supernatural material. For a discussion of Armida librettos from this period, see McClymonds, "Haydn and the Opera Seria Tradition."

89. I consulted the manuscript in F-Pn, Musique, Vm⁴ 42.

EXAMPLE 3.3 Pasquale Anfossi, *Armida*, act 2, scene 9

soporific expression. At the conclusion of act 3 Armida invokes the Furies in an accompanied recitative. Although the vocal line seems unremarkable, the accompaniment is highly expressive, with rapid sixteenth- and thirty-second-note figures, tremolos, and repeated notes, along with blaring horns and oboes to suggest the inferno. Furious stage-machine music in D major accompanies the sorceress as she flies off in her chariot. Anfossi deployed sustained notes in the horns and a pulsing bass to support the initial descending figures in the violins and violas (describing the flight of Armida?), which then play rapid tremolos against the final ascending scale in the bass.

Jommelli's setting of Saverio De Rogatis's *Armida abbandonata* (Naples, 1770, with revivals in Naples, Florence, and Lisbon) was successful if somewhat old-fashioned.[90] The magic episodes start with Rinaldo's act 1 encounter with Armida's seductive nymphs. They dance a *ciaccona*, interrupted by his comments in simple recitative. The end of act 2 shows Armida destroying her palace with thunder and lightning, then flying off in her chariot, pulled by winged dragons. The music for this scene includes instrumental passages, accompanied recitative, and an aria. After her coloratura aria "Odio, furor, dis-

90. Facsimile ed. Weimer, IO 91. I also consulted the manuscript in F-Pn, Mus. ms. D. 6218. These sources have the name Rambaldo instead of Rinaldo. In a letter to his sister from Naples dated 5 June 1770, Mozart wrote that the opera was beautiful but too elaborate, serious, and old-fashioned for the modern theater. He was not specific about what was old-fashioned here, but when compared to Gluck and Traetta, this score seems tame in affect and dominated by arias. The four brief choruses are mainly homophonic, with some short segments of polyphony. The small orchestra (oboes, horns, and strings) and single vocal ensemble may have seemed old-fashioned to the audience. The scene complexes, with their series of short contrasting segments, belong more to the realm of midcentury *feste* than to newer operas such as Gluck's *Alceste* and De Majo's *Adriano in Siria*. In a personal communication (February 2006) Marita McClymonds suggested to me that Jommelli's elaborate accompaniments, which change for each line of poetry, may have seemed dated to the audience.

petto," Armida summons the Furies in two sections of accompanied recitative, the first in a kind of coda to the aria, "Udite o furie," accompanied by strings. Here Armida sings descending octaves as she calls on the deities to listen (*udite*) and come to her command (*venite*). Her second summons, "Ecco Aletto e Meggera," is a recitative in D minor with horns, oboes, and strings that concludes the act. The piece traverses several keys, notably E-flat for the infernal imagery of the text, conveyed as well with rapid string figuration and blasts of the winds. She calls for her chariot and abducts Rinaldo. A twenty-measure *sinfonia* in D major, with rapid ascending scales, dotted figures, and arpeggios, suggests the sorceress's escape.

For Rinaldo's encounter in Armida's enchanted forest (act 3, scenes 5–6), Jommelli employed similar accompanied recitative, with cavatinas for Rinaldo and Armida and four extremely brief choral segments. A Larghetto affettuoso in D major with an oboe solo suggests the "sweet scent carried by the breeze" and the singing of birds. The scene is musically unremarkable until Rinaldo notices the monsters, at which point the sharps in the key suddenly turn to flats for a terrifying chorus of monsters in C minor using octave-and-unison sonority, descending octaves in the two vocal lines (tenor and bass), loud sustained notes on wind instruments, marcato passages, and brisk string scales. The second short chorus is in E-flat with the same sonority and descending octaves in the vocal lines. The knight then locates the magic myrtle and dispatches Armida and her specters in a short accompanied-recitative segment, a bright Allegro in D major.

Critics had high praise for Salieri's setting of Coltellini's *Armida* for Vienna in 1771,[91] and a revised score with a German translation of the text was even printed in 1783. Salieri described his opera as a spectacle "di stile magico-eroico-amoroso toccante il tragico."[92] The Franco-Italian synthesis and the influence of Gluck are apparent in the dances and choruses integrated into scene complexes and in the programmatic overture, scored for three trombones, horns, oboes, bassoons, and strings. The overture begins with a slow introduction in C minor, and leads to a C major Allegro, an Allegro assai, a Presto in G major, and a final triple-meter Andantino grazioso in C major. Salieri described these passages as making up a pantomimic prelude, with the introduction depicting the knight Ubaldo's arrival on Armida's magic island amid a thick fog, the ensuing Allegro representing the attacking monsters, and the following Allegro assai suggesting the effect of Ubaldo's magic shield as it repels the monsters. The concluding Andantino grazioso depicts the "delightful

---

91. Different versions of the opera appear in the print in F-Pn, Vm⁴ 446; the German translation and piano reduction edited by Carl F. Cramer (Leipzig: Breitkopf 1783); and the manuscript in F-Pn, D.13.587 (1–2). For details on this opera see Rice, *Antonio Salieri and Viennese Opera*, 162–75. McClymonds, "Salieri and the Franco-Italian Synthesis," also provides new research on this opera.

92. Angermüller, *Antonio Salieri*, 1:29.

tranquil serenity" of the island.[93] Salieri scored the choruses of demons with three trombones, oboes, bassoons, and strings.

Salieri's modulations enhance the expressive imagery of his *Armida*, particularly in the magical transformations, most of which occur in the recitatives (all accompanied). In act 1 the sorceress Ismene conjures Armida's demons with ungainly vocal leaps, including an ascending tenth, accompanied with octave-and-unison sonority. The ensuing scene transformation is reflected in the change from E minor to C-sharp minor as the demons arrive and sing in two unison parts with oboes, three trombones, bassoons, and strings. The "infernal" octave-and-unison accompaniment features rapid ascending scales in the violins and bass, with tremolos in the strings. The demons sing in a unison declamatory phrase, "Strazzia le fiere Eumenidi, strugga la fiamma ultrice l'incanto," as rapid ascending sixteenth-note scales seem to explode in the strings and bass. Ubaldo shows them that he has no fear, casting the demons into the air with a magic wand as the key changes from E to G to D minor in his recitative reply. Starting in the key of D minor and modulating to B-flat major, they sing a terrifying chorus, "Qual sibilo orrendo per l'aere rimbomba," with violent accompaniment of winds (including two trombones) and string tremolos. All this supports the homophonic vocal parts, with their limited range and repeated notes. Rapid descending scales in the violins and bass suggest the combat that leads to Ubaldo's triumph.

Salieri reserved his most violent music for the end of act 3, a large scene complex in which the furious Armida creates a wild storm and has her spirits (a chorus) destroy the palace. Oboes, bassoon, three trombones, and strings accompany her recitative, with descending chromatic motives and rapid thirty-second-note figures. Salieri added horns to her final aria, "Io con voi la nera face," an Allegro assai in B-flat, with a long introductory ritornello and an extended crescendo to depict her escape in the flying chariot. Octave leaps and rapid repeated notes in sextuplet rhythms lead to the repeated cadences that end the opera.

In his setting of Durandi's *Armida* for Milan just a year later, in 1772,[94] Antonio Sacchini seems to hark back to sacred polyphony by integrating complex polyphonic textures in the choruses. The act 3 chorus of magicians and priests (TTB), a Maestoso in C minor and alla breve meter, has a contrapuntal instrumental introduction with baroque-style suspensions. Sacchini generated his material through old-fashioned sequences; the segment ends with a long cadential section in octave sonority (see ex. 3.4). The triumphant final chorus of Furies in G major (SATB), an Allegro giusto with horns, oboes, and strings, employs imitative polyphony with similar suspensions. Among the instrumental

---

93. For details see Rice, *Antonio Salieri and Viennese Opera*, 162–75.

94. Manuscript in F-Pn, D. 13552[(1–3)] (without the overture). The work was thoroughly revised as *Rinaldo* in London in 1780 and as *Renaud* in Paris, 1783 (libretto by Pellegrin and Leboeuf), an unsuccessful performance subvented by Sacchini's Austrian patron, Marie Antoinette.

numbers is a *terribile* Allegro in C minor with rapid scales and tremolos (some with rising triadic figures) in the strings and sustained oboes and horns. A variety of short, rapid figures in the violins and bass add to the fantastic effect of this *sinfonia tetra*. The piece ends with a long crescendo passage that gradually rises in tessitura before beginning a seven-measure descent.

Some *Armida* operas seem tame in comparison to the one just described. Yet even an old-fashioned setting such as Johann Gottlieb Naumann's *Armida* (Padua, then Venice, 1773),[95] with its numerous da capo arias and duets, would prove influential in the handling of certain magical effects. Widely performed in Italian and German lands, *Armida* made conspicuous use not only of trumpets and timpani (unusual in Italian operas of the day), but particularly of the woodwinds. Naumann set the enchantment scene in act 1 with elegant wind music for offstage clarinets, horns, and bassoons. This effect would turn up again in numerous operas. Antonio Tozzi's score for the three-act *dramma*, *Il Rinaldo* (Venice, 1775),[96] uses similar instrumentation. Rinaldo's last aria, "Dei pietosi in tal cimento," has rapid ascending string scales at the words "Ch'io sento sia viltade osia timor" and string tremolos for the text "O pur timor." Mysliveček's setting of Migliavacca's *Armida* (1778) emphasizes coloratura arias for Armida.[97] Her bravura aria "Io non cerco ed io non amo" is an Allegro in B-flat, with *alla zoppa* syncopation, rapid figuration, and triadic themes (act 1, scene 3). The composer also deployed the terrifying musical style in recitative, with string tremolos (act 1, scene 8, Idraote's scene). In act 2, scene 6, a Furies chorus appears singing "Fuggi Amore d'Armida nel seno." Mysliveček scored this Larghetto in E-flat (3/8) with horns, and the thirty-second-note figuration leads to a violent Allegro section.

Dramma per musica, 1780–91

Composers of Italian supernatural opera in the 1780s expanded techniques developed in the previous decades. Haydn, Traetta, and Naumann, for example, typically set the most dramatic episodes as large scene complexes, combining various forces and genres to create dramatic continuity and tension. These composers also employed new expressive devices for supernatural events, particularly in the harmony and instrumental accompaniment of expansive obbligato recitative. The more substantial orchestral forces of this period provided

95. Libretto by Giovanni Bertati. The opera was also staged in Prague (1776), and Vienna (1777), then translated into German and performed in Leipzig, Dresden, Berlin, and Breslau. Manuscripts in A-Wgm (German translation, shelfmark IV 16565 H 29236) and D-B (Mus. ms. 15961), as well as two (damaged) in D-Dlb (Mus. 3480-F-10 and F-10a).

96. The libretto, by J. Durandi and F. De Rogatis, after Bertati, would also serve Haydn. Score in A-Wgm, IV 1983 H2947.

97. A manuscript score is preserved in F-Pn, D. 8196-8198 (3 vols.), but the conclusion of the opera is lost. Mysliveček also wrote an earlier sorceress opera, *La Circe,* for Venice in 1779. The music appears to be lost.

composers with the tools for imaginative exploration of timbre as an expressive device. These observations also hold true for some varieties of comic opera. In fact, large-scale comic opera would achieve equal footing with serious opera after about 1785, a significant new development in itself. Magic and supernatural events seem to have called for the same musical and expressive devices even in different genres.

Techniques for creating supernatural scenes appear not to be associated with specific cities or locales: they are common currency for composers of Italian opera, whether in German, Austrian, or Italian areas. Although most composers seem to have had access to the same repertory of compositional techniques and devices, their application is a measure of the skill and craft of the individual composer.

Mythology and Epic Romance in Italian Opera after 1780

Older librettos featuring scenes with magic continued to be recycled with new music in this decade. Thus Paisiello set Metastasio's *Alcide al bivio* for St. Petersburg (1780),[98] apparently influenced by the precepts in Gluck's *Alceste*.[99] A more thoroughgoing adoption of new techniques is exemplified by Bertoni's score of the opera seria *Armida abbandonata* (Vitturi's adaptation of the libretto by Durandi, Venice, 1780),[100] in which the composer borrowed Jommelli's approach by integrating dance and instrumental music into the action. Its incantation scene in act 2 (scene 6) is rather brief, as Armida calls forth the Furies and her monsters in a fifteen-measure recitative marked "Allegro assai" with *tremolandi* figures in the string accompaniment. On the other hand, Rinaldo's episode in the horrid grove (act 3, scene 3) is a large scene complex with short instrumental segments, dances, arias, and accompanied recitative (Bertoni uses dances where Jommelli had choral sections). Bertoni begins this episode with an instrumental introduction in the traditional infernal key of E-flat as Rinaldo enters the enchanted forest. The music builds from a soft opening to a terrifying climax with furious scales, *alla zoppa* syncopation, tremolos, and blasts of the horns with oboes. Rinaldo readies himself to encounter the monsters, and the key changes from E-flat to C minor, as a Larghetto marks his arrival at a murmuring brook. Rinaldo hears a "celestial sound," and the key changes to D major for an elegant sostenuto segment expressing the seductive

---

98. Manuscript scores in B-Bc and GB-Lbl.

99. Paisiello's *Fedra*, to a text by Luigi Salvioni after Frugoni's *Ippolito ed Aricia* (Naples, 1788) also included an underworld scene and the appearance of a sea monster. (Sebastiano Nasolini set the same libretto for Florence in 1790 as *Teseo a Stige*.)

100. Manuscripts are preserved in D-B, shelfmark KHM 319, D-Mbs, Mus. Ms. 20881 (dated 1781). Hollis, "Bertoni, Ferdinando," 1:455, states that Bertoni had composed an earlier *Armida* (Venice 1746) and cites the later Munich score erroneously. There appears to be no surviving score for the earlier opera.

powers of illusion. The nymphs appear with an Allegretto in G major, which becomes the basis of their dance. Armida enters and, in a recitative and cavatina, attempts to stop Rinaldo. The key returns to E-flat for Rinaldo's recitative, wherein the knight reacts to the frightening appearance of the Furies. The score indicates "terribile tremulandi" accompanied by a flurry of scale figures. A *ballo* for the Furies in E-flat follows, with string tremolos, descending triadic motives in dotted rhythms, and sixteenth-note ascending scales. One further marvelous transformation occurs when Rinaldo destroys the magic plant. The key changes from C minor to C major as the specters and Furies flee to the sound of sixteenth-note string figures.

Luigi Cherubini set the same adaptation of *Armida abbandonata* (Florence, 1782),[101] employing an even larger orchestra with five-part strings (two violas), winds, and timpani. Cherubini displays his mastery of musical terror in act 3, scene 4, a large scene complex with accompanied recitative, an aria, and a *ballo di furie* in D minor using rapid string figuration, loud horns, diminished chords, and *alla zoppa* syncopation. By contrast, Cimarosa's setting of Domenico Perelli's *dramma per musica La Circe* for Milan's La Scala in 1783 is mainly a number opera, with pictorial and supernatural devices employed for accompaniment in arias and accompanied recitative.[102]

Nunziato Porta probably arranged the libretto for Haydn's *Armida,* a three-act *dramma eroica* and the last opera he would compose for Eszterháza (26 February 1783).[103] The opera proved popular and was performed fifty-four times in the next five years, especially outside of Eszterháza. For this reason, and because of its intrinsic merits, it warrants detailed consideration. The initial *sinfonia* signals the main musical themes in the score. Its Allegretto section in B-flat will return in act 3, scene 2, during the scene in the enchanted grove (here in D major), along with a brief *terribile* section in D minor. As is the case with his earlier operas, arias dominate the score. By contrast with that of his contemporaries, Haydn's harmony and accompaniment for the expression of the text is, like Mozart's, often unusually original and inventive. Here his settings of three solo scenes for Armida most clearly demonstrate his considerable skill. The most dramatic of these episodes is her act 2, scene 7 accompanied recitative "Barbaro, e ardisci ancor," which leads to the E minor aria "Odio, furor, dispetto, dolor," the only minor-key aria in the opera. Marked "Presto assai" and in common time, it is a kind of infuriated incantation, with repeated motives portraying both anger and the supernatural with unison and octave sonorities, tremolos, short scalar bursts in the bass, and rapid triplet or quadruplet figures propelling the rhythm forward. Her sustained high notes over these turbulent accompaniment figures and even longer seventh chords in the

101. I consulted the manuscript score in F-Pn, D. 1964–65.

102. I consulted the manuscript score in F-Pn, D. 2083–85. Act 3 (D. 2085) is incomplete.

103. For a study on this opera and the lineage of Italian opera based on Durandi and De Rogatis composites, see McClymonds, "Haydn and His Contemporaries."

winds express an idea in the text: "ho cento smanie al cor" (I have a hundred frenzies in my heart). This line is repeated an inordinate nine times in the first part of the aria alone.

Act 3, scenes 2–3 of Haydn's *Armida* make up a long scene complex in the grove where Rinaldo has arrived to cut the magic myrtle tree, the source of Armida's power. This substantial traditional episode employs a free-fantasy style and ingenious harmonic planning. It begins with Rinaldo's recitative depicting the natural and supernatural (e.g., monsters) sights of the grove through orchestral figures and unusual harmonic changes. Haydn nicely integrated arias, arioso, and pantomime into the scene, and thus this segment of the opera owes much to the reforms promulgated by Gluck and like-minded composers. The mimetic language even seems reminiscent of Vivaldi, whose music Haydn particularly admired. Starting with a Largo in E-flat, the long introductory *sinfonia* sets an anxious tone as forte chords are answered by soft consequent phrases. A cadential passage follows, with rapid violin scales and steady sixteenth-note accompaniment. When Rinaldo goes to cut the tree there is a deceptive cadence followed by a long passage of harmonic ambiguity, dissonance, and enharmonic change from E-flat to D. Whirling motives in D minor begin, and Rinaldo sings of a sweet fragrance that swirls around him. He notices that he is weakening in his resolve, and a new *sinfonia* begins in D major, an Andante in triple meter. First heard in the overture, this simple and elegant yet captivating illusory music stops when Rinaldo resolves not to waver and steps forward to cut the tree. The nymph Zelmira now sings an aria in G in the same elegant style.

After Rinaldo's accompanied recitative and Armida's aria ("Ah non ferir"), the next recitative modulates through related keys to D minor and a fortissimo Presto instrumental segment. Here the score indicates that Armida makes signs with her wand and causes the scene to darken. She leaves Rinaldo after transforming the grove into the inferno. A magical Presto in D minor, marked by musical terror, suggests infernal imagery. The initial *alla ẓoppo* syncopated figure in the horns alternates with sustained infernal blasts set against fortissimo string tremolos and rising rapid fortissimo scales in the flutes, bassoons, violins, and basses. A fully diminished G-sharp chord is heard as the tremolos begin, and the harmonic motion quickens, moving by fifths with a series of fully diminished seventh chords. This segment continues as the key modulates first to A minor, then to E minor. The harmonic rhythm increases until a Neapolitan sixth chord commences the cadence. Haydn writes ascending scale figures to move the tonality back to D minor as Rinaldo resumes his recitative. He cries out in shock as the opening music of the Presto *sinfonia* is repeated. The sudden key changes and string tremolos seem to occasion his comment "Qual orribile suon" (What a horrible sound), and a stretto of short rapid ascending figures is heard in the winds and strings as the Furies repel his attack on the myrtle, pursuing him with rapid thirty-second-note motives in the accompaniment. The harmonic progression becomes unstable once again in this accompanied recitative in the free-fantasy style. When E-flat is reached Rinaldo exclaims his horror with diminished chords outlined in rapid octave-and-unison figures, and the tonality shifts to B-flat minor, then C minor. In the ensuing Presto he expresses his terror at the sight of the Furies, with infernal allusions in the accompaniment.

Now Rinaldo describes visions of hell as the keys quickly modulate from E-flat to F minor to G minor in the next accompanied recitative. As G minor moves back to E-flat, the hero regains his courage; he cuts the myrtle just when the E-flat is reached and an ascending scale is played in the strings. Rinaldo fights the Furies to the sound of a fully diminished leading-tone seventh chord against that same ascending E-flat scale in the bass, and this alternates with the tonic harmony as the combat ends and the scene changes to the Crusaders' camp. A diminuendo then reduces the dynamics to piano as the ascending scales and repeated notes play against the sustained E-flat chord. Three simple tonic chords in quarter notes, separated by quarter-note rests, suggest the transformation back to the reality of Rinaldo's world.

Another impressive work on the *Armida* theme is Giuseppe Sarti's setting of Coltellini's *dramma per musica Armida e Rinaldo* for St. Petersburg in 1786.[104] Scored for a large orchestra with clarinets, it deploys a variety of styles and capitalizes on the supernatural themes. Sarti's overture seems to allude to the "marvelous," with its rapid scale passages in the strings and the bass and its *alla ʒoppa* syncopation. Allusions to French pictorialism appear with the *rumor sotterraneo*, repeated three times in the overture, which forecasts its recurrence later in the opera. Supernatural scenes include act 1, scene 3, where Ismene summons his demons with his wand in a recitative accompanied with rapid scales. There follows a D minor "Coro di demoni" in the *terribile* style, with string tremolos, bursts of scales, octave-and-unison sonority, and *alla ʒoppa* figures. A second "Coro di demoni" in the same style is in the unusual key of B minor. The second act opens with an extended scene complex beginning with a "Coro con cavatina d'Armida," in F minor, in the *terribile* style. The *rumor sotterraneo* from the overture now returns in D-flat, and rapid scales and tremolos add to the violent effect. In act 2, scene 6, the *rumor sotterraneo* is heard again, and the score indicates "tempesta e venti" with piercing winds and rapid scales. Rapid thirty-second-note scales also accompany the "Coro di donzelle" as thunder is heard and the stage darkens. This chorus leads to the final, violent aria for Armida in E-flat, followed by a "Ballo della tempesta" (a *ciaccona*), and the opera concludes with a C major Allegro with rapid string figures.

Even the rather tame settings of the *Rinaldo* libretto such as Pietro Alessandro Guglielmi's (Venice, 1789) show how marvelous scenes have now become

---

104. Manuscript scores are preserved in F-Pn, D. 13726 (1-2), A-Wn, Hs. 17847, and several other libraries.

EXAMPLE 3.5 Giuseppe Gazzaniga, *La Circe*, overture

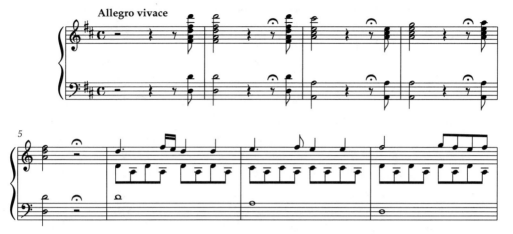

standard fare in adaptations of episodes from Tasso's epic.[105] The act 2 encounter of Rinaldo in the enchanted forest consists of a compound duple-meter Allegro in the infernal key of E-flat, an eleven-bar introduction to Rinaldo's recitative during which he remarks on the horrible sound and the descending mist that obscures his path. Guglielmi provided an original touch by punctuating string tremolos and rapid scale figures with interjecting horns and English horns, a novel combination of brass and woodwinds.

Gazzaniga's opera scores contain more supernatural musical devices. His Allegro vivace overture to Perelli's opera seria *La Circe* (Venice, 20 May 1786) has a grandiose slow introduction of eight chords in dotted rhythms, separated by fermatas (see ex. 3.5).[106] This passage recalls Traetta's overture to *Armida*, which may in turn have influenced Mozart's overture to *Die Zauberflöte*. Somber chordal beginnings seem to have had associations with grand supernatural topics. Although this score is an old-fashioned number opera dominated by arias and a few ensembles, Gazzaniga was much more ambitious with *Gli argonauti in Colco* (Venice, 1790),[107] setting large-scale accompanied recitatives for the dramatic scenes. In act 2, scene 7, Medea conjures a ghost in the presence of Jason. The key is once again E-flat. Sustained horns and strings in *alla zoppa* syncopation provide the sotto voce introduction. The earth trembles

105. I consulted the manuscript score of this two-act *dramma per musica* by Giuseppe Maria Foppa in F-Pn, D. 5149. Guglielmi also wrote *Le pazzie d'Orlando* (London, King's Theatre, 1771). Some arias from the opera were published in the same year.

106. I consulted the manuscript score of Antonio Simeone Sografi's *dramma per musica* on the myth of Jason and Medea in D-B, shelfmark K.H.M. 1609, part of the former Royal library collection. Another manuscript score is preserved in Lisbon.

107. I consulted an unusual score in two miniature volumes (175 × 115 mm) in D-Mbs, shelfmark Mus. Mss. 3728. Gazzaniga wrote earlier *seria* texts with marvelous content, for example, *Armida* (Rome, 1773), but only some arias survive.

with thirty-second-note figures in the bass before the ghost (bass) sings a recitative. The chorus then responds with cries of "che orrore" (what horror!).
Another noteworthy example of accompanied recitative is act 3, scene 2, where
Medea invokes the deities in a largo segment accompanied with oboes, horns,
and strings playing tremolo figures and vibrato.

Italian operas based on the myth of Semiramis provided opportunities for
special musical effects associated with ghosts. The first was Ferdinando Moret-
ti's *Semiramide,* with music by Michele Mortellari (Milan, 1784). Alessio Prati's setting *La vendetta di Nino* (Florence, 1786) relied on a musical convention
from comic opera: brief segments within a continuous larger ensemble scene.[108]
One striking supernatural reference occurs during the final trio in act 1, when
the ghost participates in a brief Largo section in E-flat, singing repeated-note
phrases that start with a descending octave leap, a melodic cliché for supernatural vocal utterance. The accompaniment is sustained chords in the oboes,
horns, and violas that support dotted rhythmic figures in the first violins and
thirty-second-note tremolos in the second violins. This short segment concludes with chords in *alla zoppa* syncopation in the strings.

Vienna and Dresden

An ambitious example of Viennese supernatural opera during this period is
Vincenzo Righini's 1782 setting of Coltellini's two-act *Armida,* which harks
back to its forerunner, Traetta's *Armida* of 1761.[109] Rich in vivid musical imagery, the work features an orchestra with a large wind complement (but no
trombones). The overture, in D minor, begins with a lengthy introduction
marked "Grave," with loud winds, wide melodic leaps, and chromatic passages; a D major Allegro con spirito follows. The somber music of the Grave
anticipates the material of the Andante funesto segment in act 1, scene 5, which
introduces Armida's "Coro d'ancelle." Because of its many similarities to the
overture of *Don Giovanni,* one wonders if Mozart knew Righini's *Armida.* The
first act of *Armida* has several supernatural episodes, including a nymphs' chorus (SS) and a chorus of genies in E-flat (SATB). In act 2, scene 1, Armida
and her choral retinue have a large scene complex in C minor marked "Andante maestoso," with forceful interjections by the horns and winds along with
string tremolos, all in the *terribile* style. Armida is distinguished here by her

---

108. I consulted the score in A-Wn, K.T. 460 (one of the scores in the Kärntnertortheater collection, which includes scores from various Viennese theaters). Copies are also found in Lbl, US-
Wc, and various Italian libraries. This two-act *melodrama tragico* by Pietro Giovannini after Voltaire was a widely used text. Francesco Bianchi set another version of the same libretto (Naples,
1790); a libretto by Antonio Simeone Sografi provided yet another variant and was set to music
both by Sebastiano Nasolini (Padua, 1790) and by Giovanni Battista Borghi (Milan, 1791) as *La
vendetta di Nino.*

109. I consulted the manuscript in Lbl, shelfmark Add. 16114–15.

extensive coloratura. Her recitative includes an "enchanted" wind ensemble in F minor, marked "armonia." Armida's vengeance aria, "Ingrato spiatuto mi lasci così," contains a violent instrumental section with *alla ʒoppa* syncopation, rapid scale figures, diminished-seventh sonority, abrupt rests, and long crescendos. A chorus and dance for Furies in C minor, marked "Maestoso" and with a full wind complement, string tremolos, and timpani, follows the aria. This two-part male chorus for bass voices leads to an Allegro segment in G minor, which contains the staging indication "La terra scuotasi d'averno al fremito" (In a shudder of horror, hell's earth quakes). Armida's subsequent accompanied recitative is a powerful invocation of the Furies, using a martial Allegro maestoso in C, with trumpets and timpani. A unison male chorus follows as the Furies arrive and sing "Spargan le Eumenidi" (The Eumenides scatter) in a violent F minor Allegro vivace. Armida's final accompanied recitative scene, depicting the burning of her palace, "Arda, cada, la Reggia," has running scales, bursts of short gestures in the bass, and *alla ʒoppa* syncopation. The scene builds to a furious conclusion, a C minor Allegro instrumental segment with thirty-three measures of fortissimo string tremolos, sixteenth-note ascending scales and descending arpeggios, and loud sustained notes in the trumpets and winds. This gradually subsides to a C major conclusion, first in *alla ʒoppa* syncopation, then in repeated gentle tonic chords.

Audiences in Munich were able to hear another ambitious setting of the story of Tasso's sorceress in Prati's *Armida abbandonata*, a two-act opera seria by Gaetano Sertor (1785).[110] The impressive score requires a large orchestra and features substantial instrumental writing and much variety in the arias. Vivid otherworldly musical depictions occur in the homophonic "Coro di mostri" and in the accompaniments of the recitatives, for example, Rinaldo's encounter with Armida's demons/nymphs (act 1, scene 6). He first hears magical music ("What sweet harmony!") in a *galant* Andante amoroso for oboes and strings. Act 2, scenes 4–6, is another large-scale section with accompanied recitative that features terrifying expression, an aria, and several ensemble segments. The most violent music occurs in the multipartite *scena ultima* in C minor for Armida and her chorus. The scene is full of musical terror effects such as bursts of string scales and loud winds (with trumpets and timpani).

Elsewhere in Germany, Righini set Metastasio's *Alcide al bivio* for Koblenz (1790),[111] using the winds prominently (as he did with *Armida*) and updating an old libretto with new, supernatural devices. The overture begins with a Grave introduction in D minor, leading to a D major Allegro con spirito. The thrice-repeated opening fortissimo chords in ominous dotted rhythms outline the cadence used for scenes of damnation (see ex. 3.6). These features are now

---

110. D-Mbs possesses an autograph score, shelfmark Mus. Mss. 2481. For context on this work, see McClymonds, "Carl Theodor."

111. The dated score is preserved in A-Wgm, shelfmark H 23587. See Federhofer, "Vincenzo Righini's Oper." The work was revised as a cantata for Vienna in 1804.

EXAMPLE 3.6 Vincenzo Righini, *Alcide al bivio*, overture

clearly recognizable aspects of a type of supernatural opera with terrifying scenes. This quality is apparent in scene 10, an accompanied recitative in which Alcide (tenor) confronts the specters, wonders, and monsters. Beginning in a Grave tempo in E-flat, Righini mixes arioso passages with recitative as he provides infernal imagery with sustained horn blasts and thirty-second- and sixty-fourth-note figures in the strings. The key changes to C minor as string tremolos accompany the text "Stelle! ah quale improvisa caligine profonda" (Heavens! Ah, what a sudden, deep mist), and the mode changes back to major in scene 11, when a triumphal chorus celebrates Alcide's success.

Naumann's Supernatural Operas

Joseph Gottlieb Naumann, the Saxon composer who studied with Tartini, Padre Martini, and Hasse and spent seven years in Italy, composed operas in Italian, Danish, and Swedish for stages in Venice, Palermo, Dresden, Stockholm, Copenhagen, and Berlin. Naumann's orchestrations are complex and often include powerful symphonic effects, many of which express supernatural force and terror. Naumann composed some of his earliest theater music for an Italian comic opera by Bertati and Kurz (see chapter 4), which included several supernatural episodes. In the parody of a ghost scene (act 1, scene 15), the composer may have had his first opportunity to use conventions associated with the supernatural. Unfortunately, the music is lost.

Naumann's first serious supernatural opera was *Osiride*, Caterino Mazzolà's two-act *dramma per musica*.[112] The wedding in Dresden of Prince Anton, Duke of Saxony, and Princess Caroline of Sardinia occasioned the performance at the Kleines Kurfürstliches Theater on 27 October 1781. Providing a
rare Italian example of an exotic "oriental" libretto, Mazzolà created an Egyptian fairy tale. Commentators have often compared the Egyptian setting and
fairy-tale elements in *Osiride* to that of *Die Zauberflöte*.[113] The two texts have
other elements in common as well. Like Schikaneder's and Mozart's singspiel, the libretto of *Osiride* includes moralizing speeches on enlightened rule
over a sovereign's subjects. There is also a scene in which a portrait is given
to the hero, causing him to fall in love with the beautiful image of a woman.[114]
The lovers undergo a trial of their virtue and the earth opens up and swallows
the villains at the end. The plot offers an archetypal Manichean struggle, with
light and fire symbolizing virtue. But this libretto belongs to an entirely different tradition from that of *Die Zauberflöte*. *Osiride* is a court opera, with no
comic elements and little dramatic force or tension. As such, its plot and music are tied to the traditional function of the *festa teatrale,* an obsequious moral
allegory directed at the honored nobility (the author's epilogue makes the allegory clear in its praise of the actual newlywed couple). Arranged marriage,
disdained in the libretto of *Die Zauberflöte*, is privileged in *Osiride*, which affirms the divine right of the aristocracy. Thus *Osiride* is much closer to *Alcide
al bivio* than to Schikaneder and Mozart's popular-style singspiel.

Naumann's score shows a remarkable mastery of musical terror and allusions to supernatural power.[115] Although his large orchestra is without trombones, the horns function like trombones, suggesting hellish blaring. Osiride
(Osiris), king of Egypt, rules over the realm of virtue with his spouse, Iside
(Isis). Prince Oro is their son, and Aretea, the young princess selected to be
his bride. Their education and eventual union is the main concern of this allegorical plot. Neither has ever seen the other (an allusion to the desirability of
an arranged aristocratic marriage, hardly an "enlightened" value). The difficult path of virtue becomes a harsh trial for the young couple as the evil genie
Tiphone opposes the marriage and the dissemination of goodness that it will

112. The libretto was printed in Italian with a German translation: Dresden, 1781. Manuscript
score in D-Dlb, Mus. 3480-F-21. An appendix to act 1 appears in the score, not in the libretto, and
depicts the abduction of Aretea (the original title of the opera was *Aretea*).

113. Engländer, *Johann Gottlieb Naumann,* 167–68, 326–28, 337–59, suggests that Lorenzo Da
Ponte even participated in the writing of the libretto and that Mozart knew the opera. He interprets
Masonic references in certain details of the libretto and makes the putative connections to *Die Zau-
berflöte*. Although these claims are intriguing, there is no compelling evidence to support them.

114. This scene is descriptive of the normal process of an arranged royal marriage for political
ends. Flattering portraits were commissioned and exchanged in the hope of arousing an amorous
response in a couple with no previous erotic connection.

115. A manuscript score survives in D-Dlb, Mus. c: B 524, parts: Cw 81ª. The new shelfmark
is Mus. 3480-F-21, 2 vols.

create. He intends to force Aretea to marry his own son, Gerone. In a substantial invocation scene in the grotto of Tiphone, the villains devise a scheme to sprinkle a sleeping potion on the flowers that Iside and Aretea will pluck in their garden. They will abduct Aretea and keep her imprisoned in their cave. Osiride tells Prince Oro that this is a test of their virtue and love and instructs him to go to the temple to receive the blessings of the gods. In an extended underworld scene (act 1, scene 4) Gerone (bass) sings a C minor invocation to his father and the subterranean spirits. The Adagio invocation, "con grave fiato immondo," with its portentous octave leaps in the vocal line, suggests the incantation of a sorcerer, accompanied by infernal horns playing forceful sustained notes and dotted rhythmic figures. As is the case with similar invocations, a chorus of spirits appears, singing in C minor. The terrifying ritornello has stark dynamic contrasts, pulsating rhythm, sixteenth-note scales and tremolos in the strings, and horns issuing loud blasts. The three-part chorus, "Nel sen del cupo averno la voce tua rimbomba" (In the heart of dark hell your voice resounds), then begins with a descending eighth-note scale in octave-and-unison sonority, achieving chordal harmony at the words "agita ogn'antro interno." Tiphone enters and the key modulates to E-flat. The final scene in act 1 concludes with a D minor triple-meter homophonic chorus for the subterranean voices of Gerone and Tiphone, accompanied by sixteenth-note violin figures and the full orchestra.

Naumann's score includes a new magical sleep scene that ends act 1, a scene not found in the libretto. Here Gerone, with his "chorus of evil genies," casts a spell on the unsuspecting women with a triple-meter, homophonic four-part chorus in E-flat, sung sotto voce. The accompaniment has descending triplet arpeggios in the muted violins as the flutes play staccato chords. After the women have fallen asleep, Gerone sings an obbligato recitative in a "subdued voice" (*voce sommessa*), accompanied by sustained, muted strings in the low register. An Adagio in D minor with octave-and-unison sonority follows as Gerone intones a chromatic invocation to *sdrucciolo* rhythms ("Terrai tuoi tremiti apran voragine"). The repeated cadence (i–VI–ii$^6_5$–V–i) is the same one used by Righini (*Il convitato da pietra*), Salieri (*Les Danaïdes*), and Mozart (*Don Giovanni*) for their infernal scenes. A violent abduction follows, with Gerone commanding the earth to tremble as rapid sextuplets rumble in the violins and bass. To conjure up a whirlpool and lightning, Naumann juxtaposes sixteenth-note figures in the strings against sustained whole notes in the flutes. The mutes come off the strings for the subsequent *terribile* Allegro di molto, with *alla zoppa* syncopation in the strings and a chromatic descent in the bass. There follows an extended crescendo in D major, coordinated with ascending figures in the strings, tremolos in the violas, forte horn blasts, and timpani strokes, all set to a dominant pedal as Gerone and his genies abduct Aretea and take her to a subterranean grotto. As the crescendo reaches a violent forte, a lightning bolt strikes, and ascending scales erupt in the bass, oboes, and strings. (Mozart would use a similar doubling for his lightning in the act 2 finale of *Don Giovanni*.)

Act 2 of *Osiride* begins in Tiphone's cave, where Aretea is guarded by four evil genies. She rejects Gerone's advances, and the genies take her to a subterranean vault. The opening *sinfonia* of scene 5, a D minor Adagio with ominous dotted rhythms, suggests this dark place, and Aretea's tentative steps are described in the solo oboes; her horror at seeing the genies is depicted by forte horn blasts. Gerone devises a plan to terrify Oro and render him unworthy of Aretea in her eyes. Osiride and Oro arrive, and the king gives his son a portrait of Aretea while showing him the grotto where she is imprisoned. Gerone approaches after Osiride leaves, transforming the scene into an attractive place where the spirits of Joy and Jest appear and sing a charming chorus (scene 8). A delicate, elegant march in D (marked "andante") for an enchanting wind ensemble of flutes, oboes, and horns (along with strings) evokes the change of scene, continuing with a pastoral divertissement. Gerone promises Oro a hundred beauties to compensate for his loss of Aretea, but Oro rebuffs him. The sky darkens, and Gerone transforms the scene back to the terrifying grotto with a *terribile* Allegro in D minor. Evil spirits appear from all sides, defending the entrance and threatening Oro. They repulse Oro's first attempts to enter the grotto, but eventually he succeeds in breaking into Aretea's prison. A chorus in D minor with Neapolitan harmonies leads to the rescue scene as the key suddenly changes to A minor and Gerone declares that all is lost, accompanied by forte string tremolos and a descending chromatic bass. Flames appear from the grotto as a *sinfonia* using a descending bass line (A minor–G minor–F–E–A^7–D), with rapid ascending scales and descending leaps in the strings, describes the opening of the earth and the vomiting flames. As Gerone and his evil followers fall into the abyss, a series of cadential runs forms a kind of retransition on the dominant pedal, A, leading to a scenic transformation to the splendid temple of the sun, decorated with hieroglyphics depicting various virtues. Osiride and Iside appear with their retinues for the final triumphal ensemble in D major: choruses of Virtues and Jests celebrating the triumph of good over evil and the union of Oro and Aretea.

Naumann's subsequent operas use the full range of supernatural devices. The Swedish court opera *Gustaf Wasa* (1786) has two extensive supernatural episodes, a dream scene in act 2 and a ghost scene in act 3.[116] The former (scenes 7–8) is a divertissement with pantomime, accompanied recitative, and an aria with pastoral wind instruments in appropriate major keys. The horrific ghost scene (scene 3) has *terribile* effects with string tremolos and long-

116. This is a three-act *tragédie lyrique* on a text by Johann Henrik Kellgren with some collaboration by King Gustav III. A facsimile edition (in four volumes) of a manuscript score in Stockholm's Library of the Academy of Music, is edited by Anna Johnson in Naumann, *Gustaf Wasa*. See also Åstrand, Ottenberg, and Schönfelder, *Zur Tonsetzung*.

held forte chords by three trombones; an abrupt change to the minor mode signals the transformation into darkness. The ghosts of the two Ribbings (sopranos)—Swedish heroes whom the Danish King Christiern ("the tyrant") has murdered—have an eerie Andante duet in F minor as they announce their intent of revenge in canonic texture. String tremolos begin when the bloody ghost of Sten Sture (bass), another hero of the past and a Swedish regent, appears and reveals his identity in an incantation with repeated notes in the vocal line. A chorus of ghosts then sings a powerful homophonic declamation with rapid ascending string scales, alternating with Sten Sture's declaimed incantations. Solos for other ghosts alternate with accusatory choral segments, some of these employing unison repeated notes. The solos also feature repeated notes along with descending leaps, accompanied by the trombones. The harmony in C minor, F minor, then F-sharp minor, with several diminished chords, supports bursts of octave-and-unison scales with repeated notes and tremolos in the strings. The final, violent ghost chorus has forceful repeated notes in the vocal line, accompanied by rapid string figures, unison gestures, and piercing notes in the brass.

In 1788 Naumann set Antonio Filistri's three-act opera seria *Medea in Colchide, ossia Il ritorno di Giasone in Grecia* (Berlin, 1788) with a large orchestra including clarinets and three trombones.[117] He employed a wide variety of musical styles, including the mode of terror. Act 2, scenes 1–4, comprise the powerful center of the opera when Jason wins the fleece in the primeval forest. An instrumental introduction in G minor with trombones starts the scene with the old baroque canzona motive. A unison male chorus of gnomes, imaginative harmony with altered and borrowed chords and abrupt key changes, and unison vocal exclamations recall Gluck's underworld scenes in *Don Juan* and *Orfeo ed Euridice*. Act 3 includes Medea's subterranean incantations for vengeance, an Adagio with dotted sixteenth-note motives that build to an explosion of thirty-second-note figuration and sustained blasts of the winds. In a magic-mirror scene with a sibyl, Medea sees the events in Corinth, much like scene with the magic mirror in Grétry's *Zémire et Azor*. The furious demons' dance in C minor (3/8 meter) recalls Gluck's demonic dance music, and an A minor fortissimo (vivace assai) in the terrifying musical style depicts the arrival of the Furies and their burning of the palace.

The following year Naumann provided the music for act 2 of a two-act opera seria by Gaetano Sertor, *Protesilao* (Berlin, 1789; act 1 by Johann Friedrich Reichardt).[118] This is the mythological story of the fallen Greek hero Protesilaus, who is reunited with his spouse Laodamia (here called Ersile) after her

---

117. A manuscript score is preserved in A-Wgm, D-B (Mus. ms. 15968, 3 vols., performance score), and there are two damaged manuscripts in D-Dlb, Mus. 3480-F-35 and F-36.

118. Manuscript scores are preserved in D-B (Mus. ms. 15967, 2 vols.) and D-Dlb, Mus. 3480-F-43. The myth had previously been set to music for the theater in the seventeenth century by Catherine Bernard with Bernard Le Bovier de Fontenelle, as *Laodamie, reine d'Epire* (Paris 1689),

grief moves Hermes to bring her husband back from Hades for three hours. A large orchestra with trombones supports the many supernatural episodes. The overture's initial Larghetto lugubre in C minor is the basis for the opening choral tomb scene (recalling Gluck's tomb scene and underworld chorus in *Orfeo ed Euridice*).[119] The subsequent Allegro gioioso in C major uses the music that will accompany the sleep scene (act 1, scene 6), where Mercury appears in a cloud chariot as a solo flute (with oboe and bassoon) plays melodies in soporific conjunct motion.

The seventh scene of *Protesilao* is a large complex of movements set at the gates of Hades. The initial Andante ma forte e marcato, a symphonic slow introduction in D minor for full orchestra with trombones, has slowly rising melodic lines, repetitive rhythms, and chromatic and Neapolitan harmonic inflexions. A long transition with chromatic phrases over a pedal leads to an Allegro in triple meter with trumpets and horns as Protesilaus encounters the Furies as a terrifying chorus (TTB). Naumann set one of the segments, a ballet for the Furies and deities, in B minor, an unusual key and one not generally associated with infernal scenes. In the oracle scene (act 2, scene 9), set as an accompanied recitative, the voice of the oracle (bass) announces in ungainly vocal leaps that Protesilaus has been restored to life. A modulation through a circle of fifths to G major facilitates the final scenic transformation to the temple of glory.

Haydn's Last Opera: Orfeo

Joseph Haydn's last opera, unperformed in his lifetime, was derived from the quintessential text of the operatic "marvelous," the myth of Orpheus. Carlo F. Badini wrote the libretto of *L'anima del filosofo, ossia Orfeo ed Euridice,* a *dramma per musica* in four (or perhaps five) acts.[120] Haydn composed the music for proposed London performances in 1791 (King's Theatre, Haymarket), but the production fell through when the theater's impresario was denied a license.[121] The opera may have remained unfinished, but the surviving source has a rare *fine tragico,* a violent ending with a magic storm after the murder of Orpheus by the Bacchantes and the appearance of Apollo to reclaim his son's body. *L'anima del filosofo* contains Haydn's most extensive use of musical terror and supernatural imagery. As with his *Armida,* Haydn's original approach to harmony in supernatural scenes is reminiscent of the free-fantasy style, with

---

and in the eighteenth century as an *azione teatrale* text by Mattia Verazi, *Laodamia,* 1780 (with music by his son, I. P. Verazi).

119. In 1786 Naumann set *Orpheus og Eurydike* for Copenhagen. Several scenes strongly recall Gluck's setting. For details, see chapter 5.

120. The main title refers to Euridice's father, here the philosopher Creonte (bass), who delivers moralizing texts, e.g., the act 1 aria, "Il pensier sta negli oggetti," in E major, a minuet-like Andante with the flute doubling the first violin at the octave.

121. For a recent study on this opera see Leopold, "Haydn und die Tradition."

varied and at times complex harmonic schemes to coincide with the progress of the drama. The keys are representational, with a dark C minor for the introduction to the overture and for the music for the Furies and spirits in acts 1 and 4. As in *Armida*, here Haydn chose the key of D minor for his terrifying scenes with the chorus of the Furies and the Bacchantes in act 4. Haydn's male chorus of Furies (tenors and basses) recalls Rameau's Fates in *Hippolyte et Aricie*, where men sing female supernatural roles. Here they sing for long segments in octaves, a more recent device for characters such as spirits and demons. The extensive and varied use of chorus is unmatched in any of Haydn's other operas.

The overture of *L'anima del filosofo*, including winds, brass (without trombones), and timpani, begins with a seven-measure Largo introduction in C minor, a contrapuntal fragment that prepares the succeeding cheerful Presto in C major. Like the *sinfonia* to *Armida*, this overture follows the principle enunciated by Gluck, giving the audience clues to the main expressive topics in the opera. In this case the subject seems to be the contrast of dark and the light. The first Furies' chorus in C minor recalls Gluck's scene for the Furies and Orestes in act 1 of *Iphigénie en Tauride*. Unison writing for the two choral vocal parts predominates, with octave-and-unison sonority for the orchestral accompaniment. The otherworldly allusion of the sonority is enhanced by infernal blasts of the horns, long pedals, and the rapid scale figures in the violins toward the end of the chorus.

Only a few scenes in the next two acts have supernatural content. In act 3 Orpheus (tenor) consults a spirit, who agrees to take him to the underworld (simple recitative). The spirit's C major aria, "Al tuo seno fortunato," is the opera's most brilliant display of virtuosity, with extended coloratura and military-like orchestral fanfares. Act 4 begins with an extended supernatural scene in several movements on the shores of the river Lethe. The spirit has brought Orpheus here so that he can try to retrieve Eurydice. Scene 1 begins with a chorus (SATB) for the spirits in a plaintive F minor, with Neapolitan and diminished harmonies. A short simple recitative then leads to the D minor "Coro di furie" for male voices in quadruple meter and marked "Vivace assai." The text has infernal imagery ("Urli orrendi, disperati, qui si sente ogni momento"), and Haydn utilizes the music of terror. For the desperate, horrendous howling, the composer has chosen infernal orchestration, with two trombones, horns, and trumpets, in addition to the flutes, oboes, bassoons, and strings. The Tartarean hell is depicted with forte octaves and chords on strong beats, marcato indications, octave-and-unison sonority, rapid tremolos, and brisk ascending scales. The harmony and sonority are equally potent, with diminished, Neapolitan, and dominant ninth chords, and descending augmented seconds through the modulating key scheme. A short, imitative opening introduces the rapid declamation of the tenor and basses in octave-and-unison sonority, accompanied by the same sonority in the orchestra.

Scene 3 begins with a short pastoral intermezzo for flutes doubled by oboes, with bassoons, horns, and strings. This elegant instrumental Allegretto in D major with gavotte rhythms coincides with the transformation of the scene from the gloomy Lethe to the ethereal Elysian fields. Eurydice sings a phrase that recalls the opening of Gluck's aria "Che farò senza Euridice?" This music proves irresistible, and Orpheus turns to look at her. Again Haydn uses harmony as an expressive device. The music abandons the tonal area of D, and the keys modulate by fourths, from G to C to F and then to B-flat. The accompanied recitative, marked "Allegro con brio," begins with a forceful octave-and-unison motive, followed by a consequent phrase with solo bassoon doubling the violins at the octave below. This elegant prelude clears the sonic palate of the previous key, sonority, and timbre, indicating a scenic division and a strong change of mood. Orpheus's obbligato recitative begins, accompanied by strings playing sustained notes in the low registers, an old device to suggest an otherworldly association.[122] This scene is punctuated with instrumental interludes that use the rapid string scales from the prelude.

In the final chorus the pagan priestesses (who have just poisoned Orpheus) drown in a terrible storm at sea. Haydn returns to the key of D minor with trombones, horns, trumpets, and timpani. Starting with octave-and-unison motives and a strong chromatic element, a long crescendo leads to extended instrumental storm music, with diminished chords, string tremolos, fast descending flute arpeggios (probably representing lightning), and fortissimo broken octaves in the basses to depict thunder. The storm recedes as this descriptive music grows softer and the texture becomes thinner, finally ending with six repeated Ds in octaves, marked "piano" and set off by rests.

Haydn's use of the musical conventions of magic and the supernatural was extensive but ultimately derivative. This is not to diminish his accomplishment. The expressive range and breadth of Haydn's accompanied recitatives alone distinguish the composer's mastery of one of the most difficult dramatic elements in opera. Other aspects, such as the choice of key, harmonic range, and mimetic sonic imagery, equally mark the composer's skill in their application to the text. Although Haydn did not invent these devices, he employed them at least as effectively as did his most illustrious contemporaries.

---

122. We find a confirmation of the supernatural association of this device in Haydn's oratorio *Die Schöpfung*. Here the composer writes sustained low string accompaniment during Raphael's (bass) recitative in the second part of the oratorio, "Und Gott schuf große Walfische" (And God created the great whales), when the voice of the Lord is quoted in arioso, "Seid fruchtbar alle, mehret euch!" (Be fruitful and multiply!).

CHAPTER FOUR

Italian Comic Genres

Commedia dell'arte and Early Comic Opera

Unlike *dramma per musica*, Italian musical comedy still had a place for the supernatural. Although the commedia dell'arte declined in Italy during the eighteenth century, the surviving *scenari* from this period indicate a continuing use of magical plots and characters. Among the twenty-two *scenari* preserved in the manuscript *Selva, ovvero Zibaldone di concetti comici . . . D. Placido Adriani* (1734)[1] are older works such as *L'Arcadia incantata*,[2] along with variants on common plot types such as *Pulcinella, finto prencipe*. Here a magician gives Pulcinella the appearance of the prince of Naples, and the false prince administers justice in the realm. When the true prince returns, Pulcinella is discovered and condemned as an impostor. In the end the magician saves him. The scant evidence of the Italian marionette theater suggests that it employed the fantastic plots and characters of the commedia dell'arte.[3] Commedia dell'arte plots often served as the basis of early comic opera, which continued to make use of magical content. Antonio Zaniboni's *divertimento per musica* in 3 acts, *Il mago deluso dalla magia*, with music by Giuseppe Maria Buini (lost), was produced at Bologna's Teatro Formagliari, during Carnival 1718.[4] The libretto has a sprawling plot rich in comic stereotypes: lovers (and their servants) escaping disapproving relatives meet a magician, whose magical powers are given over to the magician's foolish servant. His incompetence results in a

1. Perugia, Biblioteca comunale, Codex A.20.

2. Naples Biblioteca Nazionale, shelfmark XI.AA.ms., I, contains the same plot, 1. Cited in Parfaict and Parfaict, *Dictionnaire*, 1:157 and 3: 448; and in *Mercure de France*, 11 June 1740.

3. See Leydi and Leydi, *Marionette e burattini*.

4. Libretto, Bologna: per il Rossi e comp., n.d. [1718]; copy in Bologna, Biblioteca Universitaria, shelfmark A.V.Tab.I.G.III.35.3 [Sartori #14691]). Revived in 1735 as *Il destino trionfante e la magia delusa*. The text has no specific indications of what kind of music was included besides the arias, none of which has a supernatural text. Buini also composed *Armida delusa* (Venice, 1720).

series of bungled enchantments and transformations. Buini provided the music (also lost) for a similar libretto, *La Zanina maga par amore,* an anonymous *dramma comico per musica* of 1737.[5] The heroine, Zanina, is an illiterate peasant girl abandoned by her lover. She finds a magic wand and transforms herself into a variety of characters, correcting the flaws and weaknesses of others. The wand also creates a fire-breathing monster, imprisons her faithless lover, and transforms the scene into an enchanted grotto that she claims to be the palace of Hymen.

By the 1730s arcadian reformers advocated abolishing the marvelous and supernatural elements from comic opera.[6] This judgment seems to have been ignored. Comic operas continued to exploit the epic romance and pastoral genres for their supernatural elements. A new subgenre of opera with supernatural elements even emerged in Italy around 1735: heroic-comic opera or mock-heroic opera. One of the earliest was *Angelica ed Orlando,* a *commedia per musica* by Francesco Antonio Tullio, based on Ariosto's characters with music by Gaetano Latilla (Naples, 1735). This opera both celebrates and satirizes magic and knightly struggle. Pietro Trinchera's *commedia per musica* in three acts, *L'incanti per amore* (Naples, 1741), with music by Antonio Palella (lost),[7] is another mock-heroic plot, also drawn from the commedia dell'arte. Here the heroine, Celia, transforms herself into the sorceress Circe in order to attract the unresponsive knight-errant Olindo and to help other lovers. The comedy opens with Circe-Celia arriving on a flying chariot drawn by a dragon and culminates in a magic transformation. Celia has a magic ring that changes a person's appearance. As for music, the libretto indicates arias at the ends of scenes and short ensembles at the end of acts. Act 3, scenes 9–10, has the only specific musical indication in the libretto, "Una funesta zinfonia," when the priest enters for the last scene, a sacrifice accompanied by instrumental music (*sacrificio accompagnato con istromenti*). The anonymous three-act *dramma giocoso, La fata meravigliosa* (Venice, 1745),[8] with music by Giuseppe Scolari (lost), is another mock-heroic comic opera, recalling epic romance with its convoluted plot, disguises, and magical transformations, as well as a beautiful fairy cursed

5. Libretto, Bologna: S. Giovanni in Persiceto nel teatro de' Sig. Accademici Candidi, autumn 1737. Restaged in 1742 and 1745 (libretto, Bologna: Costantino Pisarri, n.d., and 1745 [Sartori 5, US-Wc, Schatz 1398].

6. Comedy, which had been eliminated from *dramma per musica,* was placed in *entr'acte intermezzi.* Once comic opera had achieved recognition as a genre and a respectable part of the operatic season (c. 1750), *intermezzi* gave way to ballets as *entr'actes.* Comic opera never completely eliminated magic, and by 1760 these genres included substantial supernatural scenes.

7. Libretto, Naples 1741 [US-Wc, Schatz 7712]).

8. Libretto, Venice: Appresso Modesto Fenzo, 1746 [#9805 in Sartori, US-Wc Schatz 9796]). Sartori's libretto catalog (#9806, not mentioned in NGO) cites a libretto of *La fata meravigliosa* for the Nuovo Teatro in Vienna in 1748 (Vienna: Giovanni Pietro van Ghelen, 1748), with music attribued to Ignaz Holzbauer.

with nocturnal transformation into a deadly basilisk (recalling the legend of the fairy Melusine). This enchantment can be dispelled only by the kiss of a noble knight, which occurs at the end of the opera.

Numerous comic intermezzos offered feigned conjuring by putative astrologers, magicians, and sorceresses. In Johann Adolf Hasse's *L'artigiano gentiluomo (Larinda e Vanesio)* (Naples, 1726),[9] Vanesio is furious with Larinda, and he angrily conjures the infernal spirits. Calling for music, he invokes "fagotti e timpani, violette e cembali," and he sings an invocation with descending octave leaps in *sdrucciolo* rhythm and a rising triadic clarion call on the word *sonate,* accompanied by octave-and-unison sonority. Leonardo Vinci's *L'amante geloso* (1729), Giovanni Battista Pergolesi's *Nerina e Nibbio* (Naples, 1732, music lost), and the anonymous *Vespina e Pacuvio* (Naples, 1731) all include similar episodes. For example, Pergolesi has Nerina sing a mock incantation to conjure demons from a cave, "Spirti venite dall'empio Dite."

The first two Don Giovanni operas to appear since the settings in the later seventeenth century[10] are both anonymous works: *La pravità castigata,* a *rappresentazione morale per musica* (Prague, 1730), and *La pravità castigata* (Brno, Carnival 1734), with music by Eustachio Bambini (lost). Don Juan stories seem to have been among the standard plots in the marionette repertory as well. I have listed eighteenth-century Italian settings of the Don Juan story in Appendix D, which documents the almost ubiquitous popularity of this plot.

The Gozzi-Goldoni Controversy

Italian reformers sympathetic with Enlightenment values considered the commedia dell'arte debased and outdated. Among them, the noted dramatist Carlo Goldoni derided this theatrical tradition as indecent, unrealistic, and lacking in proper moral instruction.[11] He and other "progressive" writers purged improvisatory, vulgar, and fantastic elements and produced more literary comedies. In their view the characters and situations of comedy were to be drawn from the everyday experiences of the middle classes.

9. Ed. Lazarevich in *Recent Researches in the Music of the Classical Era.*

10. *L'empio punito,* a three-act *dramma musicale* by F. Acciaiuoli and G. F. Apolloni, with music by Alessandro Melani (Rome, 1669), and *Il convitato di pietra,* a three-act *opera tragica* by Andrea Petrucci (Naples, 1678, 1690).

11. See Goldoni, *Tutte le opere,* 17:750, where Goldoni criticized the lack of rationality in Italian magic comedies: "All the servant-maids of wandering comedy troupes were somehow forced to represent *La serva maga, Lo spirito folletto,* and other similar commedia dell'arte plays, in which the servant-maid changes costumes and language as she takes up the various different roles and moral types; but there really should be a magical art that we imagine in such comedies; we really need this so they work rationally and are true to life; and ordinarily these indecent and artificial actions do not work in the bad scenes of the worst comedies. Would it not be possible, I was asking myself, to give one role to diverse characters without the dreamed-up help of magic?"

Yet even Goldoni occasionally included marvelous elements in his comic librettos such as *Il paese della Cuccagna* (Venice, Teatro Giustinian de San Moisè, Ascension Day, 1750), a *commedia per musica* with music by Baldassare Galuppi (lost). Goldoni's based his opera on the myth of the utopian land of Cocaigne.[12] The libretto was set several times over the next two decades.[13] The plot concerns a young and naive bourgeois couple, recently shipwrecked on the island of Cocaigne, an arcadian paradise where excellent food and drink are in abundance and no one has to work. They must swear an oath to obey the laws of the land, which demand a renunciation of jealousy. Soon they succumb to the society's lasciviousness, sloth, decadence, and gluttony. During one of their frequent balls an invading army easily conquers the island and forces the inhabitants to work.

While Goldoni wrote his influential comic operas, with their serious elements and more realistic plots, his great Venetian rival, Carlo Gozzi, made extensive use of fairy-tale material in his ten *fiabe teatrali* (1761–65; see table 4.1), based loosely on fantastic Parisian fair plays.[14] Gozzi's comedies exerted considerable influence in many directions. His theatrical fairy tales helped to revive the commedia dell'arte in Italy. German companies translated and performed Gozzi's *fiabe;* these adaptations may have influenced later singspiels.[15]

Unlike the middle-class Goldoni, who was the son of a doctor and himself

12. Libretto, Venice: Modesto Fenzo, 1750 [US-Wc, Schatz 3492]). This text belongs to the tradition of utopian fantasies with social or moral commentary in the frame of entertainment. For a discussion of related stories (Cucania, Cuccagna, Coquaigne, Cocagne, Cocaygne, Cockaenghen) and the sources of this myth, see Poeschel, "Das Märchen," and Cocchiara, *Il paese di Cuccagna*. Other fantastic Italian operas using utopian themes include Goldoni's *Bertoldo, Bertoldino e Cacasenno* (1738), *La favola de' tre gobbi* (1749), *Il mondo alla roversa* (1750), and *Il mondo della luna* (1750).

13. The libretto was recycled in 1750 for Rome, with music by Gerolamo Mango (lost). Mango also set the opera buffa *La mago per amore* by G. Donadini (Rome, 1776); Antonio Tozzi also set the libretto for Bologna (1771; the music is apparently lost). Tozzi set Coltellini's *Orfeo ed Euridice* (Munich, 1775; scores survive, in B-Bc, Darmstadt, Hessische Landes- und Hochschulbibliothek, D-Mbs, F-Pn), *Rinaldo* (Venice, 1775; score in A-Wgm), *Zemira ed Azor* (Barcelona, 1791 [?]) by Da Ponte (music lost), and *Lo scherzo della magia, ossia La casa incantata*, a *dramma giocoso* (Barcelona, c. 1785). A manuscript score is preserved in Palacio Liria, Madrid. Gennaro Astarita also set the libretto in Venice (1777) as *L'isola del Bengodi* (autograph score in I-Fc.) and composed an opera on an *Armida* libretto by Migliavacca (Venice, 1777); scores survive in I-Fc, Genoa, Paganini Conservatory and Lancut (Poland), Muzeum [entitled *Rinaldo*]).

14. The following sources inform this discussion: Ringger, "Carlo Gozzi's Fiabe teatrali"; Luciani, *Carlo Gozzi (1720–1806)*, 2:501–648; Fabrizi, "Carlo Gozzi e la tradizione popolare"; Nicholson, "Gozzi's *Turandot*"; Perroud, "La défense et l'utilisation des 'masques,'" 9; DiGaetani, *Carlo Gozzi: Translations;* Gozzi, *Five Tales.*

15. Several commentators have pointed to the similarities between Gozzi's tales and *Die Zauberflöte,* including Dent in his commentary on and translation of Gozzi, *The Blue Monster;* Rosen,

TABLE 4.1 Gozzi's Ten *fiabe teatrali*

1. *L'amore delle tre melarance* (The Love of Three Oranges), 1761
2. *Il corvo* (The Raven), 1761
3. *Il re cervo* (The King Stag), 1762
4. *Turandot*, 1762
5. *La donna serpente* (The Serpent Woman), 1762
6. *La Zobeide*, 1763
7. *I pitocchi fortunati* (The Fortunate Beggars), 1764
8. *Il mostro turchino* (The Blue Monster), 1764
9. *L'augellino belverde* (The Green Bird), 1765
10. *Zeim, re de' genj* (Zeim, king of the Genies), 1765

a lawyer, the playwright Carlo Gozzi came from Venice's minor aristocracy, which had fallen on hard times. He wrote his theatrical tales as a polemic on the pretensions of literary reform, criticizing the follies of the Enlightenment and its petty "paper war" waged against Venetian competitors. Gozzi employed the old commedia dell'arte, with all its exoticism, magic, and fairy-tale elements. The central polemic in Gozzi's tales concerns the theatrical reforms of Goldoni, whose comedies offered a vision of a dignified bourgeoisie in contrast with the impoverished nobility, represented as arrogant social parasites with licentious morals. Social reform was at the center of Goldoni's comedies of the middle and lower classes.

Gozzi's brother Gasparo explained the ideological substratum of Carlo's first play, *L'amore delle tre melarance* (The Love for Three Oranges, 1761), as an allegory of Venice.[16] It satirizes Goldoni and Pietro Chiari, who are portrayed as the magician Celio and the fairy Morgana, respectively. Gozzi saw Goldoni's views as a threat to the proper order of society. His target was the corrupting influence of the Enlightenment, and he spoofed modern science as the sacred cow of the Enlightenment. Gasparo's remarks make it clear that Gozzi's theater of entertainment and fantasy undermined Goldoni's assumptions about the vices of the aristocracy and the virtue of the middle class. His serious characters are aristocrats, while his comic characters are their lower- or middle-class foils. Moral issues in Gozzi's plays are often symbolized through female characters. Female villains imperil the patriarchal hierarchy and incite chaos.[17] In *La donna serpente* (The Serpent Woman) Cheristani is the figure of superhuman female power, a fairy and immortal queen of a hidden realm. She assumes

---

The Classical Style, 318–19; DiGaetani, *Carlo Gozzi: Translations*, 6–7; and Ballola, "Le fiabe di Carlo Gozzi."

16. *La gazzetta veneta* 103 (27 January 1761). The following discussion owes much to the analyses of Ted Emery in Gozzi, *Five Tales*.

17. On women and social order in Gozzi's *fiabe*, see Emery, "Autobiographer as Critic."

the shape of a serpent (like Melusine), an emblem of power. "Enlightened" sexual promiscuity threatens traditional morality, just as revealed religion is threatened by philosophical freethinking. The threat usually culminates in a physical transformation by magic. Only a heroic act or magical intervention can reverse this situation. The polemical project is most apparent in *L'augellino belverde* (The Little Green Bird), which criticizes the pernicious philosophy of the Enlightenment.[18]

Gozzi's first tale, *L'amore delle tre melarance*, was based on one of Basile's fairy tales from *Pentamerone*. It consists of a detailed *scenario* with some dialogue for the comic scenes. Gozzi wrote the next nine tales with more dialogues and progressively limited the improvisational elements. In the early decades of the eighteenth century poets of the Parisian fairs plundered fantastic oriental fairy tales for comic opera plots. Gozzi now followed their lead. With the exception of *I pitocchi fortunati* (1764), all of his *fiabe* include supernatural episodes.

Far more detailed than the ordinary *canovaccio*, Gozzi's texts depart from standard characters as well as situations. The tone is more melodramatic, with plots dominated by serious characters. Gozzi's Pantalone is a symbol of the Venetian popular virtue, a kind and simple but shrewd middle-class Venetian merchant. Elements of literary and cultural polemics complete the mixture. Rich in contemporary allusions to prominent Venetian citizens and prostitutes, the juxtaposition and jarring anomaly of serious and comic elements with exotic orientalism and farce makes for a modern quality that subverts the sanctimonious realism of his rivals.[19]

❀

In his study on Gozzi's influences Gérard Luciani identifies Lesage's *Théâtre de la foire* (mentioned in Gozzi's preface),[20] and his novels *Le diable boîteux* and *Gil Blas* as key sources. Lesage combined serious and comic elements, and drew upon oriental fairy tales. Gozzi himself relied on a number of printed "oriental" collections, especially those by Antoine Galland and Pétis de la Croix, during the five-year period when he wrote his *fiabe*. In the 1802 edition of the *Opere*, Gozzi mentions six sources:[21]

18. Jonard, "Les structures idéologiques."

19. No music survives for Gozzi's original plays, but various literary sources indicate some vocal numbers. For example, in act 3 of *L'augellino belverde*, when Truffaldino approaches the magic apples in the fairy's garden, the fruit sing a chorus, a duet, and a solo warning him to stay away. The sources also indicate instrumental music. In *Turandot* music accompanies the princess, and there are indications of music during a pantomime. In *La donna serpente* a magic sleep overcomes Farrascad. Cherestanì then appears with her retinue, transforming the scene into a garden in front of her palace. Farrascad awakes to the sound of pleasant music.

20. Luciani, *Carlo Gozzi*, 2:501–648.

21. The editions used here are Gozzi, *Opere;* Gozzi, *Opere: Teatro e polemiche teatrali;* Gozzi, *Fiabe teatrali;* Gozzi, *Five Tales;* and Gozzi, *The Blue Monster.*

PLATE 1. *Ballet du Roy des Festes de Bacchus* (1651), 24me *entrée*, "Les fées qui enfantent des esprits folets." Paris, Bibliothèque Nationale [F-Pn], Estampes, Rés. Pd 74, fol. 91. (Courtesy of Bibliothèque Nationale de France.)

PLATE 2. *Géant*. F-Pn (Opéra), Rés. D. 216 III, fol. 11. (Courtesy of Bibliothéque Nationale de France.)

PLATE 3. *Zélindor, roi des sylphes*. F-Pn (Opéra), Rés. D. 216 VII, p. 23. (Courtesy of Bibliothéque Nationale de France.)

PLATE 4. Henri Gramont, "Le tableau magique," from *Zémire et Azor*. F-Pn, MUS. 1646, Cliché B.N. RcA 13056. (Courtesy of Bibliothéque Nationale de France.)

1. Basile's *Il pentamerone* provided Gozzi with material for his *L'amore delle tre melarance*[22] and *Il corvo*.[23]

2. Pompeo Sarnelli [Marsillo Reppone], *La Posilecheata* (Naples, 1684). This source also provided elements in *Zeim, re de' genj*,[24] and *L'augellino belverde*.[25]

3. Joseph de La Porte, ed., *La bibliothèque des génies et des fées* (Paris, 1764–1765).

4. Pétis de la Croix, *Les mille et un jours*,[26] provided material for six of Gozzi's *fiabe: Il re cervo*,[27] *Turandot*, *La donna serpente*,[28] *La Zobeide*,[29] *I pitocchi fortunati*,[30] and *Zeim, re de' genj*.[31]

5. Galland, *Les mille et une nuits*, for material in *Turandot*,[32] *La Zobeide*,[33] *I pitocchi fortunati*, and *Zeim, re de' genj*.

6. Thomas-Simon Gueullette, *Les mille et un quarts d'heure*, for *Il re cervo*,[34] and *Il mostro turchino*.[35]

22. Basile, *Il pentamerone* (1925), introduction and 2:324–40.

23. Ibid., trattenimento 9, Giornata 4 (1925), 2:222–35.

24. "La Vajassa fidele," 1885 ed., 31–46. See Luciani, *Carlo Gozzi*, 2:512, 627–28.

25. "Cunto terzo, La 'Ngannatrice 'ngannata," 1885 ed., 47–67. The story involves a magic dagger from *Les mille et une nuits*, "L'Histoire des trois soeurs jalouses de leur cadette," 1838 ed., 642–67); whoever holds this dagger knows the condition of a distant beloved.

26. The references here will be to the later edition of Pétis de la Croix, *Les mille et un jours*, 1848.

27. "L'Histoire du Prince Fadallah" (1848), 84–88.

28. "L'Histoire du roi Runzvanschad et de la princesse Schehéristany," 16–29 *jours* (1848), pp. 30–33 and 24–30 *jours* (1848), 43–48. Gozzi also inserted elements from "L'histoire du jeune roi de Thibet et de la princesse des Naïmans," 19–24 *jours* (1848), 33–43, in a short recitation by Pantalone. He also borrows the name of Demogorgone from Boccaccio; Boiardo, *Orlando innamorato*, 42, verses 28–30; and Ariosto.

29. The *conte turc*, "L'histoire du prince de Carisme et de la princesse de Géorgie," and "L'histoire du prince Seyf-Elmulouk." (See Luciani, *Carlo Gozzi (1720–1806)*, 2:527).

30. "L'Histoire du prince Fadlallah," 47–55 *jours* (1848), 73–83. The story also recalls an episode from "L'histoire de Couloufe" (the 21st *jour* of *Les mille et un jours*, 1848, 73–83.), using the same material as the French comic operas *Le cadi dupé*, *Le dormier éveillé*, and *Arlequin hulla, ou La femme répudiée*.

31. "L'histoire du Prince Seyf-Elmulouk et de Bedy-Aljemal," 101–3 *jours* (1848), 141–43. This tale, also available in Galland, *Les mille et une nuits*, viii, as "L'histoire du prince Zeyn-Alasnam et du roi des genies," served as the basis of the Parisian fair play *La statue merveilleuse* (1719, 1720), with the popular magic mirror that reveals vice and virtue.

32. "L'histoire des amours de Camaralzaman, prince de l'île des Enfans de Khalédan, et de Badoure, princesse de la Chine," 211–21 *nuits*. Lesage and d'Orneval set the same story as *La princesse de la Chine* (Foire St. Laurent, 15 June 1729), published in TdlF 7 (1731).

33. "L'histoire de Beder, prince de Perse, et de Giaure, princesse du royaume de Samandal" (1848), 358–91.

34. "L'Histoire des quatre sultanes de Citor," as well as other tales, reprinted in the multivolume *Le cabinet des fées* 21, 461–80.

35. "L'histoire du centaure bleu," 47–49, and several other *contes tartares* in the collection provide elements, e.g., "L'histoire d'Outzim-Ochantey, prince de Chine" and "Le singe couleur de

Gozzi mixed elements and situations from all of these sources, adapting characters and locations freely, as Lesage had done, and as others would do in future fairy-tale works for the stage. This mixture of elements created a complex and meandering plot reminiscent of commedia dell'arte that decisively informed the *fiabe*.

※

Gozzi gave his *fiabe* several generic designations. In his preface to *La donna serpente* he referred to a "new genre of the fairy tale for the theater."[36] He called it a "tragicomic tale" and a "clear allegory on the customs of men and the false studies of the times." Gozzi also labeled *Turandot* a tragicomic tale, as well as a "seriocomic" work "without showy magic effects or transformations." He designated his *L'augellino belverde* "a philosophical tale for the theater." Gozzi discussed the use of fairy tales in the prefaces to the *fiabe* and in two nondramatic works, *Ragionamento ingenuo e storia sincera dell'origine delle mie dieci fiabe teatrali* (Ingenuous Disquisition and Sincere History of My Ten Tales for the Theater, 1772)[37] and *Memorie inutili* (Useless Memoirs, 1780).[38] In the latter two accounts Gozzi expressed disdain for the plays of Voltaire, Rousseau, and Goldoni that idealize lower-class life.

Gozzi's critics complained that his *fiabe* were too plebeian and popular, successful only because of the wit of the actors and striking theatrical effects. Gozzi answered them in his preface to *Il corvo:*

> a silly, unrealistic, puerile plot, if developed with skill, artistry, and elegance, could have an effect on the emotions of an audience, commanding their attention and moving them to tears. I wrote *Il corvo* in order to prove the truth of my proposition. The fairy tale is commonly told to children, and I took its plot from a Neapolitan book entitled "Lo cunto de li cunti."[39]

Gozzi cites Boiardo, Ariosto,[40] and Tasso as geniuses "who gave poetic truth to impossible, marvelous events, and whose work has power over the human heart." In creating the wizard of *Il corvo*, Gozzi claims to have made a noble character out of the usual silly magicians of the commedia dell'arte. In his prefaces to *La donna serpente* and *Il re cervo* Gozzi cited the *Théâtre de la foire*, Le

feu." See Luciani, *Carlo Gozzi (1720–1806)*, 2:515. This story is a variation on Beauty and the Beast. Gozzi also borrowed material from classical mythology (e.g., the hydra), Boiardo, and Ariosto, *Orlando furioso*, canto 15, stanza 66.

36. This and the following quotation are taken from *La donna serpente* in Gozzi, *Five Tales*, 185.

37. In Gozzi, *Opere edite e inedite*, 1:3–64.

38. Gozzi, *Memorie inutili*, 1:34, 2:1–5. See Emery, "Autobiographer as Critic."

39. This and the following quotations in the paragraph are taken from the introduction to *Il corvo* in Gozzi, *Five Tales*, 21–24.

40. Gozzi cites a passage from *Orlando furioso* in *La donna serpente*.

Grand, and Gherardi as precedents for his "genre of the theatrical fairy tale," taking credit for creating this new genre. He wants to retain "something of the infantile silliness of fairy tales . . . to have the freedom to invent without the limitations of literary rules and stodginess." His "new genre is free, daring, and immoderately filled with artifice and invention." Gozzi also praised the "fantastic solemnity of impossible events" and the use of an "allegorical moral lesson."[41]

Standard fairy-tale elements appear in the *fiabe*. Trials of the heroes are at the basis of several tales, such as *Turandot* and *La donna serpente*. In act 1, scene 5 of *La donna serpente* a table magically appears set with food, and a woman is enchanted into a hideous serpent. The king must kiss her in order to free her of this spell. In *Turandot* the hero, Prince Calaf, falls in love with a portrait of the Princess Turandot. An evil queen is the villain in *La donna serpente*. Truffaldino in *Il re cervo* is a bird catcher, a possible model for Schikaneder's Papageno in *Die Zauberflöte*. Dressed in an "oriental" green outfit, the bird catcher carries numerous oversized whistles tied to his chest. Gozzi clearly based the magical statue in *Il re cervo* on the magic mirror of fair plays, which in turn was derived from oriental fairy tales; it determines the truth of the statements of women (the statue smiles or laughs when the speaker lies about her virtue).

The Supernatural in Comic Opera

The comedian and playwright Joseph Felix von Kurz visited Venice in the 1760s and brought his Viennese brand of fantasy to that city. Both of his two theatrical collaborations with Giovanni Bertati included supernatural content. The first of these, a three-act *drama serio-giocoso per musica* entitled *La morte di Dimone, o sia L'innocenza vendicata*, with music by Antonio Tozzi (lost), was produced at Venice's Teatro San Cassiano in the autumn of 1763. This pastoral libretto (Venice: Paolo Colombani, 1763) includes episodes with deities, magic transformations, and machines. Kurz and his wife played Cupid and Amor. During the Carnival season of the following year Bertati and Kurz staged their three-act *Li creduti spiriti*, again at San Cassiano. The title of this *spettaculo a guisa d'intermedio* may be translated as "The Supposed Spirits." The young Johann Gottlieb Naumann and two other composers provided the music (arias, ensembles, and pantomime) for this *dramma giocoso* (lost).[42] Kurz rooted his approach in Parisian adaptations of the commedia dell'arte that had

---

41. See the preface to *Il re cervo* in Gozzi, *Five Tales*, 73.

42. Libretto, Venice: Paolo Colombani, 1764. Copies in A-Wn, F-Pn, US-Wc [Schatz 7064]. Pirker, *Teutsche Arien*, posits that Bertati may have based his *dramma giocoso* on an original German magic comedy by Kurz, but he found no direct model, only similarities with Kurz's previous Viennese comedies, especially the pantomime in act 1, which seems to have been based on the pantomime in *Der aufs neue begeisterte und belebte Bernardon* (Vienna, n.d.) in A-Wst, shelfmark 22200 A, and the manuscript in A-Wn, Handschriftsammlung, Cod. ms. 12709, 217–32.

become popular in Vienna. Although the episodic second act, with its series of colorful and diverse tableaux, suggests French fair comedies, the spectacular transformations recall Venetian opera. The recent *fiabe* by Gozzi also may have influenced Bertati, who described his piece as a purely comic entanglement of lovers, with a liberal amount of marvelous effects. Proserpina brings a spirit named Sodi (played by Kurz) out of hell and charges him with reuniting lovers with their proper mates. The businessman Mordone, disguised as a magician, instigates a long magic ballet-pantomime at the end of act 1 as he and four other magicians bring a mortal back to life after he has been murdered (his ghost sings a duet with his grieving lover). The text also includes powerful magic wands and books, a flying chariot, and a mad scene. An astrologer named Medusa makes oracular pronouncements, and Sodi performs comical magic tricks to torment his foes.

✳

The comic and the supernatural have numerous parallels in their musical style. Both utilize extreme and grotesque expression, with disjunct melody, elaborate accompanimental figures, and abrupt changes in affect. When they do occur in Italian comic opera, supernatural allusions are usually brief episodes within the rapid pace of a dramatic ensemble. But in heroic opera references to ghost scenes, musical expressions of terror, and magic vocal incantation (with descending leaps and repeated notes in the vocal line) seem to have been common. Florian Leopold Gassmann's music for Calzabigi's comedy *L'opera seria* (BT, 1769) includes one of these arias (No. 24, "Pallide ombre del misero amante" in E-flat) for the soprano Stonatrilla (her name means "tone-deaf").[43] Gassmann's pupil Salieri followed his master in his score for Giovanni Gastone Boccherini's *Le donne letterate* (BT, 1770), employing the same vocal style when Baggeo (bass) asks a ghost to come from Erebus during the duet "Credo che onori la mia tragedia."[44] At this point in the plot a librettist recites the ghost scene he has written.

The first full-length magical comic opera appears to have been *L'osteria di Marechiaro*, a *commedia per musica* in three acts by Francesco Cerlone with music by Giacomo Insanguine (lost). The premiere was in Naples at the Fiorentini Theater in 1768. The original performance run seems to have been highly successful,[45] and the libretto was revised in two acts that same year, with new music by Giovanni Paisiello.[46] With over one hundred performances, *L'osteria di Marechiaro* proved to be a popular work. Its success assured that the super-

43. Facsimile, IOB 89, ed. Weimer, 317–47. Also see Rice, *Antonio Salieri*, 94.

44. Rice, *Antonio Salieri*, 139.

45. See Scherillo, *L'opera buffa napoletana*, 309.

46. Libretto, Naples: Vincenzo Flauto, 1769. For more details and musical incipits, see Robinson, *Giovanni Paisiello: Catalogue*, 62–66. The autograph score survives in Naples, Biblioteca del

natural would have a future in comic opera, developing expressive resources in more substantial ways.

The preface to one libretto attributes the magical aspects to Luis Velez de Guevara's *Il diavolo zoppo* and Lesage's *Le diable boiteux*.[47] The main plot line concerns an ambitious widow wishing to marry a flirtatious count. True love is in need of magic powers to set things right. The supernatural material occurs in act 2, mostly in simple recitative. Although there is little overall to distinguish Paisiello's music from that in operas with more realistic plots, a few episodes warrant comment. Hearing mysterious wailing, the count discovers a little spirit (*spiritello*) in a bottle. When he releases the spirit it grants him a magic wand along with a promise of its protection. The count, impervious to gun and sword, can now transform people and the surroundings as he wishes. He renders his detractors immobile with his magic wand, making them first march in lockstep, then crawl on the ground like soldiers in battle. Paisiello gives this action marchlike music within a buffa-style quintet, a musical association of the march with trancelike movement that was rooted historically in the magic scenes of French comic opera. The spirit then returns in the form of the widow's dead husband to reprimand her for her infidelity to him and to release the count from his promise to marry her. When a small band of soldiers is about to seize the spirit and the count, the spirit flies in the air and eludes the pursuers. This vision of the dead husband returning and people flying terrifies everyone present. The voices slowly sing the text "Oh what strange terror! It seems like a dream to me!" as repeated minor and diminished chords and *alla zoppa* figures evoke the musical terror of serious opera. The count then summons another character back from Hades. Ominous repeated tonic notes in the horns lead to an incantation-like invocation to Pluto in *sdrucciolo* rhythms with the same repeated notes in the vocal line "Terrible Pluto, if you had love for the lovely, beautiful Proserpina." The horns accompany the vocal part with a sustained tonic, and the strings play "teeth-chattering" tremolo figures. The overall effect suggests a parody of an old invocation style from seventeenth-century opera.

Cerlone and Paisiello also wrote a one-act *farsetta* to be appended to the comedy *La Claudia vendicata* or *Pulcinella vendicato nel ritorno di Marechiaro*, a plot that reproduces the kind of magic scenes that occurred in act 2 of *L'osteria di Marechiaro*. The cast includes a magician who gives a magic wand to Pulcinella. He in turn banishes his enemies to Vesuvius and transforms his rival, first into an ass, then into a clock. The score too reproduces the magic scenes that occurred in the preceding opera. The magician's cavatina in B-flat begins with a monotone incantation in *sdrucciolo* rhythm ("Dal cupo barbatro") accompanied by string tremolos.

Conservatorio, with copies in Naples and Genoa. Paisiello's version truncates the material of act 3 and incorporates it into the finale of act 2.

47. Robinson, *Naples and Neapolitan Opera*, attributes the magical element to the *Arabian Nights*, but I have been unable to identify any such influence.

The score of *L'osteria di Marechiaro* makes clear that music in comic opera around 1770 lagged in inventiveness behind that of its serious counterpart. The synthesis of Italian and French musical styles from Handel to Jommelli, Traetta, and Gluck had only a small influence in the *commedia per musica*. But from this modest beginning would come a remarkable flowering of magic and supernatural allusions in the scores of comic opera, the substance of which would rival and occasionally even exceed the music of serious opera in the final fifteen years of the eighteenth century.

Comic Opera, 1771–79

In the 1770s Italian composers began to invest comic operas with substantial music for supernatural scenes using techniques honed in serious opera. Bertati's three-act *dramma giocoso L'anello incantato* (Venice, Teatro San Moisè, autumn 1771; Lisbon's Teatro della Rua dos Condes, 1772), with music by Ferdinando Bertoni, combines epic romance with commedia dell'arte in a score containing several imaginative evocations of the supernatural content.[48] The tripartite *sinfonia* (Allegro–Allegretto–Allegro) has rapid scale figures and other features common to both supernatural and comic operas. The magical scenes include an episode in act 1 where the sorceress Elisa amuses herself by invoking a spirit to enchant the gate of her rival's house with a magic circle. She waves her wand, singing an incantation with a motive consisting of repeated tonic notes and a descending octave (see ex. 4.1). The thirds in the violins provide an accompaniment used for similar invocations by composers since Handel (see the discussion of *Teseo* in chapter 3). Elisa's invocation ends with unison-and-octave sonority. The spirit appears and creates a magic circle to instrumental pantomime music consisting of simple quarter-note phrases supported by sustained notes in the winds and a pedal in the bass. Everyone who steps into the circle is forced to dance. The ensuing enchanted dance is a short three-measure segment in triple meter.[49]

In act 2 of *L'anello incantato* magical events occur in short episodes during the finale. These include *terribile* references in the vocal quartet. After the characters have witnessed the power of Elisa they exclaim "Che stravaganza orribile" to sudden triplet accompaniment, then "qual incantesimo magico" to dotted duplet chords, and finally "O caro ben terribile" to unison-and-octave sonority, followed by triplet accompaniment figures in terraced dynamics. Then Elisa reproaches the other characters with the same descending octave motive that characterized her invocation in the act 1 finale.

48. Libretto, Lisbon: Stamperia Reale, 1772, copy in US-Wc, Schatz 929. An autograph score is preserved in Ostiglia, Fondazione Greggiati, Manoscritti musiche B 228, 1–2. Unlike some other Lisbon operas in this period, this one uses both male and female singers.

49. Involuntary dancing through a magic spell is an old device found in early seventeenth-century commedia dell'arte plots. For details, see the introduction and below.

EXAMPLE 4.1 Ferdinando Bertoni, *L'anello incantato*, act 1, scene 10

Gaetano Martinelli's three-act *Le avventure di Cleomede*, with music by Jommelli (Lisbon, Ajuda Theater, 6 June 1772),[50] is another mock-heroic opera with elements of the commedia dell'arte. The magical effects in this *dramma serio-comico* include an enchanted ring that makes the wearer irresistible, a magic herb that changes the appearance of a person, a deadly plant that is the source of power for the chthonic sorceress Trivia, her magic wand, a magically set table, and numerous transformations.[51] In his *argomento* Martinelli claimed that this story was taken from Vito Amico's (1677–1762) *Cronica di Sicilia*.[52] Paralleling the Armida plot, in this story Trivia captures lovers in her enchanted forest and falls in love with the hero Cleomede, who cuts down her magic tree to liberate the captives and destroy her supernatural power. He receives help from a spirit that descends in a machine. Piremone, a cowardly and lascivious savage, and the chambermaid Ersilla provide the comic episodes. Several magical disguises and transformations occur in the plot, and the special effects include lightning, frightening noises, and thunder.

Jommelli's music for *Le avventure di Cleomede*, far more vivid in its expression than that of Bertoni in *L'anello incantato*, uses tonality and harmony as expressive devices. Like Bertoni's enchantress Elisa, Trivia sings descending octave

50. I consulted the libretto (Lisbon: Stamperia Reale, 1772) in US-Wc, Schatz 4889.

51. McClymonds, *Niccolò Jommelli*, 220–21.

52. I have not located a volume by Amico with this title. It may be that Martinelli is referring to a section of one of Amico's other works on Sicily, e.g., *Catana illustrata*, *Sicilia sacra*, or *Opuscoli di autori siciliani*.

leaps in the act 1, scene 4 duet "Ah! Domani almeno spietata," recalling incantatory vocal styles in earlier opera. Her aria (act 1, scene 14, marked "Andante ma brilliante") has bravura coloratura, which may have been an expression of her magical power in song. Several of the transformations in the libretto receive distinctive musical treatment, with pictorial elements. Some of these pieces appear to have been used in conjunction with stage machines. The expression is either a soft, elegant enchantment or a terrifying fury, as in the short pantomimic D major "Sinfonia per il Combattimento," which depicts Cleomede's battle with the monster who guards Trivia's magic plant. This triple-meter Allegro has brisk scales in the low strings moving up to the violins in broad sweeps, accompanied by punctuations of marcato notes with the oboes and horns.

In Jommelli's opera six instances of descriptive music for magic scenes occur in accompanied recitative. In act 1, scene 10, Cleomede is about to enter the dark enchanted forest when a dense cloud descends and dissolves into a luminous temple with a celestial genie. Magical transformation music is suddenly heard in the distance (called "soave armonia" in the libretto). Jommelli scored this triple-meter Larghetto, in G major, with muted violins playing in thirds and sixths; the conjunct melodic material is laden with busy ornamental figuration in dialogue with two flutes doubled by oboes and soft horns. With pizzicato bass and simple consonant sonority, this section presents an elegant decorative musical image of the luminous temple (see ex. 4.2). Sustained strings signaling a supernatural character accompany the recitative.

When Cleomede recognizes the monsters and his warriors taken captive by Trivia, flutes appear in the orchestra (act 1, scene 15). Then the score indicates "orribile armonia," a *terribile* episode starting in D minor with accented dissonance, diminished seventh chords, tremolo figures in the bass, and bellowing horns. This music depicts the howling and shrieks mentioned in the recitative. Cleomede sings of feeling his blood freezing, and brisk violin scales outline diminished chords. When he mentions "the atrocious spectacle," there is rapid string figuration in C minor. The sudden appearance of monsters corresponds to the altered chords E-flat, B-flat, and G minor, with more rapid string figures and dotted rhythms.

When Trivia transforms her statues to impress Cleomede (act 2, scene 9, [7 in the libretto]), the composer sets her incantation in a recitative with sustained strings marked "piano e tenute," creating the effect associated with oracles and ghosts. As she changes the statue of the fickle Lerteo into Cleomede, the sonority takes an unexpected turn to the major mode. The accompaniment also changes, as magical flashes of light appear in the form of quick string figures during a passage marked Allegretto.[53] In act 2, scene 15 (13 in the libretto), Trivia sings her vow for vengeance, which is filled with infernal imagery. The score is marked "Con spirito," and the accompaniment includes quick scale

53. Magically invoked thunder and lightning in the libretto (act 2, scene 12) occurs during a *recitativo semplice* with no evident correspondence in the score (act 2, scene 14).

EXAMPLE 4.2 Niccolò Jommelli, *Le avventure di Cleomede*, act 1, scene 10

figures in the strings with diminished chords in the keys of D minor and G minor. Jommelli's figures correspond to the flashes of lightning and the thunder created by the sorceress and specified in the libretto.

When Cleomede advances into the enchanted forest to battle the monster guarding the magic plant (act 3, scene 5), each mention of the horrid abyss (*orrido speco*) is represented by a short gesture in the accompaniment through a series of changing keys. In the next scene Trivia arrives after Cleomede has killed the monster. When she raises her wand and calls up a whirlwind of vapors, the key changes to the infernal E-flat. A forte section of instrumental music with short rapid scales and fanfare arpeggios accompanies her invocation of the abyss. The subsequent duet in E-flat describes horrific visions. Loud infernal sustained notes in the horns and oboes accompany the voices. An accompanied recitative concludes this scene as Trivia describes horrible images through a series of changing keys (E-flat, B-flat, C, then finally D). She throws herself into a fiery chasm to a short instrumental *sinfonia* in D major with octave-and-unison sonority and rapid passages in thirds. The final scene follows with a short chorus as the forest is transformed back into the temple of Ceres, and the people rejoice. The genie now appears, and his recitative uses the divine effect of sustained chords in the strings.

As in other Italian comic operas, most of the supernatural musical depiction in *Cleomede* occurs in the finale ensembles. In act 1 (scene 16) Dirce conjures food for the hungry Fidalmo in D minor, with oboe and flute solos. Motives in the instrumental parts mimic the gloomy gestures, actions, and expressions described in the vocal exclamations, some set to unison-and-octave sonority. Jommelli depicts flashes of lightning in the strings and winds as the actors cry out "Ahi!" During a long instrumental pedal a set table magically appears, to the stunned expressions of the actors. A minuet-like Allegretto in G major serves to express their delight, which increases with the faster surface rhythms provided by triplets in the section marked "Più allegro." This joy is interrupted by the arrival of the savage Piremone, announced by the sustained dominant notes of his "buccina," played on the solo horn. An Andante moderato in D minor changes their mood to fear, also signaled by the unison-and-octave sonority. The women escape, and Dirce turns the table into a cow before going off and leaving the men. This transformation is accompanied by a short instrumental interlude with fast ascending string scales in parallel thirds, followed by dotted rhythmic motives.

Bertati's *L'isola d'Alcina*, a *dramma giocoso* in three acts with music by Giuseppe Gazzaniga,[54] was first performed in Venice at the Teatro San Moisè in 1772 and was thereafter staged in numerous European cities such as Dresden, Paris, Vienna, and Eszterháza. Bertati borrowed elements from Ariosto in this

---

54. There are numerous librettos; I consulted one printed in Dresden 1773, US-Wc, Schatz 3666. Manuscript scores are preserved in A-Wn, Dlb, and F-Pn. Bertati's libretto was also set by Giacomo Rust for Bologna (1772).

satire, including magical sleep scenes and a fountain whose waters make one forget. If one drinks too great a quantity of the water it will cause madness. But the main point in this macaronic text is the comic contrast of various national stereotypes of lovers. The Italian Brunoro, the Frenchman La Rose, the Spaniard Don Lopez, and the Englishman James are shipwrecked on Alcina's magical island (joined later by the German baron Brick Brack). The plot evolves as the men succumb to the flirtatious but fickle sorceress, while Alcina's servant Lesbina conspires with Brick Brack to devise an escape. To resist Alcina's power Lesbina gives Brick Brack protective enchantments for his ears (virgin's wax) and his eyes (bat's blood). The baron must approach the sleeping Alcina and cut off a lock of her hair in order to free them from her enchantments. He does so, and Alcina vows vengeance by invoking the Furies in an angry aria. When her captives board a ship to take them off the island, Alcina arrives and makes a magic invocation to summon her chariot with winged dragons, threatening to pursue them and cause a storm to wreck their vessel. They sing in an ensemble that they are already free from her powers and sail off, and the raging Alcina departs in her flying chariot.

Despite all the supernatural material in the plot, Gazzaniga's music is mostly in the comic style; magical allusions are present only for humorous effect. La Rose's exaggerated *recitativo con istrumenti*, a Largo in C minor with rapid string figuration and prominent horns (a French style for the Frenchman), is an example of this comic use of the music of terror. But Gazzaniga provided no distinctive music for the magical events or for Alcina, who, along with the mortal characters, has coloratura arias.

This libretto inspired at least three other operas. *L'isola incantata*, an anonymous two-act intermedio with music by Marcello Bernardini (Rome, Teatro Capranica, Carnival, 1778),[55] is a short *farsa*, with no overture and just five vocal parts; the only supernatural episode has Alcina invoking the deities of the inferno in finale of act 2 with a repeated descending triad in a D major section, for trumpet and strings. Bruni's *L'isle enchantée* (Paris, 1789, see chapter 2), and Anfossi's *farsa La maga Circe* (Rome 1778, see below) are more substantial revisions of Bertati's libretto. Bertati would revisit this topic again in 1789 with his libretto *La fata capricciosa*, a *dramma giocoso* in two acts, with music by Francesco Gardi (lost; premiere at the Teatro Giustiniani in San Moisè, Carnival 1789).[56] In addition to the Alcina episode, where an ugly old fairy appears young and beautiful,[57] Bertati included the same device used by Casti in *La grotta di Trofonio* (1785): the magical transformation of personalities.

55. A score from Lisbon is in D-Dlb, Mus. 2671-F-1, entitled *L'isola d'Alcina*.

56. Libretto, Venice: Appresso Modesto Fenzo, 1789 (no. 9804 in Sartori). Gardi also composed the music for a two-act *Don Giovanni* (after Bertati) for Venice in 1787.

57. Other mock-heroic operas based on Ariosto include the anonymous *dramma giocoso per musica Il castello d'Atlante* (Brescia, Carneval 1791), set in the castle of Atlante with demons, and magic thunder and lightning. For details, see Döring, 279.

Bertati's two-act *dramma giocoso Il cavaliere errante [nell'isola incantata]* (known also as *Stordilano, principe di Granata*), with music by Traetta,[58] had its premiere in either Naples or Venice, c. 1777–78.[59] Other productions were staged in Vienna (1779), Parma (1780), Eszterháza (1782), Padua (1786), and Paris (1790). Traetta's impressive score has numerous supernatural elements that warrant close examination. The first segment of the tripartite overture in D major (Allegro vivace) has a series of rapid fantastic figures and slurred ascending three-note scalar bursts, suggesting that something extraordinary is at hand. Supernatural references are also apparent in the arias, ensembles, and finales.

The plot of *Il cavaliere errante* recalls chivalric fairy tales such as d'Auneuil's *Les chevaliers errans et le genie familier* (Paris: Ribou, 1709) and French fairy-tale settings for the theater such as Romagnesi and Riccoboni's *Le conte des fées* (Paris, Théâtre-Italien, 1735), using elements from epic romance and commedia dell'arte.[60] The French paladin Guido travels with his squire Calotta in search of the sorceress Melissa, who he hopes will help him find his beloved Arsinda. They arrive at a cave where Guido finds a subterranean temple vault illuminated by chandeliers. Traetta indicates a "ritornello patetico," a graceful and elegant prelude to fit the moment with highly articulated conjunct melodic motion and expressive dissonance to enhance the contrast with the predominantly consonant sonority of the thirds and sixths. A chorus of infernal spirits tries to frighten them away, but Guido persists. (The chorus in E-flat, for tenors and basses with horns, recalls Gluck's "blessed spirits" rather than the *spiriti infernali* described in the libretto.) Melissa appears and sings a sotto voce incantation in recitative, during which she makes strange gestures with her magic wand to summon her spirits. The accompaniment suggests her movements through "pantomimic" figuration in the strings, with unison-and-octave sonority (see ex. 4.3). The following trio, an Allegro moderato in B-flat with quick scale figures in the violins and bass (first heard during the instrumental introduction), includes punctuating horn interjections. Melissa starts with a comic version of a conjuring invocation for her magic circle, "Te primo invoco,

58. Manuscripts scores survive in Milan, D-Dlb, H-Bn, and US-Wc. I consulted the manuscript in F-Pn, D. 9014.

59. According to Ferrari, *Spettacoli drammatico-musicale*, Fétis cited a performance of Bertati's *Stordilano, principe di Granata*, an *opera semiseria e bernesca*, in three acts for Parma in the spring of 1760, but there is no corroborating evidence of this early date. Sartori, *I libretti italiana*, 2:97–98, lists a libretto from Rome with the date 1770. I consulted the 1780 libretto from Parma in US-Wc, Schatz 10389.

60. Italian translations of *opéra-comique* with fairy-tale content include Marmontel and Grétry's *Zémire et Azor*. The first, by Mattia Verazi (*Zemira ed Azore*, Mannheim, 1776), is a pasticcio with musical numbers by his former collaborator, the late Jommelli. Next Giuseppe Perotti composed an entirely new setting for Parma. Sartori identified librettos for performances of *Zemira e Azor* in Teatro Maccarani, Nice (1777), London's King's Theatre, Haymarket (1779, 1780, and 1783), Graz (1782), Milan (1786), and Turin (1787).

EXAMPLE 4.3 Tomasso Traetta, *Il cavaliere errante*, act 1, scene 4

Orrenda Dite, Spiriti erranti qua comparite." Her triadic melody descends an octave, and the vocal part continues with forceful, wide leaps; accompaniment includes octave-and-unison sonority, rapid scales, and *alla zoppa* syncopation. Melissa's spirits tell of Arsinda's abduction by Stordilano, the prince of Granata. Using the powers of magic incantation, Stordilano is holding her captive on a beautiful enchanted island, where he is trying to win her affection. Here Traetta constructed an oracle scene in recitative for the spirit (bass) in E-flat.

The spirit sings in normal recitative style to an accompaniment marked "Adagio staccato," with "vibrate" indicated for the notes in the violin part. When the spirit sings, the accompaniment changes to low-pitched, sustained chords in the strings, a device associated with otherworldly expression; instrumental interjections include staccato and fast scale figures. Melissa offers her help as the patron of faithful lovers. Her chariot, drawn by winged horses, will transport them to the island, and she promises to appear when Guido summons her.

On an enchanted island Arsinda's servant Dorina tells of seeing a flying chariot with winged horses carrying the evil magician Ismeno, who has come to ask the custodial spirits of the island what magic is needed to avert danger. Traetta drew upon the long tradition of magicians, such as Zoroastro in Handel's *Orlando,* when he composed the music for Ismeno. In scene 11 the magician (bass) sings a bipartite aria (Maestoso aperto in E-flat, then Allegretto agitato in the unusual key of B-flat minor), "Veggo già un nembo insorgere," describing his forecast of a horrific future. His vocal line has repeated notes (some in *sdrucciolo* rhythms) and portentous descending octave leaps. The accompaniment includes octave-and-unison sonority, trumpet-like triadic motives, short scalar bursts, and tremolos. The return of the "primo tempo" section features the addition of brief ascending scale figures in the bass and violins for a fantastic effect. In scene 12 Ismeno conjures the infernal spirits in a recitative with the strings playing thirty-second notes marked "tremolo." This response (the spirits advise Ismeno to frighten off the two strangers) is delivered in a brief *terribile* chorus in C minor (SATB) with octave-and-unison sonority, slight chromaticism, and string tremolos.

In act 2 Guido and Calotta arrive and attempt to enter the palace when darkness suddenly descends and flames block their path. Guido calls out to Melissa for help. Thunder and lightning accompany the voice of the sorceress as she instructs them to proceed without fear. Guido enters the palace and attacks Stordilano. Ismeno touches both Guido and Stordilano with his magic wand, immobilizing them. After consulting his spirits the magician enchants the two men with a new spell that makes them mad in order to prevent them from recognizing each other. Here Ismeno has a substantial invocation aria, "Vedrai, senti," with descending octave leaps and repeated notes in the vocal line. Along with string tremolos and repeated notes, Traetta gave the first violins (marked "vibrate") ornate figuration. In scene 3 he evoked earlier magic operas as the deluded Guido sings a recitative with descriptive accompaniment figures and a citation from Gluck's often quoted rondò from *Orfeo ed Euridice,* "Che farò senza Euridice." With its free formal structure and allusions to musical traditions of the past, Guido's musical expression of insanity recalls the madness scene in Handel's *Orlando.*[61]

61. The story continues with Ismeno restoring Stordilano's memory and informing him of a scheme to deceive Arsinda. Stordilano will wear Guido's helmet and Guido will wear Stordilano's cap, while Ismeno will enchant Arsinda to make her believe that Stordilano is Guido. She will

EXAMPLE 4.4 Vincenzo Righini, *Il convitato di pietra*, act 2, finale

Vincenzo Righini's music for Nunziato Porta's three-act *dramma tragicomico* on the Don Juan story, *Il convitato di pietra, ossia Il dissoluto punito* (Prague 1776, Vienna and Esterháza 1777),[62] includes a descriptive overture and supernatural episodes in the finales of acts 2 and 3. The overture, in B-flat, has segments with infernal horns, *alla zoppa* syncopation, string tremolos, and segments of stormy *terribile* music in the minor mode. The second act includes an appearance of the statue (bass) and the invitation to dinner, all set as accom-

marry him before she discovers the deception. Melissa uncovers this plan and declares that she will foil Ismeno's plot by restoring Guido's and Calotta's memories with her wand. They secretly attend the wedding ceremony, and when Arsinda addresses the prince with Guido's name, the paladin reveals himself. She refuses to believe him, and after a scuffle, Guido calls out to Melissa. The fairy then appears, dispelling Ismeno's enchantment and returning Arsinda to Guido. Melissa uses her wand to create lightning and thunder while transforming the enchanted island into an uninhabitable desert where Stordilano and Ismeno are condemned. The others leave happily on a ship that has been prepared to take them back to their native land.

62. Manuscripts survive in A-Wgm, A-Wn, and H-Bn, Mus ms OE-84 (with other material added by Haydn). The manuscript in A-Wn, shelfmark S.M. 4235, is a copy of the finales of acts 2 and 3.

EXAMPLE 4.5 Vincenzo Righini, *Il convitato di pietra*, act 3, finale

panied recitative. The eerie music for the ritornellos is in the Dorian D minor, which is associated with solemn and sacred expression. Unison-and-octave sonority, a slowly rising line, and abrupt bursts of forte followed immediately by piano dynamics all suggest something ominous and otherworldly. First scored for strings, repeated ritornellos add trumpets, horns, oboes, and finally timpani. Perhaps the composer chose the Andante sostenuto expression, the meter, and the regular rhythms in order to accompany the slow marching gait of the statue across the room (see ex. 4.4).

EXAMPLE 4.5 *(continued)*

The finale in act 3 contains the scene where Don Giovanni is taken to hell. Here Righini provided an unusual contrapuntal *coro di spiriti* (SATB) in the dark key of C minor, with strings, horns, and oboes. With its old-fashioned canzona opening and numerous suspensions, this chorus suggests the *stile antico* of contemporaneous sacred music (see ex. 4.5). The sudden bursts of forte tremolos and the phrase with octave-and-unison sonority recall Gluck's underworld imagery. The repeated minor cadence (i–VI–ii^{o6}–V–i) at measures 23–25 will be used in the infernal endings of Salieri's *Les Danaïdes* (1784), Mozart's *Don Giovanni*, and the collaborative singspiel *Der Stein der Weisen* (1790). Righini set Giovanni's tormented exclamations to wide leaps in his melody, accompanied by a steady eighth-note walking bass and suspensions in the violins.

Like Righini's opera, Giuseppe Calegari's setting of Pietro Pariati's two-act *drama giocoso* on the same subject, *Il convitato di pietra* (Venice, 1777),[63] is

63. I consulted the manuscript score in F-Pn, shelfmark, D. 1793.

mostly a conventional number opera save for the finales. The Commendatore (bass) appears at dinner in the act 2 finale. He joins the ensemble in G minor, singing "Mangia, mangia, Don Giovanni," accompanied by dotted accompaniment figures that include descending octaves. The servant Passarini's (bass) reactions are reflected in the string tremolos that depict his chattering teeth, mentioned in the text. The sonority in the accompaniment changes to octaves and unisons when the Commendatore asks for Giovanni's hand in a pledge. When they clasp hands, Giovanni (tenor) sings of a freezing cold, and thirty-second-note tremolos accompany him. At the Commendatore's call for "pentiti" the horns blare, accompanied by rapid string figures. A Largo starts as the onlookers react in horror. The music has dotted rhythmic figures, rapid scalar runs in sixty-fourth notes, and bursts of short scale figures in the strings and bass. An Allegro follows in A-flat with rapid thirty-second notes and an ostinato figure | ♩♩ ♪ ♩♩ ♪ | that is heard as Giovanni recoils from the *mostri d'averno* that tear out his viscera. He is taken to hell to the sound of sixty-fourth-note ascending runs in the strings and the bass. Then the Commendatore sings the moral to whole notes in the strings. As in Bertati's and Da Ponte's later versions of the story, Pariati has a final chorus for the characters remaining on stage to comment on the terrifying event.

Comic Opera, 1780–91

Italian comic operas with supernatural events became more common in the 1780s, with multiple settings of the Don Juan story, magic operas, and even a Viennese-style fairy-tale opera in Italian, entitled *Rübenzahl, o sia Il vero amore* (Dresden, 1789). Librettists also used supernatural devices in the *farse* of the 1780s, sometimes translating and adapting French librettos such as Favart's popular *La belle Arsène* (1789).[64] Favart's *La fée Urgèle* was likewise translated as *La fata Urgella, o sia Quel che piace alle donne in ogni tempo*, a *farsa* by G. Squilloni (Florence, Teatro Borgo Ognissanti, 26 December 1791, music lost). Even Lorenzo Da Ponte produced one work of this type when he seems to have arranged Marmontel's Beauty and the Beast libretto as a three-act *dramma giocoso* entitled *Zemira e Azor*, for either Barcelona (1791) or London (1796).[65] The overall trend in comic opera was toward an expansion that rivaled the scope of serious opera.

Some aspects of comic operas in this period stem from earlier practices. False-magic episodes are still present, for example, in Goldoni's *Il mondo della luna*, set by Haydn (1777), and in Giuseppe Palomba's *La quacquera spiritosa*,

---

64. On French librettos, see Bryant, "La Farsa musicale veneziana." On *La belle Arsène*, see Iacuzzi, *European Vogue of Favart*, 243; the subject was also set as a ballet, *La bella Arsene* in 1781; ibid., 369.

65. Stevenson and McClymonds, "Tozzi, Antonio," also cite Da Ponte's setting for Barcelona. Carter, "Da Ponte, Lorenzo," cites the London performance but not the Barcelona staging.

set by Pietro Guglielmi (1782). During Joseph Haydn's long service in Eszterháza he wrote and produced a number of operas, several with supernatural
content. He added music to Bertati and Gazzaniga's *L'isola di Alcina* (1786),
along with serious operas like Traetta's *Ifigenia in Tauride* (1786), and the pasticcio opera *Circe, ossia L'isola incantata* (1789).[66]

Haydn's first supernatural opera for Eszterháza combined satire and epic
romance in a mock-heroic text. In *Orlando paladino*, a three-act *dramma eroico-
mico* (6 December 1782), Nunziato Porta adapted an earlier libretto by Badini,
previously set to music by Guglielmi as *Le pazzie d'Orlando* in 1771.[67] The *sinfonia* starts with its mocking slurred scalar bursts in the cellos and double basses,
a device associated both with the terrifying and the Italian comic style. Alcina
has no coloratura in this number opera; she displays her power through other
musical means. The composer chose not to set a number of magical episodes
with descriptive music, for example, in act 2, when Alcina uses her powers to
turn the mad Orlando to stone and then restores him to life and locks him in a
grotto.[68]

Haydn provided a short instrumental piece for the appearance of Alcina
in act 1, scene 3, designated as "una breve orrida sinfonia." The first of two
instances of stage-machine music in the opera, this is a *terribile* Allegro in
C minor, with diminished and Neapolitan harmony, octave-and-unison sonority, pedals, rapid repeated notes, and fast descending scales in the strings
and winds. In her first aria, "Ad un guardo, a un cenno solo," Alcina vaunts
her magic powers to the distressed Angelica. With vivid musical imagery
reminiscent of Vivaldi's setting, she makes the sea rage and the earth tremble
with shudders of rapid sixteenth-note repeated chords. She then creates lightning bursts with rapid descending scales in unison-and-octave sonority. The
mode changes to minor when she commands that "greedy Fate be taken with
an icy fear," and the harmony turns to the flat side of the tonal spectrum, with
unison-and-octave sonority. It is as if her words were controlling the orchestra
by a powerful magic force.

Like that of his contemporaries, Haydn's accompanied recitative for supernatural scenes contains extreme expressive content, with fantasy style allowing for a free, episodic musical structure. In *Orlando paladino* Haydn also drew
on the French tradition (by now familiar in Italian opera) of extended instrumental segments within recitative, usually to set a mood or depict dramatic

66. Based on Anfossi's *La maga Circe*, this opera has an accompanied recitative scene by Haydn
reminiscent of his *Armida*, when in act 2 Pedrillo seeks entrance to a mysterious castle and is met
by apparitions.

67. For studies on this opera, see Geyer-Kiefl, "Joseph Haydn's vis comica," and B. A. Brown,
"*Le Pazzie d'Orlando*." Haydn's setting was staged several times in central Europe beginning in
1787.

68. I observe the scene numbering used in Haydn, *Werke*, Reihe 25, Bd. 11. Clark, "Orlando
paladino," gives different numbers.

events. Two of these *stromentati* sections involve supernatural elements. Act 2, scene 7 is an *ombra* scene for Angelica, and Haydn's music is a psychological portrait of distress, instability, and despair. It starts by depicting the enchanted forest through fantastic music in F major, with rapid appoggiaturas decorating the melody, a device later used by Mozart for the Three Boys in *Die Zauberflöte*. This music introduces Angelica's disturbed recitative, whose harmony expresses instability as it moves to borrowed and altered chords.

Haydn chose the appropriate key of E-flat to depict Orlando's deluded reactions to an imagined "mostro dell'Averno," hydra, and fire-breathing dragon (act 2, scene 10).[69] The music traverses abruptly changing keys, with unison-and-octave sonority, diminished chords, and rapid scales for the strings supported by wind chords. Short, sweeping scale figures in the violins suggest the dragon's flames. An instrumental passage creates appropriate harmonic instability as the tonic E-flat is followed by a D-flat octave sonority leading to C, then to F minor as Orlando asks "Where am I?" and "Am I delirious?" A cadence in E-flat punctuates his next question, "Or am I awake?," and the music suddenly returns to the reality of the tonic key, leading to his comic aria "Cosa vedo!," with its images of serpents, torments, and Furies.

Giovanni Battista Casti's *commedia per musica* in two acts, *La grotta di Trofonio*,[70] was set to music three times. The first, by Salieri (Vienna, BT, 12 October 1785), enjoyed great success, and the opera was popular in numerous European cities and was translated into several languages. The libretto was then reworked by Giuseppe Palomba for the Teatro de' Fiorentini in Naples (autumn 1785), with new music by Paisiello.[71] Palomba changed the names of a few characters and added some new twists to the plot. A further setting by Antonio Amicone for Rome's Teatro Valle, Carnival 1786, is apparently lost.[72] The following year Gottlieb Stephanie translated the Palomba libretto into a *komisches Singspiel* for Vienna's Burgtheater, *Die Trofonius-Höhle*, retaining the music of Paisiello.[73] The plot uses an old myth, present in earlier French

69. Act 3, scene 5 is another psychological portrait of the despairing Angelica. Haydn depicted agitated expression with rapid scale figures and abrupt tempo and key changes (E-flat–C–D–E-flat–B-flat–F). He suggested lightning with brisk descending scales.

70. Libretto, Vienna: Gius. nob. de Kurzbek, n.d. See Steptoe, *Mozart–Da Ponte Operas*, 135–36. This libretto appears to be unrelated to Piron's *L'antre de Trofonius* (February 1722; see chapter 2). The first three scenes to the one-act comedy entitled *Les antres de Trofonius* by Antoine-René de Voyes d'Argenson, the Marquis de Paulmy (active c. 1740–61), survives in Paris, Bibliothéque de l'Arsenal, shelfmark Rondel Ms. 324 (9 folios). I wish to thank David Charlton for bringing this source to my attention.

71. The libretto (Naples, 1785) indicates the original material with asterisks (US-Wc, Schatz 7680). For sources and musical incipits, see Robinson, *Giovanni Paisiello: Catalogue of His Works*, 1:358–65. I consulted the manuscript score in F-Pn, D. 10172 (1–2).

72. Libretto, Roma: Gioacchino Puccinello, 1786, US-Wc, Schatz 175.

73. 15 July 1787. The libretto survives from a performance at the Teatro di S.A.E. di Sassonia (Dresden, 1786), US-Wc, Schatz 9297/9296.

comedies and soon to make its way in another guise into *Così fan tutte*. The scene is Greece during the time of Aristotle. Aristone wants to marry off his two daughters, Ofelia and Dori. They have contrasting dispositions: the former is serious, and the latter is lighthearted and vain. Their lovers, Artemidoro and Plistine, are similarly of contrasting dispositions. A powerful hermit-magician, the philosopher Trofonius, changes the dispositions of the two suitors with an incantation to his invisible spirits in his enchanted cave. Aristone then attempts to convince his daughters to exchange their lovers. The men return to the cave and regain their original personalities, but their fiancées have also ventured into the cave and have been transformed. Trofonius appears and explains the magic of the cave, restoring the women to their former dispositions. Thus the couples gain wisdom through the experience.[74]

In Salieri's setting[75] the slow, C minor introduction of the overture will return for Trofonio's magic invocation (act 1, scene 10). This striking material begins with a triadic motive followed by a segment in *alla zoppa* syncopation, descending octave leaps, thirty-second-note scales, and unison-and-octave sonority, the basic ingredients of eighteenth-century musical incantation (see ex. 4.6). In the invocation this material is transposed to D minor, and Salieri extends it with an additional tremolo passage. Trofonio's incantation first uses ominous repeated notes and wide leaps in the vocal line, then a triadic motive. At the descending octave on the word *folgori* (thunderbolts) the basses, violins, and oboes explode in ascending thirty-second-note scale figures. As with most invocations, a chorus of spirits soon responds. The unseen male chorus sings unison phrases in a ten-measure Andante sostenuto that starts with an abrupt modulation from F major to the remote key of G-flat, accompanied by sudden string and bass tremolos with timpani rolls. Their melody (doubled by the bassoons) then begins with a descending triadic motive on E-flat minor. The line rises, accompanied by a chromatic modulation (marked "un poco di moto") until it reaches a C major chord. Now the trumpet fanfares sound as if to celebrate the arrival on the tritone (G-flat–C), the *diabolis in musica*. Trofonio then continues in a recitative, with sustained low strings and oboes providing accompaniment. The unison demons return after "un poco di silenzio" for a thirty-one-measure *terribile* chorus in D minor. The supernatural style occurs once more in the finale to act 1, when Trofonio sings a monotone recitation on the tonic in D minor with a chorus of spirits inside the grotto.

In Paisiello's setting of *La grotta di Trofonio* the supernatural material is limited to Trofonio's (bass) invocation of soprano spirits in the act 1 cavatina and chorus (Nos. 7–8). The repeated-note vocal motives, with rapid ascending scale figures in the violins and bassoons (outlining the octave), begin the cavatina invocation with a slowly rising line in octave-and-unison sonority.

---

74. See Steptoe, *Mozart–Da Ponte Operas*, 135–36.

75. I consulted the printed score (Vienna: Artaria, n.d.) in F-Pn, L. 2371, and the autograph score in A-Wn.

EXAMPLE 4.6 Antonio Salieri, *La grotta di Trofonio*, overture

Un poco adagio

EXAMPLE 4.6 *(continued)*

The potent vocal part is also characterized by octave leaps in a slow-paced, ominous incantation for the magician with traditional *sdrucciolo* rhythms (see ex. 4.7). The cavatina ends with an extravagant monotone declamation of nineteen repeated low Gs. As is usual with such an incantation, a chorus of demons responds, repeating Trofonio's opening line in unison at the upper octave.

Shortly before Da Ponte and Mozart's version would make history, Giovanni Bertati wrote a one-act *dramma giocoso* entitled *Don Giovanni, o sia Il convitato di pietra*. Set to music by Gazzaniga (Venice, 5 February 1787),[76] it is mainly a comic work with some brief allusions to the supernatural. The composer deployed musical terror in two scenes: the graveyard episode (scene 20) and the dinner scene in the closing finale. In the duet in scene 20 the statue accepts the invitation to dinner. Gazzaniga depicts his nods in descending dotted figures in the horns and violas, followed by tremolo figures in the strings that

76. For a modern edition see Gazzaniga, *Don Giovanni*.

EXAMPLE 4.7 Giovanni Paisiello, *La grotto di Trofonio*, act 1, no. 7

accompany the servant Pasquariello's fearful cries. The statue utters his words of agreement ("Ci venirò") as a syllabic ascending figure set to unison-and-octave sonority. The arrival of the "stone guest" at the dinner is signaled by a modal change, from D major to D minor, as a solemn duple-meter Largo, with stark dynamic contrasts, accompanies the walking statue's gait for five measures. The subsequent exchange between Giovanni and the Commendatore (scene 24) is set as accompanied recitative with numerous descriptive instrumental figures and changes of tempo, dynamics, and expression. The statue first sings in response to Giovanni, and the key changes to E-flat for another Largo as the statue insists that he does not eat earthly food. The pace quickens as Pasquariello sings of his feverish fear, set to rapid string figures. Giovanni asks if the statue would like some musical entertainment, and the statue answers "Do what you want" in a monotone pronouncement with a repeated A-flat. Now the servant's trembling increases, as is clearly heard in the rapid mordent string figures. The key changes but returns to the infernal E-flat when the statue demands Giovanni's hand, accompanied by unison-and-octave scalar bursts and rapid repeated-note figuration that continues as the statue tells him to repent. Giovanni refuses as he tries to break the statue's grip. The room is transformed into hell with an abrupt change to an instrumental segment in E-flat marked "furia," a triple-meter piece with ascending and descending scales in the strings and repeated blasts of the horns and oboes. The Furies arrive and torture Giovanni, who narrates his torment to the audience before descending to hell. As the scene changes back to the dining room, the key modulates to G major for the final septet.

Lorenzo Da Ponte's *dramma giocoso* in two acts *L'arbore di Diana*, with music by Vicente Martín y Soler (Vienna, BT, 1 October 1787),[77] was commissioned for the marriage celebrations of the niece of Emperor Joseph II. The story concerns a magical tree in the garden of the chaste goddess Diana that reveals both the spiritual and physical chastity of any nymph in its vicinity.[78] When a virtuous nymph passes the tree, its apples shine and pleasing music resounds. Should an unchaste nymph walk under its branches, the fruit will blacken and fall off (recalling the magic mirror of oriental fairy tales, fair plays, and Gozzi's *fiabe*). Cupid decides to undermine the power of the tree by disguising himself and enticing Diana and her nymphs. He introduces Endymion to Diana, and she falls in love with him. After the tree reveals the guilt of the goddess and her nymphs, Diana has the tree removed, and the garden is transformed into a palace of love. The composer limited musical evocations of the supernatural to the ensembles for women's voices, recalling French marvelous

77. *L'arbore di Diana* (Milan: Giov. Batista Bianchi [1788], Sartori No. 2342) was also translated as *Der Baum der Diana* (Vienna, 1787; US-Wc Schatz 6000). I consulted the manuscript score in F-Pn, L. 4684 (1–2).

78. For details on the pastoral elements here, see Link, *"L'arbore di Diana:* A Model."

opera. Unlike their French predecessors, these ensembles are relentlessly homophonic except when the soloists intervene or where there are some short exchanges required in the text, for example the act 2 trio for Cupid, Endimione, and Silvio.[79]

Among the many comic operas satirizing nationalistic stereotypes we find one that has a sorceress as its main character: *La maga Circe*, an anonymous *farsa* or intermezzo for five voices in two parts, with music by Pasquale Anfossi (Rome, Teatro Capranica, Carnival, 1788).[80] Loosely based on Bertati's popular *L'isola d'Alcina* (1772), like its model it contrasts the supposedly uncontrollable passions of the French with the more self-possessed nature of the Italians. Although the libretto has an invocation of deities and magical storms, the music only has two instances of supernatural events. The first is a parody of a conjuring scene in the finale of the second part (in the non-infernal key of B-flat!). Here the Italian Baron Nocesecca (the name means "dry nut") misunderstands the magical invocation, with its repeated-note incantation sung by Circe's confidant Lindora ("Da cocito corran tosto"). He continues to mangle the formula while trying to repeat it, changing its exotic magical imagery to that of the kitchen. The second exception is a more noteworthy allusion to the otherworld. Here Anfossi has virtuoso coloratura distinguishing the supernatural power of Circe through her demonic singing ability. In Circe's exclamation in the same finale, "Precipitosamente tutti farò perir" (I shall suddenly make everyone perish), Anfossi also uses the ominous repeated-note and descending-octave motive of fateful and oracular pronouncements and condemnations (see ex. 4.8). This repeated motive is accompanied by conjunct patterns of thirds in eighth notes and repeated sixteenth notes in the strings, an accompaniment commonly used for incantations, especially by Gluck. By this time such a melodic gesture had long had an association with magical power, having been used in this context by composers such as Handel (*Giulio Cesare*, act 1, scene 4; *Orlando*, act 1, scene 1), Ristori, and Mozart in *Don Giovanni*. Mozart would employ this device yet again, with a similar accompaniment, for Circe's memorable counterpart in *Die Zauberflöte*, the Queen of the Night.

The single instance of an Italian opera taken from a German fairy tale is *Rübenzahl, o sia Il vero amore*, Caterino Mazzolà's two-act *dramma giocoso* with music by Joseph Schuster, set for Dresden's Kleines kurfürstliches Theater

---

79. Cupid is a soprano, and Martín y Soler gives this character some of the most attractive music in the opera. His first two arias have pizzicato accompaniment and some of the childlike simplicity of Mozart's Cherubino in *Le nozze di Figaro*.

80. Libretto, Florence: Anton-Giuseppe Pagani e comp., 1789 (Sartori, No. 14661). Manuscript scores survive in Genoa (Paganini Conservatory), Rome (St. Cecilia Conservatory), US-Wc, and F-Pn. I consulted the Paris score (D 132–33). Productions were also mounted in Florence, Milan, Genova, and Pergola, where it was performed with another supernatural opera, Bertati and Gazzaniga's *Don Giovanni*.

EXAMPLE 4.8 Pasquale Anfossi, *La maga Circe*, part 2, finale

(14 February 1789).[81] The German title, *Rübenzahl,* designates the mountain spirit Ribisell, derived from a legendary imp of Silesia who was central to the published fairy tales of Johann Karl August Musäus.[82] The name comes from the German word for turnips (*Rüben*), and this is mentioned in the libretto. The locale is traditional home of Rübenzahl, the Riesenbirge (Giant Mountains) of Germany, Poland, and Bohemia. Schuster's impressive score balances the comic and serious elements created by the librettist.[83] Vivid depictions of the supernatural first occur in act 1, scene 3, at the conclusion of the *introduzione.* Rübenzahl calls up his infernal genies, waving his wand to conjure lightning and transform the rock on which they sleep into a wagon drawn by two large swans (see ex. 4.9). The incantation is sung in a slow monotone with a rising chromatic bass and abrupt dynamic changes. The chromatic progression supports the hypnotic vocal line as the compound quadruple meter creates a pulsating, triplet-like motion. The wagon's movement is depicted with the ascending sixteenth-note scale figures in the violins, set against a repeated chromatic descending figure in the violas and a bass pedal. When the bass moves up from C to D-flat (an augmented chord), the women suddenly awake. In act 1, scene 6, the spirits exclaim "Ahi!" with clarinets and horns behind the scenes, a wind ensemble suggestive of enchantment.

In scenes 8–10 of *Rübenzahl* Ferdinando and Bodino come upon a subterranean vault that emits an eerie specter of light to the sound of a descriptive instrumental prelude in E-flat. Staccato descending unison-and-octave triads yield to rapid fantastic scalar figures that suggest the darting light (see ex. 4.10). Both of these motives occur as well in the succeeding recitative as Bodino catches up to Ferdinando and reacts with fear to this strange light and

81. See Engländer, "Die Opern Joseph Schusters." As was the case with many Dresden performances, the Italian libretto was published with a German translation (Dresden, 1789 [US-Wc, Schatz 9752]). A manuscript score survives in D-Dlb, Mus. 3480-F-28. A piano-vocal score survives in A-Wgm.

82. An alternate spelling is "Rübezahl." Sources for the legend include Prätorius, *Daemonologia Rubinzalii* and *Satyrus Etymologicus,* and a number of published German stories devoted to the "Schlesischen Rübezahl." These include the version by Daniel Schiebeler in Hirschfeld, *Romanzen,* 1:53–55, and Musäus's five legends in *Volksmärchen der Deutschen* (see chapter 5). See Miller's commentary in ibid., 841–42. Rübenzahl legends continued to appear in publication, for example Fülleborn, *Volksmärchen,* vol. 6, and Naubert, *Neue Volksmärchen,* 1:1–169 (see chapter 5). The appearance of this character in the theater goes back at least to *Der Baron Hanswurst von Pikaragal,* an undated Viennese comedy from around the middle of the century (see chapter 5).

83. The manuscript is preserved in D-Dlb, Mus. 3549-F-28, Ms. Partitur, 2 vols. Like Naumann, Schuster studied in Italy (where his first operas were produced), knew Hasse, and centered his career in Dresden. Engländer, *Johann Gottlieb Naumann,* 358, notes similarities with Mozart's *Don Giovanni* and the Viennese fairy-tale operas of the 1790s. In fact there is much to contrast with Mozart's music in *Die Zauberflöte.* Each composer sets similar text with very different music. Schuster's music owes far more to Italian comic style, with its limited use of descriptive and supernatural elements. See also Engländer, "Die Opern Joseph Schusters."

EXAMPLE 4.9 Joseph Schuster, *Rübenzahl*, act 1, scene 3

clattering chains (depicted by thirty-second-note tremolos in the second violins). The unfortunate captive is the sorceress Dragontina, who asks for her freedom. Tremolos in the low-pitched strings accompany this Largo passage with its recitative vocal line in A minor (with added flats from the borrowed Neapolitan key). The mode changes to major as the winds play sustained chords. The tempo then quickens to an Allegro assai as Ferdinando approaches the gate. Suddenly a chorus of armed guardian spirits (the score refers to a chorus of giants) appears on one side, while a frightening dragon appears on the other. The two-part unison chorus of giants (TB) threatens death in a monotone declamation with *sdrucciolo* rhythms, accompanied by sustained wind chords, string tremolos, and rapid short motives, all played with forte

EXAMPLE 4.10 Joseph Schuster, *Rübenzahl*, act 1, scene 7, prelude

dynamics in the "terrifying" musical style. The mode changes back to minor as Ferdinando fights the spirits and Bodino struggles with the dragon; in each measure the dynamics alternate between piano and forte. Short scalar bursts in the bass provide a growling accent to the giants' cry of "Fuggi indietro" (Turn back), like the barking of Cerberus in Gluck's *Orfeo ed Euridice*. The voice cries out "Apri!" (Open!) as the key shifts to C, then to A minor, and finally a triumphant A major in the ensuing ensemble, which grows progressively more busy as the fighting increases. Finally overcoming the giants, Ferdinando opens the gate, and the prison is illuminated by a bright light, depicted with a short Andante passage of "dolce armonia" for an "enchanted" wind ensemble of horns, clarinets, and bassoon. Dragontina gives her magic wand to Bodino and directs them to a secret path to Rübenzahl's garden, which in turn leads to the subterranean prison of Adelaide and Geltrude. The wand will open the locked door. In the next scene Bodino tries the wand and conjures up a gruesome mountain troll who growls at him. Stuttering in fear, Bodino can barely speak ("ba ba ba ba ba ba, Signor, aiuto"). Ferdinando tells him to conjure a spirit to bring a light to lead them to the locked door. Then a small spirit with a giant lantern accosts Bodino and Ferdinando, and a two-part chorus of spirits (SA) arrives to help the frightened Bodino. He asks for more genies, and increasingly smaller ones come out of the lantern, ready to obey his command. This dainty, elegant wind music with its gavotte rhythms leads to an extended ensemble for the two men and the spirits. Scene 15 begins the long finale, when Ferdinando and Bodino enter the enchanted castle and hear Rübenzahl's invisible chorus. Rübenzahl conjures a storm to confuse his rebellious captives. The key shifts to C minor when the mountain spirit sings his invocation like a *mago*, with a slowly rising line of repeated notes in *sdrucciolo* rhythms. The basses and the horns play a pedal while the bassoon plays figures against string tremolos, always avoiding the tonic chord. Schuster set the terror-filled responses of the captives to a rising chromatic line, with pantomimic figures in the accompaniment as they grope in the dark.

During the quartet in act 2 (scene 3) Rübenzahl uncovers his magic mirror and shows Adelaide a garden scene. This recalls the magic-mirror scene in Grétry's *Zémire et Azor*, with its "enchanted" wind band (piccolo horns, flutes, oboes, and bassoon), and the musical style suggests an elegant serenade. Other magic scenes include Rübenzahl's invisible chorus and wind band performing enchanted music for Adelaide and Geltrude. In a comic episode Bodino uses the wand to transform the stool in which he sits into a large chair, with his own arms serving as the arms of the chair. Bodino then plays pranks on the evil servant, Carpio, comically grabbing food from out of his hand. Rübenzahl, who has the power to transform people into statues, also possesses a magical love potion. When despite this he fails to win Adelaide's heart, Rübenzahl turns her into a statue of their goddess. But Dragontina thwarts his plans when she enters in her flying wagon and restores Adelaide to life. Trumpets and drums announce the appearance of a triumphal arch, where Rübenzahl is in chains. Dragontina offers to forgive Rübenzahl if he changes his ways and pledges himself to be faithful to her. He agrees and is released. Rübenzahl then touches the various statues with his wand and they return to life. A chorus of revived lovers sings with the other characters, and the opera ends.

The commonalities between *Rübenzahl* and *Die Zauberflöte* (and other German operas in this decade) warrant comment. These are far more numerous than in the earlier Dresden court opera *Osiride* (1781), a work more often cited as a precedent for Mozart's singspiel. Unlike *Osiride*, *Rübenzahl* includes comic characters and scenes. Rübenzahl is the evil magician, in love with Adelaide, a princess similar to Pamina. Ferdinando is the heroic prince, much like Tamino. Geltrude is the servant of Adelaide, who is in love with Bodino. Bodino is Fer-

dinando's servant, whose ever-present interest in gratification and idle chatter
suggest Papageno's character. These four characters form contrasting pairs of
aristocratic and common lovers whose tribulations lead to success at the end.
Carpio, Rübenzahl's lecherous master of the hunt, who is in love with Geltrude, is like Monostatos in *Die Zauberflöte*. Dragontina is the beneficent sorceress, in love with Rübenzahl and recently betrayed by him. Ferdinando and
Bodino descend into a subterranean area. When they reach the door they hear
voices inside promising to rescue his beloved. The sorceress sends the two men
off with a magic implement to help them, not a flute here but a wand. Rübenzahl and Carpio meet and frighten each other, like Papageno and Monostatos. Like Papageno, too, Bodino is "locked up" by his own foolishness: he is
turned into an armchair. Ferdinando's trials, like Tamino's, include silence toward Adelaide. Adelaide has a dagger to kill Ferdinando's supposed new love,
Geltrude. Ferdinando grabs her arm and stops her. A flying wagon appears
above the stage, and Ferdinando takes the dagger and tries to kill himself because he thinks he has lost Adelaide's love. Dragontina saves him with the
words "T'arresta," much like the command of the Three Boys ("halt ein") in
Die Zauberflöte. Dragontina restores Adelaide to Ferdinando, and Rübenzahl
repents, reconciling with the sorceress.

Thus *Rübenzahl* reveals the reciprocal nature of musical practices by the
late 1780s. Until then German opera had been largely derivative, exerting little
effect on foreign stages. In this Italian comic opera with a German title, we find
the situation reversed. This tendency would only increase in the 1790s, when
German supernatural operas were translated and performed outside German-
speaking lands. The following chapter, treating magic and the supernatural
in German musical theater during the eighteenth century, demonstrates how
German opera came to achieve its appeal to wider Europe.

CHAPTER FIVE

German Musical Theater

German musical theater and comedy with supernatural content in the period 1700–1779 was based largely on Italian, French, and (to a lesser degree) English models. Only a small number of German-language stage works were derived from indigenous sources. Faust, perhaps the most traditional of German devil stories, appeared on stage relatively early in the form of *Dr. Faust,* a *Volksschauspiel* by Josef Anton Stranitzky (Vienna, 1715; revised 1736). But even in early German Faust comedies the influence of English pantomime is evident. Other German sorcerers also figured in legendary plots, for example *Heinrich der Vogler* (1718, with music by Georg Caspar Schürmann), which combined history and legend. Forest spirits (*Waldgeister*) appeared in a number of German comedies and serious plays. A rare allusion to the Silesian myth of Rübenzahl occurs in Joseph Felix von Kurz's undated comedy *Der Baron Hanswurst von Pikaragal* ("der Geist Ribisell auf der Insel Cellery und Calleraby").[1] With only a few notable exceptions, German playwrights adapted early comedies and operas from foreign-language works, performed by itinerant companies that relied on improvised comedy.

Commedia dell'arte *scenari* were known in both Western and Eastern Europe.[2] Don Juan plays became popular in Vienna starting around 1717.[3] French

---

1. A-Wn, Handschriftensammlung, Cod. 12.709, 185. Pirker, *Teutsche Arien,* lxxi (cited as vol. 4, no. 210), briefly discusses this comedy.

2. D-Dlb, shelfmark loc. Dramat. 2 u, preserves approximately 125 *scenari* in Italian, French, and Polish performed in Dresden and Warsaw (c. 1748–56). Many include magic and supernatural characters. See Korzeniewski, "Komedia dell'arte." Thirty-nine Russian- and German-language *scenari* published in St. Petersburg between 1733 and 1735 include standard plot types with supernatural and magic elements. See Peretts, *Ital'ianskie komedii i intermedii.*

3. Stephanie, preface to vol. 2 of *Sämmtliche Schauspiele,* states that the Don Juan plays have been popular in Vienna since 1717, especially on certain days every year. He was almost certainly referring to All Souls' week.

models were also prevalent. Among these, the earliest Parisian fair comedy staged in German was Johann Philipp Praetorius's *Die verkehrte Welt* (1728), a translation of Lesage, d'Orneval, and La Font's *Le monde renversé*. Georg Philipp Telemann supplied modest songs for this production, of which only a few survive.[4] In the 1730s Heinrich Rademin adapted French oriental comedies for Vienna, and translators then turned to fashionable French fairy plays of the 1740s, which sustained German-language theaters in subsequent decades, for example, Saint-Foix's *L'oracle* and Cahusac's *Zénéide*. German translations of French comic operas enjoyed widespread success starting in the 1760s, among them a good many with themes drawn from fairy tales: *La fée Urgèle*, *Le bûcheron*, *La belle Arsène*, and *Zémire et Azor* were first performed in the original French and then inspired several German translations.[5]

Although translations from English were less common, a few ballad and burlesque operas had currency in German lands, especially *The Devil to Pay* by Coffey (1728), translated as *Der Teufel ist los* by Caspar Wilhelm von Borck (1743).[6] In 1752 Heinrich Gottfried Koch had Christian Felix Weisse revise the text as a *komische Oper* for Leipzig, with new music by Johann Standfuss (1752).[7] This bawdy farce has little of the sentimentality associated with later settings of the same text in French and German. Weisse reworked it once more as *Die verwandelten Weiber*, a comic opera for the Leipzig fair (1766).

Genre designations used in German librettos rarely went beyond the most general kind of description, for example *Komödie*, *komische Oper*, [*musikalisches*] *Lustspiel*, *Schauspiel*, *Oper*, *Operetta*, *Pantomime*, [*deutsches*] *Singspiel*, and *Maschinenkomödie*, which meant a comedy on a mechanical stage with illusory effects. From such subtitles alone it is unclear whether a work featured magical scenes or special effects. More telling is the poster (A-Wt) for *Bernardons Hochzeit auf dem Scheiterhaufen, oder Ein ehrlicher Mann soll sein Wort halten* (16 July 1764), which advertised it as a comedy "mit Maschinen, Arien, und Verkleidungen vermischt." After midcentury, however, genre designations began to indicate more detail about the subject matter. Such terms as *Zauberkomödie* (c. 1760), *Zauberlustspiel* (c. 1762), and *Mährchen* (1777) make clear that, as in France, works with supernatural emphasis were beginning to count as a distinct category. Even works called *heroisch-komische Oper*, *Posse mit Gesang*, *romantisch-komische Oper*, and *romantische Oper* may also include

---

4. Some arias (along with arias from *Calypso*) appeared in Telemann, *Der getreue Music-Meister*.

5. See Smith, "Egidio Duni."

6. The piece, performed by Johann Friedrich Schönemann's company, with music by "Herr Sydow." was announced on a playbill that survives in D-Hs.

7. Schmid, *Chronologie*, traces the origins of German opera to this production. See Bauman, *North German Opera*, 22. Koch also had Weisse translate the sequel, *The Merry Cobbler*, as *Der lustige Schuster*, with music by Standfuss.

supernatural elements. An extensive list of German theatrical works with magic and supernatural content is given in Appendix E.

Mythology and Epic Romance in German Opera, 1707–79

Although in Italy many librettists working around the turn of the eighteenth century eliminated marvelous and magical episodes, north of the Alps theaters staging both Italian and German operas by such composers as Agostino Steffani, Reinhard Keiser, Schürmann, Graupner, and Telemann relied heavily on mythology and its supernatural content. Librettists favored the legends of Orpheus, Medea, Ulysses, Circe, Bellerophon, and Hercules, along with pastoral stories of Procris, Psyche, Adonis, Narcissus, and Jupiter and Semele. They also based a few operas on epic romance, such as Steffani's *Der rasende Roland* (a German translation of Mauro, *Orlando generoso;* Hanover, 1691) and Schürmann's *Orlando furioso* (Brunswick, 1722). The first eighteenth-century German Orpheus opera, Keiser's *Die biss in und nach dem Todt unerhörte Treue des Orpheus* (1709), was probably based on an earlier Brunswick Orpheus opera by Friedrich Christian Bressand (1698, revised in 1699 as *Die sterbende Euridice*).[8] The surviving score, which lacks the simple recitatives and does not name the characters or specify the events in the plot,[9] begins with a French overture and contains mostly da capo arias, many with coloratura. There are a few accompanied recitatives, ensembles, and choruses. An instrumental march (a genre often used for supernatural events) completes the score, although its placement in the opera is not clear. Keiser scored the four-part texture for oboes and strings. The bass arias are a prominent feature; perhaps some were for Pluto. But there can be no conclusive statement about the role of the "marvelous" in this music until the characters and the events have been identified.

Keiser's autograph score for a late *pasticcio*, the five-act singspiel *Circe* (Hamburg, 1734),[10] includes arias from twelve different operas by six composers, including Handel's *Rinaldo*. All German numbers were by Keiser, whose first *Circe* singspiel was mentioned earlier. The orchestra consists of four-part strings, oboes, flutes, and two *trombe di caccia*. As is typical in this period, the musical imagery is most apparent in the aria accompaniments and the *stromenti* sections in the accompanied recitatives. The violent thirty-second-note runs in Circe and Ulysses' accompanied recitative, act 2, scene 4, are especially noteworthy. Act 3 begins with simple recitative followed by a short, triple-meter *Symphonie* in B-flat, an Allegro with rapid sixteenth notes that perhaps served

---

8. Keiser also composed music for *Procris et Cephalus* (1694), *Die wunderschöne Psyche* (1701, rev. 1722), and *Minerva* (1703).

9. D-B, Mus. ms. 11486.

10. D-B, shelfmark Ms. Autog. R. Keiser.

as stage-machine music. Another "symphony" includes rapid scale passages that suggest possible supernatural subject matter (act 3, scene 10).

The myth of Jason and Medea was the subject of an early *pasticcio* by Schürmann, *Giasone* (Brunswick, 1707, based on Flaminio Parisetti's *dramma per musica*), revised in 1720 as *Jason, oder Die Eroberung des güldenen Flüsses*. Among the most widely performed and influential works on this subject was Friedrich Wilhelm Gotter's melodrama *Medea*, with music by Georg Benda (Leipzig, 1775), discussed in detail below. Perhaps the period's most varied and spectacular German treatment of the mythological sorceress Circe was staged in Hamburg in 1734. Here the text is of special interest, for the librettists Johann Philipp Praetorius and Jan Jacob van Mauritius drew on a variety of earlier sources and combined magic, mythology, spectacle, and comedy, following the Armida episode in *Gerusalemme liberata*. The music for their *Circe*, however, was of less interest; not specially composed for the occasion, it was a *pasticcio* using earlier pieces by Keiser and others.

New Influences, 1728–49

Traveling companies staged most German comic operas before 1780. The influence of Italian and Parisian comedies, along with Faust tradition,[11] meant that legends, fairy tales, and oriental stories would appear in the German comic theater. Like its Italian and French models, German improvised comedy, called *Haupt- und Staatsaktion* by modern scholars, included magic episodes and supernatural characters. The Arlecchino character was called Hanswurst, a provincial trickster whose trade was castrating livestock. Like Arlecchino, Hanswurst's comic encounters often occurred in exotic locales where he found himself the victim or fortunate recipient of magical power in plots borrowed from Italian *scenari* and *opéra-comique*. The first Hanswurst seems to have been Josef Anton Stranitzky, who performed in Vienna's Kärntnertor Theater beginning in 1709. Stranitzky produced *Dr. Faust* in 1715, and he continued to stage the story at least until 1726.[12] Gottfried Prehauser inaugurated the second era of Hanswurst (1727–69), and Johann Joseph Felix von Kurz created a variation on the Hanswurst character in the 1730s called Bernardon. Magic comedies were in his repertory by 1737. In 1744 Kurz returned to Vienna and developed the magic-burlesque comedies that came to be identified with the

---

11. Dabezies, *Le mythe de Faust*, cites performances in Graz, 1608; Dresden, 1626; Prague, 1651; Danzig, 1668 and 1679; Munich, 1669; Bremen, 1670 and 1690; Basel, 1696; and Berlin, 1703.

12. Rommel, *Die Maschinenkomödie* (1935), 36, cites this as a *Volksschauspiel*, a dubious generic category in 1715. The printed program (n.d.) for the anonymous pantomime comedy *Doktor Faust* (KT, 9 June 1731) describes this as an "Engelländerischer Pantomimien- und Italiänischer Music-Art." The program includes Italian texts and German descriptions. Bolte, "Bruchstücke einer Wiener Faust-Komödie," provides selections from several scenes.

imperial city. During his third Viennese period (1754–60), he collaborated with Haydn on the singspiel *Der neue krumme Teufel*.

Heinrich Rademin, who had translated Quinault's librettos, adapted French oriental comedies to the Viennese stage from Gherardi's popular printed anthology.[13] He was to be an important figure for the transition from the improvised *Haupt- und Staatsaktion* to more fully written comedy based on *opéra-comique*. Rademin also wrote for Franz Josef Moser's company in Prague, the forerunner of the Schulz-Menninger "Badner" company.

The 1740s began a period of sporadic experimentation in German comic opera with *Der Teufel ist los* (Berlin, 1743; Leipzig, 1752). Later Italian and French comedies influenced the German theater during this period, the end of the Gottsched era. The new French fairy story also exerted an influence through translations of plays such as Saint-Foix's *L'oracle* and Cahusac's *Zénéide* (translated by Johann Jacob Salomon in 1743).[14] The first original fairy-tale play in German appears to be Krüger's *Der blinde Ehemann* of 1744, discussed below.

Only a limited number of texts of Viennese magic comedies have survived, despite the duration of their popularity.[15] Primary source materials include manuscript collections, prints, posters, and music. Table 5.1 lists these sources. Max Pirker has documented an abundance of diverse magical elements in these comedies, including utopian stories such as the myth of *Schlaraffenland*, probably taken from the commedia dell'arte and Parisian fair comedies. Plots use oriental fantasies as well, and devil stories such as Faust, Belphegor, and Asmodeus, with magic transformations, journeys into hell, and flying machines, are common. Classical mythology provided underworld scenes and encounters with the Furies and other supernatural figures. Magic instruments, witchcraft, sorcerers, spirits, giants, dwarfs, ghosts, poltergeists, and ogres were also in the mix. One occasionally finds Egyptian motives, alchemy, and elemental spirits, along with fantastic characters and episodes from epic romance.

Rademin's *Die Königin der schwartzen Inseln*, a "musicalisch-italienische, aus denen arabischen Geschichten gezoge Zwischenspiel" (Italian-style musical intermezzo drawn from Arabian tales; composer unknown), indicates a

13. See *Höllenfahrt Bernardons*, No. 147–48, in Pirker, *Teutsche Arien*, 3, which seems to have been based on Gherardi's *La descente de Mezzetin aux enfers* and Le Grand's *Belphégor, ou La descente d'Arlequin aux Enfers* (24 August 1721). *Runtzvanscad* and Kurz's *Menschenfresser* (Pirker, *Teutsche Arien*, 1, no. 27) also seem to have been based on French sources.

14. Saint-Foix's play was translated anonymously as *Das Orackel* in 1741. Joseph Wendler reworked it as a one-act comedy (Leipzig, 1750; Brunswick and Leipzig, 1752). See Hinck, *Das deutsche Lustspiel*, 238.

15. Much research remains before any claim can be made as to a comprehensive knowledge of the surviving manuscript and printed materials for this period. Eighteenth-century German prints are the subject of an ongoing catalog; see Meyer, *Bibliographia Dramatica*, 2. Abteilung, Einzeltitel 3. Until this project is complete, the best source remains Geils and Gorzny, *Gesamtverzeichnis*. No comprehensive catalog is available for the important resources of Eastern Europe's libraries and archives.

TABLE 5.1 Sources of Viennese Magic Comedies

1. A-Wst, shelfmark A 22200: a collection of printed texts for eleven midcentury comedies, including *Neun Arien welche in der Comoedie genannt: Die Zauber=Trommel von unserm Hannswurst gesungen werden,* discussed below.

2. A-Wn, Handschriftsammlung, shelfmark Cod. 12.706–12.709: a four-volume set of manuscripts of the song texts (and a few synopses) from mid-century comedies (1737–57), originally part of the estate of Ignaz Castelli. This is the largest single collection of texts (261) from Viennese comedies.* Pirker transcribed the first volume in a modern edition (1927).

3. A-Wn, Musiksammlung, shelfmark 695.504A Musik-S.TB: five arias and synopses of two comedies. Additional prints of individual comedies include titles such as *Die bewunderungswürdige Baß-Geige* (The Marvelous Bass Viol), 448630-A.

4. Collections of theater posters, some with plot summaries, in A-Wst, A-Wn, and A-Wt.

5. The repertory catalog of comedies from the archive of the Moravian Jaromeric Castle of the Questenberg family.†

6. Music for some arias in the period 1754–58 is preserved in manuscripts in Vienna.‡

* Vol. 1 has 53 comedies, Vol. 2 has 64 comedies, Vol. 3 has 63 comedies, and Vol. 4 has 70 comedies. Asper, *Spieltexte der Wanderbühne*, 98–106, includes an index to the last three volumes of the collection, which were not included in Pirker, *Teutsche Arien*. But Asper missed a number of comedies.

† Helfert, "Zur Geschichte des Wiener Singpiels," provides a chronological list of repertory.

‡ A-Wn, Musiksammlung, shelfmark Hs. 19062 and Hs. 19603. Modern edition in *Deutsche Komödienarien, 1754–1758*.

role for an astrologer named Parpagnacco.[16] More magical references occur in the text of Rademin's *Runtzvanscad, König deren Menschen-fressern, oder Der Durchläuchtigste Gärtner* (before 15 June 1732), adapted from Dufresny and Barante's *Les fées, ou contes de ma mère l'Oye.*[17] The plot concerns Ernelinda, the daughter of King Siface of the Tartars, betrothed to an old Indostani king. A magician advises her to escape with her beloved Prince Clotinghes before the wedding. A thunderstorm then causes their ship to land on a Tartarian island ruled by Runtzvanscad, the king of a tribe of cannibals. Runtzvanscad captures the survivors, falls in love with Ernelinda, and announces his intention of making a human sacrifice of Clotinghes. Informed of the situation by the

16. See Pirker, *Teutsche Arien*, 407. A copy of the libretto (Vienna: A. Heyinger, 1731) survives in Meiningen, Thuringen Staatliche Museen, shelfmark Litt. V.o.317 (Di/II, 3C/82).

17. Libretto, Vienna: Johann Peter von Ghelen, 1732. See Rommel, *Die Alt-Wiener Volkskomödie;* and Pirker, *Teutsche Arien*, 439. Ruzvanscad is a Chinese king in "L'histoire du Roi Ruzvanscad et de la Princesse Cheheristani," from the *Les mille et un jours*. The name is also found as the hero "Runtzvanscad il Giovine" in *Arcisopratragichissima Tragedia elaborata* (Venice, 1724). Four aria texts from *Runtzvanscad, König deren Menschen-fressern* appear in Cod. ms. 12706–12709. A number of contemporary pieces about cannibals appear in various European theatrical repertories. See Pirker, *Teutsche Arien*, 437–39. The composer remains unknown, and the music is lost.

magician, King Siface rescues them. Hanswurst is the comic servant of Clotinghes. A sorcerer named Frisesomoro appears on a flying dragon, performs
a magic incantation, and gives Hanswurst a magic horn of gold that can transform people and objects.

Die Zaubertrommel (before 7 December 1737) provides an example of
Kurz's early magic comedies for Vienna.[18] Hanswurst appeared here as multiple characters, including a conjurer and an *astrologus*. The Hanswurst character also migrated to north Germany in the anonymous *deutsches Singspiel Das
ruchlose Leben und erschreckliche Ende des Welt-bekannten Erz-Zauberers D. Johann Faustus* (Opernhaus, Gänsmarkt, Hamburg, 7 July 1738, Johann Neuber
company).[19] *Hanns-Wurst neu aufgerichteter Prob-Brunnen, die Treu der Jungfrauen und Junggesellen zu erkennen,* an anonymous *operetta Bernesca,* was performed by the Schulz company of Chur-Bavarian comedians (Nuremburg, 21
August 1748). Asmodeus appears in the form of Hanswurst as a rival for Colombina's affections, and he grows small or large through a magic charm.

The popular Aladdin story from the Arabian Nights informed the anonymous comedy *Die wunderbare Lampe* (1738),[20] whose cast includes characters
with names ridiculing oriental fairy tales, such as Badruboldure, the African
magician Braxantantronopos, Rapaslipiriparides (the possessor of the magic
lamp), and two house spirits named Vizlipuzli and Smiricribri. An early description suggests French influence.[21] Other anonymous magic comedies cited
in the Questenberg catalog include *Hanns-Wurst, Hexenmeister aus Liebe* (22
July 1738, song texts in A-Wn, Cod. ms. 12706, number 18) and *Die bewunderungswürdige Baß-Geige,* also called *Plutons große bewunderungswürdige Baßgeige*
(25 April 1739),[22] whose title indicates an early example of a magic instrument.

Midcentury Developments, 1750–59

By the mid-eighteenth century many French and oriental fairy tales were available in both anonymous German translations and in editions by Johann Heinrich Voss and Friedrich Immanuel Bierling.[23] German writers first called the

18. See Pirker, *Teutsche Arien,* piece no. 2. As cited above, the text is printed in A-Wst, shelfmark A 22200, and survives in manuscript form in A-Wn, Cod. ms. 12706.

19. This information comes from a surviving theater poster in D-Hs.

20. The Questenberg catalog cites performances starting on 3 August 1738. Franz Schuch performed it in Nuremburg on 26 November 1748 under the title *L'embarras des richesses: Das ist un-
ruhiger Reichthum oder: die wunderbahre Lampe, mit dem durch ihren Besitz zum Kayser von China er-
hobenen Hannswurst.*

21. A-Wn, Cod. ms. 12706. See Pirker, *Teutsche Arien,* piece no. 5, 414. One aria features several animal sounds.

22. A printed aria book survives in A-Wn, Musiksammlung, shelfmark 448630-A, and A-Wn,
Handschriften, Cod. ms. 12706, No. 21.

23. Galland's *Les mille et une nuits* was translated anonymously and published in Leipzig in
1712. Voss's translation was published in Bremen in 1781–85, as well as other editions. Pétis de la

French stories *Feenmärchen*. One occasionally finds commentary in the publications of later German fairy tales that attempted to classify tales within poetic and aesthetic categories, making distinctions between orally transmitted *Volksmärchen* (including *Kindermärchen* and *Hausmärchen*) and *Kunstmärchen* (artistic or literary fairy tales by known authors). Although the reform-minded Gottsched disdained them as the pastime of "idle wenches and dim-witted fops,"[24] they became a source of inspiration for later writers.

❊

A magic instrument figures prominently in the anonymous pantomime *Das Zauber-Glöckel*, probably performed on 28 December 1750 at the castle theater of Prince Joseph Adam von Schwarzenberg in Český Krumlov, Bohemia.[25] A magician sets this episodic commedia dell'arte plot in motion by helping Arlequin and Colombina defeat Pantalone. He gives Arlequin a magic bell that will grant his every wish. Arlequin conjures up an enchanted roebuck to ride to the castle then plays a series of tricks on his rivals with the help of his magic bell. He creates a ladder to help Colombina escape and transforms himself into a cat, a clock, a pot, and a statue. Arlequin eventually loses his magic bell in the chaotic course of events and is tried and found guilty of sorcery. Just before the execution, the magician appears and transforms the scene. The block becomes a throne for Arlequin and Colombina, and Pantalone falls under his feet as the judge's bench changes into a dungeon.

Supernatural elements play an equally important role in the more sophisticated "moral" comedies during this decade, for example *Der blinde Ehemann*, a three-act comedy by Johann Christian Krüger (1744), revised by Johann Friedrich Jünger in 1751. It was staged numerous times in the next five decades and was even adapted as an opera libretto.[26] *Der blinde Ehemann* uses motives

---

Croix's *Les mille et un jours* was anonymously translated and published in Leipzig in 1712–14 and again in Leipzig in 1788–89. Thomas-Simon Gueulette's *Les mille et un quarts d'heure, contes tartares*, was translated anonymously and published in Leipzig in 1716–17 and in several later editions. *Le cabinet des fées* was translated into German by one Bierling and published in nine volumes as *Das Cabinett der Feen* (reviewed in *Allgemeine Deutsche Bibliothek* 6 [1768], 309–10). German writers also knew the Italian collections of Straparola and Basile. For a recent review of fairy tales in literature and theater, see Zipes, *Oxford Compendium to Fairy Tales.*

24. See Gottsched, "Von dem Wunderbaren in der Poesie," 5:183: "zum Spotte und Zeitvertriebe müßiger Dirnen und witzarmer Stutzer."

25. Preserved in two manuscripts: A-Wst, shelfmark Ja 39.543, and a copy in the A-Wst, shelfmark M 1247, Theat.-S, entitled "Pantomime des Zauber Glöckel," and dated "Wien 1773" (in pencil). For details, see Schindler, *Die Pantomime "Das Zauber-Glöckel."*

26. The text was printed (Berlin: Friedrich Maurer, 1784); a copy survives in Lbl, shelfmark 11748.f.47. A manuscript score survives in D-Hs. Bauman, *North German Opera*, found that Jünger's text was set as an *Operette* in two acts, with music by Johann Christoph Kaffka [pseud. for

from the "shipwreck-pastorals" of the Italian and Parisian comedies. Walter Hinck links the plot to the French *comédie-larmoyante*, sentimental stories where virtue and vice are clearly contrasted and fidelity rewarded.[27] Marivaux, whose *Arlequin poli par l'amour* was recently translated into German, may have influenced Krüger. The subtext of both comedies is a social critique of courtly manners, corrupt aristocracy, and the valorizing of love in the lower classes. The fairy-tale element emerges in the theme of a trial or test of virtue and in the role of the fairy. The story concerns a blind man named Astrobal (Alphonso in Jünger's setting), the half brother of the prince. The prince has fallen in love with Astrobal's beautiful and virtuous wife, Laura. The prince is the son of Oglivia, the fairy who rules over the elements and protects young women. Oglivia suffers from a decree that caused her to become ugly after she blinded Astrobal, the child of her husband's illicit union. She can regain her former beauty only when the unhappiness of her own son will result in making Astrobal the happiest of husbands. After a painful trial of her fidelity, Laura's virtue restores both Astrobal's sight and the fairy's beauty. The prince's faults are thus corrected, and all the characters proclaim Laura as a model for female virtue.

Viennese Magic Comedy, 1750–59

Although the marvelous and the supernatural were a part of north German repertories of both *dramma per musica* and German opera at midcentury, Vienna enjoyed that ubiquitous theatrical tradition of Catholic Europe, the commedia dell'arte and its French adaptation for the Parisian fairs. Catholic Vienna also had a penchant for devil stories, with their heavy-handed morals and violent punishment of sinners. One example will suffice to show the context of magic and morals in Kurz's comedies of this period. In *Die fünf kleinen Luftgeister* (c. 1750–59),[28] a sorceress named Angelica takes Hanswurst and Bernardon into her service as apprentices in order to select one of them as her husband. The two students escape and seize Angelica's magic instruments. They arrive at the deserted residence of Angelica's imprisoned daughter, Fiameta. Using Angelica's magic wand they transform a stone into a swan, which, according to an old fable, sings a song and dies. The wand transforms the dead swan into the beautiful Fiameta and the desert into a garden. The men fight over her, and the clever Hanswurst flees with Fiameta. This causes Bernardon such grief that Angelica arrives to help him. She confesses her love for him

---

J. C. Engelmann], Breslau, 1788. J. F. Drobisch also set the text for Lübeck, October 1791, but no music survives. Josef Martin Ruprecht's setting (lost?) was performed in Emanuel Schikaneder's Theater auf der Wieden in 1794.

27. Hinck, *Das deutsche Lustspiel*.

28. Kurz, *Neun Arien*. N.p., n.d. Copy in A-Wn, shelfmark 695.504-AM TB.

and transforms a rosebush into a terrifying monster and the garden back into a desert. He scorns her love but accepts her offer of help. Conjuring a large black cloud that descends and opens up to reveal the jaws of hell, she commands five sylphs (*Luftgeister*) to leap out and perform a ballet. Angelica orders the five to help Bernardon. Like Snow White's dwarfs, each represents a middle-class virtue or vice: Purzel is courteous, Mufty is ill-mannered, Corni advocates love, Mickerl argues against love, and Stinxi is an idler. A series of comic scenes ensues as Bernardon and the spirits pursue Hanswurst and Fiameta through Europe, causing Hanswurst to use the magical implements as a defense. Finally Asmodeus appears and reveals that Fiameta is Angelica's daughter. Her sister, Liseta, arrives, and there is a double wedding, Bernardon with Liseta, and Hanswurst with Fiameta.

A young Joseph Haydn composed music (lost) for *Der neue krumme Teufel*, a two-act comic opera with an appended two-act *Kinder-Pantomime, Arlequin, der neue Abgott Ram in America* (c. 1758?).[29] This is a devil story in the commedia dell'arte tradition, either identical to *Der krumme Teufel* or a sequel or revision of it. The children's pantomime is also a standard commedia dell'arte plot, where Arlequin finds himself on a savage island and becomes the deity of the primitive American inhabitants, the idol Ram. During a comic altercation between Arlequin and the magician Ronzi (who has transformed himself as a statue), the sorcerer changes into a forest spirit (*Waldteufel*) and jumps up a tree. Ronzi then returns to his natural form and approaches the terrified Arlequin, offering to protect him from the American savages. He sings and conjures six spirits on the stage and three *Maschinen*. The magician then dresses Arlequin as Ram and places him on the pedestal. The comedy continues as Arlequin plays the part of the deity. The libretto indicates five arias for the magician, and specifies "eine Musique, welche sich mit einer Mühle accompagniret" during a pantomime in which the spirits go in and out of the *Maschinen*.

Der neue krumme Teufel was revived in Vienna by the Baden theater company (29 October 1764) along with *Bernardon dem durch Zauberey glücklich gemachten Laquey*, an undated anonymous comedy.[30] Kurz's later Viennese magic comedies include *Der lebendig verbrannte Zauberer Bernardon* (1752),[31] in which Bernardon receives the help of a magician whose enchantments and

29. Rommel, *Die Maschinenkomödie* (1935), transcribed the text, which appears in facsimile in Haydn, *Werke*, Reihe 24, Bd. 2. The libretto cites Haydn as the composer. The composer's biographers Greisinger and Dies report of Haydn's composing the "Begleit- und Arienmusik" for the *Kinderpantomime Abgott Ram*. This text may have been the basis of Kurz's later comic opera, *Die Insul der Wilden, oder: Die wanckelmüthige Insulanerin mit Arlequin dem durch Zauberei zum Abgott Ram gemachten König des Insul Tschalalei* (Nuremburg, 28 August 1766). See Rommel, *Die Maschinenkomödie* (1935), 51.

30. An undated theater poster for the afterpiece (*Nachspiel*) *Die Zauber=Ruthe, oder Der gedopplte Hanswurst* survives in A-Wt, performed by the Bohemian "Baadnerischen Gesellschaft."

31. The text was published (Vienna: Trattner, 1771).

transformations confuse his beloved's father to the point of his allowing their marriage. Kurz's two-act comedy *Der sich wider seinen Willen taub und stumm stellende Liebhaber* (1755) was adapted from Gellert's translation of Saint-Foix's *L'oracle*, The undated *Der aufs neue begeisterte und belebte Bernardon* includes two magic pantomimes for Kurz's children's troupe.[32] The first, *Der durch magische Kraft und durch Würkung der Gottin Lacharis wieder aufs neue belebte Bernardon,* has an extended incantation scene with a magic caldron. Leander is the magician who restores Bernardon to life by having him hatch from a hen's egg, a device taken from the commedia dell'arte and Parisian fair plays that will be used again by Bertati and Kurz in *Li creduti spiriti* (Venice, 1764). Another undated anonymous comedy, *Das Unglück des Einen ist öfters das Glück des Andern, oder Die wolthätige Zauberin mit Hannswurst, dem tyrannischen Wallsisch-Ritter,* with music attributed to Johann Georg Heubel, has the sorceress Morgiana as the dea ex machina.[33]

The surviving sources offer little information about the nature of musical accompaniment in these comedies so rich in supernatural events and characters. German supernatural comic opera from before about 1766 also has too few surviving musical materials to form a coherent picture. As for the magic plays of Vienna's comic theaters, there remains little evidence of the musical practices for magic episodes until after about 1776.[34] The surviving music from supernatural scenes in Viennese comedies offers little indication beyond a few conventional arias and ensembles where characters reflect or express their state of mind or current condition. For example, the short, multipartite aria in G minor where Bernardon laments his fate leads to the magical appearance of a sorceress in *Bernardon auf der Gelsen-Insul, oder Die Spatzen-Zauberei mit der lustigen Regens-Chori Pantomime,* a *große Maschinen-, Flug- und Verwandlungs-Komoedie*.[35] If music accompanied magical appearances and transformations like these, it is now lost. Thus a review of music for supernatural episodes in Viennese comedy must begin in the 1760s.

The 1760s

Traveling companies continued to produce older, Italian-style comedies in this decade. *Colombina in den Elisæischen Feldern,* an anonymous three-act comedy performed by the Schulz-Menninger troupe of Baden between 1760 and

---

32. A-Wst, Musiksammlung, shelfmark A 22200 preserves this and the previous comedy; the latter also appears A-Wn, Handschriftsammlung, Cod. ms. 12709.s, 217–32, and is transcribed in Rommel, *Die Maschinenkomödie* (1935).

33. A printed aria book survives; see Kurz, *Neun Arien,* A-Wn. Musiksammlung, shelfmark 695.504A Musik-S.TB. A-Wn, Handschriftsammlung, Cod. ms. 12709. no. 51, 401–10, has some texts, a full synopsis, and a cast list.

34. Some early arias and ensembles have been edited in Glossy and Haas, *Wiener Comödienlieder;* and *Deutsche Komödienarien.*

35. *Deutsche Komödienarien,* pt. 1, 1–3.

1770,[36] has this kind of sprawling, convoluted plot. The characters Colombina and Maga, the abused man turned magician for revenge, and the two magic rings given to Hanswurst and Colombina by the magician clearly belong to this tradition. In 1768 Johann Laroche (1745–1806) joined the Baden troupe, which began producing successful magic comedies called *Maschinenkomödie*, *Zaubercomödie*, and *Zauberlustpiel*. One of these uses a devil story: *Belfagor der befreyte Teufel, oder die dem Hannswurst erwiesene höllische Dankbarkeit*, an undated (c. 1760–70) *Zaubercomödie*.[37] The surviving theater poster (in A-Wt) indicates that Hanswurst outwits the devil. The same troupe performed *Die Zauber=Ruthe, oder Der gedoppelte Hannswurst*, an undated afterpiece (also c. 1760–70).

The improvisational comic actor Prehauser died in 1769, and Kurz returned to Vienna to enjoy a second period of success. But when the Baden troupe attempted to become the permanent company of the Kärntnertor Theater, the official censor, Joseph von Sonnenfels, convinced Joseph II to once again limit improvised comedy. In March 1770 the emperor required all publicly performed plays be submitted to Sonnenfels. Kurz was his first casualty, and the actor left for Warsaw. Soon after that he retired from the stage.

Like its French counterpart and model, German comic opera in the 1760s seems to have had a greater musical component than in previous decades. One of the earliest surviving examples with supernatural content confirms this, a setting of Weisse's *Die verwandelten Weiber, oder Die Teufel ist los* (Leipzig, 1766).[38] This revision owes much to Sedaine's more refined translation of 1756. Johann Adam Hiller's score includes an invocation for the magician in act 2, a strophic D minor Grave ma non lento, "Auf naht euch, ihr dienstbaren Geister, hinzu er schein jetzt." The brief, dramatic instrumental introduction and conclusion suggest recitative. The magician summons his magical spirits with a combination of octave-and-unison accompaniment, tritone leaps, and darkly evocative D minor harmony.

One can learn more about music in this decade by examining scores of new pantomime-ballets in two German-speaking locations, Vienna and Stuttgart. Composers employed varied expressive styles in this genre (see chapter 3 for the contributions of Gluck and his colleagues in Vienna). Jean-Joseph Rodolphe set Etienne L'Auchery's heroic ballets for Stuttgart,[39] including *Rinaldo*

36. Schindler, *Stegreifburlesken der Wanderbühne*, 41–46, transcribed the undated manuscript source, which survives in A-Wn, Cod. 13.609.

37. The Faust tradition informed *Bernardon der dumme Nachfolger Dr. Faustus*, performed in Frankfurt am Main in 1767. See Rommel, *Die Maschinenkomödie* (1935), 36.

38. The music survives in a piano-vocal score (Leipzig: J. F. Junius, 1770), RISM H 5276, A-Wst, Musiksammlung, 48979 M, and in manuscripts in D-B (reduced score, Mus. ms. 1190) and in Munich and Kaliningrad. See Bauman, *North German Opera*, 28–34.

39. Charles-Théodore [or Jean-Baptiste] Toeschi and Jean-François Regnard also set Etienne l'Auchery's *ballet-héroique Roger dans l'île d'Alcine* [*Rogerius auf der Insel der Alcina*] for Mannheim (4 November 1772). The libretto to *Themistocles* by Apostolo Zeno (music by J. C. Bach) includes

und Armida (1761; Kassel, 1769),[40] *La mort d'Hercules* (1762), and *Medea und Jason* (1763). Florian Johann Deller also set a short *Orpheus und Eurydice* for the same Stuttgart performance as Rodolphe's *Medea und Jason*.[41] These works include segments of musical terror, with its special keys, figures, tremolos, rapid figurations, and use of brass (usually horns) in infernal scenes. Similar music occurs at the end of *Rinaldo und Armida* with rapid sixteenth-note runs and tremolo string accompaniments. *Medea und Jason* includes a scene where Medea conjures chthonic spirits, accompanied by somber dotted figures alternating with ascending sixteenth-note scales and rapid short gestures. Rodolphe sets a similar furious ending to tremolos and sixteenth-note scales as the sky darkens, the earth trembles, the palace crumbles, and Medea flies away in her chariot.

٭

Philipp Hafner's three- act *Megära, die fürchterliche Hexe, oder Das bezauberte Schloß des Herrn von Einhorn* enjoyed its first success in the early 1760s and would remain a familiar subject on German stages through the early nineteenth century,[42] offering a Viennese parallel to the Parisian sorceress Coraline. The success of his *Zauberlustpsiel* inspired Hafner to write a sequel, *Der förchterlichen Hexe zweyter Theil; unter dem Titel: Die in eine dauerhafte Freundschaft sich verwandelnde Rache* (1764). The original music for *Megära* is lost; it consisted of only four arias, some brief songs, and perhaps instrumental pieces (Stieger attributes the music to Johann Heinrich Böhm).[43] The episodic text

---

a description (Mannheim: Hof-und Akademiebuchdruckerei, 1772); cited in Sonneck, *Catalogue of Opera Librettos*, 1058.

40. A program was printed in Kassel: D. Estienne, 1769. A modern edition of the music is in Abert and Moser, *Ausgewählte Ballette*.

41. Also in Abert and Moser, *Ausgewählte Ballette*. See Hansell, "Opera and Ballet," 289–303, 1017–1051.

42. The libretto was published (Vienna: Joseph Kurzböck [c. 1764]), A-Wst, shelfmark A 13 387. Editions include Haffner, *Philipp Hafners gesammelte Schriften*, 2; Hafner, *Gesammelte Werke*, 1:71ff.; and Rommel, *Die Maschinenkomödie* (1935). Rommel designates this a *Zauberburleske*, his own term for a transitional piece between the improvised theater and the more literary productions of the later eighteenth century. These transitional works moved away from the "baroque tradition" of improvisation and toward the more literary comedy of manners. Rommel also suggests influences from Kurz, Molière, and others. An incomplete anonymous Viennese manuscript score of *Megära*, with numerous performance indications, survives in the castle archive at Český Krumlov (Czech Republic), shelfmark 49b/1-2 K17. The watermarks in the paper are contemporary with scores from the late 1790s. The manuscript comprises three arias and the finale (nos. 12–16) from act 1 (in a particell score), all of act 2 (a terzetto, four arias, and the finale, in full score), and all of act 3 (a duet, three arias, and the finale, in full score).

43. *Megära*, a *Lokalstück*, was performed at BT, 31 May 1765 (part 1) and 23 August 1765 (part 2). Stieger lists another *Megära*, an *Oper* in three acts for Berlin, Koch's theater, 27 July 1774. The productions of *Megära* at LT during the 1780s probably had new music, perhaps by Wenzel Müller.

and long philosophical exchanges on love and money clearly owe much to the French tradition of Italian-style comedy. Some standard comic scenes, with an undercurrent of cruelty, betray Italian roots; Hafner's few scenes in short synopses suggest improvised dialogue.

The plot concerns Oboardo von Einhorn, a former salesman who has become a miserly nouveau riche. His daughter Angela and the young nobleman Leander are in love, but Oboardo wants her to marry Anselmo, a rich old widower. Megära is the beneficent sorceress of the title who helps the lovers, along with Angela's servant Colombine and Leander's servant Hanswurst.[44] She appears when invoked with the word "Schlickziroschuraskas" and uses her wand to create a storm at sea and a volcano and to make devils and dead souls to rise out of the earth.[45] She transforms a rock into a woman, and she creates two giants and two dwarfs, followed by two dragons and various crawling creatures. With her help Leander and Hanswurst carry out a series of deceptions, first pretending to have died, then frightening their opponents by appearing as ghosts. In one comic episode Megära touches the hump of Oboardo's servant Riepel with her wand and enchants him so that he can only say "schmecks." Megära transforms her appearance into that of a rich young cavalier named Graf von Ganßbiegel from "Malta, in upper Austria." He proposes to marry Oboardo's daughter and endow him with a large fortune. Angela agrees on the condition that Colombina be allowed stay with her as her servant. Hanswurst then requests the hand of Colombina, and she also agrees. Graf von Ganßbiegel transforms the scene to a splendid ballroom with Oboardo and his helpers suspended like hanging lights. Megära then reveals her true identity and compels Oboardo to allow Angela to marry Leander.

Daniel Schiebeler's *romantisch-komische Oper* in two acts *Lisuart und Dariolette, oder die Frage und die Antwort* (25 November 1766), with music by Hiller,[46] was another popular work with French roots. Based on Schiebeler's dramatic epilogue (a spoken afterpiece) of 1763–64,[47] the libretttist expanded it once again in 1767 into three acts. The success of Favart and Duni's *La fée Urgèle*

---

44. Megaera, one of the Furies in Greek mythology, is evoked in Renaissance poetry: she is "a female heretic arming her vipers with poison" in Chiabrera's canzonetta "Qual sulla cetera," *Canzonette* (Rome, 1625), 6, and also appears in Venetian baroque opera (*Ercole in Tebe*, Moniglia/Boretti, 1671).

45. Schlickziroschuraskas (*Schlick* = slime) was the magician who fell in love with and abducted Megära and eventually taught her magic.

46. Hiller and Schiebeler again collaborated on a short afterpiece, *Die Muse* (3 October 1767), a false-magic story.

47. The two-act version of the libretto was printed in the *Hamburgische Unterhaltungen* in 1766. The three-act libretto (Frankfurt am Main, 1776, US-Wc, Schatz 4726) and a full manuscript score (horns, flutes, oboes, bassoons, and strings) survive of the three-act version with thirteen parts (D-Hs, shelfmark ND VII 187). A manuscript short score (two accompanying parts and voices) in D-B, Mus. ms. 10636 (copies in US-Wc, M 1500 H65L6, and Kaliningrad), gives indications of some parts for flutes, oboes, horns, and bassoons. Another manuscript score is in B-Bc, Cons. ms.

probably influenced the revisions: both share the same sources, traced back to Chaucer's "The Tale of the Wife of Bath."[48] The story was recycled as *Das Rätsel, oder Was dem Frauenzimmer am meisten gefällt*, a one-act comedy by Johann Friedrich Löwen (Hamburg, before August 1767).[49] The names Lisuart and Dariolette had long been familiar from the epic *Amadis de Gaula*.[50] A number of elements here suggest that this work may have served as a model for later fairy-tale librettos, including *Die Zauberflöte*.[51]

Queen Ginevra grieves over the loss of her daughter Dariolette, who has been absent for two years. Her ladies remind her that the playful fairy Serena, sister of Merlin, is sworn to protect her family. Ginevra tells of the knight Lisuart and his shield bearer Derwin, who violated the code of the Round Table by trying to abduct one of Ginevra's ladies. Both face death unless they meet one of two conditions: either they find the princess or answer a riddle: "What is it that women desire most ardently?" The queen has granted them a year and a day before they must return, with either Dariolette or the solution to the riddle. Today their time is up and they have failed on both counts. In a secluded forest Lisuart withdraws a small portrait of Dariolette that the queen gave him. Having fallen in love with the image, he sings an aria ("O Bild voll göttlich hoher Reize!"). An impoverished old peasant woman approaches and offers to help solve the riddle if they will each agree to grant her a single request. Lisuart agrees, and she whispers the answer in his ear and leaves. Lisuart then returns

---

24 10. Several arias were published (for details, see Bauman, *North German Opera*). The piano-vocal score lacks the overture (Leipzig: Breitkopf 1768, 2nd ed., 1769, RISM H 5267).

48. For details on the German translations and adaptations of *La fée Urgèle*, see Busch, "Daniel Schiebeler, Schikaneder und Mozarts Berlin-Besuch." Schiebeler discussed his sources in "Anmerkung zu Lisuart und Dariolette," *Wöchentliche Nachrichten und Anmerkungen die Musik betreffend*, 2 November 1767, 135–39. He acknowledged the debt of comic operas such as *Lisuart und Dariolette* to *Feyenmährchen*, also citing epic romance as an influence.

49. Lessing discussed the work in the *Hamburgische Dramaturgie*, 7 August 1767, referring to it as a *Hexenmärchen*. See Iacuzzi, *European Vogue of Favart*, 199ff. It was translated into Danish by Johann Hermann Wessel as *Feen Ursel, eller Hvad der behager Damerne* (music by Duni), 1783, and by Thomas Thaarup (based on Wessel) as *Feen Ursel* (music by Johann Abraham Peter Schulz), 1792.

50. See Schmidtmann, "Daniel Schiebeler," 104.

51. In both operas the queen's ladies sing an ensemble at the beginning of act 1 in which they mourn the abduction of the queen's daughter. The naive knight Lisuart (tenor), like Tamino, sings a portrait aria. The comic bass Derwin is his cowardly companion and shield bearer. The fairy Serene has a retinue of sylphs and sylphids. Dariolette has been transformed into an old woman. A *fürchterliche Zwerg*, much like Monostatos, is one of the villains. The work ends with a similar triumphal ballet and chorus in praise of the sun ("Lässt glänzend die Sonne, ihr Antlitz sehn, so strahlt nach langen Tagen, im schwartzen Gram verlebt"). Emanuel Schikaneder in fact performed this work in 1777. Numerous performances occurred in places where both Schikaneder and Mozart would have had opportunity to attend. Calmus, *Die ersten deutschen Singpiele*, also points out elements here that may have influenced the text of *Die Zauberflöte*. *La fée Urgèle* was also produced in Vienna in 1780.

to the queen and her court, where he answers the riddle correctly: women desire most of all to have supremacy. Astonished, Ginevra grants him clemency and freedom. Lisuart confesses love for Dariolette and pledges to continue the search. When Lisuart encounters the old woman again, she demands that he grant her request, namely his hand in marriage. He is incredulous until she shows him a letter bearing the magic seal of the fairy Serena and declaring that Ginevra can be reunited with her daughter only when the old woman is granted two requests: Lisuart must marry her, and the queen's ladies must tear thirty-six hairs out of Derwin's mustache. The ladies seize Derwin, tie him up, dance around him, and pull out the hair. Lisuart then agrees to marry the old woman. Suddenly thunder rolls, and the old woman turns into the beautiful Dariolette. Soft music announces the appearance of Serena in a cloud chariot, a Grave "Entrée der Fée Serena in Wolken" recalling something of the elegant French "marvelous," with its refined ornamental style, conjunct motion, and consonant sonority. Hiller scores the *sanfte Musick* specified in the libretto for muted strings and a solo cello, repeated with flutes at the upper octave.[52] Serena explains that the fairy Morosa, the enemy of all women, captured Dariolette in order to force her to marry Morosa's ugly son, Bubu. She refused, and Morosa transformed her into an old hag. This spell would remain until a handsome knight accepted her as his bride. Serena knew that Lisuart had fallen in love with the picture and was to return today to Ginevra's court. Although Morosa was making a magic potion, she removed Dariolette from her prison and told her the situation. Ginevra declares that Lisuart and Dariolette should be married, and they celebrate in a final ensemble and chorus.

Two intriguing fairy-tale singspiels followed the model of *Lisuart und Dariolette*, *Walmir und Gertraud* and *Je unnatürlicher, je besser,* both by Johann Benjamin Michaelis. These librettos invoked the terms *romantisch* and *heroisch*, the former suggesting fanciful, complex plots, epic romance, and fantastic elements. Neither work appears to have been performed. In 1766 Michaelis wrote the three-act *Operette Walmir und Gertraud, oder Man kann es ja probieren.*[53] Anton Schweitzer composed music, but owing to the difficulties of its staging, the Seyler troupe did not perform the opera (two arias were later published).[54] In his preface Michaelis mentions the exclusion of divinities from singspiels and the addition of the "marvelous" (*Wunderbare*), presented here in the "most believable manner possible." This sentimental libretto, with its theme of female

---

52. Another instance of "marvelous" music occurs in the act 3 chorus "Wenn vor dem Donner wagen," which depicts a magic storm with rapid sixteenth-note figures.

53. Published in Michaelis, *Einzelne Gedichte.*

54. They appear in the *Gothaer Theater Kalender* (Gotha, 1776). For details, see Bauman, *North German Opera.* Poštolka, "Wranitzky, Paul," reports a setting of this libretto by Paul Wranitzky in a manuscript score in Prague, Národní Muzeum, Hudební Oddůleni (National Museum, Music Department), and suggests that it may have been set for Vienna c. 1791. However, the catalogs of this museum include no such score.

virtue, incorporates fairy-tale elements, mock-heroic romance (the knight is evil, corrupt, and less than chivalric), and characters from Shakespeare's *A Midsummer Night's Dream*. The plot concerns testing Gertraud's love for her husband, Walmir, who has been transformed into a statue. She resists the entreaties of a rich knight named Marbott and the urging of the magician Nadoboi. Their demands turn to threats against her and her two ,children Philibert and Adelgunde. When she refuses to be unfaithful the villains place all three on a sacrificial altar. A fire is lit, and suddenly the scene changes to a temple. Nadoboi, Marbott, and his squire, Turban, turn into Oberon, Titania, and Puck, with their retinue of fairies and spirits. The statue of Walmir returns to life ("Wo bin ich? Ich lebe?"), and Oberon and Titania explain that this was a trial of Gertraud's virtue, initiated by a wager over the fidelity of women.

Michaelis borrowed from the French episodic satire and the fairy story in his *Je unnatürlicher, je besser*, a three-act *komische Oper*.[55] A magician falls in love with his ward, Irene, who is affiancéed to the insipid and pedantic Philint, the son of Armide. Armide places Irene under a spell that can only be broken when someone locates the most unnatural thing on earth. The magician orders his spirits to produce a series of odd persons—a shepherd poet, a chivalric knight, and Robinson Crusoe. Philint ultimately breaks the spell when he proves himself to be more unnatural than any of the characters the magician can find. The text also includes elemental spirits, spells, vanishing objects and people, and Armide's chariot, drawn by dragons.

The 1770s

By the end of the 1770s itinerant theater companies began to establish themselves at courts or in major cities. Abel Seyler's company was active in northern Germany, especially in Gotha. With the help of his wife, the actress and author Friedericke Sophie Hensel Seyler, they adapted fairy-tale operas such as *Die verwandelten Weiber*, *Lisuart und Dariolette*, *Zemire und Azor*, *Der Holzhauer*, and other German translations of *opéra-comique*. Companies in Berlin and other locations performed this repertory as well. Large-scale fairy-tale singspiels became fashionable beginning around 1779.

Adaptations of the Faust legend continued to be popular. The Baden and Prague company of Johann Matthias Menninger (the Schulz-Menninger troupe) performed *Hoffart kommt vor dem Fall: Doctor Johann Fausts* in the Leopoldstadt's Czernin palace (poster in A-Wt, dated 22 January 1770). In the following month the company staged a *Maschinenkomödie* entitled *Der neue Doctor Faust, oder Kasperle der Zauberer wider seinen Willen*, in the same location (poster in A-Wt, dated 19 February 1770). Based on an "alte Märchen von dem be-

---

55. Published in Michaelis, *Einzelne Gedichte*, and *Sämtliche poetische Werke*, 77–190. Christian Gottlob Neefe apparently set two arias from the libretto in 1773. See Bauman, *North German Opera*, 412.

rühmten Doctor Faust," the poster announced many "Maschinen, Arien, [and] Fluchwerken." *Johann Faust*, a five-act singspiel by Paul Weidmann, with music by Joseph Christian Willibald Michl, was staged in Munich (16 May 1776).

Melodrama, a new theatrical genre with musically accompanied dialogue, utilized supernatural stories. Rousseau's melodrama *Pygmalion*, translated by Joseph G. Laudes, with music by Franz Aspelmayr, was staged at Vienna's Kärntnertor Theater (19 February 1772, manuscript score in A-Wn). Another version of *Pygmalion*, with music by Anton Schweitzer (lost), was produced at Weimar (13 May 1772). The potent new musical style of Gluck and his contemporaries influenced Georg Benda's melodramas (see below).

Early German Comic Opera and the Marvelous from Foreign Sources

Gozzi's works exerted an influence on German writers such as Lessing, Goethe, and Tieck.[56] The translation of Gozzi's dramatic works in the 1770s helped to disseminate the *fiabe* in German-speaking areas.[57] In the preface to his *Das wütende Heer, oder Das Mägden im Thurme* (1779), Christoph Friedrich Bretzner categorized his own libretto as a *Märchen*, acknowledging Gozzi as his model. The first Gozzi play in German was based on the only *fiaba* without supernatural elements, *I pitocchi fortunati* (1764), and was entitled *Die glücklichen Bettler* (Gotha, 1777). *I pitocchi fortunati* was also the source of a two-act *Schauspiel mit Gesang* by Johann Friedrich Wilhelm Gotter, *Das tartarische Gesetz*.[58] Johann André set the music, and the work had its premiere in Mannheim, followed by productions in Berlin, Hamburg, Hanau, Weimar, and probably Vienna. Both Hiller and Seydelmann (the latter in Dresden) composed music for this libretto in 1779. Around the same time Johann Friedrich Schmidt translated Gozzi's *Turandot* as *Hermannide, oder Die Rätsel*, calling it an old *fränkisches Märchen* (BT, 14, 16, and 25 October 1777).[59] Friedrich Eberhard Rambach arranged *Turandot* as a *Tragikomödie* entitled *Die drei Räthsel* (Leipzig, 1779).[60]

56. See Rusack, *Gozzi in Germany*.

57. Gozzi, *Theatralische Werke*. The translator, Werthes, was a protégé of Wieland.

58. Leipzig: Dyk, 1779. A copy survives in US-Wc, Schatz 190, and in Wolffenbüttel. Gotter also produced a comedy, *Juliane von Lindorak*, based on Gozzi's *Doride* (based in turn on Calderón's *El secreto a voces*) for Hamburg (1778) that was later produced in Berlin, Gotha, Bonn, Leipzig, Vienna, Salzburg [by Schikaneder; see Blümml, *Aus Mozarts Freundes- und Familienkreis*, 145], Mannheim, and Munich. Emanuel Schikaneder staged Werthe's translation of *Le due notte affannose*, entitled *Peter der Grausame, oder die zwei schlaflosen Nächte*. Mozart wrote an aria for it (see Blümml, *Aus Mozarts Freundes- und Familienkreis*, 145). In 1784 Gozzi's *La principessa filosofa* was translated and produced as *Die philosophische Dame*. Emanuel Schikaneder staged it in Regensburg in 1787.

59. See Alth, *Burgtheater*, 15, and Hadamowsky, *Die wiener Hoftheater*, Teil 1, 62. A libretto was printed (Vienna: Logenmeister, 1777).

60. *Die 3 Räthsel. Tragikomödie in 5 A. nach Gozzi* (Leipzig, 1779; Graz, 1800). See Alth, *Burgtheater*, 15.

Gozzi was not the only Italian source for the German "marvelous." The Baden troupe adapted the commedia dell'arte play *Il finto prencipe* as *Der durch Zauberey auf wunderbare und lächerliche Art, zum Fürsten gemacht Hannswurst* (poster in A-Wt, dated 3 February 1770). As is typical for the genre, magic facilitates the reversal of social positions. The printed text for *Harlequin Friseur, oder Die Zaubertrompete* reveals yet another Viennese commedia dell'arte pantomime with a magical instrument (1778).[61] A number of Don Juan adaptations were also staged in the 1770s, including Justinus Knecht's *Don Juan, oder Das klägliche Ennde eines verstockten Atheisten* (28 December 1772) and Gluck's ballet (Munich, 1777).[62]

�֍

Translations of *opéra-comique* with supernatural episodes continued to be popular on the German stage. *Le bûcheron* (1763) became *Der Holzhauer [oder Die drei Wünsche]*, published anonymously in Berlin and Riga in 1772 (the opera was also performed in the original French in Vienna in 1768 and 1773).[63] Johann Joachim Eschenburg made a new translation, set to music by Johann August Christoph Koch (Berlin, 1774), and Johann Friedrich Reichardt composed a version sometime in the 1770s.[64] In Friedrich Gottlob Fleischer's modest vocal score of Christian Fürchtegott Gellert's adaptation of Saint-Foix's *L'oracle*, the sorceress has forceful da capo arias with a little coloratura. Stieger cites a performance of *Das Orakel* with music by Anton Laube in Prague's Kotzentheater (8 August 1771). A playbill in Hamburg documents a performance of *Das Orackel* on 9 April 1788, and manuscript materials in Hamburg include a prompter's book and an orchestral score of scenes 1 and 2 only, labeled "Parte prima."[65] The musical style seems dated as well, with da capo arias and rhymed verse dialogues. One short instrumental piece at the end of the manuscript is intriguing. This untitled number, which does not appear in the

61. Lbl, shelfmark 11746.ee.22.(7.).

62. C. Russell, *Don Juan Legend*, 453–54. Russell calls the Knecht work a "musical farce." He also mentions a ballet entitled *Don Juan, oder Der steinerne Gast*, performed by Johannes Böhm's troupe in Salzburg, Frankfurt am Main, and other German-speaking cities (1781–90).

63. The French theater in Vienna staged musical comedies beginning in the 1750s, including *Zéneide, Arlequin poli par l'amour, L'oracle, La sylphide, L'île de Merlin, ou le monde renversé*, and *Le diable à quatre, ou La double métamorphose*. French fairy-tale comedies and fairy plays were also printed in Vienna, for example, *La belle Arsène* (Kurzböck, n.d.). For details, see Witzenetz, *Le théâtre français de Vienne*, and Brown, *Gluck and the French Theatre*.

64. Manuscripts survive in Lüneberg and US-Wc.

65. D-Hs preserves both the playbill and these manuscripts. The score is preserved in the Musiksammlung, shelfmark ND VII-126; the prompter's book, dated 1788, is found in the Theaterbibliothek, shelfmark 567, Nr. 91. The score has no overture. The orchestra consists of flutes, horns, oboes, bassoon, and strings. A printed vocal score also survives: Fleischer, *Das Orackel;* RISM F 1119, copy in F-Pn, D. 4153.

EXAMPLE 5.1 Friedrich Gottlob Fleischer, *Das Orackel*, scene 2

printed vocal score, is a duple-meter binary in A major scored for two flutes and "violin primo." The instrumentation, conjunct motion, and consonant sonority all suggest the "marvelous," perhaps in a sleep or transformation scene (see ex. 5.1).

✻

Johann Heinrich Faber translated *Zemire und Azor* in 1775, as did Moritz August von Thümmel, a version that was set by Christian Gottlob Neefe (Leipzig, 1776; Vienna, 1778).[66] Karl Emil Schubert adapted *Zemire und Azor* as a *romantisch-komische Oper* with music by Gotthilf von Baumgarten. First performed by the Wäser troupe at Breslau (18 May 1776), the music survives in a keyboard score, edited by one "Wolf."[67] Baumgarten, a Prussian lieutenant residing in Silesia, set all of Marmontel's musical numbers. Like Grétry, he uses an *entr'acte* depicting the magic cloud machine that transports Sander and Ali (Baumgarten borrows the key and melodic motive of the first aria for this episode). Although the *Zwischenmusik* to act 2 and the storm music toward the end of the opera evince something of the terrifying style, Baumgarten's keyboard score does not include music for the magic-mirror episode.[68]

66. Libretto, Frankfurt and Leipzig: 1776, in D-B, Mus. Tm 110. Viennese audiences also attended performances of Grétry's original opera starting in 1776.

67. Breslau: Korn, 1775; RISM B 1375–76. I consulted the copy in F-Pn, D. 736(1).

68. Grétry's original music survives in a Viennese manuscript, A-Wn, Musiksammlung, K.T. (K.T. = Kärntnertor Theater Collection) 475, with an anonymous undated German translation of Marmontel's text, certainly based on the Faber translation. This undated manuscript must date from after 1771 (the year of Grétry's original). Bauer, *Opern und Operetten*, 112, cites a 1780–81 performance of the Grétry opera at the Kärntnertor Theater. A Viennese libretto survives from 1779 for a production at the Nationaltheater, published by Logenmeister without attribution of au-

Faber translated Favart's *La fée Urgèle* as *Die Fee Urgele, oder Was den Damen gefällt* (1772), using both Schiebeler's and Löwen's models, with the original music of Duni. Karl [?] Goedecke's *Die Fee Urgele, oder Was den Damen gefällt* was set for Eszterháza as a marionette *Operette* (November 1776), probably arranged by Karl Michael von Pauersbach, with music by Ignaz Pleyel.[69] Pleyel's score is a bright, *galant* setting. Favart's *La belle Arsène* was also performed with its original music; it was set as a three-act singspiel, *Arsene* or *Die schöne Arsene*, and in a four-act version by Johann Heinrich Faber (1776). Pasquale Bondini's company at Dresden produced a translation by August Gottlieb Meissner in four acts (1779), with music by Johann Nikolaus Franz Seydelmann,[70] later performed in Leipzig and Berlin. Hadamovsky documents a staging in Vienna (BT, 4, 8, and 25 August 1786). Seydelmann's instrumental music includes *Zwischenaktmusik* to acts 2, 3, and 4; the music in act 4 depicts a storm in G minor. Seydelmann does little with the supernatural scenes in his score; the fairy's music is indistinguishable from that of the mortal characters. A double chorus for nymphs seems somewhat unusual, but the musical style is nondescript.

In March 1776 Joseph II allowed the free establishment of theaters in Vienna (the *Spektakelfreiheit*), and the first suburban theaters opened soon thereafter. The combination of supernatural and comedy continued to be a feature of the Viennese suburban theater, where translations of French texts were as popular as Italian adaptations. Comedies with titles such as Gottlieb Konrad Pfeffel's *Der Zaubergürtel* (1779) suggest magic and an origin in *opéra-comique*.[71]

❋

Original German fairy-tale operas enjoyed their first success in the last half of the 1770s. The earliest of these appears to be *Der Schiffbruch*, a *Mährchen* in four acts by Graf von Spaur. First performed in Königsberg in 1778, with music by Nikolaus Mühle (lost), a libretto survives from the 1778 Frankfurt production,[72] with music by Franz Hugo, Freiherr von Kerpen (music also lost).[73]

---

thor, translator, or composer. J. B. Wallishausser reprinted the libretto (Vienna, 1790), almost certainly for a performance in the imperial city.

69. An autograph score, in four volumes, is preserved in A-Wn, Ms. 15560.

70. The vocal score (Leipzig: Breitkopf, 1779; RISM [S 2864]) was consulted (A-Wst, Musiksammlung, M.S. 11017), along with two damaged manuscripts in D-Dlb, Mus. 3550-F-1, and Mus. 3550-F-1a (only acts 1, 2, and 4 are intact). Johann André composed yet another setting of the opera (Offenbach, 1779).

71. Cited in Blümml and Gugitz, *Alt-Wiener Thespiskarren*, 517.

72. Frankfurt am Main: mit Andreäischen Schriften, 1778; US-Wc, Schatz 5142.

73. Stieger cites this production at Mainz in January 1778. There exists some confusion over various librettos by this name. Stieger and NGO cite an opera with this title based on Shakespeare's *The Tempest* (*Die bezauberte Insel*) with music by Franz Anton Hoffmeister (Stieger, *Opernlexikon*, and Bauer, *Opern und Operetten*, give Vienna, 1783, and NGO gives 1792. Stieger cites an opera

One of the first instances of the use of *Märchen* as a genre designation, this Egyptian fairy tale borrows elements from the commedia dell'arte,[74] Greek tragedy, and the biblical account of Joseph.[75] The lengthy text emphasizes dialogue over music, which consists of arias, songs, ensembles, choruses, and instrumental numbers.

The plot concerns the Egyptian king Malsora and his brother Maken, a virtuous magician. Owing to the slander of the corrupt high priest Osis, Malsora has unjustly banished Maken from Egypt. Maken abducts Malsora's daughter Selma, who is in love with the Egyptian prince Medon. Malsora and Medon then attempt to rescue Selma, but they cannot overcome Maken's magic power. Only when Malsora is willing to sacrifice himself to save his people and his daughter do the gods forgive his injustice against his brother. The opera has magic transformations, spells, storms, and a cloud chariot. A chorus of priests accompanies a ceremony leading to an abstruse oracle (a "dumpfer unverständlicher Gesang und Mischmasch der Priester"), and a magic obelisk with illuminated hieroglyphics foretells the future. Thus *Der Schiffbruch* has aspects in common with *Die Zauberflöte*.

Bretzner's *Operette* in three acts, *Der Irrwisch, oder Endlich fand er sie* (or *Das Irrlicht*), proved to be the most popular large-scale fairy-tale German libretto, inspiring as many as eight different musical settings.[76] Friedrich Preu's setting for Leipzig (1779) is mainly a number opera with no music to depict magical events. The other two surviving settings, discussed in detail below, have more distinctive musical settings. The libretto, which owes much to the sentimental, erotic French fairy stories of the 1740s, concerns Alwin, the prince of the Green Island, who suffers from a dreadful enchantment incurred

---

by J. J. Pfeiffer, music by Bernhard Romberg, Bonn, 1791. No music apparently survives for any of these performances. An unrelated *Trauerspiel* in five acts by Johann Christian Brandes also has this title (a manuscript libretto survives in Mannheim's Reiß-Museum). NGO makes no mention of the Mühle or Hugo settings.

74. Particularly the "naufrage" plot, where a magician causes a shipwreck.

75. Bauman, *North German Opera*, believes the author borrowed heavily from Shakespeare's *The Tempest*, but these motives come from the commedia dell'arte and are found in numerous other sources. I found very little similarity to Shakespeare's play.

76. Bretzner, *Operetten*, vol. 1 (US-Wc, Schatz 8464), and two Stuttgart prints. The original music was composed by Friedrich Preu for Leipzig's Theater am Rannstädter Tor, 1779 (an orchestral score and parts survive in D-Hs, shelfmark ND VII 315). A version by O. F. Holly for Breslau (1779) appears to be lost. Otto Carl Erdmann, Freiherr von Kospoth, composed a version for Berlin's Döbbelin's Theater (2 October 1780). Nikolaus K. Mühle composed a four-act setting for Königsberg (1780, lost), and Christian Ludwig Dieter's setting for Stuttgart, Kleines Theater (23 September 1782) was published (Stuttgart: Christoph Gottfried Maentler, 1782). The manuscript score in Darmstadt was destroyed in World War II. Gottlieb Stephanie revised the opera as *Das Irrlicht*, with music by Ignaz Umlauf (BT, 17 January 1782); see below. Stieger cites two additional settings, one by Anton Mayer (Cologne, c. 1783) and the other by a composer named Schön (Innsbruck, 1787).

as punishment for his youthful dalliances. Each night he becomes the epony-
mous will-o'-the-wisp, a specter that hovers over the swamp. He can be freed
from this spell only if an innocent and virtuous maiden loves him for himself
and not for his position or wealth. Disguised as a shepherd, he travels in search
of this maiden. One night the *Irrwisch* encounters a beauty named Blanka and
falls in love with her. Alwin invites her to the Green Island, where her virtue
must be tested before an oracle in a temple. Her stepparents, a poor fisherman
named Berthold and his wife, Rosa, force her to go, hoping to acquire wealth.
Blanka meets the prince in his disguise as a flute-playing shepherd and soon
falls in love with him. A magic white dove also appears to Blanka as an omen.
At the ceremony Rosa wears an opaque veil, attempting to deceive Alwin and
take Blanka's place. But when Rosa approaches the altar lightning strikes, ex-
tinguishing the magic flame and throwing the room into darkness. The guilty
couple admit their deception, and the officials summon Blanka to the temple.
Alwin's friend Count Sever greets Blanka and welcomes her in the place of his
own daughter, who was lost in a flood as an infant. As she approaches the altar, the flame expands into a huge fire. Pleasant music accompanies two small
genies with a laurel wreath and the white dove in their hands. The prince enters and removes Blanka's veil. The enchanted dove flies to her, and the officials place it on the altar to still the flame. When Blanka looks perplexed by the
prince's familiar appearance, Alwin reveals himself as the shepherd. Berthold
then tells Alwin how he found Blanka as a baby, washed ashore in a storm. He
produces the cross that she wore around her neck, and Sever recognizes it as
the one that his baby daughter wore when she was lost. The happy characters
then celebrate in the final chorus.

 Das wütende Heer, oder Das Mägden im Thurme, another *Operette* in three
acts by Bretzner from the same period (1779),[77] proved to be almost as popular as *Der Irrwisch,* with five different musical settings (see below). The supernatural aspects include a maiden turned to marble, an enchanted dove, a magic
blue flame, and an oracular voice singing backstage. The storm music and chorus of the *wütende Heer,* a supernatural army of vengeful hunters that wanders
through the lands of an ancient feudal estate, are dramatic features that seem to
have been widely imitated.

The Bendas

The Bohemian brothers Friedrich Wilhelm Heinrich Benda and Georg Anton Benda were both successful composers who developed the impassioned
expressive style made popular by Gluck. Georg Benda set the comic opera *Le
búcheron* as *Der Holzhauer* (1778) and the melodramas *Ariadne auf Naxos* (1775),
Medea (1775), *Pygmalion* (1779), and *Almanzor und Nadine* or *Philon und Theone* (c. 1780). Friedrich set the mythological German operas *Orpheus* (1785)

77. The libretto was printed in the Bretzner, *Operetten,* vol. 1 (US-Wc, Schatz 9777).

and Wieland's *Alceste* (1786, music lost). The melodramas employed instrumental music as an enhancement to the spoken dialogue, using vivid, sometimes violent musical imagery to depict inner turmoil as well as external (sometimes supernatural) events. Benda favored the keys of E-flat, C minor, and D minor in the supernatural episodes, with *alla zoppo* syncopation, tremolos, octave-and-unison sonority, and rapid scale figures. Both *Adriadne auf Naxos* and *Medea* have *terribile* death scenes in D minor, probably inspired by Gluck's *Don Juan*.

Georg Benda's first and best-known melodrama was Johann Christian Brandes's one-act duodrama, *Adriadne auf Naxos* (Gotha, 27 January 1775).[78] Although Benda mostly employed vivid musical imagery to portray psychological turmoil, he also set a storm scene in D minor, several oracle scenes in E-flat and C minor (with the voice of Oreade), and Ariadne's D minor suicide scene at the conclusion, all in the terrifying style. Less than six months later he set Friedrich Wilhelm Gotter's one-act *Medea* (Leipzig, 1 May 1775).[79] The melodrama was then staged at Gotha, Berlin, Hamburg, Prague, and Mannheim, where Mozart saw it and said that it had "the most splendid effect." Again Benda employed the musical mode of terror mostly for psychological portrayal, but he also found it appropriate for the oath scene in G, which leads directly to a storm scene in C minor (Allegro furioso), and an invocation to the Furies (no Furies actually appear in the play). The D minor instrumental *Eingang*, marked "un poco grave e maestoso," suggests musical terror, with bursts of octave-and-unison figures in the strings, flutes, and bassoons. Act 1 starts with the same D minor music, which then shifts to an elegant minuet-like Allegro in D major as Medea appears in her cloud chariot drawn by flying dragons. The D minor music returns at a few key points in the play, particularly for the suicide scene at the end.

Benda set Friedrich Wilhelm Gotter's (with J. G. von Wulff) translation of *Le bûcheron* as *Der Holzhauer, oder Die drei Wünsches* for Gotha's castle theater (Abel Seyler troupe, 2 January 1778).[80] The singspiel apparently was not successful. The accompanied recitative for the magic appearance of Mercury is longer than Philidor's original. An eighteen-measure instrumental introduction for flutes, horns, trumpets, bassoon, strings, and timpani heralds the arrival of the deity with fanfare motives, dotted rhythms, and rapid ascending scales. Later string tremolos accompany Mercury's (low tenor) recita-

78. For a modern edition see *Musica antiqua bohemica*. The printed score (Leipzig, c. 1781) and manuscript (D-B) have numerous variants.

79. For the modern edition, see Gotter, *Medea*. Benda revised the work several versions times over a ten-year period with many variants and stylistic differences. Manuscript copies survive in D-B (including two autographs), Darmstadt (missing, only photographs survive), and Brno, and there is a print of a keyboard reduction (Leipzig: Schwickert, 1778).

80. A reduced score survives (Leipzig: Schwickert, 1777; RISM B 1876, F-Pn, Vm³ 114). Manuscripts survive in D-B, Mus. ms. 1356; D-Dlb, Mus. 3107-F-17; and the Boston Public Library, M.320.6.

tive, whose vocal line has no distinguishing supernatural features. Gotter and Benda added a new touch here: choral interjections with the marvelous exclamation "O Himmel, was ist das?" As in the original setting, one finds a comic septet where the enchanted Brigitte can only sing "heing heing" in eighth-note interjections.

The following year Benda set Karl Wilhelm Ramler's translation of Rousseau's one-act monodrama *Pygmalion* (Gotha, 20 September 1779), a brief score of only some fifteen pages.[81] The composer depicts Pygmalion's inner turmoil with musical terror after his rejection of love. When the statue Galathee comes to life, there is a key change to C major, and the terrifying music resumes when she first speaks. As she begins to move, the key changes to E-flat for a *galant* Allegretto.[82]

Haydn's Puppet Plays

Eszterháza staged elaborate marionette productions and the few surviving musical scores suggest proportions comparable to contemporary German comic opera. Several of these were fairy-tale or magical texts with music by Haydn and Pleyel.[83] Haydn composed the music for the Eszterháza marionette plays some twenty years after his two early singspiels (c. 1773–79), which also included supernatural episodes. Unfortunately, the music for these works is lost, fragmentary, or of questionable authenticity. But the surviving texts of most of these works indicate that Haydn composed instrumental and vocal music for magic events and transformations.

Philemon und Baucis, oder Jupiters Reise auf die Erde, a one-act marionette opera by Gottlieb Konrad Pfeffel (27 June 1773), began with a *Vorspiel* entitled *Der Götterrat*, whose second scene has stage-machine music for the arrival of Diana. Haydn composed a binary form in D major for this "Gottheit anspielende Musik," with horn-call motives, gigue rhythms, and oboes and horns that suggest the association of Diana with hunting.[84] Haydn's biographer Dies (1810) mentioned another two-act marionette opera, *Hexenschabbas* (?1773, lost), with a title suggestive of magic content. Although the authenticity of the manuscript score discovered by H. C. Robbins Landon is doubtful, the two-act marionette singspiel *Die Feuersbrunst* (?1775–78) has been published in the complete-works edition.[85] The music includes an aria for the ghost, a lyric piece in E-flat for tenor with no allusions to the marvelous. The *Drachen-*

81. A printed vocal score survives (Leipzig: Schwickert, 1780; Lbl, F. 386.(2.)).

82. Friedrich Wilhelm Heinrich Benda, *Pygmalion*, Lbl, shelfmark E. 929a, is a cantata, probably written in 1783, for one soprano; the musical style has no supernatural elements.

83. Librettos survive in three Eisenstadt archives. See Robbins Landon, "Haydn's Marionette Operas."

84. Modern edition in Haydn, *Werke*, Reihe 24, Bd. 1.

85. Modern edition in Haydn, *Werke*, Reihe 24, Bd. 3.

musik is more telling and might suggest some of the styles used in Haydn's lost setting of *Die bestrafte Rachbegierde* (see below). This Allegro in D minor evinces the terrifying style of Traetta and Gluck, with its rapid sixteenth-note figures in the strings punctuated by blaring infernal winds (flutes, oboes, bassoons, horn, trumpets) and timpani. The harmony in this *sinfonia* modulates to F and C minor through diminished seventh chords; augmented sixth chords also color the sonority. An unusual retransition to the repeat has an ascending chromatic passage in octave-and-unison sonority leading from a dominant (G) in C minor to the leading tone in D minor (C-sharp), with a prominent use of the interval of an augmented second from B-flat to C-sharp. Perhaps this alluded to some event on the stage. Hanswurst's fearful bass aria "Da ist die Katz" has some of the same elements as the *Drachenmusik*. Both pieces are in D minor with unusual harmonic juxtapositions, touching on C minor, D, E, and A; the harmony changes abruptly, using motives in octave-and-unison sonority, diminished chords, and repetitive phrases. The initial motive begins with rapid slurred scalar figures in the strings and bass, a figure that composers employed to suggest supernatural force. The final ritornello ends with a powerful descending scale in string tremolos.

Although Haydn's music for Philipp Georg Bader's three-act marionette opera *Die bestrafte Rachbegierde* (?1779) is lost, the libretto offers intriguing details on the decorations, transformations, and music.[86] This farce has numerous supernatural elements, including good and bad fairies, a chorus of fairies, magicians, genies, Furies, and a fire-breathing dragon. The combination of commedia dell'arte and the aristocratic *festa teatrale* seems unusual and noteworthy. Standard carnivalesque inversions and comical dialogues combine cant and proverb with absurdity. The ugly and foolish old fairy Furette, a comic distortion of Armida and Alcina, is a standard villain of eighteenth-century fairy stories. The libretto includes descriptions of a well that changes into a fiery mountain and an apple orchard enchanted into a dragon. Scenes occur in a dark forest, a magic grotto, and a deserted area with ruins. The magician either appears in a cloud chariot or rides a *Waldteufel* (forest spirit or devil). Liebhold, the capricious young king of Utopia, desires a queen and an heir to his throne. His intended bride is Lucinde, the princess of Kockligallinien. Liebhold assembles his ridiculous retinue of courtiers for their advice and flattery. Furette is in love with him, and she soon frustrates his plans. An evil old magician who was banished by Liebhold's father is in love with Lucinde and seeks revenge on Liebhold. Furette and the magician conspire to force the two nobles to marry them. If they refuse they will be destroyed through magic. Hanswurst comes as an envoy and attracts Liebhold to Furette's house by the promise of meeting a rich and beautiful young woman who is love with the king. The fairy transforms herself into a beautiful young girl and then transforms the room to im-

---

86. For a facsimile of the libretto see Haydn, *Werke*, Reihe 34, Bd. 2, *Textbücher verschollener Singspiele* (Munich: Henle, 1989).

press him. But the king has been raised to reject the seductions of magic, and he resists Furette's advances. She then punishes him by covering his body with hair and bristles and then tormenting him with other cruel magical transformations. The magician enters with the lost Lucinde and transforms her into a similar creature when she refuses his demands. The good fairy Candide then appears in a cloud chariot, restoring the former appearance of the noble pair and punishing Furette and the magician with hellish torment. The third act is a series of scenes celebrating the union of the royal pair, culminating in a fireworks display with festive orchestra. The text specifies appropriate (*analogue*) music for magical invocations and transformations. The opening of the singspiel indicates that "fairies and magicians arrive with soft, appropriate music," a reference to the long tradition of soft music accompanying the appearance of a deity. The second scene in act 2 indicates a terrifying scenic transformation with appropriate "horrid" music ("unter einer widerwärtigen analoguen Music verwandelt sich der Rubefelsen in eine Schreckenmaschine"). The libretto indicates ensembles and choruses of fairies, magicians, and genies. Had it survived, all of this music would have provided important early examples of Haydn's approach to the "marvelous" well before his Italian operas.

The Emergence of German Fairy Tales in the 1780s

Praise for folk legends and fairy tales by such luminaries as Herder and Wieland demonstrated a new attitude toward "natural" literature among German literati.[87] Their fascination with the unsophisticated spirit of popular narrative, as personified by the now-common use of the term *Volk*, was also a reaction against the restraints of contemporary German literature, with its heavy reliance on the models of classical antiquity. A specifically German narrative tradition, more difficult to trace than French or oriental tales, figures prominently in the earliest published German fairy tales. Found in almanacs, collections of legends,[88] and seventeenth-century chapbooks,[89] these tales made their way into more serious German literature starting with Johann Karl August Musäus's *Volksmärchen der Deutschen* (Gotha, 1782–87), the first modern German fairy-tale collection. Musäus transformed the tales into a genre of the Enlightenment, employing literary allusions, allegory, recent history, and

87. See Herder, *Märchen und Romane*, in *Adrastea*, 3. Stück (Leipzig, 1801), in *Sämmtliche Werke*, 23:273–97. See Andrae, "Studien zu den Volksmärchen," 4–5. On Wieland, see K. Otto Mayer, "Das Feenmärchen," 386. For a more recent discussion of Wieland's sources, see Craig, "Themes and Style." For a detailed treatment of the literary and aesthetic context of Wieland's tales, see Nobis, *Phantasie und Moralität*.

88. Among the tales of elves, ghosts, witches, and other spirits is the Silesian sprite Rübezahl, who figures in several prints of Johannes Praetorius (1662, 1671–73). For details see Grätz, *Das Märchen in der deutschen Aufklärung*, 381–82.

89. Goethe recalled these in his early youth and considered them "schätzbare Überreste der Mittelzeit." See Andrae, "Studien zu den Volksmärchen," 3.

TABLE 5.2 The Contents of *Dschinnistan*

VOLUME 1 (1786)

Vorrede

[1.] "Nadir und Nadine"

[2.] "Adis und Dahy"

[3.] "Neangir und seine Brüder, Argentine und ihre Schwestern"

[4.] "Der Stein der Weisen, oder Sylvester und Rosine"

[5.] "Timander und Melissa"

VOLUME 2 (1787)

[6.] "Himmelblau und Lupine"

[7.] "Der goldene Zweig"

[8.] "Der Druide, oder Die Salamandrin und die Bildsäule"

[9.] "Aboflede"

[10.] "Pertharit und Ferrandine"

[11.] "Der Zweikampf" (Einsiedel)

[12.] "Das Labyrinth" (Einsiedel)

VOLUME 3 (1789)

Der Herausgeber an die Leser

[13.] "Der eiserne Armleuchter: Ein türkisches Märchen"

[14.] "Der Greif vom Gebürge Kaf"

[15.] "Die klugen Knaben" (Einsiedel)

[16.] "Die Prinzessin mit der langen Nase" (Einsiedel)

[17.] "Der Korb" (Liebeskind)

[18.] "Der Palast der Wahrheit"

[19.] "Lulu, oder Die Zauberflöte" (Liebeskind)

topical humor, thereby improving the literary quality, like earlier French writers.[90] Similar collections of German fairy tales appeared later in the decade, such as the *Ammenmärchen* by Johann Ferdinand Roth,[91] Wieland's *Dschinnistan* (1786–89),[92] and three other contemporary collections.[93] *Dschinnistan* is a collection of nineteen stories with a preface and further editorial remarks at the beginning of the third volume.[94] Wieland included two stories by August Jacob Liebeskind, his son-in-law, and four stories by the Weimar Chamberlain, Friedrich Hildebrand von Einsiedel (see table 5.2). Liebeskind is in fact the au-

90. See ibid.; Bleich, "Die Märchen des Musäus"; and Musäus, *Volksmärchen der Deutschen*. Musäus's *Volksmärchen* had a decisive influence on Wieland.

91. Roth, *Vom Könige Artus*.

92. Wieland, *Dschinnistan*.

93. Günther, *Kindermärchen;* Fülleborn, *Volksmärchen;* and [Naubert], *Neue Volksmärchen*.

94. The title *Dschinnistan* [= Genie-stan] refers to a mythical land of the genies commonly mentioned in oriental fairy tales.

thor of the story "Lulu, oder die Zauberflöte," which Schikaneder used as the basis of *Die Zauberflöte*. The quality of the stories in the collection is uneven, owing to the less polished contributions by Einsiedel and Liebeskind.[95]

Wieland's sources included *Le cabinet des fées* and the translations of Galland and Perrault. He adapted his sources freely, following much the same pattern as Musäus in supplementing, deleting, and rearranging the preexisting material. Also like Musäus, he highlighted moralistic and allegorical elements related to the Enlightenment, stressing reason over superstition and criticizing oppressive authoritarian rule. Fairy tales improved the behavior of both adults and children; they instructed and amused in order to better us and eliminate bad habits. Wieland also noted that unusual elements may be introduced in a tale, including intellectual, allegorical, naive, and satirical features, along with esoteric philosophy, perhaps an allusion to the hermetic references in Wieland's original fairy tale "Der Stein der Weisen."

In 1789, just as the fairy-tale singspiel was reaching its apogee in Vienna, an anonymous essay on fairy tales and *Märchenoper* appeared in the *Kritisches Theater-Journal von Wien*, along with a scornful review of the Leopoldstadttheater's *Feenmärchen Das Glück ist kugelrund, oder Kaspars Ehrentag* (Happiness Is Roly-poly, or Kaspar's Day of Glory).[96] The essay is entitled "The Thoroughly False Ideas about Fairy Tales in General: An Investigation of Their Peculiar Nature and Their Worth or Lack of Worth. Afterwards We Hope to Justify Their Applicability for the Stage." In his discussion of "the marvelous, the delightful, and the terrifying" (*das Wunderbare, Entzücken, und Schrecken*) the author appears to be attacking the notion of delight and terror advanced by John Aiken and others. Fairy tales are said to usurp the only legitimate use of the marvelous element, that of religion. Only in religion (here the writer almost certainly means Roman Catholicism) does "one acknowledge the truth before seeking to be convinced by reason. Because we doubt the truth of the supernatural outside of religion, it cannot be effective in literature or the theater. Only the common rabble enjoy fairy tales, and they harm these people." Fairy tales also damage children by "filling their heads with far-fetched ideas that continually haunt them and spoil their enjoyment and appreciation of the delights of the real world." These children grow up, he claims, to be superstitious and fearful adults: "When happiness resides in that which is unattainable,

95. The language of the Einsiedel and Liebeskind contributions is not as refined, and there is not as much cohesion in their story lines. Liebeskind's "Lulu, oder Die Zauberflöte," is one of the less artful stories in its language and plot.

96. *Kritisches Theater-Journal*, zweites Vierteljahr, Viertes Stück, 28 February 1789, 72–80: "Die durchaus falschen Begriffe von den Märchen überhaupt; werden nach folgender Untersuchung über ihr eigentlichen Wesen, dem Werthe oder Unwerte derselbe, und ihre Anwendbarkeit für die Bühne, hoffentlich rechtfertigen." A single bound copy of this journal survives in Vienna, Österreichische Nationalbibliothek, Sammlung von Inkunabeln, alten und wertvollen Drucken, shelfmark 6.080-A Alt.

all joy will die." Because fairy tales do not present a clear moral truth, as in the case of *Das Glück ist Kugelrund,* they have no value as art.

The tensions of the Austrian Enlightenment emerge when this writer suggests that fairy tales are appropriating a sphere reserved for established religion. Employing arguments about verisimilitude and the use of reason, the writer exempts religion (and, by implication, divine-right monarchy) from his critique of the marvelous element. In effect he can have it both ways, as a rationalist and as a man of faith. The attack on fairy tales and fairy-tale opera as damaging to children and to the "common rabble" is revealing of yet another tension. The effects of the marvelous are no longer seen as incredible and affirming of the established order, as asserted by Rousseau, Grimm, and Diderot. For the writer of this review they are in fact a danger to that order. In light of events in France in this same year of 1789, an infantile, superstitious, fearful, and joyless rabble was a serious concern to that established order.

Genres and Foreign Models in German Musical Theater

Despite their interest in *Volk* narrative, writers for German musical theater continued to employ relatively few indigenous sources. Exceptions include the occasional Faust staging and the anonymous *Die sieben Schwaben* (1786), based on a Bavarian folktale that would be included in a nineteenth-century anthology by the Grimm brothers.[97]

The new genre designations in the period indicate more detail about the subject matter. These designations make it clear that the supernatural was beginning to be treated as a distinct category: *Feenmärchen* (1785), *Feenkomödie, große Oper* (1791), *Lust- und Zauberspiel* (1790), and *Zauberspiel* (1787). Works called *heroisch-komische Oper, orientalisches Scherzspiel* (1791), and *romantische Oper* often included supernatural elements.

Adaptations of foreign-language works continued to figure prominently in German repertories. The most popular of these were French, including *L'oracle, La fée Urgèle,* and *Zémire et Azor.*[98] Italian supernatural operas were translated into German, for example, Casti's *La grotta di Trofonio* and Da Ponte's *L'arbore di Diana.* Gozzi's *fiabe* remained a favored source of translated comedy and comic opera, with numerous settings of *I pitocchi fortunati* as *Das tartarische Gesetz* in Stuttgart (1780), Hanau (1780), Frankfurt (1782), Bonn (1782), Gotha (1787), and Mannheim (1787, with music by Georg Benda). An anonymous *Maschinenkomödie* in three acts, *Zween Wunderdinge des Zauberers*

97. Grimm and Grimm, *Kinder- und Hausmärchen,* 1, no. 119. Early sources include a song by Hans Sachs and a story by Hans Wilhelm Kirchhoff in his book *Wendunmuth* (1563). The humor here is at the expense of Swabians, and the moral instruction is based on improbable situations rather than the supernatural.

98. On German translations of Saint-Foix's *L'oracle,* see Busch, "'Da der Gesang eine große Gewalt über unser Herz hat,'."

Durandarte, oder Der König Tiger (Leopoldstadt, 10 February 1781, performed by the Baden company, poster in the A-Wt), was based on Gozzi's *Il re cervo*. The comic hero Kasperle is a *glückliche Vogelfänger,* like Gozzi's bird catcher Truffaldino. Stieger cites *Das blaue Ungeheuer,* an anonymous singspiel probably based on *Il mostro turchino* with music by Joseph Schubert, staged at the private theater of Margrave Friedrich Heinrich of Schwedt in 1781. Another German opera based on *Il mostro turchino* was produced in Dresden in 1786 as *Das Ungeheurer, oder Liebe aus Dankbarkeit,* a *komisches Singspiel* by Caterino Mazzolà with music by Franz Seydelmann. Goethe, who saw Gozzi's plays and knew his work, directed *Die glücklichen Bettler* in Weimar (1778), followed by stagings of *Das grüne Vögelchen* (*L'augellino belvedere*) in 1780 and *Zobeis* (*La Zobeide*) in 1783. Goethe's *Triumph der Empfindsamkeit* (1777) seems to have had a segment inspired by Gozzi's *L'amore delle tre melarance.*

Der Triumph der Tugend, oder Der Mund der Wahrheit, a spectacular "Chinese" ballet in two acts by "Herr Sacco" (Hamburg, 1782), borrowed elements from several Gozzi *fiabe.* The plot concerns an emperor who is trying to find a spouse who honestly loves him. A magic statue helps him in his quest, revealing the truth of the women who speak before it by smiling when they lie. Andreas Romberg also composed music for three later operatic adaptations of Gozzi's *fiabe* by Walter Anton Schwick (Hamburg, 1791–93). Gozzi's plots also served as the basis *Das Reh* by one Herr Schmohl (c. 1790). Ludwig Tieck wrote a number of works that utilize the fairy-tale elements from Gozzi's *fiabe.*[99]

The traditional sources of supernatural plots, mythology and epic romance, continued to be the bases of singspiels and melodramas after 1780, particularly the myths of Orpheus, Circe, Medea, and Ulysses.[100] Peter Winter composed several pastoral and mythological singspiels for Munich, and Tasso's epic poem provided the subject for Winter's *Reinhold und Armida* (1780) as well as Johann Rudolf Zumsteeg's *Armida* (Stuttgart, 1785).[101]

Large-scale German Opera in the 1780s

By the early 1780s the era of Saxon opera was at an end and Prussian domination of the genre was beginning with composers such as Johann André. Fairy-tale singspiels in Berlin and Vienna now had substantial musical components with a larger orchestra and prominent wind writing, allowing for more expres-

99. See Marelli, *Ludwig Tiecks frühe Märchenspiele.*

100. *Medea und Jason,* a melodrama by Anton Klemens, Graf von Törring-Seefeld, for Munich, c. 1789, appears to be lost. For works based on the story of Ulysses, see, for example, *Circe und Ulisses,* a singspiel with music by Joachim Albertini for Hamburg, 1785. Albertini also set a Polish *Don Giovanni* in Warsaw, 1783.

101. Johann Adolf Hasse's *Rinaldo und Armida,* "eine dramatische Cantate" by Christopher Petri, was published in a vocal score (Leipzig: The author, 1782; Lbl, shelfmark F. 386.(1.)). The text appeared in the *Musenalmanach,* 1778. There are two choruses of sylphs and sylphids, recitatives, duets, and arias.

EXAMPLE 5.2 Otto Carl Erdmann Freiherr von Kospoth, *Der Irrwisch*, overture

sive devices, mimetic effects, and allusions to supernatural events and characters. The increased use of these devices can be seen in the three surviving
settings of Bretzner's popular fairy-tale libretto *Der Irrwisch* (three other settings are lost). The supernatural element in Otto Carl Erdmann Freiherr von
Kospoth's score (Berlin, 1780) is apparent only in the E-flat overture, with
its *alla zoppa* syncopation and sustained wind phrases (see ex. 5.2).[102] Gottlieb
Stephanie revised the libretto as *Das Irrlicht*, with Ignaz Umlauf providing a

---

102. Librettos in US-Wc (1784, 1787, Schatz 5218); two manuscripts and parts survive in D-F,
dated 1 April 1780, Berlin. Bauman, *North German Opera*, cites various excerpts, especially the songs
from *Favorit Gesänge aus den Opern* [RISM K 1349]. These range from simple lieder to bravura arias.

substantial musical setting (BT, 17 January 1782).[103] Mozart recounted in a letter (6 October 1781) that Umlauf claimed the opera required a year to compose, a claim Mozart doubted. *Das Irrlicht* is basically a number opera in which little attempt is made to use music to propel the action. Marvelous musical references include the one short instrumental Adagio for clarinets, horns and bassoons in E-flat, which serves as celebratory temple music in act 2, scenes 5 and 6. This "enchanted" wind ensemble, with a consonant, serenade-like style and marked "dolce," evokes the soft music long associated with supernatural episodes. Act 3 also has temple music in the form of two choruses for temple virgins, with colorful instrumental introductions and accompaniments. Violent storm music in C minor occurs during the opening *Sinfonia* of act 2.

Two other influential fairy-tale operas were staged in 1780. Ludwig Zehnmark's *romantische Oper Was erhält die Männer treu?*, with music by Joseph Martin [Stephan?] Ruprecht (BT 30 March or 1 May), was also known as *Das Raethsel*. It was later produced in Hamburg (28 January 1784, poster in D-Hs).[104] Zehnmark borrowed elements from diverse sources. The story concerns a fairy who educates innocents in the ways of love and a young suitor who has to solve a riddle. Magic devices include enchanted sleep, soft magic music, and an obelisk that rises from the earth. The score is another number opera; the choruses (even those for the fairies) are modest homophonic pieces. The first act ends with an imposing tempest scene where Ruprecht depicts thunder and lightning with rapid sixteenth-note arpeggios and scales set against syncopated accompaniment. As the storm recedes, the dynamics gradually diminish to pianissimo.

Bretzner's *Das wütende Heer, oder Das Mädgen im Thurme*,[105] was another

---

103. The libretto was published (Vienna: Logenmeister, 1785). Three manuscript scores are preserved in A-Wn, Musiksammlung, Mus. Hs. 16521, Mus. Hs. 17901, and K.T. 227, along with two scores of the Romanze "Zu Stephen sprach im Traume" and various printed arias. Manuscript scores also survive in A-Wgm and D-Hs. For details on the work, see de Groat, "Leben und Singspiele," 177–217. Mannheim (1786), Hamburg (1787), and Riga (1786) staged performances. See also Umlauf, *Die Bergknappen*.

104. The libretto (Vienna: Logenmeister, 1780) survives in A-Wn (Musiksammlung), 629.128 B.Th, and A-Wt, Mus., 647.433-AM TB, and in US-Wc, Schatz 9161. I consulted the manuscript score in A-Wn, Mus. Hs. 16519. Ruprecht originally sang the role of Passerdo, the comic servant. He also composed music for *Der blinde Ehemann*, produced at Schikanender's Wiennertheater in 1794.

105. The first setting, by Anton Schweitzer, was never performed (the music is lost). A manuscript score survives for Johann André's setting for Berlin's Döbbelin Theater (22 November 1780) in D-B, Mus. ms. 607. See Bauman, *North German Opera*, 181–82. Johann Friedrich Kaffka set the libretto for the Wäser troupe in Breslau (January 1782, now lost, formerly in Berlin, Staatliche Hochschule für Musik und darstellende Kunst). Another libretto (Vienna: Logenmeister, n.d.), revised as a *heroisch-komisches Singspiel* in two acts with music by Joseph Martin [or Stephen] Ruprecht (KT, 1 June 1787), survives in A-Wn, shelfmark 641.433 A.M. TB IX/5. The manuscript score survives in A-Wn, Musiksammlung, K.T. 205. Friedrich Franz Hurka set the libretto for Schwedt (1788; only the libretto survives). Stieger cites additional settings by Gottfried Rieger (Brno, 1787) and Johann Baptist Lasser (Landständisches Theater, Graz, 1789).

popular *Märchenoper* set by several composers. The story combines Teutonic legend, fairy tale, and gothic romance. The "raging army" of the title is a supernatural troop of angry dead hunters, wandering through the lands of the ancient feudal estate of Count Conrad. Laura, Conrad's daughter, loses her way in a forest and is taken captive by the army. She remains imprisoned in the tower of their castle. A number of knights have tried to free her after seeing her portrait, but all have failed or died. The knight Albert also falls in love with her portrait and sets out to liberate her, accompanied by his cowardly squire, Robert. When they reach the tower a terrible storm begins. Thunder and lightning accompany the army of dead hunters, who sing a chorus amid terrible cries, hounds baying, and blasts of hunting horns. After the storm passes they hear a disembodied female voice sing that only a faithful husband can free Laura. He must catch a snow-white dove at midnight and remove two of its feathers. These will open the gates of the tower. The moon shines again, revealing a white dove. Robert catches it and removes two feathers. Lightning disperses the clouds from around the tower, and the men release Laura from her captivity. But Laura has been enchanted: after being kissed she turns into a marble statue. In despair and grief the squire Robert takes out the dove and stabs it with his dagger. A blue flame suddenly rises from behind the statue and Laura slowly returns to life. After a joyful reunion with her father the opera ends in a final triumphal chorus.

André's score for the Berlin production (November 1780) has a descriptive tripartite *Overtura*, starting with a D minor Allegro section with tremolos, rapid scales, and a series of opening crescendos expressing terror (see ex. 5.3).[106] A Larghetto segment in D minor follows, and the overture concludes with a triumphant Allegretto in D major with trumpets and timpani. A supernatural chorus in C minor, "Heraus! Heraus! Heraus! o wütend' Heer zur Jagd" (act 2, scene 17), returns to the terrifying style of the overture. Piccolos, horns, bassoons, and strings accompany a three-part chorus situated behind the stage. The vocal parts are to be sung in a "terrifying, strong, hollow voice" (*fürchterlicher, starker hohler Stimme*), the melody employing a single-line declamation in octaves that recalls chant recitation. Numerous diminished seventh chords, abrupt harmonic and dynamic shifts, rapid scales, and string *tremulandi* enhance the supernatural nature of the scene.[107]

Johann Abraham Peter Schultz set Favart's popular *La fée Urgèle* as a German *Operette* (?Rheinsberg, 1782; Kiel, 1784; and Berlin, 1789).[108] The overture, in D major, begins with a slow introduction followed by a Molto vivace with *tremulandi* and rapid scales. The remaining music seems to lack clear supernatural allusions with the exception of the scene where the fairy first ap-

106. A manuscript score survives in D-B, Mus. Ms. 607.

107. Bauman, *North German Opera*, 189–91, transcribes forty measures of the chorus.

108. A vocal score survives, D-B, Mus. ms. 20411/2, with occasional indications of instruments (flutes, trumpets, clarinets, horns, oboes, bassoons, and strings). A score copy survives in Copenhagen, Konigelige Bibliotek.

EXAMPLE 5.3 Johann André, *Das wütende Heer*, overture

pears. A stormy Allegro in G major, with episodes in the parallel minor, seems
to be music for a mechanical stage scored for horns, trumpet, oboe, bassoons,
and strings, with repeated pitches in sixteenth-note rhythms. The instrumental
prelude to the fairy's accompanied recitative, marked "Andante," begins with
an ascending major triad spanning two octaves. Trumpets and oboes double
the violins. The fairy sings a forceful melodic figure accompanied by pizzicato
bass and motives with trilled thirds. Her aria ends with a short instrumental
passage on a tonic chord, using *alla zoppa* syncopation over a tonic pedal, apparently more stage-machine music (see ex. 5.4). This style came to be a con-

EXAMPLE 5.4 Johann Abraham Peter Schultz, *La fée Urgèle*, no. 26

vention for magic scenic transformations in Wiednertheater operas, for example, the entrance of the Queen of the Night in act 1 of *Die Zauberflöte*.

Friedrich Maximilian Klinger's five-act comedy *Der Derwisch* (1780),[109] based on Henri Pajon's fairy tale,[110] is one of the earliest examples of an oriental plot type that would soon become popular for German librettos. The sultan's sister Ginerva, an enchanted princess who lost one of ninety-nine diamonds in her possession, is condemned to continually count them. She cannot marry, and her fate is tied to the liberation of two Illyrian princesses transformed into pocket watches by the powerful magician Primrose. One of Ginerva's suitors, Prince Mustapha, and his cousin Oronoko unsuccessfully attempt to save the princesses. The beggar Derbin finally frees the two princesses; the ninety-ninth diamond appears in the fold of one of the slips of the Princess Rose. Klinger added a subplot about a magician and a dervish with magic powers to revive the dead.

❊

The Josephinian theatrical reform of 1776 encouraged the flourishing of Vienna's suburban theaters.[111] Karl Marinelli's new Theater in der Leopoldstadt opened on 20 October 1781 with Johann Laroche's Kaspar (or Kasperl) character as the leading comic attraction. (The itinerant Schultz-Menninger or Baadner company, of which Marinelli and Laroche were members, had been performing in this district at the Czernin Garden Palace for over ten years.) Some of the first productions at the new theater were singspiels based on fairy tales and similar fantastic material. *Megära* singspiels remained popular at the theater, and new *Maschinenkomödien* such as *Die Fee Angelika* became repertory pieces for several seasons. Beginning with the comedy *Don Juan, oder der steinerne Gast* by Karl Marinelli (31 October 1783, and repeated 1–3, 10, and

109. Ormus, 1780; copy in D-Hs, shelfmark A/13 641.

110. "L'histoire des trois fils d'Hali Bassa de la mer et des filles de Siroco, gouverneur d'Alexandrie" (attributed to M. Jaques, a pseudonym) in *Mercure de France*, August–December 1745, and printed in *Le cabinet des fées* 34 (1786), 119–236, and as "Néangir et ses frères, Argentine et ses soeurs," in La Porte, *Bibliothèque*. Wieland adapted the tale in his first volume of *Dschinnistan* (1786). For details, see Mayer, "Die Quellen zu Klingers Derwisch," 356–62; and Hinck, *Das deutsche Lustspiel*.

111. Tomek, "Die Musik an den Wiener Vorstadttheatern," is a brief review mostly based on secondary sources.

23 November),[112] performances of Don Juan operas and comedies around the time of All Souls' Day became a tradition at this theater; they continued regularly for some forty years.[113] (This was also the case at Schikaneder's Theater auf der Wieden, which staged Mozart's *Don Giovanni* in German during the All Souls' period, starting in 1792.)[114]

The actress and director Barbara Fuhrmann produced a series of anonymous magic singspiels and comic pantomimes at the Kärntnertor Theater starting in 1783,[115] including *Pierot, die bezauberte Baberl, oder Arlekin der Narrenmaler* and *Arlequin der bezauberte Zauberer, oder Die fliehende Totentruhe,* with music by Johann Friedrich Reichardt. Other anonymous magic pieces at this theater include a two-act singspiel by Gensicke (first name unknown), *Die bezauberte Jagd,* with music by Franz Anton Hoffmeister (lost); *Die musikalische Zaubertrommel des Phöbus,* a four-act comedy "mit Flugwerken"; and *Der verliebte Zauberer,* a three-act *Lustspiel mit Gesängen und Chören,* based on a märchen of Count Friedrich Franz Johann von Spauer of Wetzlar.

The Burgtheater also produced occasional fairy-tale singspiels, for example *Das Irrlicht,* discussed above. Smaller theaters staged similar kinds of singspiels such as the two-act anonymous *Die Zauberrose* (lost) at Vienna's Theater zum weißen Fasan am Neustift (11 November 1783).[116]

✳

Unlike Georg Benda's other melodramas, the anonymous one-act *Almanzor und Nadine* (or *Theone*) is an oriental fairy tale with dramatic action depicted

112. Marinelli, "Dom Juan."

113. Wenzel Müller's autograph diary of the Theater in der Leopoldstadt, the "Kaiserköniglich priviligirtes Theater in der Leopoldstadt in Wien" [1781–1830], in A-Wst, shelfmark Ja 51926, 14, records the first performance on 31 October 1783 of "Don Juan oder der steinerne Gast, 1ste mal." Müller lists further performances for 1784 (9 January, 1 February, 20 July, 12 October, 1 November, and 18 December), 1785 (6, and 9 November), 1786 (1, 2, and 4 November), 1787 (2, 6, and 13 November), 1788 (2, 3, and 7 November), 1789 (2 and 3 November), 1790 (31 October and 1, 2, and 8 November), 1791 (31 October and 1 and 2 November), 1792 (1, 2, and 7 November), etc. This seasonal performance tradition continued until 1822. See also Price, "Don Juan: A Chronicle," 92.

114. On 5 November 1792 and 31 October 1793. A poster in A-Wgm for the latter includes the following notice: "Es dient ergebenst zur Nachricht, daß diese Oper mit dem Trauerspiel das Schwerdt der Gerechtigkeit abwechselnd bloß diese 8 Tage hindurch aufgeführt wird, und dann wieder bis künftiges Jahr verschoben bleibt." Schikaneder's tragedy *Das Schwerdt der Gerechtigkeit,* which included a ghost scene, had been performed regularly during the octave of All Souls' since 1790. According to the surviving theater posters in A-Wgm, other religious holidays also had special pieces in the repertory, e.g., Palm Sunday, Carnival, and fast days. Punderlitschek, "Das Freyhaus-Theater auf der Wieden," gives the entire repertory from 1795 to 1801.

115. Various Viennese periodicals give this information. See Blümml and Gugitz, *Alt-Wiener Thespiskarren,* 145–49.

116. Cited in Bauer, *Opern und Operetten* (no. 4778), 112, and Tomek, "Die Musik an den Wiener Vorstadttheater," 241.

in music. Although other melodramas contain more violent expression, their music depicts psychological states rather than stage action. The text was perhaps translated and adapted from the French by Karl Leopold Rollig.[117] The primary sources include a manuscript of a French libretto and four German translations, along with other related materials, including a printed page where the glass-harmonica virtuoso Rollig claims to be the originator of the idea of setting this *Geniewerk* as a melodrama.[118] Rollig names the composer Wenzel Müller and suggests a performance in the Kärntnertor Theater. Although the premiere of this melodrama with choruses remains unknown, Wenzel Mihule's company performed the work at Prague's Nationaltheater in 1791.[119] According to the synopsis in the French libretto, Zelmore, the queen of the sylphs, creates a series of trials for Prince Almanzor and his beloved Nadine, a Persian princess descended from sylphs. Escaping Zelmore, Almanzor takes Nadine on a ship. A storm drives him to seek safety on a deserted island, where he loses Nadine. After another series of trials (including a terrifying cavern and an enchanted sleep scene), Zelmore brings the lovers back together.

The work's harmony and style suggest supernatural events. The overture begins with a C minor Andante in the terrifying style with thirty-second-note scales, followed by a short Allegro in D minor. The choruses are for two soprano parts and solo (Nadine), and a mixed final chorus (SATB). Benda scored the conventional magic sleep music for solo flute and strings, then solo bassoon. The music starts in B-flat, but when the score indicates a "dream," the key and mode suddenly change to F minor.

❧

The year 1784 marks the beginning of the era of fairy-tale singspiels in Vienna, especially at the Theater in der Leopoldstadt, where revivals of *Don Juan*, *Megära*, and *Zemire und Azor* were mounted along with an extensive series of new works called *Maschinenkomödie*, *Feenmärchen*, and *Zauberkomödie*.[120] Karl

---

117. The manuscript score in A-Wn, Musiksammlung, Hs. 18522, cites Rollig on the first page. In addition to this contemporary copy, the Musiksammlung possesses an autograph score (Hs. 18521) with the title [*Philon und*] *Theone*. The date "July, 1779" has been added to the score. The manuscript copy bears the title *Almansor und Nadine*. Bauman, "Benda, Georg," cites additional music not by Benda. Also see Schimpf, *Lyrisches Theater*, 233.

118. All the materials are in A-Wn, Handschriftsammlung, Cod. Ser. u. 218. A later one-act comedy, *Almanzor et Nadine*, by Fonpré de Fracansalle, Th. de Grand Danseurs, 6 December 1787, F-Pn, n.a.f. 2857, seems to be related to this text.

119. Cited in *Theater Kalendar* (Gotha, 1792), 304. I wish to thank Alena Jakubcová for making me aware of this performance.

120. See Appendix E for a full list. The information here comes from Müller's "Kaiser-Königlich privil: Theater in der Leopoldstadt in Wien" and a smaller Müller autograph diary from 1781–89 (A-Wst, Ja 40426), and accounts in various periodicals such as *Das Wienerblättchen*, *Die Wiener Zeitung*, and *Kritisches Theater-Journal von Wien*. Also see Rommell, *Die Alt-Wiener Volkskomödie*, 542.

Friedrich Hensler's three-act *Feenmärchen mit Maschinen, Flugwerken, und lustigen Charakteren*, titled *Philibert und Kaspar im Reiche der Phantasey, oder Weiber sind getreuer als Männer* (20 January 1785), was one of the first with the genre designation *Feenmärchen*. The poster in A-Wt, 31 March 1785, gives the cast of characters of this popular piece: the fairy Chlorinde, her *Zichtochter* Kunigunda, wild men, Furies, two dwarfs, and a monster. An evil magician named Kronoxos has abducted Chlorinde's daughter. A Frankish prince named Philibert and his squire, Kaspar, rescue her using a magic talisman. Philibert tests the fidelity of his intended bride by approaching her unrecognized. Along the way he falls in love with the Princess Kantilde, whom he also liberates from captivity. No music has survived.

During this period the Kärntnertor Theater also continued to stage new and larger fairy-tale operas such as *Die schöne Melusina*, a five-act *Feenmärchen* (16 December 1784), and *Zemire und Azor* (1 January 1785, also 5 or 6 December).[121] La Roche's Kaspar character figured in anonymous *Zauberkomödien* such as *Kasperl der Rauchfangkehrer als Fürst und der Fürst als Rauchfangkehrer* (30 July 1785) and *Kasperl ein Originalgenie* (29 August and 1 September 1785). The periodical *Das Wienerblättchen* cites all of these comedies. New theaters in the Wieden, Josefstadt (1787), Mariahilf, Spitalberg, and Landstrasse districts also mounted productions based on fairy tales. These include several ambitious, large-scale operas as well as smaller singspiels. The Burgtheater produced Favart and Monsigny's popular *opéra-comique La belle Arsène* on 4, 8, and 25 August 1786.

Paul Weidmann's three-act *Der Ring der Liebe, oder Zemirens und Azors Ehestand*, with music by Umlauf (KT, 3 October 1786),[122] was a sequel to Grétry's *Zemire und Azor*, set twelve years after the events in the original opera.[123] Although it appears not to have been successful,[124] *Der Ring der Liebe* provides an important example of a large-scale operatic setting of a fairy tale in Vienna before the era of the Theater auf der Wieden. After their marriage the fairies transported Zemire and Azor from Persia to the Isle of Whimsy (Grillen In-

---

121. A score, without an indication of date or theater, survives in A-Wn, Musiksammlung, shelfmark K.T. 475. This may have been used for performances at the Burgtheater. The Kärntnertor Theater was closed from 6 February 1788 to June 1791.

122. A printed libretto survives (Vienna: Logenmeister, 1786); it states that the music is based on a *Wälsch* (meaning foreign, often Italian) singspiel. Manuscript copies of an aria and duet are found in A-Wgm. A full manuscript score survives in A-Wn, Musiksammlung, K.T. 385. See de Groat, "Leben und Singspiele," 244–75.

123. The story strongly recalls the plot of *Le roi de cocagne*, a three-act comedy in free verse with prologue and divertissements by Marc-Antoine Le Grand, with music by Jean-Baptiste-Maurice Quinault. The comedy premiered at the Comédie Française on 31 December 1718 (see chapter 2). It was also set by Jan Stefani in Polish for the National Theater in Warsaw, 3 February 1787, entitled *Król w kraju rozkoszy*.

124. F. C. Kunz, *Almanach der National Schaubühne in Wien auf das Jahr 1788* (Vienna: J. Gerold), 55, discusses the reception; see de Groat, "Leben und Singspiele," 244–45.

sel), the realm of the fairies, where Azor was made king. Zemire accidentally lost the ring that Cupid gave her as a token of fidelity. Fernando and Isabella, a pair of Spanish lovers who have fled their disapproving parents, swim ashore after a shipwreck, along with their comic servants Pedro and Grazioso.[125] They eat some enchanted figs and fall asleep to magic music. A cloud chariot then appears carrying Cupid, who berates Zemire for losing the ring and says he will use these strangers to punish her. The ring will now cause anyone who wears it to go mad. This begins a series of comic episodes as Grazioso, Isabella, and Azor undergo radical personality changes while wearing the ring. Confusion reigns until six voices intone that Cupid has decided to spare Azor's realm from chaos. Azor returns to his original state, reuniting Isabella with Fernando. The statue of Cupid speaks and brings Zemire to Azor, giving them a new golden ring and allowing them to resume their vows of fidelity. Umlauf's impressive score for a large orchestra shows little attempt to suggest the supernatural quality of the text in the arias, choruses, and long finales. He restricted otherworldly musical references to a few accompaniment figures in arias and ensembles.

Josef Martin Ruprecht's score of *Das wütende Heer, oder Das Mädgen im Thurme,* for Vienna's Kärntnertor Theater (1 June 1787), has a greater expressive range than *Der Ring der Liebe.*[126] The descriptive overture begins with an ominous opening Adagio in C minor that leads to a comic Allegro in C major. The short ascending scalar bursts in the bass and strings, set against repeated notes and dotted rhythms, suggest the otherworldly topic. The supernatural hunters' chorus does not bring back the music of the overture, although it is in C major. Instead, it offers a kind of grotesque gigue in 6/8 meter, steadily building from a quiet beginning for strings to a violent fortissimo with sixteenth-note surface rhythms, octave-and-unison sonorities, timpani rolls, and horn calls. The dance at first seems a pastoral allusion to the hunt, but the above-mentioned features and the chromatic inflections and harmony, borrowing heavily from the minor mode with segments in E-flat, A-flat, B-flat, and G minor, suggest something unearthly. Ruprecht depicted another magical event in act 2, scene 3, at the conclusion of Aria no. 13. Here the final word, "death" (*Tod*), is set as a supernatural echo. Finally, in act 2, scene 15, a soprano voice delivers the oracular pronouncement sotto voce. The accompaniment is an enchanted wind ensemble of clarinets, horns, and bassoons playing sustained chords and repeated notes (see ex. 5.5).

That same month the Kärntnertor Theater revived Grétry's *Zemire und Azor* (19 June), performed by the same National Singspiel troupe that mounted

---

125. Grazioso, a typical comic servant, harks back to Arlecchino, and is the basis of characters like Papageno. He provides jokes and sarcastic remarks, and is mainly concerned with his immediate gratifications.

126. I consulted the manuscript score in A-Wn, Musiksammlung, K.T. 205.

EXAMPLE 5.5 Josef Martin Ruprecht, *Das wütende Heer,* act 2, scene 15

the work in the Burgtheater that year. In addition to reviving the *Don Juan* comedy and the *Megära* singspiels, the Theater in der Leopoldstadt produced new fantastic operas such as Ferdinand Eberl's *Kaspar der gefoppte König auf den grünen Wiesen,* with music by Wenzel Müller (30 January 1788, revived 26 September 1788).[127] Hensler's four-act *Feenmarchen Das Glück ist Kugelrund, oder Kaspers Ehrentag,* with music by Müller (17 February 1789), had numerous revivals. The cast includes the fairy Roxalina and a chorus of nymphs.[128]

Karl Mayer's company at the new Theater in der Josefstadt also produced fantastic Kaspar plays such as *Kaspar auf den Sprung,* an anonymous *Zauberspiel* (15 April 1787). The poster in A-Wt indicates that the cast includes a magician named Ossbock. Christian Rosbach's company at the Theater auf dem

127. Bauer, *Opern und Operetten;* Stieger, *Opernlexikon;* and Branscombe, "Müller, Wenzel," in NGO 3:514, cite the premiere as 30 January 1788.

128. No libretto or music is known to have survived. A poster survives in A-Wt, as well as a review in *Kritisches Theater-Journal von Wien* (1789), 72–80.

Spitalberg produced the anonymous magic ballet *Der bezauberte Wald, oder Der dankbare Geist* on 11 July 1787.

✹

Southern German cities also produced serious and comic operas with supernatural content. Johann Rudolf Zumsteeg's setting of Johann Christoph Bock's three-act singspiel *Armida* (Stuttgart, 1785), based on Bertati's *Rinaldo,* survives in one incomplete manuscript copy.[129] Zumsteeg employs the techniques of Italian epic romance opera of the 1770s, setting important scenes in extended accompanied recitative and having the main characters sing demanding coloratura arias (Rinaldo is a castrato role). The supernatural nature of the text is mostly in evidence in these recitatives, with their substantial instrumental segments, varied accompaniments, numerous expressive techniques, and colorful instrumentation (e.g., the "enchanted" wind ensembles).

In this same period the court opera in Munich staged mythological singspiels by Peter Winter: *Bellerophon* (text by Johann Friedrich Binder von Kreigelstein, 29 July 1785), *Circe* (text by Domenico Perelli, 1788, lost), and *Medea und Jason* (1789). Munich was also the location of one of the first local *Volksmärchen* operas, the anonymous *Die sieben Schwaben,* set as a one-act *Operette* (composer unknown). The publication of vocal texts in 1786 indicates a performance run.[130] But this was apparently not the first theatrical setting of the story; Mozart and his family attended a ballet with this title in 1783.[131] The plot revolves around the sighting of a rabbit and its being mistaken for a monster. The foolish Swabians prepare to do battle with the beast after much boasting and anxious chatter. In the end they discover the monster is merely a rabbit. In the final chorus they agree to keep their folly a secret for the sake of the honor of the Swabian nation.

✹

Although the 1780s was a period of decline in the output of north German opera, with only six new works a year as compared to eleven in the previous decade, theaters continued to stage magic comedies, pantomimes, and singspiels. A poster for Hamburg's city theater, preserved in the Theatersammlung of D-Hs, announces an anonymous *grosse komische Pantomime in drei Aufzügen,*

129. Preserved in Stuttgart's Württembergische Landesbibliothek, shelfmark Cod. Mus. II 2° 11 a.b.

130. *Musiktext zur Operette Die sieben Schwaben,* (no publication information, dated 1786), preserved in Munich's Theatermuseum (Clara Ziegler Stiftung), shelfmark 18 592.

131. See Bauer-Deutsch 6, *Kommentar,* p. 156. Nannerl Mozart's diary, October 1783, refers to going to the theater and seeing a singspiel (presumably *Adrast und Isadore*) and this ballet. The performers would have been the troupe of Ernst Kuhne, which was in Salzburg at the time.

Die Zaubereyen, oder Arlekins Schicksale, with music by Sedlaczek (first name unknown; 17 June 1784). The roles include Pantalon, Colombina, Arlekin, Pierot, and a magician named Dollore, who suddenly emerges from a tree on which Arlekin tries to hang himself. Dollore gives Arlekin magical powers to use against his enemy Pantalon, and the rest of the pantomime consists of a series of episodes in which Arlekin transforms people and various inanimate objects to do his bidding. Surviving posters in Hamburg (D-Hs) also document performances of *Die schöne Arsene* and *Zemire und Azor* in 1784.

Gottfried Ferdinand von Lindemann's three-act singspiel *Orpheus,* with music by Friedrich Benda, was a more traditional form of the "marvelous," inspired by mythology and epic romance (Berlin, Corsika'scher Saal, 16 January 1785). The surviving piano-vocal score seems rather old-fashioned.[132] Act 2 begins in Pluto's black palace as the Furies rush past in flaming wagons on the Styx. Orpheus's first aria, "Habt Dank, ihr fürchterliche Wellen," sung as he rises out of Charon's barque, is an A major Andante grazioso whose only possible magic allusion is the scoring with flutes. His accompanied recitative, "Wie schrecklich!," leads to the stormy D minor Allegro where the Furies try to repel him with unison exclamations as he plays his lyre and attempts to placate them. A march in the unusual key of E-flat minor, described as "eine fürchterliche majestätische Musik," then announces the arrival of the Hadean deities with Pluto. Benda conveyed the underworld with an unusual combination of regal pomp and parody through the repetition of a short four-note motive in dotted rhythm (see ex. 5.6). Pluto appears and delivers his edict in a dramatic Larghetto recitative in B-flat, with dotted rhythmic figures and ascending sixty-fourth-note bursts in the bass and violins.

In this period Vulpius continued to write fairy-tale works. His three-act singspiel *Der Schleyer,* with music by the Saxon-Weimar composer Ernst Wilhelm Wolf (lost), was staged at Weimar's Herzogliche Komödiehaus in 1786.[133] The singspiel was also produced in Hamburg on 22 May 1788 but had little success (poster in D-Hs). This fairy-tale libretto combines chivalric and oriental motives, as well as references to ancient Egypt. The cast includes a good fairy named Marzinde who sends her nephew, a Gallic prince named Markomir, on a quest to find the ideal woman. The fairy's supernatural implements include a magic wand, a magic veil that grants eternal beauty to the most innocent and virtuous of women, a magic mirror that can show images from other locations, and a magic ring that reveals infidelity in one's spouse. The plot concerns a curse of the Soldan Issuf, the king of Egypt, who rejected the love of the fairy Morgalinde. When the king married Mandane, the princess of Tschirkassien,

132. Berlin: The author, n.d. [1787 is printed in the dedication]; Lbl, shelfmark E. 929.

133. Three librettos were published: Vulpius, *Opern* (US-Wc, Schatz 11084a), *Gesänge aus dem Singspiele: Der Schleyer* (US-Wc, Schatz 11084); and *Der Schleyer* (Yale University School of Music Library). Vulpius later wrote an *allegorisches Vorspiel mit Gesang, Die Feyer im Reich der Feen,* for Weimar in 1787; cited in Grätz, *Das Märchen,* 109, 392.

EXAMPLE 5.6 Friedrich Benda, *Orpheus*, act 2, "Marcia"

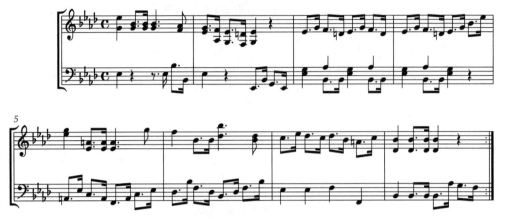

he received a wedding gift from Morgalinde, a beautiful but enchanted crown. He wore the crown during his wedding ceremony only to find that any attempt to remove it resulted in great pain. Only a knight whose lady is faithful in both deed and thought can remove it. One maiden is that virtuous: Issuf's sister Bellamira, who is engaged to the evil Moorish magician Mervillo. Many knights have attempted to help the king, but none has succeeded because Mandane, a lascivious and unfaithful queen, has love affairs that undermine the removal of the king's curse. With the help of Marzinde's magic, Markomir wins the love of Bellamira and vanquishes Mervillo and his spirits. Markomir removes the crown and the king grants him the hand of Bellamira. Soft music announces the arrival of Marzinde, who gives a magic ring to the king; its jewel will remain clear so as long as his spouse remains virtuous. Queen Mandane curses this day and its unfortunate outcome for her.

Johann Gottlieb Naumann's *Orpheus og Euridyke,* a three-act singspiel (Copenhagen, 31 January 1786; Hamburg, 1787), was set to a Danish text by Charlotte Dorothea Biehl, based on Calzabigi's Italian libretto and the German setting by Gottfried Ferdinand von Lindemann.[134] The Adagio introduction to the overture in C minor introduces infernal imagery with piercing fortissimo winds and sweeping scale figures. The first act ends with Orpheus singing of Cerberus, and the horns blare out a motive in quarter notes as the strings play descending scalar bursts, like the barking gesture from the underworld chorus in Gluck's *Orfeo ed Euridice.* Naumann scored winds and trombones in the distance during the scene complex in a tomb.[135] The second act, set in Hades with Pluto, Cerberus, and the Furies, begins with a segment of musical terror in

134. A segment of the area near Hamburg belonged to Denmark. Danish operas, although rare, were occasionally produced in this area. Manuscript scores for this opera are preserved in Copenhagen, D-B, and D-Dlb, Mus. 3480-F-30. I consulted the latter two for this study.

135. Engländer, *Johann Gottlieb Naumann,* suggests Hasse's oratorio *Elena al calvario* (1772) as a possible model.

C minor with winds and two trombones. Naumann constructed the scene complex along the same lines as Gluck's setting, with a similar refrain structure.

As for comic operas with supernatural content in northern Germany, *Doktor Fausts Leibgürtel*, a two-act singspiel by Bernhard Christoph d'Arien (based on J.-J. Rousseau and Wilhelm Christoph Siegmund Mylius), with music by Karl Hanke (lost), was produced in Hamburg in 1786.[136] Heinrich Gottlieb Schneider's four-act opera *Doktor Faust*, with music by Ignaz Walter (lost), was mounted in Bremen (28 December 1787). Berlin's National Theater produced *Was den Damen gefällt*, a anonymous singspiel based on *La fée Urgele*, with music by Johann Abraham Peter Schulz (28 April 1789).[137]

Along with Breslau, Brno and Prague produced new singspiels for their German-speaking audience. The libretto *Selim und Zelide, oder Die Macht der Feen*, an anonymous two-act *romantisch-komische Oper*, by composer(s) unknown, was published (Breslau and Hirschberg: Korn der Ältere, 1788; US-Wc, Schatz 11463), and Joseph Emanuel Diesbach in Prague printed the vocal texts the next year. The title page of the songbook gives the performance date as 30 November 1789, directed by [Wenzel] Mihule and Johann Butteau at the Kleinseitner Theater in Prague.[138] The plot concerns an evil fairy Murza, who demands that the successful trader Selim marry her. He must reject his beloved Zelide to save her life. Murza condemns Zelide to death when Selim refuses to marry. Orkanm, the overseer of the slaves, helps the lovers. At the end the fairy Amine restores Zelide to life. The score consisted of arias; duets; trios; choruses for sylphs, sylphids, and priests; a funeral chorus (*Trauerchor*); and an ensemble of Furies. Prague also produced German melodramas such as Václav Praupner's *Circe* (Prague, 1789), a familiar mythological subject. The composer used the expressive musical language of his fellow Bohemians Gluck and Georg Benda, with violent, dramatic force.

Johann Christoph Kaffka (a pseudonym for J. C. Engelmann) provided music for a 1788 production of Johann Christian Krüger's *Der blinde Ehemann* in Breslau.[139] Although this score has a significant amount of music, the single example of a supernatural scene occurs in the second-act finale. According to the text, solemn (*feyerliche*) music announces the arrival of the fairy, who descends in a cloud chariot in her full splendor and beauty. This ceremonial music is a triple-meter, D major instrumental prelude, beginning softly with a repeated ascending triadic bass figure and accompanied by *alla zoppa* synco-

---

136. Rönnau, "Hanke, Karl."

137. Iacuzzi, *The European Vogue of Favart*, 199. A manuscript piano vocal score survives in D-B.

138. Although Bauman, *North German Opera*, 414, states that this opera was never performed, the *Nurnberger Theater-Journal vom Anfang des Jahres 1795 bis zum Schluß desselben*, 1795 [12], indicates a performance of *Selim und Zelide*, an opera in two acts, on 16 September 1795 by the Wenzel Mihule company. A copy of printed vocal texts survives in A-Wt, shelfmark 620065-A-Th.S.

139. I consulted the score in D-Hs, shelfmark ND VII 199.

pation in the strings. The strings have ascending triadic figures as a crescendo leads to a fanfare section for flutes, trumpets, and timpani. A short segment for two flutes follows; the dynamics diminish, and the interlude ends on the dominant with the strings playing *alla zoppa* figures accompanied by trumpets and timpani marked "piano." The finale then continues with an elegant Andantino aria for the fairy in D major, accompanied by solo oboe and flutes.[140]

Oberon

Librettists and impresarios seem to have taken a special interest in Wieland's epic poem *Oberon* as a source for singspiels in early 1789,[141] although operas had already appropriated elements of the Oberon and Titania episodes from Shakespeare's *A Midsummer Night's Dream*, for example, Michaelis's *Walmir und Gertraud*. The first singspiel plot loosely based on Wieland's *Oberon* may have been *Der Triumph der Treue*, an *ernsthaftes Singspiel in drey Aufzügen* probably by Johann Friedrich von Binder, with music by Franz Danzi (lost) for Munich's Churfürstliche Nationaltheater (early 1789).[142]

Around the same time Jens Emmanuel Baggesen was preparing a Danish opera on this same subject. His protagonist was not Wieland's Huon, but the traditional Danish hero of the title, *Holger Danske*. With music by Friedrich Ludwig Aemilius Kunzen, the opera was performed at Copenhagen's Royal Theater on 31 March 1789. Apparently it was not successful, although it seems to have aroused considerable interest.[143] Kunzen portrayed numerous super-

---

140. A manuscript score, formerly in Berlin's Staatliche Hochschule für Musik und Darstellende Kunst until 1945, is today lost. Kaffka also set Bretzner's three-act *romantisch-komische Oper* in three acts, *Der Talisman* (1789). It was produced as *Der seltene Spiegel* in Bremen.

141. Wieland based his poem on a thirteenth-century *chanson de geste* (in the Geste du Roi, the Elfking is Auberon [= Alberich]) and another chanson, *Huon de Bordeaux*. There are references in English literature to the Elfking from at least Chaucer. The first reference to Oberon is the translation of *Huon* by Lord John Bourchier Berner, *The Boke Huon of Bordeuxe*, 1534. A number of subsequent writers used these themes and characters, including Shakespeare in *A Midsummer Night's Dream* (Titania was taken from Ovid). Wieland relied on Shakespeare but also added fantastic elements from oriental tales, especially the testing of the fidelity of a mortal couple (Huon and Amande) by a supernatural couple (Oberon and Titania).

142. According to Joseph Bellomo's printed catalog of German operas for Graz (1797, A-Wn. Hs. 8953) Friedrich Hildebrand von Einsiedel's *Die Zauberirrungen, oder Die Irrthümer der Zauberei*, with music Ernst Wilhelm Wolf (Weimar, 24 October 1785, directed by Bellomo), was also based on Wieland's poem. The surviving playbill suggests a debt to Shakespeare's *A Midsummer Night's Dream*.

143. German translations of this work were published in 1788–89, one by [?] Schultz and another by Carl Friedrich Cramer in *Cramer's Musik* (Copenhagen 1789, US-Wc, Schatz 5321, ML 4. M3.). Two manuscript scores survive in Copenhagen's Royal Library, an autograph (shelfmark C II.116) and a copy (C II.116tv). A piano-vocal score was published (Copenhagen: S. Sönnischsen n.d., RISM K 3031), as well as a similar score in a German translation, ed. Carl Friedrich Cramer, *Holger Danske, oder Oberon. Eine Oper in drey Acten* (Copenhagen: S. Sönnischsen 1790, RISM K

natural events in the music, both in traditional and in novel ways. Elegant and graceful wind music suggests benevolent magic, while musical terror evokes dark forces and storms. The magic instrument here is the horn, first heard play- ing an initial long note in the overture, a presto *contradanse*-like movement in D major that will accompany the magic dance scene in act 1. The overture's slow movement, an elegant Larghetto in D for winds and solo violin, also serves as the music accompanying the magic appearance of Oberon in act 1, scene 2. Holger describes this music as "heavenly tones." An Allegro moder- ato in D minor follows this segment, a short foreboding transition whose trem- olos in the bass and strings build to the final Allegro molto in D minor, which serves as terrifying storm music in scenes 1 and 2.

Kunzen scored Oberon's pronouncements with either enchanted wind en- semble or sustained strings in the low register. When in act 1 Oberon punishes Holger's squire Kerasmin for his cowardice, he forces the squire to dance by playing the enchanted horn with music from the opening of the overture.[144] Oberon then presents Kerasmin with a magic drink to increase his courage. As he drinks the potion the low strings play a short interlude in octave-and-unison sonority, continuing as the accompaniment to his recitative. In act 2, scene 3, Holger and Rezia avoid capture by the slaves when they play the horn (one long note on G), enchanting the soldiers to dance. The music for this panto- mime, marked "Molto vivace" and in C minor, suggests a *contradanse*. A series of dancing scenes follows. Finally the dance slows down again and Kerasmin blasts the horn to conjure ghosts; now the music evokes the terrifying style in an episode in B-flat and D minor.

Friederike Sophie Seyler's *Hüon und Amande,* a *romantisches Singspiel* in five acts with music by Karl Hanke (lost), was performed at Schleswig in 1789 and appears to have had more success. Librettos survive from Flens- burg, Schleswig, and Leipzig (1789). The plot concerns Prince Huon, exiled by King Childerich (in the original poem Huon was a German knight exiled by Charlemagne), who demands almost impossible conditions for his forgive- ness. Huon must retrieve four teeth from Mahmud, the sultan of Egypt, along with a tuft of his beard. He must also bring back the sultan's daughter Amande as his bride. On his way to Baghdad Huon meets Scherasmin, who joins Huon on his quest. Titania and her nymphs magically appear, narrating how she pro- tected an errant slave; Oberon swore an oath not to see her again until he finds

---

3032). A modern edition was published (Copenhagen: Elektra, 1941) and a compact disc (1995) has been issued (Dacapo/Marco Polo, 8.224036). For details and bibliography see Barford, "Holger Danske."

144. Implements that cause involuntary dancing are found in old commedia dell'arte plots (see the introduction) and reappear in Italian opera such as *L'anello incantato,* by Bertati and Bertoni (1771). See chapter 4 for details. The horn derives from Ariosto's *Orlando furioso,* where the sound of a magic horn renders all hearers helpless with terror. The horn functions in this manner in Sey- ler's *Hüon und Amande.*

two chaste mortal lovers whose fidelity would endure the most rigorous test. She has come here to consult the oracle and learn whether Oberon has been successful. Magical music begins, and the oracle announces that Oberon has found a worthy pair of mortals, Huon and Amande. Meanwhile, Oberon arrives in a cloud chariot as Huon's guardian spirit and demonstrates his power by making a troupe of Musselmen dance involuntarily with the touch of his magic lily stalk. They grab the terrified Scherasmin and force him to dance with them until Oberon renders them immobile. He then gives the two men a magic goblet and horn to help them on their quest. The horn will make men immobile when blown softly and will summon Oberon when blown loudly. The goblet will fill with wine for an honest person and burn the lips of a dishonest one. Huon and Scherasmin then depart for Bagdad in the cloud chariot.

In Baghdad Amande tells her servant, Fatime, about a dream of a strange young man. She is apprehensive concerning her arranged marriage to Babekan, whom she has not yet seen. Huon and Scherasmin then land in the nearby forest, where Oberon's genies present them with Turkish clothes and horses. Huon and Scherasmin enter the sultan's court disguised as a wealthy landowner and his servant. Huon and Amande immediately recognize each other from their dreams; they know they are destined to be united and call out to each other. Huon identifies himself as a Christian destined to marry Amande. Mahmud orders Huon and Amande put to death, but as Babekan draws his saber, the knight plays his magic horn and immobilizes them. Scherasmin then enters and says that Fatime has prepared an escape. Huon demands four of the sultan's teeth and hair from his beard for King Childerich. Mahmud orders his men to capture Huon, but Scherasmin blasts the horn and Oberon appears with a thunderbolt. The sultan and his court fall to the earth immobile. Oberon blesses the union of Huon and Amande and presents Huon with a small box containing the words he must speak to the king in order to be released from his exile. Scherasmin, Fatime, Huon, and Amande escape.

After a storm causes their ship to founder, Huon, Scherasmin, and Fatime swim to the Tunisian shore. Pirates have captured Amande and sold her into the harem of the Pasha Almansor. Scherasmin tells Huon that has he has lost the magic horn. The pasha's wife Almansaris sees Huon, who is pretending to be a poor slave. She becomes enamored of him and orders Huon and Scherasmin to serve Osmin, the guardian of the harem. She tries to seduce Huon, but he remains faithful to Amande. Almansoris draws a dagger to stab him and when he seizes the knife, his cap falls off, revealing his full head of hair (this signifies that he is a Christian). Almansor then enters and sees Huon with the dagger in his hand. Almansoris tells him that Huon tried to rape her. The pasha has him condemned to torture and death. Almansor desires Amande, but she refuses his advances. The pasha condemns both Huon and Amande to the stake. A thunderbolt strikes a moment before their execution, and pleasant music begins; Huon and Amande are magically freed as Oberon appears in his cloud chariot and plays the magic horn, causing the villains to dance.

Titania's march returns as she appears on a splendid ship with her retinue of fairies.

The most successful Oberon opera was certainly *Oberon, König der Elfen,* with music by Paul Wranitzky (7 November 1789).[145] Emanuel Schikaneder commissioned the opera for his initial season as director of the Theater auf der Wieden, and the singspiel would be the first of many successful fairy-tale operas at the Wiednertheater. The actor and writer Karl Ludwig Giesecke arranged the text as a three-act *romantisch-komische Oper,*[146] based on Seyler's *Hüon und Amande.* Commentators have observed numerous textual and musical affinities between *Oberon* and *Die Zauberflöte.*[147] Some of the same principals sang in *Die Zauberflöte:* Josepha Hofer (the Queen of the Night) sang Oberon, Benedikt Schack (Tamino) was Huon, Franz Xaver Gerl (Sarastro) sang Almanzor and the oracle, Barbara Gerl (Papagena) sang Titania, and Anna Gottlieb (Pamina) was Amande. Schikaneder may have sung the role of Scherasmin, although he did not participate in the May 1790 revival, which provides the earliest surviving cast list. Hofer was given coloratura in her B-flat aria "Dies ist des edlen Huon's Sprache." (Mozart would also provide Hofer's Queen of the Night with a B-flat coloratura aria.)[148] Like Mozart, Wranitzky gave the superhuman characters Titania and Oberon elaborate coloratura. There is also solemn (*feierlich*) music for ceremonial scenes, for example, the Andante con moto affetuoso in act 1 (No. 4),[149] a movement similar to the Priests' March in *Die Zauberflöte.* Act 3 has a march and an Andante con moto chorus for the

145. For details, see Fellinger, "*Oberon* im achzehnten Jahrhundert"; Komorzynski, "'Zauberflöte' und 'Oberon'"; Kielbasa, "Paul Wranitzky's *Oberon*"; and Wranitzky, *Oberon; König der Elfen.* The earliest surviving librettos are from Augsburg and Hamburg (1792). A later Viennese libretto for a performance at the Theater in der Leopoldstadt survives in Vienna and US-Wc (Vienna: Wallishausser, 1806).

146. He omitted thirteen numbers from Seyler's original text, revised six numbers, and added new finales. By the time Giesecke was done with it, only seven of Seyler's numbers were left intact. He also supplied additional numbers for the comic pair Scherasmin and Fatime.

147. Mozart owned a copy of Wieland's poem and heard this opera at the Nationaltheater in Frankfurt (15 October 1790) if not in Vienna. See Schmid, *Ein schwäbisches Mozartbuch,* 465, n. 761.

148. F. L. Schröder heard *Oberon* and wrote that Hofer did not have the range for the role (she "squeaked"). He was also annoyed by Schack's Austrian dialect and suburban declamation. See Meyer, *Friedrich Ludwig Schröder,* 2: 85.

149. References to the music in this discussion refer to the modern edition, based on the Viennese manuscript score formerly in Donaueschingen, Fürstliche Fürstenbergische Hofbibliothek, and now in Karlsruhe, Badische Landesbibliothek: Wranitzky, *Oberon; König der Elfen.* The surviving sources include piano-vocal scores printed in Mannheim, n.d. (RISM W2014) and Worms, n.d., (RISM W2015). No autograph survives. Other copies of the full orchestral score are in Hamburg, Munich, Prague (3), Weimar, Frankfurt, Paris, Stuttgart, Regensburg, Berlin (2), Dresden (2), and Neuenstein. The author also located copies in D-Hs, ND VII 450 (1-3) and ND VII 451, recently returned from St. Petersburg, where it had been kept since World War II. There are substantial new arias in ND VII 450 by Carl David Stegmann. Almansor's aria "So viel Reizen spröde

Musselmen guarding Huon, who is tied to a stake. The opening of the second act of *Die Zauberflöte* has something of the spirit of this sacrificial prayer.

Oberon is more of a number opera than later Wiednertheater singspiels such as *Der Stein der Weisen* and *Die Zauberflöte*. The score (for trumpets, horns, flutes, oboes, clarinets, bassoons, strings with two viola parts, timpani, and bass drum, cymbals, and triangle for the Turkish scenes) has fewer instances of recalled material or interconnected motives. There are no large scene complexes, trios, quartets, or quintets. The introduction in act 1 and the finales are relatively brief, especially in comparison to operas that would be produced in this theater in the future. But the act 1 overture and the act 3 sinfonia are both substantial movements. The overture begins with bursts of ascending scale figures in the bass and strings, both a comic and a "supernatural" motive; it continues with comic-style music, with solos for oboe, flute, and the "enchanted" horn. The splendid development section has passages with string tremolos, rapid scales, wind ensembles, and stormy music in the minor mode. The act 3 sinfonia begins with an Allegro assai in C minor, violent storm music that introduces an Allegro non troppo in the parallel major mode.

The supernatural material in act 1 includes Titania's ensembles with her two-part nymphs' chorus, "Hör' o Schicksal meine Klagen." The oracle (bass) addresses Titania in a simple recitative with the strings playing low sustained notes. Oberon appears in a cloud chariot accompanied by an elegant binary Andante in F major (no. 6), scored for horns, oboes, and bassoons, an "enchanted" wind ensemble that returns in act 3, where it is labeled "Marche." This solemn march recalls those used for similar scenes by a variety of composers since Lully. Oberon's aria (Allegro maestoso in B-flat) fits her supernatural character, beginning with an unusually large ritornello. In this virtuoso coloratura cavatina with an extended closing section, the vocal line has wide ascending and descending leaps, as much as two octaves. The accompaniment is highly varied, with running scale figures and wind motives. This segment leads to a short but dramatic accompanied recitative where Oberon boasts of magic powers.

The dervish chorus for unison basses in D minor (act 1, no. 8, "Heil, heil allen Menschenkinder, unsre Wallfahrt ist vollbracht") uses an ascending walking-bass motive in eighth notes. This may have inspired Mozart's similar motive for the scene in *Die Zauberflöte* with the two men in black armor (act 2, scene 28). When Oberon first hears this, he calls it "feierliche Musik." The exotic serpentine scale figures in the strings occur again in the first Turkish chorus of Schikaneder's *Der wohltätige Derwisch* of 1791 After the chorus Oberon uses his lily stalk to create a magic trance that forces the group to dance. The libretto calls for a "wild dance" or a "waltz"; the score has a triple-meter Presto in C minor. The melody (doubled at the octave above and below) is made up

---

sein" (no. 23) appears only in published keyboard reduction (Mannheim: Götz, 1799) and in the Weimar manuscript.

entirely of leaps in a wide melodic range. The harmony features an abrupt change to E-flat, then to C major in a binary middle section. The waltz here seems to evoke reeling passion and a dizzying trance, an association consistent with later descriptions of the dance.[150]

In act 2 most of the supernatural material occurs in dialogues during a melodrama in E-flat. Act 3 opens with an extended sinfonia, called an "Entracte Pantomime" in some manuscript scores. (Giesecke eliminated the storm scene.) The sound of Oberon's march from act 1 (now an Adagio in E-flat) announces the appearance of the deity in his cloud chariot. Huon and Amande are released, and Oberon blows his horn. An Allegro dance in A minor ensues, and the villains dance involuntarily while the keys modulate by thirds. Oberon declares that his own oath to Titania is now fulfilled. Another magic march begins as Titania and her fairies appear.

Wranitzky's *Oberon* and the Viennese fairy-tale operas that followed it would form the core of a German repertory that endured through the first two decades of the nineteenth century. This is the first German operatic repertory that would be the subject of translation into other languages. Less than a year after its Viennese premiere, *Oberon* was staged at Frankfurt's Nationaltheater, 9 October (as reported in Steiger) or 15 October 1790, for the coronation of Leopold II. The opera had new musical contributions by Heinrich Schmieder, Carl David Stegmann, and Ignaz Walter. It was revived frequently in Frankfurt.[151] The Hamburg City Opera mounted a highly successful production on 17 October 1791, with Stegmann's new arias (poster in D-Hs). A printed libretto (Hamburg: Herold Buchhandlung, 1792) survives. *Oberon* became the most popular opera in Hamburg in the 1790s and remained so well in the early nineteenth century. Numerous cities mounted successful performance runs as well.

Fairy-Tale Operas in Suburban Vienna, 1790–91

After the success of the Wiedertheater production of *Oberon*, oriental fairy tales became a frequent inspiration for new singspiels at Schikaneder's theater. Some of these singspiels were full-length operas such as *Der Stein der Weisen* and *Die Zauberflöte*. Others had less music and more dialogue, for example, *Die schöne Isländerin, oder Der Muffti von Samarkanda*, a three-act *Zauberkomödie mit Arien und Chören* by Emanuel Schikaneder, with music by unknown composers (lost). The premiere (22 April 1790) is listed in Schikaneder's *Allmanach für Theaterfreunde* of 1791, but the only available information on this work comes from a poster announcing a revival on 21 July 1791.[152] Schikaneder and

150. Marx, *Die Lehre von der musikalischen Komposition*, 2:55–56, describes the dance as swinging, spirited, rustic, and raw.

151. Saure, "Die Geschichte der Frankfurt Oper," 240–41.

152. The poster survives in A-Wgm. See Blümml, *Aus Mozarts Freundes- und Familienkreis*, 204 n. 48, and Deutsch, *Das Freihaustheater auf der Wieden*, 31.

the *Kapellmeister* Johann Baptist Henneberg (if he joined the company this early) may have written some of the music along with two other composer-singers in the company, Benedikt Schack and Franz Xaver Gerl. The story takes place in Samarkanda (the location used in Gozzi's *I pitocchi fortunati*). The cast list included the singers who created the roles in *Oberon, Der Stein der Weisen, and Die Zauberflöte,* suggesting that the music might have included some demanding numbers. Several of these performers have parallel roles in other magic singspiels at this theater. Gerl would represent other magicians and Schack would sing the part of numerous princes, Anna Gottlieb numerous princesses, Johann Nouseul the exotic characters such Monostatos, Schikaneder the comic servants, and Hofer the authoritative coloratura soprano roles.

Der Stein der Weisen, oder Die Zauberinsel (11 September 1790) was the first singspiel that Schikaneder based on Wieland's *Dschinnistan.*[153] It was revived frequently at the Wiednertheater and was performed in several German theaters outside Vienna (it was performed in Czech starting in 1795). The title was taken directly from the Wieland tale of the same name,[154] but as he would do for *Die Zauberflöte,* Schikaneder plundered several *Dschinnistan* stories for *Der Stein der Weisen.* He drew the main plot and characters from "Nadir und Nadine," the first story in the collection:[155] the magician Astromonte ("Astramond" in *Dschinnistan*), Sadik (Nadine's father and Nadir's stepfather), the cloud chariot, the magic ring, the magic sword, the magic bird, and the pastoral setting with its shepherds and shepherdesses. The unusual reversal of plot

153. Manuscript librettos survive in D-Hs (shelfmark M. 721), and D-B (Mus. ms. 861), along with *Rollenhefte* in D-F, Mus Hs Opern 508. The poster advertised a printed songbook for the premiere, but no copy seems to have survived. The *Allmanach für Theaterfreunde auf das Jahr 1791* (Vienna: Matthias Ludwig, 1791), A-Wst, G83479, contains the earliest surviving song texts. *Arien und Gesänge aus Dem Stein der Weisen oder: Die Zauberinsel; Eine heroisch = komische Oper in zwei Aufzügen* (Frankfurt am Main, 1796) printed all the musical numbers for a revival of the opera at Frankfurt's *Nationaltheater* (US-Wc, shelfmark ML 48 Schatz 9570). Another songbook, *Gesaenge zur heroisch-comischen Oper, Der Stein der Weisen,* was published in 1802, without indication of the city or publisher. A copy survives in Regensburg's Proskesche Musikbibliothek, shelfmark Mus. tx. 116/9. A third songbook in D-Mbs, *Gesänge aus der Oper Der Stein der Weisen oder Die Zauberinsel* (no publication information), bears the indication "Musik gesetzt von Herrn Mozart" (shelfmark L. eleg m.3170v). One song was printed in *Sechs schöne neue Weltliche Lieder aus der Oper des Steins der Weisen* (Vienna: Anton Leitner, n.d.), A-Wst, E 80360. For a critical edition and study of the libretto see Buch and Jahrmärker, *Schikaneders heroisch-komische Oper.*

154. Wieland's "Der Stein der Weisen," one of the more original contributions in *Dschinnistan,* contrasts with the free translations of preexisting fairy tales that make up most of the other stories in the collection. It is quite different from the singspiel. Wieland concentrates mainly on "a narration" of King Mark of Cornwall and his advisor Misfragmutosiris, an initiate in the Egyptian hermetic mysteries, which include trials of fire and water. References to initiation, Egyptian lore, and alchemy are more apparent in *Die Zauberflöte* than in *Der Stein der Weisen.*

155. Based on Claude Paujon's "L'enchanteur, ou la bague de puissance," in *Le cabinet des fées* (1785–89), 34:58–199.

in "Nadir und Nadine," where a supposedly evil magician kidnaps a virtuous maiden but turns out to be a good character, probably provided *Die Zauberflöte* with its similar plot twist. In the original story the villain is Astromond's evil brother, Neraor. Schikaneder changed the name to Eutifronte, a variant of Euthyfron, which was taken from another *Dschinnistan* story, "Timander und Melissa." Schikaneder reduced the narration of the fairy tale to a simple plot line, alloyed elements from a commedia dell'arte type that involves a shipwreck on a remote magic island, and added the comic pair of commoners. He employed a similar process of adaptation for the other *Dschinnistan*-based operas, particularly *Die Zauberflöte*. *Der Stein der Weisen* has a surprising number of similarities in structure and language to Mozart's opera, suggesting that the earlier singspiel was the model for *Die Zauberflöte*. Both text and musical materials would be recycled in *Die Zauberflöte:* a contrasting pair of lovers, an evil magician who kidnaps the young princess but turns out in the end to be good, comic ensembles for a character who cannot speak, a scene where an ensemble of women fight over who is the most innocent, a rescue from suicide, and long flute solos.

The opera begins in an arcadian land where the elder Sadik leads a sacrificial ceremony to the guardian spirit, Astromonte. Sadik's two foster children, the lovers Nadir and Nadine, are missing. They soon appear with their rustic friends, the newlyweds Lubano and Lubanara. The audacious Lubanara, dreaming of flying in Astromonte's cloud chariot, persuaded the simple forester to participate, but the couple's presence desecrates a ceremony reserved for virgins. Sadik metes out a mild punishment, warning Nadir and Nadine of coming danger, when enchanting music heralds the arrival of Astromonte's genie in a cloud chariot. The genie carries a cage that contains a magic bird and announces Astromonte's imminent appearance. The bird will identify the most virtuous and innocent maiden by its song, and Astromonte will take her with him. In a series of comic scenes with Lubano and Lubanara, the woodsman locks his wife in their hut and she invokes the evil spirit Eutifronte, who appears with thunder and lightning. He frees her, but Lubano returns to find his wife with the soot-covered demon. Eutifronte takes Lubanara into the abyss (fig. 5.1) and enchants Lubano so that he has a set of antlers on his head, the sign of cuckoldry. Eutifronte's supernatural hunters then chase Lubano. Meanwhile, Nadir and Nadine plan an escape, but the unseen voice of Astromonte warns them to stay. Sadik returns and orders the ceremony to begin. Each maiden holds the bird, but it remains silent until Nadine takes it. Lubano then runs in, chased by the hunters, and hides behind the pyramid. Astromonte descends in his cloud chariot and accepts the offerings of the people. As he is about to leave he hears the bird singing and sees Nadine. He takes them both in his chariot and flies away. The arcadians then decide to sail to the magic island to free Nadine.

In act 2 Eutifronte causes a storm to wreck the ships, but Nadir and Lubano swim to the enchanted island. Eutifronte overhears Nadir dreaming and

FIGURE 5.1. *Allmanach für Theaterfreunde,* plate 11 (fol. 39 recto): "He! schwarzer Kerl!" from *Der Stein der Weisen,* 11 September 1790, act 1, scene 14. From left to right: Barbara Gerl as Lubanara, Franz Xaver Gerl as Eutifronte, and Emanuel Schikaneder as Lubano. Vienna, Stadt- und Landesbibiliothek, Druckschriftensammlung, G.83.479EK.

decides to use the young man's anger toward Astromonte for his own evil purposes. Eutifronte narrates his story to Nadir: Astromonte and he are brothers, the sons of a great sorcerer who taught them both the magic arts. Their father discovered the greatest of all magic secrets, the philosopher's stone. He offered his sons an equal share of his wealth, but Astromonte, as the firstborn, was to receive the stone. Eutifronte could not accept this slight, and he cursed his brother. On hearing this, their father decided that neither son should have the stone and summoned an eagle to take it away. It would some day be given to the most worthy of their sons. At that time the two brothers loved the same beautiful princess. She chose Astromonte, and they had a son. Realizing that this son might receive the philosopher's stone, Eutifronte ordered his henchmen to

FIGURE 5.2. *Allmanach für Theaterfreunde,* plate 12 (fol. 42 recto): "Fort in die Abgründe der Hölle," from *Der Stein der Weisen,* 11 September 1790, act 2, scene 10. From left to right: child actors as Eutifronte's dwarfs, Anna Schikaneder as the genie, and Barbara Gerl as Lubanara. Vienna, Stadt- und Landesbibiliothek, Druckschriftensammlung, G.83.479EK.

suffocate the boy. Soon after learning of her child's disappearance, the princess died of grief. To assuage his unhappiness, their father gave Astromonte a magic bird that would identify the most virtuous maiden: this proved to be Nadine. Eutifronte then tells Nadir that he must murder Astromonte in order to save her.

Lubano receives instructions from Astromonte's genie. Eutifronte's dwarfs arrive and tempt him with food until Lubanara interrupts. She tells him of Eutifronte's plans, but before she can tell Nadir, Eutifronte overhears them and bewitches her so that she can only meow like a cat. Eutifronte summons his subterranean spirits, who forge a magic sword with which Nadir can kill Astromonte. A dwarf appears and presents Nadir with Eutifronte's magic bow and lethal arrows, and Nadir sets out for Astromonte's palace. Lubano searches for Lubanara, who was saved from the dwarfs by the genie (fig. 5.2). Eutifronte seizes him and pulls him into the abyss. Outside Astromonte's palace Nadir hears the bird sing and he shoots the magic arrow. Nadine cries out that she is fatally wounded and dies. The genie comes and takes Nadir away before he is overcome by suicidal despair. The dwarfs imprison Lubano in a cage and Eutifronte declares that Lubano will die by Nadir's hand. But before Nadir can kill Lubano, Astromonte appears disguised as an old man holding the bird. He asks for Eutifronte's sword, promising that the bird will return Nadine to him, along with Sadik and all the lost arcadians. He reveals Nadir's true identity as Astromonte's son, saved after Eutifronte's companions threw him into the sea. Eutifronte tries to persuade Nadir that Astromonte is the enemy, but Nadir is not fooled, and he presents the sword to the old man. An eagle flies in carrying a vessel; the genie declares that this is the philosopher's stone, delivered to Nadir, the worthy son, just as Astromonte's father had predicted. Nadine is restored to life along with the other arcadians, and Astromonte removes his disguise. Eutifronte and his spirits sink down into the abyss, and the scene changes into a splendid temple where all give thanks to Astromonte and plan the marriage of Nadir and Nadine.

The music in *Der Stein der Weisen* was something of a mystery until a Viennese score, thought to be lost, was returned to Hamburg in 1991 from Russia. That score,[156] copied by six scribes associated with the theater, contains composer attributions in the hand of the fourth copyist, the actor and singer Kaspar Weiss. Weiss attributes much of the music to Henneberg, along with attributions to Mozart, Schack, Gerl, and Schikaneder.[157] Mozart's attributions are in the second act: the duet "Nun liebes Weibchen," K.625/592a,[158] and two segments in the finale (the beginning section and the Moderato sec-

156. Three Viennese manuscript scores of the opera survive: D-B, Mus. Ms. anon. 1451 (olim, 15,156), 2 vols.; D-Hs, ND VII 174, 2 vols.; and D-F, Mus Hs Opern 508, 2 vols., with parts and other materials from a performance in Frankfurt c. 1795–96. Theater auf der Wieden scribes copied the latter two scores in the early to middle 1790s; For details on the Frankfurt materials, see Didion and Schlichte, *Thematischer Katalog*, 251. A fourth manuscript, a piano-vocal score from the early nineteenth century with several new musical segments, survives in I-Fc, shelfmark Ms. FPT 738.

157. Weiß had been in the company since early 1790, He was apparently Schikaneder's agent in selling scores and librettos. The poster from the premiere (A-Wgm) and the revival on 12 May 1791 (A-Wst, 77250 C) indicates no composers. (Schikaneder began crediting his composer "teams" in 1791.) The cast list names Schikaneder as Lubano, Barbara Gerl as Lubanara, Schack as Astromonte, Anna Gottlieb as Nadine, Gerl as Eutifronte, Anna Schikaneder as the genie, and Johann Michael Kistler as Nadir.

158. The act 2 duet, "Nun liebes Weibchen," K.625/592a, survives in a partial Mozart autograph now in P-Fn, Musique, Ms. 247. The edition in *W. A. Mozart: Werke*, Ser. 6, Bd. 47 (Leipzig: Breitkopf & Härtel, 1881), was based on an inaccurate copy made by Aloys Fuchs. The duet is not yet published in the New Mozart Edition. For details see Buch, "On Mozart's Partial Autograph."

tion in C minor for the genie and Nadir that occurs about halfway into the finale).[159] Weiss attributed one aria to Schikaneder, as well as much of the melodic material in the first finale. This collaboration was probably the result of the pressing schedule of new singspiels, as related in an anonymous Viennese article from 1794,[160] where several individuals, including Schack and Gerl, are cited as the composers of *Der Stein der Weisen* and *Der wohltätige Derwisch*.

Several distinguishing musical characteristics first appear in this opera, and these will continue to be features of Wiednertheater fairy-tale opera. First is the "romantic" style, reflected in the minimal repetition of text; the limited use of instrumental ritornellos except for staging purposes and important scenes; the mixing of conventions from comic, court, and serious opera; and the abruptly episodic finales, which, unlike in Italian opera, are assemblies of short, contrasting tableaus. To match the succession of magic, comic, sentimental, and solemn scenes, the composers supplied choruses, solos, recitatives, ensembles, and instrumental pieces, ending with a triumphal final chorus. Instrumental music to accompany magic episodes and transformations with machines is a prominent feature in *Der Stein der Weisen*. The *feierlich* style, denoting a solemn, ceremonial expression associated with the grand royal occasions so popular in imperial Vienna, employed sacred or mythological symbolism, most often to affirm the divine right of the Habsburgs. The term *feierlich* occurs in the librettos of *Oberon*, *Der Stein der Weisen*, and *Die Zauberflöte*. In the review of *Der Stein der Weisen* for the Altona performance in 1800, the *feierlich* effect is the dominant quality for which the two finales are praised.[161]

The two overtures, both substantial Allegro movements with slow introductions, contain supernatural allusions. The first overture, attributed to Henneberg, begins with a solemn Andante maestoso in D minor that leads to a D major Allegro; initial antecedent-consequent motives have the winds answering the dotted repeated-note figures in the strings. The agitated *alla zoppa* syncopated accompaniment, the stark dynamic contrasts, the blaring brass, the severe Dorian key and the Neapolitan harmony had been used for infernal scenes since the 1760s. The overture to the second act portrays a violent storm

159. For basic background material on *Der Stein der Weisen* and Mozart's participation, see Buch, "Mozart and the Theater auf der Wieden," and "*Der Stein der Weisen*, Mozart, and Collaborative Singspiels." Also see Edge, "Mozart's Viennese Copyists," chap. 10.

160. "Ueber den Stand der Musik in Wien" in *Wiener Theater Almanach* (Vienna: Kurzbeck, 1794), 188: "Bey den sechs Theilen der beyden Anton oder des dummen Gärtners . . . , bey den der Schellenkappe oder dem Derwisch, und bey dem Stein der Weisen componirten mehrere zugleich, man arbeitete an diesen Operetten wie an einem Hause, und es ist nicht zu läugnen, dass diese Manier die allerbeste ist, wenn eine Oper bald zu Stande gebracht seyn soll."

161. *Hamburgisch- und altonaische Theater- und Litteratur-Zeitung*, Ser. 4, Bd. 32 (Altona: Friedrich Bechtold, 1800); preserved in D-Mbs, shelfmark Per. 190 ef), 119–22 (9 August 1800). In a letter to his wife (8–9 October 1791), Mozart uses the phrase "der feyerlichen Scene" to describe the first scene in act 2. The unnamed author (probably Julius Friedrich Knüppeln) of the *Vertraute Briefe*, 2: 52, praises Sarastro's aria and the priests' chorus for their *feierlich* quality.

at sea, beginning with a recitative-like Larghetto in E-flat with dotted figures and rapid short scalar figures in the violins, answered by chords in the winds (clarinets, oboes, horns, and bassoons). Traces of this opening solemn music will return in the second finale for the funeral chorus. The ensuing Allegro assai in C minor, with its extended initial crescendo, rising pitch level, and octave sonority, develops into a fully fledged storm, with violent bursts of scale figures in the strings, abrupt dynamic contrasts, piano timpani rolls, and *alla zoppa* syncopated accompaniment figures. The movement leads to a C minor chorus for the sailors and passengers. The comic pantomime for Eutifronte's dwarfs in act 2, marked "Marsch" in the Hamburg score, is the other instrumental number in the act. This comic movement is a binary form in B-flat for flutes and strings, with a humorous trio in E-flat featuring added bassoons and horns.

A number of short instrumental segments accommodate supernatural scenes and stage-machine music. The first finale has a short repeated instrumental section for flute solo, accompanied by strings, when a magic bird determines the most virtuous maiden. This music returns when the bird reappears in the second finale. The instruments imitate the bird with trills and repeated notes, while tutti refrains allow for the characters to mime the action. The instrumental introduction to Schack's act 1 chorus (no. 4) also serves as magic music as it announces the solemn arrival of the genie ("Welch' reizende Musik erhebt die Herzen feierlich!"). Scored for two clarinets doubled by flutes at the upper octave, horns, and bassoons in C major, it is a traditional wind ensemble in the elegant marvelous style, a gentle sonic image of enchantment in *siciliano* rhythms. Astromonte's magic appearance in the first finale, scene 21, also has stage-machine music, a prelude in E-flat for winds and strings with syncopated figures in the flutes; sustained chords in the clarinets, horns, and second bassoon; and a quarter-note pulse in the first bassoon. This leads to an accompanied recitative and bipartite aria, culminating in a coloratura Allegro section in B-flat. This scene may have inspired Mozart's similar episode for the Queen of the Night in act 1 of *Die Zauberflöte*.

The composers employed underworld instrumentation in three appropriate choruses, scored with horns, trumpets, trombones, and timpani. The supernatural hunters' chorus in act 1 (no. 7 and the first finale) may have been inspired by a similar scene in Ruprecht's *Das wütende Heer* of 1787. The "Chor der Geister" in C minor, attributed to Schack ("Astromont' stirbt durch uns," act 2, no. 7), is an Adagio scored for muted horns, muted trumpets, trombones, bassoons, basses, and timpani. The old-fashioned suspensions, the low, muted winds, and the dark timbre all suggest a Hadean character. Some choruses employ the terrifying style, with rapid slurred scale figures, string tremolos, octave-and-unison sonority, and *alla zoppa* syncopation (e.g., act 2, no. 1; act 2, no. 7; and the choral segments in the second finale).

In the duet attributed to Mozart, Lubanara has been enchanted so that she can only meow like a cat. The point here is humor rather than supernatural

EXAMPLE 5.7 Johann Baptist Henneberg, *Der Stein der Weisen*, act 1, finale

force. The disjunct (but always consonant) meowing, accompanied by winds with chromatic inflections, suggests an animal.[162] This contrasts with the verbal singing of her husband, who has a conjunct melody with diatonic string accompaniment.

Some arias have supernatural expression, for example, Eutifronte's underworld aria in act 1, "In finstrer Höhlenkluft verschlossen" (no. 6, attributed to Gerl), scored with trombones, horns, oboes, bassoons, and strings playing *alla zoppa* syncopation. The aria was probably based on Gluck's "Ombre, larve" from *Alceste* (see chapter 3). These features, along with the ominous declamatory repeated notes in the vocal line, are indicative of a supernatural villain. The genie's aria in the act 1 chorus (no. 4) is an elegant minuet that expresses his divine and noble character.

The supernatural characters Astromonte, Eutifronte, and the genie all have special accompanied recitatives that feature sustained chords (in obbligato recitative) or tremolos in the strings. The recitative of the underworld deity Eutifronte (act 1, no. 6) has trombones, as does his subsequent aria. Astromonte's first appearance in the act 1 finale begins with an instrumental prelude for winds and strings playing triadic figures with *alla zoppa* syncopation in E-flat, stage-machine music to facilitate his magic entry (see ex. 5.7). Act 1, no. 9 is a dream episode in recitative, with the unseen deity Astromonte addressing his son, Nadir. The key is C minor, and the strings play dotted figures set against *alla zoppa* accompaniment.

The two finales are long, episodic structures, with much dramatic action determined by the abruptly changing events. The supernatural scenes in the

162. The comic ensemble with a character who can no longer speak goes back to *Le bûcheron* (1763; see chapter 2). A similar ensemble occurs in *Die Zauberflöte*, where, during the act 1 quintet, Papageno has a lock on his mouth and can only hum inarticulately.

first finale include the segment with the magic bird in scene 19, the repeat of the hunters' chorus in the same scene, and Astromonte's magic arrival and departure in scene 21. The comic beginning of the second finale, also attributed to Mozart, recalls the "cat" duet in act 2. It commences with Lubanara meowing as Lubano searches for her. As in their earlier act 2 duet (no. 4), the disjunct meowing by Lubanara contrasts with Lubano's conjunct singing. Eutifronte suddenly appears and drags the terrified Lubano into the underworld with the music of a headlong *contradanse*. After Nadir accidentally kills Nadine with a magic arrow, a solemn chorus sings "Jüngling! Nadine ist todt!," accompanied by trombones and based on the opening of the act 2 overture. The chorus repeats its pronouncement in a C minor Grave segment, leading to a violent segment for the text "Donner brüllet, Stürme brauset," with its rapid scale passages, blasts of the trumpets, horns and trombones, and repeated timpani strokes. The next section is a duet in the heroic style attributed to Mozart, a Moderato in triple meter for the genie and Nadir ("Fort, armer Jüngling, eile von hier"). The stormy beginning in C minor, with its short scalar burst and its encouraging modulation to E-flat, suggest both a supernatural event and a rescue scene (the genie persuades Nadir not to commit suicide). Eutifronte's next entrance (with his spirits) brings stormy music in C minor with tremolos, fast scales, trombones, and timpani. Nadir and Astromonte alternate calm E-flat duet segments with the increasingly violent music of Eutifronte and his spirits. When Nadir rejects Eutifronte, the spirits cry out "O weh!" in their infernal key of C minor. In a short accompanied recitative passage, the genie announces the appearance of the philosopher's stone with trumpet fanfares, and Nadine now returns to life (presumably through the life-giving power of the magic stone). Astromonte chastises Eutifronte and his spirits; they rush back into their subterranean caverns with exclamations in C minor, using a cadence favored for damnation scenes (i–VI–ii$_5^6$–V–i). The wealth of comic, sentimental and supernatural allusions in this score are breathtaking and indicative of the ambitious operas to come.

Some six months after *Der Stein der Weisen*, Schikaneder staged another theatrical adaptation from Wieland's *Dschinnistan*, a *Lust- und Zauberspiel* in three acts entitled *Der wohltätige Derwisch, oder Die Schellenkappe*. A diary entry by Count Karl Zinzendorf documents a performance on 14 March 1791.[163] Commentators have described *Der wohltätige Derwisch* as having been devised to reproduce the success of *Die Zauberflöte*.[164] With the correction of Deutsch's

163. Zinzendorf wrote that he heard "Den [*sic*] Derwisch [,] farce singulière avec les nés qui viennent aux hommes et femmes." See Link, *National Court Theatre*, 372. Lorenz Lausch advertised arias and ensembles in *Die Wiener Zeitung*, 9 April 1791. In his 1937 study on the Theater auf der Wieden, Deutsch incorrectly cites the premiere as 10 September 1793.

164. Komorzynski, *Emanuel Schikaneder* (1901), 140, and (1951); and Honolka, *Papageno*, 187, among other authors, refer to the opera in this manner. Komorzynski, *Emanuel Schikaneder* (1951), 272–81, gives the plot based on the Mannheim libretto, cited in Komorzynski (1901), 140 n. 1.

error, the situation is actually reversed; *Die Zauberflöte* owes something to *Der wohltätige Derwisch*. Manuscript librettos survive from performances in Frankfurt, Altona, Český Krumlov, and Mannheim,[165] along with several printed collections of vocal texts.[166] The singspiel was frequently revived at the Wiednertheater in the 1790s, and then at the Theater an der Wien in 1803. It was also performed on a variety of other German stages through the first two decades of the nineteenth century, as well as in translation (Czech and Hungarian). It was revived at Vienna's Theater in der Josefstadt as *Die Zaubertrommel* (18 March 1807) and staged in various theaters at least until 1817.

Like *Der Stein der Weisen* and *Die Zauberflöte*, Schikaneder relied primarily on a single story from *Dschinnistan*, drawing details from other tales in the collection. The primary source of *Der wohltätige Derwisch* is Einsiedel's "Die Prinzeßin mit der langen Nase." The plot concerns Prince Sofrano, the son of King Almandor (Sofrano seems a variant of the name Sofra from Einsiedel's tale "Die klugen Knaben"). After stealing the magic goblet from his enemy, Sheik Abukaf of Basora, Almandor pretends to have died. He returns to his son disguised as an ailing, impoverished dervish whom Sofrano nurtures back to health.[167] Sofrano is in love with the evil Princess Zenomide, who steals his precious legacy: a magic pouch that produces gold and a magic

165. Hamburg (D-Hs, Theaterbibliothek Nr. 142), Frankfurt (D-F, Mus Hs Opern 509), and Český Krumlov's castle archive (shelfmark 49a K17). The Theatersammlung of Mannheim's Reiss-Museum possesses a manuscript libretto from a four-act revision, shelfmark M. 371, for a single performance in Mannheim's Nationaltheater on 2 December 1806. Franz Gerl, who left the Wiednertheater in 1793 to move to Brno, settled in Mannheim in 1802. His presence may have instigated the later revival and revision. (The Mannheim libretto is incorrectly cited as the now defunct Wissenschaftliche Staatsbibliothek und Universitätsbibliothek in Branscombe, "Gerl, Franz Xaver," and Tyler, "Schack, Benedikt.") Walter, *Die Bibliothek des Großh. Hof = und Nationaltheaters*, 2:179, cites a score and orchestral parts that existed before the destruction of this library in World War II. There are two new arias in the Mannheim libretto.

166. In the first print, *Arien und Duetten aus dem wohltätigen Derwisch, oder Die Schellenkappe* (Vienna: Mathias Ludwig, 1791, in A-Wt, 698.427 A.Th. 239, the work has the genre designation of *Lust- und Zauberspiel*. A later songbook, *Arien zur Zaubertrommel oder Der wohltätigen Derwisch* (Augsburg, 1793), attributes the music to "Herrn Schak," and the genre is now a *grosses [sic] komisches Singspiel*. This edition includes more choruses along with changes to the aria and ensemble texts. A copy survives in D-B, shelfmark Ts 282, and in US-Wc, Schatz 9571. The opera, performed by Wenzel Mihule's traveling company, was now entitled *Die Zaubertrommel*. The following year there appeared a songbook for a four-act revision of the singspiel, *Gesänge zu der großen komischen Oper in vier Aufzügen, genannt Die Schellenkappe, oder Die Zaubertrommel*, A-Wn, 641.433 A.M. xviii.8. Two other songbooks also survive in D-Mbs from performances in Altona (Altona: Ecksdorff, n.d., with music attributed to Schack, shelfmark Her. 1972), and Frankfurt (1794, shelfmark Her. 344).

167. Schikaneder borrowed the dervish and his situation from Wieland's "Der eiserne Armleuchter: ein türkisches Märchen." The dervish is also a character in the tale "Neangir und seine Brüder." Perhaps Schikaneder also was inspired by Klinger's fairy-tale comedy *Der Derwisch* (1780).

drum that conjures an army of warriors. Sofrano's comic companion is Mandolino, a henpecked fisherman (played by Schikaneder) who finds a fool's cap with magic bells that conjure a troupe of dervishes. Using the bells, Mandolino helps Sofrano and the dervish. They trick Zenomide and her court into eating enchanted fruits that cause them to grow long noses. Sofrano and Mandolino then come disguised as two farmers with flasks of curative water. They retrieve the pouch and drum, leaving Zenomide and Mandolino's shrewish wife with their disfigured faces. There are scenes with magic music and two incantations in pseudo-Turkish by a chorus of whirling dervishes. The moralizing content in the dervish's arias and recitative prefigure the speeches of Sarastro and the Speaker in *Die Zauberflöte*.

Like many singspiels at this time that emphasized spoken text over large-scale musical numbers, *Der wohltätige Derwissch* was less a full-scale opera than a three-act play with substantial incidental music.[168] No specific attributions for the music are known, although eighteenth-century sources attribute the music to Henneberg, Gerl, and Schack. Perhaps Schikaneder or others helped with the music.

The score of this singspiel is less ambitious than that of *Der Stein der Weisen*. Instrumental numbers include two "magic marches," a serenade for wind ensemble, and a pantomime for the sea battle. The two brief men's choruses for the whirling dervishes in pseudo-Turkish are both magical numbers, occurring when Mandolino shakes the bells on his enchanted fool's cap. This seems a precursor to the scene with Papageno's magic bells in the first finale of *Die Zauberflöte*. (The bells also conjure the dervishes for March no. 12, and three beats of Sofrano's enchanted drum invoke March no. 6.) The Turkish musical style dominates in the first chorus (no. 7), while the second (no. 21), "Nino pani Turco cani," has more of a supernatural character, with its enchanted wind ensemble (clarinets, bassoons, and horns), cellos, and basses. The music is concise, with a limited range for the three male voice parts. But when performed repeatedly at a rapid pace (or at an increasingly faster tempo), this chorus of-

168. Early Viennese performing parts, perhaps from the Wiednertheater, survive in the archive of the Theater an der Wien, now in A-Wn, Fonds 116, TW 546A. A Viennese prompter's book survives in A-Wst, MH 10691. Of the four surviving full scores, the Frankfurt (D-F, Mus Hs Opern 509), Budapest (H-Bn, IV S II E 197-1), and Český Krumlov copies (castle archive, shelfmark 49 K17) are Viennese in origin. The music is attributed to Henneberg in the Budapest score, which has the name of the impresario Ferenc (Friedrich) Bulla on the title page, with the date 1791. Mozart's name appears twice on the binding of the Frankfurt score. A copy in D-Mbs, shelfmark St. Th. 382, not Viennese, is anonymous. A label on the binding appears to have attributed the music to Mozart. This was later erased and replaced with "W. Müller," and the library has erroneously catalogued it as an opera by Wenzel Müller. Parts attributed to Wenzel Müller survive in D-Hs, ND VII 277; the score is lost. Müller is also cited as the composer on the title page of the manuscript libretto in Mannheim. The attribution to Müller is probably the result of an early error. An engraved edition of "Wir sind die zwei lustigen Leutchen vom Land" (Dresden: Hilscher, n.d., copy in Prague's National Music Museum, shelfmark XLC.197) falsely attributes the duet to Müller.

fers an effective evocation of whirling dervishes. Its wit resides in the shifting rhythmic patterns in the almost steady eighth-note surface rhythm. The "pa-pa-pa" text may have inspired the comic encounter between Papageno and Papagena in the second finale of *Die Zauberflöte*.[169]

One of the intriguing roles in this singspiel is the magician-king disguised as a dervish. Franz Gerl, the original Sarastro, almost certainly created the role. His two moralizing arias, his magical appearance in the powerful accompanied recitative in C minor (no. 20), and his part in the first duet (with Sofrano) are all in the solemn ceremonial (*feierlich*) style; they probably influenced Mozart when he composed Sarastro's music. The duet actually contains a melodic phrase that Mozart quotes in the first finale of *Die Zauberflöte*. The dervish sings "Du reichtest Trank und Speise mir" in F major; this is the same melody in the same key as Sarastro's line "Ein Mann muss eure Herzen leiten" (act 1, scene 18). The first aria, "So bald der Mann ist all zu gut," an Adagio in E-flat, is a moralistic admonition. The second aria, the substantial bipartite "Bald wird auch dieser Traum vorübergehn," begins as a slow prayer. The bravura Allegro section has repeated incantatory motives with dotted rhythms and descending octave leaps.

Ludwig Herzog von Steiermark, oder Sarmäts Feuerbär, a four-act play "arranged from an old folk fairy tale" (*alten Volksmärchen*), by Eleonore and Emanuel Schikaneder (3 August 1791),[170] included some anonymous songs and instrumental music (lost). Fairy tales, Shakespeare, *Sturm und Drang*, and gothic horror all contribute to the story, which, like other "enlightened" theatrical fairy tales, concerns the proper use of aristocratic divine right, here in a medieval setting. Karlmann, the corrupt young cousin of Duke Ludwig, has usurped the duchy. Only one count has remained loyal, Ernst. Ludwig is imprisoned and Ernst condemned to death. Only the powerful magician Sarmät can save them. He reads the future in his magic mirror and conjures magic fire. Sarmät also possesses a magic shawm, a powerful wand, and a hammer that can make one mad or restore sanity. A terrifying "fire bear" guards his enchanted cavern in the Styrian Alps, and Sarmät appears with thunder, lightning, and a magic fire log that is not consumed. The peasant dairyman Mathies and his wife Trautel help him to restore the duke to power and punish Karlmann. The tone, characters, and wording are like Schikaneder's other librettos, for example the *geharnischten Männer* and the comic episodes. Less than

169. See the musical example in Buch, "Mozart and the Theater auf der Wieden," 228–29.

170. Published in *Emmanuel Schikaneders sämmtliche theatralische Werke* (Vienna: Aloys Doll, 1792), 2:5–119. The frontispiece of the volume is an engraved illustration by Clemens Kohl from act 4, scene 3, showing Trautel with Ludwig. The fire bear and the cave appear in the background. A poster dated 2 August 1791 and preserved in A-Wgm announces the *ganz neues Schauspiel* for the next day and attributes it to Eleonore Schikaneder. Deutsch, *Die Freihaustheater*, states that the work was performed in the presence of Leopold II and the Archduke Franz but offers no documentation of the visit. Komorzynski, *Emanuel Schikaneder*, 356, cites it as a work written in 1781 but provides no evidence for this date, which contradicts Schikaneder's own poster.

two months after the premiere of *Ludwig Herzog* Schikaneder introduced his new *große Oper* in two acts with music by Mozart, *Die Zauberflöte*.[171]

Schikaneder's main competition continued to be the Theater in der Leopoldstadt, which produced revivals of earlier singspiels as well as new works, many of which used fairy tales and other supernatural sources. The company revised *Die Hexe Megäre*, an anonymous setting probably based on Hafner's play, with new music by Anton [Franz Josef] Eberl (3 July 1790).[172] In 1791 a young librettist named Joachim Perinet produced his first singspiel, *Kaspars Zögling, oder Der Sieg der Beständigkeit [sic; Bescheidenheit] auf der Insel des Vergnügens*, with music by Ferdinand Kauer (1 February 1791).[173] Karl Friedrich Hensler wrote a four-act *Zauberoper* entitled *Kasperl, der glückliche Vogelkrämer*, with music by the theater's *Kapellmeister*, Wenzel Müller (3 March 1791). The text and music for all three of these singspiels appear to be lost. Another fairy-tale singspiel by Perinet would become one of the most popular in the era, *Kaspar der Fagottist, oder Die Zauberzither*, with music by Müller (8 June 1791). The premiere occurred a few months after that of *Der wohltätige Derwisch* and capitalized on Schikaneder's success with Wieland's *Dschinnistan*. The opera was performed forty-five times in the second half of 1791 and continued to be a favorite in German theaters well into the nineteenth century. The literary quality was criticized, and later writers revised the text (Munich, 1795; Rostock, 1796).[174] Mozart tersely dismissed the opera in a letter to his wife (12 June 1791): "there is nothing to it." Was he referring to the music, the text, or perhaps both? The similarities between this libretto and *Die Zauberflöte* result from their common source, "Lulu, oder die Zauberflöte" in *Dschinnistan*. But compared to Schikaneder's librettos, *Der Fagottist* seems more episodic, disconnected and haphazardly constructed, as the synopsis demonstrates.

Armidoro, the prince of Eldorado, and his comic companion Kaspar Bita, encounter Perifirime, the starry queen (her name was derived from the Persian *peri*), during a hunt. Emerging from a rock, she tells them of her enemy, the evil magician Bosphoro, who stole her magic tinderbox and abducted her beautiful daughter Sidi. She gives Armidoro a magic ring that will change his appearance and a magic zither that arouses and calms emotion. If they ever find themselves in trouble they have only to call the name of her tiny genie, Pizichi,

---

171. Schikaneder continued to produce similar fairy-tale singspiels, including a three-act *Feenmärchen mit Maschinen und Gesäng [sic] und Chören* by Friedrich Spengler, *Der Zauberdrachen, oder Etwas für den Fasching* (no composer indicated, January 1792). The cast includes a Persian prince, a magician, a genie, and a tiny ghost. Giesecke wrote a heroic-comic opera in two acts, *Das Schlaraffenland*, that has a utopian fairy-tale plot and music by Schack and Gerl (23 June 1792). The singspiel appears to have been unsuccessful, and no text or music survives.

172. See White, "Eberl, Anton." The partial score at Český Krumlov, shelfmark 49b/1-2 K17, may be the music of Eberl.

173. Janetschek, "Joachim Perinet."

174. The libretto was published in the *Marinellische Schaubühne* (Vienna: Schmidt, 1791); Rommel, *Die Maschinenkomödie* (1935), 206–62, gives the text in a modern edition.

and she will send help to them. She conjures an air balloon that takes them to Bosphoro's residence, where they meet the portly guardian of the harem, Zumio. Armidoro transforms himself into an old man and sings with the zither, which enchants the birds. When the angry magician appears, Armidoro placates his fury with another song. This induces the magician to hire Armidoro as a court musician, hoping he can help to render women tractable. Although alone, Kaspar calls out "Pizichi," and a tiny genie appears with a large bassoon. Kaspar sings as he plays the instrument, accompanied by Pizichi, who plays on his own small bassoon. Zumio secretly listens and invites Kaspar to perform for the women of the harem, whom he torments as they spin. The magician enters with Armidoro and Kaspar; the latter makes seductive gestures to Palmire (Bosphoro's favorite) before he slips into the kitchen to eat. Armidoro then sings a ballad to Sidi, narrating a story about an abducted maiden. Kaspar emerges from the kitchen and plays a waltz that gradually enchants them all to dance. Bosphoro and Zumio even kiss each other, and soon Armidoro and Sidi are embracing, as are Kaspar and Palmire. Armidoro then suggests that Bosphoro dress more fashionably, and the magician and Zumio leave. Now Armidoro uses his ring to reveal his identity to Sidi. She tells him that Bosphoro keeps the magic tinderbox on his person at all times. Palmire warns them that Zumio and Bosphoro are returning. When the magician and the guardian try to kiss Sidi and Palmire, Armidoro and Kaspar play their instruments, and the music immobilizes the two men so that the women can escape their grasp. Bosphoro then wants to go sailing and reveals the magic tinderbox, with which he conjures a throng of spirits to prepare a seaside celebration. He is now suspicious of Armidoro and Kaspar, and he orders Zumio to drown them on their sea voyage after he conjures a storm.

As Kaspar flirts with Palmire, he invokes Pizichi to play the bassoon and enchant her. When Zumio interrupts them, Kaspar insists that he is giving Palmire a music lesson. Zumio demands a lesson as well, and the celebrated comic bassoon duet follows. Pizichi warns Kaspar of Bosphoro's plans to kill them, and the genie gives him a lock of hair that when wrapped around his little finger will save him from danger. Armidoro tells Kaspar of a small magic ball that will protect him. Pizichi gives them two shields that will make the men invisible. Kaspar and Armidoro escape with the women, but Bosphoro pursues them. Perifirime appears in a cloud and invokes a storm, destroying the boats with a thunderbolt. Pizichi makes the storm recede, and the Tritons save them from drowning.

Bosphoro now plans to poison the two musicians at a feast. Pizichi informs Armidoro of the poisoned food and drink and tells him how to counteract the effect of the poison. Bosphoro's slaves attack Kaspar, who plays his bassoon to make them to stop. When Zumio then attacks him, four little genies play their bassoons, enchanting the slaves. They seize Zumio, toss him in the air, and spin him around until he collapses. The genies blast their bassoons in Zumio's ears, and he staggers into Bosphoro's dining room, where the magician has prepared a feast for the harem and the court. Bosphoro summons Armidoro and Kaspar, and a set table rises from the earth. He commands the two musicians to play cheerful music, and Zumio sings as the women dance in a circle. Bosphoro then insists that they drink the poisoned wine, but Armidoro and Kaspar play a lullaby that puts all the people to sleep. Armidoro takes the magic tinderbox from Bosphoro. When the guardian spirits awake and see Armidoro with the magic tinderbox, they sink to their knees in obedience. Armidoro turns his ring and restores his appearance, then awakens the others. Bosphoro and Zumio awake and try to attack the lovers, but the guardian spirits defend them. Armidoro holds out the tinderbox and declares that Perifirime has been avenged. Thunder announces the arrival of Perifirime and Pizichi. The fairy condemns the magician and Zumio to three hundred years in the depths of the earth. They sink with the table in a thick cloud amid a great clatter. The fairy awards Armidoro the hand of Sidi, who will become the queen of Eldorado. The stage changes into the palace of Perifirime; the lovers embrace, and all celebrate their triumph in the final chorus.

Der Fagottist was more of a number opera than either *Der Stein der Weisen* or *Die Zauberflöte*.[175] Despite the large orchestra (flutes, oboes, clarinets, bassoons, trumpets, horns, strings, timpani, and a *tambura grande*), this is a relatively modest score with relentless diatonic sonority relieved only by occasional dramatic moments where minor modes or chromatic inflections occur. The choruses use only homophonic textures. However, the music has its virtues, despite several trite numbers. Müller's memorable overture has a freshness and playfulness that should endear it to modern audiences. One finds only a few instances of musical representation of the many supernatural effects required by the libretto. These include the use of bassoons and horn as magic instruments. A magic bassoon appears in act 2, scene 12, where Kaspar gives a comic music lesson to the bumbling Zumio.[176] In act 3, scene 14, Kaspar plays his magic bassoon and repulses Zumio's slaves (*Geister* in the vocal score), forcing them to sing the two-part chorus "Faß an, faß an, trala la la," scored for flutes, horns, oboe, bassoons, strings, and *tambura grande*. Four little genies with their bassoons force Zumio to spin until he falls exhausted. The indication is "attacca Fagotti," and a monophonic marchlike piece serves as magic music,[177] followed by a few measures of orchestral music in waltz rhythms (see ex. 5.8).

175. The surviving musical sources include a full orchestral score, a late eighteenth-century Viennese manuscript in A-Wn, Mus. Hs. 25253. An early nineteenth-century Viennese piano-vocal score survives in A-Wst, M.H. 227. There are number of divergences between the orchestral score and the printed vocal score. Subsequent librettos published for productions in different locations also indicate changes. The 1795 revised text with new musical additions was prepared for Frankfurt. An early nineteenth-century score (c. 1805) and performing materials survive in D-F, Mus Hs Opern 406. An orchestral score from c. 1795 survives in D-Hs, ND VII 270.

176. A piano-vocal score of this number is in Glossy and Haas, *Wiener Comödienlieder*, 50–57.

177. The Wiednertheater composers also use the march similarly. In *Die Zauberflöte* Mozart suggests a lockstep trance in the scenes with the magic bells and in the duet of Papageno and Papagena in act 2 (see chapter 6 for details).

EXAMPLE 5.8 Wenzel Müller, *Kaspar der Fagottist*, act 3, scene 14

An aria and chorus for Kaspar and the slaves follow, "Pack an, faß an trala la la, pack an, faß an, he hopsasa." Magic sleep music occurs in act 3 (no. 22), starting with a slow duet for Armidoro's bassoon and Kaspar's zither (played by pizzicato strings in triplets). Horns, flutes, oboes, clarinets, bassoons, and strings then accompany the duet. An Andantino section in 3/4 features the clarinets and bassoons playing a conjunct melody in octaves with violas, for which cellos and basses provide the support. The violins join the accompaniment for the repeat, then the flutes, followed by the oboes and the horns. The harmony is elementary and the melodies are consistently symmetrical, so the listener's attention focuses on the changing timbres. Thus Müller, like the Wiednertheater composers, knew how to create inventive, popular-styled music to please his audience, even if it was more or less pedestrian.

German Opera in the North

Northern German theaters also produced oriental fairy-tale singspiels. Ludwig Tieck began writing his fairy-tale plays in 1790,[178] and Anton Walter Schwick translated Gozzi's *fiabe* for Bonn in the same year.[179] The fairy-tale singspiels of August von Kotzebue enjoyed greater success. Viennese singspiels such as *Oberon* may have inspired Kotzebue's three-act opera *Der Spiegelritter,* with music by Ignaz Walter (Frankfurt, National Theater, 11 September 1791).[180] In his preface Kotzebue notes that his opera is "in the contemporary style" (*nach heutigem Zuschnitt*), and indeed, this oriental fairy-tale plot recalls the material from *Dschinnistan* that Schikaneder borrowed for his *Der wohltätige Derwisch.*[181] At times the librettist parodies the fairy-tale genre, using extreme images in odd juxtapositions while ridiculing the lack of verisimilitude.

178. See Zeydel, *Ludwig Tieck,* 24–25.

179. These include *Die wiedergefunde Statue,* with music by Bernhard Heinrich Romberg (text and music lost), 1790. See Stephenson, "Romberg, Bernhard Heinrich." According to Stephenson, "Romberg, Andreas Jakob," the three-act singspiel *Das blaue Ungeheuer,* with music by Andreas Jakob Romberg (1790–93), was never performed. Stieger, *Opernlexikon,* Teil II, 3:941, cites *Der Rabe,* a four-act singspiel by Walter Anton Schwink with music by Andreas Jacob Romberg (1791). *The Mellen Opera Reference Index,* 4:1542, cites a performance in Hamburg's Deutsches Nationaltheater on 7 April 1794 as a three-act *tragi-kom. Märchen.* Incomplete parts survive in D-Hs, shelfmark ND VII 329. The exact date of origin is uncertain. No score or libretto has been located. Several instrumental numbers appear in the parts, for example "Das Racheopfer," a "Marcia," and melodramas in acts 1 and 3.

180. Full scores survive in D-F, Mus Hs Opern 600; and D-B, Mus. ms. 22520, D-Hs (ND VII 417). Walter also wrote music for another magic singspiel, Wilhelm Schreiber's *Die Harfe* 1793 (lost).

181. The libretto (N.p., n.d., US-Wc, Schatz 10865a) includes an engraving of the scene with the dead giant and a short biographical essay on the life of Musäus. The Reiß-Museum has two manuscript librettos from a performance in Mannheim on 2 November 1793. Bauman, *North German Opera,* 277–78, provides a brief synopsis and cites a contemporary criticism of its low literary

The opera begins on the seashore of Dunnistan, where a ship is being loaded. Prince Almador stands in his armor with his father, the king, and his court. The king has ordered his pampered son to pursue a dangerous quest in order to learn virtue and experience true love. The king asks him to select a shield bearer from the pages. Almador selects the cowardly and boastful Schmurzo. An old magician named Burrudusussusu appears and gives Almador a blue shield with a magic mirror that darkens when danger is near. Almador travels to the Black Island, where the giant Kroxbox guards the palace of the beautiful Queen Milmi. An evil magician whom Milmi rejected has enchanted the queen, turning her into a cannibal with a raging hunger for human flesh. A storm wrecks Almador's ship, and the prince uses his shield to defeat the queen's dragon. Almador and Schmurzo then swim ashore and meet Kroxbox. Almador fights the giant, using his shield to stun and then kill him. Almador and Schmurzo attempt to enter the palace but are refused. The women lower food and wine to them, but Almador consults his shield and learns that the food is poisoned. Next a dwarf appears with silver dishes and a gold goblet, offering them refreshment. Almador refuses this poisoned food as well. Finally they enter the palace and arrive in a splendid bedchamber provided with more poisoned food. Schmurzo invokes Burrudusussusu, and a small genie appears with safe food and drink. They eat and two maidens arrive with a zither, saying the queen sent them for entertainment. After they sing the men to sleep, Milmi enters with two other maidens carrying daggers. Milmi tries to stab Almador, but the prince awakes and stops her. Milmi swears vengeance and falls into a faint. The maidens now tell of Milmi's curse, a spell that will not be broken until Milmi sees herself in a mirror as a bride. The queen awakes and sings of her rage until Almador lifts his shield in front of her. The music suddenly changes to a "soft, melting Adagio," and her song becomes blissful. She asks Almador to rule the island as her bridegroom, and the curse is dispelled. Almador's parents appear with their court, led by Burrudusussusu. All thank the magician, and a chorus and ensemble end the opera.

Although the libretto reveals the growing influence of popular Viennese fairy-tale opera in northern Germany, Walter's score departs from those of most of his Viennese counterparts. The composer employed the Italian style in his ensembles and finales, written as a series of fluid, rapidly unfolding episodes that stress continuity over the Viennese romantic contrast of abruptly changing tableaus and musical styles. Walter interweaves references to supernatural images in the continuous musical discourse. Even the bass voices of the magician Burrudusussusu and the giant Kroxbox have music that is only rarely different from that of the human characters. There is no musical accompaniment to the scene where Almador kills the dragon; it is reported rather than depicted onstage.

---

value in the *Zeitung für Theater und andere schöne Künste* 7 (1793): 129–30. Carl Christian Agthe (Ballenstädt, 1795) and August Himbert Hinze (Waldenburg, 1797) also set the libretto.

In the act 1 finale the magician appears and gives the shield with its magic mirror to Almador, accompanied by a D major fanfare with trumpets, horns, and timpani added to the strings. The magician reappears at the end of the act 3 finale, during an Allegro molto in A major, with no magical allusions in the score. The giant Kroxbox enters at the end of the ensemble in act 2, no. 11, depicted by sixteenth-note string tremolos and timpani rolls. The trumpets play in dotted rhythms on his word "Sturm," and the strings have rapid ascending scales. Kroxbox's threatening aria (no. 12) is in C major, marked "Allegro maestoso" and scored for horns, trumpets, timpani, and strings. With its ritornello and repeated text, the number recalls Italian rage arias. Walter accompanies the leaps in the vocal line with rapid descending and ascending scales, dotted repeated-note figures for strings and trumpets, and timpani rolls. The unusual harmonic progression here also seems inspired by the grotesquely threatening nature of the giant (C–G–E-flat–G minor–G). The C major duet (No. 15) for Kroxbox and Schmurzo has a dancelike 3/8 meter (Andante poco focoso) with sixty-fourth-note figures in the violins and thirty-second-note figures in the trumpets and horns to suggest Schmurzo's trembling. Kroxbox sings a short exclamation at the end of the duet, "Ha! Ein Spiegel!," as he looks into the mirror and is stunned. Ascending scalar figures for the bass and violins introduce this segment, leading to a C minor episode when Almador kills the giant to the sound of repeated sixty-fourth notes. A decrescendo depicts his death. Although the music for the dwarf (soprano) in the finale of act 3 seems unremarkable, the duet segment for Schmurzo and the raging Milmi is noteworthy. She sings a curse much like Mozart's Queen of the Night, "Fluch über Dich! den bittersten Fluch," a quadruple-meter Allegro in D major with a descending vocal line marked by wide leaps and a long coloratura passage. Almador disenchants Milmi with the magic mirror, and her music returns without the coloratura and accompanied by rapid descending violin scales. An Allegro molto duet for Milmi and Schmurzo (scored with trumpets and timpani) soon changes to a duple-meter Adagio in F major, an enchanted wind ensemble with flutes, clarinets, horns, and bassoons (marked "piano e dolce"). On hearing this magical music Milmi sings "Ha! How soft and lovely!" The libretto specifies that the music immediately becomes the most soft and liquid ("sanfteste, schmelzendste") Adagio.[182]

---

182. Kotzebue wrote another successful fairy-tale opera, *Sultan Wampum, oder Die Wuensche*, a three-act *orientalisches Scherzspiel* with music by the tenor Carl David Stegmann (lost), set for Mainz National Theater, 3 December 1791 (Stieger), and performed in Hamburg in 1792. This is a darkly comic story based on a commedia dell'arte plot in which magic rings change the appearance of those who wear them. A libretto from a 1794 performance survives in US-Wc, Schatz 10042, and Schatz 11749 (N.p., n.d.).

✦

CHAPTER SIX

The Supernatural in the Operas of Mozart

Having firsthand knowledge of opera, ballet, comedy and pantomime in Italy, France, and German lands, Mozart skillfully utilized the full range of expressive musical devices in his operas, including otherworldly imagery. His expressive range also incorporated the "learned style" and other features associated with sacred music (e.g., chant and modal sonority), which could be employed for supernatural episodes. Although Mozart's awareness of the recent Franco-Italian synthesis in opera is perhaps most apparent in *Lucio Silla* and *Idomeneo*, *Don Giovanni*, and *Die Zauberflöte* also contain elements of the French "marvelous," which few commentators have identified or discussed in depth.[1] Indeed, Mozart's student Joseph Frank recalled that the composer studied the French operatic scores of Grétry, Gluck, Piccinni, and Salieri for their dramatic effects.[2] Mozart mentions a number of supernatural operas in his letters, including Grétry's *Zémire et Azor*, Prati's *Armida abbandonata*, Jommelli's opera of the same title, Piccinni's *Roland* (1778), Umlauf's *Das Irrlicht* (1781–82), and Müller's singspiel *Kaspar der Fagottist* (1791). He also saw a pantomime ballet of the fairy tale *Die sieben Schwaben* in Salzburg, Wranitzky's *Oberon, König der Elfen* in Frankfurt, and fairy-tale operas in Vienna.

Although Leopold Mozart disdained the fairy-tale and supernatural elements of Viennese musical comedy, his son appears to have enjoyed them. In his letter to Lorenz Hagenauer (30 January–February 1768)[3] Leopold provides a list of reprehensible elements on the Viennese stage, deriding the "närrisches

---

1. Although Mozart's *Così fan tutte* is not a supernatural opera, the composer used devices associated with the marvelous genres. I discuss this in Buch, *"Così fan tutte, La scuola degli amanti and L'école des amans."*

2. Deutsch, *Mozart: Die Dokumente*, 476.

3. See Bauer-Deutsch, 4:254.

zeug, tanzen, teufel, gespenster, Zaubereyen, Hanswurst, Lipperl, Bernardon, Hexen, und Erscheinungen" (foolish implements, devils, ghosts, magic, Hanswurst, Lipperl, Bernardon, witches, and apparitions). Like audiences in Catholic Vienna and Prague, Wolfgang had a taste for the fantastic and the supernatural,[4] of which Mozart's own attempt at a magic comedy, *Die Liebesprobe,* is the best evidence. This draft begins with comic scenes for a dwarf, a giant, and a sorceress.[5] His interest in Schikaneder's Wiednertheater is evident in a letter to his wife in the spring (2 June?) of 1790, where he expressed a preference for *Die zween Anton* over Schikaneder and Schack's sequel to Martín y Soler's *Una cosa rara,* entitled *Der Fall ist noch weit seltner* (May 1790).[6]

Of course *Die Zauberflöte* testifies to Mozart's interest in Viennese fairy-tale opera, but Mozart was also involved to some degree in providing the music of Schikaneder's fairy-tale singspiel *Der Stein der Weisen, oder Die Zauberinsel.* There is yet more evidence of Mozart's taste for fairy tales. The composer knew and admired Wieland, the editor of *Dschinnistan,* the fairy-tale collection from which Schikaneder created the librettos of *Der Stein der Weisen* and *Die Zauberflöte,* and he owned a copy of Wieland's epic poem *Oberon.* Mozart praised the popular collection of oriental fairy tales *A Thousand and One Nights,*[7] and an account printed in 1799 tells of Constanze Mozart reading fairy tales to her husband on the night before the premiere of *Don Giovanni.* The two specified tales, "Aladdin's Lamp" and "Aschenputterln" (Cinderella), represent both Arabian and French types of fairy tales.[8]

Mozart's Early Operas

The early operas of Mozart show a variety of marvelous and supernatural devices, both in comic and serious works. Mozart's first German comic opera, *Bastien und Bastienne,* K. 50 (46b), an adaptation by Friedrich Wilhelm Weiskern and Johann Müller of Rousseau's *Le devin du village* of 1752 (and the Favart parody), was composed for Vienna sometime in 1768. Mozart sets the

4. Pezzl, *Skizze von Wien,* noted that Vienna was still in its initial stages of giving up its prejudices and remained staunchly unenlightened. Cited in Braunbehrens, *Mozart in Vienna: 1781–1791,* 128.

5. Bauer-Deutsch, 4:168–73.

6. *Die zween Anton* refers to the series of comic operas entitled *Der dumme Gärtner aus dem Gebürge, oder Die zween Antons,* parts 1–3.

7. In his letter of 21 July 1770, Mozart writes to his sister: "ich habe die Tausend und eine Nacht in italienischer Sprache von unserer Hausfrau zu Rom schenken bekommen; es ist recht lustig zu lesen." For details on Mozart's literary tastes, see Valentin, "Mozart und die Dichtung," 90.

8. A report in the *Allgemeine Musikalische Zeitung* 19 (6 February 1799), col. 290, attributed to Constanze Mozart, reports that Mozart enjoyed fairy tales. Translated in Eisen, *New Mozart Documents,* 78.

false-magic incantation by Colas as an aria, "Diggi, daggi, schurry, murry" (no. 10). Johann Andreas Schachtner text combined nonsense language and garbled, fragmentary Latin ("quid quo pro"). Mozart's accompaniment to the Andante maestoso in C minor ridicules the operatic style of invocation. A steady pulsating bass in eighth notes supports a slow and simple vocal line with repeated notes and pompously wide leaps. The two oboes play mostly whole and half notes, enhancing the ominous bass line with sustained winds. The strings accompany with rapid scalar figures and repeated notes, reminiscent of a *bruit souterrain;* a few measures with polyphony in the inner voices may actually parody Rameau's counterpoint.

Mozart's first serious opera, *Mitridate, rè di Ponto,* K. 87/74a, on a text by Amadeo Cigna-Santi for Milan (1770), contains an *ombra* scene in act 3 for Aspasia (no. 21), a cavatina enclosed by two accompanied recitatives. The C minor aria in act 3 for Sifare quotes Gluck's *Orfeo ed Euridice* ("Che fiero momento") during an Allegro agitato, with syncopated rhythms and strong dissonance. Mozart's awareness of Gluck's most celebrated supernatural music is not surprising. Although not an opera, Mozart's 1771 oratorio for Salzburg, the text of which is Metastasio's *Betulia liberata,* K. 188/74c, begins with a tripartite D minor *overtura.* This piece culminates in a final section in 2/4 that recalls Gluck's infernal scene in *Don Juan.*

The composer's first major operatic success was *Lucio Silla,* K. 135, with a libretto by Giovanni De Gamerra (Milan, 1772), which contains two *ombre* scenes. Giunia first invokes the ghost of her dead father in the act 1 aria in E-flat, "Dalla sponda tenebrosa" (no. 4). But the true *ombra* episode follows the next aria, set in a tomb for Roman military heroes (scenes 5–8). Beginning with an Andante instrumental prelude (in A minor, but starting on the Neapolitan, B-flat), a solemn funeral march commences with striding, processional rhythms. Short ascending scale bursts soon accompany the obsessive repeated notes; then the music explodes with blasts of infernal brass, which will become the punctuating instrumental interjections in the interpolated accompanied recitative for Cecilio, "Morte, morte fatal." When Cecilio enters the music modulates to C minor, continuing with violent scale figures, unstable modulation, and dotted rhythms. Sighing figures and ascending crescendo passages complement Cecilio's evocation of death and entombment. A violent passage signals his surprise as his beloved Giunia enters the tomb with her retinue. The chorus then sings their *lugubre canto,* "Fuor di queste urne," a dirge that begins with the Hadean horn chords of the previous number. Ascending scale bursts in the violins accompany the angry demand for revenge. In the following segment Giunia addresses her dead father, begging for pity in a soaring solo. Sustained strings accompany the following obbligato recitative, addressed to the deceased ("Tu pura ombra adorata"). The second *ombra* scene occurs in act 3, Giunia's scena and aria "Fra i pensier più funesti di morte" (no. 22).

Thamos and *Idomeneo*

The first stage music that Mozart wrote when he came of age was incidental music for Tobias Philipp Gebler's five-act play *Thamos, König in Ägypten*, K. 345/336a (Salzburg, 1776; rev. 1779–80). Never was the composer closer to Gluck's and Benda's expression of violent force than in this music, particularly the choruses and melodramas. Mozart had been impressed by this use of instrumental accompaniment to spoken text, and he composed similar symphonic music in the terrifying style for the entr'actes (*Zwischenakten*). Using the keys of C minor, E-flat, G minor, and D minor, he employs the full range of infernal and storm imagery, with portentous opening chords in dotted rhythms, octave-and-unison sonority, rapid scales, chromatic passages, blaring winds, and string tremolos. For the final punishment of the deities (in D minor), the composer writes characteristic explosive scale figures in the basses, which are then imitated in the upper strings.

Mozart's *Idomeneo*, K. 366 (1780–81), masterfully exploits the new expressive force that Jommelli, Traetta, and Gluck developed in their theatrical music. Two supernatural episodes in acts 1 and 3 can serve as examples. The first, a storm at sea, is actually anticipated by the psychological storm expressed in Elettra's accompanied recitative and aria "Tutte nel cor vi sento," addressed to the Furies (scene 6). This vengeance aria is a terrifying invocation of forces from the underworld, set in the Dorian D minor, with eighth-note "murky" bass figures, scales in the flutes (perhaps suggestive of lightning?), string tremolos with a crescendo, bellowing horns, and *alla zoppa* syncopation. The vocal line has an obsessive repetition of motives, with leaps and *sforzandos*. The midway point is a fully diminished seventh chord that leads to a repeat of the opening material, now in C minor, anticipating the key of the choral storm scene that follows the aria. This harmonic relationship reinforces the impression that Elettra's violent emotions invoke divinely guided forces in nature. Two male choruses, one near and the other at a distance, cry out for divine mercy. The scene culminates in a pantomime where Neptune appears and calms the seas, depicted in the short instrumental interlude that begins scene 8; this modulates to a serene E-flat recitative that leads to Idomeneo's *ombra* aria in C major.

The second supernatural episode, recalling a traditional oracle scene (act 3, scene 10, no. 28), is in C minor. Scored with three trombones, two horns, and bass voice, it begins with three sustained wind chords, C minor–D^7–G, a quasi-modal, somber sonic image that continues throughout the number.[9] The

9. There are four different settings of this scene, one of them without trombones. Leopold Mozart mentions the scene in a letter of 29 December 1780, in which he advises his son to choose "very deep wind instruments to accompany the subterranean voice" and suggests dramatic crescendos and decrescendos to "almost inspire terror" (*bis ins Schröckliche*); Bauer-Deutsch 3, no. 572, 73–75. Mozart wrote back on 3 January 1781 that he accompanied the subterranean voice

choice of three flats here is consistent with the key used for underworld scenes and supernatural references in Italian and French opera. The harmony is disorienting; perhaps it evoked an association of supernatural Italian court opera of the seventeenth century. This harmony, along with the trombones and the oracular bass voice, appears to have served as a model for the graveyard scene in *Don Giovanni*.[10]

Inferno in the Comic Theater: *Il dissoluto punito o sia il Don Giovanni*

Most nineteenth-century commentators saw Don Giovanni as a heroic character, irresistible to women and personifying courage in the face of death and damnation.[11] No such interpretations existed in the eighteenth century, when Don Juan was described as anything but admirable. For La Serre in 1734, Don Juan was simply a villain, made more odious by his black deeds and hypocrisy.[12] Cailhava de l'Estandoux (1772) finds Don Juan to be "a man hateful for his crimes."[13] For the late eighteenth-century writer Johann Friedrich Schink, he was

> the craziest, most nonsensical malformation of an errant Spanish fantasy. A most lewd, base, nefarious fellow, whose life is an unbroken series of infamies, murders, and seductions of innocents. A hypocrite and religious scoffer, an abject rake, a crafty deceiver, double-dealer and a fop, the most treacherous, cruel *beast,* a villain without conscience or honor. He commits the greatest atrocities as coolly as if he were drinking up a glass of water; he stabs a man as if he were going to a dance, seduces and betrays

---

with three trombones and two French horns, placed near the vocalist (Bauer-Deutsch 3, no. 574, 79–80).

10. Other musical devices in *Don Giovanni* recall *Idomeneo*, e.g., the repeated descending-octave incantation motive sung by Idomeneo in the act 3 quartet ("Nettun spietato!"), and in the second finale of *Don Giovanni*, especially for the statue's music. The vocal line of the infernal spirits in the second finale of *Don Giovanni* recalls the unison monotone recitation of the priests in the aria with chorus, "Accogli, o rè del mar" (act 3, scene 7).

11. For an accurate edition of Da Ponte's libretto with its variant readings in the printed sources and autograph manuscript, see Da Ponte, *Il Don Giovanni*.

12. De La Serre, *Mémoires*, xxxi: "un scélérat odieux par ses noirceurs et par son hypocrisie." Cited in Lagrave, "Don Juan," 267. Lagrave states that the church and the moralists consistently condemned the story, asserting that it not only represented "les vices les plus horribles," but also taught the audience how to commit them.

13. Cailhava de l'Estandoux, *De l'art de la comédie*, 2:191. (Page numbers here and in other citations refer to the 1970 edition.) Cailhava regards the Don Juan story as absurd, superstitious, and supernatural. He blames the superstitious nature of Italians and Spanish for the interest in the story, and he believes that the plot's lack of verisimilitude consists as much in the ill-mannered behavior in which the Don indulges as in the supernatural element. As an example, he notes that a nobleman simply would never do such things as sit with his servant.

female virtue as if he were taking a pinch of snuff. And all these abomina-
tions amuse him, he thinks all these *bestialities* a lot of fun.[14]

The Don Juan story originated in a tradition of demonic morality plays;
early titles such as *L'ateista fulminato* stressed the theological aspect. Thomas
Shadwell claimed to have based his five-act tragedy *The Libertine* (London, 1675) on *L'ateista fulminato*, a play that he was told was performed in
"Churches, on Sundays, as a part of Devotion."[15] *Le festin de pierre* comedies
and pantomimes were common at the fair theaters in Paris, which were active
in yearly periods linked to the church calendar. Devil and ghost plays such as
the Don Juan plays functioned in a quasi-religious context in Vienna (and in
other cities of the Austrian Empire), often performed during the autumn octave of All Souls' Day, when the Requiem mass was sung. Opera in Italy also
was linked to the church calendar, particularly during Carnival season (Bertati's *Don Giovanni* was first performed in Venice during Carnival). Underworld
scenes occur in the comic traditions of various Catholic centers of Europe, and
the large number of musical stage works with these episodes detailed in chapter
5 demonstrates that the Viennese had a particular taste for them.[16]

Seventeenth-century versions of the Don Juan story from Tirso de Molina
to Molière offered a similar series of episodes demonstrating Don Juan's various sins. In the course of the eighteenth century many of these episodes van-
ished as the theological aspect receded into the background in favor of comedy, spectacle, and music. By the 1780s the Don Juan story was outdated but
still familiar. This is apparent in the model for Da Ponte's setting, Bertati's *Don
Giovanni Tenorio, o sia Il convitato di pietra*. This opera was the second of a pair
of one-act operas by Bertati, the first being the prologue entitled *Il capriccio
drammatico*. In this "dramatic caprice" a troupe of Italian actors in Germany
debates the merits of the Don Juan story. The singer Ninetta objects, saying:
"The plot is improbable. The libretto does not follow the rules. The music cannot be described." For an enlightened comedy troupe, *Don Giovanni* was a con-
cession to the "rabble" (*popolazzo*). Rather than a novelty, it was "rather an old
thing, moreover an invention about [hell's] roasting pit" (*vecchia all'opposto,
più ancor dell'invenzion del Menarosto*).

The title of Da Ponte's text, *Il dissoluto punito, o sia Il Don Giovanni*, departs
from the model of Bertati's *Don Giovanni, o sia Il convitato di pietra* by stressing
the punishment of the dissolute sinner. The term "Il dissoluto" was taken from

14. From Schink, *Dramatische Monate*. Translations in Nagel, *Autonomy and Mercy*, 112, and in
Braunbehrens, *Mozart in Vienna: 1781–1791*, 306–7.

15. From the preface to Shadwell, *The Libertine*, 27. Quoted in Russell, *The Don Juan Legend*, 15.

16. After the demons take Giovanni to hell, Leporello refers to "fumo e fuoco," while Bertati's
Pasquariello refers to "I Diavoli, il foco, il Commendatore . . . sentite il fetore," presumably the
stench of sulfur, which remained on his clothing.

Goldoni, who took it from Molière's "le dissolu." Da Ponte's text is at times more serious than Bertati's, and he reintroduces the older moralistic demonstrations of sin, such as the graveyard scene where Don Giovanni strikes the tombstones (in Tirso de Molina's play he pulls the statue's beard). This text, along with the vivid music supplied by Mozart, makes this opera somewhat atypical for the period.

In the earliest version of his memoirs, Da Ponte recounts that Mozart received the *Don Giovanni* commission in the form of the one-act *dramma giocoso* by Bertati.[17] Both men would have known that this opera might be especially popular in Vienna during the week of All Souls' Day. Mozart probably found Bertati's short libretto inadequate and turned to Da Ponte, commissioning the writer to expand the text into two acts. The librettist's challenge was to vary the hackneyed plot by adding new twists that would entertain an audience already familiar with the story. This challenge is also evident in the Bertati model, as the one-act prefatory opera, *Il capriccio drammatico*, makes clear. Thus, like Bertati, Mozart and Da Ponte introduced new material.[18] Both librettist and composer enhanced the serious moral component, adding new comic elements and increasing the incipient horrific aspect of the piece.

Like the connection of Don Juan to All Souls' Day, Da Ponte's addition of moralistic material in the libretto seems to have been neglected in modern commentary, as has Mozart's use of supernatural musical conventions in the score, found primarily in the overture and the second finale. By examining these aspects one sheds new light on the persistent question of the degree to which Mozart invested the work with "serious" musical elements, a claim made by Da Ponte himself.[19] One can partially answer this question by assessing the moral and religious references in both the music and the text. Although these elements operate in the background of this mostly "comic" libretto, they offer insight into a unique balance of comedy and terror.

✳

The juxtaposition of comic and terrifying music is striking in *Don Giovanni*, and Mozart again would effectively employ this opposition in *Die Zauberflöte*. Humor sets off the serious moments in the opera and relieves the tension aroused by the display of violence, terror, and erotic passion. Perhaps the best example

17. See Heartz, *Mozart's Operas*, 158.

18. For example, the musical citations in the so-called banquet scene (act 2, finale). See Armbruster, *Das Opernzitat*.

19. Francis, *Old New York*, 265–66; cited in Heartz, *Mozart's Operas*, 174. Da Ponte told Francis that Mozart conceived of *Don Giovanni* as a serious opera, while Da Ponte insisted on the comic elements, citing "Batti, batti," and "Là ci darem la mano" as examples of the latter. The classification of the act 1 duet as a comic number contradicts the received interpretation of it as a love duet where the seductive powers of Giovanni work their magic on the innocent Zerlina.

is the second finale, beginning with a comic parody that leads to the stunning damnation scene and a concluding ensemble that is first humorous, then sentimental, and finally moralizing. Compared to the comic librettos set by Bertoni, Cherubini, Sarti, Righini, and Naumann, Da Ponte's *Don Giovanni* seems to have greater contrasts, at once more comic and yet also more serious at appropriate moments. Mozart invested the libretto with music to match, starting with a violent and somber tone in the first bars of the overture, and employing conventions from recent French and Italian serious operas.

Which elements might a Prague audience on 29 October 1787 have perceived as "serious" in this opera? Which characters, episodes, or musical elements would have been seen as distinct from the comedy? Judging from his music, it is difficult to imagine that the Commendatore was an object of ridicule for the audience. Donna Anna, Donna Elvira, and Don Ottavio also seem to have received serious treatment by Mozart, if not in Da Ponte's text. (In the Don Juan literary tradition they can be parodies of the aristocracy, so one doesn't know if they always are to be taken at face value.) In any event, Da Ponte appears to have emphasized their serious character. The Commendatore, Anna, Elvira, and Ottavio all express sentiments from serious opera. Da Ponte even creates a direct contrast in the oaths of Ottavio and Giovanni (see below). And even if the court poet meant the righteous indignation and moralistic pronouncements of these serious characters to be taken as parody, Mozart provided some of his most profoundly serious music for these passages.

❋

Before he converted to Catholicism as a teenager, Da Ponte was Emmanuele Conegliano, the son of a Jewish tanner. He probably had a basic Jewish education as a child, before he trained as a priest and took orders in the church. Although this may not be the reason he enhanced the moralizing aspects over Bertati's libretto, it certainly provided him with the tools to do so. His main vehicles for moralizing are Anna and Elvira, with Leporello and the statue also contributing indignant comments.[20] Donna Elvira's line "Da quel ceffo si dovria la ner'alma giudicar" in the act 1 quartet hints at a diabolic image in describing Giovanni's face as revealing of his black soul (the word "ceffo" can denote an animal's snout). In act 2, scene 11, she delivers another moral condemnation with a vivid image when she refers to his remaining in the "foul stink, a horrible example of iniquity." The penultimate time she sings this line Mozart gives her a traditional incantation motive of infernal condemnation marked by descending octaves. Later the statue will sing this same motive, and it will be varied by the *coro di spiriti*. Unlike the light celebratory ending of

---

20. Leporello's humorous "libro stampato" comment (act 1, scene 4) is a response to Elvira's statement about Giovanni transgressing the laws "of earth and heaven."

the Bertati text, Da Ponte provides a moral to conclude the final sextet, which does not belong to the realm of enlightened thought, but to that of moralizing religion.

The Don Juan story concerns the sinful abuse of privileges by a member of the class endowed by heaven with those privileges. Da Ponte adheres to this older convention by demonstrating a number of sins for which the title character earns his damnation. At least six categories of infractions against Holy Scripture and humanity can be identified in the libretto. Da Ponte and Mozart's emphasis on only one sin, the final one that warrants the terrible punishment, is unique. Here then is *il catalogo* of the crimes of Da Ponte's Don Giovanni:[21]

1. The attempted rape of Donna Anna and Zerlina.
2. False oaths and feigned repentance. In act 1, scene 4 Giovanni takes an oath, "Lo giuro sul mio onore" (exactly as Ottavio did in the previous scene), and then promptly breaks his word. Later (act 2, scene 2) Giovanni proclaims falsely that "pentito io son già," words that he refuses to say when his life and soul depend on it in the finale. (The statue's repetitive demands and Giovanni's refusals to repent were not in the Bertati model.)
3. Blasphemy and abusing the secular and religious authority of the Commendatore and the ghost statue. In act 2, scene 11 he beats the tombstones with his sword, and the ghost of the Commendatore that inhabits the statue admonishes him (this action is not in the Bertati model). After receiving the statue's agreement to come to dinner, Giovanni remains undaunted. When the statue appears Giovanni sings, "I would not have believed it if I did not see it myself." Da Ponte has Giovanni scoffs at the statue, parodying its call to repent by rhyming with it ("Pentiti, scellerato!"—"No, vecchio infatuato!"). Mozart enhances this musically by having Giovanni throw the same melodic figure back at the Commendatore. In the course of the finale he mocks three ascending levels of existence: first he derides the lowborn in the figure of the servant Leporello, then he mocks his own aristocratic class in the form of Donna Elvira, and finally he scorns divinity in the form of the ghost of the Commendatore.
4. The abuse of the sacrament of marriage. Giovanni has committed both adultery and polygamy, and he has falsely promised marriage to hundreds of women. He reveals his strategy for seduction in an act 1 encounter with Zerlina, based on the Maturina episode in Bertati, which is, in turn, based on earlier models. Da Ponte calls this a comic duet for good reason. Although Giovanni sweetens the deal with flattery, from the beginning it is the promise of marriage and social elevation that interests Zerlina. This is apparent from the text in both the duet and the preceding recitative ("ci sposeremo"). Giovanni does not se-

---

21. I do not include the killing of the Commendatore among the crimes. This was a duel that Giovanni tried to avoid.

duce through revealing his heart or even some "irresistible charm," although directors usually stage the duet to suggest this. He seduces through lies, appealing to weaknesses that are not necessarily sexual in nature. Zerlina acquiesces only after she has extracted the promise of social elevation. Economics is the main aphrodisiac here, and Zerlina is also a manipulator.

5. Cruelty toward those in his service. He abuses Leporello throughout the opera. In act 1 he falsely accuses him of attempting to rape Zerlina. In act 2, scene 11, he tells Leporello that he would have no objection to seducing his wife. In act 2, scene 13, he torments the hungry Leporello, eating a meal in front of him and telling the audience how he enjoys watching his servant suffer. In act 2, scene 4, he tells a group of peasants how to find and brutally beat Leporello, disguised as his master.

Despite these transgressions the ghost still offers Don Giovanni the opportunity to repent and presumably absolve himself of guilt after suffering death and some form of purgatory in the afterlife. One final sin seals his terrible fate in eternal damnation, and this is so serious that it requires a public intervention by divine forces, a revelation of the existence of God in the earthly world:

6. In both Bertati's and Da Ponte's libretto it is Giovanni's refusal to repent for his sins that justifies his fate. Giovanni violates an essential tenet of Catholic faith, the most serious infraction in the opera: the principle of repentance through the confession of sin. Here is the linchpin of Catholic salvation. In refusing to repent for his sins, Giovanni threatens the cosmology and must incur its greatest punishment. In fact characters twice offer Giovanni the opportunity to repent, first Elvira and then the statue (in Tirso's story and many subsequent versions, Don Juan asks to repent by confessing, but the statue refuses him). In Bertati's libretto he does not respond to the statue's demand that he repent of his sins. Only in Da Ponte's text is there an extended and emphatic series of refusals by Giovanni to the statue's *sdrucciolo* demands of "Pentiti!" Da Ponte stresses repentance for the remission of sin by having the statue sing that eternal damnation is not certain. He may still be forgiven through a declaration of repentance and willingness to "change his life." But Giovanni willfully declares his devotion to evil, even in the presence of an oracular miracle before three human witnesses, a sight that leaves aristocrat (Elvira) and commoner (Leporello) screaming in terror. The apparition has little effect on Giovanni, who cavalierly issues a retort and then calmly asks his servant to set another place. Even after feeling the freezing cold of the statue's grip, Giovanni remains firm in his resolve not to repent. This moment of conviction seems out of character for a liar and opportunist, and it occasioned the later reading of Giovanni as heroic in nature. The statue declares that Giovanni's time for repentance is over ("Ah, tempo più non v'è"). The earth quakes. and the fires of hell appear as a chorus of spirits sings from below with "voci cupe." Giovanni

sings of horrible pain and anguish, but he utters not the slightest word of contrition.

Here then is the crime: the violation of man's pact with the medieval Christian deity and the willful devotion to evil and pleasure in the presence of proof of the existence of God and hell. It is a crime of arrogant modernity that warrants this horrific fate from which there can be no absolution. This sin demands the intervention of divinity in a public display. Giovanni's crime is the violation of the crux of Catholic faith, the confession of sin. This display affirms a belief that derives from the fear of death, an anxiety that no degree of Enlightenment could erase from the eighteenth-century mind.[22] By having the villainous Giovanni deride religion in the face of a divine presence, the audience is put in the position of assuming the opposite point of view, seeing such behavior as utterly despicable. As such, this is a conservative, moralistic work, even anti-Enlightenment in fundamental ways. It affirms aristocratic power in demonstrating divine punishment for its abuse. And that is why the audience, some of whom certainly committed sins equal to those of Giovanni's, could distinguish themselves from the *dissoluto punito*.

✻

Audience members in 1787 would have known that this Don Juan opera was something different the moment they first heard the violent and portentous introduction of the overture. The powerful opening burst of D minor, the ominous dotted rhythmic figures, the abrupt dynamic contrasts, the descending octave leap (as well as the other wide leaps), the *alla zoppa* syncopation, the chromatic harmony and melodic figures,[23] and the octave-and-unison sonorities were all references to the otherworld. The audience would have recognized the topic of terror here and its association with the infernal scene of the opera's conclusion. Some listeners might even have recalled the ending of Gluck's *Don Juan* ballet (Vienna, 1761). One reviewer in 1789 referred to Mozart's otherworldly music and the terrifying plot as

> a legend in the manner of Father Kochem, to which Mozart's splendid (and occasionally too artificial) music is equally fitting as Raphael's style is to a Teniers and a Calot. Despite the whole thing's being a friar's farce, I have

22. Mozart's comment to his father regarding how Voltaire "died like a dog" is also indicative of the anti-Enlightenment sentiment that was common in the period.

23. Chromatic harmony and melodic figures have numerous precedents in underworld scenes, e.g., Rameau's three Fates in *Hippolyte et Aricie* (1733), Wagenseil's *Euridice* and *Armida placata* (both Vienna, 1750), Hasse's *Alcide al bivio* (Vienna, 1760), Monsigny's *L'île sonnante* (Paris, 1767), Salieri's *Armida* (1771), and Sacchini's *Renaud* (Paris, 1783), among others.

to admit that the scene in the churchyard gripped me with horror. Mozart appears to have learned the language of ghosts from Shakespeare. A gloomy, horrific sound from the grave seemed to come out of the ground; I believed I saw the spirits of the departed rising out of their tombs.[24]

Such an overture might have been expected in serious supernatural operas such as Righini's *Armida* (Vienna, 1782), whose D major overture begins with a similar introduction in the parallel minor mode. Although a serious overture in a comic setting would not be traditional, it was not entirely new. Salieri used a similar overture (but less powerful, and in the keys of C minor and C major) for his *La grotta di Trofonio* (BT, 1785). Mozart's overture might have recalled Salieri's recent integration of potent supernatural expression in opera buffa.

Like Salieri's opera, the *terribile* material returns in Mozart's opera, specifically at the point in the second finale when the statue comes to dinner and Giovanni meets his fate. Mozart adds another supernatural reference in having the statue sing his text with a kind of incantation. This vocal style was prepared in the graveyard scene, where Mozart employed the instrumentation and incantation associated with oracles and deities, almost identical to the scene for the oracular voice in *Idomeneo,* which in turn seems based on the oracle scene in Gluck's *Alceste.* In the finale the statue is no longer an oracle but a powerful *mago* who invokes the infernal spirits. The spirits respond and sing in kind with a unison incantation, not far removed from the chant recitation. Mozart's allusions to archaic and religious musical styles are especially noteworthy. Another surviving Don Juan uses the sacred style: Righini's *Il convitato di pietra* (Prague, 1776; Vienna, 1777) has a contrapuntal infernal chorus. Mozart's setting is unusual in the extent of the application of both sacred styles and the mode of terror associated with such composers as Gluck and Benda to the fate of a comic character, the dissolute aristocratic seducer and scoundrel Don Juan.[25] There had been nothing quite like it in opera.

The opera has several prominent musical motives first heard in the overture, an established practice in serious opera that also dates back to Gluck. (Mozart would do this again in his next two comic operas, *Così fan tutte* and *Die Zauberflöte.*) One of these motives involves the leap of a descending octave, doubled by several instruments for emphasis. This is the motive sung by the statue in his declaration "Don Giovanni, a cenar teco, m'invitasti e son venuto!," and was earlier heard in Elvira's condemnation. Mozart also uses this interval in comic contexts, for instance the end of the Catalogue Aria and at the start of the final sextet, when it appears devoid of harmonic filler, providing welcome relief from the demonic tumult of the chromatic harmonies in the previous scene.

24. From *Dramaturgische Blätter* (Frankfurt am Main, 13 March 1789, 116), in Deutsch, *Mozart: Die Dokumente,* 299.

25. Contemporary critics compared Mozart to Benda and Gluck and considered their expression more strong and stirring. See Fellerer, "Zur Mozart-Kritik."

The Ghost in the Statue

Two supernatural scenes occur in the second act, the first in a graveyard, where Giovanni and Leporello encounter the statue of the Commendatore; and the second in Giovanni's residence, where he receives the nocturnal visit from the statue and meets his fate. The Commendatore first appeared in act 1, scene 1, when Giovanni killed him during a duel. Mozart composed the Commendatore's music here in a lyrical style. Don Giovanni takes up the Commendatore's first melodic material in his response, suggesting they belong to the same human realm. When the Commendatore dies, Giovanni embellishes his motive with sighing figures, and Leporello inverts the same motive during the ensemble. Again this music indicates the Commendatore's participation in human events. This will not be the case when he reappears as the statue in act 2.

The next appearance of the Commendatore is in the graveyard scene, when his ghost has inhabited a statue that was being prepared in his honor before his death, circumstances not explained in Da Ponte's libretto.[26] When he proclaims, "You will have laughed for the last time before dawn," he has a new accompaniment: three trombones, oboes, clarinets, bassoons, and cellos with basses, Hadean instrumentation suggestive of early *intermedi* and Italian opera. This is not Gluck's terrifying trombone music, with its hellish blaring. The graveyard scene recalls more the underworld orchestra of the *intermedio*, with a regal formality expressed through the pompous style of a slow instrumental canzona with modal sonorities and instrumentation associated with solemn religious and ceremonial occasions.

The Commendatore's vocal style has changed, along with his accompaniment, to that of the quasi-religious incantation of an oracle or ghost, based in the long tradition of French tragic opera.[27] With its scoring and its repeated A's, a traditional chant dominant for the D minor Dorian mode, we find the quasi-religious style used by Mozart for the voice of Neptune in *Idomeneo* (there in a modal C minor). When Giovanni starts beating the gravestones with his sword, demanding "Who goes there?," the statue's response, "Audacious scoundrel, leave the dead in peace," again suggests an oracle. The melody recalls an incantation in a quasi-religious Renaissance modal style of otherworldly character, accompanied by Hadean instrumentation.

The final appearance of the Commendatore as a statue occurs in the remarkably violent finale (act 2, scene 15), which brings back the explosive music of the overture's introduction. The scene is a veritable catalog of marvelous and terrifying musical devices with some novel twists added by Mozart.

26. Don Ottavio explains the situation in Bertati's libretto: the statue was constructed while the Commendatore was still alive.

27. Some recent commentators have interpreted this as "statuesque" music, owing to the lack of movement in melody line. For a more historical discussion of the derivation of this style, see Wood, "Orchestra and Spectacle."

This segment reflects a contemporary trend toward greater violence in operas, discussed in earlier chapters. The choice of the key of D minor is appropriate here. In the course of the 1760s the key of D minor began to compete with E-flat and C minor as the infernal key of choice, especially after Gluck's widely performed *Don Juan* ballet.[28]

Wye Allanbrook uses the term "archaic solar tonality" to describe the unrelenting D minor with itinerant, short harmonic sallies into other tonal areas, possible allusions to older modal sonorities.[29] Her extensive and perceptive harmonic analysis need not be rehearsed here, but a review of the marvelous allusions provides some context for Allanbrook's discussion. Although finales have the greatest harmonic freedom in Italian comic opera, the unusual amount of chromatic material here is rare for comic opera. It permeates other parts of the opera as well, such as the end of the duet in act 1 and the sextet in act 2.

After a cadence in F major, a first-inversion mediant chord (voiced to emphasize the medieval octave-and-fifth sonority) seems to take the tonality toward some archaic modal realm as Don Giovanni opens the door and sees the statue (scene 15). The orchestra then explodes with a fully diminished seventh chord, a leading tone to the dominant A in D minor, followed by a dominant seventh chord that confirms the new key of D minor. (Fully diminished seventh chords accompany the next five entries of the statue's voice.) The statue then sings a slow declamation with the emblematic descending octave leap, accompanied by the infernal instrumentation playing the repeated obsessive dotted rhythms from the overture. As *alla zoppa* syncopation begins in the strings, Giovanni responds with quicker eighth-note declamations of disbelief. The

---

28. One can find D minor underworld scenes in the early eighteenth century, e.g., Lacoste's *Philomèle* (1705). Rameau employed the key in several works for similar effect. But it was with Gluck's ballets *Don Juan* and *Sémiramis*, as well as his opera *Alceste*, that this key began to be strongly associated with the otherworld. Salieri (*Armida*) and others use the key for their infernal scenes, e.g., Rodolphe's *L'aveugle de Palmyre*, with its D minor invocation by Alibeck at the end of act 2, "Astre éternel et des mers brillant." Composers also chose the key for parodies of infernal invocations in comic operas like Paisiello's *L'osteria di Marechiaro*. In his *Die verwandelten Weiber* (1766) Hiller composed an act 2 incantation for the magician in D minor. Georg Benda's melodramas exploit the key, mostly for the portrayal of psychological distress. *Adriadne auf Naxos* has a storm scene in D minor, the same key as Ariadne's suicide. *Medea* has D minor *terribile* music at various points in the play, especially for Jason's suicide scene. Benda also uses a *terribile* D minor episode in *Almanzor und Nadine*.

29. In her *Rhythmic Gesture in Mozart*, 277–328, Allanbrook borrows the concept of "solar tonality" from Ratner, *Classic Music*, 48–51, in analyzing this scene. (Ratner describes this scene as a "full-scale key-area fantasy," *Classic Music*, 410.) For Allanbrook this is an *ombra* scene that relates to earlier underworld scenes dating back to Monteverdi's *L'Orfeo*. But there is no *ombra* scene like this in all of opera. Magic incantation scenes with demons are more relevant here than ghost scenes. Although aspects of the statue's vocal writing are similar to the writing for ghosts in earlier French opera, here Mozart uses a style closer to the incantation of a *mago*.

"enlightened" scoundrel then commands Leporello to get another plate, and the servant now uses his master's vocal style in his fearful declamations, accompanied by "trembling" sixteenth-note motives in the violins ♪ ♫.[30] The statue then orders Leporello to stay with a descending octave leap and goes on for another ten measures with the ungainly leaps associated with older fugal subjects, an allusion to the archaic baroque sacred style ("Non si pasce di cibo mortale chi si pasce di cibo celeste"). Obsessive dotted rhythms persist throughout much of the scene until the demons take Giovanni to hell.[31]

The statue then sings, "Another concern, more grave than this, another mission, brought me down here," in the quasi-religious incantation style of an oracle, sung on A, the dominant of the tonic D minor Dorian. Leporello responds in terror with triplets to depict his "feverishly trembling limbs." Giovanni sings with calm resolve in a recitative style that features the rhythms of speech. His music suggests that he is unimpressed and unmoved by this apparition. The statue continues its slow cantillation on B-natural, with half-note and dotted-quarter-note punctuation for "I'll speak, you listen. My time is short" as the two other men retain their individual vocal styles. The first of three cadences in this section common in damnation scenes is i–VI–ii$^{o6}_{5}$–V–i.[32] (The spirits will sing the same cadence as they take Giovanni down to hell.)

A long chromatic ascent accompanies the statue's next statement in a monotone cantillation, "You invited me to dine," this time with dotted repeated-note figures and a descending octave leap, long associated with the invocation of a magician.[33] Initially sung by Elvira in her moral condemnation, the statue takes up the motive with greater emphasis. By now this is no oracle or ghost singing, but a *mago* invoking his *spiriti*. The obsessive figures in the bass add to a growing sense of an impending event of terrible moment. The statue demands a response from Giovanni ("Rispondimi") with the ungainly leaps that recall old contrapuntal subjects. Leporello interjects with an excuse that his master has no time for a dinner with the statue, set to octave-and-unison sonority. The same dotted figures continue to accompany the statue when he asks Giovanni to decide if he will reciprocate by accepting the dinner invitation ("Risolvi: Verrai?"), once again with archaic leaps in the vocal line. After another "damnation cadence" in G minor, the statue requests Giovanni's hand and a pledge to honor his promise to come to dinner. (Why is this requested?

---

30. Mozart uses these same figures in the Queen of the Night's act 1 aria ("Noch seh' ich ihr Zittern mit bangem Erschüttern").

31. In Gluck's *Iphigénie en Tauride* the obsessive figures represented the conscience of Orestes.

32. For example, Righini's *Il convitato di pietra* (Prague, 1776; Vienna, 1777), Salieri's *Les Danaïdes* (Paris, 1784), and *Der Stein der Weisen* (Vienna, 1790).

33. For example, Zoroastro in Handel's *Orlando* (London, 1734) and Doro in Ristori's *Le fate* (Dresden, 1736). Later examples include Anfossi's *La maga Circe* (1788) and Mozart's Queen of the Night, in her second aria for the text "Verstoßen sie auf ewig."

Giovanni is a proven liar who has already broken his oath repeatedly.) The statue sings this passage in style of a slow and emphatic incantation.

A new section begins when their hands meet. The surface rhythms and tempo increase as string tremolos play a fully diminished seventh chord, suggesting the freezing cold of the statue's hand. The statue now sings in faster rhythms his demand that Giovanni repent. With the text "change your life, it is your final moment" the harmonic rhythm increases and the key moves back to the G minor of the statue's previous demand. Rapid ascending scale figures in the bass articulate the chord progression as the statue demands repentance with a persistent dotted rhythmic pattern and a descending octave leap at the end of the motive.[34] Giovanni's refusal uses motives of almost equal force. In a moment of comic macabre, the statue insults Giovanni, saying "Repent, you scoundrel," but the young man does him one better, returning the insult ("No, you old fool") with a diminution of the statue's previous music, musically thumbing his nose at the statue.[35] This gesture recalls the parallel scene in Gluck's ballet, where Don Giovanni "mocks and imitates all the movements of the specter."[36]

The insult will be Giovanni's last. It may be coincidence, but this melodic diminution uses the same obsessive dotted rhythm motive that underpins the scene. The statue sings archaic descending leaps to the repeated calls for repentance while the dotted rhythm and the growing harmonic tension build to a climactic peak. Sweeping gestures in the bass increase as the scene continues, reinforcing the sense of a cumulative drive to the finish with a circle of fifths leading to the Neapolitan key, the infernal E-flat, on the statue's descending octave leap for the command "Pentiti." At Giovanni's final refusal the music suddenly stops for a half-note rest, possibly when Giovanni breaks free of the statue's grip (no source actually indicates this action). The statue then declares "Ah, there is no more time," sung to the slowest rhythm in the scene, with whole-note leaps and a descending tritone of D to G-sharp (the *diabolus in musica*), accompanied by the ominous octave-and-unison sonority of emphatic resolve.

The statue leaves, and the accompaniment starts again at a frenetic pace, with *alla zoppa* syncopation, timpani rolls (the libretto says that the earth quakes), and sweeping figures in the violins suggesting the flames indicated in

34. These sweeping rapid ascending scale figures are associated with the "marvelous" and were heard earlier at the flashing swords of their act 1 duel, but in the violins.

35. Mozart and Da Ponte employed mocking earlier in the finale. Da Ponte has Leporello mock Giovanni's words in an aside by imitating his syllable count and rhyme ("Ah che piatto saporito!"—"Ah che barbaro appetito"). Mozart also uses a sarcastic imitation of melodic material when Giovanni boasts to his servant, referring to the first finale of *Una cosa rara* ("Bravi! 'Cosa rara!'—Che ti par del bel concerto?"). Leporello's bold retort "è conforme al vostro merto" signals that he is willing to give as good as he gets.

36. Reported by Karl von Zinzendorf. Cited in Gluck, *Don Juan/Sémiramis*, in *Sämtliche Werke*, Ser. 2, Bd. 1, xi.

the libretto. Giovanni sings with greater urgency of the fiery torments that sear him. Using the dotted rhythms of the ominous accompaniment, he describes his experience of the assailing spirits and horrible flames with an almost dispassionate accuracy, evidenced earlier in his description of the slow death agony of the Commendatore. Mozart then adds syncopated *alla zoppa* figures in the strings and a few bars of sixteenth-note tremolos to the obsessive rhythmic accompaniment and the flame motives.

The incantation of the statue has had its effect: a chorus of infernal spirits has been conjured,[37] and they take up where the statue left off. The spirits sing their muffled unison bass line in simple incantation mostly on one note, with the obsessive dotted rhythmic figure ("All this is nothing compared to your sins. Come, there is worse torment"), accompanied by sixteenth-note figures in the violins. These figures begin with two-measure motives that include an octave leap, in a measure of *alla zoppa* syncopation and a measure of rapid descending scales, highlighted by the flute—a musical depiction used for flames and lightning. Don Giovanni continues describing his agony to the same accompaniment. He sings of his soul being torn from his body, his viscera becoming agitated, and of madness, terror, and the inferno. Simultaneously Leporello describes his master's appearance in the same musical and narrative style. The *coro* returns and joins for an *archistrepitoso* drive to the final "damnation" minor-key cadence, the most impressive one yet, based on the obsessive rhythmic figure, now played at full force with the entire orchestra subito forte. Don Giovanni screams "Ah!" on a sudden modal change to D major. Leporello's scream follows, held twice as long as his master's. Perhaps Mozart wanted to express the doubling of fear in the heart of a coward.

The Infernal Scene

No surviving operatic scene dating from before Mozart's *Don Giovanni* can match the force and violence in the finale of act 2, even taking into account the most violent Parisian operas of the 1780s. Theaters certainly staged more horrific librettos and with longer segments in the terrifying style. But the musical devices in these scenes were often repetitive and monotonous, the key schemes simple and predictable, and the stylistic range far more limited. Mozart employed more *terribile* devices than his contemporaries, and he used them in ingenious ways.

The most likely model for Mozart's scene of the statue's visit and the succeeding swallowing up of Giovanni by the spirits from hell was not the Gazzaniga version, but that extremely popular and controversial Parisian *tragédie*

---

37. The demonic chorus is from hell, but the Commendatore made it clear that he was from heaven when he sang that he partakes of celestial nourishment ("pasce di cibo celeste"). But they sing the same music, showing that when it comes to Giovanni's condemnation, both heaven and hell can agree.

lyrique of 1784, Salieri's *Les Danaïdes*. Like *Don Giovanni,* Salieri's opera begins with an overture that starts with a D minor fortissimo Andante introduction that leads to a D major Allegro section in sonata form. I briefly mentioned the similarities of Salieri's horrific hell scene to Mozart's finale in chapter 1. These include the same final "damnation" cadence that Mozart repeats for Don Giovanni's descent to hell, with a similar trombone accompaniment. We find yet another correspondence in Mozart's autograph manuscript, where he added an identical harmonized "Ah!" in a closely voiced D major triad for the arriving protagonists in bar 595 (probably meant for bar 596), which he crossed out after rejecting the idea.[38] This is exactly the scoring for the identical "Ahs" in *Les Danaïdes.*

The final sextet also contains another reference to the otherworld: "So that rascal remains with Proserpina and Pluto," in octave-and-unison sonority with sweeping accompaniment figures of the marvelous style. After the words "ripetiam allegramente l'antichissima canzon" Mozart provides an "old song" in species counterpoint for the first of two moralizing ideas: "This is the end that befalls those who do evil." But the singers deliver the final moral, "and the scoundrel's death always conforms to his life," in the bustling homophony of the buffa finale, affirming both the operatic genre and the simplistic pedagogy of its text.

Die Zauberflöte: Schikaneder's Libretto

The review presented in this book demonstrates that many of the basic elements in *Die Zauberflöte* are clearly present in previous supernatural operas, ballets, comedies, and pantomimes. These works situate *Die Zauberflöte* in an accurate theatrical context and provide much-needed perspective on the question of symbolism, which has dominated scholarly discussions of Mozart's singspiel. Although a few lines seem to be based on sources used by Freemasons,[39]

---

38. Commentators often cited this as proof that Mozart planned to delete the final sextet from the Viennese performance of the opera in 1788, as the libretto from that year seems to suggest. But there is no convincing evidence for this assumption, and other explanations are equally plausible. The ensemble cry of "Ah" begins the *scena ultima* in the libretto, and therefore Mozart may have been intending to start the scene here, using the cry to indicate the entrance of the other characters just after Giovanni is swallowed up by the infernal forces. When they ask "Dove è il perfido, dov'è l'indegno?" they may have even witnessed his sinking into the earth and be asking in amazement, "Where is the traitor?" Moreover, one should remember that Masetto is not a part of this ensemble cry. The same singer, Giuseppe Lolli, performed the role of the Commendatore, so he may not have had the time to change his costume from that of the statue. This may have been the reason Mozart changed his mind and started the next scene after the last chord of the infernal music—to allow Lolli enough time to change his costume and enter with the other characters as the libretto specifies.

39. Some of the words sung by the two armored men in the act 2 finale and in Sarastro's hymn with chorus (act 2, scene 1) seem paraphrased from Terrasson, *Sethos,* book 1, hymn 1, and book 3,

the notion of a complex network of hidden symbols and a coherent Masonic al-legory does not withstand scrutiny.[40] Schikaneder's popularly styled singspiel was intended to appeal to a general audience at the Theater auf der Wieden.

The sources of the libretto have a hierarchical priority. At the first level of influence are indisputable sources such as the fairy tales from *Dschinnistan* and the fairy-tale operas that preceded *Die Zauberflöte* in the Theater auf der Wieden. Schikaneder exploited a stock of characters and situations that he frequently recycled. Scholars unaware of this content have emphasized more peripheral sources that bear some resemblance to plot elements or characters in Schikaneder's libretto. But the myths of Orpheus and Cupid and Psyche, the Spanish plays of Calderón, the story of Sethos, and Shakespeare's *The Tempest* seem to be at least three steps removed from those at the first level of influence. The second level is occupied by magic and supernatural operas from German, French, and Italian traditions, works that were known in the period throughout Europe. The following discussion will review the sources and the influences on these first two levels, then briefly assess some tertiary sources and their implications.

Dschinnistan

The most important literary sources for *Die Zauberflöte* were the *Dschinnistan* stories by Wieland, Einsiedel, and Liebeskind, which provided the basic fairy-tale material for several Schikaneder productions, both before and after *Die Zauberflöte*. Liebeskind's "Lulu, oder Die Zauberflöte," supplied only some of these motives, while other stories contain additional material, particularly Wieland's "Der Stein der Weisen," "Nadir und Nadine," "Timander und Melissa," "Der Druide," "Adis und Dahy," and Einsiedel's "Die klugen Knaben." Egon Komorzynski has demonstrated the close relationship of *Die Zauberflöte* to Wieland's collection as a whole, identifying motifs borrowed from other stories in the collection, as well as from the Wieland's *Oberon*.[41] Yet Komorzynski did not recognize some of the more important motives. Enumerating small details of language, plot, and locale, he concentrated on the characters from the stories. He identified the boys in "Die klugen Knaben" as the model for the three boys in *Die Zauberflöte*. Both tell the hero to be "steadfast, patient, and silent," hold golden palm leaves, and arrive as dei ex machina in a cloud chariot. The repulsive Moorish slave is a character in "Adis und Dahy."

---

hymn 1. The material sometimes attributed to Born, "Über die Mysterien der Ägyptier," seems more tenuous. For a review of these passages, see Branscombe, *W. A. Mozart: Die Zauberflöte*, 10–18. Pirker, *Teutsche Arien*, demonstrated that references to Egyptian lore and alchemy have a long history in the Viennese theater, well before the rise of Freemasonry in Vienna.

40. For a detailed discussion of this topic and a review of the various allegorical theories and interpretations, see Buch, "Die Zauberflöte, Masonic Opera, and Other Fairy Tales."

41. Komorzynski, "'Zauberflöte' und 'Dschinnistan,'" and "'Zauberflöte' und 'Oberon.'"

A queen, a wise man, and the initiation trials of fire and water all appear in "Der Stein der Weisen." One finds the wise, older mentor and the hero who falls in love with the heroine's portrait and sets off to rescue her in "Neangir und seine Brüder."

The first story in *Dschinnistan*, "Nadir und Nadine," which served as the basis of Schikaneder's earlier singspiel, *Der Stein der Weisen*, employs the same plot reversal found in *Die Zauberflöte*. Identifying the source of the plot reversal is significant because much has been made of its awkward effect. Commentators still cite the apocryphal account of how Schikaneder had to suddenly reconstruct the plot after discovering that a rival theater was staging the same story. Hence Schikaneder is supposedly to have turned the villain Sarastro into a benevolent wise man and the good queen into the source of evil.[42]

Some elements that modern writers often designate as Masonic in *Die Zauberflöte* appear in these fairy tales without such meaning. Komorzynski mentions the similar trial scene in "Der Stein der Weisen," as well as the Egyptian references. Also depicted here is an exclusively male ritual. In "Der Druid" an enlightened group of older males instruct a headstrong youth; Egyptian symbols also appear in this story. In "Der Palast der Wahrheit" the hero is warned against "women's falsehoods." In "Der Zweikampf" the hero accepts a required vow to renounce associating with women. This is the same misogynistic tone that we find in *Die Zauberflöte*, clearly a part of the Middle Eastern exotic flavor and not necessarily a Masonic reference.

In addition to the boys in the story "Die klugen Knaben," we encounter wise, magic boys in two other stories. "Timander und Melissa" has a small vehicle with silver-plated oars, rowed on each side by "drei Knaben, schön wie Liebesgötter." In "Das Labyrinth" four boys serve as guardian spirits to a young prince who pursues the daughter of a queen, similar to the situation in *Die Zauberflöte*. The queen even promises the princess to him in a scene that parallels that in the opera. "Das Labyrinth" also has an awesome midnight scene: a mysterious table set with food and drink appears, as it does for Tamino and Papageno in *Die Zauberflöte*. Another of these scenes of terror appears in "Der eiserne Armleuchter" when a weak-willed young man finds himself alone and terrified in a dark underground cavern, exactly as Papageno does in the opera. Rescues from suicide attempts (most often by knife or sword) in "Das Labyrinth" and "Die klugen Knaben" recall both Pamina's and Papageno's suicide attempts in *Die Zauberflöte*.

Thus the plot of Schikaneder's opera combines elements from several *Dschinnistan* fairy tales and, much as he had done with his previous fairy-tale singspiels, *Der Stein der Weisen* and *Der wohltätige Derwisch*. The librettist drew the basic situation from "Nadir und Nadine": a pair of young, innocent, and virtuous lovers (Tamino and Pamina) are deceived by an evil magician (the Queen of the Night) whom they believe to be good; their putative enemy,

42. Treitschke, "Zauberflöte, Dorfbarbier, Fidelio."

another magician (Sarastro), turns out to be their benefactor. The enlightened initiation of an innocent (Nadir in *Stein*, Sofrano in *Derwisch*, and Tamino in *Zauberflöte*) is at the core of all three *Dschinnistan* librettos by Schikaneder. He also added characters from other stories: "Lulu, oder Die Zauberflöte" provided the Queen of the Night and the magic flute (although these elements have numerous precedents in German opera, as remarked in the discussion above). Monostatos has many forerunners as well,[43] but his most direct model comes from *Dschinnistan*. As in his two previous Wieland adaptations and virtually all of his comedies, Schikaneder interpolated episodes for his own character, the simple but goodhearted rustic trickster with a female counterpart whose name is a feminine derivative of his own.

Wiednertheater Operas

The Wieland fairy-tale operas of the Wiednertheater are the immediate theatrical context for *Die Zauberflöte*. The first of these operas, *Oberon, König der Elfen* (7 November 1789), was certainly known to Mozart. Like *Die Zauberflöte*, *Oberon* centers on an initiatory trial for the lovers Huon and Amande. Oberon acts like Sarastro, a wise and beneficent guide; Huon is a prince who has been promised a princess, as Tamino has been promised Pamina. Scherasmin is the Papageno character, a cowardly servant whose main concern is for food, wine, and a woman. When Scherasmin meets Huon he exclaims "Ich bin ein Mensch, wie ihr," almost the identical words that Papageno utters. Scherasmin has an aria similar to Papageno's "Vogelfänger" song, with the words "heissa, lustig, ohne Sorgen." A set table emerges magically from a trap door; there is a cloud chariot, a solemn male chorus singing a prayer, and a magic horn that renders listeners immobile or forces them to dance involuntarily. Two genies are in the cast, and one gives a little box with magic words to Scherasmin. The retinue of Queen Titania is an ensemble of nymphs.

Schikaneder's next fairy-tale singspiel, *Die schöne Isländerin, oder Der Muffti von Samarkanda* (22 April 1790), was a tale of a noble prince, a magician, a mufti, a young maiden, and a comic servant. Schikaneder's first libretto based on Wieland's *Dschinnistan*, *Der Stein der Weisen, oder Die Zauberinsel* (9 September 1790), seems the most direct model for *Die Zauberflöte*, with elements that will continue to be used in later fairy-tale operas:

1. A heroic and a comic pair of lovers.
2. A beneficent wise man with supernatural power.
3. The same plot reversal as in "Nadir und Nadine."
4. The opposition of good and evil, night and day, light and dark (personified by the "black devil" Eutifronte), hypocrisy and truth.

43. See Enzinger, "Randbemerkungen"; Krüger, "Das Urbild des 'Zauberflöte'"; Leeuwe, "Monostatos."

5. Women presented either as seductresses or pure, virtuous maidens.

6. A magical appearance by the deity in act 1, with similar recitatives and coloratura arias.

7. Armored men (*geharnischte Männer*).

8. Musical texts with rhymed poetry in loosely metered verse, with the same varied use of interlocking rhymes to reflect character and situation. Characters interlock rhymes as their interests coincide; Eutifronte grabs Lubano by the horns and the woodsman takes up his rhyme, meter, and syllable count. Schikaneder mostly wrote the few recitatives in prose.

9. Finales conceived as a series of contrasting episodes with magic scenes, comic episodes, and tableaus with solemn, ceremonial (*feierlich*) expression; this structure necessitated a quickly changing mixture of ensembles, solos, recitatives, instrumental music, and choruses.

As in his later fairy-tale works, Schikaneder's plot here offers a series of changing tableaus, freely mixing comic and serious elements. An anonymous reviewer of *Der Stein der Weisen* in Altona in 1800 characterized the opera as "romantic [with] images quickly appearing and receding, like an optical or shadow box [*optischen Kasten*]; spirits come and then vanish, people travel on the water and on clouds; there is thunder and lightning, and so there is always something for the ear and for the eye."[44] The term *romantic*, first associated with medieval epic poetry, was often applied to fairy-tale operas in the late eighteenth century. If such operas had less than perfectly coherent plot lines and required a somewhat strenuous suspension of disbelief, they were consistent with their literary traditions: epic romance, fable, and fairy tale. In Schikaneder's fairy-tale singspiels the main problem for the protagonists is to correctly determine who is bad and who is good. That recognition happens in a later act, when the riddles and dilemmas posed in the first act are resolved through surprising developments or revelations in a speech. Schikaneder's musical plan adheres to a pattern as well: he usually has two acts, the first beginning with an ensemble introduction. Each act of a full-scale opera ends with a lengthy finale, made up of a series of short, active tableaus that further the plot. The arias include both comic and serious types; comic arias use strophic form with paired lines in metered rhyme; there is usually one major virtuoso aria in each act, as well as occasional accompanied recitative; and there are also ensembles, both comic and serious. In his elemental use of meter and imagery and

---

44. *Hamburgisch- und altonaische Theater- und Litteratur-Zeitung.* The critic asked to be excused from detailing the plot because "der Stoff nicht mythologisch, blos romantisch ist, Bilder schnell vorgerückt und wieder weggezogen werden, grade wie in einem optischen Kasten: . . . Geister erscheinen und verschwinden, die Menschen fahren bald auf den Wasser bald auf Wolken daher, Donner und Bliz ist auch nicht vergessen, und so ist denn alles angebracht, dessen sich Operndichter bedienen, um die Gehör[-] und Gesichtsnerven der Zuschauer abwechselnd zu beschäftigen."

abundance of cant and cliché, Schikaneder rarely attempted to be profound. But his distinct blend of humor, mystery, and plot intrigue produced some of the most lively and entertaining German operas of his day. The best of them have spontaneity and dramatic flair. Schikaneder's substitute verses, improvised dialogues, and comic pantomimes were reflected in the fast-paced music and the keyboard variations used in segments of *Der wohltätige Derwisch* and *Die Zauberflöte* that exude a spirit of improvisation.[45]

Schikaneder's fairy-tale librettos typically exploit the theme of initiation, derived from court operas based on myths like Orpheus, where a youth first must learn to rule his own emotions before he can rule others. This is the predicament of the heroes Nadir in *Der Stein der Weisen* and Sofrano in *Der wohltätige Derwisch*. It is Tamino's greatest trial and the one for which Pamina is the essential element. *Die Zauberflöte* exploits another theme from court opera, the topic of arranged royal marriage. This was often the event that occasioned supernatural Italian court operas such as *Osiride,* another Egyptian story (Dresden, 1781). The portrait scene is standard here because this was the means of first introducing the royal couple. Flattering portraits would be commissioned and sent to the prospective spouse. It was this image that was to spark initial interest and, it was hoped, lead to erotic attachment. In *Die Zauberflöte* Schikaneder made this element an Enlightenment theme of sentiment where loving freely is the basis of marriage, as shown in the contrast between Sarastro and the queen's intentions for Pamina. Thus Salieri's description of *Die Zauberflöte* was no empty compliment; when he told Mozart that his was an opera "worthy to be performed at the greatest festivity before the greatest of monarchs," he was acknowledging the allusions to court opera.

Schikaneder's next fairy-tale singspiel based on *Dschinnistan, Der wohltätige Derwisch, oder Die Schellenkappe* (early 1791) has an initiation plot similar to *Die Zauberflöte,* where a young prince must learn to control his emotions before he can rule others. The opposition of good and evil, night and day, light and darkness, and hypocrisy and falseness are again central themes. The two female characters are both evil: a fairy princess who seduces men only to destroy them (Zenomide) and a violent dominatrix (Mandolina). The poetic conventions and use of rhyme are typical of Schikaneder; he poses riddles and dilemmas in the first act that are resolved later. Comic scenes are complemented by serious moralizing arias, one recitative, and speeches sung by the dervish (performed by Gerl).[46] The most conspicuous similarity is in the scenes with the magic bells when the characters are enchanted by the sound. As in *Die Zauberflöte,* the bells occasion enchanted vocal ensembles.

45. For a discussion of improvisation in Schikaneder's singspiels, see Buch, "On the Context of Mozart's Variations."

46. Gerl's characters also sang similar arias in *Die zween Anton* singspiels, for example, "Das was ich that vor Menschenpflicht" in the first sequel, called *Die verdeckten Sachen* (26 September 1789).

Earlier Fairy-tale Operas

The previous chapter demonstrated that German operas relied heavily on foreign models, especially *opéra-comique*.[47] Schikaneder's fairy-tale librettos blend a variety of elements from Italian and French sources. Some of the elements in *Die Zauberflöte* were already evident in earlier singspiels that certainly were known to Schikaneder, for example, Schiebeler's *Lisuart und Dariolette* (1766).

The Graf von Spaur's *Mährchen* singspiel *Der Schiffbruch* (1778) has numerous aspects in common with *Die Zauberflöte*. Both are Egyptian fairy tales, with beneficent magicians that set the plot in motion and a story that concerns an abducted princess and a cowardly slave in love with the princess. The musical texts include quasi-religious songs and comic arias for the secondary characters. As in *Die Zauberflöte*, there are also a suicide scene with a dagger and trials in which the heroic characters must prove themselves virtuous.

In Bretzner's popular *Das Irrlicht* one finds a flute-playing prince, a "Mann und Weib" duet, trials held within the temple, prayerlike hymns, and two young genies. The cast of Zehnmark's *Was erhält die Männer treu?* (1780) includes a frightening dwarf as the villain and a powerful fairy. Like *Die Zauberflöte*, the work ends with a triumphal ballet and chorus celebrating the sun ("Läst glänzender die Sonne, Ihr Antlitz sehn. / So strahlt nach langen Tagen, im schwartzen Gram verlebt"). Vulpius's *Der Schleyer* (1786) has an evil queen, initiatory trials for both the noble and the comic couples, magic implements, and villains that are swallowed up by the earth at the end.

At least two similar fairy-tale operas were produced in close proximity to *Die Zauberflöte*. Perinet's *Kaspar der Fagottist, oder Die Zauberzither* (1791) was modeled on the same *Dschinnistan* fairy tale used for *Die Zauberflöte* and has much in common with Mozart's opera. Kotzebue's *Der Spiegelritter* (1791) also relied on *Dschinnistan*. It too has many elements found in *Die Zauberflöte*, as well as in *Der wohltätige Derwisch*. As in *Die Zauberflöte*, Kotzebue's moralizing libretto stresses the battle between good and evil magic. Again a prince undergoes trials by being offered food and wine (on a magically set table) by the evil dwarfs and beautiful maidens of the enchantress Milmi, who make seductive proposals. One also finds a group of four prattling ladies who have an ensemble scene with the comic companion, as in *Die Zauberflöte*. Milmi sings a coloratura passage swearing vengeance that recalls the Queen of the Night's second aria. There is also a scene with a dead giant, similar to the dead serpent

47. Several modern commentators have suggested a direct influence of Gozzi's ten *fiabe teatrale*, e.g, Rosen, *Classical Style*, 317–21. DiGaetani, *Carlo Gozzi: Translations*, 6–7, states that "Gozzi's fairy-tale plays helped to create the Viennese magic plays and singspiels of the late eighteenth century. Mozart and Schikaneder's *Die Zauberflöte* (1791) is the most famous opera of this genre and it was certainly influenced by Gozzi." The review of Gozzi's here suggests that Gozzi was less an originator or popularizer of fairy-tale theater, and more a late adapter of a well-known tradition that still thrived in many European centers.

scene in *Die Zauberflöte*. The music includes prayers of thanks to heavenly powers that recall the music of Sarastro and his priests.[48]

Fairy Tales

Die Zauberflöte contains some of the most frequently encountered fairy-tale motifs. These include magic instruments and objects that have the power to change the hero's life, sagacious magicians, severe tests and trials, secret orders of initiates, temples, a pair of contrasting comrades on a mutual quest, and young couples, generally a prince and a princess.[49] The matching male and female forms of characters' names are typical. Plots often have heroes captured and then liberated. Humor is a common element, as are admonishing tales of drunkenness, lying, and exaggeration (Papageno's vices). Cowardice and talkativeness are punished by the loss of speech (Papageno's punishment).

Fairy tales contain characteristic plot situations that Schikaneder exploited in his librettos. In the story "The Raven," a queen's daughter is held captive and turned into a raven. Her young rescuer is warned that he must remain awake and not eat or drink anything that an old woman will bring to him.[50] He promises but fails, like Papageno with his "old woman," the disguised Papagena. The dangers and wiles of women are common themes in exotic oriental stories. In the myth of Psyche and Eros, Psyche sets out on a journey, only to become prey to a serpent. Eros saves her and keeps her hidden in his castle. Her sisters talk her into killing Eros with a knife they give her. She cannot kill him, so she tries to kill herself instead. She is saved when Zeus comes down to make Psyche and Eros immortal. In one contemporary version of the myth published in Göttingen, the story is designated a *Feenmährchen*.[51]

Characters in fairy tales are divided into clear opposites, reflecting the capacity of children (the intended audience) to understand moral and ethical issues only in simple, unambiguous relationships. A recurrent fairy-tale motif has two youths (often brothers) starting out together on a quest—the initiatory archetype.[52] They separate, having different fates according to their opposite natures—one noble and the other controlled by his animal desires. Tamino and Papageno do just this, embodying the striving for independence and self-assertion, along with their opposites, the need for dependence and the fear of separation aroused by such desires.

48. Although it is not a fairy-tale opera, Karl Friedrich Hensler's *Das Sonnenfest der Braminen* (LT, 9 September 1790, with music by Wenzel Müller) may have also inspired Schikaneder and Mozart to include similar *feierlich* music and high-minded choral texts.

49. For details, see Thompson, *Motif Index of Folk Literature* and *Types of Folktale*.

50. See Bettelheim, *Uses of Enchantment*, 187.

51. Apuleius, *Pysche*. For a discussion of the oral tradition of Apuleius's stories, see Scobie, *Apuleius and Folklore*. Hoevels, *Märchen und Magie*, offers a discussion of the story as it relates to archaic ritual, contemporary developments in intellectual history, and psychoanalytic theory.

52. See Bettelheim, *Uses of Enchantment*, 90–102.

Among the other fairy-tale motifs in the libretto is the common mother-and-daughter conflict. An evil queen who is jealous of her virtuous young daughter suspects the princess of desiring to surpass her. She attempts to arrest her daughter's development and increasing independence. The relationship of Pamina and the Queen of the Night reflects this archetype (a motif also used in Wieland's tale "Pertharit und Ferrandine"). The typical fate of evil characters is to be eaten up by the earth, the fate of Eutifronte in *Der Stein der Weisen* and the Queen of the Night in *Die Zauberflöte*.

In many initiatory fairy tales (including those in Wieland's collection), an older man's realm must be given over to a youthful successor who proves his worth through meriting a virtuous spouse. In the story "The Goose Girl" a widowed queen (like the queen in *Die Zauberflöte*) has a beautiful daughter who finds herself in an alien land. A headstrong young man suspects an older mentor (or his father) of cheating him out of his rightful partner. This is not unlike Tamino's situation in act 1.[53] In fact, the central quest and the trial or testing of the hero and heroine propel the action in *Die Zauberflöte*.

Contemporary Social Values

Schikaneder's fairy-tale librettos contain the middle-class assumptions that were also a feature of German fairy tales.[54] In one sense the German fairy tale is a symbolic attempt to come to terms with the rising middle class and its new but less elegant literary forms developing out of the market system. French fairy tales are related (but not identical) to late eighteenth-century German fairy tales, which also expressed nostalgia for an older and simpler kind of society. But the values of hard work, the renunciation of impulses, delayed gratification, and success through discipline and obedience are more prevalent in German fairy tales and fairy-tale librettos. Failure in life is associated with acting upon base and basic impulses such as lust, hunger, sexual desire, addiction to alcohol, idle chatter, lying, and laziness. Like the heroes of court opera, the protagonists of Schikaneder's plots are solid citizens and faithful spouses with the virtues deemed necessary in both political and family roles. The noble prince, Tamino, develops these qualities as he progresses through the opera. Sarastro teaches him the self-control of impulses and the discipline necessary for middle-class success. Pamina, a virtuous young princess, is captured so as to remove the evil influence of her mother and enable the young woman fulfill her role as a queen in her own right. The Queen of the Night is a subversive force; she threatens this natural order by her unnatural ambition.

In contrast with Tamino, the commoner Papageno has clear problems with

53. Ibid., 136–43.

54. For a general discussion of these aspects as they influenced the Grimm stories, see Zipes, *The Brothers Grimm*, especially the essays "Dreams of a Better Bourgeois Life: The Psycho-social Origins of the Tales," 28–42, and "The German Obsession with Fairy-Tales," 75–95.

self-control, renunciation of physical impulses, and delay of gratification. The struggle with his impulses is continuous, and he is easily discouraged. He is a child in this regard, and his lack of obedience and self-discipline gets him into trouble when he tries to restrain his speech, hunger, thirst, and lust. Although Papageno recognizes the proper values, he cannot always live by them. The more extreme example of vice is the repugnant Monostatos, a primitive, non-Caucasian character whose attributes conform to some common racial stereotypes. He is a villain, and Sarastro orders him to be punished with lashes on the soles of his feet (a sentence later suspended). His self-control is even less developed than Papageno's, and his motivation is strictly the sensual gratification of impulses. Thus he (like, to a lesser degree, Papageno) represents dangerous inner forces that the middle class believed most threatening to its tenuous position on the social ladder. Although in *Die Zauberflöte* these feared forces were projected onto a foreign race,[55] it is not clear that this is a particularly European prejudice, for this element comes from the oriental fairy tale itself.

Die Zauberflöte has a stable hierarchy of characters with clear class strata: the aristocrats are never comic characters and comic characters are never aristocrats. A strong influence of Enlightenment thought is apparent, for a corrupt monarchy, headed by the queen and her ladies, promises to wreak havoc on the natural and proper order of things. This is apparent when the queen promises her daughter Pamina to the slave Monostatos, a violation of the contemporary social order. Tamino, Pamina, Sarastro, and his priests represent the virtuous nobility. The simple Papageno is a kind of tradesman, lacking the virtues of the nobility. Like that of *Don Giovanni,* this libretto tells us that although individual aristocrats may be evil, the aristocratic social order is basically beneficent.

Two aspects of this libretto are most troublesome to modern sensibilities: a few misogynistic passages and the deprecatory references to the skin color of Monostatos. The review presented in this book suggests that such expressions have more to do with the fairy-tale sources than any prevailing contemporary view of women or Africans. Only Schikaneder's exotic fairy-tale singspiels contain such references,[56] for example, *Der wohltätige Derwisch,* where evil women, motivated by gynecocratic ambition, attempt a disruptive domination by the female sex. When Sarastro sings "Ein Mann muss eure Herzen leiten," he espouses joint rule by a virtuous couple as an ideal. It is the heart

---

55. For a discussion of this aspect, see Schwartz, "Cultural Stereotypes and Music."

56. For example, *Es giebt doch noch treue Weiber!,* a *Schauspiel* in three acts "nach einer wahren Geschichte bearbeitet von Karl Ludwig Giesecke" [Vienna, 1790] (A-Wn, Theater Museum, shelf-mark 820365-A ThS), tells of two friends at the university, Metzler (Giesecke's real name was Johann Georg Metzler) and Karl von Freyberg. Experience has taught the misogynistic Metzler to doubt the virtue of women. Freyberg has fallen in love with Emilie, the wife of his friend Weilen. In the end Freyberg turns out to be Emilie's long-lost brother and Metzler comes to realize that women can be as virtuous as men.

that concerns Sarastro, not the domination of a mind, soul, or body. That the male also must have the female as his partner in order to achieve the necessary balance is evident when Tamino relies upon Pamina for success in his trials. The misogyny of *Die Zauberflöte* results from the exotic Middle Eastern fairy-tale world of the Arabian and Persian Nights, a literary tradition where women could be depicted as dangerous, seditious, and seductive villains.[57] The rather harsh pronouncements against women in this libretto are rare in eighteenth-century operas, as is the negative view of dark-skinned Moors. This aspect was also probably carried over from the oriental fairy tales that served as the basis for these librettos. These details come from the conveying of the exotic world of the orient, and from a harsher view of a culture that Europeans considered less civilized. The accusation of misogyny should be viewed in the context of the postmodern critique of the libretto. The earlier criticism of Schikaneder's verses for their vulgarity and popular appeal have yielded to the identification of inconsistencies in ethics, such as Sarastro's being a slave-holder and the charge of misogyny.[58] These reveal disillusionment with the basic intellectual background of the libretto, the Enlightenment, which was believed to have failed in its high-minded goals. Such critiques stem from anachronistic judgments on a text taken out of context and measured against the values of the current age. Slaves were a part of the ancient society depicted in the fairy tale. Sarastro's fair and enlightened treatment of his subjects is praised here ("er lohnet und strafet in ähnlichem Kreise"). As for Tamino, his role concerns the initiation and proper morals of a prince, selected by divine forces for rule over a people he does not know. Thus Emperor Leopold and Vienna's clergy could attend *Die Zauberflöte* without fear of seditious subtexts. Sarastro's instruction to his wise men is one of submission to authority: teach the initiates "the duty of Mankind, teach them to acknowledge the power of the gods" (act 2, scene 1).

Die Zauberflöte: Mozart's Score

Die Zauberflöte was the most substantial supernatural libretto set by Mozart, the fourth in a series of fairy-tale singspiels at the Wiednertheater based on Wieland's writings, and the third to be derived from *Dschinnistan*. Chapter 5 demonstrated that Schikaneder had a similar approach in *Der Stein der Weisen* (and, to a lesser degree, *Der wohltätige Derwisch*). Mozart drew upon earlier fairy-tale singspiels from this theater, even quoting them. *Der Stein der Weisen* was the most direct model for *Die Zauberflöte*, and Mozart himself contributed music to the earlier singspiel. Both *Der Stein der Weisen* and *Die Zauberflöte* have a similar two-act structure with an *introduzione*, large-scale episodic fi-

57. For examples, see Elisséeff, *Thèmes et motifs*, 139–40.

58. See Braunbehrens, *Mozart in Vienna, 1781–1791*, 393–401.

EXAMPLE 6.1a Franz Xaver Gerl, *Der Stein der Weisen*, act 1, duet

EXAMPLE 6.1b W. A. Mozart, *Die Zauberflöte*, act 1, quintet

nales, and similar arias and ensembles. Both operas offer a romantic mixture of solemn, comic, magic, and love scenes. Both have musical segments for the working of the mechanical stage and for magic episodes. One finds traditional supernatural devices in both operas, for example the enchanted march music, magical wind ensembles, and the use of descending octave leaps for magic invocations. A striking similarity occurs in the appearance of Astromonte, almost certainly the model for the scene with the Queen of the Night in act 1. Both scenes begin with preludes in syncopated *alla zoppa* rhythm, music to facilitate the mechanical devices in scenes that feature a deus ex machina. In both operas the prelude leads to an accompanied recitative, followed by a two-part aria ending in a B-flat Allegro coloratura section. The choral scene in act 1 (no. 4), attributed to Schack, has a segment where four *Mädchen* argue over who is the most worthy to be the beloved of Astromonte, much as the three ladies in the *introduzione* to *Die Zauberflöte* argue over Tamino. Both scenes have imitation, stretto, sequences, and dramatic climaxes, although the music attributed to Schack is more modest than Mozart's. Of particular interest are the direct musical citations in *Die Zauberflöte* from *Der Stein der Weisen* (there is also a citation from *Der wohltätige Derwisch*). The music for Lubano's exclamations in the first finale probably inspired Papageno's "O wär' ich eine Maus, wie wollt ich mich verstecken" in the first finale of *Die Zauberflöte*, with its similar sonority, orchestration, and pitch contour. Also we find a phrase from Gerl's act 1 duet in *Der Stein der Weisen* in the act 1 quintet of *Die Zauberflöte* (see ex. 6.1), where Mozart also quotes one of Henneberg's children's songs.[59] Here the common conceit is a padlock. In the duet Lubano (Schikaneder) places a padlock on the door of his cabin, and in the quintet a padlock has just been removed from Papageno's mouth.

There are differences as well. Unlike *Die Zauberflöte*, *Der Stein der Weisen* has no independent trios or quintets but includes a comic aria in the buffa style (no. 2). *Der Stein* also contains no coloratura soprano arias, perhaps because Josepha Hofer, later the Queen of the Night, was on maternity leave. There are fewer old-fashioned supernatural devices in Mozart's opera than in *Der Stein der Weisen*, for example, the elegant wind music (usually scored with a pair of flutes in thirds playing a conjunct melody) for the arrival of the deity Astromonte (act 1, finale) and his genie (act 1, no. 4). Mozart's vocal music, particularly his arias, has a minimal repetition of text, somewhat less than that in earlier Wiednertheater fairy-tale singspiels such as *Der Stein der Weisen* and *Der wohltätige Derwisch*. This adds to the episodic, romantic quality of this genre discussed in chapter 5, in which the textual and musical imagery continually change in a series of contrasting episodes.

❄

For Schikaneder *Die Zauberflöte* was clearly a special occasion. He commissioned an imperial court composer, created new sets, and printed an impressive libretto with two engraved scenes from the opera. The name of an opera often indicates of its main subject. Unlike his earlier fairy-tale operas, here Schikaneder's title emphasizes the subject of music. The text draws a parallel to the transforming power of music with the enlightenment of its two central characters, Tamino and Pamina. And transformation is most apparent in the scenes with magic music for the flute and bells.

Mozart's music for this *große Oper* is more substantial than that for earlier Wiednertheater singspiels, and the orchestra is larger. In introducing conventions from church and public spectacle, Mozart both invokes and departs from earlier Wiednertheater practices. His undisguised quotation of a chorale melody and extensive use of the sacred contrapuntal style were not typical devices in the theater. His magnificent overture, with trombones added to the solemn opening chords, embodies the solemn ceremonial style (*feierlich*), as does the contrapuntal presentation and development of the primary theme. Several other numbers also employ the solemn style to a greater degree than in earlier Wiednertheater operas, owing to the emphasis placed on this in the libretto.

Mozart was not original in choosing marches for his magic scenes, with their

59. The last four measures (for solo piano) of Henneberg's song "Das Veilchen und der Dornstrauch" from the *Liedersammlung für Kinder und Kinderfreunde* (Vienna: Alberti, 1791), a collection that included three children's songs by Mozart, K. 596–98. See Tyson, "Two Mozart Puzzles."

lockstep power through that most basic rhythm of motion. His original touch is evident, on the other hand, in the way his magic bells present music: they provide only variations, and after hearing the variation the enchanted characters magically recognize the theme and sing it out, displaying enchantment purely through musical means. Mozart's ingenuity in these and other instances should not surprise us, for ultimately his virtuosity is also a topic here. Although the Wiednertheater repertory included operas with substantial musical settings, *Die Zauberflöte* seems more ambitious than its generic predecessors. Mozart's critics were correct in perceiving that in his theatrical compositions he placed his own musical virtuosity at the center of the audience's attention.

Music and Genre

The first printed libretto and the original playbill of *Die Zauberflöte* call it a *große Oper*, a term also used to describe *dramma per musica* in Vienna during this period.[60] But this is no opera seria, although the Queen of the Night's coloratura arias derive from a musical style associated with serious opera. When Mozart entered the work in his own catalog he called it a *teutsche Oper*, referring simply to the language of the libretto. For the Berlin *Musikalisches Wochenblatt*, [10] December 1791, it is a *Maschinenkomödie*, a common term for supernatural singspiels in Vienna. Mozart reported in a letter dated 14 October 1791 that Antonio Salieri and Caterina Cavalieri used the Italian term *operone* in praising the opera. Both this term and the designation *große Oper* suggest grandeur in subject and music. The surviving evidence suggests that *Die Zauberflöte* was the grandest Wiednertheater singspiel to date. But Mozart's opera is not so far removed from its predecessors. An unusual variety in musical style figures in the scores of the Wiednertheater, including Italian vocal writing, comic conventions, and marvelous or terrifying effects. Mozart adds some novel elements to this romantic mixture, especially styles derived from church music. Contemporaries acknowledged still another musical style called the *feierlich*, a term used to denote the solemn expression that was associated with the grand ceremonial occasions in Vienna.

The previous chapters make clear that the main outline of the plot and the characters are conventional, mostly derived from fairy-tale *opéras-comiques* of earlier decades, works that in turn have their roots in commedia dell'arte plays that feature magic. But Mozart's musical setting here is not always conventional, although it has clear links to traditional approaches and techniques for musical decoration and mimetic depiction with "sonic imagery." From a historical perspective *Die Zauberflöte* is a kind of ambitious German version of

60. See Rice, "Leopold II, Mozart, and the Return." The term *große Oper* is also a translation of the French *grand opéra*, a designation used in Paris since 1782 for post-Gluck *tragédie-lyrique*. This is no more a "grand opera" than an opera seria, although there are musical elements clearly derivative of Gluck, Piccinni, and their Parisian followers.

recent *opéra-comique* with an oriental fairy-tale text.[61] The commedia dell'arte characters and situations, the essential material given in dialogue as much as in music, the fairy-tale plot and archetypal characters, and the popular style of language and humor (with matching musical components) all point to the French comic legacy. The magically set table, the trials, Papageno's comic suicide scene, the magic instruments, Papageno's locked-mouth humming (derived from the ever-popular *Le Bûcheron* by Philidor and its German version, *Der Holzhauer*) would have been as familiar to audiences in Paris as to those in Vienna.

Like *Don Giovanni*, this text juxtaposes comic and serious elements, using both convention and novelty.[62] And like *Don Giovanni*, this opera offers more substantial music than is usual for the genre. Schikaneder's libretto has more low comedy and uses less sophisticated language than Da Ponte's, and early commentators attacked it for its poor quality, along with the more common critique that supernatural opera was lacking in verisimilitude.

Orchestration

The variety of timbre combinations in *Die Zauberflöte* is unique in Mozart's operas, particularly the scoring with low strings and winds. One finds similar orchestration in the earlier Wiennertheater operas, particularly *Der Stein der Weisen*. Mozart's distinctive use of the basset horns, often with three trombones and low strings, contributes to the unusual sonority and complements the sacred references and keys associated with otherworldly expression.[63] The trombones and key associations have precedent in earlier operas, including the supernatural scenes in Mozart's *Idomeneo* and *Don Giovanni*. Trombones suggest solemn and ceremonial expression in many scenes in *Die Zauberflöte*, starting with the first chords of the overture. Mozart also uses these instruments in scenes with the three boys, in music for the priests, in the *schrecklicher*

61. The sizable music that adorns this text is not without precedent in recent supernatural *opéra-comique*, e.g., Grétry's *Raoul, Barbe-bleue* (1789), Bruni's *L'île enchantée* (1789), and Langlé's *Corisandre* (1791).

62. One novel aspect of the libretto is the moral ambiguity in the first act. The Queen of the Night first appears to be virtuous, but her virtue is seriously questioned during the first finale. Sarastro's character is similarly unclear. The three boys are also ambiguous characters, at first oracles in the service of the Queen, then Cupid-like agents furthering the objectives of Sarastro, who intends to unite Tamino and Pamina. For all their innocence, they are as seditious as the Queen, only they are on the side of right. All this creates tension and suspense, for things are not as they seem. But this ambiguity is also somewhat confusing, as the real intentions are not clear until the Sarastro's speech in act 2, scene 2.

63. Only two trombones are used in *Der Stein der Weisen*. Three trombones doubling vocal parts is an old convention in Austrian church music. Mozart employs this convention in the priests' chorus (act 2, scene 20) and the scene for the two armored men (act 2, scene 28), which recalls Gluck's underworld scene in the opening of the second act of *Orfeo ed Euridice*.

Accord at the end of act 2 (scene 25), in the magic trial music of act 2 (scene 28), for the destruction of the Queen of the Night (along with her three ladies and Monostatos), and in the triumphal end of the finales in both acts. Some fantastic scenes such as the *introduzione* and the Queen of the Night's second aria (act 2, scene 14) use horns, trumpets, and timpani (without trombones). In several sections the orchestral accompaniment employs the expression of musical terror associated with storms and horror. The flute is clearly magical, as are the bells; both instruments have a long history of supernatural association.

The Overture

The first music in Mozart's score is a series of solemn chords. The initial timbre suggests the otherworldly, with a large wind complement that includes trombones and basset horns. The orchestration is the prominent feature here, and the chords form an invocation of sorts, what the French called an *annonce*. These chords serve as a kind of motto in the opera, returning not only for the three-fold chords in act 2, but also in the introduction to Pamina's address to Sarastro in the first finale, "Herr, ich bin zwar Verbrecherin." Modern commentators have speculated that this emblematic gesture was intended to suggest Freemasonry. But the combination of winds and low-pitched strings is less Masonic than it is exotic and otherworldly. Mozart also used this combination in his religious music, for example the Requiem. Composers of earlier Wiednertheater singspiels such as *Der Stein der Weisen* also used this kind of orchestration.

Rather than referring to a hypothetical Masonic style, these are probably references to the "marvelous." The overture starts with material that recalls Traetta's *Armida*, an *azione teatrale per musica* that was performed as late as 1780 in Vienna (see chapter 3). Both the slow introduction and the Allegro use material similar to Traetta's overture. Gazzaniga's three-act opera seria *La Circe* (1786) has a similar opening, suggesting that this may have been associated with marvelous operas about a powerful sorceress. But operas without supernatural references also use these kinds of opening chords, for example Cimarosa's *Il matrimonio segreto* (BT, 1792).

The main melody for the contrapuntal Allegro section is a cliché used by numerous composers of that time, not just by Muzio Clementi in his Allegro con brio movement from the B-flat Piano Sonata, op. 24, no. 2.[64] The motive suggests the idea of flight and exhibits Mozart's compositional virtuosity in a contrapuntal treatment that is rare in contemporary opera overtures. The form of the overture actually recalls something of the French overture, with its slow introduction and faster contrapuntal section, and suggests the source of operatic "marvelous," the French *tragédie en musique*. Rameau's overture to *Zoroastre* has a fast contrapuntal movement with intermittent sections of wind mu-

64. Jahn, *W. A. Mozart*, 4:612, cites another similar theme from J. H. Collo's cantata *Lazarus Auferstehung* (Leipzig, 1779).

sic. The contrapuntal texture here suggests the learned style of church music, a frequent reference in Mozart's supernatural music. The key of E-flat also suggests the infernal topic, used by composers from Lully to Gluck. Gluck's music in fact plays a role in this score, both with direct citations and general stylistic similarities.[65]

Alfred Einstein suggested that an autograph sketch for a very different overture in E-flat (K. 620a = Anh. 102) was an earlier version of an overture to *Die Zauberflöte*. This music seems to have been based on the well-known aria "Ombre, larve," from Gluck's *Alceste* of 1767 (act 1, scene 5). If this really is an earlier version of the overture to this opera, then it would confirm both the supernatural association and the link to Gluck.[66]

Music for the Mechanical Stage

Stage machines and supernatural effects were prominent features in Schikaneder's theatrical productions. These aspects distinguish this opera among Mozart's works, because the composer provided music to accompany the machinery, just as his predecessors at the Wiednertheater had done. Examples include:

65. In the quartet of the second finale (act 2, scene 26), Pamina sings a lamenting phrase in F minor on the text "bald werden wir, bald werden wir, vermählet sein." This music recalls a passage a trio in Gluck's *Armide* (act 3, scene 2), when Phénice sings to Armide, "Lorsqu'il était le plus terrible de touts vos ennemis." The priests' march in act 2 of *Die Zauberflöte* has a beginning identical to that of the *Hymne*, "Chaste fille de Latone," from Gluck's *Iphigénie en Tauride* (act 4, scene 2; originally composed for *Sémiramis*). Mozart employs this common musical material in the Kyrie of his Mass in C Major, K. 220/196b. The style strongly recalls the march in *Idomeneo* (act 3, scene 7). Mozart's second aria for the Queen of the Night includes another citation from *Iphigénie en Tauride* (act 1, scene 4), discussed below. Still more traces of Gluck's music are found in the score. The violent end of the Queen of the Night and her retinue recalls the opening of *Iphigénie en Tauride*. Precedents for Sarastro's aria with chorus "O Isis und Osiris" can be found in earlier fairy-tale operas for the Wiednertheater, which included bass arias for Franz Gerl, the singer and composer who sang the role (e.g., his two arias in *Der wohltätige Derwisch*). But these arias do not include choral segments. This kind of piece is more common in French *grand opéra*, e.g., Gluck's *Iphigénie en Aulide* (Paris, 1774), an opera that Mozart knew. Here the priest Calcas has a solemn *air* in the hymn style, "Au faîte des grandeurs" (act 1, scene 4). A choral refrain, "Que d'attraits," encloses the *air*. Gluck also employs this music for the chorus of priestesses in *Iphigénie en Tauride*, act 2, scene 6. Mozart's apparent use of musical citation may not be intentional; it may instead be an instance of cryptomnesia, a process in which one hears, forgets, and then recalls something as an original idea. See Tenpenny et al., "In Search."

66. The aria was revised as "Divinités du Styx" in the French version staged in 1776 (act 1, scene 7). For a modern edition of the sketch, see Heartz, *Mozart's Operas*, 271. The opening of the overture was to begin with a direct citation from Alceste's powerful B-flat aria, with its ascending bass arpeggios, trombones, and *alla zoppa* syncopation in the strings. Even the flutes have material recalling Alceste's opening vocal line of. I am indebted to Michel Noiray for pointing out this connection.

Act 1, scene 1: The beginning of the opera uses the *terribile* style to accompany the serpent's pursuit of Tamino, with rapid scales, tremolos, abrupt dynamic shifts, and *alla zoppa* syncopation.[67]

Act 1, scene 6: The first appearance of the Queen of the Night begins with an instrumental prelude to an accompanied recitative, long associated with *tragédie en musique,* and transformed by Gluck into striking mood-setting music for his accompanied recitatives.[68] Here Mozart uses syncopated figures and a long crescendo for the mechanical device that conveyed the Queen and changed the set to a starry night. Jahn observed that this prelude is a paraphrase of music that accompanies the rising sun in Georg Benda's *Ariadne auf Naxos.*[69] The scene and its music have a direct model in *Der Stein der Weisen,* where Astromonte makes his magical appearance. Instrumental preludes commonly accompany dei ex machina. Fairy-tale operas such as *La fée Urgèle,* with music by Johann Schultz (1782, 1784, and 1789) included such pieces. The extensive use of the bassoon here (and elsewhere) in the score recalls French marvelous opera, beginning with Rameau.[70] After the recitative, the first section of this multipartite aria has bursts of string scales to highlight the word "Bösewicht." Sixteenth-note figures in the violins show Pamina's trembling and shuddering just as she sings of them.[71] The second section, where tragic narration changes to a call-to-arms, has the long coloratura with which Mozart defined this supernatural character through her unusual musical power. This was also the case with Astromonte in the parallel scene in *Der Stein der Weisen.* The final ritornello is another example of stage-machine music as the Queen of the Night and her Ladies leave the stage and the scenery returns to its previous appearance. Short bursts of ascending scale figures in the basses and the

---

67. The initial music recalls a melody in Josef Myslive Ček's oratorio *Isacco figura del redentore* (Florence, 1776), a work performed by Schikaneder in Budapest in 1785. Mozart may also have heard this popular oratorio or seen the score. The music occurs in an accompanied recitative for Abraham. After an angel has told him that he will have to sacrifice his son, the patriarch expressed his conflicting emotions ("Eterno Dio! Che inaspettato è questo, che terribil commando!"). Pečman, *Josef Mysliveček,* 155, first discussed this connection. I would like to thank James Ackerman for pointing it out.

68. Accompanied recitative plays an important role in *Die Zauberflöte,* e.g., the long scene for Tamino and the Speaker (called the Old Priest in the score), and the scene for Pamina and for Sarastro (act 1, scene 18, finale). The earlier fairy-tale operas in the Wiednertheater used this device as well.

69. Otto Jahn, *W. A. Mozart* 4: 644.

70. Mozart also uses the bassoon in comic situations and for ironic effect, for example, in the first quintet (act 1, scene 7), when the instrument doubles Papageno's inarticulate utterances. The bassoon is also one of the solo instruments in Pamina's moving aria "Ach, ich fühl's."

71. Mozart accompanied Leporello's frightened exclamation ("Ah padron, siam tutti morti") in the second finale of *Don Giovanni* with these figures and composed a similar accompaniment for Pamina's narration in the finale (act 1, scene 18), where she refers to her mother and the duty of a daughter.

bassoons, along with descending scales in the violins and oboes, again suggest the supernatural.

Act 1, scene 15 (finale): The music for the three boys as they lead Tamino to the three temples is a processional march (marked "Larghetto") with dotted rhythms and scored with an array of winds, including three trombones, trumpets, and timpani. More often than not Mozart used the march for his magic stage music, a common convention of the "marvelous" that dates back to French baroque opera.

Tamino's flute solo in this scene is also a magical device that may have been aided by stage machines, as in the second finale. It demonstrates the mystical ethos of music as Pamina and Papageno proclaim after witnessing the effects of the magic bells (act 1, scene 17): "Only the harmony of friendship alleviates hardships; without this sympathy there is no happiness on earth." Similar flute music occurs in the magic bird scenes in both finales of *Der Stein der Weisen.* The long tradition of magic flutes in the theater dates back at least to the early seventeenth century.[72]

Act 2, scene 16: Mozart uses enchantment music for the appearance of the three boys in their flying machine, one that suits their function in the plot as cupids. They offer moralizing admonitions to Tamino and Papageno in a popular song style. Fantastic ornamental appoggiaturas in the violins (derived from French serious opera) accompany this compound duple-meter allegretto. Similar music occurs in the opening and closing ritornellos, as the flying machine enters and exits, and when the three boys prepare a set table. This seems to allude to childhood, with the flutes and bassoons highlighting fussy string arpeggios decorated with ornaments.

Act 2, scene 26: An enchanted wind serenade, marked "Andante" and "sotto voce," accompanies the descent of the three boys in their flying machine. Again, Mozart provides a marchlike processional with dotted rhythms. This episode begins a long and fluid dramatic scene that leads to Pamina's attempted suicide and concludes with a happy resolution as the boys tell her that Tamino loves her. After the final waltz or *Ländler* section in E-flat, a concluding ritornello bears the indication "Verwandlung" for the scenic transformation to the awesome site of the trials.

Other instances of music for the mechanical stage and scenic transformation include:

Act 2, scene 27: The magic trial scene invokes the four elements of nature, long familiar in supernatural representations. The music, specifically indicated as a *Marsch,* sets the pace and mood for Tamino and Pamina's procession

---

72. Especially Jean Millet, *Pastorale ou tragicomédie de Janin, ou de la Hauda,* performed in Grenoble, 1635 (see the Introduction).

through their trials. Trombones, horns, and timpani accompany the flute. This unusual combination of instruments complements the special effects noted in the libretto and autograph score.

Act 2, scenes 27–28: Mozart provides transformation music for the scene where the earth swallows up the villains and daylight breaks through the darkness of night. This begins with rapid ascending scales in the strings that introduce the climactic violent episode (*zerschmettert*) for the full orchestra with three trombones. This music recalls the beginning of Gluck's *Iphigénie en Tauride* and the opening of the second act of *Der Stein der Weisen*, with thunder, lightning, and a storm depicted with diminished harmonies, timpani rolls, string tremolos, syncopation, and sustained wind blasts. The scenic transformation has a series of modulations by fifth as the villains sink into the earth. A gentle descending melodic idea forms a transition as the light returns in the form of a large sun, and Sarastro sings an accompanied recitative to introduce the final triumphal chorus in E-flat.

Ensembles for Supernatural Characters and Events

The libretto calls for ensembles that include supernatural characters such as the queen, the three boys, and the three ladies. Mozart's musical settings here are often displays of compositional mastery; as such, they recall some ensembles in Italian and French comic opera of the 1760s,[73] along with more recent French *grand opéra*.[74] The immense trio for the three ladies in the first act's *introduzione* is a remarkably ambitious composition with inventive virtuoso vocal writing (the original setting included a cadenza for the three voices that Mozart later canceled) and intricate instrumental accompaniment. Somewhat similar scenes occur in both comic and serious French opera, such as the trio of Greeks at the beginning of Gluck's *Iphigénie en Aulide* (act 1, scene 5). But the length and the combination of comic and serious episodes in a dramatically unfolding ensemble make Mozart's trio distinctive. After the three ladies kill the serpent, they express a complex series of reactions to the attractive young man who has fallen unconscious (another association with Armida, who falls in love with the sleeping Rinaldo).

The first of two remarkable multipartite quintets (act 1, scene 7) in the opera begins with the humming of Papageno, who has been rendered speechless by an enchanted lock on his mouth. The ensemble continues as the three ladies remove the lock, delivering an admonishing moral. The two men join them

---

73. One might compare Mozart's ensembles with the complex textures of the nine ensembles in Monsigny's *L'île sonnante* (Paris, 1768), a neglected opera that has some elements in common with *Die Zauberflöte*.

74. Rameau wrote these kinds of ensembles in his later *tragédies* and his "comédie-ballet" *Les Paladins* (1760).

for further admonitions (like most of the other morals in the opera, Mozart marks the passage "sotto voce"). In the next section the three ladies present the magic flute and bells to the men. This segment has an array of abruptly changing affects and styles, freely mixing comedy, the supernatural, and moral pronouncement. The keys seem to have been selected purposefully in the rapidly progressing segment of mm. 165–90. Papageno expresses his anxiety about Sarastro in G minor, the ladies' presentation of the magic bells turns to the supernatural key of E-flat, and the reassuring farewell is in a more neutral B-flat. In the final segment the ladies mention the three boys for the first time. Here Mozart employs a childlike allusion with "dolce" and "piano" indicated for the pizzicato strings and sustained winds that accompany the simple periodic melody sung sotto voce. The instrumental ending quotes a children's song by the theater's *Kapellmeister*, Henneberg.

Like the first quintet, the second (act 2, scene 5) is a complex ensemble with a rapid progression of comic and serious moments for the same five characters (again with moral pronouncements sung sotto voce). The ending segment employs the *terribile* style as the priests warn (in octaves) that the presence of the three ladies has profaned the temple. The ladies hear repeated sixteenth notes (the libretto specifies "a terrifying chord with all the instruments; thunder, lightning and a crash"), a *bruit souterrain;* they exclaim "O weh" and sink into a trap door to the sound of a descending sixteenth-note phrase in the violins.

The scene for the men in black armor (act 2, scene 28) begins with an Adagio in C minor. The first six measures recall the beginning of act 2 of Gluck's *Orfeo ed Euridice* (also an underworld scene) and the beginning of the act 1 overture in *Der Stein der Weisen*. This segment introduces an unusual fugato, scored with low-pitched strings, trombones, and winds. With a slow homophonic introduction and a contrapuntal texture for the second section, Mozart has returned to the style of the overture. The composer employs some unusual sacred references: Heinrich Biber's third Kyrie from the *St. Henry Mass* and the chorale tune "Ach Gott, vom Himmel sieh darein, und lass dich doch erbarmen." Although a two-part male chorus singing in octaves or unison is not uncommon for supernatural characters, a duet for tenor and bass soloists singing in octaves is rare in fairy-tale operas.[75]

The "Nur stille, stille, stille" quintet (act 2, scene 29) starts with an octave-and-unison motive in C minor along with the sound of thunder and rushing water. Diabolical music for Monostatos follows ("Dort wollen wir sie überfallen") and leads to an equally menacing song of praise ("Dir, große Königin

75. Unlike many fairy-tale operas, the choruses here are not for supernatural characters. They use both homophony for expression of uniformity of opinion, e.g., act 1, scene 19 (finale), and polyphony (act 2, scene 30). The homophonic chorus for the priests (act 2, scene 20), scored with winds and trombones, seems to represent night and day through the opposition of sharps and flats.

der Nacht").[76] This style here, with its hypnotic repetition of single notes, recalls *falsobordone*. After a cadence, rapid string scales interrupt their song and announce their terrible fate.

The Invocation Aria

The Queen of the Night's second aria belongs to a tradition of incantation sung by the great enchantresses of the lyric theater, Medea, Circe, Alcina, and Armida. The furious *terribile* style, the minor key with chromatic inflexion, the demonic coloratura, and the fantastic figuration in the accompaniment are all conventional elements of infernal incantation. The aria contains the longest coloratura in the opera; its extravagant embellishment defines her character as powerful, violent, and angry. A long coloratura passage on the word "nevermore" (*nimmermehr*) seems intended to overwhelm Pamina with her mother's murderous demands. In the second coloratura, with its triplets on the word "Bande" she drives home her vow to destroy the bonds of nature between mother and daughter. This passage recalls Handel's coloratura for his sorceress Medea in the aria "Sibillando, ululando, fulminate" in *Teseo* (see chapter 3).

The melodic gesture of condemnation beginning with the text "Verstoßen sei auf ewig" is the same as that used for the condemnation by the statue and the chorus from hell in *Don Giovanni* (motives previously sung by Donna Elvira in her condemnation of Giovanni). The queen sings the incantation motive three times, followed by a threefold repetition of the octave leap from the end of the motive. This repeated incantation motive seems to have been a cliché for an angry supernatural character cursing or casting a spell. It dates back to early eighteenth-century opera. Handel uses it several times, for example in *Rinaldo, Giulio Cesare,* and *Orlando.* The repeated descending octave motive is also a traditional gesture of supernatural force in eighteenth-century Italian opera, as seen in the examples by Handel, Ristori, and Bertoni, discussed in chapters 3 and 4. Mozart accompanies this melodic cliché with running parallel thirds and accented wind blasts. In *La maga Circe* Anfossi gave this same figure an almost identical accompaniment in Circe's exclamation "Precipitosamenta, tutti farò perir." The previous chapters demonstrated that composers often accompanied incantations and expressions of anger in this manner, dating back at least to Gluck.

The queen ends her aria proper with the words "Sarastro wird erblassen!,"

---

76. Monostatos's origin has been the subject of speculation. A villainous Moorish slave appears in several *Dschinnistan* stories as well as other operas with fairy-tale or oriental subjects. One intriguing possibility is Arlequin, who wears a dark mask, is a coward, and is unable to endure deprivations or delay gratification. He often serves a wealthy patron. Sarastro's punishment of Monostatos, seventy-seven lashes on the soles of his feet, occurs in oriental fairy tales and at least one French comedy derived from those tales, *Le combat magique* (Théâtre des Grands-Danseurs [1772–91]), preserved in an undated anonymous manuscript in F-Pn, f.f. 9257, fols. 159–79.

set to a musical quote from Gluck's *Iphigénie en Tauride* (act 1,scene 4), where the Furies sing to the aghast Orestes "il a tué sa mère!" (a motive that Gluck uses to end emphatic phrases in other operas as well). Mozart's quotation of Gluck here is a clever reversal of context. Gluck had the Furies sing it to summon the memory of a mother to her offspring. Mozart has a mother sing it to summon the Furies in front of her offspring. It is as if the Queen of the Night quotes a powerful operatic invocation to the Furies in order to get their attention, an invocation in the Furies' own musical language. She states this intention literally in the next phrase, addressed to the Furies and set in accompanied recitative, as she invokes the Eumenides to witness her oath, "Hört, hört, hört, Rachegötter, hört der Mutter Schwur!" Mozart changed the original text here ("Rache! Götter!") to make his point.

Another small recollection from *Don Giovanni* occurs in the accompaniment of this recitative segment. Mozart uses the same emphatic scalar figures in the bass that he used for the statue's loud knocks in the second finale of *Don Giovanni*, punctuating the "Hört" exclamations with supernatural emphasis.

The Enchanted March

Mozart's music for the magic flute and that for the magic bells have one thing in common: the march. This style apparently offered the composer advantages in constructing a dramatic sequence of events in music. The march moves steadily forward, imparting a sense of linear progression. It may employ various types of stepwise movements and gestures, pacing a scene in a sort of temporal underpainting. Moreover, the march ideally suits magical scenes because it seizes the attention in a distinctive manner. In its original military association the march sets individuals in motion, compelling a kind of lockstep response. The repetition of its short duple-meter phrase units can also create a trancelike effect, suggesting enchantment and magic spells.

Sulzer and Kirnberger discussed the march as a primitive precursor of dance with the "ability to control and direct the body."[77] This lockstep quality was observed in southern Germany by Charles Burney, who expressed amazement at the soldiers he saw in military formation in Ludwigsburg and Würzburg. They appeared "disciplined like clockwork,"[78] and Burney had never seen such "mechanical exactness in animated beings . . . one would suppose that the author of *Man a Machine* had taken his idea from these men."[79]

77. Sulzer and Kirnberger, *Allgemeine Theorie der schönen Künste* (1970), 3:394–95. Koch and Rousseau discuss the march as well (see Allanbrook, *Rhythmic Gesture*, 46). Mattheson, *Der vollkommene Capellmeister*, describes the march as suitable for a military style, and he refers to ceremonial marches where characters merely stride slowly and nobly.

78. Burney, *Present State of Music*, 103.

79. Burney is referring to Julien Offray de La Mettrie, *L'homme machine* (Leyden, 1748), translated as *Man a Machine* (1912).

We first encounter Mozart's magic march music in the act 1 finale (scene 15, no. 8), with the magic flute solo by Tamino, an ornamented march that enchants the animals, recalling Orpheus and his lyre. Scene 16 continues the march rhythms in a faster tempo (Andante, G major) for Pamina and Papageno's text "Schnelle Füsse, rascher Mut." In scene 17 Monostatos and the slaves capture Pamina and Papageno ("Ha! Hab ich euch noch erwischt!"), and the pace quickens to an Allegro. The key modulates from G to C as Papageno invokes the magic bells with mock triadic fanfares in his vocal line, recalling the clarion-call magic invocations in grand opera ("Komm, du schönes Glockenspiel"). Papageno's invocation has the rhythm of a simple march as the key returns to G. Papageno plays the magic-bell music, and the libretto specifies that Monostatos and his slaves "gehen unter dem Gesang marschmäßig ab."[80] The little march seizes Monostatos and the slaves just as they are about to tie up Papageno and Pamina. Its military association makes it the perfect choice for magic music, forcing the villain and his slaves into lockstep like toy soldiers.

Mozart's harmony is simple, consisting of only three chords. He starts with a variation on a theme not yet heard (most of the magic music in the opera is a variation rather than a theme). Here the variation, an act of freedom for the performer, is the end of free will and liberty for the victim of its allure. The magic of this scene occurs in a purely musical fashion. Once they hear the variation, Monostatos and his slaves magically recognize the theme, singing it together in three-part harmony. Mozart uses this original device again in a parallel scene for the magic bells in the second act (see below).

The dancing-slave scene has precedents, as detailed in the previous chapters. But here only the beauty of the music causes the trance that forces its victims to sing its praises. It is no coincidence that this sounds like an improvised variation, or that Mozart enjoyed playing the bell music behind the scenery.[81] The music playfully seizes its listeners and compels admiration and astonishment, two key elements of the "marvelous." This seems appropriate for a man who enjoyed playing ingenious musical games and making jokes. Mozart even included an additional ironic figure in the form of a short eighth-note embellishment in the fourth measure of the variation. This is the musical equivalent of a child's taunt, wagging a finger or thumbing one's nose at one's adversaries.

80. A magic spell that forces its victims to dance occurs in commedia dell'arte plots, for example, *Rosalba incantatrice, Il theatro delle favole* . . . (Venice, 1611), Giornata xliiii, *Li tre satiri*, Rome, Biblioteca Corsiniana, Ms. 45 G. 5 and 6, i, 9, and Rome, Biblioteca Casanatense, F. IV, 12–13, now codices 1211, 1212, ii, 28 [1622]. *The Necromancer*, Lincoln's-Inn-Fields, 1723, translated as *Le docteur Faustus* for Paris, 1740, has a magic dance where Arlequin appears and strikes his magic wand, making the characters dance by enchantment. Italian comic operas such as *L'anello incantato* by Bertati and Bertoni (Venice, 1771) also employed this device. Bertati's *La fata capricciosa* (Venice, 1789) also has a scene with a dance that dispels a magic enchantment.

81. Mozart's letter to Constanze of 8–9 October 1791 describes a performance of the opera where he played the keyed glockenspiel part during Papageno's aria "Ein Mädchen oder Weibchen" from behind one of the flats.

The Magic Bells

Bells, clocks, and carillons have a long historical association with the super-natural. They could symbolize eternity or immortality by virtue of tones that seem to continue to ring without cease. Early Christian communities thought bells "spoke," and thus they were sometimes baptized. Communities rang bells on occasion to counter the effects of nature, for instance during violent storms. In opera magic bells date back at least to early eighteenth-century France. Fuzelier's comic opera *Mélusine* (1719) includes scenes with *L'horloge de la verité d'amour, les cloches,* and *les carilloneurs*. Rameau composed descriptive panto-mime music for an enchanted *horloge* in *Les Boréades* (1764). The comic fairy-tale opera *Fleur d'Épine* (1776) has a magic carillon that rings its two thousand bells when a captive tries to escape. In Dezède's *opéra-féerie Alcindor* (1788), a magic carillon reveals the truth by sounding whenever a woman lies about her virtue. The pantomime *Das Zauber-Glöckel,* probably performed on 28 December 1750 at the Schwarzenberg castle in Krumau (today Česky Krum-lov), then in Vienna in 1773,[82] has scenes with magic bells that grant the wishes of their possessor. Schikaneder's direct predecessor of *Die Zauberflöte* in the Wiednertheater, *Der wohltätige Derwisch* (late winter, 1791), featured a fools' cap with magic bells. The cap was worn and used by Mandolino, the comic companion of the princely hero. This role directly parallels that of Papageno, who will also be given a set of magic bells.

I have already discussed the magic-bell music as a march variation in act 1. In act 2 the bells appear in two scenes. In scene 21 the bells play a theme and two variations for Papageno's strophic aria "Ein Mädchen oder Weibchen." Mozart wrote these variations as an accompaniment to Schikaneder's quasi-improvised pantomime of Papageno's intoxication and bell playing. Scene 29 is another instance of enchantment, starting with Papageno calling out for his lost mate, Papagena. The musical style recalls the gigue, a compound-duple-meter dance, here marked "Allegro" and in the major mode. When Papageno contemplates and attempts suicide however, he sings another theme in gigue rhythms, now marked "Andante" and in the key of G minor, parodying Pami-na's aria in the same key and meter (also somewhat reminiscent of the Commen-datore's death music in *Don Giovanni*). This episode recalls the mock-heroic suicide scenes of Arlequin in the commedia dell'arte and in *opéra-comique*. Mo-zart's simple melody and his sparse accompaniment during this episode also suggest parody, as does Papageno's line "Gute Nacht du falsche Welt," which lacks the poignancy and chromatic pain of Pamina's aria "Ach, ich fühl's."

As they had done with Pamina, the three boys rescue Papageno from sui-cidal despair. They descend and announce their intentions with an abrupt change of tempo (Allegretto) and an unprepared change of key. The boys have become pastoral cupids since stopping Pamina's suicide; once again they

82. For details, see chapter 5.

function to further the cause of love. Entering stealthily, they repeat a simple fanfare-like call on the dominant seventh chord of the new key of C ("Halt ein, Halt ein, Halt ein"). Mozart then sets the rest of the line ("o Papageno, und sei klug, man lebt nur einmal dies sei dir genug") with a short motive and a repeated cadence in the popular lieder style. Most important, he brings back the meter of a march, his rhythm of musical enchantment. Papageno acknowledges this by taking up the boys' meter and motive. But he does not yet share their optimism, for he returns to the former key of G, singing that although they can joke, they would also seek girls if they felt as passionate as he does. Here Papageno varies the boys' melodic material but uses the same phrase structure and cadence in the same popular style. Mozart's accompaniment is now spinning off into effusive variation and fantasy, exactly where Papageno's mind should be (the boys have just told him to wise up ["sei klug"]). The boys now seem to rejoice in Papageno's getting their message as they extend his musical response into their own new contrasting section. They refuse his key (G) and move back to their own (up a fourth to C). Accented accompaniment in the military style brings the march character into sharp focus as the boys remind Papageno of his magic bells, the source of his first magic march ("So lasse deine Glöckchen klingen, dies wird dein Weibchen zu dir bringen"). He now repeats their magic-bell motive in their key as he admits to having foolishly forgotten about his *Zauberdinge*. He then further varies the material by once more using the popular-song style, here commanding the bells to play with a melodic figure that includes martial dotted rhythms.

Now the music has finally settled into the boys' key of C, and the tempo changes to allegro for the solo of the magic bells. This solo is a highly ornamental march variation whose original theme would be indecipherable to listeners, except for Papageno. He demonstrates this magic recognition by singing the simple tune immediately after the variation. This is an act of pure musical magic, exactly the same kind that occurred with the bells in act 1. The enchanted listener intuitively hears the melody by listening to the variation, something possible only with supernatural power.

While Papageno and his bells are alternating musical parlays, the libretto specifies that the boys run to their flying machine and bring out the woman (perhaps an ironic touch in the libretto, since they had told Papageno that the magic bells would bring Papagena). After the final cadence of the magic-bell episode with Papageno, the boys change the key once more, this time back to Papageno's key, G major. They instruct Papageno to turn around and see what they (and not the bells, as they have said) have brought him. The boys then ascend in their cloud chariot, and Papageno turns to look at Papagena. Here the libretto specifies another pantomime: "Beide haben unter dem Ritornell komisches Spiel." For this Mozart provides a new parody march, one that brings Papagena into erotic lockstep with her mate. Their stupefied repetition of each other's name (or is she really mocking him?) and their preoccupation with the results of their union leave little doubt as to the nature of their trance. Perhaps Schikaneder or Mozart meant the "pa-pa-pa" reiterations by the birdlike couple to be a musical interpretation of erotic foreplay, recalling Mozart's own childlike games of erotic stimulation in sound.

The idea of erotic play permeates this scene as one march inspires another and one phrase stimulates a new variation. This is Mozart's personal fantasy style, very different from that of C. P. E. Bach or Haydn. As with the Fantasy for Piano in C Minor, K. 475, Mozart creates not jarring juxtapositions of material with abrupt interruptions, but new symmetries with intimately related material. This subtle transformation of material is Mozart's real magic, and characters such as Papageno show it as they create new ideas and vary older material. They seem lifelike to us because they appear to have the creative instinct in their music. Invention, improvisation, variation, play, and fantasy are regenerative elements in Mozart's music, closely allied to his own creative and carnivalesque inclination. His use of the march is yet another imaginative twist on an old convention from marvelous opera and ballet.

Thus Mozart's supernatural music features a limited number of motives developed in a controlled fantasy style for long scenes of continuous action with changing musical references. Mozart is one of the few composers to relate the stylistic approach of magic to the fantasy style of quasi-improvised, preludial music. Haydn does this as well. Although Salieri attempted a similar technique, he does not often connect his scenes through related motives or with a sense of playful improvisation. Music rarely propels the scenic progression in earlier Viennese fairy-tale works such as *Der Ring der Liebe, Das wütende Heer, Der Irrwisch,* and *Kaspar der Fagottist.* The Wiednertheater productions seem to have done more with this aspect, especially *Der Stein der Weisen.* Mozart's dismissive comment on the popular *Kaspar der Fagottist* ("there is nothing at all to it") probably refers in part to the lack of dramatic substance in the music. One only has to compare Müller's score to that of *Der Stein der Weisen* and *Die Zauberflöte* to confirm the truth of Mozart's assessment.

∶✦∶

The Significance & Influence
of Supernatural Topics

In this book I have demonstrated that music for magic and supernatural events was significant in the context of the overall achievement of major European opera composers in the eighteenth century. This significance is not just a matter of the quantity of supernatural events on the stage, but the result of qualitative changes in musical style and their influence beyond the theater. Composition of theater music starts with a libretto or a plot scenario, and it is clear that the composer had a degree of freedom in setting the music. The evidence presented here indicates that although some composers did not musically distinguish divine characters from mortals, or supernatural episodes from natural ones, others, such as Mouret, Rameau, Monsigny, Traetta, Jommelli, Gluck, J. C. Bach, Haydn, and Mozart, chose a different path. Rather than neglecting the original magic association of music, they transformed it in new directions.

For much of the seventeenth century the mere presence of music was evidence of a magical or divine event on the stage. The act of singing alone could indicate and justify the divine nature of a character. With the Enlightenment a kind of disenchantment of music occurred—its presence alone no longer indicated a supernatural character or event. Music moved to the mortal, rational, and natural realm. In response to this change some composers developed procedures to distinguish the divine from the mortal, the supernatural from the natural, the magic from the rational. Even more significantly, the disenchantment of music eventually meant that magical and supernatural events in a libretto could become the stimulus and the source of inspiration for the artistic imagination to represent the transcendental element with special musical techniques. In doing so the composer took on attributes of the magus, casting sonic spells through what I call "mimetic engineering". By taking on this role, by creating music that represented metaphysical beings and events, composers assumed the creative force associated with the divine. This assumption is an essential basis of the sublime in music.

Magic musical expression penetrated other, nonmagical situations far from vocal music and deep into the realm of an instrumental repertory associated with the sublime. An understanding of this influence has been hampered by ignorance of supernatural musical references, which have remained unacknowledged, even in detailed analytical studies that stress "topics." The mode of terror (*terribile*) has been misunderstood and dubbed the so-called Sturm und Drang style. This was not a musical expression of a literary movement, but the participation of instrumental genres in the new expressive mode of ballet and opera. Profiting from new styles in Italian and French stage music, composers adapted the mode of terror and the "marvelous" into their instrumental music. The suggestion of tempest scenes and of fateful encounters with the underworld inspired eighteenth-century composers such as Haydn to write instrumental works with more powerful and energetic expression.

Mozart followed Haydn in this regard, applying the older composer's application of theatrical conventions to his instrumental music. His Symphony no. 25 in G Minor, K. 173d/183 (October 1773), is an early example. The first movement has *alla zoppa* syncopation, string tremolos, rapid descending and ascending scales, octave-and-unison sonority, a disjunct baroque "subject," infernal blasts of the winds (oboes, horns, and bassoons), and sweeping gestures in the bass. All of these devices suggest an infernal scene or a tempest invoked by a divine or magical character with supernatural power. This music would have served especially well for a *Don Juan* ballet, and Gluck is a probable influence. There are similar references in the other movements as well, such as the minuet, with its emphatic unisons and chromatic touches recalling Gluck's *Don Juan*. Even the wind band in the trio evokes contrasts similar to those in the Gluck ballet.

During Mozart's stay in Paris in the summer of 1778, the composer heard the latest French *grand opéra* during the height of the Gluck-Piccinni controversy. At least one work composed in this period, the first movement of the Piano Sonata no. 8 in A Minor, K. 310/300d, is redolent with the stormy Parisian opera style of Gluck and Piccinni, beginning with its bold, accented strokes and sweeping gestures. The development section in particular suggests infernal images with persistent dissonance, trills, and a final chromatic sweep into the recapitulation. The piano's idiomatic imitation of the string tremolo and abrupt diminished chords in the recapitulation also bring the supernatural to mind.

The two piano concertos in minor keys are especially evocative of the new operatic mode of the supernatural and the terrifying. The composer who longed to write opera is displaying his theatrical capabilities before the Viennese public with these concertos. Mozart filled his Piano Concerto no. 20 in D Minor, K. 466 (February 1785), with allusions to the supernatural and later employed the same short, powerful ascending glissandos in the bass as emphatic knocks in *Don Giovanni* and explosive curses in the Queen of the Night's second aria. The concerto's vividly pictorial music is also heard in the sweeping string figures. Mozart's seems to borrow from Gluck's *Don Juan* here, mixing the demonic D minor with abruptly contrasting moments of a more tender expression for wind ensemble. The Piano Concerto no. 24 in C Minor, K. 491 (March 1786), features string tremolos, baroque-style themes with wide leaps, and blaring brass, all suggestive of the operatic inferno. The waltzlike phrases in the minor mode bring to mind the demonic triple-meter episodes of the second finale in *Don Giovanni*. Sweeping string gestures of the "marvelous" are now transmuted into piano virtuosity, and the torturous chromatic lines parallel those in *Don Giovanni*.

This style of expression had implications for sacred vocal music as well. Aspects of the Requiem, K. 626, seem suggestive of supernatural opera. The Dies irae has an abundance of terrifying musical imagery, beginning with rapid figuration, string tremolo, *alla zoppa* syncopation, and choral exclamations suggesting the anguished cries of the damned in an infernal scene from contemporary opera. (Both Joseph Eybler and Franz Xaver Süßmayr added blaring winds and punctuating brass and timpani in their completions.) At the final cadence of the initial segment of the Dies irae (m. 57) the words "cuncta stricte discussurus" (judge all things severely) are set to a variation of the cadence used for damnation scenes (here with a Neapolitan chord in the repeat at m. 63). This cadence, found in several operas discussed in the previous chapters, confirms the allusion to condemnation in this most *terribile* of all texts in the liturgy. The violent opening sections of both the Rex tremendae and the Confutatis could easily be operatic scenes with the Furies. Thus in his last composition Mozart incorporated dramatic elements of stage music to create a complex and vivid portrayal of supernatural events, as he had in *Idomeneo, Don Giovanni*, and *Die Zauberflöte*.

Without this legacy of marvelous, supernatural, and terrifying topics, Beethoven might not have developed his own powerful expression in instrumental music (one need only recall his piano and symphonic music in D minor, C minor, and F minor). Neither would Carl Maria von Weber or Richard Wagner have had as rich a musical vocabulary upon which to draw when creating their operas. Just as fairy tales influenced their texts, the musical traditions of the eighteenth century bequeathed to them an expressive sonic land of fantasy, marvel, enchantment, and terror.

Chronological List of Operas, Ballets, *Comédies*, *Féeries*, Pantomimes & Other Plays with Magic & Supernatural Content, 1699–1791

1699–1714

Tragédies, Ballets, Celebratory Works, Etc.

La réjouissance des fées, dramatic dialogue by Hubi, for the birth of the Duke of Bretagne, 1704

Alcine, tm, A. Danchet, mus. A. Campra, PO, 15 Jan. 1705

Philomèle, tm, P.-C. Roy, mus. L. de Lacoste, PO, 20 Oct. 1705

Alcyone, tm, A. Houdar de Lamotte, mus. M. Marais, PO, 18 Feb. 1706

Manto la fée, opéra, [?] Mennesson, mus. J.-B. Stück, PO, 29 Jan. 1711

Jérusalem délivrée, tl, H.-B. Requelayne, Fontainebleau, 17 Oct. 1712

Mélusine, tragédie, A.-L. Lebrun, pub. Paris, 1712

Medée et Jason, tm, S.-J. Pellegrin, mus. J.-F. Salomon, PO, 24 Apr. 1713

Le comte de Gabalais et les peuples élémentaires, divertissement, P.-F. Godard de Beauchamps, mus.
   T. L. Bourgeois, Château de Sceaux, Oct. 1714

At the Comic Theaters

Les fées, oc, F.-C. Dancourt, Fontainebleau, 24 Sept. 1699; C.-Fr., 29 Oct. 1699

Le diable boiteux, oc, F.-C. Dancourt, C.-Fr., 1 Oct. 1707

Le second chapitre du diable boiteux, oc, F.-C. Dancourt, C.-Fr., 20 Oct. 1707

Le fée bien-faisante, c, le Chevalier La Beaume, Th. de Grenoble, 7 July 1708

Arlequin à la guinguette, divertissement, Simon-Joseph Pellegrin, St. Laurent, 25 July 1711

Arlequin au sabat, pant, J.-A. Romagnesi, mus. de la Croix, St. Germain, 3 Feb. 1713

La bague enchantée, oc, S.-J. Pellegrin, St. Germain, 3 Feb. 1713

Arlequin fille malgré lui, oc, P.-F. Dominique, called Biancolelli, 22 July 1713

Arlequin invisible chez le roi de Chine, oc, A.-R. Lesage, St. Laurent, 30 July 1713

Le festin de pierre, pant, Le Tellier, performed 1713–21

La matrone d'Ephèse, oc, L. de Fuzelier, St. Germain, 2 Feb. 1714

Arlequin favori de la fortune, oc, [?] Duvivier de Saint-Bon, St. Germain, 3 Feb. 1714

Arlequin Mahomet, oc, A.-R. Lesage, mus. J.-C. Gilliers, St. Laurent, 25 Sept. 1714

Griselde, ou La princesse de Saluces, oc, L.-G. Gillot, Mme de Sainctonge, Dijon, 1714

La coupe enchantée, oc, L. Fuzelier, St. Laurent, 1714

1715–19

Tragédies, Ballets, Celebratory Works, Etc.

Le palais d'Urgande, intermède, P.-C. Roy, mus. J. J. Mouret, Château de Sceaux, 15 Feb. 1715

Sémiramis, tm, P.-C. Roy, mus. A. Destouches, PO, 4 Dec. 1718

At the Comic Theaters

Les eaux de Merlin, oc, Lesage, mus. Gilliers, St. Laurent, 25 July 1715

La ceinture de Venus, oc, Lesage, mus. Gilliers, St. Germain, 1715

L'école des amans, oc, Lesage and Fuzelier, mus. Gilliers, St. Germain, 3 Feb. 1716

Arlequin, jouet des fées, ou Les folies de Rosette, oc, Fuzelier, St. Germain, 3 Feb. 1716

L'Arcadie enchantée, c, anon, Th.-It., 3 Feb. 1717

Les anneaux magiques, canevas, anon, 13 May 1717

Les avantures de Cythére, c, J. Charpentier, St. Laurent, 1717

Pierrot furieux, ou Pierrot Roland, oc, Fuzelier, Pontau, Pannard, St. Germain, 1717

Le métempsychose d'Arlequin, canevas by Lelio, with French scenes by Dominique. Th.-It., 19 Jan. 1718

La château des lutins, oc, Lesage, St. Germain, 3 Feb. 1718

Les animaux raisonnables, oc, Fuzelier, M.-A. Legrand, St. Germain, 25 Feb. 1718

Arlequin, valet de Merlin, oc, Lesage, St. Germain, 1 Mar. 1718

Le monde renversé, oc, Lesage, d'Orneval, La Font, mus. Gilliers, St. Laurent, 2 Mar. 1718

Les comédiens par hazard et l'anneau de Brunel, oc, T.-S. Gueullette, Th.-It., 15 Mar. 1718

La princesse de Carisme, oc, Lesage and d'Orneval, mus. Lacoste, St. Laurent, July 1718

La fiancée du roy de Garbe, oc, S.-J. Pellegrin, Aug. 1718

Le roi de Cocagne, c, M.-A. Le Grand, mus., Quinault, C.-Fr., 31 Dec. 1718

Les lunettes magiques, ou Les enchantemens, oc, Meunier, Th.-It., 1718

Arlequin Pluton, c, T.-S. Gueullette, mus. Mouret, Th.-It., 19 Jan. 1719

Arlequin libérateur, ou La caverne des Baigards, oc, anon, 27 Aug. 1719

La fée Mélusine [or *Mélusine*], oc, Fuzelier, Th.-It., 3 Dec. 1719

La statue merveilleuse, oc, Lesage, mus. Gilliers, St. Germain, 1719, and St. Laurent, 1720

1720–29

Tragédies, Ballets, Celebratory Works, Etc.

Renaud, ou La suite d'Armide, tm, Pellegrin, mus. Desmarest, PO, 14 May 1722

La reine de péris, comédie-persanne, Fuzelier, mus. J. Aubert, PO, 10 Apr. 1725

Pirame et Thisbé, tm, de La Serre, mus. Rebel and Francœur, PO, 15 Oct. 1726

At the Comic Theaters

Arlequin roi des ogres, ou Les bottes de sept lieues, oc, Fuzelier, Lesage, d'Orneval, St. Germain, 3 Feb. 1720

La queuë de verité, oc, Fuzelier, Lesage, d'Orneval, St. Germain, 3 Feb. 1720

L'isle de Gougou, oc, Lesage, d'Orneval, St. Germain, 2 Mar. 1720

L'âne du Daggial, oc, Lesage, d'Orneval, St. Germain, 27 Mar. 1720

Arlequin poli par l'amour, c, Marivaux, Th.-It. (Hôtel de Bourgogne), 17 Oct. 1720

La fôret de Dodone, oc, Lesage, Fuzelier, d'Orneval, mus. Gilliers, St. Germain, 3 Feb. 1721

La guitare enchantée, oc, D. Carolet, G.-A. Dupuy, St. Laurent, 5 July 1721

Belphégor, ou La descente d'Arlequin aux enfers, oc, M.-A. Le Grand, St. Laurent, 24 Aug. 1721

Le fleuve d'oubli, oc, M.-A. Le Grand, St. Laurent, 12 Sept. 1721

Magotin, oc, Lesage, d'Orneval, St. Germain 1721

Arlequin dans l'isle enchantée, canevas italien, anon, 4 Feb. 1722

Arlequin camarade du diable, oc, L. Rustaing de Saint-Jorry, Th.-It., 4 Feb. 1722

Le jeune vieillard, oc, Fuzelier, Lesage, d'Orneval, mus. Mouret, St. Laurent, 25 July 1722

La foire des fées, oc, Fuzelier, Lesage, d'Orneval, St. Laurent, 8 Aug. 1722

Tirésias, oc, A. Piron, St. Laurent, Sept. 1722

Tirésias aux quinze-vingt, oc, D. Carolet, St. Laurent, 1722

Le lutin amoureux, oc, anon, 28 Nov. 1722

Arlequin amoureaux par enchantement, oc, P.-F. Godard de Beauchamps, Th.-It., 16 Dec. 1722

L'Endriaque, oc, A. Piron, airs by J.-P. Rameau, St. Germain, 3 Feb. 1723

L'oracle muet, pièce en écriteaux, Lesage, d'Orneval, St. Laurent, July 1724

La reine de péris, [oc], Lesage, d'Orneval, undated parody of the Fuzelier/Aubert opera

Pierrot fée, oc, J. de La Font, St. Laurent, 17 July 1726

Arlequin Bellérophon, c, Dominique and Romagnesi, Th.-It., 7 May 1728

La princesse de la Chine, oc, Lesage and d'Orneval, mus. Gilliers, St. Laurent, 15 June 1729

La noce angloise, ballet-pantomime, [?] Roger, St. Laurent, 16 Aug. 1729

1 7 3 0 − 3 9

Tragédies, Ballets, Celebratory Works, Etc.

Hippolyte et Aricie, tm, Pellegrin, mus. Rameau, PO, 1 Oct. 1733

La féerie, entrée in *Les Romans*, M. de Bonneval, mus. Niel, PO, 30 July 1736

Les génies, ballet, Fleury de Lyon, mus. Mlle. Duval, PO, 18 Oct. 1736

Sethos, tragédie, A. Tanevot, based on Terrasson, 1738

Dardanus, tm, C.-A. Le Clerc de La Bruère, mus. Rameau, PO, 9 Nov. 1739

At the Comic Theaters

La pantoufle, oc, M. Marignier, St. Germain, 30 Mar. 1730

La sylphide, c, Dominique and J.-A. Romagnesi, Th.-It., 11 Oct. 1730

Le prince de Noisy, c, Jean du Mas d'Aigueberre, C.-Fr., 4 Nov. 1730

L'esprit aérien, ou La petite sylphide, c, Bartholomé, 1730

Roger de Sicile, surnommé le roi sans chagrin, oc, Lesage, d'Orneval, St. Laurent, 28 July 1731

Polichinelle, roi des Silphes, pièce, anon, St. Laurent, 8 Aug. 1731

Arlequin Amadis, c, Dominique and J.-A. Romagnesi, Th.-It., 27 Dec. 1731

Le sejour enchanté, oc, anon, Foire St., 1731

Le parterre merveilleux, oc, D. Carolet, mus., Gilliers, St. Laurent, 1731

Le palais de l'ennuy, ou le triomphe de Polichinelle, marionette pièce, D. Carolet, St. Laurent, 1731

Polichinelle, Amadis, marionette pièce, Carolet, St. Germain, Mar. 1732

Les épreuves des fées, oc, Fuzelier, St. Laurent, 28 July 1732

Les sinceres malgré eux, oc, Fuzelier, St. Laurent, 28 July 1733

La fée Marote, oc, Soulas d'Allainval, St. Laurent, 28 Aug. 1734

Le palais enchanté, oc, Nicolas [de] La Grange, St. Germain, 27 Feb. 1734

La miroir magique, oc, F.-A. Lesage, called Pittenec, St. Germain, 7 Apr. 1734

Le conte de fée, c, J.-A. Romagnesi and A.-F. Riccoboni, Th.-It., 26 May 1735

L'isle des fées, ou Le géant aux marionnettes, oc, anon, St. Laurent, 12 July 1735

Le songe agréable, ou Le rêve de l'Amour, oc, anon, St. Laurent, 1735

Les amours magiques, pièce à machines, A. Pavy, Chambéry (Hôtel de Bellegarde), Jan. 1736

Les fées, c, M. Procope Coltelli and J.-A. Romagnesi, Th.-It., 14 July 1736

Pierrot valet de magicien, oc, Lesage, St. Laurent, 27 July 1736

Belphégor dans Marseille, c, J.-B.-P. Baco, Marseilles, 1736

Polichinelle, roi des fées, marionette pièce, anon, St. Germain, 4 Feb. 1737

Le rien, oc, C.-F. Panard, Boizard de Pontau ou Vadé, and Fagan, St. Germain, 1 Mar. 1737

Le palais de l'illusion, oc, Laffichard and Valois, St. Laurent, 1 July 1737

L'amant genie, c, La Borde Montibert, Metz, 6 Aug. 1737

Le rejeunissement inutile, c, N. La Grange, mus. Brulart, C.-Fr., 27 Sept. 1738

Grisélidis, c, anon, Avignon, Sept. 1738

Les métamorphoses d'Arlequin, canevas italien, anon, St. Laurent, 13 Mar. 1739

Les âges, ou La fée du Loreau, c, A.-C.-P. de Tubières Grimoard de Pestels de Lévis, comte de Caylus, Château de Morville, 20 Sept. 1739. With a divertissement, *Le prince pot à thé*

Arlequin magicien, c, anon, The Hague, c. 1739

Le songe de Pierrot, marionette pièce, anon, Foire, 1739

1740−49

Tragédies, Ballets, Celebratory Works, Etc.

La princesse de Navarre, comédie-ballet, Voltaire, mus. Rameau, Versailles, 23 Feb. 1745

Zélindor, roi des silphes, ballet féerie, Moncrif, mus. Rebel and Francœur, Versailles, 17 Mar. 1745

La féerie in *Les festes de Polimnie*, ballet-heroïque, Cahusac, mus. Rameau, PO, 12 Oct. 1745

Zélinsca, comédie-ballet, de La Noue, mus. Jélyote, Versailles, 3 Mar. 1746

Scylla et Glaucus, tm, d'Albaret, mus. J.-M. Leclair, PO, 4 Oct. 1746

Les festes de l'Hymen et de l'Amour, ou Les Dieux d'Egypte, opéra-ballet, Cahusac, mus. Rameau, Versailles, 15 Mar. 1747

Zaïs, ballet-héroïque, Cahusac, mus. Rameau, PO, 29 Feb. 1748

Pigmalion, acte de ballet, Ballot de Sauvot, mus. Rameau, 27 Aug. 1748

Aeglé, ballet-héroïque, P. Laujon, mus. P. de La Garde, Versailles, 1748 and 1750

Le prince de Noisy, ballet-héroïque, C.-A. Leclerc de La Bruere, mus. Rebel and Francœur, Versailles, 13 Mar. 1749

Zoroastre, tl, Cahusac, mus. Rameau, PO, 5 Dec. 1749

At the Comic Theaters

Arlequin dans le château enchanté, c, J.-A. Romagnesi, Th.-It., 17 Mar. 1740

L'oracle, c, G.-F. Poullain de Saint-Foix, mus. N. Ragot de Grandval, C.-Fr., 17 Apr. 1740

Le naufrage d'Arlequin, ou L'Arcadie enchantée, c, anon, Th.-It., 11 June 1740

Le docteur Faustus, c, anon, dated 1740

Les métamorphoses de Polichinelle, marionette c, anon, St. Germain, 1740

Amour pour amour, c, P.-C. Nivelle de La Chaussée, mus. N. R. de Grandval, C.-Fr., 16 Feb. 1742

L'île des talents, c, B.-C. Fagan de Lugny, Th.-It., 19 Mar. 1743

Zénéïde, c, L. de Cahusac, mus. N. R. de Grandval, C.-Fr., 13 May 1743

Arlequin et Scapin, magiciens par haʒard, c, anon, Th.-It., 15 July 1743

Le combat magique, canevas italien, anon, Th.-It., 12 Sept. 1743

La miroir véridique, oc, Lesage, 1743 revival of *La statue merveilleuse*

Acajou, oc, C.-S. Favart, mus. Blaisé, St. Germain, 18 Mar. 1744

Coraline esprit follet, c, Carlo A. Véronèse, Th.-It., 21 May 1744

Coraline magicienne, c, C. A. Véronèse, mus. Blaisé, Th.-It., 2 July 1744

Polichinelle gros Jean, marionette pièce, anon, St. Germain, 1744

Polichinelle, maître maçon, marionette pièce, anon, St. Germain, 1744

La fée Acarenne, oc, anon, St. Laurent, Aug. 1745

Les métamorphoses de Scaramouche, ou La vengeance de Scaramouche, c, Gandini, Th.-It., 13 Sept. 1745

Coraline protectrice de l'innocence, c, anon, Th.-It., 28 Sept. 1745

Les folies de Coraline, c, anon, Th.-It., 8 Jan. 1746

Le fée Carabosse, oc, anon, St. Germain, 19 Feb. 1746

Le puits enchanté, c, anon, Th.-It., 28 Feb. 1746

La félicité, c, anon, Th.-It., 20 Apr. 1746

Coraline fée, c, C. A. Véronèse, Th.-It., 23 May 1746

La Barbe-bleüe, oc, A.-J. Valois d'Orville, St. Laurent, 3 July 1746

La fée Manto, ou Le chien qui secoue des pierreries, oc, anon, St. Laurent, 15 Aug. 1746

Le prince de Salerne, canevas italien, anon, 24 Sept. 1746

L'amour et les fées, c, F.-Jo. de Pierres, Cardinal de Bernis, C.-Fr., 1 Oct. 1746

Arlequin apprenti magicien et cocher par amour, oc, Restier, St. Germain, 20 Mar. 1747

Ninna, oc, anon, St. Laurent, 28 June 1747

L'Arcadie enchantée, c, anon, mus. Blaisé, 13 July 1747

Le miroir, c, "Mr. Petit, médicin," 28 Aug. 1747

Les métamorphoses d'Arlequin, canevas italien, anon, 30 Aug. 1747

Les metamorphoses, ou les amants parfaits, c, G.-F. Poullain de Saint-Foix, Th.-It., 25 Apr. 1748

L'année merveilleuse, c, anon, mus. Blaisé, Th.-It., 18 July 1748

Les fées rivales, c, Véronèse, mus. Blaisé, Th.-It., 18 Sept. 1748

Le palais des fées, 1749, oc, anon, Th. de Nicolet, Feb. 1755

1750–59

Tragédies, Ballets, Celebratory Works, Etc.

Ismène, pastorale-héroïque, F.-A. Paradis de Moncrif, mus. Rebel and Francœur, Versailles, 20 Dec. 1747, PO, 28 Aug. 1750

Le génie, ballet, 4 parties, [?] Dupré, Collège Louis-le-Grand, Aug. 1751

La guirlande, ou Les fleurs enchantées, acte de ballet, J.-F. Marmontel, mus. Rameau, PO, 21 Sept. 1751

Acante et Céphise, ou La sympatie, pastorale-héroïque, Marmontel, mus. Rameau, PO, 18 Dec. 1751

Le fôret enchantée, spectacle à machines, J.-N. Servandoni, mus. F. Geminiani, Tuileries, 21 Mar. 1754

Le ballet de fées, comédie-ballet, A. Houdar de La Motte, 1754

La constance couronnée, spectacle à machines, J.-N. Servandoni, mus. Carlo Sodi, Tuileries, 27 Mar. 1757

At the Comic Theaters

Arlequin et Scapin morts vivans, canevas italien, anon, 20 Feb. 1750

Le songe vérifié, canevas italien, anon [from Mme. de Caillerie], 13 Oct. 1751

Le jardin des fées, ballet-pantomine, anon, mus. C. Sodi, St. Laurent, 13 Jan. 1752

Les Thessaliennes, ou Arlequin au sabat, c, Pierre Prévost and Cazanove, Th.-It., 24 July 1752

Le miroir magique, oc, J. Fleury (based on Lesage), St. Laurent, 25 July 1752

Arlequin génie, c, C. A. Véronèse, Th.-It., 14 Aug. 1752

La baguette, c, anon, Th.-It., 18 July 1753

La coupe enchantée, oc, Rochon de la Valette, M.-A.-J. Rochon de Chabannes, St. Laurent, 19 July
1753

Zélide, c, Paul Barett, Chateau de Berny, 1753 or 1755

Arlequin génie, c, J.-B Dehesse [dit Deshayes], Th.-It., 14 Jan. 1754

Zélide, ou L'art d'aimer et l'art de plaire, c, J.-J.-C. Renout, C.-Fr., 26 July 1755

Le palais des fées, oc, anon, Th. de Nicolet, Feb. 1755 [1749?]

Le diable à quatre, oc, Sedaine, St. Germain, 1756

Les métamorphoses d'Arlequin, c, anon, Th.-It., 5 May 1757

Nina, ou La mitaine enchantée, c, C.-H. Fusée de Voisenon, Th.-It., 14 Jan. 1758

Coraline et Camille fée, c, [C. Véronèse] Th.-It., 23 or 24 Aug. 1758

Cendrillon, oc, L. Anseaume, mus., J.-L. Laruette, St. Germain, 21 Feb. 1759

L'amant statue, oc, J.-F. Guichard, mus., C. de Lusse, St. Laurent, 18 Aug. 1759

Le masque enchanté, farce, E.-L. Billardon de Sauvigny, Th. de Lyon, 28 Aug. 1759

1760–69

Tragédies, Ballets, Celebratory Works, Etc.

Les paladins, comédie-lyrique attrib. to Duplat de Monticourt and others, mus. Rameau, PO,
12 Feb. 1760

Le prince de Noisy, ballet-héroïque, C.-A. Leclerc de La Bruere, mus. Rebel and Francœur, PO,
16 Sept. 1760

Les Boréades, tm, anon, mus. Rameau, rehearsed Apr. 1763

At the Comic Theaters

Le bûcheron, ou Les trois souhaits, c, J.-F. Guichard, mus. F.-A. Danican Philidor, Th.-It., 28 Feb.
1763

Pierrot, roi de Cocagne, pant, [Laurent Dubut] Th. de Nicolet, 10 Jan. 1764 (or 25 Nov. 1764)

La fée Urgèle, ou Ce qui plaît aux dames, c, C. S. Favart, mus. E. Duni, Fontainebleau, 26 Oct. 1765,
and Th.-It., 4 Dec. 1765

La Barbe-bleu, c, G. Delautel, Th. de Nicolet, 1766

L'aveugle de Palmyre, c, F.-G. Fouques Deshayes, dit Desfontaines, mus. J.-J. Rodolphe, Th.-It.,
5 Mar. 1767

Le turban enchanté, c, Véronèse, fils, Th.-It., 14 July 1767

L'île sonnante, c, C. Collé, Monsigny, Villers-Cotterêts, chez Mme. De Montesson, Aug. 1767,
Th.-It., 4 Jan. 1768

Arlequin recruteur, oc, anon, St. Laurent, c. 1768

Le petit poucet, c, L.-C. Carmontelle, before 1769

Tanzaï et Néadarné, c, C. Collé, pub. 1768

Arlequin financier, ou Le mariage par magie, c, Pagnier, ms. dated 1769

La table enchantée, c, L.-J. Mancini Mazarini, duc de Nivernois, chez Mme. de Caraman, pub.
1769

La ceinture enchantée, c, F.-H. Barthélemon, called Bartlemain, Th. de Bordeaux, 1769

Le bouquet enchanté, oc, anon, Th. de Nicolet, 1769

1770–79

Tragédies, Ballets, Celebratory Works, Etc.

La tour enchantée, ballet-figuré, N.-R. Joliveau or Laval, mus. d'Auvergne, Versailles, 20 June
    1770

Pygmalion, scéne lyrique by Jean-Jacques Rousseau (1762), set by Horace Coignet (Lyon, 1770)

Amadis de Gaule, tm, P.-M. Berton, after Quinault, mus. J.-B.-F. La Borde, PO, 26 Nov. 1771

Isménor, drame héroïque, Desfontaines, mus. Rodolphe, Versailles, 17 Jan. 1773

Sabinus, tl, M.-P.-G. de Chabanon, mus. F.-J. Gossec, Versailles, 4 Dec. 1773

Iphigénie en Aulide, tragédie, M. F. L. G. Roullet, mus. Gluck, PO, 19 Apr. 1774

Orphée et Euridice, tragédie-opéra, P. L. Moline, mus. Gluck, PO, 2 Aug. 1774

Azalon, ou Le serment indiscret, ballet- héroïque, Lemonnier, mus. Floquet, PO, 15 Nov. 1774

Alceste, tragédie, M. F. L. G. Roullet, mus. Gluck, PO, 2 Aug. 1776

La féerie, entrée in *Les Romans*, ballet-héroïque, Michel de Bonneval, mus. J.-J. Cambini, PO,
    2 Aug. 1776; revision of Niel's ballet, PO, 30 July 1736

Armide, drame héroïque, revision of P. Quinault, mus. Gluck, PO, 23 Sept. 1777

Roland, tl, Marmontel, after Quinault, mus. N. Piccinni, PO, 27 Jan. 1778

Jérusalem délivrée, ou Renaud et Armide, pant, J.-J. Le Boeuf, mus. J.-B. Rochefort, Th. des élèves
    de l'opéra, 7 Jan. 1779

Amadis de Gaule, tragédie-opéra, Vismes du Valgay, after Quinault, mus. J. C. Bach, PO, 14 Dec.
    1779

At the Comic Theaters

L'arbre enchanté, pièce italienne, anon, Th.-It., 19 Jan. 1770

L'Arcadie enchantée, c, C. A. Véronèse, Th.-It., 1770

La baguette merveilleuse, ou La magicienne confondue, pièce à changements, A. L. B. Robineau,
    called Beaunoir, Th. de Nicolet, 1770 (1771)

Arlequin et les fées, drame, anon, c. 1770

Riquet à la houpe, c, Toussaint-Gaspard Taconet, Th. de Nicolet, 1770

La belle au bois dormant, pant, J.-F. Mussot, called Arnould (other sources cite F. Huguet, called
    Armand) Ambigu-comique, 1770, revised 1776

Arlequin Mahomet, ou Le cabriolet volant, drame, J.-F. Cailhava de L'Estendoux, Th.-It., 13 Mar.
    1770

Zémire et Azor, comédie-ballet, J.-F. Marmontel, mus. A.-E.-M. Grétry, Fontainebleau, 9 Nov.
    1771, Th.-It., 16 Dec. 1771

Arlequin au sabbat, pant, anon, Th. de Nicolet, 1771

Le petit poucet, c, J.-J.-C. Renout, Ambigu-comique 1771

Le chat-botté, pant, J.-F. Musset, called Arnould, or P.-J.-B. Nougaret, Chois-le-roi ambigu-
    comique, 8 Apr. 1772

L'amant voleur, ou La Bégueule, c, A.-L.-B. Robineau, called Beaunoir, Th. des grands-danseurs
    du Roi, 1772 (1773)

Le bouquet enchanté, c, Louis-Carrogis Carmontelle, c, 1772

La lanterne magique, ou les pourquoi, c, [?] Maille de Lamalle, en Provinçe, 1772

Les mannequins, ou Le sculpteur, c, J.-F. Mussot, called Arnould, Ambigu-comique, 23 June 1773

La belle Arsène, comédie-féerie, C.-S. Favart, mus. Monsigny, Th.-It., 6 Nov. 1773

La haine par amour, féerie en dialogue, Fanny de Beauharnais, 1773

Le rosier parlant, féerie en dialogue, Fanny de Beauharnais, 1773

La Barbe bleue, pant, anon, Th. des grands-danseurs du Roi, cited in *Almanach forain*, 1773

Riquet à la houpe, pièce, J.-F. Mussot, dit Arnould, Ambigu-comique, 5 Dec. 1774

Le petite chaperon rouge, pièce, [?] Mension, Ambigu-comique, 1774

Fleur d'épine, oc, C.-H. Fusée de Voisenon, mus. M.-E. Bayon, Th.-It., 19 Aug. 1776

Les quatres Arlequins, ou Les quatre filles à marier, pant, Th. des grands-danseurs du Roi, 1776

Les effets de la haine et de la constance, ou Asmodée diable boiteux, opéra-féerie, Verteuil l'aîne, mus. Guillmino, Comédiens de Toulouse in 1777, then in Marseilles

[*Les statues*, c, J. F. Marmontel, mus. Grétry, c. 1777 (planned but never completed)]

Matroco, drame burlesque, P. Laujon, mus. Grétry, Fontainebleau, 3 Nov. 1777, then Th.-It., 4 Feb. 1777

Les petits lutins, pant, anon, Ambigu-comique, 1778

Les héroïnes, ou Les soldats magiques, pant, anon, Ambigu-comique, Feb. 1778

Madame Hautaine, ou L'amant voleur, pant, anon, Th. des grands-danseurs du Roi, Feb. 1778

Le jugement de Midas, c, Thomas Hale, mus. Grétry, Th.-It., 27 June 1778

Le magicien de village, ou L'âne perdu et retrouvé, pant, N.-M. Audinot, mus. Papavoine, Th. des petits comédiens du Bois de Boulogne, 18 Sept. 1779

Les amours de la fée Carabosse, ou Le bouquet enchanté, pant, anon, Th. des grands-danseurs du Roi, 13 Sept. 1779

La Barbe-bleue, pant, anon, Apr. 1779

La pantoufle de Cendrillon, pant, anon, Th. des Elèves de l'Opéra, 13 Sept. 1779

1780–84

Tragédies, Ballets, Celebratory Works, Etc.

Atys, tl, Marmontel, after Quinault, mus. N. Piccinni, PO, 2 Feb. 1780

Iphigénie en Tauride, tl, A. Du Congé Dubreuil, mus. N. Piccinni, PO, 23 Jan. 1781

Thésée, tl, E. Morel de Chédeville, mus. F.-J. Gossec, PO, 1 Mar. 1782

Renaud dans la forêt enchantée, ballet-héroïque, E. l'Auchery, Kassel, 1782

Renaud, tl, J.-J. le Bœuf, N.-E. Framéry, after Pellegrin, mus. A. Sacchini, PO, 25 Feb. 1783

Les Danaïdes, tl, M.-F. Louis Gand Roullet and Tschudi, after Calzabigi, mus. A. Salieri, PO, 4 Apr. 1784

At the Comic Theaters

Barbe-bleue, pant, anon, Th. des élèves de l'opéra, 1 Jan. 1780

Les métamorphoses d'Arlequin, pant, anon, Th. des grands-danseurs du Roi, 19 June 1780

Rosanie, c, A.-M.-D. de Vismes de Saint-Alphonse, mus. H.-J. Rigel, Ambigu-Comique, 24 July 1780

Le géant désarmé par l'amour, pant, anon, Ambigu-comique, 15 Aug. 1780

La corbeille enchantée, ou La pays des chimères, c, L.-F.-A. Dorvigny, Th. de variétés-amusantes, 4 Sept. 1780

Le débarquement, ou Les trois géants, ou Le serpent magicien, pant, anon, Th. des grands-danseurs du Roi, 19 Oct. 1780

Le prince noir et blanc, féerie, N.-M. Audinot, J.-F. Mussot, called Arnould, Ambigu-comique, 11 Dec. 1780

Les étrennes de Mercure, ou Le bonnet magique, oc, P.-A.-A. de Piis and P.-Y. Barré, Th.-It., 1 Jan. 1781

Blanche et Vermeille, comédie-pastorale, J.-P. Claris de Florian, mus. H.-J. Rigel, Th.-It., 5 Mar. 1781 and 26 May 1781

Le combat magique, pièce, anon, Th. des grands-danseurs du Roi, 21 May 1781

Les deux sylphes, c, B. Imbert, mus., M.-A. Desaugiers, Th.-It., 18 Oct. 1781

Le baiser, ou La bonne fée, c, J.-P. Claris de Florian, mus. S. Champein, Th.-It., 26 Nov. 1781 and
    28 Nov. 1782

La bégueule, c, J. Mague de Saint-Aubin, Ambigu-comique, 27 Nov. 1781

Les deux génies, ou Le faux et le vrai bonheur, conte dramatique, L.-P. de Ségur, 1781

La caverne enchantée, ou Rien n'est difficile en amour, pant, anon, Th. des grands-danseurs du Roi,
    7 Sept. 1782

Le diable-boiteux, ou La chose impossible, divertissement, C.-N.-J. Favart [fils], Th.-It., 27 Sept.
    1782

La Barbe-bleue, tragédie burlesque, F.-M. Poultier, called Delmotte, Th. de Lunéville [1782?]

Arlequin protégé par l'amour magique, pant, anon, Th. des grands-danseurs du Roi, 6 Apr. 1783

Arlequin volant, pant, anon, Th. des grands-danseurs du Roi, 20 May 1783

Les amours de la fée Doyenne, pant, anon, Th. des grands-danseurs du Roi, 21 May 1783

Arlequin protégé par la harpie dans la caverne enchantée, pant, anon, Th. des grands-danseurs du
    Roi, 24 Nov. 1784

1785–91

Tragédies, Ballets, Celebratory Works, Etc.

Alcine, opéra, M. Sedaine and N.-E. Framery, mus. le comte Bernard-Germain-Étienne Lacé-
    pède, 1785

Les Horaces, tl, N. F. Guillard, after P. Corneille, mus. A. Salieri, Versailles, 2 Dec. 1785

Œdipe à Colone, opéra, N. F. Guillard, mus. A. Sacchini, Versailles, 4 Jan. 1786

La toison d'or, tl, P. Desriaux, mus. J. C. Vogel, PO, 5 Sept. 1786

Tarare, opéra, P.-A. Caron de Beaumarchais, mus. A. Salieri, PO, 8 June 1787

Alcindor, opéra-féerie, M.-A.-J. Rochon de Chabannes, mus. N. Dezède, PO, 17 Apr. 1788

Corisandre, ou Les fous par enchantement, comédie-opéra, A.-F. Lebailly, mus. H.-F.-M. Langlé,
    PO, 8 Mar. 1791

At the Comic Theaters

L'arbre enchanté, ou Le batelier désobligeant, c. anon, Th. des associés, 19 Jan. 1785

Belphégor, ou Le diable à Florence, c, L.-C.-P. de Bérainville, Th. des Beaujolais, 10 Mar. 1785

Arlequin roi dans la lune, c, N.-M.-F. Bodard de Tezay, Th. des variétés-amusantes, 17 Dec. 1785

La magi blanche, pant. anon, Th. des grands-danseurs du Roi, 30 Sept. 1785

Cendrillon, pièce-féerie, Maillé de Marencourt, Th. de Séraphin, 1785

Le petit poucet, pièce-féerie, Maillé de Marencourt, c. 1785

L'antre magique, ou Le péruvien triomphant de l'héroïne americaine, pant, F.-M. Mayeur de Saint-
    Paul, Th. des grands-danseurs du Roi, 2 Apr. 1786

Le calife Arbroün, c, P.-L. Moline, Th. des Associées, 1786

Urbélise et Lanval, ou La journée aux aventures, comédie-féerie, A.-J. Bourlin, called Dumaniant,
    Th. des variétés-amusantes, 28 Apr. 1787, Th. du Palais-Royale, 30 Apr. 1788

Les jeunes vieillards, féerie, anon [after Lesage?], Th. des Beaujolais, 5 May 1787

Almanzor et Nadine, c, Fonpré de Fracansalle, Th. des grands-danseurs du Roi, 6 Dec. 1787

Les deux fées, c, P.-A.-L.-P. Plancher, called Valcour, Th. délassements, 1787

Les mannequins de la bonne fée, c, S. Constant de Rebecque, before 1787

Lanval et Viviane, ou Les fées et les Chevaliers, comédie-héroïque-féerie, P.-N.-A. de Murville,
    mus. S. Champein, Théâtre de l'Odéon, 13 Sept. 1788

Le chevalier errant, ou Le palais enchanté, oc, H.-M. Dorvo, Th. patriotique, 1788

Urgande et Merlin, c, J.-M. Boutet de Monvel, mus. N.-M. Dalayrac, written c. 1788, perf. Th. Favart, 1793

Belphégor, ou La descente d'Arlequin aux enfers, c, Le Grand, mus. F. Beck, Bordeaux, 9 Feb. 1789

Raoul, Barbe-bleue, c, M.-J. Sedaine, mus. A.-E.-M. Grétry, Th.-It., 2 Mar. 1789

Cora, ou La prêtresse du soleil, drame, J.-L. Gabiot de Salins, mus. J. J. Cambini, Th. de Beaujolais, 25 Mar. 1789

L'isle enchantée, oc, J.-F. Sedaine de Sarcy, mus. A. B. Bruni, Th. de Monsieur, 3 Aug. 1789

Le menuisier de Bagdad, c, C.-J. Guillemain, Th. de Beaujolais, 22 Dec. 1789

Aʒélie [=*Rosanie*], comédie féerie, A.-M.-D. de Vismes, mus. H.-J. Rigel, Th. de Monsieur, 14 July 1790

Les trois bossus de Damas, ou Le mauvais frère, c, J. Roger d'Orléans, pub. 1790

Les bourse magique, ou Bon cœur vaux mieux que richesse, drame féerie, J. Roger d'Orléans, pub. 1790

Les deux génies, c, Sc. de Meissner, tr. Rauquil-Lieutaud; place and date of performance unknown [other works c. 1790]

La sopha, opéra-féerie, Crébillon fils, mus. E. Scio, Marseilles, 26 Aug. 1791

UNDATED EIGHTEENTH-CENTURY WORKS

Aladin, ou La lampe merveilleuse, pièce, Amédée Noisette, Th. de Séraphin

L'anneau magique, c. anon, F-Pn, f.f. 9284, fols. 154–67

Les antres de Trofonius, c, A.-Re. de Voyes d'Argenson, marquis de Paulmy (active c. 1740–61)

Arlequin financier, ou Le mariage par magie, c, Pagnier, F-Pn, n.a.f. 2865, fols. 206–40

Arlequin génie, c, P.-C.-F. Aunillon (1684–1760). Ms. Arsenal 2757, pp. 1–97

Arlequin génie, pant, anon, F-Pn, n.a.f. 2866, fols. 1–5

Arlequin, jouet des fées, c, anon, F-Pn, f.f. 9310, fols. 126–60. Probably based on Fuzelier, St. Germain, 3 Feb. 1716

Arlequin mort supposé, squelette et dogue, parade, anon, F-Pn n.a.f. 2866, fols. 79–101

Arlequin nécromancien, pant, anon, Th. des grands-danseurs du Roi

Arlequin valet enchanté, c, anon

Artus et Lanval, comédie-féerie, Jean Monnet, based on Imbert and used as the basis of *Lanval et Viviane*

La baguette enchantée, pant, anon, F-Pn, n.a.f. 2871, pp. 66–80

La belle Fortuna, ou Le palais des nains, pant, anon, F-Pn, Ms. n.a.f. 2873, fols. 221–29

Le bon-homme Cassandre aux indes, parade, T.-S. Gueullette or J.-A. Sallé, F-Pn, f.f. 9341 and printed sources

Caracataca et Caracataqué, parade, T.-S. Gueullette, Arsenal Ms. 9445 and prints (1756)

Ce qui plaît aux dames, oc, A.-J.-P., vicomte de Ségur, Ms. Arsenal 94901

La colonie, ou L'isle des roses, comédie-féerie, anon, F-Pn, f.f. 9256, fols. 210–32

Le combat magique, pièce, anon, F- Pn, f.f. 9257, fols. 159–79, Th. de Sr. Nicolet

La constance récompensé, ou le magicien impuissant, c, Antoine Pavy

Les enchantements de la fée Biscaroux, pièce, anon, F-Pn f.f. 9241, fols. 1–8

Le festin de pierre, c, anon, Ms. f.f. 25480

Le génie rose et le génie bleu, ou les vieilles femmes rajeunées, pant, anon

L'isle d'amour, comédie-féerie, anon, F-Pn, f.f. 9280, fols. 45–54 [postdates *La belle Arsène* (1772)]

L'isle désert, ou Le naufrage, opuscule dramatique, M.-L. de Sacy, pub. Paris 1775 and 1778

Merlin précepteur, opuscule dramatique, M.-L. de Sacy, pub. Paris, 1775 and 1778

Le naissance des fées, ballet-comique, Thomas Laffichard

Le palais des génies, pièce, Hyp. Marvint

Polichinelle, marionette pièce, anon, F-Pn Ms ThB 2076

Polichinelle magicien, marionette pièce, anon, 1695–1712

Prologue d'Arlequin Cendrillon, [?] Ourry

La reine des sylphides, comédie-ballet, anon

Le trois talismans, ou Le pied de nez, c, anon, F-Pn, n.a.f. 3004, fols. 220–25

Selected Italian Circe, Medea & Orpheus Operas, 1700–1791

CIRCE

Circe delusa, drama, G. A. Falier, mus. G. Boniventi, Venice, 1711 (lost)

Circe delusa, drama, G. A. Falier, mus. A. Orefice, Naples, 1713, music lost; 3 Mar. 1734

Ulisse errante, G. Badoaro, mus. G. Sciroli, Palermo, 1749, music lost

La Circe, dm, D. Perelli, mus. J. Mysliveček, Venice, 1779, music lost

La Circe, dm, D. Perelli, D. Cimarosa, Milan, 1783

Circe, os, D. Perelli, mus. Gazzaniga, Venice, 1786

Circe, os, D. Perelli, mus. Peter Winter, Munich, 1788, not performed

Circe, ossia L'isola incantata, past, 1789

JASON AND MEDEA

Medea e Giasone, os, G. Palazzi, mus. F. Brusa, Venice, 1726 (lost)

Giasone e Medea, os, mus. G. Andreozzi, ? St. Petersburg, 1785

Gli Argonauti in Colco, dm, S. A. Sografi, mus. Gazzaniga, Venice, 1790

Medea in Colchide, os, A. Filistri, mus. Naumann, Berlin, 1788

Medea und Jason, mus. P. Winter, Munich, 1789

ORPHEUS

Euridice, D. Lalli, mus. T. Orgiani, Obizzi/Padua, 1712

Orfeo ed Euridice, componimento da camera per musica, P. Pariati, mus. J. J. Fux, Vienna, 1715

Orfeo, past, mus. J. A. Hasse, F. Araia, et al., London, 1736

I lamento di Orfeo, festa da camera, Pasquini, mus. G. A. Ristori, Dresden, 1749

Euridice, past, mus. Bernasconi, Wagenseil, Jommelli, etc., Vienna, 1750

L'Orfeo, os, L. de Villati, mus. C. H. Graun, Berlin, 1752

Orfeo ed Euridice, azione teatrale, R. Calzabigi, mus. Gluck, Vienna, 1762

Orfeo ed Euridice, tragédie, M. Coltellini, after Calzabigi, mus. A. Tozzi, Munich, 1775

Orfeo ed Euridice, dm, Calzabigi, mus. F. Bertoni, Venice, 1776

Orfeo, opera, mus. L. Torelli, St. Petersburg, 1781

Orfeo ed Euridice, burlesque op, Houlton, mus. T. Giordani, London, 1784

Le tre Orfei, intermezzo, mus. Marcello Bernardini, Rome, 1784

Orfeo, dm, Calzabigi, mus. F. Bertoni and J. F. Reichardt, Berlin, 1785

Orfeo, mus. Giuseppe Amendola, Palermo, 1788

Orfeo negli Elisi, azione teatrale, mus. Vittorio Trento, Venice, 1789

L'anima del filosofo, ossia Orfeo ed Euridice, dm, C. F. Badini, mus. J. Haydn, London, 1791

Operas Based on Ariosto & Tasso, 1700–1791

Note: This list excludes the Ginerva, Ariodante, Olimpia, and Ruggiero episodes that lack supernatural materials.

OPERAS BASED ON ARIOSTO

L'Orlando, overo La gelosa pazzia, dm, Carlo Sigismondo Capeci, mus. A. Scarlatti, Rome, 1711

Orlando furioso, dm, Grazio Braccioli, mus. Alberto Ristori, Venice, 1713

Orlando furioso, dm, Braccioli, Venice, 1714 (a revision of Ristori by Vivaldi)

Rodomonte sdegnato, dm, Braccioli, mus. M. A. Gasparini, Venice, 1714

Orlando finto pazzo, dm, Braccioli, mus. Vivaldi, based on Boiardo, Venice, Nov. 1714

La pazzia d'Orlando, tragicomedia, Domenico Lalli, Venice, 1715

Ariodante, dm, Antonio Slavo, based on Braccioli, 1716 (set as *Ginerva, principessa di Scorzia* by Vivaldi, 1736)

Angelica vincitrice de Alcina, festa musicale, Pietro Pariati, mus. J. J. Fux. Vienna, 1716 (Vienna: Ghelen, 1716)

Angelica, serenata, P. Metastasio, mus. N. Porpora, Naples, 1720

Orlando furioso, dm, Braccioli, mus. Schürmann, Brunswick, 1722

Angelica e Medoro, comedia de magia, Canizares, composer unknown, Madrid, 1722

Orlando furioso, dm, Braccioli, mus. Bioni, Guckuksbade, 1724

Orlando furioso, dm, Braccioli, mus. O. Polaroli, Mantua, 1725

Alcina delusa da Rugero, dm, Antonio Marchi, mus. Albinoni, Venice, San Cassiano, 1725 (revived as *Gl'evenimenti de Rugero,* 1732)

Alcina maga, past, anon, various composers, perf. Bologna, 1725

Orlando furioso, dm, Braccioli, mus. Vivaldi, Venice, 1727

Orlando furioso, dm, Braccioli, various composers, Brussels, 1727

L'isola di Alcina, dm, Antonio Fanzaglia, mus.Riccardo Broschi (lost), Rome, 1728

L'avenimenti di Ruggiero, dm, Antonio Marchi, 1732; revival of Marchi's *Alcina delusa da Rugero*

Orlando, dm, anon setting of *L'Orlando,* Carlo Sigismondo Capeci (Rome, 1711); mus. Handel, London, 1733

Alcina, dm, anon, based on Broschi's *L'isola di Alcina,* 1728

Alcina, dm, mus. Handel, based on Marchi's *Alcina,* London, 1735

Le fate, dm, Stefano Benedetto Pallavicini, mus. Giovanno Albero Ristori, Dresden, 10 Aug. 1736

Angelica, Carlo Vedova, based on Braccioli, mus. G. B. Lampugnani, Venice, 1738

Angelica e Medoro, C. Vedova, mus. Pescetti, London, 1739

L'Angelica, anon, mus. I. Fiorillo, Padua, 1744

Orlando furioso, dm, anon, composer unknown, Venice, 1746

Angelica e Medoro, festa teatrale, Metastasio, mus. G. B. Mele, Madrid, 1747

La Bradamante, L. Bergalli, pub. and perf. Venice, 1747

Angelica e Medoro, dm, L. de Villati, mus. Graun, Berlin, 1749

Angelica, festa teatrale, Metastasio, composer unknown, Wolfenbüttel, 1751

L'Angelica, festa teatrale, Metastasio, mus. F. Brusa, Venice, 1756

Il nuovo Orlando, opera buffa, anon, mus. N. Piccinni, Modena, 1764

Il Ruggiero, opera seria, C. Mazzolà, mus. P. A. Guglielmi, Venice 1769

Il Ruggiero, ovvero L'eroica gratitudine, Metastasio, pub. Vienna, 1771; perf. Milan, 1771

Alcina e Ruggiero, opera seria, Amedeo Cigna-Santi, Torino, Teatro Regio, 1775

Rinaldo, dm. G. F. Tenducci, mus. Antonio Tozzi, Venice, 1775

L'isola di Alcina ossia Alcina e Ruggiero, dm, V. Cigna-Santi, mus. F. Alessandri, Torino, 1775

I furori di Orlando, dramma semigiocoso, D. Friggieri, mus. J. Touchemoulin, Regensburg, 1777

L'Angelica, festa teatrale, Metastasio, mus. J. de S. Carvalho, Lisbon, 1778

Bradamante, dm, Mazzolà, mus. J. Schuster, Padua, 1779

L'isola d'Alcina, anon, various composers, Naples, 1785

Il castello d'Atlante, librettist and composer unknown, Brescia, 1791

Angelica e Medoro, dm, G. Sertor, mus. Andreozzi, Venice, 1791

ARMIDA OPERAS BASED ON TASSO

Armida abbandonata, dm, F. Silvani, mus. Ruggieri, Venice, 1707

Armida al campo, dm, F. Silvani, mus. Boniventi, Venice, 1708

Rinaldo, os, Aaron Hill, from Giacomo Rossi, mus. Handel, London, Queen's Theatre, Haymarket, 24 Feb. 1711 (with numerous revivals and adaptations)

Armida in Damasco, dm, G. Braccioli, mus. Rampini, Venice, 1711

Armida abbandonata, dm, F. Silvani, mus. G. M. Buini, Bologna, 1716

Armida al campo, dm, F. Silvani, mus. Sarro, Naples, 1718

Armida al campo d'Egitto, dm, G. Palazzi, mus. Vivaldi, Venice, 1718

Armida abbandonata, dm, F. Silvani [?], mus. Falco, Naples, before 1719

Armida delusa, text and mus. G. M. Buini, Venice, 1720

Armida abbandonata, dm, F. Silvani, mus. Bioni, Prague, 1725

Il trionfo di Armida, dm, Colatelli, mus. Albinoni, Venice, 1726

Armida al campo, dm, F. Silvani, mus. Bioni, Breslau, 1726

L'abbandono di Armida, trattenimento scenico de cantarsi, Boldini, mus. A. Pollarolo, Venice, 1729

Armida, os, Bartolomeo Vitturi, mus. Bertoni, Venice, 1746 (revised as *Armida abbandonata* in 1780)

Armida placata, os, G. Migliavacca, mus. Mele, Madrid, 1750

Armida placata, [past], Vienna, 1750, mus. G. C. Wagenseil, Predieri, Hasse,[1] Bonno, and Abos

---

1. Hasse composed music for *Rinaldo und Armida,* a dramatic cantata by Christopher Petri. The piano-vocal score (Leipzig: The author, 1782) survives in Lbl, shelfmark F. 386.(1.). The text

L'Armida, dm, L. de Villati, based on Quinault, mus. Graun, Berlin, 1751

Armida abbandonata, dm, L. de Villati, mus. Sarti, Copenhagen, 1759

Armida, azione teatrale per musica, Giovanni Ambrogio Migliavacca and Giacomo Durazzo after Quinault, mus.T. Traetta, Vienna, BT, 3 Feb. 1761

Armida, dm, Coltellini, mus. G. Scarlatti, Vienna, c. 1766

Armida, dm, Jacopo Durandi, mus. P. Anfossi, Turin, carn., 1770

Armida abbandonata, dm, Francesci Saverio De Rogatis, mus. N. Jommelli, Naples, 1770

Armida, dm, J. Durandi, mus. Manfredini, Bologna, 1770

Armida, dm, 3, Carlo Cotellini, mus. A. Salieri, Vienna, 1771

Armida, dm, J. Durandi, mus. A. Sacchini, Milan, 1772 (revived as *Rinaldo* in London 1780 and as *Renaud* in Paris, 1783, *livret* by Pellegrin and Leboeuf)

Gli amori de Armida e Rinaldo, dm, G. Migliavacca, mus. Astarita, Livorno, 1773 (revised as *Armida*, Venice, 1777)

Armida, dm, anon, mus. G. Gazzaniga, Rome, Teatro Della Torre Argentina, 1773

Armida, dm, G. Bertati, mus. J. G. Naumann, Padua, 1773; revised as *Armida*, Leipzig, 1780

Armida, dm, G. De Gamerra, mus. L. Gatti, Mantua, 1775

Rinaldo, dm, Bertati, Durandi, De Rogatis, mus. A. Tozzi, Venice, 1775

Armida, os, Durandi, De Rogatis, mus. Mortellari, Modena, 1776

Armida, os, G. Migliavacca, mus.J. Mysliveček, Lucca, 1778, and Milan, 1779

Armida abbandonata, os, Vitturi, mus. L. Cherubini, Florence, 1782

Armida, dm, Coltellini, mus. V. Righini, Vienna, 1782 (revised as *La Gerusalemme liberata*, Berlin, 1799)

Armida, dramma eroica, N. Porta, mus. Haydn, Eszterháza, 1783

Armida abbandonata, anon, mus. Mortellari, Florence, 1785

Armida abbandonata, dm, G. Sertor, mus. Prati, Munich, 1785

Armida e Rinaldo, dm, Coltellini, mus. Sarti, St. Petersburg, 1786

Armida, anon, mus. Zingarelli, Rome, 1786

Rinaldo, Domenico Chelli and Leboeuf, mus. P. Skokoff, Naples 1788

Rinaldo, dm. G. M. Foppa, mus. P. A. Guglielmo, Venice, carn., 1789

SOME COMIC AND PARODY LIBRETTOS BASED ON ARIOSTO

Angelica e Orlando, opera buffa, F. A. Tullio (Tertulliano Fonsaconico), mus. G. Latilla, Naples 1735

La pazzi di Orlando, C. F. Badini, mus. P. A. Guglielmi, London, 1771; revised as *Orlando Paladino,* Nunziato Porta, Prague, 1775, Vienna, 1777, mus. J. Haydn, Eszterháza, 6 Dec. 1782

L'isola d'Alcina, G. Bertati, mus. G. Gazzaniga ,Venice, S. Moisè, 1772, mus. G. Rust, Bologna 1772

Il castello d'Atlante, dg, anon., carn., Brescia, 1791

---

appeared in the *Musenalmanach*, 1778. There are two choruses of "Sylphen und Sylphiden," recitatives, duets, and arias.

Some Eighteenth-Century Italian
Don Juan Settings

La pravità castigata, rappresentazione morale per musica, Prague, 1730

Don Giovanni Tenorio, c, Carlo Goldoni, 1736

La pravità castigata, opera, Brno, Moravia, carn., 1734, librettist unknown [Antonio Denzio?], mus. Eustachio Bambini (lost); Strasbourg, 1750

Don Juan de Espina en Madrid, c, anon, mus. Francesco Corradini, 1740 and 1741

Don Juan, ou Le festin de pierre, ballet, Gluck, Parma, 1765 (based on 1761, Vienna); Cremona, 1783; Pavia, 1784; Milan, 1785; as *Il convitato*, ballet, Bologna, spring, 1787

Il convitato di pietra, ballet, G. A. Le Messier (based on Gluck, Turin, 1766)

Don Giovanni Tenorio, ballet, anon, Naples, 1769

Il convitato di pietra, ballet, anon, Padua, Oct. 1775

Il convitato di pietra, ossia Il dissoluto punito, drama tragicomico, Nunziato Porta, mus. Vincenzo Righini, Prague, 1776; also Vienna, 1777, and Eszterháza, 1781–82, with additions by Haydn and perhaps other composers. Also Budapest,[1] Eisenstadt, Warsaw, and Brunswick, 1782; Hanover, 1783 or 1784

Il convitato di pietra, ballet, anon, Florence, carn., 1777–78

Il convitato di pietra, dg, 2, [Pietro Pariati?], mus. Giuseppe Calegari, Venice, 1777

Il convitato di pietra, ballet, composer unknown, Como, carn., 1780

Il convitato di pietra, ballet, composer unknown, Florence, carn., 1780

Il convitato di pietra, ballet, composer unknown, Naples, carn., 1781

Don Juan, Albo Libertyn Ukarany, opera, Wojtech Boguslawskj or Bogusìawskj (adapted from Porta), mus. Gioacchino Albertini, Warsaw, 23 Feb. 1783

Il convitato di pietra, farsa, Giambattista Lorenzi, mus. Giacomo Tritto, Naples, carn., 1783; Palermo, 1784; Naples, 1791

Il convitato di pietra, ballet, anon, Milan, 1783

Il convitato di pietra, ballet, anon, Novara, spring, 1783

Il convitato di pietra, ballet, anon, Parma, carn., 1784

Il convitato di pietra, ballet, mus. Luigi Marescalchi, Rome, carn., 1784

---

1. A score survives from a revision for Eszterháza by Haydn (Budapest, Országos Széchényi Könyvtára). Manuscript of the finales to acts 2 and 3 are in A-Wn.

Don Giovanni, o sia Il gran convitato di pietra, ballet, anon, Verona, carn., 1784

Il convitato di pietra, ballet, anon, Florence, carn., 1785

Il convitato di pietra, ballet, anon, Lodi, spring, 1785

Il convitato di pietra, ballet, anon, Mestre, spring, 1785

Il convitato di pietra, ballet, anon, Treviso, spring, 1785

Il convitato di pietra, ballet, anon, Undine, summer, 1785

Il convitato di pietra, ballet, anon, Carrara, carn., 1786

Don Giovanni, o sia Il convitato di pietra, dg, Giovanni Bertati, mus. Giuseppe Gazzaniga. Venice,
    5 Feb. 1787, Varese, autumn, 1787; Bergamo, 1788; Bologna, 1788; Cittadella, 1788; Cremona,
    1788; Treviso, 1788; Udine, 1788; Cremona, 1788; Padua, 1788; Corfù, carn., 1789; Ferrara,
    1789; Modena, 1789; Reggio Emilia, 1789; Forlì, 1789; Trento, 1789; Bagnacavallo, 1789;
    Fuime, 1789; Milan, 1789; Turin, 1789; Faenza, 1790; Forlì, 1790; Imola, 1790; Pisa, 1790;
    Verona, 1790; Lucca, 1790; Brescia, 1791; Florence, 1791; Pergola, 1791; Crema, 1791

Don Giovanni, o Il nuovo convitato di pietra, drama tragicomico, Giuseppe Foppa [?], based on Bertati, mus. Franceso Gardi, Venice, 1787; Milan, 1791

Il convitato di pietra, ballet, anon, Cento (Ferrara), summer, 1787

Il convitato di pietra, ballet, anon, Lugo (Ravenna), summer, 1787

Il convitato di pietra, dg, Giambattista Lorenzi, mus. Vincenzo Fabrizi,[2] Rome, 1787; Fano, 1788;
    Civitavecchia, 1788; Milan, 1789; Fano, 1789; Florence, 1789; Livorno, 1789; Siena, 1789; Naples, 1790; Barcelona, 1790; Perugia, 1790; Bologna, 1791

Il dissoluto punito, o sia Il Don Giovanni, dg, 2, Lorenzo Da Ponte, mus. Mozart, Prague, 1787; Vienna, 1788

Il dissoluto, ballet, anon, Livorno, carn., 1788

Il convitato di pietra, ballet, anon, Vicenza, carn., 1788

Il convitato di pietra, ballet, anon, Milan, La Scala, spring, 1788

Il dissoluto, ballet, anon, Singaglia, summer, 1788

Il convitato di pietra, past, Albano, autumn, 1788

Il convitato di pietra, past, Rome, autumn, 1788

Il nuovo convitato di pietra, c, F. Cerlone, pub. Bologna, 1789

Il convitato di pietra, past, Pavia, carn., 1789

Il convitato di pietra, past, Rovereto, spring, 1789

Il convitato di pietra, ballet, anon, Vercelli, summer, 1789

Il convitato di pietra, past, Bolzano, autumn, 1789

Il convitato di pietra, past, Racunigi, autumn, 1789

Il convitato di pietra, past, Rivarolo, autumn, 1789

Il convitato di pietra, past, Rome, autumn, 1789

Il convitato di pietra, past, mus. attrib. to Cimarosa and Paisiello, Macerata, carn., 1790

Il convitato, past, Pinarolo, carn., 1790

Il convitato di pietra, dg, anon, Rieti, 1790

Il convitato di pietra, dg, anon, Capua, 1791–92

Il convitato di pietra, past, Ancona, carn., 1791

Il convitato di pietra, ballet, anon, Padua, 1791

2. Manuscript scores in Lbl (selections), Rome, Massimo collection (private) and Conservatorio di Musicao S. Cecilia.

Chronological List of German Theatrical Works with Magic & Supernatural Content, 1728–92

Note: Revivals are indicated in brackets; e.g., [–1805] means that the piece was performed through the year 1805.

1728–59

Dr. Faust, Volksschauspiel, K, J. A. Stranitsky (1715, revised 1736)

Die verkehrte Welt, [kO?], J. P. Praetorius (based on Lesage), mus. G. P. Telemann, 1728

Die Königin der schwartzen Inseln, Zwischenspiel, H. Rademin, Vienna, c. 1731

Runtzvanscad, König deren Menschen-fressern, oder Der Durchläuchtigste Gärtner, Sch, H. Rademin, Vienna, 1732

Doktor Faust, pant, anon, KT, 9 June 1731

Circe, spl, J. P. Praetorius and J. J. van Mauritius, mus. Keiser et al., Hamburg, 3 Mar. 1734

Die Zaubertrommel, K, J. F. von Kurz, before 7 Dec. 1737

Das ruchlose Leben und erschreckliche Ende des Welt-bekannten Erz-Zauberers D. Johann Faustus, spl, anon, Opernhaus, Gänsmarkt, Hamburg, 7 July 1738

Die wunderbaren Lampe, K, anon, 3 Aug. 1738

Hannswurst, Hexenmeister aus Liebe, K, anon, 22 July 1738

Die bewunderungswürdige Baß-Geige, K, anon [Questenberg catalog lists as *Plutons große bewunderungswürdige Baßgeige*], 25 Apr. 1739

Der Teufel ist los, K, C. W. von Borck (Coffey), mus. [?] Sydow, Berlin, 1743

Hannswurst neu aufgerichteter Prob-Brunnen, die Treu der Jungfrauen und Junggesellen zu erkennen, operetta Bernesca, anon, Nuremburg, 21 Aug. 1748

Das Zauber-Glöckel, pant, anon, Česky Krumlov, Bohemia, 28 Dec. 1750

Der blinde Ehemann, L, J. C. Krüger (1744), adapted by J. F. Jünger (Sch), 1751

Die verkehrte Welt, L, J. U. von König, Dresden, 1749

Das Orakel, L, Jos. Wendler (Saint-Foix), Leipzig 1750; Brunswick and Leipzig, 1752

Der neue krumme Teufel, spl, J. F. von Kurz, mus., F. J. Haydn, ?1752

Der lebendig verbrannte Zauberer Bernardon, K, anon, perf. 1752

Der sich wieder seinen Willen taub und stumm stellende Liebhaber, L, J. F. von Kurz, Vienna, 1755

Die fünf kleinen Luftgeister, Zauberkomödie, K, J. F. von Kurz, c. 1750–59

Bernardon der ruchlose Juan del Sole, K, J. F. von Kurz, c. 1750–59

Das steinerne Gastmahl, oder die redende Statua samt Arie welche Hannswurst singet nebst dene Verserin Der Eremiten, anon, undated prints (2), Vienna, 1760

Der neue krumme Teufel, spl, with Kinder-Pantomime, *Arlequin, der neue Abgott Ram in America*, by J. F. von Kurz, mus. F. J. Haydn, Vienna, ?1752

Der lebendig verbrannte Zauberer Bernardon, K, J. F. von Kurz, Vienna, 1752

Der sich wieder seinen Willen taub und stumm stellende Liebhaber, L, J. F. von Kurz, Vienna, 1755

Der aufs neue begeisterte und belebte Bernardon, K, J. F. von Kurz, c. 1750–59

Der Baron Hanswurst von Pikaragal, K, anon, c. 1750–59

Das Anglück des Sinen ist öfters Gas Glück des Andern, oder Die wolthätige Zauberin mit Hannswurst, Den tyrannischen Wallsisch-Ritter gesungen werden, K, anon, mus. J. G. Heubel, c. 1750–59

1760–79

Don Juan, ou Le festin de pierre, ballet, Calzabigi, Angiolini, mus. Gluck, BT, Oct. 1761

Rinaldo und Armida, ballet héroïque, E. l'Auchery, mus. Rodolphe, Stuttgart, 11 Feb. 1761

Megära, die fürchtliche Hexe, oder Der bezauberte Schloß des Herrn von Einhorn, Zauberlustspiel, Philipp Hafner, mus. J. H. Böhm [?], BT, late 1762 or 1763

Megära, Lokalstück, BT, 1 May 1765

Der förchterlichen Hexe zweyter Theil; unter dem Titel: die eine dauerhafte Freundschaft sich verwandelnde Rache, spl, P. Hafner, BT, 1764

Die neue krumme Teufel, oder Bernardon dem durch Zauberey glücklich gemachten Laquey, K, anon, Baadnerische Gesellschaft, 29 Oct. 1764

Die verwandelten Weiber kO, Weisse, mus. J. A. Hiller, 28 May 1766

Lisuart und Dariolette, oder Die Frage und die Antwort, rkO, D. Schiebeler, mus. J. A. Hiller, 25 Nov. 1766

Die Insul der Wilden, oder Die wanckelmüthige Insulanerin mit Arlequin dem durch Zauberei zum Abgott Ram gemachten König des Insul Tschalalei, kO, J. F. von Kurz, Nuremburg, 28 Aug. 1766

Bernardon der dumme Nachfolger Dr. Faustus, kO, anon, Frankfurt am Main, 1767

Maschinen-ballet Don Juan, ballet, J. F. von Kurz, Cologne, 1768

Don Juan, oder Der steinerne Gast, ballet, anon, Vienna, Leipzig, 1769, Gluck (?)

Je unnatüralicher, je besser, kO, J. B. Michaelis, pub.1769

Colombina in den Eliscæischen Feldern, K, Schulz-Menninger troupe (Baadnerische Gesellschaft), ms., c. 1760–70

Belfagor der befreyte Teufel, oder Die dem Hannswurst erwiesene höllische Dankbarkeit, Zaubercomödie, Baadnerische Gesellschaft, c. 1760–70

Die Zauber-Ruthe, oder Die gedoppelte Hannwurst, Nachspiel following *Die wandernde Rache*, Baadnerische Gesellschaft, c. 1760–70

Hoffart kommt vor dem Fall: Doctor Johann Fausts, Pragerische Gesellschaft, Vienna, 22 Jan. 1770

Il finto prencipe, oder Der durch Zauberey auf wunderbare und lächerliche Art, zum Fürsten gemacht Hannswurst, Sch, Baadnerischen Gesellschaft. 3 Feb. 1770

Der Neue Doctor Faust, oder Kasperle der Zauberer wider seinen Willen, Mk, Baadnerische Gesellschaft, Leopoldstadt, 19 Feb. 1770

Das Orakel, Opr, C. F. Gellert (Saint-Foix), mus. F. G. Fleischer. Brunswick 1771

Das Gespenst, spl, 3, K. F. Henisch, mus. O. F. Holy, Prague, Kotce, 13 March 1771

Pygmalion, melodrama, J.-J. Rousseau, mus. F. Aspelmayr, KT, 19 Feb. 1772

Pygmalion, melodrama, J.-J. Rousseau, mus. A. Schweitzer, Weimar, 13 May 1772

Der Holzhauer, oder Die drei Wünsche, kO, anon transl. of Castet and Guichard, 1772, mus. J. F. Reichardt (c. 1775, no known perfornance)

Der Zauberer, spl, K. F. Henisch, mus. O. F. Holy, Prague, 1772

Don Juan, oder Das klägliche Ennde eines Verstockten Athiesten, musical farce, J. Knecht, 28 Dec. 1772

Philemon und Baucis, oder Jupiters Reise auf die Erde, marionette spl, G. K. Pfeffel, mus. F. J. Haydn, Eszterháza, 27 June 1773, with a Vorspiel titled *Die Götterrat*

Hexenschabbas, marionette spl, Kurz, mus. F. J. Haydn, Eszterháza, ?1773

Der Holzhauer, oder Die drei Wünsche, kO, J. J. Eschenburg, mus. J. A. C. Koch, Berlin, Theater in der Behrenstrasse, 20 Feb. 1774

Megära, spl, P. Hafner, mus. J. Böhm, Berlin, Koch's Theater, 27 July 1774

Die Feuersbrunst, marionette spl, Haydn, Eszterháza, ?1775–78

Adriadne auf Naxos, melodrama, J. C. Brandes, mus., G. A. Benda, Gotha 1775

Medea, melodrama, F. W. Gotter, mus. G. A. Benda, Leipzig, 1775

Zemire und Azor, rkO, K. E. Schubert, mus. G. von Baumgarten, Wäser company, Breslau, 18 May 1776

Die Fee Urgele, oder Was den Damen gefällt, a marionette spl, probably by K. M. von Pauersbach, mus. I. J. Pleyel, Eszterháza, 1776

Arsene or *Die schöne Arsene,* spl, J. H. Faber (Favart), 1776

Johann Faust, spl, P. Weidmann, mus. J. C. W. Michl, Munich, Salvator, 16 May 1776

Die glücklichen Bettler, K [based on Gozzi], Gotha, 1777

Hermannide, oder Die Rätsel, Märchen, J.F. Schmidt (Gozzi), BT, 25 Oct. 1777

Don Juan, ballet, mus. Gluck, Munich, 1777

Der Holzhauer, J. F. W. Gotter, mus. G. A. Benda, Gotha, 2 Jan. 1778

Die glücklichen Bettler, K [based on Gozzi], Wiemar, 1778

Der Schiffbruch, Märchen, H. Graf von Spaur, Königsberg, 1778

Harlequin Friseur, oder Die Zaubertrompete: Eine Pantomime in drey Acten, pub. 1778

Pygmalion, melodrama, J.-J. Rousseau (transl. K. W. Ramler), mus. G. A. Benda, Gotha, 20 Sept. 1779

Die schöne Arsene, spl, A. G. Meissner, mus. F. Seydelmann, Dresden, churfürstliches kleines Theater, 3 Mar.1779

Das tartarische Gesetz, Sch, J. F. W. Gotter, mus. J. André, Berlin, Döbbelin's Theater, 31 May 1779

Das Irrwisch, oder Endlich fand er sie (Das Irrlicht), Opr, C. F. Bretzner, mus. F. A. Holly (Breslau, 1779); another setting by F. Preu, Leipzig, Theater am Rannstädtertor, 1779

Pygmalion, melodrama, J.-J. Rousseau, transl. K. W. Ramler, mus. G. A. Benda, Gotha, 20 Sept. 1779

Die bestrafte Rachbegierde, marionette spl, P. G. Bader, mus. F. J. Haydn, Eszterháza, c. 1779

Die drei Räthsel, K, F. Rambach, Leipzig, 1779

Der Zaubergürtel, L, G. K. Pfeffel, Josefstadt, 1779

1780–83

Was erhält die Männer treu? rO, L. Zehnmark, mus. Ruprecht, BT, 30 Mar. [or 1 May] 1780

Reinhold und Armida, melodrama, J. M. Babo, based on Tasso, mus. P. Winter, Munich, 30 Apr. 1780

Das Irrwisch, spl, C. F. Bretzner, mus. O. C. Erdmann Freiherr von Kospoth, Berlin, Döbbelin's Theater, 2 Oct. 1780

Das wütende Heer, oder Das Mädgen im Thurme, Opr, C. F. Bretzner, mus. J. André, Berlin, Döbbelins Theater, 22 Nov. 1780

Der Derwisch, L, F. M. Klinger, Ormus and Prague, 1780

Das Irrwisch, spl, Bretzner, mus. Nikolaus K. Mühle, 1780

Das grüne Vögelchen, based on Gozzi's *L'augellino belvedere*, Weimar, 1780

Almanzor und Nadine, melodrama, mus. G. Benda, c. 1780

König Rabe, spl, mus. F. A. Martelli, Münster, c. 1780

Zween Wunderdinge der Zauberers Durandarte, oder Der König Tiger, Mk, based on Gozzi, LT, 10 Feb. 1781

Die drei Rätsel, Mk, anon, LT, 15 Nov. 1781[–84]

Die Zauberrose, spl, LT, 18 Nov. 1781[–85]

Der Edelmann und die Bauer in dem Reiche der Feen, Mk, anon, LT, 22 Nov. 1781[–84]

Die Zauberspiegel, oder: Kasperle der verstellte Hassa von Hassabassa, spl, anon, LT, 26 Nov. 1781[–1805]

Die Ungetreue oder: Die Zauberin aus Liebe, K, anon, LT, 5 Dec. 1781[–1804]

Die neue Megära, spl, anon, LT, 9 Dec. 1781[–95].[1]

Das blaue Ungeheuer, spl (based on Gozzi), anon, mus. Joseph Schubert, Schwedt, 1781

Die Entzauberung, spl, anon, mus. Joseph Schubert, Schwedt, 1781

Das Irrlicht, Opr, G. Stephanie (based on Bretzner), mus. I. Umlauf, BT, 17 Jan. 1782

Die Gelseninsel, oder: Kaspars Spatzenzauberei, spl, anon, LT, 17 Jan. 1782[–87]

Das wütende Heer, oder Das Mädgen im Thurme, Opr, Bretzner, mus. Johann Friedrich Kaffka, Wäser troupe, Breslau, Jan. 1782

Die Fee Angelica, oder: Karlin und Kaspar von ungleicher Geschicklichkeit, Mk, anon, LT, 11 Apr. 1782[–85]

Das Irrwisch, spl, Bretzner, mus. Christian Ludwig Dieter, Stuttgart, kleines Theater, 23 Sept. 1782

Der krumme Teufel, spl, anon, LT, 4 Nov. 1782[–83]

Der Triumph der Tugend, oder Der Mund der Wahrheit, ballet, Sacco (based on Gozzi), Hamburg, 1782

Merkur der Neumodezauberer, oder: Kaspars Hochzeit nach seinem Tode, Mk, anon, LT, 28 Feb. 1783[–1800]

Arlequin der bezauberte Zauberer, oder Die fliehende Totentruhe, pant, anon, mus. Johann Friedrich Reichardt, KT, 29 Aug. 1783

Der Zauberei Quintessenz, L, anon, KT, 13 Sept. 1783

Der bezauberte Kürbis, pant, anon, KT, 3 Oct. 1783

Die musikalische Zaubertrommel des Phöbus, L, anon, KT, 5 Oct. 1783

Der Weinkeller in der Hölle, oder Keinen Rausch mehr liebes Weiberl, spl, anon, KT, 19 Oct. 1783[2]

Der verliebte Zauberer, L, anon, KT, 28 Oct. 1783

Don Juan, oder Der steinerne Gast ein Lustspiel nach Molieren . . . bearbeitet, mit Kaspars Lustbarkeit, K, Karl Marinelli, 31 Oct. 1783[–1821]

Der Zauberrose, spl, anon, Vienna, Theater beim Fasan am Neustift, 11 Nov. 1783

1. Wenzel Müller's catalog indicates several different titles for Megära operas: *Die Hexe Megära* (5 Feb., 28 Oct., and 18 Dec. 1782; 30 Nov. 1783), *Die neue Megära* (9 Dec. 1781; 19 Jan., 10 July, and 26 Dec. 1783), *Die alte Hexe Megära* (5 Sept. 1784), and *Megära* (13 Sept. 1787; 4 May and 6 July 1788; and 1 June 1789). Hadamowsky, *Die wiener Hoftheater (Staatstheater)*, treats these as identical works, but they may be different. Some sources give the title as *Die neue Megäre, oder Kasperl der Schüler der Frau Megäre* (2 Dec. 1784).

2. Blümml and Gugitz, *Alt-Wiener Thespiskarren*, 146, 153–54.

Arlequin im Mausoleum, pant, anon, KT, 21 Nov. 1783

Pirot, die bezauberte Baberl, oder Arlekin der Narrenmaler, pant, anon, KT, 4 Dec. 1783

Alceste. Ein Opera Seria 3, Lustig bearbeitet wobei Kasperle den Höllengott spielen wird, 11 Dec. 1783[–95]; cited in *Das Wienerblättchen*

Zobeis, K, anon (based on Gozzi), Weimar, 1783

Oberon und Titania, oder Jubelfeier der Versöhnung, Vorspiel, C. A. Vulpius, Weimar, 1783

Das Irrwisch, spl, Anton Mayer, Cologne, c. 1783

Der Trank der Unsterblichkeit, Vorspiel, C. A. Vulpius, mus. I. Walter, Prague, 1783

Die bezauberte Jagd, spl [?], Gensicke, mus. F. A. Hoffmeister (lost), KT, 1783

Die Wassergeister, Opr, F. Hildebrand von Einsiedel (publ. Dessau 1783-84)

1784 – 85

Das Schwartzkünsters, erster Theil, oder Kasperl der Zauberer wider seinen Willen, Mk, anon, LT, 4 Jan. 1784[–93]

Der Streit zwischen dem Zauberer Scionco, und der Fee Galantine, oder Kasperl' bleibt Kasperl! Mk, anon [?K. Marinelli], mus. Ferd. Kauer, 3 Feb. 1784[–99]

Die Zaubereyen, oder Arlekins Schicksale, pant, anon, mus. Sedlaczek, Hamburg, 17 June 1784

Die schöne Melusina, Feenmärchen, anon, KT, 16 Dec. 1784

Die Reiche des Schwannen und Pfauen, oder Die Königin Blandine, Feenkomödien, anon, Vienna, 1784

Doktor Faust, parodie, anon, mus. W. Müller, Brno, Krautmarkt, 1784

Zemire und Azor, anon transl. of Marmontel, mus. Grétry, KT, 1 Jan. 1785

Orpheus, spl, G. F. von Lindemann, mus. Friedrich Benda, Berlin, corsika'scher Saal, 16 Jan. 1785

Philibert und Kaspar im Reiche der Phantasey, oder Weiber sind getreuer, als Männer, Feenmärchen, K. F. Hensler, LT, 20 Jan. 1785[–93]

Zemire und Azor, anon transl. of Marmontel, mus. Grétry, KT, 1780/81, BT, 29 March 1785

Armida, J. C. Bock's transl. of Bertati's *Rinaldo*, mus. J. R. Zumsteeg, Stuttgart, 24 May 1785

Kasperl der Rauchfangkehrer als Fürst und der Fürst als Rauchfangkehrer, Mk, anon, KT, 30 July 1785

Kasperl ein Originalgenie, Zauberkomödie, anon, KT, 29 Aug. 1785

Die Zauberirrungen, oder Die Irrthümer der Zauberei, Sch, Hildebrand Freiherr von Einsiedel, mus. E. W. Wolf, Weimar, 24 Oct. 1785

1786 – 89

Kasperle als Amor: Ein Maschinenkomödie 2 mit Gesängen, anon, 16 Feb. 1786[–88]

Der Ring der Liebe [*oder*] *Zemirens und Azors Ehestand*, spl, P. Weidmann, mus. I. Umlauf, KT, 3 Oct. 1786

Doktor Fausts Leibgürtel, spl, Bernhard Christoph d'Arien, mus. Karl Hanke, Hamburg, 1786

Der Schleyer, spl, C. A. Vulpius, mus. E. W. Wolf, Weimar, Herzogliche Komödiehaus, 1786

Die sieben Schwaben, Opr, anon, publ. Munich, 1786

Kaspar auf den Sprung, Zauberspiel, anon, Neustift beim weißen Fasan, 15 Apr. 1787; poster, A-Wt

Das wütende Heer, oder Das Mädgen im Thurme, Opr, Bretzner, mus. J. M. (or Stephen) Ruprecht, KT, 1 June 1787

Zemire und Azor, Faber (transl. of Marmontel), mus. Grétry, KT, 19 June 1787

Der bezauberte Wald, oder Der dankbare Geist, ballet, Rosbachischen Theater auf dem Spitalberg, 11 July 1787

Doktor Faust, O, H. G. Schneider, mus. I. Walter, Bremen, 28 Dec. 1787

Die Feyer im Reich der Feen, allegorisches Vorspiel, C. A. Vulpius, Weimar, 1787

Das Mädchen im Eichtale, spl, anon, mus. [?] Schön, Innsbruck, 1787; cited in Stieger

Das Irrwisch, spl, mus. [?] Schön, Innsbruck, 1787

Das wütende Heer, oder Das Mädgen im Thurme, Opr, Bretzner, mus. Gottfried Rieger, Brno, 1787

Don Juan, oder der steinerne Gast: Ein Kassastück, Anton Cremeri (Frankfurt/Leipzig, n.d. [Vienna, c. 1787])

Kaspar der gefoppte König auf der grünen Wiese [spl], [?F. Eberl] mus. Wenzel Müller, LT, 30 Jan. 1788

Die Elektrisiermaschine, spl, F. Eberl, mus. Wenzel Müller, LT, 13 Nov. 1788[–89]

Das wütende Heer, oder Das Mädgen im Thurme, O, Bretzner, mus. Friedrich Franz Hurka, Schwedt, 1788

Das wütende Heer, oder Das Mädgen im Thurme, O, Bretzner, mus. J. B. Lasser, Graz, Landständisches Theater, c. 1788

Das Orackel, anon transl. Saint-Foix's *L'oracle*, Hamburg, 1788; poster in D-Hs

Der Triumph der Treue, spl, J. F. von Binder [?], mus. F.Danzi (lost), Munich, [?7 Feb.] 1789

Das Gluck ist Kugelrund, oder Kaspers Ehrentag, Feenmärchen, K. F. Hensler, mus. W. Müller, LT, 17 Feb. 1789[–98]

Holger Danske, O, J. E. Baggesen (Wieland), mus. F. L. A. Kunzen, Copenhagen, Kg. Th., 31 March 1789

Was den Damen gefällt [spl], anon transl. of Favart, mus. J. A. P. Schultz, Berlin, National Theater, 28 Apr. 1789

Hüon und Amande, romantisches spl, F. S. Seyler, mus. K. Hanke, Schleswig, 1789

Oberon, König der Elfen, rkO, arr. K. L. Giesecke, mus. P. Wranitzky, WT, 7 Nov. 1789[–95]

Selim und Zelide, oder Die Macht der Feen, rkO, anon, [Prague] Kleinseitner Theater, 30 Nov. 1789

Der Talisman, C. F. Bretzner, mus. J. C. Kaffka (also called *Der seltene Spiegel*, *Die seltsamen Spiegel*, and *Der seltsame Spiegel*), rkO, anon, Breslau, 1789

Circe, melodrama, anon, mus. Václav Praupner, Prague, 1789

1 7 9 0 – 9 2

Harlekins Zauberzweig, wobei Kasperle den Harlekin spielen wird, pant, anon, 21 Apr. 1790

Die schöne Isländerin, oder Der Mufti von Samarkanda, Zauberkomödie, E. Schikaneder, WT, 22 Apr. 1790

Der Stein der Weisen, oder Die Zauberinsel, rkO, E. Schikaneder, mus. J. B. Henneberg, B. Schack, F. X. Gerl, W. A. Mozart, and E. Schikaneder, WT, 11 Sept. 1790[–99]

Die weidergefunde Statue [spl], W. A. Schwick (based on Gozzi), mus. B. H. Romberg, Bonn, 1790

Der ausgeprügelte Teufel, [spl], anon, mus. I. Walter, 1790

Harlequins Grabmahl, Opernpantomime, anon, mus. [?] Ditta, Vienna, Theater zum weißen Fasan, 1790

Das Rätsel, kO, Heinrich Schmieder, mus. Fr. H. von Kerpen, Mainz, Dec. 1790

Das blaue Ungeheuer [spl], W. A. Schwick (based on Gozzi), mus. A. J. Romberg, Bonn, 1790–93

Kaspars Zögling, oder Der Sieg der Bescheidenheit, auf der Insel des Vergnügens, spl, J. Perinet, mus. F. Kauer, LT, 1 Feb. 1791[–92]

Kasperl' der glückliche Vogelkrämer, oder: Das Glück kennt seine Lieblinge! Feenmärchen, K. F. Hensler, mus. W. Müller, LT, 3 March 1791[–96]

Der Wohltätigige Derwisch, oder Die Schellenkappe, Lust- und Zauberspiel, E. Schikaneder, [mus. probably by Henneberg, Schack, Gerl], WT, late winter, 1791[–99]

Kaspar der fagottist, oder Die Zauberzither, spl, J. Perinet, mus. W. Müller, LT, 8 June 1791[–1819]

Ludwig Herzog von Steiermark, oder Sarmäts Feuerbär, Sch, E. Schikaneder, WT, 3 Aug. 1791

Der Spiegelritter, O, A. von Kotzebue, mus. I. Walter, Frankfurt, National Theater, 11 Sept. 1791

Die Zauberflöte, große Oper, E. Schikaneder, mus. W. A. Mozart, WT, 30 Sept. 1791

Vormals half noch Zauberei, oder der Alt' und Neue Kasperle, Mk, anon, 18 Nov. 1791[–92]

Sultan Wampum, oder Die Wuensche, ein orientalischer Scherzspiel, A. von Kotzebue, mus. C. D. Stegmann, Mainz National Theater, 3 Dec. 1791

Der Rabe, spl, W. Schwink, mus. A. Romberg, Bonn, 1791

BIBLIOGRAPHY

Aarne, Antii. *The Types of the Folktale: A Classification and Bibliography; Antti Aarne's* Verzeichnis Der Märchentypen. Translated and enlarged by Stith Thompson. Helsinki: Suomalainen Tiedeakatemia, 1961.

Abert, Hermann. *W. A. Mozart*. Leipzig: Breitkopf & Härtel, 1924.

Abert, Hermann, and Hans Joachim Moser, eds. *Ausgewählte Ballette Stuttgarter Meister aus der 2. Hälfte des 18. Jahrhunderts. Florian Deller—Johann Joseph Rodolphe*. Denkmäler der Deutscher Tonkunst, 1. Folge, vols. 43–44. Wiesbaden: Breitkopf & Hartel, 1958.

Abnot, James Fullarton. "Shakespeare and the Marvellous." *Revue de la Société d'Histoire du Théâtre* 15, no. 1 (1963): 21–28.

Adams, Hazard. *Critical Theory since Plato*. New York: Harcourt, Brace, Jovanovich, 1971.

Addison, James. "On the Pleasures of the Imagination." *Spectator* 418 (30 June 1712). Reproduced in *Critical Theory since Plato*, edited by Hazard Adams. New York: Harcourt, Brace, Jovanovich, 1971. 292.

Aikin, John. "On the Pleasure Derived from Objects of Terror." In *Miscellaneous Pieces [in Prose]*. London: J. Johnson, 1773; repr., 1775, 1792.

Algarotti, Francesco, *Saggio sopra l'opera in musica: Le edizioni di Venezia (1755) e di Livrono (1763)*. Edited by Annalisa Bini. Lucca: Libraria Musicale Italiana Editrice, 1989.

Allanbrook, Wye Jamison. *Rhythmic Gesture in Mozart*. Chicago: University of Chicago Press, 1983.

Allmanach für Theaterfreunde auf das Jahr 1791. Vienna: Matthias Ludwig 1791. [Copy in A-Wst, shelfmark G83479.]

Almanach forain, ou Les différens spectacles des Boulevards et des Foires de Paris. Paris: Valleyre, 1773.

Alth, Minna von. *Burgtheater, 1776–1976*. Edited by Gertrude Obzyna. Vienna: Ueberreuter, [1979].

Amico, Vito. *Catana illustrata*. 3 vols. Catania: S. Trento & J. Pulejo, 1740–41.

———. *Opuscoli di autori siciliani*. 19 vols. Panormo, 1758.

———. *Sicilia sacra*. 2 vols. Panormo: Apud haeredes P. Coppulae, 1733.

Amusement des companies, ou nouveau recueil des chansons choisis, tome premier. The Hague: Grosse & van Daalen, 1761.

Andrae, Richard. "Studien zu den Volksmärchen der Deutschen von J. K. A. Musäus." Ph.D. diss., University of Marburg, 1897.

Andries, Lise. *La bibliothèque bleue au dix-huitième siècle: Une tradition éditoriale*. Studies on Voltaire in the Eighteenth Century 270. Oxford: Voltaire Foundation at the Taylor Institution, 1989.

Angermüller, Rudolph. *Antonio Salieri: Sein Leben und seine weltlichen Werke unter besonderer Berücksichtigung seiner "großen" Opern*. 2 vols. Munich: Emil Katzbichler, 1974.

Anthony, James R. *French Baroque Music from Beaujoyeulx to Rameau*. Revised ed. New York: Norton, 1981.

Apuleius. *Psyche: ein Feenmährchen des Appulejus: Lateinisch nach Oudendorps und Ruhnkes Recension*. Göttingen: Vandenhoeck und Ruprecht, 1789.

Ariosto, Ludovico. *The Frenzy of Orlando*. Ferrara, 1516. Translated by Barbara Reynolds. Harmondsworth and Baltimore: Penguin, 1975.

Aristotle. *Poetics: English and Greek*. Translated by Stephen Halliwell. 2nd ed. Cambridge, MA: Harvard University Press, 1995.

Armbruster, Richard. *Das Opernzitat bei Mozart*. Schriftenreihe der Internationalen Stiftung Mozarteum Salzburg 13. Kassel: Bärenreiter, 2001.

Armeno, Christoforo. *Peregrinaggio di tre giovani figliuoli del re di Serendippo, per opra di M. Christoforo Armeneo dalla persiana nell'italiana lingua trapportato*. Venice, 1557; repr., Erlangen: Fr. Junge, 1891.

Arteaga, Stefano. *Le rivoluzioni del teatro musicale italiano dalla sua origine fino al presente opera*. 3 vols. Bologna: Carlo Trenti, 1783–88.

Asper, Helmut G. *Spieltexte der Wanderbühne: Eine Verzeichnis der Dramenmanuskripte des 17. und 18. Jahrhunderts in Wiener Bibliotheken*. Quellen zur Theatergeschichte 1. Vienna: Verband der Wissenschaftliche Gesellschaften Österreichs, 1975.

Assier, Alexandre. *Bibliothèque bleue depuis Jean Oudot 1er jusqu'à M. Baudot*. Paris, 1874; repr., Nîmes: Lacour, 1991.

Åstrand, Hans, Hans-Günther Ottenberg, and Gerd Schönfelder. *Zur Tonsetzung vom "Gustav Wasa": Beiträge zur Biographie J. G. Naumann's*. Stockholm: Kungl. Musikaliska akademien, 1991.

Aubert, Jacques. *La reine des péris*. Paris: The author, 1725.

Aureli, Aurelio, and Francesco Lucio. *Il Medoro*.Venice, 1658. Facsimile ed., edited by Giovanni Morelli and Thomas Walker, Drammaturgia musicale veneta 4, Milan: Ricordi, 1984.

Aureli, Aurelio, and Antonio Sartorio. *L'Orfeo*. Introduction by Ellen Rosand. Facsimile ed. Drammaturgia musicale veneta 6. Milan: Ricordi, 1983.

Bach, Johann Christian. *The Collected Works of Johann Christian Bach, 1735–1782*. Edited by Ernest Warburton. New York: Garland, 1984–.

Baggesen, Jens Emmanuel. *Holger Danske*. Transl. Carl Friedrich Cramer in *Cramer's Musik*. Copenhagen, 1789.

Baggio, Pauline. "The Ambiguity of Social Characterization in Lesage's Théâtre de la Foire." *French Review* 55, no. 5 (1982): 618–24.

Bakhtin, Mikhail. *Rabelais and His World*. Translated by Helene Iswolsky. Bloomington: Indiana University Press, 1984.

Ballola, Giovanni Carlo. "Le fiabe di Carlo Gozzi nelle strutture teatrali della *Zauberflöte*." In *Europa im Zeitalter Mozarts*, edited by H. Haslmayr and A. Rausch. Schriftenreihe der Österreichischen Gesellschaft zur Erforschung des 18. Jahrhunderts 5. Vienna: Böhlau, 1995. 167–70.

Balmas, Enes. *Il mito del Don Giovanni nel seicento francese*. 2 vols. Rome: Lucarini, 1986.

Balsano, Maria Antonella, and Thomas Walker, eds. *Tasso, la musica, i musicisti*. Florence: L. S. Olschki, 1988.

Barberet, Victor. *Lesage et le Théâtre de la foire*. Nancy, 1887; repr., Geneva: Slatkine, 1970.

Barbier, Pierre. "La pastorale au XVIe et au XVIIe siècles." *Annales de la Société d'Émulation de l'Ain* 5 (1875): 259–89.

Barchilon, Jacques. *Le conte merveilleux français de 1690 à 1790: Cent ans de féerie et de poésie ignorées de l'histoire littéraire*. Paris: Honoré Champion, 1975.

———. "Uses of the Fairy Tale in the Eighteenth Century." *Studies on Voltaire* 24–27 (1963): 111–38.

Barford, Esther. "Holger Danske." In *Pipers Enzyklopädie des Musiktheaters*, edited by Carl Dahlhaus. Munich: Piper, 1989. 3:380–82.

Barthélemy, Maurice. "L'opéra francais et la querelle des anciens et des modernes." *Les lettres romanes* 10 (1956): 379–91.

———. "Alexis Piron et l'opéra-comique." In *Grétry et l'Europe de l'opéra-comique*, edited by Philippe Vendrix. Liège: Mardaga, 1992. 191–200.

Bartlet, M. Elizabeth. "Pièce à machines." In NGO 3:1008.

Baselt, Bernd. *Händel-Handbuch*. 5 vols. Kassel: Bärenreiter, 1978–.

Basile, Giambattista. *Il pentamerone o Lo cunto de li cunti*. Original ed., 1634–36; Naples, 1644. Edited by Benedetto Croce as *Il pentamerone, ossia La fiabe delle fiabe*, 2 vols., Bari: Laterza, 1925–57.

Batteux, Charles. *Les beaux-arts réduits à un même principe*. Paris, 1746; repr., Geneva: Slatkine, 1969.

———. *Cours de belles-lettres distribué par exercises*. Paris: Desaint & Saillant, 1747.

Bauer, Anton. *Opern und Operetten in Wien*. Wiener Musikwissenschaftliche Beiträge 2. Graz: Hermann Bohlaus, 1955.

Bauman, Thomas. "Benda, Georg." In NGO 1:399–401.

———. *North German Opera in the Age of Goethe*. Cambridge: Cambridge University Press, 1985.

Baumgarten, Gotthilf von. *Zemire und Azor*. Breslau: Korn, 1775.

Bayon, Marie-Emmanuelle. *Airs détachés de Fleur d'épine*. N.p., n.d.

———. *Fleur d'épine: Comédie en deux actes*. Paris: Huguet, [c. 1776].

Beagle, Nancy Sue. "The Théâtres de la Foire in Early 18th-Century France: Analysis of *La Ceinture de Vénus* by Lesage." D.M.A. diss., Stanford University, 1985.

Beall, Chandler B. *La fortune du Tasse en France*. Studies in Literature and Philology 4. Eugene: University of Oregon Press, 1942.

Beat, Janet E. "Monteverdi and the Opera Orchestra of his Time." In *The Monteverdi Companion*, edited by D. Arnold and Nigel Fortune. New York: Norton, 1972. 277–301.

Beattie, James, [and Anna Barbauld]. *Dissertations Moral and Critical*. London, 1783; Philadelphia: Hopkins & Earle, 1809.

———. *Essays*. Edinburgh, 1776; repr., New York: Garland, 1971.

Benda, Friedrich Wilhelm Heinrich. *Orpheus*. Berlin: The author, [1787?].

———. *Pygmalion, eine Kantate im Clavierauzuge*. Dessau: Verlagskasse für Gelehrte und Künstler, 1784.

Benda, Georg Anton. *Adriadne auf Naxos*. Leipzig: Schwickert, 1778.

———. *Adriadne auf Naxos*. Edited by Jan Trojan. Musica antiqua bohemica, ser. 2, vol. 10. Prague: Editio Supraphon, 1984.

———. *Der Holzhauer oder Die drei Wünsche*. Leipzig: Schwickert, 1777.

———. *Medea*. Edited by Jan Trojan. Musica antiqua bohemica, ser. 2, vol. 8. Prague: Editio Supraphon, 1976.

————. *Pygmalion*. Leipzig: Schwickert, 1780.

Berger, Peter L. *The Sacred Canopy*. Garden City, NY: Doubleday, 1967.

Bergerac, Cyrano de. *L'autre monde, ou Histoire comique des états et empires de la lune*. Paris, 1662. New ed., Paris: Cercle du livre de France, [c. 1940].

Bergman, Gösta M. "La grand mode du pantomime à Paris vers 1740 et les spectacles d'optique Servandoni." *Recherches théâtrales* 2 (1960): 71–81.

Bernard, Catherine. *Inés de Cordoue: Nouvelle espagnole*. Paris, 1697.

Bertati, Giovanni. *L'anello incantato*. Lisbon: Stamperia Reale, 1772.

————. *La fata capricciosa*. Venice: Modesto Fenzo, 1789.

Bertati, Giovanni, and Joseph Felix von Kurz. *I creduti spiriti*. Venice: Paolo Colombani, 1764.

————. *La morte di Dimone, o sia L'innocenẓa vendicata*. Venice: Paolo Colombani, 1763.

Bertoni, Ferdinando. *Orfeo ed Euridice*. Bibliotheca musica bononiensis, sez. 4, no. 5. Bologna: Forni, 1970.

Bettelheim, Bruno. *The Uses of Enchantment: The Meaning and Importance of Fairy Tales*. New York: Vintage, 1977.

Betzwieser, Thomas. "Exoticism and Politics: Beaumarchais' and Salieri's *Le Couronnement de Tarare* (1790)." *Cambridge Opera Journal* 6, no. 2 (1995): 91–112.

Bianconi, Lorenzo. *Music in the Seventeenth Century*. Translated by David Bryant. Cambridge: Cambridge University Press, 1987.

Bibliothèque universelle des romans. Paris: Au bureau, 1789.

Bila, Constantin. *La croyance à la magie au XVIIIe siècle en France dans les contes, romans et traités*. Paris: J. Gamber, 1925.

Bleich, Ernst. "Die Märchen des Musäus vornehmlich nach Stoffen und Motiven I." *Archiv für Deutschen Literature [Herrig's Archiv]* 108 (1902): 273–87.

————. "Die Märchen des Musäus vornehmlich nach Stoffen und Motiven II." *Archiv für Deutschen Literature [Herrig's Archiv]* 109 (1902): 5–32.

Blümml, Emil Karl. "Ausdeutungen der 'Zauberflöte.'" *Moẓart-Jahrbuch* 1 (1923): 111–46.

————. *Aus Moẓarts Freundes- und Familienkreis*. Vienna: Strache, 1923.

Blümml, Emil Karl, and Gustav Gugitz. *Alt-Wiener Thespiskarren; Die Frühẓeit des Wiener Vorstadtbühnen*. Vienna: Anton Schroll, 1925.

Böhme, Jakob. *Sämtliche Schriften: Faksimile-Neudruck der Ausgabe von 1730*. 11 vols. Edited by Will-Erich Peuckert. Stuttgart: F. Frommann, 1955.

Boileau [Despreaux], Nicolas. "Dissertation sur Joconde." In *Œuvres complètes*, introduction by Antoine Adam, edited by Françoise Escal. Paris: Gallimard, 1966. 309–28.

Bolte, Johannes. "Bruchstücke einer Wiener Faust-Komödie vom Jahre 1731." *Euphorion: Zaitschrift für Literaturgeschichte* 21 (1914): 129–36.

Boretti, Giovanni Antonio. *Ercole in Tebe*. Facsimile edited by Howard Mayer Brown. IO 6, 1977. Libretto, IOL 5, 1978.

Born, Ignaz von. "Über die Mysterien der Ägyptier." *Journal für Freimaurer* (1784): 17–132.

Bottigheimer, Ruth B. "Straparola's *Piacevoli Notti*: Rags-to-Riches Fairy Tales as Urban Creations." *Merveilles & Contes* 7 (1994): 281–95.

Bottrigari, Ercole. *Il Desiderio, overo De' concerti di varii strumenti musicali*. 1594; facsimile repr., 1924; translated into English by C. MacClintock, [Rome]: American Institute of Musicology, 1962.

Bouissou, Sylvie. *Jean-Philippe Rameau: Les Boréades, ou la tragédie oubliée*. Paris: Meridiens Klincksieck, 1992.

————. "Mécanismes dramatiques de la tempête et de l'orage dans l'opéra français à l'âge baroque." In *D'un opéra l'autre: Hommage à Jean Mongrédien*, edited by Jean Gribenski, Marie-

Claire Mussat, and Herbert Schneider. Paris: Presses de l'Université de Paris-Sorbonne, 1996. 217–30.

Branscombe, Peter. "Gerl, Franz Xaver." In NGO 2:384.

———. "Müller, Wenzel." In NGO 3:514.

———. *W. A. Mozart: Die Zauberflöte*. Cambridge Opera Handbook. Cambridge: Cambridge University Press, 1991.

Braunbehrens, Volkmar. *Mozart in Vienna, 1781–1791*. Translated by Timothy Bell. New York: Grove Weidenfeld, 1989.

Brenner, Clarence D. *A Bibliographical List of Plays in the French Language, 1700–1789*. Berkeley: University of California Press, 1947.

———. *Dramatization of French Short Stories in the Eighteenth Century: With Special Reference to the "Contes" of La Fontaine, Marmontel, and Voltaire*. University of California Publications in Modern Philosophy 33. Berkeley: University of California Press, 1947.

Bretzner, Christoph Friedrich. *Operetten*. Leipzig: Carl Friedrich Schneider, 1779; Leipzig: C. F. Schneidern, 1788.

Brockett, Oscar G. "The Fair Theaters of Paris in the Eighteenth Century: The Undermining of the Classical Ideal." In *Classical Drama and its Influences: Essays presented to H. D. F. Kitto*. Edited by M. J. Anderson. New York: Barnes and Noble, [1965]. 249–70.

Brophy, Brigid. *Mozart the Dramatist: The Value of His Operas to Him, His Age and to Us*. New York: Da Capo Press, 1988.

Brown, Bruce Alan. *Gluck and the French Theater in Vienna*. Oxford: Oxford University Press, 1991.

———. "*Le Pazzie d'Orlando, Orlando Paladino*, and the Uses of Parody." *Italica* 64, no. 4 (1987): 583–605.

Brown, Howard Mayer. *Sixteenth-century Instrumentation: The Music for the Florentine Intermedii*. Musicological Studies and Documents 30. [Rome]: American Institute of Musicology, 1973.

Bruni, Antonio Bartolomeo. *L'isola incantata, ou L'isle enchantée: Opera bouffon en trois actes*. Paris: Le Duc, n.d.

Bryant, David. "La Farsa musicale veneziana." In *I vicini di Mozart* 2. Florence: L. S. Olschki, 1989.

Buch, David J. "*Così fan tutte, La scuola degli amanti* and *L'école des amans*." In *Festschrift Tomislav Volek*. Special issue, *Hudební věda* 3–4 (2001): 313–20.

———. *Dance Music from the Ballets de cour, 1575–1651: Historical Commentary, Source Study, and Transcriptions from the Philidor Manuscripts*. Dance and Music Series 7. Stuyvesant, NY: Pendragon Press, 1994.

———. "Mozart and the Theater auf der Wieden: New Attributions and Perspectives." *Cambridge Opera Journal* 9, no. 3 (1997): 195–232.

———. "On Mozart's Partial Autograph of the Duet 'Nun, liebes Weibchen,' K. 625/592a." *Journal of the Royal Musical Association* 124 (1999): 53–85.

———. "On the Context of Mozart's Variations on the Aria 'Ein Weib ist das herrlichste Ding auf der Welt,' K. 613." *Mozart Jahrbuch 1999*, 71–80.

———. "*Der Stein der Weisen*, Mozart, and Collaborative Singspiels at Emanuel Schikaneder's Theater auf der Wieden." *Mozart Jahrbuch 2000*, 89–124.

———. "*Die Zauberflöte*, Masonic Opera, and Other Fairy Tales." *Acta Musicologica* 76 (2004): 193–219.

Buch, David J., and Manuela Jahrmärker. *Schikaneders heroisch-komische Oper* Der Stein der Weisen*: Modell für Mozarts* Zauberflöte*; Kritische Ausgabe des Textbuchs*. Göttingen: Hainholz Verlag, 2002.

Burke, Edmund. *A Philosophical Inquiry into the Origin of Our Ideas of the Sublime and Beautiful.* London, 1757; revised 1759.

Burney, Charles. *A General History of Music from the Earliest Ages to the Present Period* [London, 1789]. Edited by Frank Mercer. 2 vols. New York: Harcourt, Brace, 1935.

————. *The Present State of Music in Germany, the Netherlands and United Provinces.* London: T. Becket, 1773.

Busch, Gudrun. "'Da der Gesang eine große Gewalt über unser Herz hat . . .': Die musikalische Rezeption der Dichtungen Gellerts." In *"Ein Lehrer der ganzen Nation": Leben und Werk Christian Fürchtegott Gellerts,* edited by Bernd Witte. Munich: Wilhelm Fink, [c. 1990]. 192–99.

————. "Daniel Schiebeler, Schikaneder und Mozarts Berlin-Besuch 1789, oder: 'kein Ende' der Quellen des 'Zauberflöten'-Librettos?" *Mozart-Jahrbuch 1991,* 963–68.

Butler, Margaret Ruth. *Operatic Reform at Turin's Teatro Regio: Aspects of Production and Stylistic Change in the 1760s.* Lucca: Libreria Musicale Italiana, 2001.

Das Cabinett der Feen. Nuremberg: Gabriel Nicolaus Raspe, 1761–66.

Le cabinet des fées, ou Collection choisie des contes des fées et autres merveilleux. 9 vols. Amsterdam: Michel Charles le Cene, 1735. Expanded by Charles-Joseph, Chevalier de Mayer, 41 vols. Amsterdam and Paris: Hôtel Serpente, 1785–89.

Caccini, Francesca. *La liberazione di Ruggiero dall'isola d'Alcina.* Edited by Doris Silbert. Smith College Music Archives 7. Northhampton, MA: Smith College, 1945.

Cahusac, Louis de. "Ballet." In *Encyclopédie ou Dictionnaire raisonné* 2:42–46.

————. "Féerie." In *Encyclopédie ou Dictionnaire raisonné* 6:464.

————. *La danse ancienne et moderne, ou Traité historique de la danse.* The Hague: Jean Neaulme, 1754.

————. "Decoration, opéra." In *Encyclopédie ou Dictionnaire raisonné* 4:701–2.

————. "Enchantement." In *Encyclopédie ou Dictionnaire raisonné* 6:619.

Cailhava de l'Estandoux, Jean-François. *De l'art de la comédie, nouvelle édition.* Paris, [1786]; repr., Geneva: Slatkine, 1970.

Calmus, Georgy. *Die ersten deutschen Singspiele von Standfuss und Hiller.* Publikationen der Internationalen Musik-Gesellschaft, Beihefte 6. Leipzig: Breitkopf & Hartel, 1908.

Calvino, Italo. *Italian Folktales.* Translated by George Martin. New York: Harcourt, Brace, Jovanovich, 1980.

Calzabigi, Ranieri de'. *Scritti teatrali e letterari.* Edited by Anna Laura Bellina. 2 vols. Testi e documenti di letteratura e lingua 13. Rome: Salerno Editrice, 1994.

Campardon, Émile. *Les spectacles de la Foire depuis 1595 jusqu'à 1791.* 2 vols. Paris, 1877; repr., Geneva: Slatkine, 1970.

Campra, André. *Le carnaval de Venise.* Edited by James Anthony. French Opera in the 17th and 18th Centuries 17. Stuyvesant, NY: Pendragon, 1989.

Carmontelle, Louis-Carrogis. "Le petit poucet." In *Amusements de société, ou Proverbes dramatiques.* 6 vols. Paris: Merlin, 1768–69. 3:65–100.

Carroll, Charles M. "François Danican Philidor: His Life and Dramatic Art." 2 vols. Ph.D. diss., Florida State University, 1960.

Castelnau, Henriette-Julie de, Comtesse de Murat. *Contes des fées.* Paris, 1698.

————. *Nouveaux contes des fées.* Paris, 1698.

Casti, Giovanni Battista. *La grotta di Trofonio* Vienna: Gius. nob. de Kurzbek, n.d.; Rome: Gioacchino Puccinello, 1786. Arranged by Guiseppe Palomba, Naples, 1785.

Carter, Tim. "Arisoto, Ludovico." In NGO 1:191–92.

————. "Da Ponte, Lorenzo." In NGO 2:1075.

————. Review of Balsano and Walker, *Tasso, la musica. Journal of the Royal Musical Association* 115 (1990): 258–61.

————. "Tasso, Torquato." In NGO 4:656–57.

Cavalli, Francesco. *Il Giasone* (1649). Edited by Robert Eitner. Publikationen älterer praktischer und theoretischer Musikwerke 12 [Die Oper 2]. Berlin, 1883; repr., New York: Broude Brothers, 1966.

Cerlone, Francesco. *L'osteria di Marechiaro.* Naples: Vincenzo Flauto, 1769.

Cesti, Marc Antonio. *Il Pomo d'oro.* Edited by Guido Adler. Denkmäler der Tonkunst in Österreich, Jahrg. 3, no. 2 [vol. 6]). Vienna: Artaria 1896; Jahrg. 4, no. 2 [vol. 9]. Graz: Akademische Druck- und Verlagsanstalt, 1959.

Chailley, Jacques. *La flûte enchantée: Opéra maçonnique; Essai d'explication du livret et de la musique.* New ed., Paris: Robert Laffont, 1983.

Champion, Pierre. *Ronsard et sa temps.* Paris: E. Champion, 1925.

Chantler, Abigail. "The *Sturm und Drang* Style Revisted." *International Review of the Aesthetics and Sociology of Music* 34, no. 1 (June 2003): 17–31.

Chaponnière, Paul. *Alexis Piron: Sa vie et ses oeuvres.* Geneva: Imprimerie du Journal de Genève, 1910.

Charlton, David. "Dezède, Nicolas." In NGO 1:1152–53.

————. *Grétry and the Growth of Opéra-comique.* Cambridge: Cambridge University Press, 1986.

————. "The Overture to Philidor's *Le Bûcheron* (1763)." In *D'un opéra l'autre: Hommage à Jean Mongrédien,* edited by Jean Gribenski, Marie-Claire Mussat, and Herbert Schneider. Paris: Presses de l'Université de Paris-Sorbonne, 1996. 231–42.

Charpentier, Marc-Antoine. *David et Jonathas.* Edited by Jean Duron. Musique française aux XVIIe XVIIIe siècle 1. Paris: Editions du Centre Nationale de la Recherche Scientifique, 1981.

————. *Medée.* Paris, 1694; repr., Farnsborough, Hants: Gregg Press, 1968. Modern edition, edited by Edmond Lemaître, Paris: Editions du Centre Nationale de la Recherche Scientifique, 1987.

————. *Orphée descendant aux enfers.* Facsimile in *Œuvres complètes: Fac-similé du manuscrit Paris, Bibliothèque Nationale, Rés. Vm1 259.* Meslanges Autographes 6. Geneva: Minkoff, 1996. Edited by John S. Powell in *Marc-Antoine Charpentier: Vocal Chamber Music,* Recent Researches in the Music of the Baroque Era 48, Madison, WI: A-R Editions, 1986.

Le Chevalier de Mailly. *Les illustres fées: Contes galans.* Paris, 1698.

Christensen, Thomas. *Rameau and Musical Thought in the Enlightenment.* Cambridge: Cambridge University Press, 1993.

————. "The *Règle de l'octave* in Thorough-Bass Theory and Practice." *Acta Musicologica* 64 (1992): 91–117.

Christoforo, Armeno. *Peregrinaggio di tre giovani figliuoli del re di Serendippo, per opra di M. Christoforo Armeneo dalla persiana nell'italiana lingua trapportato.* Venice, 1553; repr., Erlangen: Fr. Junge, 1891.

Christout, Marie-Françoise. *Le ballet de cour de Louis XIV, 1643–1672.* Vie musicale en France sous les Rois Bourbons 12. Paris: J. Picard, 1967.

————. *Le merveilleux et le "théâtre du silence" en France à partir du XVIIe siècle.* The Hague: Mouton, 1965.

Claris de Florian, Jean-Pierre. *Théâtre.* Paris: Didot l'aîné, 1782.

Clark, Caryl. "Orlando paladino." In NGO 3:758–60.

Clubb, Louise George. "The Making of the Pastoral Play: Italian Experience between 1573 and

1590." In *Petrarch to Pirandello: Studies in Italian Literature in honour of Beatrice Corrigan*, edited by Julius A. Molinaro. Toronto: University of Toronto Press, 1973.

Cocchiara, Giuseppe. *The History of Folkore in Europe*. Translated by John N. McDaniel. Philadelphia: Institute for the Study of Human Issues, 1981.

———. *Il paese di Cuccagna e altri studi di folklore*. Turin: Boringhieri, 1980.

Coeyman, Barbara. "The Stage Works of Michel-Richard de Lalande in the Musical-Cultural Context of the French Court, 1680-1726." Ph.D. diss., New York University, 1987.

Collé, Charles. *L'île sonnante*, Paris: G. Hérissant, 1768.

Collins, Michael, and Elise K. Kirk, eds. *Opera & Vivaldi*. Austin: University of Texas Press, 1984.

Conant, Martha Pike. "The Oriental Tale in England in the Eighteenth Century." Ph.D. diss., Columbia University, 1908.

Il corago, o vero Alcune osservazioni per metter bene in scena le composizioni drammatiche. Edited by Paolo Fabbri and Angelo Pompilio. Florence: L. S. Olschki, 1983.

Couvreur, Manuel, and Philippe Vendrix. "Les enjeux théoriques de l'opéra-comique." In *L'opéra-comique en France au XVIIIe siècle*, edited by Philippe Vendrix. Liège: Mardaga, 1992. 213–81.

Craig, Charlotte Marie. "Themes and Style in Christoph Martin Wieland's 'Fairy Tales': A Comparison of Sources." Ph.D. diss., Rutgers University, 1964.

Crosby, Clare. "The Fairy Tale on the Old Viennese Stage." Ph.D. diss., University of St. Andrews, 1986.

Cusick, Suzanne G. "Caccini, Francesca." In NGO 1:669.

Dabezies, André. *Le mythe de Faust*. Paris: A. Colin, 1972.

Danchet, Antoine. *Alcine*. Paris: Ribou, [1705].

Dancourt, Florent-Carton. *Les fées*. Paris: Ribou, 1699.

———. *Œuvres de théâtre: Nouvelle edition, revue & corrigée*. Paris, 1760; repr., Geneva: Slatkine, 1963.

Da Ponte, Lorenzo. *L'arbore di Diana*. Milan: Giov. Batista Bianchi, [1788]. Translated as *Der Baum der Diana*. Vienna, 1787.

———. *Il Don Giovanni*. Edited by Giovanna Gronda. Collezione di teatro 354. Milan: Giulio Einaudi, 1995.

Darton, F. J. Harvey. *Children's Books in England: Five Centuries of Social Life*. 3rd ed. Revised by Brian Anderson. Cambridge: Cambridge University Press, 1982.

Darnton, Richard. "Peasants Tell Tales: The Meaning of Mother Goose." In *The Great Cat Massacre and Other Episodes in French Cultural History*. New York: Basic Books, 1984. 9–72.

d'Aulnoy, Comtesse [Marie Catharine Jumelle de Berneville]. *Les contes des fées*. Paris, 1696.

———. *Contes nouveaux, ou Les fées à la mode*. Paris, 1698.

Dean, Winton. *Handel and the Opera Seria*. Berkeley: University of California Press, 1969.

———. *Handel's Operas, 1726–1741*. Woodbridge: Boydell Press, 2006.

Dean, Winton, and John Merrill Knapp. *Handel's Operas, 1704–1726*. Oxford: Clarenden Press 1987.

Decroix, Jacques Joseph Marie. *L'ami des arts, ou Justification de la pratique de la musique*. Amsterdam: Marchands, 1776.

de Groat, James E. "Leben und Singspiele des Ignaz Umlauf." Ph.D. diss., University of Vienna, 1984.

Delaporte, P. V[ictor]. *Du merveilleux dans la littérature française*. Paris: Retaux-Bray, 1891.

Delarue, Paul, and Marie-Louise Tenèze. *Le conte populaire français: Catalogue raisonnée des versions de France et des pays de langue française et d'outre-mer*. Paris: Maisonneuve & Larose, 1976.

De La Serre, Jean-Louis-Ignace. *Mémoires sur la vie et les ouvrages de Molière.* Paris, 1734.

Desaugiers, Marc-Antoine. *Les deux sylphes: Comédie sémi-lyrique, en un acte en vers.* Paris: The author, [1781].

Desboulmiers [Jean-Auguste Jullien]. *Histoire anecdotique et raisonné du Théâtre Italien depuis son rétablissement en France (1717) jusqu'à l'année 1769.* 7 vols. Paris, 1769; repr., Geneva: Slatkine, 1968.

Desmarets, Henry. *Circé.* Paris: Ballard, 1694.

———. *Renaud, ou La suite d'Armide.* Paris: Ballard, 1722.

Destouches, André Cardinal. *Amadis de Grèce.* Paris: C. Ballard, 1699. Facsimile of the 3rd ed. of the score (Paris, 1712), Farnsborough, Hants.: Gregg Press, 1967.

———. *Issé.* Facsimile ed. Edited by Robert Fajon. French Opera in the 17th and 18th Centuries 14. New York: Pendragon, 1984.

———. *Sémiramis.* Paris: Ballard, 1718.

Deutsche Komödienarien, 1754–1758. 1. Teil. Edited by Robert Haas. Denkmäler der Tonkunst in Österreich 64. Vienna: Universal Edition, 1926; repr., Graz: Akademische Druck- und Verlagsanstalt, 1960. Zweiter Teil, edited by Camillo Schoenbaum and Herbert Zeman, Denkmäler der Tonkunst in Österreich 121, Graz: Akademische Druck- und Verlagsanstalt, 1971.

Deutsch, Otto Erich. *Die Freihaustheater auf die Wieden, 1787–1801.* 2nd ed. Vienna: Deutscher Verlag für Jugend und Volk, 1937.

———. *Mozart: Die Dokumente seines Lebens.* Neue Mozart-Ausgabe, Ser. 10, Werkgruppe 34. Kassel: Bärenreiter, 1961.

Diderot, Denis. *Entretiens sur le fils naturel.* Paris, 1757. In *Œuvres esthétiques,* edited by Paul Venière. Paris: Garnier Frères, 1968. 77–178.

Didion, Robert, and Joachim Schlichte. *Thematischer Katalog der Opernsammlung.* Katalog der Stadt- und Universitätsbibliothek Frankfurt am Main 9. Frankfurt: V. Klostermann, 1990.

Dieter, Christian Ludwig *Der Irrwisch.* Stuttgart: Christoph Gottfried Maentler, 1782.

DiGaetani, John Louis. *Carlo Gozzi: Translations of "The Love of Three Oranges," "Turandot," and "The Snake Lady" with a Bio-critical Introduction.* Contributions in Drama and Theatre Studies 24. New York: Greenwood Press, 1988.

Dominique, dit Biancolelli, Pierre-François, and Jean-Antoine Romagnesi. *La sylphide.* Paris: Delatour, 1730.

Donà, Mariangela. "Dagli Archivi Milanesi: Lettere di Ranieri de' Calzabigi e di Antonia Bernasconi." *Analecta Musicologica* 14 (1974): 268–300.

Döring, Renate. *Ariostos "Orlando Furioso" im italienischen Theater des Seicento und Settecento.* Hamburger Romanistische Dissertationen 9. Hamburg: Romanistisches Seminar der Universität Hamburg, 1973.

Doutrepont, Georges. *Les mises en prose des épopées et des romans chevaleresques du XIVe au XVIe siècle.* Brussels, 1939; repr., Geneva: Slatkine, 1969.

Drake, Nathan. *Literary Hours, or Sketches Critical and Narrative.* Sudbury: J. Burkitt, 1798.

Dramaturgischen Blättern. Frankfurt am Main (13 March 1789), 116, cited in *Mozart: Dokumente,* 299.

Dubos, Jean-Baptiste. *Réflexions critiques sur la poésie et sur la peinture.* Paris, 1719; repr., Geneva: Slatkine, 1967.

Dubugrarre, François. *Méthode plus courte et plus facile que l'ancienne pour l'accompagnement du clavecin.* Paris, 1754; repr., Geneva: Minkoff, 1972.

Duclairon, Antoine Maillot. *Essai sur la connaissance des théâtres français.* Paris: Prrult [Prault], 1751.

Dufrenoy, Marie-Louise. *L'orient romanesque en France, 1704–1789*. 3 vols. Montreal: Beauchemin, 1946–48.

Dugat, Gustave. *Histoire des orientalists de l'Europe du XIIe au XIXe siècle*. Paris: Maissonneuve, 1868–70.

Duni, Egidio Romualdo. *La fée Urgèle*. Paris: The author, n.d.

———. *La fée Urgèle*. Paris: Bignon, n.d.

d'Urfé, Honoré. *L'astrée*. Paris, 1607–24. Edited by Hughes Vaganay in 5 vols., Lyons, 1925–28; repr., Geneva: Slatkine, 1966.

Duval, Mlle. *Les Génies, ou Les caractères de l'amour*. Paris: The authors, n.d.

Edge, Dexter. "Mozart's Viennese Copyists." Ph.D. diss., University of Southern California, 2001.

Einsiedel, Friedrich Hildebrand, Frieherr von. "Die Wasser-Geister." In *Neueste vermischte Schriften*. Dessau, 1784. 2:129–210.

Eisen, Cliff. *New Mozart Documents*. New York: Macmillan, 1991.

Elisséeff, Nikita. *Thèmes et motifs des Mille et une nuits: Essai de classification*. Beirut: Institut Français de Damas, 1949.

Emery, Ted. "Autobiographer as Critic: The Structure and 'Utility' of Gozzi's *Useless Memoirs*." *Italian Quarterly* 154 (1983): 43–49.

Encyclopédie, ou Dictionnaire raisonné des sciences, des arts, et des métiers. Edited by Denis Diderot, Jean d'Alembert, et al. Paris: Briasson, Le Breton, etc., 1751–65; suppls., Amsterdam and Paris: M. M. Roy, 1776–77, 1780; repr., Elmsford, NY: Pergamon Press, [1969].

Engländer, Richard. *Johann Gottlieb Naumann als Opernkomponist, 1741–1801*. Leipzig: Breitkopf & Härtel, 1922.

———. "Die Opern Joseph Schusters, 1748–1812." *Zeitschrift für Musikwissenschaft* 10 (1928): 257–91.

Enzinger, Moriz. "Randbemerkungen zum Textbuch der 'Zauberflöte.'" In *Sprachkunst als Weltgestaltung: Festschrift für Herbert Seidler*, edited by Adolf Haslinger. Munich: Anton Pustet, 1966. 49–74.

Fabrizi, Angelo. "Carlo Gozzi e la tradizione popolare (a proposito de 'L'amore delle tre melarance')." *Italianistica* 7 (1978): 336–45.

La fata benefica. Venice, n.d.

La fata meravigliosa. Venice: Appresso Modesto Fenzo, 1746.

Favart, Charles-Simon. *La belle Arsène*. Paris: Houbaut, 1775.

———. *La fée Urgèle, ou Ce qui plaît aux dames*. Paris: Christophe Ballard, 1765; Paris: Veuve Duchesne, 1765; Paris: The author, n.d. [c. 1766].

Favorit Gesänge aus dem Opern "Adrast und Isadoro und dem Irrwisch," für's Clavier und Gesang eingerichtet. Berlin: Rellstab, n.d.

Federhofer, Hellmut. "Vincenzo Righni's Oper *Alcide al bivio*." In *Essays Presented to Egon Wellesz*, edited by Jack Allan Westrup. London: Oxford University Press, 1966. 130–44.

Fellerer, Karl Gustav. "Zur Mozart-Kritik im 18./19. Jahrhundert." *Mozart-Jahrbuch 1959* (1960): 80–94.

Fellinger, Robert. "*Oberon* im achzehnten Jahrhundert." *Die Musik* 24 (1934): 915–19.

Ferrari, Paolo-Emilio. *Spettacoli drammatico-musicale e coreografici in Parma dal 1628 al 1883*. Parma, 1884; repr., Bologna: Forni, 1969.

Fleischer, Friedrich Gottlob. *Das Orackel: Ein Operette vom Herrn Professor Gellert*. Brunswick: Fürstliche Waisenhaus-Buchhandlung, 1771.

Flemming, Willi. *Geschichte des Jesuitentheaters in den Landen deutscher Zunge*. Schriften der Ge-

sellschaft für Theatergeschichte 32. Berlin: Selbstverlag der Gesellschaft für Theatergeschichte, 1932.

———. "Le merveilleux sur la scêne du baroque en Allemagne." *Revue d'histoire du théâtre* 6
(1963): 13–20.

Fleury de Lyon, Mlle. *Les génies, ou Les caractères de l'amour.* Paris: J. B. C. Ballard, 1736.

Fouques, François-George [Desfontaines]. *L'aveugle de Palmyre.* Paris: Veuve Duchesne, 1767
[music by Jean-Joseph Rodolphe]. Score: Paris: La Chevardiere, n.d.

Fox, Leland. "*La Belle Arsène* (1773) by Pierre-Alexandre Monsigny." *Recherches sur la musique
française classique* 9 (1969): 141–44.

———. "Dezède, Nicolas." In *The New Grove Dictionary of Music,* edited by Stanley Sadie.
20 vols. London and New York: Macmillan, 1980. 5:412–13.

Francis, John W. *Old New York, or Reminiscences of the Past Sixty Years.* New York: W. J. Wid-
dleton, 1866.

Frati, Lodovico. "Torquato Tasso in musica." *Rivista musicale italiana* 30 (1923): 389–400.

Freeman, Robert S. *Opera without Drama: Currents of Change in Italian Opera, 1675–1725, and
the Roles Played Therein by Zeno, Caldara, and Others.* Ann Arbor: UMI Research Press,
1981.

Friedrich, Ernst. *Die Magie im französischen Theater des XVI. und XVII Jahrhunderts.* Münchener
Beiträge zur romanischen und englischen Philologie 41. Leipzig: A. Deichert'sche Verlags-
buchhandlung, 1908.

Fritz, Gérard. *L'idée de peuple en France du XVIIe siècle au XVIIIe siécle.* Strasbourg: Presses universitaires de Strasbourg, 1988.

Frugoni, Carlo-Innocenzo. *Ippolito ed Aricia.* Facsimile edited by Howard Mayer Brown. IO 14,
1983.

Fülleborn, Georg Gustav. *Volksmärchen des Deutschen.* Halle: Franck & Bispink, 1789.

Fux, Johann Joseph. *Orfeo ed Euridice.* Fascimile edited by Howard Mayer Brown. IO 19, 1978.

Fuzelier, Louis de. *La reine des péris.* Paris: Veuve de Pierre Ribou, 1725.

Galland, Antoine. *Les mille et une nuits: Contes arabes traduits en François.* 12 vols. Paris/Lyon:
Barbin/Florentin Delaulne/Briasson, 1704–17.

———. *Les mille et une nuits, contes arabes, traduits en français,* nouv. éd. [. . .] avec notes de A.
Loiseleur-Deslong-Champs. Paris: Desrez, 1838.

Gamerra, Giovanni de. *L'Armida.* Milan: Giuseppe Galeazzi, 1771.

Gardner, Edmund G. *The Arthurian Legend in Italian Literature.* London: J. M. Dent, 1930.

Garin, Eugenio. *Science and Civic Life on the Italian Renaissance.* Translated by Peter Munz. Garden City, NY: Doubleday, 1969.

Garlington, Aubrey S. Jr. "'Gothic' Literature and Dramatic Music in England, 1781–1802."
Journal of the American Musicological Society 15, no. 1 (1962): 48–64.

———. "*Le merveilleux* and Operatic Reform in 18th-Century French Opera." *Musical Quarterly* 49 (1963): 484–97.

Gassmann, Florian Leopold. *Amore e Psiche.* Facsimile edited by Eric Weimer. IO 87, 1983.

———. *L'opera seria.* Facsimile edited by Eric Weimer. IO 89, 1982.

Gazzaniga, Giuseppe. *Don Giovanni, o sia Il convitato di pietra.* Edited by Stefan Kunze. Kassel:
Bärenreiter, 1974.

Geils, Peter, and Willi Gorzny, eds. *Gesamtverzeichnis des deutschsprachigen Schrifttums (GV),
1700–1910.* 160 vols. Munich: K. G. Saur, 1979–87.

Genlis, Stéphanie-Félicité Ducrest de Saint-Aubin. *Dictionnaire critique et raisonné des étiquettes de
la cour.* Paris: P. Mongrié aîné, 1818.

————. *Théâtre à l'usage des jeunes personnes.* Vol. 2. Paris: Lambert, 1783.

Geyer-Kiefl, Helen. *Die heroisch-komische Oper, ca. 1770–1820.* 2 vols. Würzburger Musikhistorische Beiträge 9. Tutzing: Hans Schneider, 1987.

————. "Joseph Haydn's vis comica." *Österreichische Musik Zeitschrift* 37, no. 5 (1982): 225–33.

Gherardi, Evaristo. *Théâtre italien; ou, Le recueil de toutes les scènes françaises qui ont été jouées sur le Théâtre Italien de l'Hôtel de Bourgogne.* Paris: Guillaume de Luyne, 1694. Repr. as *Le théatre italien, ou le recueil général de toutes les comédiens italiens du Roi.* Paris, 1741; repr., Geneva: Slatkine, 1969.

Gieseke, Karl Ludwig. *Oberon, König der Elfen.* Vienna: Wallishausser, 1806.

Glossy, Blanka, and Robert Haas. *Weiner Comödienlieder aus drei Jarhhunderten.* Vienna: Anton Schroll, 1924.

Gluck, Christoph Willibald. *Sämtliche Werke.* Edited by Rudolf Gerber et al. Kassel: Bärenreiter, 1951–.

Goldoni, Carlo. *Il paese della Cuccagna.* Venice: Modesto Fenzo, 1750.

————. *Tutte le opere di Carlo Goldoni.* [Venice: G. B. Pasquali, 1761–78], edited by Giuseppe Ortolani. [Verona:] Arnaldo Mondadori, 1935–56. 4th ed., 1959, 14 vols.

Gotter, Johann Friedrich Wilhelm. *Medea.* Edited by Jan Trojan. Musica antiqua bohemica, ser. 2, vol. 8. Prague: Editio Supraphon, 1976.

————. *Das tartarische Gesetz.* Leipzig: Dyk, 1779.

Gottsched, Johann Christoph. *Von dem Wunderbaren in der Poesie.* Vol. 5 of *Versuch einer critischen Dichtkunst für die Deutschen.* Leipzig, 1751; repr., Darmstadt: Wissenschaftliche Buchgesellschaft, 1962.

Gozzi, Carlo. *The Blue Monster: A Fairy Play in Five Acts.* Translated by Edward J. Dent. Cambridge: Cambridge University Press, 1951.

————. *Fiabe teatrali: Testo, introduzione e commento.* Edited by Paolo Bosisio. Biblioteca di Cultura 261. Rome: Bulzoni, 1984.

————. *Five Tales for the Theatre.* Edited and translated by Albert Bermel and Ted Emery. Notes by Ted Emery. Chicago: University of Chicago Press, 1989.

————. *Memorie inutili.* Edited by Domenico Bulferetti. 2 vols. Turin: Unione tipografico-editrice torinese, 1923.

————. *Opere.* 7 vols. Venice: Colombani, 1772.

————. *Opere edite e inedite.* 14 vols. Venice: G. Zanardi, 1801.

————. *Opere: Teatro e polemiche teatrali.* Edited by Giuseppe Petronio. Milan: Rizzoli, 1962.

————. *Theatralische Werke.* 5 vols. Translated by Friedrich August Clemens Werthes. Bern, 1777–79.

Grandval, Nicolas Ragot de. *L'oracle.* Paris: Prault fils, 1764.

Grattan-Guinness, I. "Counting the Notes: Numerology in the Works of Mozart, especially *Die Zauberflöte.*" *Annals of Science* 49 (1992): 201–32.

Grätz, Manfred. *Das Märchen in der deutschen Aufklärung: Vom Feenmärchen zum Volksmärchen.* Germanistische Abhandlungen 63. Stuttgart: J. B. Metzler, 1988.

Graun, Carl Heinrich. *Duetti, terzetti, quintetti, sestetti ed alcuni chori dell opere.* Berlin: Georg Jacob Decker & Gottlieb Leberecht Hartung, 1773.

Greene, Thomas M. "Magic and Festivity at the Renaissance Court." *Renaissance Quarterly* 40 (1987): 636–59.

Greg, Walter Wilson. *Pastoral Poetry and Pastoral Drama.* London: A. H. Bullen, 1906.

Grenet, François-Lupien. *Le triomphe de l'harmonie.* Paris: The author, n.d.

Grétry, André-Ernest-Modeste. *Collection complète des œuvres.* Leipzig: Breitkopf & Härtel, 1884–1936.

———. *De la vérité: Ce que nous fûmes, ce que nous sommes, ce que nous devrions être*. 3 vols. Paris: The author, 1801.

———. *Le jugement de Midas*. Paris: Houbart, [1779].

———. *Mémoires, ou Essais sur la musique*. 3 vols. Paris: Imprimerie de la République, an 5 [1797].

———. *Raoul, Barbe-bleue*. Paris: The author, [1790].

———. *Zémire et Azor*. Paris: Houbart, 1772.

Grewe, Andrea. *Monde renversé—théâtre renversé: Lesage und das Théâtre de la Foire*. Bonn: Romantischer Verlag, 1989.

Grimm, Friedrich Melchior. "Poème lyrique." In *Encyclopédie, ou Dictionnaire raisonné*, vol. 12 (1765), 828–30; reproduced in Grimm, "Poème lyrique," in *Encyclopédie méthodique*. Paris: Chez Panckoncke, 1791, 1, 3e partie, 102.

Grimm, Friedrich Melchior, et al. *Correspondance littéraire, philosophique et critique*. Edited by Maurice Tourneux. 16 vols. Paris: Garnier, 1877–82.

Grimm, Jacob, and Wilhelm Grimm. *Kinder- und Hausmärchen*. 2nd ed. Berlin, 1819.

Gueullette, J.-E. *Un magistrate du XVIIIe siècle: Thomas-Simon Gueullette*. Paris: E. Droz, 1938.

Gueullette, Thomas-Simon. *Les mille et un quarts d'heure, contes tartares*. 2 vols. Paris: J. B. Mauzel, 1712.

———. *Notes et souvenirs sur le Théâtre Italien au XVIIIe siècle, publiés par J.-E. Gueullette*. Paris: Droz, 1938; repr., Geneva, 1976.

Günther, Christoph Wilhelm. *Kindermärchen, aus mündlichen Erzählungen gesammelt*. Erfurt: Georg Adam Keyser, 1787.

Haas, Robert. *Gluck und Durazzo im Burgtheater*. Vienna: Amalthea, 1925.

Hadamowsky, Franz. *Die wiener Hoftheater (Staatstheater), 1776–1966: Verzeichnis der aufgeführten Stücke mit Bestandsnachweis und täglichem Spielplan*. 2 vols. Vienna: Georg Prachner, 1966. 1:1776–1810.

Hafner, Philipp. *Megära, die fürchtliche Hexe, oder Der bezauberte Schloß des Herrn von Einhorn*. Vienna: Joseph Kurzböck, [ca.1764]. Printed in *Philipp Hafners gesammelte Schriften*, Vienna: J. B. Wallishausser, 1812, vol. 2; and in Philip Hafner, *Gesammelte Werke*, edited by Ernst Baum in *Schriften des Literarischen Vereins in Wien*. Vienna: Verlag des Literarischen Vereins, 1914–15, vol. 1.

Hammerstein, Reinhold. "Invokation—Göttersprach—Orakel: Zur Topik des Wunderbaren in Bühnenwerken von J.-Ph. Rameau." In *Studien zur Musikgeschichte: Eine Festschrift für Ludwig Finscher*. Kassel: Bärenreiter, 1995. 222–37.

Handel, Georg Frideric. *Hallische Händel-Ausgabe*. Im Auftrage der Georg Friedrich Händel-Gesellschaft. Edited by M. Schneider et al. Kassel: Bärenreiter, 1955–.

———. *Werke*. Ausgabe der Deutschen Handelgesellschaft. Edited by Friedrich Chrysander. 94 vols. and 6 suppls. Leipzig: Breitkopf & Härtel, 1858–1902.

Hanlon, Kenneth M. "The Eighteenth-Century Trombone: A Study of Its Changing Role as a Solo and Ensemble Instrument." D.M.A. diss., Peabody Conservatory of Music, 1989.

Hansell, Kathleen Kuzmick. "Opera and Ballet at the Regio Ducal Teatro of Milan, 1771–1776: A Musical and Social History." Ph.D. diss., University of California, Berkeley, 1980.

———. "Theatrical Ballet and Italian Opera." In *Opera on Stage*. Vol. 5 of *The History of Italian Opera*, edited by Lorenzo Bianconi and Giorgio Pestelli. Chicago: University of Chicago Press, 2002. A revised English version of "Il ballo teatrale e l'opera italiana," in *La spettacolarità*, Storia dell'opera italiana 5. Turin: Edizioni di Torino, 1988. 175–306.

Hansell, Sven. H. "Ferdinando Bertoni's Setting of Calzabigi's *Orfeo ed Euridice*." In *Venezia e il melodramma nel Settecento*, edited by Maria Teresa Muraro. Florence: Olschki, 1981. 185–211.

————. "Mythological Subjects in Opera Seria." In Collins and Kirk, eds., *Opera & Vivaldi*, 41–53.

Harf-Lancner, Laurence. *Les fées au moyens âge: Morgane et Mélusine; La naissance des fées*. Geneva: Slatkine, 1984.

Harris, Ellen T. "Eighteenth-Century Orlando: Hero, Satyr, and Fool." In Collins and Kirk, eds., *Opera & Vivaldi*. Austin: University of Texas Press, 1984.

————. *Handel and the Pastoral Tradition*. Oxford: Oxford University Press, 1980.

————. "*L'Orfeo:* The Metamorphosis of a Musical Myth." *Israel Studies in Musicology* 2 (1980): 101–20.

————. Preface to Aureli and A. Sartorio, *L'Orfeo*.

Hasse, Johann Adolf. *Alcide al bivio*. Facsimile edited by Howard Mayer Brown. IO 81, 1983.

————. *L'artigiano gentiluomo (Larinda e Vanesio)*. Edited by Gordana Lazarevich. Recent Researches in the Music of the Classical Era 9. Madison, WI: A-R Editions, 1979.

Haydn, Joseph. *Werke*. Herausgegeben vom Joseph-Haydn-Institut. Munich: Henle, 1962–.

Hayes, Deborah. "Marie-Emmanuelle Bayon, later Madame Louis, and Music in Late Eighteenth-Century France." *College Music Symposium* 30 (1990): 14–33.

Hazard, Paul. *La pensée européenne au XVIIIe siècle: De Montesquieu à Lessing*. Paris: Boivin, 1946.

Heartz, Daniel. *Haydn, Mozart and the Viennese School, 1740–1780*. New York: Norton, 1995.

————. "*Les Lumières:* Voltaire and Metastasio; Goldoni, Favart and Diderot." In *International Musicological Society: Report of the Twelfth Congress, Berkeley, 1977*. Kassel: Bärenreiter, 1981.

————. *Mozart's Operas*. Berkeley: University of California Press, 1990.

————. *Music in European Capitals: The Galant Style, 1720–1780*. New York: W. W. Norton, 2003.

————. "Operatic Reform at Parma: *Ippolito ed Aricia*." In *Atti del Convegno sul Settecento parmense nel 2o Centenario della morte di C. I. Frugoni*. Parma: Deputazione di Storia Patria delle Province Parmensi, 1969. 271–300.

————. "Traetta in Vienna: Armida (1761) and Ifigenia in Tauride (1763)." *Studies in Music from the University of Western Ontario* 7 (1982): 65–88.

Heck, Thomas. *Commedia dell'arte: A Guide to the Primary and Secondary Literature*. Garland Reference Library of the Humanities 786. New York: Garland, 1988.

Helfert, Vladmir. "Zur Geschichte des Wiener Singspiels." *Zeitschrift für Musikwissenschaft* 5 (1922–23): 194–209.

Herder, Johann Gottfried. *Sämmtliche Werke*. Edited by Bernard Suphan. Hildesheim: G. Olms, 1967–68.

Hedelin d'Aubignac, François. *La pratique du théâtre*. Paris: De Sommaville, 1657.

Hiller, Johann Adam. *Le diable à quatre*. Leipzig: J. F. Junius, 1770.

————. *Lieder für Kinder*. Leipzig: Weidmanns, Erben, & Reich, 1769.

————. *Lisuart und Dariolette*. Leipzig: Breitkopf, 1768. 2nd ed., 1769.

————. *Die verwandelten Weiber, oder Die Teufel ist los*. Leipzig: J. F. Junius, 1770.

Hinck, Walter. *Das deutsche Lustspiel des 17. und 18. Jahrhunderts*. Germanistische Abhandlungen 8. Stuttgart: J. B. Metzler, 1965.

Hirschfeld, Christian Cajus Lorenz, ed. *Romanzen der Deutschen*. Leipzig: Christian Gottlieb Hertel, 1774.

Hoevels, Fritz Erik. *Märchen und Magie in den Metamorphosen des Apuleius von Madaura*. Studies in Classical Antiquity 1. Amsterdam: Rodopi, 1979.

Hollis, George Truett. "Bertoni, Ferdinando." In NGO 1:455–56.

Honolka, Kurt. *Papageno: Emanuel Schikaneder, der große Theatermann der Mozart-Zeit*. Salzburg: Residenz Verlag, 1984.

Hortschansky, Klaus. *Parodie und Entlehnung in Schaffen Christoph Willibald Glucks*. Analecta musicologica 13. Cologne: Hans Gerig, 1973.

Iacuzzi, Alfred. *The European Vogue of Favart: The Diffusion of the Opéra-Comique*. New York, 1932; repr., New York: AMS Press, 1972.

Irmen, Hans-Josef. *Mozart: Mitglied geheimer Gesellschaften*. [Zülpich]: Prisca, 1988.

Isherwood, Robert M. *Farce and Fantasy: Popular Entertainment in Eighteenth-century Paris*. New York: Oxford University Press, 1986.

———. *Music in the Service of the King: France in the Seventeenth Century*. Ithaca, NY: Cornell University Press, [1973].

———. "Popular Music Entertainment in Eighteenth-Century Paris." *International Review of the Aesthetics and Sociology of Music* (1978): 295–310.

———. "The Third War of the Musical Enlightenment." In *Studies in Eighteenth-Century Culture*, vol. 4, edited by Harold E. Pagliaro. Madison: University of Wisconsin Press, 1975. 223–45.

Ivy, Frederick Maurice. "The Development of Pre-Romantic Elements in Wieland's Work as Illustrated in His Fairy Tales." Ph.D. diss., University of Louisiana, 1966.

Jackson, James L. "Palella, Antonio." In NGO 2:831.

Jahn, Otto. *W. A. Mozart*. Leipzig, 1859; repr., Hildesheim: Georg Olms, 1976.

Jameson, Frederic. "Magical Narratives: Romance as Genre." *New Literary History* 7 (1975): 135–63.

Janetschek, Karl Ludwig. "Joachim Perinet: Eine zusammenfassende Darstellung seiner Bedeutung auf Grund seiner Lebensgeschichte und seiner Werke." Ph.D. diss., University of Vienna, 1924.

Jensen, H. James. *The Muses' Concord: Literature, Music and the Visual Arts in the Baroque Age*. Bloomington: Indiana University Press, 1976.

Johnson, James H. *Listening in Paris: A Cultural History*. Berkeley: University of California Press, 1995.

Jommelli, Niccolò. *Armida abbandonata*. Facsimile edited by Eric Weimer. IO 91, 1983.

———. *Fetonte: Dramma per musica*. Edited by Hermann Abert. 2 vols. Denkmäler deutscher Tonkunst, ser. 1, vols. 32–33. Leipzig, 1907; repr., Graz: Breitkopf & Härtel, 1958.

Jonard, Norbert. "Les structures idéologiques de *L'augellino belverde* de C. Gozzi." *Romantische Zeitschrift für Literaturgeschichte* 2 (1978): 10–20.

Jünger, Johann Friedrich. *Der blinde Ehemann*. Berlin: Friedrich Maurer, 1784.

Keightley, Thomas. *The Fairy Mythology*. London, 1850; repr., New York: Haskell House, 1968.

Kielbasa, Marilyn. "Paul Wranitzky's *Oberon, König der Elfen:* The Historical Background of the Opera and Its Composer, and Its Influence on Mozart's *Die Zauberflöte*." Master's thesis, University of Southern California, 1975.

Kiepert, Willy. *Fletcher's "Women Pleased" und seine Quellen*. Halle, 1903.

Kintzler, Catherine. "Du merveilleux et du sublime: Nature lacunaire, surnature, contre-nature." In *D'un opéra l'autre: Hommage à Jean Mongrédien*, edited by Jean Gribenski, Marie-Claire Mussat, and Herbert Schneider. Paris: Presses de l'Université de Paris-Sorbonne, 1996. 413–20.

———. *Poétique de l'opéra français de Corneille à Rousseau*. Paris: Minerve, 1991.

Kirk, Carolyn. "The Viennese Vogue for Opéra-Comique, 1790–1819." Ph.D. diss., University of St. Andrews, 1983.

Klinger, Friedrich Maximilian. *Der Derwisch*. Ormus, 1780.

Köhler, Reinhold. *Aufsätze zum Deutschen Märchen*. Berlin: Weidmann, 1894.

[Knüppeln, Julius Friedrich?]. *Vertraute Briefe zur Charakteristik von Wien*. Görlitz: Hermsdorf & Anton, 1793.

Komorzynski, Egon. *Emanuel Schikaneder*. Berlin: B. Behr, 1901; revised, Vienna: Ludwig Doblinger, 1951.

———. "'Zauberflöte' und 'Dschinnistan.'" *Mozart-Jahrbuch 1954*, 177–94.

———. "'Zauberflöte' und 'Oberon.'" *Mozart-Jahrbuch 1953*, 150–61.

Kopp, James Butler. "The 'Drame lyrique': A Study in the Aesthetics of Opéra-Comique, 1762–1791." Ph.D. diss., University of Pennsylvania, 1982.

Korzeniewski, Bohdan. "Komedia dell'arte w Warszawie." *Pamiętnik teatralny* 3, nos. 3–4 (1954): 29–55.

Kotzebue, August von. *Der Spiegelritter*. N.p., n.d. [US-Wc, Schatz 10865a].

———. *Sultan Wampum, oder Die Wuensche*. N.p. n.d. [US-Wc, Schatz 10042 and 11749].

Koyré, Alexandre. *Mystiques, spirituels, alchemistes*. Paris: Colin, 1955.

Kritisches Theater-Journal von Wien. Vienna: Matthias Ludwig, 1789.

Krüger, Walther. "Das Urbild des "Zauberflöte"-Mohren: Mozarts Freimaurer-Cafetier." *Neue Zeitschrift für Musik* 118, no. 4 (1957): 237–39.

Kunz, F. C. *Almanach der National Schaubühne in Wien auf das Jahr 1788*. Vienna: J. Gerold, 1788.

Kunzen, Friedrich Ludwig Aemilius. *Holger Danske*. Copenhagen: S. Sönnischsen, n.d. German translation, edited by Carl Friedrich Cramer, Copenhagen: S. Sönnischsen, 1790. Modern edition, Copenhagen: Elektra, 1941.

Kurtz, Benjamin P. *Studies in the Marvellous*. University of California Publications in Modern Philology 1, no. 2. Berkeley: University of California Press, 1910. 69–244.

Kurz, Joseph Felix von [Bernardon]. *Der lebendig verbrannte Zauberer Bernardon*. Vienna: Trattner, 1771.

———. *Neun Arien welche in der Comodie Die funf kleinen Lust-Geister oder die wunderliche Reisen des Hannswurst und Bernardons nacher Hungarn, Italien, Holland, Spanien, Türkey und Frankreich als zwey undankbare Schüler einer grossmütigen Zauberin von solcher auf das lächerlichste ausgezahlet werden*. N.p., n.d.

La Borde, Jean Benjamin de. *Essai sur la musique et moderne*. Paris: Ph. D. Pierres, 1780.

La Chaussée, Pierre-Claude Nivelle de. *Amour pour amour*. Paris: Prault, 1742.

———. *Œuvres de théâtre*. 3 vols. Paris: Prault, 1741–47.

Lacoste, Louis de. *Philomèle*. Paris: Christophe Ballard, 1705.

Lacroix, Paul. *Ballets et mascarades de cour*. 6 vols. Paris, 1868–70; repr., Geneva: Slatkine, 1968.

La Force, Charlotte-Rose Caumont de. *Les contes des contes*. Paris, 1697.

La Gorce, Jérôme de. "L'opéra sous le regne de Louis XIV: Le merveilleux ou les puissantes surnaturelles (1671–1715)." 3 vols. Thesis, University of Paris (Sorbonne), 1978.

Lagrave, Henri. "Don Juan au siècle des lumières." In *Approches des lumières: Mélanges offerts a Jean Fabre*. Paris: Klincksieck, 1974. 257–76.

La Laurencie, Lionel de. "*L'Orfeo nell'inferni* d'André Campra." *Revue de musicologie* 9 (1928): 129–33.

La Mettrie, Julien Offray de. *L'homme machine*. Leyden, 1748. Translated as *Man a Machine*. Chicago: Open Court, 1912.

Langlé, Honoré-François-Marie. *Corisandre, ou Les fous par enchantement*. Paris: le Duc, n.d.

La Porte, Joseph de, ed. *Bibliothèque des génies et des fees*. Paris, 1764–65.

Laruette, Jean-Louis. *Cendrillon*. Paris: The author, [after 1762].

La Taille, Jean de. *Œuvres*. Edited by René de Maulde. Paris: L. Willem, 1878–82.

L'Auchery. Etienne. *Rinaldo und Armida*. Kassel: D. Estienne, 1769.

Laufer, Roger. *Lesage, ou Le métier de romancier.* Paris: Gallimard, 1971.

Laurent de Béthizy, Jean. *Exposition de la théorie et de la pratique de la musique.* Paris: Lambert, 1754.

Lea, Kathleen Marguerite. "The Bibliography of the Commedia dell'arte." *Library* 9 (1930): 1–38.

———. *Italian Popular Comedy: A Study in the Commedia dell'arte, 1560–1620.* 2 vols. Oxford: Clarendon Press, 1934.

Lebègue, Raymond. "Le merveilleux magique en France dans le théâtre baroque." *Revue d'histoire du théâtre* 1 (1963): 7–12.

Leblond, Gaspard Michel. *Mémoires pour servir a l'histoire de la révolution [opérée] de la musique par M. Chevalier Gluck.* Naples, 1781; repr., Amsterdam: Antiqua 1967.

Le Boeuf, Jean-Joseph. *Jérusalem délivrée, ou Renaud et Armide.* [Paris]: de Lormel 1779.

Lebrun, Antoine-Louis. *Mélusine* in *Théâtre lyrique . . .* Paris: Ribou, 1712. 123–54.

Leclair, Jean-Marie. *Scylla et Glaucus.* Paris: The author, Boivin/Le Clerc, n.d.

Lecomte, Natalie. "L'orientalisme dans le ballet aux XVIIe et XVIIIe siècles." 2 vols. Thesis, University of Paris (Sorbonne), 1981.

Leeuwe, Hans de. "Monostatos: Zur Deutung einer Rolle in Mozarts 'Zauberflöte.'" *Mitteilungen der Internationalen Stiftung Mozarteum* 38, nos. 1–4 (1990): 123–36.

Le Grand, Marc-Antoine. *Le roi de Cocagne.* Paris: P. Ribou, 1719.

Leopold, Silke. "Haydn und die Tradition der Orpheus-Opern." *Musica* 36 (1982): 131–35.

Le Roux, Philibert-Joseph. *Dictionnaire comique, satyrique, critique, burlesque, libre et proverbial.* Amsterdam: Charles Le Cene, 1718; Lyon: Héritiers de Beringos frates, 1735.

Lesage, Alain-René. *Gil Blas.* Paris, 1715. Modern edition, Paris: Éditions du Club français du Livre, 1958.

Lesage, Alain-René, and [Jacques Philippe] d'Orneval. *Le théâtre de la foire, ou L'opéracomique . . . aux foires de S. Germain et S. Laurent.* 10 vols. Paris, 1721–37; repr. in 2 vols., Geneva: Slatkine, 1968.

Lesueur, Jean-François. *Exposé d'une musique.* Paris: Veuve Hérissant, 1787.

Leydi, Roberto, and Renata M. Leydi. *Marionette e burattini.* Milan: Avanti, 1958.

L'Héritier [de Villandon], Marie-Jeanne. *Œuvres meslées.* Paris, 1695.

Lindsay, Frank Whiteman. *Dramatic Parody by Marionettes in Eighteenth-Century Paris.* New York: King's Crown Press, 1946.

Link, Dorothea. "*L'arbore di Diana:* A Model for *Così fan tutte.*" In *Wolfgang Amadé Mozart: Essays on His Life and on His Music,* edited by Stanley Sadie. Oxford: Clarendon Press, 1996. 362–73.

———. *The National Court Theatre in Mozart's Vienna: Sources and Documents, 1783–1792.* Oxford: Oxford University Press, 1998.

Locke, John. *Two Treatises of Government.* Rev. ed. Edited by Peter Laslett. Cambridge: Cambridge University Press, 1960.

Luciani, Gérard. *Carlo Gozzi (1720–1806): L'homme et l'œuvre.* Paris: Champion, 1977.

Lusse, Charles de. *Ariettes de L'amant statue.* Paris, n.d.

Lüthi, Max. *The European Folktale: Form and Nature.* Translated by John D. Niles. Philadelphia: Institute for the Study of Human Issues, 1982 [orig., *Das europäische Volksmärchen: Form und Wesen.* Munich, 1981].

Lynch, Robert Donald. "Opera in Hamburg, 1716–1738: A Study of the Libretto and Musical Style." Ph.D. diss., New York University, 1979.

Mably, [Gabriel Bonnet], de. *Lettres à Madame la marquise de P*** sur l'opéra.* Paris, 1741; repr., New York: AMS Press, 1978.

Macchia, Giovanni. *Vita avventure e morte di Don Giovanni*. Turin: G. Einaudi, 1978.

Macmillan, Dougald, ed. *Catalogue of the Larpent Plays in the Huntington Library*. San Marino, CA, 1939. Texts reproduced in *Three Centuries of Drama*, edited by Henry Willis Wells. New York: Readex Microprint, 1963–69.

MacNeil, Anne. "A Modern *Centaur:* Musical Representations of Genre in Early Seicento Theater." Paper read at the annual meeting of the Society for Seventeenth-Century Music, Danville, KY, 30 April 1995.

La maga Circe. Florence: Anton-Giuseppe Pagani e comp., 1789.

Magné, Bernard. "Le chocolat et l'ambroisie: Le statut de la mythologie dans les contes de fées." *Cahiers de littèrature du XVIIe siècle* 2 (1980): 95–146.

———. *Crise de la littérature française sous Louis XIV: Humanisme et nationalisme*. 2 vols. Paris: Champion, 1976.

Magnin, Charles. *Histoire des marionnettes en Europe depuis l'antiquité jusqu'à nos jours*. Paris: Michel-Lévy, 1862.

Mallet, Edme. "Fée." In *Encyclopédie ou Dictionnaire raisonné* 6:464.

———. "Fée, féerie." In [A. A. F. Babault et al.], *Annales dramatiques, ou Dictionnaire général des theaters*. 9 vols. Paris: Babault, 1808–12. 4:65–67.

Mamczarz, Irène. *Les intermèdes comiques italiens au XVIIIe siècle en France et en Italie*. Paris: Editions du Centre National de la Recherche Scientifique, 1972.

———. "Quelques aspects d'interaction dans les théâtres italien, français et polonais des XVIe et XVIIe siècles: Drame humaniste, comédie dell'arte, théâtre musical." In *Le théâtre italien et l'Europe, XVe–XVIIe siècles*. Paris: Presses Universitaires de France, 1983.

Marelli, Adiana. *Ludwig Tiecks frühe Märchenspiele und die goʒʒische Manier: Eine vergleichende Studie*. Cologne: A. Wasmund-Bothmann, 1968.

Marinelli, Karl. "Dom Juan, oder Der steinerne Gast: Lustspiel in vier Aufzügen nach Molieren, und dem Spanischen des Tirso de Molina." In *Deutsche Literatur in Entwicklungsreihen, Reihe Barock, Barocktradition im Österreichisch-Bayrischen Volkstheater*. 2nd ed. Edited by Otto Rommel. Leipzig: Philipp Reclam, 1936. 3–96.

Marmontel, Jean-François. "Dénouement." In *Encyclopédie ou Dictionnaire raisonné* 4:832.

———. *Eléments de littérature*. 3 vols. Paris: Chez Née de la Rochelle, 1787; repr., Paris: Didot, 1846.

———. "Merveilleux." In *Supplément à l'encyclopédie*, 906–8.

———. *Poétique françoise*. Paris: Lesclapart, 1763.

Marsan, Jules. *La pastorale dramatique en France à la fin du XVIe et au commencement du XVIIe siècle*. Paris, 1905; repr., Geneva: Slatkine, 1969.

Martello, Pier Jacopo. *Scritti critici e satiri*. Edited by Hannibal S. Noce. Bari: G. Laterza, 1963.

Martinelli, Gaetano. *Le avventure di Cleomede*. Lisbon: Stamperia Reale, 1772.

Martino, Pierre. *L'orient dans la littérature française au XVIIe et au XVIIIe siècle*. Paris, 1906; repr., Geneva: Slatkine, 1970.

Marx, Adolf Bernhard. *Die Lehre von der musikalsichen Komposition*. 2 vols. Leipzig: Breitkopf & Härtel, 1837–38.

Mattheson, Johann. *Der vollkommene Capellmeister*. Hamburg, 1739; facs. Kassel: Bärenreiter, 1959.

Maury, Louis Ferdinand Alfred. *Les fées du moyen-age: Recherches sur leur origin, leur histoire et leur attributs pour servir à la connaissance de la mythologie Gauloise*. Paris, 1843. Revised as *Croyances et légendes du moyen âge*, edited by A. Longnon and G. Bonet-Maury. Paris, 1896; repr., Geneva: Slatkine, 1974.

Mayer, K. Otto. "Das Feenmärchen bei Weiland." *Vierteljahrschrift für Litteraturgeschichte* 5 (1892): 374–408, 497–533.

———. "Die Quellen zu Klingers *Derwisch*." *Zeitschrift für deutsche Philologie* 25 (1893): 356–62.

Maynadier, G[ustavus] H[oward]. *The Wife of Bath's Tale: Its Sources and Analogues*. London, 1901; repr., New York: AMS Press, 1972.

Mazzacurati, Giancarlo. "La narrativa di G. F. Straparola e l'ideologia del fiabesco." In *Forma & ideologia*. Naples: Liguori, 1974. 67–113.

Mazon, [?]. "Une collaboration inattendue au XVIIe siècle: L'abbé de Choisy et Charles Perrault." *Mercure de France* (2 January 1928).

Mazzolà, Caterino. *Osiride*. Dresden, 1781.

———. *Rübenzahl, o sia il vero amore*. Dresden, 1789.

McClelland, Clive. "*Ombra* Music in the Eighteenth-Century: Context, Style and Signification." 3 vols. Ph.D. diss., University of Leeds, 2001.

McClymonds, Marita P. "Algarotti and Voltaire in Berlin." Paper read at L'Europe Galante [symposium honoring Daniel Heartz]. 5 October 2003. University of California, Berkeley.

———. "Carl Theodor, the Munich Theatrical Establishment, and the Franco-Italian Synthesis in Opera: The Sertor/Prati *Amida abbandonata* of 1785." In *Mozart's Idomeneo und die Musik in München zur Zeit Karl Theodors*, edited by Theodor Göllner and Stephan Hörner. Munich: Bayerischen Akademie Wissenschaften, 2001. 143–50.

———. "Haydn and the Opera Seria Tradition: *Armida*." In *Napoli e il teatro musicale in Europa tra Sette e Ottocento: Studi in onore di Friedrich Lippmann*, edited by Bianca Maria Antolini and Wolfgang Witzenmann. Florence: Olschki, 1993. 191–206.

———. "Haydn and His Contemporaries: *Armida Abbandonata*." In *Joseph Haydn: Proceedings of the International Joseph Haydn Congress, Vienna 1982*, edited by Eva Badura-Skoda. Munich: G. Henle, [c. 1986]. 325–32.

———. "Mannheim, *Idomeneo*, and the Franco-Italian Synthesis in Opera Seria." In *Mozart und Mannheim: Kongreßbericht Mannheim 1991*, edited by Ludwig Finscher et al. Quellen und Studien zur Geschichte der Mannheim Hofkapelle 2. Frankfurt am Main: Peter Lang, 1994. 187–96.

———. "*La morte di Semiramide ossia La vendetta di Nino* and the Restoration of Death and Tragedy to the Italian Operatic Stage in the 1780s and 90s." In *Atti del XIV Congresso della Società Internazionale di Musicologia*, vol. 3. Turin: EDT, [c. 1990]. 285–92.

———. *Niccolò Jommelli: The Last Years, 1769–1774*. Studies in Musicology 23. Ann Arbor: UMI Press, 1980.

———. "Opera Reform in Italy, 1750 to 1880." In *"Et facciam dolci canti": Studi in onore di Agostino Ziino*, edited by Bianca Maria Antolini et al. Lucca: Libreria musicale italiana, 2003. 895–911.

———. "The Role of Innovation and Reform in the Florentine Opera Seria Repertory 1760 to 1800." In *Music Observed: Studies in Memory of William C. Holmes*, edited by Colleen Reardon and Susan Parisi. Warren, MI: Harmonie Park Press: 2004. 281–99.

———. "Salieri and the Franco-Italian Synthesis: *Armida* and *Europa riconosciuta*." Paper read at the conference Antonio Salieri (1750–1825) e il teatro musicale a Vienna. Legnago, Italy, 18–20 April 2000.

———. "Traetta, Tommaso." In NGO 4:776–79.

———. "Verazi, Coltellini, and the Mannheim-Vienna Connection." In *Mannheim—Ein 'Paradies der Tonkunstler'? Kongressbericht Mannheim 1999*, edited by Ludwig Finscher et al. Frankfurt am Main: Peter Lang, 2002. 307–16.

McClymonds, Marita P., and Daniel Heartz. "Opera Seria." In NGO 3:698–707.

McGowan, Margaret M. *L'art du ballet de cour en France, 1581–1643*. Paris: Editions du Centre National de la Recherche Scientifique, 1963.

McGrane, Bernard. *Beyond Anthropology: Society and the Other*. New York: Columbia University Press, 1989.

Melani, Jacopo. *Ercole in Tebe*. Facsimile edited by Howard Mayer Brown. IO 4, 1978. Libretto, IOL 5 [= vol. 55], 1978.

The Mellen Opera Reference Index: Opera Composers and Their Works. Edited by Charles H. Parsons. 23 vols. Lewiston: Edward Mellen Press, 1986.

Mélusine. Troyes: N. Oudot, 1624.

Ménéstrier, Claude-François. *Des balets anciens et modernes selon les règles du théâtre*. Paris, 1682; facsimile repr., Geneva: Minkoff, 1972.

———. *Des réprésentations en musique anciennes et modernes*. Paris, 1681; repr., Geneva: Slatkine, 1972.

Menesson, [?]. *Manto la fée*. Paris: Christophe Ballard, 1710.

Mercier, Louis-Sébastien. "Poémes lyriques." *Tableau de Paris* 654 (1783). Modern edition in *Tableau de Paris* 2, edited by Jean-Claude Bonnet. Paris: Mercure de France, 1994.

Metastasio, Pietro. *Alcide al bivio*. Facsimile edited by Howard Mayer Brown. IOL 11, 1984.

Meyer, Reinhardt, ed. *Bibliographia Dramatica et Dramaticorum: Kommentierte Bibliographie der im ehemaligen deutschen Reichsgebiet gedruckten und gespielten Dramen des 18. Jahrhunderts*. Tübingen: Max Niemeyer, 1986–.

Meyer, Freidrich Ludwig Wilhelm. *Friedrich Ludwig Schröder: Beitrag zur Kunde des Menschen und des Künstlers*. 2 vols. Hamburg: Hoffmann & Campe, 1819.

Michaelis, Johann Benjamin. *Einzelne Gedichte, Erste Sammlung*. Leipzig: Crusius, 1769.

———. *Sämtliche poetische Werke*. Vienna: Schrämbl, 1791.

Minniear, John Mohr. "Marionette Opera: Its History and Literature." Ph.D. diss., North Texas State University, 1971.

Mirollo, James V. *The Poet of the Marvelous: Giambattista Marino*. New York: Columbia University Press 1963.

Misrahi, Jean. *Le roman des sept sages*. Paris, 1933; repr., Geneva: Slatkine, 1975.

M. L. M. D. M. *Le roman de Mélusine*. Paris, 1637.

Molainville, Bathélemy d'Herbelot de. *Bibliothèque orientale*. Paris, 1697.

Moland, Louis. *Molière et la comédie italienne*. Paris: Didier, 1867.

Monelle, Raymond. "Gluck and the 'festa teatrale.'" *Music and Letters* 54 (1973): 308–25.

Monsigny, Pierre-Alexandre. *La belle Arsène*. Paris: Houbaut, 1775.

———. *L'île sonnante*. Paris: Herissant, n.d.

Montfaucon de Villars, Nicolas-Pierre-Henri. *Le comte de Gabalis; ou, Entretiens sur les sciences secretes*. Amsterdam [i.e., Geneva]: Jacques Le Jeune, 1671.

Moore, Robert E. *Henry Purcell and the Restoration Theatre*. London, 1961; repr., Westport, Conn.: Greenwood Press, [1974].

Mouret, Jean-Joseph. *Cinquième recueil des divertissements*. Paris: The author, n.d.

———. *Nouveau recueil des chansons choisies*. Vol. 5. The Hague: P. Gosse & J. Neaulme, 1732.

———. *Nouveau recueil des chansons choisies*. Vol. 6. The Hague: P. Gosse & J. Neaulme, 1732.

———. *Premier recueil des divertissements de nouveau théâtre italien*. Paris: The author, n.d.

———. *Quatrième recueil des divertissements*. Paris: The author, n.d.

———. *Sixième recueil des divertissements*. Paris: The author, n.d.

Mozart, Wolfgang Amadeus. *Mozart: Briefe und Aufzeichnungen*. Edited by Wilhelm Bauer, Otto Erich Deutsch, and Heinz Eibl. 7 vols. Kassel: Barenreiter, 1962–75.

————. *Neue Ausgabe sämtlicher Werke*. Edited by E. F. Schmid et al. Kassel: Barenreiter, 1955–.

————. *Werke*. Edited by Ludwig von Köchel et al. Leipzig: Breitkopf & Härtel, 1877–83.

Müller, Wenzel. "Kaiser-Königlich privil: Theater in der Leopoldstadt in Wien [1781–1830]." [In A-Wst, shelfmark Ja 51926, a smaller Müller autograph diary from 1781–89 (A-Wst, Ja 40426).]

Murata, Margaret. *Operas for the Papal Court, 1631–1688*. Ann Arbor: UMI Press, 1981.

Murville, Pierre-Nicolas-André de. *Lanvale et Viviane*. Paris: Prault, 1788.

Musäus, Johann Karl August. *Volksmärchen der Deutschen*. 5 vols. Gotha: Carl Wilhelm Ettinger, 1782–87. Modern edition with historical essay by Norbert Miller, Munich: Winkler, [1961].

Musiktext zur Operette Die sieben Schwaben. N.p., [1786]. Copy in Munich, Theatermuseum (Clara Ziegler Stiftung), shelfmark 18 592.

Nagel, Ivan. *Autonomy and Mercy: Reflections on Mozart's Operas*. Translated by Marion Faber and Ivan Nagel. Cambridge, MA: Harvard University Press, 1991.

[Naubert, Christiane Benedikte.] *Neue Volksmärchen der Deutschen*. Leipzig: Weygandschen Buchhandlung, 1789–92.

Naudé, Gabriel. *Apologie pour tous les grands personnages qui ont esté faussement soupçonnez de magie*. Paris: F. Targa, 1625.

Naumann, Johann Gottlieb. *Gustaf Wasa*. Edited by Anna Johnson. Monumenta musicae svecicae 12. Stockholm: Reimers, 1991.

Neun Arien welche in der Comoedie genannt: Die Zauber=Trommel von unserm Hannswurst gesungen werden. N.p., n.d.

Neun Arien welche in der Machinen-Comoedie betittult Das Anglück des Sinen ist öfters Gas Glück des Andern. . . . N.p., n.d.

Nicholson, David. "Gozzi's *Turandot:* A Tragicomic Fairy Tale." *Theatre Journal* 31, no. 4 (1979): 467–78.

Niel, Jean-Baptiste. *Les Romans*. Paris: Boivin, [c. 1736].

Nissard, Charles. *Histoire des livres populaires, ou De la littérature du colportage depuis le xve siècle jusqu'a l'établissement de la Commission d'examen des livres de colportage*. Paris: Amyot, 1854.

Nivelle de La Chaussée, Pierre-Claude. *Amour pour amour*, Paris: Prault, 1742. Repr. in vol. 3, *Oeuvres de théâtre*. Paris: Prault, 1747.

Nobis, Helmut. *Phantasie und Moralität: Das Wunderbare in Wielands Dschinnistan und Der Geschichte des Prinzen Biribinker*. Kronberg: Scriptor, 1976.

Nodot, Paul-François. *Histoire de Mélusine, tirée des chroniques de Poitou, et qui sert d'origine à l'ancienne maison de Lusignan*. Paris: Claude Barbin, 1698.

Noiray, Michel. "La dramaturgie musicale de Gluck." In *Gluck: Iphigénie en Tauride*. L'avant-scène opéra 62. Paris, 1984.

Nougaret, Pierre-Jean-Baptiste [pseud. P.-J. Discret]. *De l'art du théâtre en général . . . et des observations sur ses différents genres reçus au théâtre*. 2 vols. Paris, 1769; repr., Geneva: Slatkine, 1971.

Nouveau cabinet des fées, ou Collection choisie des contes des fées, et autres merveilleux. 18 vols. Paris, 1785–89; repr., Geneva: Slatkine, 1978.

Noverre, Jean-George. *Lettres sur la danse, et sur les ballets*. Stuttgart and Lyon: Delaroche, 1760. Modern edition, Paris: Ramsay, 1978. Facsimile, New York: Broude, [1967].

Osthoff, Wolfgang. "Musica e versificazione: Funzioni del verso poetico nell'operea italiana." In *La drammaturgia musicale*, edited by Lorenzo Bianconi. Bologna: Il mulino, 1986. 126–32.

Palisca, Claude. *Baroque Music*. 3rd ed. New York: Norton, 1991.

Pallavicini, Benedetto. *Le fate*. Dresden: Vedova Stössel, 1736.

Pallavicino, Carlo. *La Gerusalemme liberata*. Edited by Hermann Abert. Denkmäler Deutscher Tonkunst, 1. Folge, vol. 55. 1916. Revised ed., Graz: Breitkopf & Härtel, 1959.

Pandolfi, Vito. *La commedia dell'arte: Storia e testo*. 6 vols. Florence: Sansoni, 1957–61.

Paracelsus, Theophrastus. *Werke*. Edited by Will-Erich Peuckert. Basel: Schwabe, [1964–68].

Parfaict, François, and Claude Parfaict. *Histoire de théâtre français*. 15 vols. Paris: P. G. Le Mercier, 1735–49; repr. in 3 vols., Geneva: Slatkine, 1967.

———. *Dictionnaire des théâtres de Paris, contenant toutes les pièces*. . . . 7 vols. Paris: Lambert, 1756; repr., Geneva: Slatkine, 1967.

Parker, Cynthia May. "Pastoral Drama, Masque, and Epic Romance: Studies in Non-Aristotelian Sources of Seventeenth-century Opera." Ph.D. diss., Indiana University, 1980.

Pauly, Reinhard G. "Benedetto Marcello's Satire on Early 18th-Century Opera: Part 1." *Musical Quarterly* 34 (1948): 222–33, 371–403.

———. "Benedetto Marcello's Satire on Early 18th-century Opera: Part 2." *Musical Quarterly* 35 (1949): 85–105.

Pečman, Rudolph. *Josef Mysliveček*. Prague: Editio Supraphon, 1981.

Peretts, Vladimir Nikolaevich. *Ital'ianskie Komedii i intermedii predstavlennye pri dvore Imperatricy Anny Ioannovny v 1733–1735 godakh*. Teksty. Petrograd: Akademiia nauk, 1917.

Perinet, Joachim. *Kaspar der Fagottist, oder Die Zauberzither* in *Marinellische Schaubühne*. Vienna: Schmidt, 1791. Modern edition in Rommel, *Die Maschinenkomödie* (1974), 206–62.

Perrault, Charles. *Histoires ou contes du temps passé: Avec des moralitez*. Paris: Claude Barbin, 1697. Modern edition, edited by Gilbert Rouger, Paris: Garnier, 1967.

———. *Parallèle des anciens et des modernes*. 2nd ed. 4 vols. Paris, 1692; repr., Geneva: Slatkine, 1971.

Perrotta, Romolo. "Gnostiche 'Ethos' im Textbuch der 'Zauberflöte." *Mozart Jahrbuch 1997*, 45–67.

Perroud, Robert. "La défense et l'utilisation des 'masques' de la commedia dell'arte dans l'œuvre de Carlo Gozzi." In *Das Ende des Stegreifspiels, die Geburt des Nationaltheaters: Ein Wendepunkt in der Geschichte des europäischen Dramas*. Munich: Wilhelm Fink, 1983. 9–16.

Pétis de la Croix, François. *Les mille et un jours: Contes persans traduits en françois*. 5 vols. Paris: Barbin/Gosselin/Goeffrey, 1710–12. Modern edition, Paris: V. Lecou, 1848; published as *Les mille et un jours: Contes persans, texte établi, avec une introduction, des notices, une bibliographie, des jugements et une chronologie par Paul Sebag*, Paris: C. Bourgois, [c. 1980].

Les petits spectacles de Paris, ou Calendrier historique et chronologique de ce qu'ils offrent d'intéressant, septieme partie; huitième partie. Paris: Chez Guillo, 1786–87.

Petri, Christopher. *Rinaldo und Armida*. Leipzig: The author, 1782.

Pezzl, Johann. *Skizze von Wien: Ein Kultur- und Sittenbild aus der josefinischen Zeit*. Vienna, 1786–90. Modern edition, edited by Gustav Gugitz and Anton Schlossar, Graz: Leykam, 1923.

Philidor, François-André Danican. *Le bûcheron, ou Les trois souhaits*. Paris: The author, n.d.

———. *Le soldat magicien*. Paris: The author, n.d.

———. *Le sorcier*. Paris: Chevardiere, n.d.

Piccinni, Niccolo. *Atys*. Facsimile edited by Julian Rushton. French Opera in the 17th and 18th Centuries 65. Stuyvesant, NY: Pendragon Press, 1991.

———. *Iphigénie en Tauride*. Paris: Chez le Suisse de l'hôtel de Noailles, 1781.

———. *Roland*. Paris: The author, 1778.

Pirker, Max. *Teutsche Arien, welche auf dem Kayserlich-privilegirten Wienerischen Theatro in unterschiedlich producirten Comoedien, deren Titul hier jedesmahl beigeruket, gesungen worden: Cod. ms. 12706–12709 der Wiener Nationalbibliothek*. Vienna, Prague, Leipzig: Strache, 1927.

Pirrotta, Nino. *Don Giovanni's Progress: A Rake goes to the Opera*. Translation by Harris S. Saunders, Jr., as *Don Giovanni in musica* (Venice, 1991); New York: Marsilio, 1994.

———. *Music and Theatre from Poliziano to Monteverdi*. Cambridge: Cambridge University Press, 1982.

Pitou, Spire. *The Paris Opéra: An Encyclopedia of Operas, Ballets, Composers, and Performers*. 3 vols. Westport, CT: Greenwood Press, 1983.

Poeschel, Johannes. "Das Märchen vom Schlaraffenlande." *Beiträge zur Geschichte der deutschen Sprache und Literatur* 5 (1878): 389–427.

Poggioli, Renato. *The Oaten Flute: Essays on Pastoral Poetry and the Pastoral Ideal*. Cambridge, MA: Harvard University Press, 1975.

[Poitevin, Auguste]. *Le théâtre de la foire: La comédie italienne et l'opéra comique . . .* Paris: Firmin-Didot, 1889.

Poštolka, Milan. "Wranitzky, Paul." In NGO 4:1180.

Prätorius, Johannes. *Daemonologia Rubinzalii*. 3 vols. Leipzig: J. H. Ellingen, 1663.

———. *Satyrus Etymologicus oder Der Reformierende und Informierende Rüben-Zahl*. Leipzig: J. H. Ellingen, 1672.

Préchac, Jean de. *Contes moins contes que les autres: Sans parangon et La reine des fées*. Paris, 1698.

Pré, Corinne. "Le livret d'opéra-comique en France de 1741 à 1789." Thesis, University of Paris (Sorbonne), 1981.

Price, Elizabeth. "Don Juan: A Chronicle of His Literary Adventures in Germanic Territory." Ph.D. diss., Washington University, 1974.

Programme du Chat-Botté, pantomime, à choisi devant sa majesté par les enfans de l'Ambigu-comique . . . Paris, n.d.

Prunières, Henry. *Le ballet de cour en France avant Benserade et Lully*. Paris: H. Laurens, 1914.

Punderlitschek, Stephan. "Das Freyhaus-Theater auf der Wieden: Das Tagebuch von Ignaz Ritter von Seyfried 1795 bis 12. Juni 1801." Master's thesis, University of Vienna, 1997.

Quinault, Jean-Baptiste-Maurice. *Le roi de Cocagne*. Paris, n.d.

Rademin, Heinrich. *Die Königin der schwartzen Inseln*. Vienna: A. Heyinger, 1731.

———. *Runtzvanscad, König deren Menschen-fressern, oder Der Durchläuchtigste Gärtner*. Vienna: Johann Peter von Ghelen, 1732.

Rambach, Friedrich Eberhard. *Die 3 Räthsel: Tragikomödie in 5 A. nach Gozzi*. Leipzig, 1779.

Rameau, Jean-Philippe. *Achante et Céphise*. Paris: Boivin, Le Clerc, n.d.

———. *Achante et Céphise, ou La Sympathie*. Edited by Robert Fajon. *Opera Omnia*, sér. 4, vol. 21. RCT 29. Paris: Gérard Billaudot, 1998.

———. *Les Boréades*. Facsimile ed. Paris: Stil, 1982.

———. *Erreurs sur la musique dans l'Encyclopédie*. Paris: S. Jorry, 1755; repr., New York: Broude, 1969.

———. *Les festes de Polimnie*. Paris: Ballard, n.d.

———. *La Guirlande, ou Les fleurs enchantées*. 1751. Modern edition, edited by Georges Beck, Le pupitre 62, Paris: Heugel, 1981.

———. *Œuvres complètes*. General editor Camille Saint-Saëns. Paris, 1895–1924; repr., New York: Broude Brothers, 1968.

———. *Opera omnia*. Paris: G. Billaudot, 1996–.

———. *Les Paladins*. Facsimile ed. Edited by R. Peter Wolf. French Opera in the 17th and 18th Centuries 44. Stuyvesant, NY: Pendragon Press, 1986.

———. *Zaïs*. Paris: Delormel, n.d., edited in *Œuvres complètes*, vol. 16.

———. *Zoroastre*. Paris: Veuve Boivin, n.d. [c. 1749]. Modern edition of the 1756 revision *Zo-*

roastre: Tragédie lyrique de L. de Cahusac, restored by *Françoise Gervais*. Paris: Éditions Françaises de Musique, 1964.

———. *Zoroastre (version 1749)*. Edited by Graham Sadler. *Opera Omnia*, sér. 4, vol. 19. RCT
62A. Paris: Gérard Billaudot, 1999.

Ranke, Kurt, et al., eds. *Enzyklopädie des Märchen*. Berlin: Walter de Gruyter, 1978–.

Ratner, Leonard. *Classic Music: Expression, Form, and Style*. New York: Schirmer, 1980.

Rebel, François, and François Francoeur. *Pirame et Thisbé*. Paris: Carfour & Boivin, 1726.

———. *Le Prince de Noisy*. Paris: The authors, n.d.

———. *Zélindor, roi des sylphes*. Paris: Madame Boivin, le Sieur le Clerc, 1745.

Rice, John A. *Antonio Salieri and Viennese Opera*. Chicago: University of Chicago Press, 1998.

———. "Danaïdes, Les." In NGO 1:1058.

———. "Leopold II, Mozart, and the Return to a Golden Age." In *Opera and Enlightenment*,
edited by Thomas Bauman and Marita P. McClymonds. Cambridge: Cambridge University
Press, 1995. 277–78.

Riccoboni, Luigi. *Le nouveau théâtre italien, ou Recueil général des comédies, nouvelle édition*.
10 vols. Paris: Briasson, 1753; repr., Geneva: Slatkine, 1969.

———. *Réflexions historiques, et critiques sur les différents théâtres de l'Europe*. Paris, 1738.

Rigel, Henri-Joseph. *Airs détachés de Rosanie, comedie lyrique en trois actes*. Paris: The author, n.d.

———. *Blanche et Vermeille: Comedie-pastorale en 2 actes et en prose: Mise en musique et dédie à
Monsieur le Cavalier de Florian. Par H. J. Rigel*. Paris: Lauriers, n.d.

Ringger, Kurt. "Carlo Gozzi's *Fiabe teatrali:* Wirklichkeit und romantischer Mythos."
Germanisch-romantisch Monatsschrift, neue Folge 18 (1968): 14–20.

Robbins Landon, H. C. "Haydn's Marionette Operas." In *Haydn Yearbook* 1. Bryn Mawr, PA:
T. Presser, 1962. 111–93.

Robert, Raymonde. *Le conte des fées littéraire en France de la fin du XVIIe à la fin du XVIIIe siècle*.
Nancy: Presses Universitaires de Nancy, 1982.

Robinson, Michael F. *Giovanni Paisiello: A Catalogue of his Works*. Vol. 1, *Dramatic Works*.
Stuyvesant, NY: Pendragon Press, 1991.

———. *Naples and Neapolitan Opera*. Oxford: Clarendon Press, 1972.

Rochefort, Jean-Baptiste. *Jérusalem délivrée, ou Renaud et Armide*. Paris, 1779.

Rochemont, [?] de. *Réflexions d'un patriote sur l'opéra français et sur l'opéra italien, qui présentent le
parallèle du goût des nations dans les beaux-arts*. Lausanne, 1754.

Rochon de Chabannes, Marc-Antoine-Jacques. *Alcindor*. Paris: Delormel, 1787.

Rodolphe, Jean-Joseph. *L'aveugle de Palmyre*. Paris: La Chevardiere, n.d.

———. *Medea und Jason*. In *Ausgewählte Ballette Stuttgarter Meister aus der 2. Hälfte des 18.
Jahrhunderts: Florian Deller—Johann Joseph Rodolphe*, edited by Hermann Abert and Hans
Joachim Moser. Denkmäler der Deutscher Tonkunst, 1. Folge, vols. 43–44. Wiesbaden:
Breitkopf & Hartel, 1958.

Röhrich, Lutz. *Sage und Märchen: Erzählforschung heute*. Freiberg im Breisgau: Herder, 1976.

*Le roman de sept sages de Rome: A Critical Edition of the Two Verse Redactions of a Twelfth-Century
Romance*. Prepared by Mary B. Speer. Lexington, KY: French Forum, 1989.

Rommel, Otto. *Die Alt-Wiener Volkskomödie: Ihre Geschichte vom barocken Welt-Theater bis zum
Tode Nestroys*. Vienna: Anton Schroll, 1952.

———. *Die Maschinenkomödie*. Deutsche Literatur in Entwicklungsreihen, Reihe Barock,
Barocktradition im Österreichisch-Bayrischen Volkstheater 1. Leipzig, 1935; repr., Darmstadt: Wissenschaftliche Buchgesellschaft, 1974.

Rönnau, Klaus. "Hanke, Karl." In NGO 2:637.

Rosand, Ellen. Introduction to A. Aureli and A. Sartorio, *L'Orfeo*. Drammaturgia musicale veneta 6. Milan: Ricordi, 1983.

———. *Opera in Seventeenth-Century Venice: The Creation of a Genre*. Berkeley: University of
California Press, 1991.

———. "Orlando in *Seicento* Venice: The Road Not Taken." In Collins and Kirk, eds., *Opera &
Vivaldi*, 87–104.

Rosen, Charles. *The Classical Style: Haydn, Mozart, Beethoven*. New York: Viking, 1971.

Rospigliosi, Giulio. *Erminia sul Giordano*. Rome, 1637. Facsimile, Bibliotheca musica bononiensis, sez. 4, no. 12. Bologna: Forni, [1969].

———. *Il palazzo incantato, ovvero La guerriera amante*. Facsimile edited by Howard Mayer
Brown. IO 2, 1977. Libretto, IOL 8, 1979.

Roth, Johann Ferdinand. *Vom Könige Artus und von dem bildschönen Ritter Wieduwilt*. Leipzig,
1786.

Roth, Thomas. *Der Einfluss von Ariost's "Orlando Furioso" auf das französische Theater*. Leipzig,
1905; repr., Geneva: Slatkine, 1971.

Rousseau, Jean-Jacques. *Dictionnaire de musique*. Paris: Veuve Duchesne, 1768. Edited by J.-J.
Eigeldinger et al. in *Œuvres complètes* 5, *Ecrits sur la musique, la langue et le théâtre*, edited by
Bernard Gagnebin, Marcel Raymond et al. Paris: Gallimard, 1995.

Rousseau, Jean-Jacques, and Horace Coignet. *Pygmalion* [1770]. Facsimile with introduction by
Emilio Sala. Drammaturgia musicale Veneta 22. Milan: Ricordi, 1996.

Rusack, Hedwig Hoffmann. *Gozzi in Germany: A Survey of the Rise and Decline of the Gozzi Vogue
in Germany and Austria*. New York: Columbia University Press, 1930.

Rushton, Julian. "Floquet, Etienne-Joseph." In NGO 2:231–32.

———. "Music and Drama in the Académie Royale de Musique, Paris, 1774–1789." Ph.D. diss.,
University of Oxford, 1970.

———. "Salieri's *Les Horaces:* The Study of an Operatic Failure." *Music Review* 37, no. 4 (1976):
266–82.

———. "The Theory and Practive of Piccinnism." *Proceedings of the Royal Musical Association*
98 (1971–72): 31–46.

Russell, Charles C. *The Don Juan Legend before Mozart*. Ann Arbor: University of Michigan
Press, 1993.

———. "The Libertine Reformed: *Don Juan* by Gluck and Angiolini." *Music & Letters* 65, no. 1
(1984): 17–27.

Russo, Paolo. "Visions of Medea: Musico-dramatic Transformations of a Myth." *Cambridge Opera Journal* 6 (1994): 113–24.

Sadie, Julie Anne. "*Musiciennes* of the Ancien Régime." In *Women Making Music: The Western
Art Tradition, 1150–1950*, edited by Jane Bowers and Judith Tick. Urbana: University of Illi-
nois Press, 1987. 191–223.

Sadler, Graham. "Rameau." In *The New Grove French Baroque Masters*. New York: Macmillan,
1986. 205–308.

———. "Rameau and the Orchestra." *Proceedings of the Royal Musical Association* 108 (1981–82):
47–68.

Saint-Évremond, Charles de Marguetel de Saint Denis, Seigneur de. "Sur les opéra: à M. le Duc
de Buckingham" [1684]. In *Œuvres meslées de Mr. de Saint-Evremond*, nouvelle éd. Amsterdam: Mortier, 1706. 3:230–46.

Saint-Foix, Germaine-François Poullain de. *L'oracle*. Paris: Prault fils, 1740.

Saint-Mard, Raymond de. *Réflexions sur l'opéra*. The Hague: Neaulme, 1741.

Salieri, Antonio. *Armida*. Leipzig: Breitkopf, 1783.

———. *La grotta di Trofonio*. Vienna: Artaria, n.d.

———. *Les Danaïdes*. Paris: Des Lauriers, n.d.

———. *Tarare*. Edited by Rudolph Angermüller. 2 vols. Die Oper 2. Munich: Henle, 1978.

Salomon, Joseph-François. *Médée et Jason*. Facsimile ed. Edited by Leslie Ellen Brown. French Opera in the 17th and 18th Centuries 28. Stuyvesant, NY: Pendragon Press, 1991.

Sarnelli, Pompeo. *Posilecheata*. Edited by Enrico Malato. Rome: G. & M. Benincasa, 1986.

Sartori, Claudio. *I libretti italiana a stampa dalla origini al 1800: Catalogo analitico con 16 indici*. 7 vols. Milan: Bertola & Locatelli, 1990.

Saure, Wolfgang. "Die Geschichte der Frankfurt Oper von 1792 bis 1880." Ph.D. diss., University of Cologne, 1959.

Scenarios of the Commedia dell'Arte: Flaminio Scala's "Il teatro delle favole rappresentative." Translated by Henry F. Salerno, with a foreword by Kenneth McKee. New York: New York University Press, 1967.

Scherillo, Michele. *L'opera buffa napoletana durante il Settecento: Storia letteraria*. 2nd ed. Milan: R. Sandron, 1917.

Schiebeler, Daniel. "Anmerkung zu Lisuart und Dariolette." *Wöchentliche Nachrichten und Anmerkungen die Musik betreffend* (2 November 1767): 135–39.

———. *Lisuart und Dariolette, oder die Frage und die Antwort*. Frankfurt am Main, 1776.

Schikaneder, Emanuel. *Arien und Duetten aus dem wohltätigen Derwisch, oder Die Schellenkappe*. Vienna: Mathias Ludwig, 1791.

———. *Arien zur "Zaubertrommel, oder Der wohltätigen Derwisch."* Augsburg, 1793.

———. *Arien und Gesänge aus "Dem Stein der Weisen, oder: Die Zauber=insel": Eine heroisch=komische Oper in zwei Aufzügen*. Frankfurt am Main, 1796.

———. *Gesaenge zur heroisch-comischen Oper, "Der Stein der Weisen."* N.p., 1802.

———. *Gesänge aus der Oper "Der Stein der Weisen, oder Die Zauberinsel."* N.p., n.d.

———. *Gesänge zu der großen komischen Oper in vier Aufzügen, genannt "Die Schellenkappe, oder Die Zaubertrommel."* [Vienna], 1794.

———. *Sämmtliche theatralische Werke*. 2 vols. Vienna: Alois Doll, 1792.

Schimpf, Wolfgang. *Lyrisches Theater: Das Melodrama des 18 Jahrhunderts*. Göttingen: Vandenhoeck & Ruprecht, 1988.

Schindler, Otto G. *Stegreifburlesken der Wanderbühne: Szenare der Schulz-Menningerschen Schauspielertruppe*. St. Ingbert: Röhrig, 1990.

———. *Die Pantomime "Das Zauber-Glöckel" und die Hanswurstspiele von Böhmisch Krumau: Spieltexte vom Schloßtheater des Fürsten Joseph Adam von Schwartzenberg; Vortrag, gehalten am 30. September 1993*. České Budejovice: Památkovy ústav, 1993.

Schink, Johann Friedrich. *Dramatische Monate*. Hamburg, 1790. Cited in *Mozart: Die Dokumente*, 310–13.

Schmid, Christian Heinrich. *Chronologie des deutschen Theaters*. [Leipzig], 1755. Repr. in *Christian Heinrich Schmids "Chronologie des deutschen Theaters,"* edited by Paul Legband. Berlin: Gesellschaft für Theatergeschichte, 1902.

Schmid, Ernst Fritz. *Ein schwäbisches Mozartbuch*. Lorch-Stuttgart: Alfons-Bürger, 1948.

Schmidt, Carl B. "Antonio Cesti's *Il pomo d'oro*: A Reexamination of a Famous Hapsburg Court Spectacle." *Journal of the American Musicological Society* 29 (1976): 381–412.

———. "Pomo d'oro, Il." In NGO 3:1051–54.

Schmidt, Johann Friedrich. *Hermannide, oder Die Rätsel*. Vienna: Logenmeister, 1777.

Schmidt, Leopold. *Zur Geschichte der Märchen-Oper*. Halle: Otto Hendel, 1896.

Schmidtmann, Gottfried. "Daniel Schiebeler." Ph. D. diss., University of Götttingen, 1909.

Schneider, Marcel. *La littérature fantastique en France*. Paris: Fayard, 1964.

Schreiber, Heinrich. *Die Feen in Europa: Eine historisch-archäologische Monographie*. Freiburg, 1842; repr., Allmendingen, 1981.

Schubart, Christian Friedrich Daniel. *Ideen zu einer Ästhetik der Tonkunst* [c. 1784–85]. Vienna, 1806; repr., Leipzig: Wolkenwanderer-Verlag, 1924.

Schuhl, Pierre Maxime. *Le merveilleux, la pensée et l'action*. Paris: Flammarion, 1952.

Schwartz, Judith L. "Cultural Stereotypes and Music in the 18th Century." *Studies on Voltaire and the Eighteenth Century* 151–55 (1976): 1989–2013.

Scobie, Alex. *Apuleius and Folklore*. London: Folklore Society, 1983.

Scott, Virginia. *The Commedia dell'arte in Paris, 1644–1697*. Charlottesville: University Press of Virginia, 1990.

Sechs schöne neue Weltliche Lieder aus der Oper des Steins der Weisen. Vienna: Anton Leitner, n.d.

Seeber, Edward D. "Le 'Conte de la Femme de Bath' en français au XVIIIe siècle." *Revue de littérature comparée* 9 (1929): 117–40.

―――. "Sylphs and Other Elemental Beings in French Literature since *Le Comte de Gabalis* (1670)." *Publications of the Modern Language Association* 59 (1944): 71–83.

Selfridge-Field, Eleanor. "The Viennese Court Orchestra in the Time of Caldara." In *Antonio Caldara: Essays on His Life and Times*, edited by Brian W. Pritchard. Aldershot, England: Scholar Press, 1987. 117–51.

Les sept Sages de Rome: Roman en prose du xviiie siècle. Nancy, 1981.

Sévigné, [Marie de Rabutin-Chantal] Madame de. *Lettres*. Edited by Gérard Gailly. Paris: Gallimard, 1953.

Seydelmann, Franz. *Die schöne Arsene*. Leipzig: Breitkopf, 1779.

Shadwell, Thomas. *The Libertine*. The Complete Works of Thomas Shadwell 3. Edited by Montague Summers. London: Fortune Press, 1927.

Shah, Idries. *La magie orientale*. Paris: Payot, 1957.

Shimp, Susan. "Women, Magic, and Incantation in Counter-Reformation Rome: Domenico Mazzocchi's *La Catena d'Adone*." Paper presented at annual meeting of the Society for Seventeenth-Century Music, Danville, KY, 30 April 1995.

Sidney, Philip. *Arcadia* [c. 1590]. Paris: Toussaint du Bray, 1624.

Simpson, Joyce G. *Le Tasse et la littérature et l'art baroques en France*. Paris: A. G. Nizet, 1962.

Smith, Kent M. "Egidio Duni and the Development of the Opéra-comique, 1753–1770." Ph.D. diss., Cornell University, 1980.

Sografi, Simeone Antonio, and G[iovanni] B[attista] Cimador. *Pimmalione*, [1790]. Facsimile with introduction by Emilio Sala. Drammaturgia musicale Veneta 22. Milan: Ricordi, 1996.

Sonneck, O[scar] G. T. *Catalogue of Opera Librettos Printed before 1800*. 2 vols. Washington, DC: Government Printing Office, 1914.

Soriano, Marc. *Les contes de Perrault: Culture savante et traditions populaires*. Paris: Gallimard, 1968.

Spada, Stefania. *Domenico Biancolelli, ou L'art d'improviser*. Naples: Insitut Universitaire Oriental, 1969.

Spaur, H. Graf von. *Der Schiffbruch*. Frankfurt: Andreäische Schriften, 1778.

Spaziani, Marcello. *Il teatro minore de Lesage: Studi e richerche*. Rome: A. Signorelli, [c. 1957].

―――. *Teatro della Foire: Dieci commedie de Alard, Fuzelier, Lesage, d'Orneval, La Font, Piron*. Rome: Edizioni dell'Ateneo, 1965.

―――. *Don Giovanni dagli scenari dell'arte alla "foire."* Rome: Edizioni di storia e letteratura, 1978.

―――. "Don Juan à la foire." In *L'opéra au xviiie siècle: Actes du colloque organisé à Aix-en-*

Provence par le Centre Aixois d'études et de recherches sur le xviiie siècle . . . 1977. Marseilles: J. Laffitte, 1982. 111–41.

Les spectacles des foires et des boulevards de Paris et des principales villes de l'Europe, ou Calendrier historique et chronologique des forains, cinquieme partie. Paris: J. Fr. Bastien, 1777.

Spiess, Johann. *Historia von Dr. Johann Fausten.* Frankfurt, 1587.

Spitzer, John, and Neal Zaslaw. "Orchestration." In NGO 3:719–28.

Steblin, Rita. *A History of Key Characteristics in the Eighteenth and Early Nineteenth Centuries.* Ann Arbor: UMI Press, 1983.

Steffani, Agostino. *Ausgewählte Werke.* Edited by Hugo Riemann. Denkmäler der Tonkunst in Bayern 23, Jahrg.12, no. 2. Braunschweig: H. Littolff, 1912.

———. *La lotta d'Hercole con Acheloo.* Handel Sources 9. New York: Garland, 1986.

Stein, Louise. *Songs of the Mortals, Dialogues of the Gods: Music and the Theater in Seventeenth-century Spain.* Oxford: Oxford University Press, 1993.

Stephanie, Gottlieb (the Younger). *Sämmtliche Schauspiele.* 2 vols. Vienna: Ghelen, 1774.

———. *Der Irrwisch.* Vienna: Logenmeister, 1785.

———. *Die Trofonius-Höhle.* Dresden, 1786.

Stephenson, Kurt. "Romberg, Bernhard Heinrich." In NGO 4:22.

———. "Romberg, Andreas Jakob." In NGO 4:21.

Steptoe, Andrew. *The Mozart–Da Ponte Operas: The Cultural and Musical Background to "Le nozze di Figaro," "Don Giovanni," and "Così fan tutte."* Oxford: Clarendon Press, 1988.

Sternfeld, Frederick W. "Orpheus." In NGO 3:776–78.

———. "Orpheus, Ovid, and Opera." *Journal of the Royal Musical Association* 113 (1988): 172–202.

Stevenson, Robert, and Marita P. McClymonds. "Tozzi, Antonio." In NGO 4:776.

Stieger, Franz. *Opernlexikon.* 11 vols. Tützing: Hans Schneider, 1975.

Storer, Mary E. *Un épisode littéraire de la fin du XVIIe siècle: La mode des contes de fées (1685–1700).* Paris: Edouard Champion, 1928.

Straparola, Giovanni Francesco. *Piacevoli notti.* Venice, 1550–53. Modern edition, Rome: Gius. Laterza, 1975.

———. *The Facetious Nights of Straparola.* Translated by W. G. Waters. 4 vols. London: Society of Bibliophiles, 1897. 2nd ed., 1909.

Striker, Ardelle. "The Theater of Alain-René Lesage." Ph.D. diss, Columbia University, 1968.

Strohm, Reinhard. *Italienische Opernarien des frühen Settecento (1720–1730).* 2 vols. Analecta Musicologica 16. Cologne: Arno Volk, 1976.

———. "Comic Traditions in Handel's *Orlando.*" In *Essays on Handel and Italian Opera.* Cambridge: Cambridge University Press, 1985. 249–67.

Strunk, Oliver, ed. *Source Readings in Music History.* New York: Norton, 1950.

Sulzer, Johann Georg. *Allgemeine Theorie der schönen Künste.* 2nd ed. Leipzig: Wiedmann, 1786–87.

Sulzer, Johann Georg, and Johann Philipp Kirnberger. *Allgemeine Theorie der schönen Künste.* Frankfurt and Leipzig, 1798; repr., Hildesheim: G. Olms, 1970.

Tarr, Edward H. amd Thomas Walker. "'Bellici carmi, festivo fragor': Die Verwendung der Trompete in der italienischen Oper des 17. Jahrhunderts." *Hamburger Jahrbuch für Musikwissenschaft* 3 (1978): 143–203.

Tasso, Torquato. *Jerusalem Delivered: An English Prose Version.* Translated by Ralph Nash. Detroit: Wayne State University Press, 1987.

———. *Discourses on the Heroic Poem.* Translated by Mariella Cavalchini and Irene Samuel. Oxford: Clarendon Press, 1973.

Telemann, Georg Phillipp. *Der getreue Music-Meister.* Hamburg: The author, 1728–29.

Tenpenny, Patricia L., et al. "In Search of Inadvertent Plagarism." *American Journal of Psychology* 111, no. 4 (22 December 1998): 529–59.

Terrasson, Jean. *Sethos, histoire, ou Vie tirée des monuments, anecdotes de l'ancienne Égypte d'un manuscrit grec.* 3 vols. Paris, 1731, Amsterdam, 1732; German trans., Mathias Claudius, 1777.

———. *Dissertation critique sur l'Iliade d'Homère.* Paris, 1715, repr., Geneva: Slatkine, 1971.

Thayer, Alexander Wheelock. *Salieri: Rival of Mozart.* Edited by Theodore Albrecht. Kansas City, Mo.: Philharmonic of Greater Kansas City, 1989.

Thomas, Keith V. *Religion and the Decline of Magic.* London: Weidenfeld & Nicolson, 1971.

Thompson, Stith. *Motif Index of Folk Literature: A Classification of Narrative Elements.* 6 vols. 2nd ed. Folklore Fellows' Communications 106–11. Copenhagen: Rosenkilde & Bagger, 1955–58.

Till, Nicolas. *Mozart and the Enlightenment: Truth, Virtue and Beauty in Mozart's Operas.* London: Faber & Faber, 1992.

Tomek, Peter. "Die Musik an den Wiener Vorstadttheater, 1776–1825: Theatermusik und Zeitgeist; Eine Bestandsaufnahme." Ph.D. diss., University of Vienna, 1989.

Tomlinson, Gary. *Music in Renaissance Magic: Toward a Historiography of Others.* Chicago: University of Chicago Press, 1993.

Traetta, Tomasso. *Ausgewählte Werke.* Edited by Hugo Goldschmidt. Denkmäler der Tonkunst in Bayern 25, Jahrg. 14, no. 1. Leipzig: Breitkopf & Härtel, 1914.

———. *Iphigenia in Tauride.* Facsimile edited by Howard Mayer Brown. IO 47, 1978.

———. *Ippolito ed Aricia.* Facsimile edited by Eric Weimer. IO 77, 1982.

Treitschke, Georg Friedrich. "Zauberflöte, Dorfbarbier, Fidelio." *Orpheus: Musikalisches Taschenbuch* 2 (1841): 239–64.

Trinchera, Pietro. *L'incanti per amore.* Naples. 1741.

Trott, David. "Louis Fuzelier et le théâtre: vers un état présent." *Revue d'histoire littéraire* 83, no. 4 (1983): 604–17.

———. "Pour une histoire des spectacles non-officiels. Louis Fuzelier et le théâtre à Paris en 1725–26." *Revue d'histoire du théâtre* 37, no. 3 (1985): 255–75.

Trowell, Brian. "Libretto (ii)." In NGO 2:1191–1252.

Tyler, Linda. "Schack, Benedikt." In NGO 4:211.

Tyson, Alan. "Two Mozart Puzzles: Can Anyone Solve Them?" *Musical Times* 129 (March 1988): 126–27.

Umlauf, Ignaz. *Die Bergknappen.* Edited by Robert Haas. Denkmäler der Tonkunst in Österreich 17. Graz: Akademische Druck- und Verlagsanstalt, 1959.

Valentin, Erich. "Mozart und die Dichtung seiner Zeit." *Neues Mozart-Jahrbuch* 1 (1942): 79–113.

van der Meer, John Henry. *Johann Josef Fux als Opernkomponist.* 4 vols. Utrechtse Bijfragen tot de Musiekwetenschaf 2. Bilthoven: A. B. Creyghton, 1961.

Vasari, Giorgio. *Vite scelte di Giorgio Vasari.* Edited by Anna Maria Brizio. 2nd ed. Turin: Unione tipografico-editrice torinese, [1964].

Vismes du Valgay, Alphonse-Denis-Marie de. *Amadis de Gaule.* Paris: Lormel, 1779; facsimile in J. C. Bach, *Collected Works,* 45.

Vivaldi, Antonio. *Griselda.* Facsimile edited by Howard Mayer Brown. IO 25, 1978. Modern edition, edited by R. Fasano, Palermo: Enchiridion, [1985].

Vogel, Johann Christoph. *La toison d'or.* Paris: Clochet, n.d.

Vogt, George McGill. "'The Wife of Bath's Tale,' 'Women Pleased,' and 'La fée Urgèle': A Study in Transformation of Folklore Themes in Drama." *Modern Language Notes* 37 (1922): 339–42.

Voisenon, Claude-Henri Fusée de. *Fleur d'épine*, Paris: Duchesne, 1777.

Vulpius, Chistian August. "Die Feyer im Reich der Feen." *Ephemeriden der Litteratur und des Theaters* 23 (1787): 353–60.

———. *Gesänge aus dem Singspiele: Der Schleyer.* Hamburg: Johann Matthias Michaelsen, 1788.

———. *Opern.* Bayreuth and Leipzig, 1790.

———. *Der Schleyer.* Bayreuth and Leipzig: J. A. Lübecks Erben, 1789.

Wagenseil, Georg Christoph. *Euridice.* Facsimile edited by Eric Weimer. IO 75, 1983.

Walker, D[aniel] P[ickering]. *Spiritual and Demonic Magic from Ficino to Campanella.* London: Warburg Institute and University of London, 1958.

———, ed. *Musique des intermèdes de "La Pellegrina."* Paris: Editions du Centre National de la Recherche Scientifique, 1963.

Walker, Thomas. "Cavalli." In *The New Grove Italian Baroque Masters.* New York: Macmillan, 1984. 137–78.

Walter, Friedrich. *Die Bibliothek des Großh. Hof= und Nationaltheater.* Leipzig: S. Hirzel, 1899. 2 vols.

Weaver, Robert L. "*Il Girello:* A Seventeenth-century Burlesque Opera." *Quadrivium* 12 (1971): 141–64.

———. "The Orchestra in Early Italian Opera." *Journal of the American Musicological Society* 17 (1964): 83–89.

———. "Sixteenth-century Instrumentation." *Musical Quarterly* 47 (1961): 363–78.

Weber, Max. *The Protestant Ethic and the Spirit of Capitalism.* New York: Scribner, 1958.

———. *The Sociology of Religion.* Boston: Beacon Press, 1963.

Weber, William. "*La musique ancien* in the Waning of the Ancien Régime." *Journal of Modern History* 56 (1984): 58–88.

Weidinger, Hans Ernst. "*Il Dissoluto punito:* Untersuchungen zur äußeren und inneren Entstehungensgeschichte von Lorenzo da Ponte und Wolfgang Amadeus Mozarts *Don Giovanni.*" Ph.D. diss., University of Vienna, 2002.

Weidmann, Paul. *Der Ring der Liebe, oder Zemirens und Azors Ehestand.* Vienna: Logenmeister, 1786.

Weise, Christian. *Bauernkomödie von Tobias und der Schwalbe.* 1682. Modern edition, Berlin: Hofmann, 1882.

Weiss, Harry B. *A Book about Chapbooks: The People's Literature of Bygone Times.* Hatboro, PA: Folklore Associates, 1969 [orig. 1942].

Weiss, Piero. "Sciroli, Gregorio." In NGO 4:272.

Weiss, Piero, and Richard Taruskin, eds. *Music in the Western World: A History in Documents.* New York: Schirmer, 1984. 201–3.

Weller, Philip. "Aubert, Jacques." In NGO 1:247.

Westrup, Jack, et al. "Aria." In NGO 1:169–77.

White, A. Duane. "Eberl, Anton." In NGO 2:3.

Wieland, Christoph Martin. *Dschinnistan, oder auserlesene Feen- und Geistermärchen.* Winterthur: Heinrich Steiner, 1786, 1787, and 1789. Modern edition, edited by Gerhard Seidel, Berlin: Rütter and Loening, 1968.

Wiener Theater Almanach. Vienna: Kurzbeck, 1794.

Winkler, Klaus. "Die Bedeutung des Posaune im Schaffen von Johann Joseph Fux." *Alta Musica* 9 (1987): 177–99.

Winter, Marian Hannah. *The Pre-Romantic Ballet.* London: Pitman, 1974.

Witzenetz, Julia. *Le théâtre français de Vienne, 1752-1772.* Études françaises publiées par l'Institut Français de l'Université de Szeged 6. Szeged, 1932.

Wood, Caroline. "Jean-Baptiste Lully and His Successors: Music and Drama in the *tragédie en musique*, 1673–1715." Ph.D. diss., University of Hull, 1981.

———. "Orchestra and Spectacle in the *Tragédie en Musique*, 1673–1715: Oracle, *sommeil* and *tempête*." *Proceedings of the Royal Musical Association* 108 (1981–82): 25–46.

Wranitzky, Paul. *Oberon, König der Elfen: Singspiel in drei Akten*. Edited by Christoph-Hellmut Mahlung and Joachim Veit. 2 vols. Die Oper 4. Munich: Henle, 1993.

Yates, Frances A. *Giordano Bruno and the Hermetic Tradition*. London: Routledge and Kegan Paul, 1975.

Zaniboni, Antonio. *Il mago deluso dalla magia*, Bologna: per il Rossi e comp., n.d. [1718].

La Zanina maga par amore. Bologna: Costantino Pisarri, n.d.

Zaslaw, Neal. "Leclair's 'Scylla et Glaucus.'" *Musical Times* 120 (1979): 900–904.

Zehnmark, Ludwig. *Was erhält die Männer treu?* Vienna: Logenmeister, 1780.

Zelm, Klaus. *Die Opern Reinhard Keisers: Studien zur Chronologie, Überlieferung und Stilentwicklung*. Munich: Katzbichler, 1975.

Zeno, Apostolo. *Themistocles*. Mannheim: Hof- und Akademiebuchdruckerei, 1772.

Zeydel, Edwin H. *Ludwig Tieck, the German Romanticist*. 2nd ed. Hildesheim and New York: G. Olms, 1971.

Zipes, Jack David. *The Brothers Grimm: From Enchanted Forests to the Modern World*. New York: Routledge, 1988.

———, ed. *The Oxford Compendium to Fairy Tales*. Oxford: Oxford University Press, 2000.

INDEX

Italicized page numbers refer to examples, figures, and tables.